International and European Disability Law and Policy

In this first textbook on international and European disability law and policy, Broderick and Ferri analyse the interaction between different legal systems and sources. Guided by the global legal standards of the CRPD, students are equipped with the necessary theoretical and conceptual background on disability, and are given a comprehensive overview of the international and European legal and policy frameworks on disability.

The narrative maintains the important balance between theory and practice, focusing on both the legal framework and challenges in the realm of policy-making, as well as ensuring that students are aware of current legal debates and controversial issues in the field. Accommodating different learning styles, the book employs a range of accessible features, which include learning outcomes at the start of each chapter, problem questions, thought bubbles, group activities, extracts from legal debates and a variety of textboxes.

Including case studies and examples from countries around the world, this book has a truly global perspective that is suitable for introductory and advanced modules in law departments, as well as interdisciplinary courses.

Andrea Broderick is an Assistant Professor at the Department of International and European Law, Maastricht University, and obtained the Edmond Hustinx Prize for Science in 2018.

Delia Ferri is a Lecturer in Law at Maynooth University Department of Law, and is a qualified lawyer and member of the Italian Bar.

International and European Disability Law and Policy

Text, Cases and Materials

Andrea Broderick
Maastricht University, The Netherlands

Delia Ferri
National University of Ireland, Maynooth

CAMBRIDGE
UNIVERSITY PRESS

CAMBRIDGE
UNIVERSITY PRESS

University Printing House, Cambridge CB2 8BS, United Kingdom

One Liberty Plaza, 20th Floor, New York, NY 10006, USA

477 Williamstown Road, Port Melbourne, VIC 3207, Australia

314–321, 3rd Floor, Plot 3, Splendor Forum, Jasola District Centre,
New Delhi – 110025, India

79 Anson Road, #06–04/06, Singapore 079906

Cambridge University Press is part of the University of Cambridge.

It furthers the University's mission by disseminating knowledge in the pursuit of education, learning, and research at the highest international levels of excellence.

www.cambridge.org
Information on this title: www.cambridge.org/9781108418195
DOI: 10.1017/9781108289450

First published 2019

Printed in the United Kingdom by TJ International Ltd. Padstow Cornwall

A catalogue record for this publication is available from the British Library.

Library of Congress Cataloging-in-Publication Data
Names: Broderick, Andrea, author. | Ferri, Delia, author.
Title: International and European disability law and policy : text, cases and materials / Andrea Broderick, Universiteit Maastricht, Netherlands; Delia Ferri, National University of Ireland, Maynooth.
Description: Cambridge, United Kingdom ; New York, NY : Cambridge University Press, 2019.
Identifiers: LCCN 2019013613 | ISBN 9781108418195 (hardback : alk. paper) | ISBN 9781108406604 (pbk. : alk. paper)
Subjects: LCSH: People with disabilities–Legal status, laws, etc. | Capacity and disability. | Convention on the Rights of Persons with Disabilities and Optional Protocol (2007 March 30) | People with disabilities–Legal status, laws, etc.–European Union countries.
Classification: LCC K637 .B76 2019 | DDC 346.01/3087–dc23
LC record available at https://lccn.loc.gov/2019013613

ISBN 978-1-108-41819-5 Hardback
ISBN 978-1-108-40660-4 Paperback

Scribendum ergo quam diligentissime et quam plurimum.
Nam ut terra alte refossa generandis alendisque seminibus fecundior,
sic profectus non a summo petitus studiorum fructus
et fundit uberius et fidelius continet.

(Quintilianus, *Institutio Oratoria* X, 3, 2)

CONTENTS

FOREWORD

As the introduction to this book remarks: 'In the last decade, disability law has emerged as a distinct and dynamic field of international and European action, and as an evolving academic discipline'. Consequently, it is not surprising that disability law, whether in the form of international, European or comparative law, is increasingly being taught in stand-alone courses at universities as well as within broader human rights courses, and that there is increasing demand for training and knowledge in this area among practitioners, policy-makers and civil society. Such a discipline demands a textbook, which acknowledges its status as a comprehensive body of law that has matured into a coherent discipline. This book by Andrea Broderick and Delia Ferri is the first such textbook to be published. It reflects the truly global nature of disability human rights following the adoption of the UN Convention on the Rights of Persons with Disabilities. The textbook covers both international and European disability human rights law, as well as including chapters on disability rights within the Inter-American and African human rights systems.

This book is an impressive achievement – as noted above, not only is it the first such publication, but its scope is very broad and the authors have taken different pedagogical approaches and learning styles into account, thereby enabling the book to be used to support different teaching activities and styles. Such detailed attention to how a book will actually be used by students and tutors is sometimes missing from textbooks, and this thoughtfulness is to be applauded. However, given its comprehensive and detailed scope, the book will be of value not only to students and tutors, but to legal practitioners, civil society organisations and policy-makers and civil servants who work for States Parties to the UN Convention on the Rights of Persons with Disabilities.

The field of disability human rights law has 'come of age'. It requires not merely a chapter or two in textbooks covering international law as was previously the case, but a textbook of its own. Andrea Broderick and Delia Ferri have met this challenge and written an excellent textbook, for which there is now a clear need.

Lisa Waddington
European Disability Forum Chair in European Disability Law,
Maastricht University

PREFACE

This textbook addresses international and European disability law and policy, highlighting, in a comparative fashion, the interaction between different sources of law and legal systems. It aims to describe the principles embraced by the human rights model of disability and by the social model, as opposed to the outdated medical model, in order to equip students with the necessary theoretical and conceptual background on disability. Furthermore, it aims to provide a comprehensive overview of the international legal and policy framework on disability, including regional systems for the protection of disability rights. By including chapters on the European Union (EU) and the Council of Europe (CoE), the Inter-American and the African systems as well as on the protection of the rights of people with disabilities in Asia, this textbook aims to achieve a global focus. This is strengthened by the addition, where appropriate, of case studies and examples of good practice from different countries around the world.

The textbook is divided into three main parts, preceded by an introductory chapter that lays down the methodology and pedagogical approach of the book. The first part examines the development of international standards on disability, focusing on the United Nations Convention on the Rights of Persons with Disabilities (CRPD or the 'Convention'). The general comments and decisions of the United Nations Committee on the Rights of Persons with Disabilities (CRPD Committee) are also addressed, among other sources. The second part analyses EU disability law and policy, paying attention to the role of the Court of Justice of the EU (CJEU) in protecting the rights of EU citizens with disabilities. Since the CRPD is the first human rights treaty that the European Union has concluded, this textbook critically assesses the status and effects of the CRPD in the EU legal order. The third part of the textbook covers the role of regional systems, such as the CoE and the Inter-American and African human rights systems, as well as other transnational regimes, in protecting and promoting the rights of people with disabilities.

The textbook is premised on the idea that it should address a diverse readership. It aims to be usable by students at different levels, while maintaining academic rigour. Written in an accessible style, the textbook blends legal and policy analysis, and it makes extensive references to relevant primary and secondary sources. All topics included in the book are broken down into easy-to-read sections, with clear headings. In addition, the textbook aims to maintain a balance between theory and practice. This combination makes the textbook suitable for purely legal programmes as well as interdisciplinary courses in disability studies.

The textbook includes special pedagogical features, summaries and activities. Textboxes and extracts from various sources are also included. In addition, the textbook contains several flow charts and diagrams, which are specifically designed to facilitate the understanding of key issues, and 'thinking points' for reflection, in order to test one's knowledge and foster critical thinking. Further reading lists on selected topics are supplied at the end of each chapter, to deepen the reader's knowledge. On the whole, the textbook aims at inspiring students to reflect on the *status quo* of the law and to challenge existing paradigms, motivating them to explore the subject matter in a deeper manner.

It is important to point out that this textbook builds directly on the authors' teaching experience in both undergraduate and postgraduate classes, as well as their experience with students from different cultural and linguistic backgrounds. In order to accommodate diverse learning styles, the textbook strikes a careful balance between the need to address technical topics in a comprehensive fashion and the need to ensure readability. It is intended to be a flexible instrument that is targeted at introducing the foundations of disability law and policy and, at the same time, presenting specialist knowledge and highlighting current developments in the field.

This textbook is the product of a close collaboration between the authors and of a joint process of reflection and elaboration. However, Andrea Broderick wrote Chapters 2, 4, 6, 8, 11 and 14, while Delia Ferri wrote Chapters 3, 5, 7, 10, 12 and 15. This preface, the introductory chapter as well as Chapters 1, 9 and 13 have been written jointly by the authors.

Finally, it is important to bear in mind that this textbook takes into account legal developments and judicial decisions up to 1 December 2018.

ACKNOWLEDGEMENTS

We first spoke about writing a textbook on disability law and policy three years ago, in order to facilitate the studies of our own students and to allow them to engage in a more comprehensive and cross-cutting manner with the rights of persons with disabilities. The process of writing this textbook has been a long and demanding one, but we are extremely proud of the fact that we have compiled the first academic textbook on international and European disability law. This textbook is being published at an opportune moment in time, ten years after the entry into force of the United Nations Convention on the Rights of Persons with Disabilities. We feel that this is the ideal moment to take stock of the extent to which the Convention has influenced regional and domestic legal and policy systems, as well as the system of international human rights protection on the whole.

Compiling this volume was indeed a challenging endeavour, but we would not have been able to do so without the support of the many people with whom we have worked closely along the way. We are indebted, first of all, to the wonderful academics who have inspired us, although in very different ways and capacities, to pursue research in the field of disability law: Professor Lisa Waddington, Professor Anna Lawson and Professor Gerard Quinn. Your work in the field is much admired. Special thanks also go to the three anonymous reviewers who helped to streamline the research objectives at the beginning of the writing process, and to the four anonymous reviewers who gave their helpful feedback on selected chapters at a later stage.

This book would not have been possible without the support of Marta Wallowiak of Cambridge University Press, who strongly believed in the project from its inception and supported us in advancing the textbook. Our gratitude also goes to Caitlin Lisle, Lisa Pinto, Melissa Shivers and the whole publishing team at Cambridge University Press for their advice and patience as well as their management skills. A word of special thanks also goes to Claire McGovern, PhD candidate at the Department of Law of Maynooth University, who acted as our editorial assistant in the very last phase of the project. In this respect, we also want to acknowledge the support that we attained from the Maynooth University Publication Fund, which allowed us to avail of such editorial assistance and to complete the book in a timely fashion.

Finally, we are very grateful to our close friends and colleagues who supported us along the way. There are too many of you to name, but please know that we appreciate your support more than words can express. Andrea would like to thank her father for setting her on this academic path and for being so wise and supportive. She would like to thank her mother for her untiring support and for her admirable strength of character. Andrea would also like to thank her husband for his patience and dedication. Last but not least, she is indebted to Delia for being not only an inspiring person and a very kind friend but also a commendable academic. Delia's special thanks go to her father for his many words of wisdom and constant support, and to Andrea for being such a fantastic co-author and a wonderful friend.

ABBREVIATIONS

AAC	Alternative and Augmented Communication
ACDEG	African Charter on Democracy, Elections and Governance
ACE	Arts Council of England
ACHPR	African Commission on Human and Peoples' Rights
ACHR	American Convention on Human Rights
ACRWC	African Charter on the Rights and Welfare of the Child
Action Plan	Council of Europe Disability Action Plan 2006–2015
ADA	Americans with Disabilities Act
African Charter	African Charter on Human and Peoples' Rights
African Court	African Court on Human and Peoples' Rights
African Decade	African Decade of Persons with Disabilities 1999–2009
African Decade 2010–2019	African Decade of Persons with Disabilities 2010–2019
African Women's Protocol	Protocol to the African Charter on Human and Peoples' Rights on the Rights of Women in Africa
AHRD	ASEAN Human Rights Declaration
AICHR	ASEAN Intergovernmental Commission on Human Rights
ANED	Academic Network of European Disability Experts
AODA	Accessibility for Ontarians with Disabilities Act
ARI	African Rehabilitation Institute
ASEAN	Association of Southeast Asian Nations
AT	Assistive Technologies
AU	African Union
AYC	African Youth Charter
Auslan	Australian Sign Language
AVMS	Audiovisual Media Services Directive
Bali Declaration	Bali Declaration on the Enhancement of the Role and Participation of the Persons with Disabilities in ASEAN Community
B2C	Business-to-Consumers

CAHDPH	*Comité Ad Hoc sur les droits des personnes handicapées* (Ad-Hoc Committee of Experts on the Rights of Persons with Disabilities)
CAT	Convention against Torture and Other Cruel, Inhuman or Degrading Treatment or Punishment
CEDAW	Convention on the Elimination of All Forms of Discrimination against Women
CEDAW Committee	Committee on the Elimination of Discrimination against Women
CEDDIS	*Comité Interamericano para la Eliminación de Todas las Formas de Discriminación contra las Personas con Discapacidad* (Inter-American Committee for the Elimination of All Forms of Discrimination against Persons with Disabilities)
CEN	European Committee for Standardization
CENELEC	European Committee for Electrotechnical Standardization
CERD	International Convention on the Elimination of All Forms of Racial Discrimination
CESCR	UN Committee on Economic, Social and Cultural Rights
CHRC	Canadian Human Rights Commission
CIADDIS	*Convención Interamericana para la Eliminación de Todas las Formas de Discriminación contra las Personas con Discapacidad* (Inter-American Convention on the Elimination of All Forms of Discrimination against Persons with Disabilities)
CJEU	Court of Justice of the European Union
CoE	Council of Europe
CoE CoHR	Council of Europe Commissioner for Human Rights
CoM	Committee of Ministers of the Council of Europe
Continental Plan	Continental Plan of Action of the African Decade of Persons with Disabilities 2010-2019
COs	Concluding Observations
CRC	UN Convention on the Rights of the Child
CRC Committee	Committee on the Rights of the Child
CRPD	UN Convention on the Rights of Persons with Disabilities
CRPD Committee	UN Committee on the Rights of Persons with Disabilities
CRTH	Centre de Ressources Théâtre et Handicap
CteAT	UN Committee against Torture
DGCS	Directorate-General for Development Cooperation
DPOs	Disabled Peoples' Organisations

EAA	European Accessibility Act
EAFRD	European Agricultural Fund for Rural Development
EASPD	European Association of Service Providers
EC	European Community
ECHR	European Convention on Human Rights
ECSR	European Committee of Social Rights
ECtHR	European Court of Human Rights
EDF	European Disability Forum
EDS	European Disability Strategy 2010–2020
EEC	European Economic Community
EEOC	Equal Employment Opportunity Commission
EFA	Education for All
EIDD	European Institute for Design and Disability
EMFF	European Maritime and Fisheries Fund
ENIL	European Network on Independent Living
EPSR	European Pillar of Social Rights
ERDF	European Regional Development Fund
ESC	European Social Charter
ESCAP	UN Economic and Social Commission for Asia and the Pacific
ESCWA	UN Economic and Social Commission for Western Asia
ESF	European Social Fund
ESOs	European Standardisation Organisations
ETSI	European Telecommunications Standards Institute
ETUC	European Trade Union Confederation
EU	European Union
EU CFR	Charter of Fundamental Rights of the European Union
EU DAP	European Union Disability Action Plan
EURES	Regulation on a European Network of Employment Services
FRA	European Union Agency for Fundamental Rights
GBER	General Block Exemption Regulation
GDP	Gross Domestic Products
HRC	Human Rights Committee
HRW	Human Rights Watch
IACHR	Inter-American Commission on Human Rights
IACtHR	Inter-American Court of Human Rights
IAHRS	Inter-American System for the Protection of Human Rights
ICCPR	International Covenant on Civil and Political Rights
ICESCR	International Covenant on Economic, Social and Cultural Rights

ICF	International Classification of Functioning, Disability and Health
ICIDH	International Classification of Impairments, Disabilities and Handicaps
ICT	Information and Communications Technologies
IDC	International Disability Caucus
IEC	International Electronic Commission
ILO	International Labour Organization
Incheon Strategy	Incheon Strategy to 'Make the Right Real' for Persons with Disabilities in Asia and the Pacific
INGOs	International Non-Governmental Organisations
ISO	International Organization for Standardization
IVF	In vitro fertilisation
Kampala Convention	AU Convention on Internally Displaced Persons in Africa
LAS	League of Arab States
LFS-AHM	EU Labour force survey
MCSS	Multi-Country Survey Study on Health and Responsiveness
MDAC	Mental Disability Advocacy Center
MDGs	Millennium Development Goals
MDRI	Mental Disability Rights International
Mobilisation Framework	Mobilisation Framework of the ASEAN Decade
MoU	Memorandum of Understanding
NCVS	National Crime Victimization Survey
NHRIs	National Human Rights Institutions
NGOs	Non-Governmental Organisations
OAS	Organization of American States
OAS Charter	Charter of the Organization of American States
OECD	Organisation for Economic Co-operation and Development
OHCHR	Office of the United Nations High Commissioner for Human Rights
OIE	International Organisation of Employers
OJ	Official Journal of the European Union
OP-CRPD	Optional Protocol to the Convention
PA	Parliamentary Assembly of the Council of Europe
PAD	Program of Action for the Decade of the Americas for the Rights and Dignity of Persons with Disabilities
PO	Personal Ombudsmen
PWDA	People with Disability Australia

Revised Charter	Revised European Social Charter
RPDA Protocol	Protocol to the African Charter on Human and Peoples' Rights on the Rights of Persons with Disabilities in Africa
SAM	State Aid Modernisation
SCTS	Scottish Courts and Tribunals Service
SDGs	Sustainable Development Goals
SSOs	Standard-Setting Organisations
Standard Rules	Standard Rules on the Equalization of Opportunities for Persons with Disabilities
TEN-T	Trans-European Transport Network
TEU	Treaty on European Union
TFEU	Treaty on the Functioning of the European Union
TSI	Technical Specifications for Interoperability
UD	Universal Design
UDHR	Universal Declaration of Human Rights
UN	United Nations
UNCHR	UN Commission on Human Rights
UNDG	UN Development Group
UNDP	UN Development Programme
UNESCO	UN Educational, Scientific and Cultural Organization
UNGA	UN General Assembly
UNPRPD	UN Partnership on the Rights of Persons with Disabilities
UPIAS	Union of Physically Impaired People Against Segregation
USID	User-Sensitive Inclusive Design
WDE	World Declaration on Education
WG	Working Group
WHO	World Health Organization
WIPO	World Intellectual Property Organization
WPA	World Programme of Action Concerning Disabled Persons
1996 Strategy	1996 European Community Disability Strategy

TABLE OF LEGISLATION

INTERNATIONAL AND REGIONAL INSTRUMENTS

EUROPEAN UNION

Treaties

Regulations

Directives

Decisions

NATIONAL LEGISLATION

Austria

Bulgaria

Canada

Estonia

Finland

France

Gambia

Germany

Hungary

Ireland

Mauritius

Netherlands

Norway

Oman

South Africa

Spain

United Kingdom

United States

Venezuela

TABLE OF CASES

INTERNATIONAL AND REGIONAL CASES

African Commission of Human and People's Rights

African Court on Human and Peoples' Rights

CRPD Committee

European Committee of Social Rights

European Court of Human Rights

European Court of Justice

Inter-American Court of Human Rights

NATIONAL CASES

Australia

Belgium

Canada

United Kingdom

FIGURES

Introduction

1 CENTRAL ISSUES OF THE TEXTBOOK

This textbook conceptualises disability law as a comprehensive body of rules that has matured as a coherent discipline. Specifically, this book addresses international and European disability law and policy, a discipline which has been influenced by disability studies, the disability rights movements and disabled peoples' organisations (DPOs). The textbook highlights, in a comparative fashion, the interaction between different sources of law and legal systems. It examines the most recent disability-related developments at the international, European Union (EU) and regional levels, with the United Nations Convention on the Rights of Persons with Disabilities[1] (CRPD or the 'Convention') serving as the global standard on disability rights.

This textbook maintains a balance between theory and practice and focuses on the relevant legal frameworks, their interpretation and application, as well as on current challenges in the realm of international and regional policy-making in the disability context.

This chapter introduces the reader to the textbook itself and to the novelties and intricacies inherent in international and European disability law and policy. In that regard, the chapter begins with an overview of the developments that led to the emergence of disability law as an academic discipline. Thereafter, the chapter briefly discusses how the language of disability has changed over time. It then goes on to provide an account of the aims and objectives of this textbook, and it outlines the guiding perspective and the methodological approach adopted in the book. Finally, the chapter ends with an outline of the structure of the textbook as a whole.

[1] UN Convention on the Rights of Persons with Disabilities, 13 December 2006, in force 3 May 2008, UN Doc. A/RES/61/106, Annex I.

2 DISABILITY LAW AS AN ACADEMIC DISCIPLINE

In the last decade, disability law has emerged as a distinct and dynamic field of international and European action, and as an evolving academic discipline. This is part of a broader phenomenon related to the expansion and specialisation of international law, which has gradually been divided into various sub-disciplines (e.g. human rights law, international trade law, international investment law and international environmental law, among others). Each area has its own rules, principles and institutions. At the European level, the emergence of disability law is also linked to the development of the EU and the expansion of its competences.

The emergence of international disability law as an academic discipline correlates with the emergence of a comprehensive disability agenda within the United Nations (UN), culminating in the approval of the first comprehensive legally binding instrument on disability rights – the CRPD. The Convention, adopted by the UN General Assembly (UNGA) in 2006, entered into force in 2008, together with its Optional Protocol (OP-CRPD).[2] Under the OP-CRPD, the UN Committee on the Rights of Persons with Disabilities (CRPD Committee) is charged with the task of considering communications from, or on behalf of, individuals or groups of individuals subject to its jurisdiction who claim to be victims of a violation by a State Party of the provisions of the Convention.

The CRPD is the first international human rights treaty that seeks to ensure the protection and promotion of the rights of persons with disabilities on an equal basis with others. The primary aim of the CRPD was, arguably, not to create new rights but to ensure that existing human rights were made equally effective for persons with disabilities. However, as Mégret points out and as will be discussed in the first part of this textbook, the CRPD 'also subtly reformulates and extends existing human rights to take into account the specific experience of persons with disability'.[3]

As will be further examined in Chapters 1 and 3 of this textbook, the CRPD also represents the culmination of previous efforts to shift the perception of disability from the outdated individual, or medical, model to the social model of disability. The Convention embodies what can be termed the 'social-contextual model of disability'.[4] That model goes further than the 'pure' social model, which attracted many criticisms on account of the fact that it focused

[2] Optional Protocol to the Convention on the Rights of Persons with Disabilities, note 1, Annex II.

[3] Frederic Mégret, 'The Disabilities Convention: Human Rights of Persons with Disabilities or Disability Rights?' (2008) 30(2) *Human Rights Quarterly* 494. See below Chapter 3, section 3.

[4] Andrea Broderick, *The Long and Winding Road to Equality and Inclusion for Persons with Disabilities: The United Nations Convention on the Rights of Persons with Disabilities* (Cambridge-Antwerp: Intersentia, 2015), p. 77.

on societal barriers (physical, attitudinal and legislative, among others) and neglected the role of impairment in disabling the individual concerned.[5] According to the social-contextual model, disability is perceived as an interactive process between people with impairments and societal barriers. This contrasts sharply with the medical model of disability, which views disability as a 'problem' stemming from the functional limitations of the disabled person rather than as a societal problem arising from disabling and discriminatory barriers. The paradigm shift from the medical model to the social model has also been accompanied by a shift from a social welfare perspective that viewed persons with disabilities as objects of charity towards a human rights-based approach to disability. These paradigm shifts are encapsulated in the CRPD, which requires States Parties to ensure the provision of reasonable accommodation (i.e. adjustments to existing environments, policies and practices, with a view to enabling the participation and inclusion of disabled individuals in society); to take measures to facilitate accessibility; and to raise awareness of the capabilities of disabled persons.

The CRPD attracted a high number of signatories and ratifications on a global scale within a short period of time. The EU officially became a Party to the CRPD on 23 December 2010.[6] It became the first regional integration organisation to ratify a human rights treaty and to take on its binding obligations.

The EU's accession to the CRPD has marked a definite step forward in the development of a comprehensive EU disability policy informed by the social model.[7] As Chapter 10 will discuss in detail, the CRPD has become an integral part of EU law and, due to its sub-constitutional status, it now represents the benchmark against which EU disability initiatives must be assessed. On foot of the momentum generated by the CRPD, the EU has adopted the European Disability Strategy 2010–2020 (EDS 2010–2020),[8] which attempts to mainstream disability in all EU policy fields and aims to ensure that people with disabilities can exercise their rights on an equal basis with others. The EU legal framework currently includes disability-related provisions in various areas,

[5] For a critique of the social model of disability, see, among others, Deborah Marks, 'Dimensions of Oppression: Theorising the Embodied Subject' (1999) 14(5) *Disability and Society* 611.

[6] Council Decision 2010/48/EC of 26 November 2009 concerning the conclusion, by the European Community, of the United Nations Convention on the Rights of Persons with Disabilities, OJ 2010 No. L23/35. See below Chapter 10.

[7] In this book, the social-contextual model is referred to in connection with the CRPD, denoting the focus of the CRPD on the individual's impairment in interaction with external barriers in society. By contrast, the social model is referred to in the chapters on EU law, since, as will be argued in Chapter 11, the case law emerging from the Court of Justice of the European Union (CJEU) appears not to be fully in line with the CRPD's social-contextual model.

[8] Commission Communication of 15 November 2010, 'European Disability Strategy 2010–2020: A Renewed Commitment to a Barrier-Free Europe', SEC (2010) 1324 final.

such as in the fields of transport; public procurement; and electronic communications, networks and services, among others. However, at the time of writing this textbook, the Employment Equality Directive,[9] which requires EU Member States to adopt legislation prohibiting discrimination on the basis of disability in the context of employment and vocational training, remains the primary legislative enactment protecting and promoting the rights of people with disabilities. Significant reforms are underway in the EU in the context of disability. A directive on the accessibility of the websites of public sector bodies was approved in 2016.[10] A proposal for a new non-discrimination directive is under discussion, to tackle discrimination, *inter alia*, on the basis of disability outside the labour market.[11] Moreover, a 'European Accessibility Act' (EAA),[12] which would impose obligations to provide accessible goods and services, is, at this moment in time, in the final stage of the legislative procedure.

There have also been considerable reforms in the disability context within the Council of Europe (CoE) in the period preceding the CRPD and in the period following its adoption. Furthermore, there has been a significant increase in the amount of disability-related cases heard by the European Court of Human Rights (ECtHR), and the Court is increasingly referring to the CRPD as a guide to interpreting the rights contained in the European Convention on Human Rights (ECHR). Regional systems for the protection of human rights – the inter-American and African systems – as well as other transnational regimes, such as the League of Arab States and the Association of Southeast Asian Nations (ASEAN) are also demonstrating an increased recognition of the rights of persons with disabilities, especially since the entry into force of the CRPD.

In attempting to situate disability in a global context, the textbook is underpinned by an understanding of the power relations between the Global North (i.e. Western Europe and North America) and the multifaceted Global South,[13] and of the complexities related to socio-economic development in

[9] Council Directive 2000/78/EC of 27 November 2000 on establishing a general framework for equal treatment in employment and occupation, OJ 2000 No. L303/16.

[10] Directive (EU) 2016/2102 of the European Parliament and of the Council of 26 October 2016 on the accessibility of the websites and mobile applications of public sector bodies, OJ 2016 No. L327/1.

[11] Proposal for a Council Directive on implementing the principle of equal treatment between persons irrespective of religion or belief, disability, age or sexual orientation, COM (2008) 426 final.

[12] Proposal for a Directive of the European Parliament and of the Council on the approximation of the laws, regulations and administrative provisions of the Member States as regards the accessibility requirements for products and services, COM (2015) 615 final.

[13] The term 'Global South' is used to refer to post-colonial territories and peoples who are negatively impacted by contemporary capitalist globalisation. For discussion of the term, see, among others, Russell West-Pavlov, 'Toward the Global South', in Russell West-Pavlov (ed.), *The Global South and Literature* (Cambridge: Cambridge University Press, 2018),

post-colonial contexts.[14] While the textbook does not undertake an extensive analysis of the academic discourse related to development and disability, it provides a comprehensive account of current issues in disability law and policy at the international, European and regional levels. It also highlights and critically analyses the various challenges encountered to date and those which may be encountered in the future in the implementation of the CRPD.

3 DISABILITY LAW AND THE LANGUAGE OF DISABILITY

The adoption of the CRPD, together with various developments that took place before the CRPD,[15] has made disability a human rights issue. These developments in disability law have contributed to extending the 'language of rights' to disability law and to placing disability firmly within the realm of human rights discourse. This 'language of rights' goes hand in hand with the use of the so-called 'people-first language',[16] which is currently used in several international law documents, in the CRPD itself[17] and in the English versions of EU legislation and case law.[18] The Convention refers to 'persons with disabilities', as did the Standard Rules on the Equalization of Opportunities for Persons with Disabilities (Standard Rules),[19] which were adopted by the UN before the CRPD.

The language of academic discourse on disability has greatly evolved. Linguistic stereotyping and the use of negative terms relating to disability have long been a focus of scholarly attention and criticism. Furthermore, the use of words and phrases such as 'the retarded', 'the handicapped', 'mentally

pp. 1–20. See also Anne Garland Mahler, 'Global South' (2017) *Oxford Bibliographies in Literary and Critical Theory*; Vera Chouinard, 'Living on the Global Peripheries of Law: Disability Human Rights Law in Principle and in Practice in the Global South' (2018) 7(1) *Laws* 8.

[14] Benedicte Ingstad, 'Disability in the Developing World', in Gary Albrecht, Katherine Seelman and Michael Bury (eds.), *Handbook of Disability Studies* (California: Sage, 2001), pp. 219–51; Helen Meekosha, 'Decolonising Disability: Thinking and Acting Globally' (2011) **26**(6) *Disability and Society* 667; Clare Barker, 'Interdisciplinary Dialogues: Disability and Postcolonial Studies' (2010) 3 *Review of Disability Studies: An International Journal* 6; Shaun Grech, 'Disability, Poverty and Development: Critical Reflections on the Majority World Debate' (2009) **24**(6) *Disability and Society* 771.

[15] For further discussion on these developments, see below Chapter 2.

[16] Phil Foreman, 'Language and Disability' (2005) **30**(1) *Journal of Intellectual and Developmental Disability* 57.

[17] The French text of the CRPD still uses the word '*personnes handicapées*'. For an overview of the CRPD in French, see Mamoud Zani, 'La Convention de l'O.N.U. relative aux droits des personnes handicapées' (2008) 3 *Revue de droit international et de droit comparé* 551.

[18] In the French and Italian versions of EU legislation (e.g. the Employment Equality Directive), the words '*handicap*' and '*personnes handicapées*' are still used.

[19] Standard Rules on the Equalization of Opportunities for Persons with Disabilities, 20 December 1993, UN Doc. A/RES/48/96.

sub-normal' and 'mental deficiency' (all of which evoked pity, fear or even shame) have almost disappeared. Anglo-Saxon literature tends to refer to a 'disabled person', evoking the role of societal and environmental barriers in disabling the individual. However, several scholars, including legal scholars, prefer to use the so-called 'people-first language', referring to a 'person with a physical disability', a 'child with an intellectual disability', a 'person with Down syndrome', a 'person with a learning disability' or, most frequently, simply a 'person with a disability'. This language reflects the view that disability is just one of an individual's many characteristics rather than his or her defining characteristic, or his or her problem, and does not imply any generalised lack of ability or incapacity. The language of rights and 'people-first language' are in accordance with the CRPD.

In this book, the term 'persons/people with disabilities' will be used for the most part. The term 'disabled persons/people' might be used occasionally, but always in line with the idea that people who have (or are perceived to have) 'impairments' are 'disabled' by social structures and systems. This textbook fully embraces the language of human rights and, in that vein, it avoids language that presents people with disabilities as victims of their impairment, who are in need of assistance.

In line with the CRPD, this textbook does not discuss the relevant legal instruments by type of disability. It does, however, embrace the view that disability can arise from the interaction between different impairments (i.e. physical, mental, intellectual or sensory impairments) and external barriers. While acknowledging that terminology can be very problematic, since meanings vary from jurisdiction to jurisdiction, this textbook refers to intellectual disabilities in its broadest meaning, encompassing cognitive and learning disabilities. The use of the term 'mental' in the CRPD seems to refer to persons with psychosocial disabilities. In that vein, this textbook also uses the term 'psychosocial disability' to refer to psychological (mental) impairments, which, in interaction with other barriers, give rise to a disability. As noted by Bell and Waddington, 'examples of conditions that may give rise to a psychosocial disability include: depression, anxiety, stress, addictions, phobias, eating disorders, schizophrenia, post-traumatic stress disorder, bipolar disorder and personality disorders'.[20]

4 AIMS AND OBJECTIVES OF THE TEXTBOOK

The primary aim of this textbook is to inform the studies of university students who follow basic and advanced programmes in international and European

[20] Mark Bell and Lisa Waddington, *The Employment Equality Directive and Supporting People with Psychosocial Disabilities in the Workplace: A Legal Analysis of the Situation in the EU Member States* (Luxembourg: Publications Office of the European Union, 2016), p. 7.

disability law and policy at both undergraduate and postgraduate level. It is intended to be a flexible instrument, written in an accessible style for students generally. However, it is also meant to serve as a useful resource for professional courses and for a range of different educational initiatives and training in the field.

The textbook aims to impart basic knowledge to readers by introducing topics. At the same time, it presents specialist knowledge and outlines current developments and controversial issues in the field. This textbook interacts with the reader and complements existing learning/teaching strategies, including problem-based learning systems. In that regard, the textbook contains a variety of resources and activities, such as problem questions ('group projects'), essay questions and 'thinking points' for reflection, in order to test the reader's knowledge and foster critical thinking.

A further objective of this textbook is to stimulate independent research. For that purpose, further reading lists are provided at the end of each chapter on selected topics, in order to deepen the reader's knowledge. All of those readings are in English, but they have been chosen to be accessible to non-native readers. Additional scholarship in languages other than English is referred to in the footnotes in various parts of the textbook.

Apart from its primary objective to inform the studies of university students, this textbook is also intended as a comprehensive guide to the field of international and European disability law and policy for practitioners, policy-makers and non-governmental actors. By virtue of the large number of case studies and the extensive legal and policy analysis included, lawyers and policy-makers can use this textbook to advance the disability rights agenda at the national, EU and international levels.

On the whole, this textbook can be seen as a valuable tool that can be used to improve the understanding of the rights of persons with disabilities and the challenges associated with the practical implementation of those rights.

5 GUIDING PERSPECTIVE AND METHODOLOGY OF THE TEXTBOOK

Against this background and with the foregoing objectives in mind, this textbook adopts a traditional legal doctrinal approach to jurisprudence and legal literature. An extensive range of primary sources is drawn on in the book and critically analysed. The textbook also builds upon a wide range of secondary sources. To achieve a global focus, it refers to scholarship in English and other languages.

Positioning itself primarily as an educational tool, this textbook is designed to support different teaching activities and styles. It is informed by the

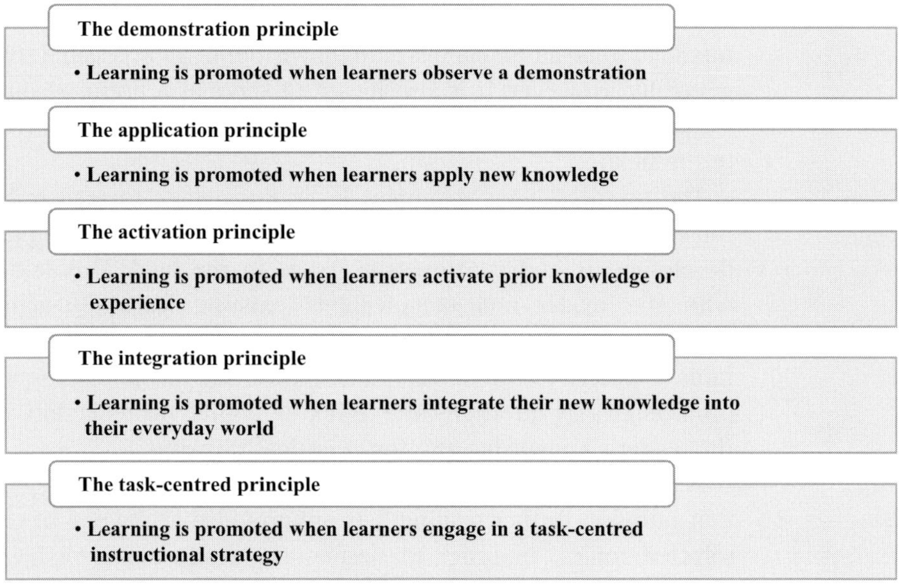

Figure A Merrill's Pedagogy

principle of constructive alignment.[21] Thus, it aims to encourage coherence between intended learning outcomes and teaching as well as assessment strategies.[22] The textbook also attempts to accommodate different learning styles and techniques,[23] based on the understanding of learning and teaching as a student-centred activity. Furthermore, it is informed by the five-pronged approach to pedagogy advocated by Merrill, as illustrated by Figure A.[24]

[21] See, for instance, John Biggs, *Teaching for Quality Learning at University – What the Student Does* (Buckingham: Open University Press, 2003); see also John Biggs and Catherine Tang, *Applying Constructive Alignment To Outcomes-Based Teaching and Learning* (2009) available at https://drjj.uitm.edu.my/DRJJ/MQAGGPAS-Apr2011/What-is-CA-biggs-tang.pdf. Tang and Biggs affirm that the term 'constructive' refers to 'the idea that students construct meaning through relevant learning activities'. Furthermore, the term 'alignment' refers to 'the situation when teaching and learning activities, and assessment tasks, are aligned to the intended learning outcomes'.

[22] John Biggs and Catherine Tang, *Applying Constructive Alignment to Outcomes-Based Teaching and Learning*, note 21.

[23] John Dunlosky, Katherine Rawson, Elizabeth Marsh, Mitchell Nathan and Daniel Willingham, 'Improving Students' Learning with Effective Learning Techniques: Promising Directions from Cognitive and Educational Psychology' (2013) **14**(1) *Psychological Science in the Public Interest* 14.

[24] David Merrill, 'First Principles of Instruction', in Charles Reigeluth and Alison Carr (eds.), *Instructional Design Theories and Models: Building a Common Knowledge Base* (New York: Routledge Publishers, 2009), vol. 3; David Merrill, 'First Principles of Instruction: A Synthesis', in Robert Reiser and John Dempsey (eds.), *Trends and Issues in Instructional Design and Technology*, 2nd edn (Upper Saddle River, NJ: Merrill-Prentice Hall, 2007), vol. 2, pp. 62–71.

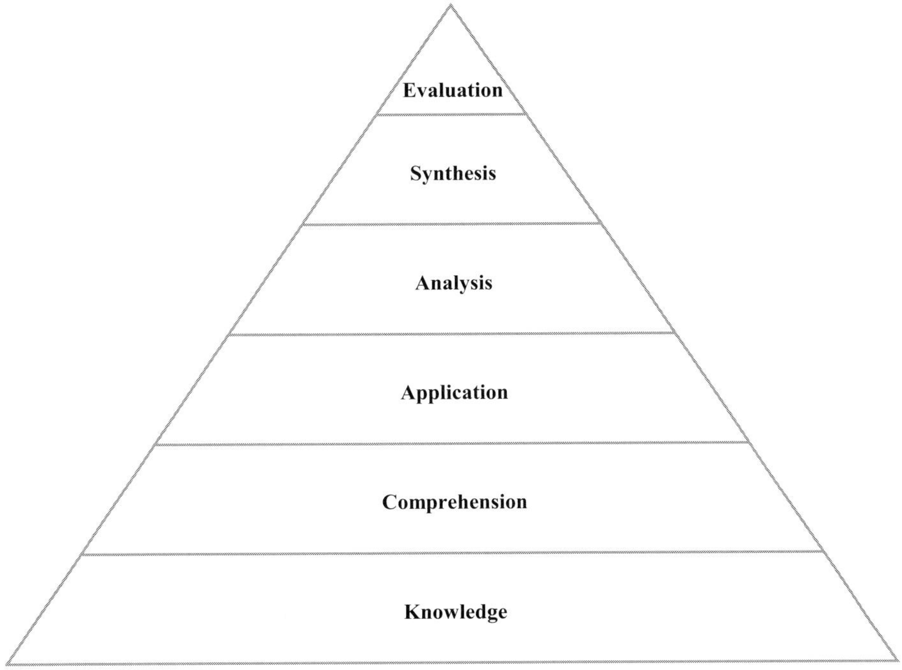

Figure B Learning Levels

This textbook is also informed by Bloom's taxonomy[25] of educational objectives, and it is written in accordance with the six levels of intellectual behaviour that are deemed to be important for learning in the cognitive domain (Figure B).

This textbook works from the starting point of the various pedagogical theories highlighted above, in order to provide the reader with the most reliable and comprehensive knowledge in the field of international and European disability law and policy.

In line with the approach adopted, the textbook includes specific pedagogical features. At the beginning of every chapter, clear learning outcomes are delineated, and, at the end of each chapter, a brief summary is provided, which sets out the key issues and the most important concepts discussed. In addition, the textbook includes special 'Did you know that . . .?' boxes and other textboxes. These contain, for example, extracts from soft law, general comments of UN bodies, literature in the field and relevant policy documents, as well as case studies on specific countries. The sources for all of the

[25] Benjamin Bloom, Max Engelhart, Edward Furst, Walker Hill and David Krathwohl, *Taxonomy of Educational Objectives: The Classification of Educational Goals*, Handbook I: Cognitive Domain (New York: David McKay Company, 1956). For a simplified explanation of the taxonomy, see, *inter alia*, www.nwlink.com/~donclark/hrd/bloom.html.

material drawn on are included in the corresponding textboxes. The textbook also contains 'thinking points' in the form of bubbles. These are designed to foster reflection and to enhance critical thinking. The number of pedagogical features included in each chapter varies according to the nature of the topic under discussion. Additionally, as mentioned above, every chapter includes activities to help students to reflect on the content, in line with Merrill's application and activation principles. Review questions, essay questions and group projects support the student's learning experience and help students to test their knowledge and understanding, to apply the new knowledge that they have acquired and also to activate prior experience.

To increase readability, the textbook includes a list of abbreviations and acronyms at the outset. In addition, in every chapter, acronyms and abbreviations are spelled out, to facilitate ease of reading.[26]

6 STRUCTURE OF THE TEXTBOOK

This textbook is divided into three main parts. The first part addresses the international framework on disability law and policy, focusing specifically on the CRPD. The second part addresses EU disability law and policy, while the third part centres on regional systems for the protection of disability rights.

Part I of the textbook begins with Chapter 1, which builds the foundations of the textbook as a whole. It addresses the various theoretical models of disability that have been delineated by scholars in the field. It also outlines several core foundational themes in disability law and policy. Finally, the chapter briefly describes the emergence of international disability law.

Chapter 2 addresses the protection of the rights of persons with disabilities under binding international human rights law before the adoption of the CRPD. In that regard, it draws links between human rights law and disability, and it outlines the role of the UN, the International Labour Organization (ILO) and the World Health Organization (WHO) in the development of binding standards for disabled persons.

Chapter 3 provides a comprehensive overview of the negotiation sessions that led to the conclusion of the CRPD. It also provides an account of the structure of the CRPD, its main features and its component parts. Another key focus of Chapter 3 is the monitoring system of the CRPD. Finally, Chapter 3

[26] With the exception of: the United Nations, which is referred to as the 'UN'; the UN Convention on the Rights of Persons with Disabilities, which is referred to as the 'CRPD' throughout the textbook; and the European Union, which is always indicated as 'EU'.

turns its attention to the pivotal role played by persons with disabilities and DPOs in implementing the Convention.

Chapter 4 examines the CRPD's equality and non-discrimination norms. In that connection, an overview is provided of the constituent elements of Article 5 CRPD. The concept of 'reasonable accommodation' is discussed in detail, including the definition and scope of the duty, its objectives and limitations. Thereafter, the concept of 'positive action' is examined. Attention is also paid to the CRPD's provisions related to multiple and intersectional discrimination. The chapter concludes with a theoretical and comparative perspective on the model of equality embodied in the CRPD.

Chapter 5 addresses one of the core principles of the CRPD, namely accessibility. The chapter starts off by addressing the concept of 'accessibility' generally, before focusing on the scope of the accessibility norm in the CRPD. The chapter then links back to Chapter 4 in dealing with the relationship between the duty to reasonably accommodate and the accessibility obligation.

Chapter 6 provides an account of the core norm of legal capacity. It focuses on supported decision-making, and it outlines the connection between legal capacity and independent living, as well as family life.

Chapter 7 focuses on access to justice, and it also addresses the rights of people with disabilities as victims of crimes or as offenders.

Chapter 8 discusses the right to work. It focuses on Article 27 CRPD, which requires States Parties to create an open, inclusive and accessible labour market. The chapter also examines the types of positive measures that States Parties to the CRPD should implement to promote employment of persons with disabilities.

Chapter 9 concludes Part I of the textbook. It addresses core policy issues in relation to a selection of CRPD rights, namely, the rights to education, access to culture and political participation.

Part II of the textbook deals with the EU framework of disability law and policy.

Chapter 10 provides an account of current EU disability law and policy. Since the CRPD is the first human rights treaty that the EU has concluded, the chapter also provides a critical assessment of the status of the CRPD in the EU legal order. Additionally, it focuses on the implementation of the Convention at the EU level.

Chapter 11 examines the relevance, from a disability perspective, of the Employment Equality Directive and the proposed non-discrimination directive. It discusses relevant CJEU case law on disability pre- and post-CRPD ratification.

Chapter 12 links back to the CRPD's core obligations, by dealing with accessibility issues at the EU level and examining pertinent provisions included in EU legislation.

The third and final part of the textbook focuses on regional disability law and policy.

Chapter 13 evaluates the role of the CoE in shaping European disability policy. The chapter addresses the disability case law of the ECtHR. The chapter also analyses the provisions of the Revised European Social Charter (Revised Charter) and the views of the European Committee of Social Rights (ECSR) as they apply to disability.

Chapter 14 deals with the key features of the inter-American system in protecting and promoting the rights of people with disabilities.

Finally, Chapter 15 outlines developments in the African human rights system, in the League of Arab States and in the Asian transnational regime as they relate to disability law and policy.

Part I

The International Framework

1 Building the Foundations: Disability Theory and Core Themes

LEARNING OUTCOMES

- ✓ Describe the key models of disability.
- ✓ Identify turning points in the process of elaboration of different models of disability.
- ✓ Understand the reasons for the development of the social model of disability.
- ✓ Comprehend the main criticisms of the social model of disability.
- ✓ Identify the significance of the human rights model of disability.
- ✓ Understand the relevance of the capabilities approach in relation to disability.
- ✓ Demonstrate awareness of the core foundational themes in the field of disability law and policy.
- ✓ Describe the emergence of disability law as a field of study and practical application.

[Disability stems from] the failure of a structured social environment to adjust to the needs and aspirations of citizens with disabilities rather than from the inability of the disabled individual to adapt to the demands of society.[1]

1 INTRODUCTION

In western culture, disability was traditionally viewed as a medical problem or a 'personal tragedy'.[2] In particular, disability was conceived of as an individual deficit that derives from a disease, trauma or health condition that impairs or disrupts physiological or cognitive functioning.[3] This 'medical model' focused on the actual health condition of the person in question and on the treatments that could be provided to 'fix the problem' or alleviate the impairment. As a reaction to the individualised, or medicalised, vision of disability, from the late 1960s onwards, scholars and disability activists elaborated the 'social model of disability', which perceives disability as a societal construction.[4] In particular, disability is viewed under the social model as the consequence of environmental, attitudinal or other barriers. Thus, impairment is seen as comprising the functional limitations of the individual, while disability is conceived of as 'the loss or limitation of opportunities to take part in the normal life of the community on an equal level with others due to physical and social barriers'.[5]

Theoretical reflections on the social model are still evolving, and different conceptualisations of the social model have been developed by various authors. There are several 'social models' of disability that are variants of the primary social model. These include the 'social-contextual' model, the 'legal rights' model, the 'minority group' model and the 'affirmative model' of disability. There are also a number of models of disability that take elements of the medical and social models of disability and integrate them. Two

[1] Harlan Hahn, 'Public Support for Rehabilitation in Programs: The Analysis of US Disability Policy' (1986) 1(2) *Disability and Society* 121, at 128.

[2] Among others, Colin Barnes, 'Understanding the Social Model of Disability: Past, Present and Future', in Nick Watson, Alan Roulstone and Carol Thomas (eds.), *The Routledge Handbook of Disability Studies* (London/New York: Routledge, 2012), pp. 12–29.

[3] See further Charles Drum, 'Models and Approaches to Disability', in Charles Drum, Gloria Krahn and Hank Bersani, *Disability and Public Health* (Washington: American Public Health Association/American Association on Intellectual and Developmental Disabilities, 2009). See also Julie Smart, 'Models of Disability: The Juxtaposition of Biology and Social Construction', in T.F. Riggar and Dennis R. Maki (eds.), *Handbook of Rehabilitation Counseling* (New York: Springer, 2004) pp. 25–49.

[4] See below section 2.2.

[5] Colin Barnes, *Disabled People in Britain and Discrimination* (London: Hurst and Co., 1991).

significant examples are the 'Nagi model'[6] and the 'bio-psycho-social model' of disability, based on the International Classification of Functioning, Disability and Health (ICF) promoted by the World Health Organization (WHO).[7]

The social model has not escaped scholarly criticism.[8] In spite of growing critiques regarding its content, relevance and practical application, it remains the dominant paradigm in understanding disability. It has inspired the disability agenda at the European and international levels for the last thirty years. The CRPD also marks a clear shift away from the individual model of disability towards a social model of disability. During the negotiation sessions leading up to the adoption of the CRPD, States Parties were eager to avoid making reference to the 'pure' social model of disability in the Convention. One of the 'inherent limitations' of a strict version of the social model stems from the fact that it is 'not well disposed to accommodate disadvantages that result directly from an impairment, as opposed to those which arise from a socially-constructed barrier'.[9] The understanding of disability espoused by the Convention is one that is based on the interactional relationship between people with impairments and the wider environment. This has been termed 'a social-contextual understanding of disability'.[10] Consequently, the CRPD recognises that 'disability stems primarily from the failure of the social environment to meet the needs and aspirations of people with impairments'.[11]

This chapter provides the theoretical backdrop to the foregoing developments in international and European disability law and policy. In addition to this brief introduction, the chapter is divided into two main sections. Section 2 focuses on the various theoretical approaches that have dominated the discourse surrounding disability in the last few decades. In section 3, the key

[6] In a nutshell, the 'Nagi model' promotes a social and cultural relativistic view of disability. See Saad Nagi, 'Some Conceptual Issues in Disability and Rehabilitation', in Marvin Sussman (ed.), *Sociology and Rehabilitation* (Washington: American Sociological Association, 1965), pp. 100–13.

[7] For an analysis of the different approaches mentioned, see, among others, Maria Giulia Bernardini, *Disabilità, Giustizia, Diritto. Itinerari tra filosofia del diritto e Disability Studies* (Torino: Giappichelli, 2016), pp. 10 et seq.; on the affirmative model, see John Swain and Sally French, 'Towards an Affirmative Model of Disability' (2000) 15(4) *Disability and Society* 569, at 569.

[8] See below section 2.3.

[9] Andrea Broderick, *The Long and Winding Road to Equality and Inclusion for Persons with Disabilities: The United Nations Convention on the Rights of Persons with Disabilities* (Antwerp: Intersentia, 2015), p. 28; see further on this point, Jenny Morris (ed.), *Pride against Prejudice: Transforming Attitudes to Disability – A Personal Politics of Disability* (London: Women's Press, 1991), p. 10.

[10] Broderick, *The Long and Winding Road to Equality and Inclusion for Persons with Disabilities: The United Nations Convention on the Rights of Persons with Disabilities,* note 9, p. 77.

[11] Lisa Waddington and Andrea Broderick, *Disability Law and the Duty to Reasonably Accommodate Beyond Employment: A Legal Analysis of the Situation in EU Member States* (Luxembourg: Publications Office of the EU, 2016), p. 38.

foundational themes that have inspired developments in disability law and policy at the international and European levels are outlined.

2 THEORETICAL MODELS OF DISABILITY

Although the terminology referring to disability has not always been used consistently in legal scholarship, this section of the chapter aligns to the majority of the existing scholarship and, in that vein, it identifies and analyses four main theoretical models of disability: the medical model (often called the 'charity' or 'individual' model), the social model, the human rights model and the capabilities approach. These models have superseded the oldest paradigm, i.e. the so-called 'moral or religious model' of disability, which still exists in South Asia and in certain parts of Africa.[12] The religious model perceives disability as an act of God, or a curse inflicted upon an individual by an external, supernatural force.[13]

DID YOU KNOW THAT ...?

Models of disability:

provide definitions of disability
are based on (perceived) needs
provide explanations of causal attribution and responsibility attributions
guide the formulation and implementation of policy
are not value neutral
shape the self-identity of people with disabilities
can cause prejudice and discrimination

For further discussion, read Julie Smart, 'Models of Disability: The Juxtaposition of Biology and Social Construction', in T.F. Riggar and Dennis R. Maki (eds.), *Handbook of Rehabilitation Counseling* (New York: Springer, 2004) pp. 25–49.

2.1 The Medical Model of Disability

As outlined above, disability was traditionally conceived of, by academics and professionals alike, as a medical, or individual, welfare issue. The functional limitations of disabled persons were viewed as having flowed directly from a given impairment and, therefore, life situations and outcomes were seen as being directly dependent on the impairment itself. The medical model of

[12] See below Chapter 15.

[13] Arie Rimmerman, *Social Inclusion of Persons with Disabilities: National and International Perspectives* (New York: Cambridge University Press, 2013), p. 24.

disability focuses on the health status or biological characteristics of the individual and on attempts to 'cure' the functional limitations of the disabled person in question, in order to bring the individual in line with the non-disabled 'norm'. Since the medical model views disabled people as being the ultimate source of the 'problem', the primary tools used to drive legal and policy analysis under the medical model are rehabilitation and the prevention of disability.

Within the medical model, structural inequalities and inaccessibility are not taken into account, nor are they addressed as possible factors in the process of disablement. In fact, the medical model requires the disabled individual to fit into society rather than requiring society to adapt to the individual.

Degener[14] summarises the two core features of the medical model of disability as follows:

i. Disabled persons are people in need of shelter and welfare.
ii. Impairment can hinder the exercise and enjoyment of legal capacity.

These assumptions legitimise, on the one hand, segregated facilities for disabled persons, such as special schools, institutions or sheltered employment, and, on the other hand, guardianship laws based on the deprivation of legal capacity. Overall, the result of this approach to disability is segregation from mainstream society, as those who are considered 'deviant' from the norm and 'incompetent' are excluded. The medical model of disability is disempowering, and it reinforces stigmatisation as well as unequal structures in society. It has been criticised for 'its debilitating emphasis on physical limitations and low expectations'.[15]

When legislators and policy-makers rely on medical definitions of disablement, the result is a 'labelling' approach, segregated structures and alternative services. The medical model is often referred to as a 'charity model' because the state has the responsibility to compensate the disabled person through welfare payments.[16]

2.2 The Social Model of Disability

As a result of the weaknesses inherent in the medical model of disability, the social model emerged as the 'Big Idea'[17] of the UK Disabled People's

[14] Theresia Degener, 'Challenges and Compliance of the UN CRPD', in Dorothy Estrada-Tanck (ed.), *Human Rights of Persons with Disabilities in International and EU Law* (AEL Working Papers, 2016/01) available at http://cadmus.eui.eu/bitstream/handle/1814/41985/WP_2016_01.pdf?sequence=1&isAllowed=y.

[15] Simon Brisenden, 'Independent Living and the Medical Model of Disability' (1986) 1(2) *Disability and Society* 173, at 177.

[16] Gerard Quinn and Eilionóir Flynn, 'Transatlantic Borrowings: The Past and Future of EU Non-Discrimination Law and Policy on the Ground of Disability' (2012) 60 *American Journal of Comparative Law* 23, at 23.

[17] Frances Hasler, 'Developments in the Disabled People's Movement', in John Swain, Vic Finkelstein, Sally French and Mike Oliver (eds.), *Disabling Barriers, Enabling Environments* (London: Sage, 1993); see also, Jerry Allen Winter, 'The Development of the Disability Rights Movement as a Social Problem Solver' (2003) 1 *Disability Studies Quarterly* 33.

Movement. The lack of control over the support they received, combined with the restriction of choice, independent living and self-determination, led many disabled individuals to question the principles underlying the medical model.

The social model of disability was first articulated in the mid-1970s by the Union of Physically Impaired People Against Segregation (UPIAS), a British organisation advocating for the rights of people with physical disabilities. Several scholars and activists – such as Michael Oliver, Paul Hunt, Vic Finkelstein, Paul Abberley and Colin Barnes – played central roles in the development and extension of this model to other forms of disability. According to the interpretation provided by UPIAS, society disables people with impairments, and a distinction needs to be made between the 'impairment' itself and the social 'situation' of people with impairments,[18] the latter giving rise to a 'disability'. Under the social model, disabled people are, therefore, viewed as an oppressed group in society.

> Read the full policy statement of UPIAS. Do you agree with its core principles?

In essence, the social model of disability identifies societal barriers (in the form of environmental, attitudinal and legislative obstacles) as the main factor in disabling people with impairments. This is illustrated in Figure 1.1. In other words, a wheelchair user is disabled in circumstances where buildings do not have accessible entrances or where ramps are not provided; and a Deaf person is disabled by virtue of the fact that service providers do not provide devices such as translation services or other aids.

The social model essentially maintains that responsibility lies with national governments and society as a whole to remedy the disadvantage and inequalities faced by persons with disabilities. It mandates that the needs of persons with disabilities are incorporated into all aspects of law- and policy-making. This is achieved through giving voice to, and facilitating the participation of, disabled individuals or their representative organisations in law- and policy-making negotiations.

Lang asserts that the social model 'should not be considered as a monolithic entity, but rather as a cluster of approaches to the understanding of the notion

[18] UPIAS, *Fundamental Principles of Disability* (London: The Disability Alliance, 1975), p. 4.

Figure 1.1 Societal Barriers

of disablement'.[19] The social model is responsible for redefining the concept of 'disability' itself (in terms of the social environment) and also for redefining the responsibility for overcoming disabling factors in society.

While there are several formulations of the social model and there has been fierce discussion among disabled peoples' organisations (DPOs) regarding its correct interpretation, there are several key features common to the variant streams of the social model. These key features are outlined hereunder:

i. The central tenet of the social model of disability is the rejection of impairment as a 'personal tragedy' and the shifting of accountability to national governments to rectify disabling barriers as a matter of social justice. Disabled people are now entitled to provision as a matter of right, not charity.

[19] Raymond Lang, 'The Development and Critique of the Social Model of Disability' (University of East Anglia, 2001), p. 2, available at www.ucl.ac.uk/lc-ccr/lccstaff/raymond-lang/DEVELOPMMENT_AND_CRITIQUE_OF_THE_SOCIAL_MODEL_OF_D.pdf.

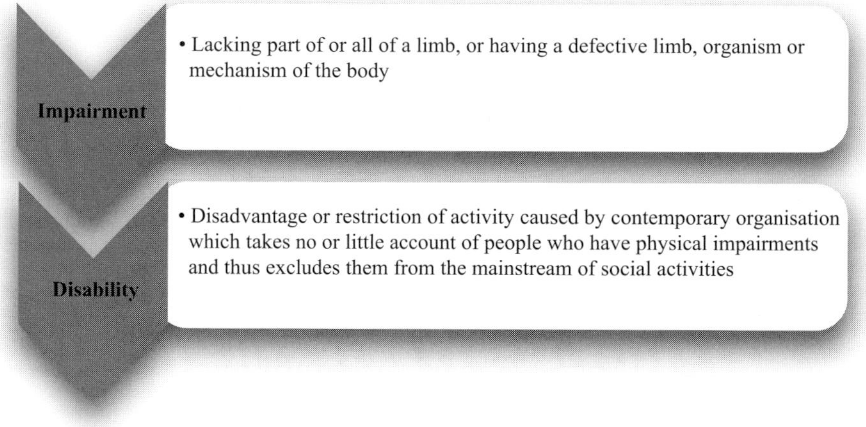

Figure 1.2 Distinction between Impairment and Disability

ii. The social model acknowledges a clear distinction between impairment (physical, psychosocial, intellectual, cognitive and sensory limitations) and disability (in terms of exclusion from society). The UPIAS definitions of 'impairment' and 'disability' are outlined in Figure 1.2.[20]
iii. The social model adheres to the notion that disabled people are an oppressed group in society and are systematically discriminated against.
iv. The social model asserts that societal barriers prevent disabled persons from gaining equal access to education, employment, public transport, housing, information and recreational opportunities.
v. The social model gives precedence to the importance of 'politics, empowerment, citizenship and choice'.[21] Ensuring the participation of disabled persons and their representative organisations is key in implementing the social model.

2.3 Criticisms of the Social Model of Disability

Many criticisms of the 'pure' social model began to emerge within the disability movement in Britain and also within the sphere of disability studies on a global scale. In spite of establishing itself as the dominant paradigm in disability research, there have been calls for the social model to be abandoned in its entirety[22] and criticisms related to the fact that it is a product of the Global North.[23]

[20] UPIAS, *Definition of Impairment and Disability*, note 18. [21] Ibid. p. 4.

[22] See, for instance, Tom Shakespeare and Nicholas Watson, 'The Social Model of Disability: An Outdated Ideology?' (2001) 2 *Research in Social Science and Disability* 9.

[23] Among many others, Shaun Grech, 'Disability, Poverty and Development: Critical Reflections on the Majority World Debate' (2009) 24(6) *Disability and Society* 771.

The criticisms have focused primarily on the appropriateness of the social model as a theoretical tool to explain the multifaceted dimensions of disability, and on how the model can be applied in any given situation. In particular, certain authors criticise the social model due to the fact that it downplays the role of impairment and illness in restricting physical activity and life outcomes. For instance, the disabled feminist scholar Jenny Morris highlights that 'while environmental barriers and social attitudes are a crucial part of our experience of disability – and do indeed disable us – to suggest that this is all there is is to deny the personal experience of physical and intellectual restrictions, of the fear of dying'.[24] In other words, she claims that 'there is a tendency within the social model to deny the experiences of our own bodies'.[25] In the same vein, Crow emphasises the importance of the impairment in the experience of disability.[26]

A further critique of the 'pure' social model relates to the fact that it is impossible to create the so-called barrier-free 'utopia' that is implicit in social model reasoning, in light of differences between various types of disabilities as well as lack of resources and other constraints. However, the response of proponents of the social model to these criticisms is that the social model of disability is 'about nothing more complicated than a clear focus on the economic, environmental and cultural barriers experienced by people who are viewed by others as having some form of impairment – whether physical, sensory or intellectual'.[27] In other words, the social model is not viewed as 'an all-encapsulating'[28] theory of disability but as a framework through which disability can be recognised as a social process.

Some authors maintain that the future of disability theory lies not in the social model but in what has been termed the 'affirmative model of disability',[29] which celebrates the differences that characterise the lives of persons with disabilities. Swain and French argue that, while 'the social model disassociates impairment from disability', it still 'leaves the possibility that even in an ideal world of full civil rights and participative citizenship for disabled people, an impairment could be seen as a personal tragedy'.[30] For this reason, the social model, in itself, may be viewed as being deficient as a theoretical tool for understanding disability. By 'embracing an affirmative model, disabled individuals assert a positive identity, not only in being disabled, but also

[24] Morris (ed.), *Pride against Prejudice: Transforming Attitudes to Disability – A Personal Politics of Disability*, note 9, p. 10.

[25] Ibid.

[26] Liz Crow, 'Including All of Our Lives: Renewing the Social Model of Disability', in Colin Barnes and Geof Mercer (eds.), *Exploring the Divide: Illness and Disability* (Leeds: The Disability Press, 1996), pp. 55–73, p. 58.

[27] Mike Oliver, 'The Social Model in Action: If I had a Hammer', in Colin Barnes and Geof Mercer (eds.), *Implementing the Social Model of Disability: Theory and Research* (Leeds: The Disability Press, 2004), pp. 18–31.

[28] Mike Oliver, *Understanding Disability: From Theory to Practice* (London: Macmillan, 1996), p. 30.

[29] Swain and French, 'Towards an Affirmative Model of Disability', note 7.

[30] Ibid. at 571.

in being impaired'.[31] In affirming this positive identity, persons with disabilities 'are actively repudiating the dominant view of normality'.[32]

This affirmative model can be seen as a close relation of what has been termed the 'social-contextual model of disability',[33] which, as outlined above, conceives of disability as an interactive process between persons with impairments and societal barriers. The social-contextual model of disability fosters a deeper understanding of disability and complementary approaches, such as the human rights model of disability and the capabilities approach to disability, which are discussed in the sub-sections below.

2.4 The Human Rights Model of Disability

As outlined above, conceptualisations of disability have evolved significantly in recent decades. Disability is now seen through the lens of human rights and equality. In other words, persons with disabilities are viewed as holders of rights, entitled to exercise and enjoy human rights guarantees on an equal basis with others.

The Convention endorses what the CRPD Committee and several scholars[34] term the 'human rights model' of disability. In the Committee's view, the human rights model of disability 'requires the diversity of persons with disabilities to be taken into account [recital (i) of the Preamble] together with the interaction between individuals with impairments and attitudinal and environmental barriers [recital (e) of the Preamble]'.[35] The CRPD Committee notes that the human rights model recognises disability as a 'social construct', but it also acknowledges the relevance of impairment.[36] To this extent, the social-contextual model overlaps with the human rights model. Moreover, this model acknowledges the fact that persons with disabilities are holders of rights

[31] Ibid. [32] Ibid.

[33] Broderick, *The Long and Winding Road to Equality and Inclusion for Persons with Disabilities: The United Nations Convention on the Rights of Persons with Disabilities*, note 9, p. 79; on contextual factors, see Peizhong Peter Wang, Elizabeth Badley and Monique Gignac, 'Exploring the Role of Contextual Factors in Disability Models' (2006) 28(2) *Disability and Rehabilitation* 135.

[34] Broderick, *The Long and Winding Road to Equality and Inclusion for Persons with Disabilities: The United Nations Convention on the Rights of Persons with Disabilities*, note 9, p. 79; other authors highlight the CRPD's 'disability human rights paradigm', see Michael Ashley Stein and Penelope Stein, 'Beyond Disability Civil Rights' (2007) 58 *Hastings Law Journal* 1203, at 1224; see also, Theresia Degener, 'A New Human Rights Model of Disability', in Valentina Della Fina, Rachele Cera and Giuseppe Palmisano (eds.), *The United Nations Convention on the Rights of Persons with Disabilities: A Commentary* (Cham: Springer, 2017), pp. 41–59.

[35] CRPD Committee, *S.C. v. Brazil*, Communication No. 10/2013, UN Doc. CRPD/C/12/D/10/2013, para. 6.3.

[36] CRPD Committee, General Comment No. 6, 26 April 2018, UN Doc. CRPD/C/GC/6, paras. 9 and 73(b).

on an equal basis with others and that they are not objects of charity. The human rights model also affirms that 'disability is one of several layers of identity. Hence, disability laws and policies must take the diversity of persons with disabilities into account'.[37]

The human rights model of disability is not a new one, having been acknowledged by Quinn and Degener before the CRPD came into force.

G. Quinn and T. Degener, *Human Rights and Disability: The Current Use and Future Potential of the United Nations Human Rights Instruments in the Context of Disability* (New York/Geneva: United Nations 2002), p.14.

The human rights model focuses on the inherent dignity of the human being and subsequently, but only if necessary, on the person's medical characteristics. It places the individual centre-stage in all decisions affecting him/her and, most importantly, locates the main 'problem' outside the person and in society. The 'problem' of disability under this model stems from a lack of responsiveness by the State and civil society to the difference that disability represents. It follows that the State has a responsibility to tackle socially created obstacles in order to ensure full respect for the dignity and equal rights of all persons. The end goal from the perspective of the human rights model is to build societies that are genuinely inclusive, societies that value difference and respect the dignity and equality of all human beings regardless of difference.

Degener highlights the fact that, whereas the 'pure' social model explains disability, the human rights model acknowledges the human dignity of disabled persons and values human difference.[38] Moreover, while the social model underpins mainly an anti-discrimination policy, the human rights model of disability is wide-ranging, because it embraces the whole spectrum of human rights – civil and political, as well as economic, social and cultural rights.[39] Finally, the human rights model acknowledges that persons with disabilities are a heterogeneous group, that disability is a multidimensional experience, and that impairments (in interaction with external barriers) create varying disabilities (i.e. they can be visible or invisible; temporary or long term; static or deteriorating) and, sometimes, intersectional disadvantage.

While there were elements of the human rights model of disability in the Standard Rules for the Equalization on Opportunities for Persons with Disabilities (Standard Rules),[40] that model has been fully embedded in the CRPD,

[37] Ibid. [38] See above Degener, 'Challenges and Compliance of the UN CRPD', note 14.

[39] Ibid.

[40] Standard Rules on the Equalization of Opportunities for Persons with Disabilities, 20 December 1993, UN Doc. A/RES/48/96. See below Chapter 2.

which represents the culmination of the evolution of disability rights at the international level.[41]

2.5 The Capabilities Approach

The capabilities approach was developed by economist-philosopher Amartya Sen[42] and it was refined significantly by philosopher Martha Nussbaum,[43] among others. The first basic conceptual distinction within the framework of the capabilities approach is between capabilities, on the one hand, and functionings and resources, on the other hand. Capabilities represent the innate potential of each human being, defined as 'what people are actually able to do and to be'[44] when given real opportunities. Functionings represent the various activities that a person can undertake, resulting in a particular outcome or achievement (reading, writing, communication, etc.), while 'resources' are the means by which to achieve the outcome. The capabilities approach highlights several 'conversion factors', such as environmental factors and social norms. These factors may affect the rate of conversion of resources into functionings.

> Did you have pre - conceived ideas about people with disabilities and their capabilities? Have these changed after reading this chapter?

In Nussbaum's work, in particular, the capabilities approach is also defined as linking human vulnerability, interdependence and dignity. Nussbaum develops her theory by affirming that society should enable citizens to flourish on their own terms. The capabilities framework incorporates the idea of 'equality of capabilities' in a wide range of areas that are deemed to be of central importance to the quality of human life. Public policies can foster capabilities, and individuals can also influence the scope of public policy (through public debate).

[41] See below Chapter 3.

[42] Amartya Sen, 'Development as Capability Expansion' (1989) 19 *Journal of Development Planning* 41; in addition, see Amartya Sen (ed.), *Development as Freedom* (Oxford: Oxford University Press, 1999).

[43] Martha Nussbaum, 'Capabilities and Human Rights' (1997) 66(2) *Fordham Law Review* 273; see also Martha Nussbaum, *Creating Capabilities: The Human Development Approach* (Cambridge/London: Harvard University Press, 2011).

[44] Martha Nussbaum, *Women and Human Development* (Cambridge/New York: Cambridge University Press, 2001), p. 5.

According to Trani et al., the capabilities approach has the merit of placing disability 'within the wider spectrum of human development, shifting the focus from the specificities of the disabling situation to looking at establishing equality in terms of possibilities and choices'.[45]

The capabilities approach is interlinked with the social and human rights models of disability.[46] Furthermore, the essential principles underlying the capabilities approach can be found in the CRPD.[47] In that regard, Harnacke notes that 'according to the CRPD and the capabilities approach, a society is just if the state guarantees for all citizens the social basis of their capabilities, regardless of existing impairments'.[48]

3 CROSS-CUTTING THEMES IN DISABILITY LAW AND POLICY

Having discussed the key theoretical models of disability, this section aims to identify certain cross-cutting themes that will be explored throughout the textbook.

3.1 Disability on the Global Scale

According to the World Report on Disability, published by the WHO[49] and the World Bank, more than a billion people worldwide have a disability.[50] According to other statistics, approximately 10 per cent of the global population, i.e. 650 million people, live with a disability.[51] According to the UN Development Programme (UNDP), 80 per cent of persons with disabilities live in developing countries. The latest statistics from the EU reveal that approximately 40 million EU citizens have a disability.[52]

45 Jean Francois Trani, Parul Bakhshi, Nicolo Bellanca, Mario Biggen and Francesca Marchetta, 'Disabilities through the Capability Approach Lens: Implications for Public Policies' (2011) 5 (3) *ALTER – European Journal of Disability Research / Revue Européenne de Recherche sur le Handicap* 143.

46 Tania Burchardt, 'Capabilities and Disability: The Capabilities Framework and the Social Model of Disability' (2004) 19(7) *Disability and Society* 735; see also Carolyn Baylies, 'Disability and the Notion of Human Development: Questions of Rights and Capabilities' (2002) 17(7) *Disability and Society* 725.

47 See below Chapter 3.

48 Caroline Harnacke, 'Disability and Capability: Exploring the Usefulness of Martha Nussbaum's Capabilities Approach for the UN Disability Rights Convention' (2013) 41 *Journal of Law, Medicine and Ethics* 768, at 777.

49 On the role of the WHO, see below Chapter 2.

50 WHO and World Bank, *World Report on Disability* (2011) available at www.who.int/disabilities/world_report/2011/en/.

51 Disabled World, 'Disability Statistics: Information, Charts, Graphs and Tables', available at www.disabled-world.com/disability/statistics/.

52 See at http://ec.europa.eu/eurostat/statistics-explained/index.php/Disability_statistics_-_prevalence_and_demographics.

DID YOU KNOW THAT ...?

According to the WHO World Report on Disability (www.who.int/disabilities/world_report/2011/en/), ageing has a major influence on global disability trends. There is a higher risk of disability in older age. Higher disability rates among older people reflect an accumulation of diseases, injuries and chronic illnesses. Older women tend to have higher rates of disability than older men. According to the report, environments also have a huge effect on disability trends. Environmental changes, caused by natural disasters or conflict situations, affect the prevalence of disability not only by causing impairments but also by creating barriers in the physical environment.

Both UN and EU statistics reveal that people with disabilities have lower educational achievements, lower rates of economic participation and higher rates of poverty than people without disabilities. Moreover, the World Bank estimates that 20 per cent of the world's poorest people are disabled.[53] In the EU, the highest prevalence of disability was observed among individuals with the lowest educational attainments.[54] Unemployment levels among people with disabilities are also extremely high, and this is linked to the low educational achievements as well as the high levels of exclusion that are associated with disability. In 2013, approximately 30 per cent of the population of the EU aged 16 or over and having a disability was at risk of poverty or social exclusion, compared with 22 per cent of those with no impairments.[55]

3.2 Core Themes in Current Disability Law and Policy

This detrimental situation experienced by people with disabilities is the result of decades of policies based on the medical model, and of laws ignoring disabled people or even negating their rights. Historically, until the Industrial Revolution, individuals with disabilities were, for the most part, integrated into society (albeit in a climate of oppression and social stigma). With the advent of industrial capitalism, a series of discriminatory policies and practices (justified by currents of thought based on liberal utilitarianism, Social Darwinism and eugenics) became prevalent. From the early 1980s, with the shift to the social model, the first forms of international protection for the rights of persons with disabilities were established and, as a consequence, the first national laws were enacted. As will be discussed in Chapter 2, the World

[53] WHO and World Bank, *World Report on Disability*, note 50.

[54] These statistics can be viewed at http://ec.europa.eu/eurostat/statistics-explained/index.php/Disability_statistics_-_poverty_and_income_inequalities.

[55] Ibid.

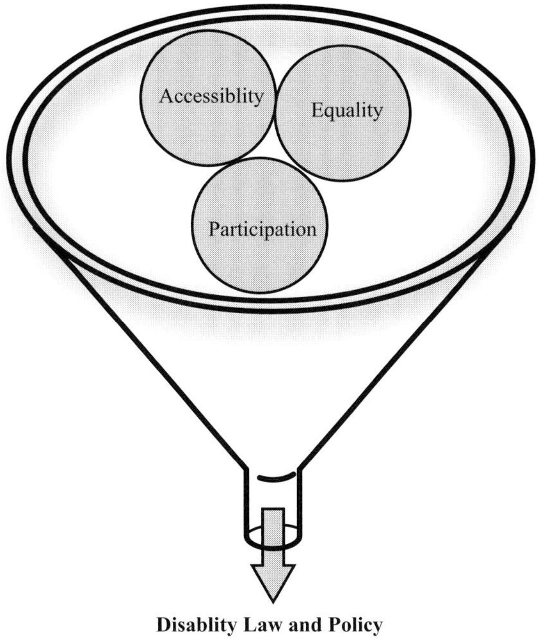

Figure 1.3 Core Themes in Current Disability Law

Programme of Action Concerning Disabled People (1982)[56] and, later, the Standard Rules (1993) integrated disability within the UN human rights agenda. The CRPD is, as mentioned above, the culmination of a long process of the emergence of disability human rights. In turn, the international human rights agenda has influenced a slow change in approach to disability in national legislation, and several countries on a global scale began to adopt disability discrimination legislation during the 1990s. The primary example of this change was the enactment of the Americans with Disabilities Act (ADA) in 1990,[57] which was designed to prohibit discrimination on the ground of disability and to reaffirm the civil rights of people with disabilities. Current disability law is mainly centred on ensuring equality and on dismantling environmental and societal barriers[58] (See Figure 1.3.). Accessibility has also become a key issue in current disability policy, because it is perceived as a precondition for people to access and enjoy their rights.[59]

[56] UN General Assembly (UNGA), World Programme of Action concerning Disabled Persons, 3 December 1982, UN Doc. A/RES/37/52.

[57] Americans with Disabilities Act of 1990, 42 USC § 12101.

[58] Vlad Perjul, 'Impairment, Discrimination, and the Legal Construction of Disability in the European Union and the United States' (2011) 44 *Cornell International Law Journal* 102.

[59] See below Chapters 5 and 12.

3.3 The CRPD as the Roadmap of Current Disability Policy

As recounted in the Introduction, and as will be discussed further in Chapter 3 of this textbook, the CRPD was adopted by the UN General Assembly (UNGA) on 13 December 2006, together with its Optional Protocol (OP-CRPD). It was opened for signature on 30 March 2007 and quickly entered into force on 3 May 2008, as did the OP-CRPD. Irrespective of the fact that the Convention imposes onerous obligations on States Parties (as it requires them to challenge and ultimately change their disability laws and policies), the CRPD has obtained a high number of ratifications.

The CRPD is innovative because it aims to ensure the active participation of persons with disabilities in political, economic, social and cultural life by accommodating their difference. It obliges States Parties to guarantee equality and to protect the rights of every person to participate and be included in society on an equal basis with others. The CRPD is built on the core tenets of dignity, autonomy and self-determination, and it is underpinned by the principles of non-discrimination and equality, which encompass the right to reasonable accommodation. According to Article 2 CRPD, reasonable accommodation refers to 'necessary and appropriate modification and adjustments not imposing a disproportionate or undue burden, where needed in a particular case, to ensure to persons with disabilities the enjoyment or exercise on an equal basis with others of all human rights and fundamental freedoms'.[60] The CRPD also acknowledges that protection against discrimination and promotion of autonomy and legal capacity are not enough to accommodate the 'differences' that people with disabilities live with. In that regard, it lays down the principle of accessibility – the process of making structures inclusive of persons with disabilities through the removal of barriers, which requires wide-ranging changes to the environment, facilities and services, among others. Ultimately, the CRPD, its principles and its focus on the societal dimension of rights, must be considered to represent the legal cornerstone of current disability law and policy. For this reason, the Convention is the point of reference of this entire textbook.

3.4 Disability and Sustainable Development

3.4.1 *From the Millennium Development Goals to the 2030 Agenda*

While the CRPD can be considered as the roadmap of current disability policy globally, the UN policy work on sustainable development has been a complementary framework in ensuring that the rights of persons with disabilities are translated into reality in developing countries and in what is often termed the 'Global South'.[61]

[60] See below Chapter 4. [61] See above the Introduction, note 13.

A comprehensive UN development policy dates back to the 1980s, 'when the global community became more attuned to issues of intra-country social justice in both high- and low-income countries'.[62] The third (1980–1990) and fourth (1990–2000) UN development decades, as well as the Copenhagen Summit on Social Development (1995) identified the need to tackle social exclusion and lack of participation as factors generating poverty on a global scale. In 2000, following the adoption of the UN Millennium Declaration by the UNGA,[63] the Millennium Development Goals (MDGs) were adopted. They set out eight objectives for the year 2015: to eradicate extreme poverty and hunger; to achieve universal primary education; to promote gender equality and empower women; to reduce child mortality; to improve maternal health; to combat HIV/AIDS, malaria and other diseases; to ensure environmental sustainability; and to develop a global partnership for development. Like previous initiatives, the MDGs did not address disability explicitly. More generally, as noted by Stuart and Woodroffe,[64] while they gave rise to substantial progress, this progress did not reach the poorest and most marginalised individuals. Poverty and disability are closely intertwined, and persons with disabilities are more likely to face socio-economic disadvantage. However, the MDGs failed to address the specific barriers encountered by disabled people, and they did not fully address the causes of long-term impairments, such as lack of nutrition and diseases. The lack of reference to disability in the MDGs also resulted in the exclusion of persons with disabilities from a wide range of initiatives and in the lack of opportunities for their voices to be heard. During the 2012 UN Conference on Sustainable Development, UN Member States agreed to launch a process to develop a more comprehensive set of Sustainable Development Goals (SDGs) to supersede the MDGs, and to address, in a complementary way, the three dimensions of sustainable development (environmental, economic and social). The 2030 Agenda on Sustainable Development – Transforming our World 2015–2030 (2030 Agenda) was finally adopted in 2015.[65]

[62] Gabriele Koehler, 'The 2030 Agenda and Eradicating Poverty: New Horizons for Global Social Policy?' (2017) 17(2) *Global Social Policy* 210.

[63] UNGA, Resolution No. 55/2 without reference to a Main Committee (A/55/L.2) United Nations Millennium Declaration, 8 September 2000, available at www.un.org/millennium/declaration/ares552e.htm.

[64] Elizabeth Stuart and Jessica Woodroffe, 'Leaving No-One Behind: Can the Sustainable Development Goals Succeed where the Millennium Development Goals Lacked?' (2016) 24(1) *Gender and Development* 69.

[65] UNGA, Resolution No. 70/1 on Transforming our World: The 2030 Agenda for Sustainable Development, 21 October 2015, available at www.un.org/ga/search/view_doc.asp?symbol=A/RES/70/1&;referer=/english/&Lang=E. In 2018, the UN released the first report that examines disability and the Sustainable Development Goals (SDGs) of the 2030 Agenda for Sustainable Development at the global level. The report reviews data, policies, programmes and

Read the SDGs and identify the most relevant ones from a disability perspective.

The 2030 Agenda is informed by the overarching goal of 'leaving no one behind'. This means that the needs of the most marginalised and discriminated individuals (including persons with disabilities), who had previously been excluded, must be addressed. In addition, SDG 10 is of key importance, as it aims to tackle inequality within and between countries. Among other things, it calls on the international community to reduce inequality by empowering and promoting the social, economic and political inclusion of all, including persons with disabilities. In doing so, the 2030 Agenda is consonant with the CRPD, which, as mentioned before, is underpinned by the concepts of 'non-discrimination' and 'equality'. The terms 'disability' and 'persons with disabilities' are mentioned eleven times in the 2030 Agenda and, besides SDG 10, they are referred to in SDGs 4, 8, 11 and 17. SDG 4 (on inclusive and equitable quality education and promotion of life-long learning opportunities for all) focuses on eliminating gender disparities in education and ensuring equal access to all levels of education and vocational training, including for persons with disabilities. In addition, SDG 4 calls for the building of 'education facilities that are child, disability and gender sensitive and provide safe, non-violent, inclusive and effective learning environments for all'. SDG 8 (on decent work and economic growth) calls on the international community to achieve full and productive employment and decent work for all women and men, including for persons with disabilities, and equal pay for work of equal value. SDG 11 aims to make cities and human settlements inclusive, safe and sustainable. To realise this goal, UN Member States are called upon to provide access to safe, affordable, accessible and sustainable transport systems, with special attention to the needs of persons with disabilities. In addition, SDG 11 calls for universal

identifies good practices; and uses the evidence it reviewed to outline recommended actions to promote the realisation of the SDGs for persons with disabilities (Division for Inclusive Social Development (DISD) of the United Nations Department for Economic and Social Affairs, *UN 2018 Flagship Report on Disability and Development*, available at www.ohchr.org/Documents/HRBodies/CRPD/UN2018FlagshipReportDisability.pdf.

access to safe, inclusive and accessible green and public spaces, particularly for persons with disabilities. Finally, SDG 17 stresses that the collection of data and monitoring of the SDGs' implementation are crucial. To enhance capacity-building support to developing countries, SDG 17 also highlights the importance of increasing the availability of high-quality, timely and reliable data disaggregated, by among other things, disability, in line with Article 31 CRPD.[66]

3.4.2 *The UN Development Programme and Disability*

The UNDP, the global development network administered by Vice-Chair of the UN Development Group (UNDG),[67] supports the implementation of the 2030 Agenda and helps States Parties to the CRPD to implement it. In particular, the UNDP supports countries to develop and strengthen disability law and policy, improve accessibility, social protection, livelihood opportunities, and promote the participation of persons with disabilities in public life.[68]

The UNDP also hosts the secretariat of the United Nations Partnership on the Rights of Persons with Disabilities (UNPRPD). The latter brings together UN entities,[69] governments, DPOs and civil society to advance disability rights around the world. The overall goal of the UNPRPD is to develop the capacities of national stakeholders, particularly governments and DPOs, for the effective implementation of the CRPD, with a view to triggering systemic change and strengthening the participation of persons with disabilities.[70] Several projects have been financed under the UNPRPD, in particular in African and Asian countries.[71]

[66] See below Chapter 3, section 6.

[67] UN Development Group, 'UNDG at The Global Level', available at https://undg.org/about/undg-global/.

[68] UN Development Programme, 'Disability-inclusive Development', available at www.undp.org/content/undp/en/home/democratic-governance-and-peacebuilding/rule-of-law–justice-security-and-human-rights/disability-inclusive-development.html.

[69] The UN entities participating in the UNPRPD are the International Labour Organization (ILO), the OHCHR, the United Nations Department for Economic and Social Affairs (UNDESA), the United Nations Development Programme (UNDP), the United Nations Educational, Cultural and Scientific Organization (UNESCO), the United Nations Population Fund (UNFPA), the United Nations Children's Fund (UNICEF), the United Nations Entity for Gender Equality and the Empowerment of Women (UN Women), the World Health Organization (WHO).

[70] UN Partnership to promote the Rights of Persons with Disabilities Multi-Donor Trust Fund (UNPRPD MDTF), available at http://mptf.undp.org/factsheet/fund/RPD00.

[71] UNPRPD, *Connections. An overview of results from the first UNPRPD Funding Round Building partnerships for disability rights* (2016), available at https://global-health.tcd.ie/assets/doc/UNPRPD%20REPORT-CONNECTIONS%202016%20(3).pdf. See also Chapter 15, section 5.

SUMMARY

- **In western culture, disability has traditionally been viewed as an individual, medical 'problem', and it has been conceived of as an individual deficit, deriving from a disease or health condition. This perception of disability was embodied in the medical model, which focused on the actual health condition of the disabled person and on the treatments that could be provided to 'cure' the person in question.**
- **As a reaction to the perceived limitations and weaknesses of a medicalised construction of disability, scholars and disability activists elaborated the social model of disability in the late 1960s.**
- **According to the social model, disability is perceived as arising from barriers – environmental, attitudinal and legislative barriers. Theoretical reflections on the social model of disability are still evolving, and the social model itself has been the subject of scholarly criticism.**
- **For decades, disability has been regulated from a welfare perspective. However, since the 1990s, the UN has started to address the rights of persons with disabilities as part of its system of human rights protection, prompting a global change in the approach to disability.**
- **Current disability law and policy is firmly anchored to the core themes of equality, accessibility, participation and inclusion, and it is highly influenced by the CRPD. The Convention has, in fact, become the legal cornerstone for the development of national disability laws and policies.**
- **The CRPD has obtained widespread support from several states all over the world. It was, in fact, the most rapidly negotiated UN treaty.**
- **The 2030 Agenda calls on the international community to reduce inequality, by empowering and promoting the social, economic and political inclusion of all, including persons with disabilities. In doing so, it is consonant with the CRPD.**

ACTIVITIES

REVIEW QUESTIONS

1. How has disability law emerged as a distinct discipline of academic study, and what have been the main turning points in the field?
2. What are the main criticisms of the social model of disability, and how have these been articulated in the relevant literature?
3. Why is it important that disability laws and policies adopt a human rights model and a capabilities approach?

ESSAY QUESTIONS

1. 'Impairment is an important but tangential aspect of disability'. *Discuss.*
2. 'Disabling and discriminatory barriers are the main cause of disability'. *Discuss.*

GROUP PROJECT

Make a table related to the various ways in which you could ask someone about their disability and how it affects their life. Break the table into three columns related to the medical model, the social model and the capabilities approach. When you are finished making your table, look at the table produced by T. Burchardt, 'Capabilities and Disability: the Capabilities Framework and the Social Model of Disability' (2004) 19(7) *Disability and Society* 735–51, p. 741.

FURTHER READING

Anastasiou, D. and Kaufmann, J., 'The Social Model of Disability: Dichotomy between Impairment and Disability' (2013) 38(4) *Journal of Medicine and Philosophy* 441–59.

Barnes, C. and Mercer, G., 'Theorising and Researching Disability from a Social Model Perspective', in Barnes, C. and Mercer, G. (eds.), *Implementing the Social Model of Disability: Theory and Research* (Leeds: The Disability Press, 2004), pp. 1–18.

Cuenca Gomez, P., 'Human Rights and Disability: a Theoretical Analysis (2015) 4 *The Age of the Human Rights Journal*, 34–59.

Dewsbury, G., Clarke, K., Randall, D., Rouncefield, M. and Sommerville, I., 'The Anti-Social Model of Disability' (2004) 19(2) *Disability and Society* 145–58.

García Iriarte, E., McConkey, R., and Gilligan, R. (eds.), *Disability and Human Rights: Global Perspectives* (London-New York: Palgrave, 2016).

Harpur, P., 'From Disability to Ability: Changing the Phrasing of the Debate' (2012) 27(3) *Disability and Society* 325–37.

Humphrey, J. C., 'Researching Disability Politics, Or, Some Problems with the Social Model in Practice' (2000) 15(1) *Disability and Society* 63–86.

MacLachlan, M. and Swartz, L., 'From the Local to the Global: the Many Contexts of Disability and International Development', in MacLachlan, M. and Swartz, L. (eds.), *Disability & International Development. Towards Inclusive Global Health* (Cham: Springer, 2009), pp. 1–11.

Mitra, S., 'The Capability Approach and Disability' (2006) 16(4) *Journal of Disability Policy Studies* 236–47.

Morris, J., *Pride Against Prejudice: Transforming Attitudes to Disability – A Personal Politics of Disability* (London: The Women's Press, 1993).

Oliver, M., *Understanding Disability: From Theory to Practice* (Basingstoke: Macmillan, 1996).

'The Social Model in Action: If I Had a Hammer', in C. Barnes and G. Mercer (eds.), *Implementing the Social Model of Disability: Theory and Research* (Leeds: The Disability Press, 2004), pp. 18–31.

'The Social Model of Disability: Thirty Years On' (2013) 28(7) *Disability and Society* 1024–6.

Rembis, M. et al. (eds.), *The Oxford Handbook of Disability History* (Oxford University Press, 2018).

Stein, M. A., 'Disability Human Rights' (2007) 95 *California Law Review* 75–121.

Thomas, C., 'How is Disability Understood? An Examination of Sociological Approaches' (2004) 19(6) *Disability and Society* 569–83.

Tregaskis, C., 'Social Model Theory: The Story so Far' (2002) 17(4) *Disability and Society* 457–70.

2 The Protection of the Rights of Persons with Disabilities under International Human Rights Law before the Adoption of the United Nations Convention on the Rights of Persons with Disabilities

LEARNING OUTCOMES

- ✓ Understand the developments that took place before the adoption of the CRPD.
- ✓ Identify the shift towards the human rights perspective in the UN.
- ✓ Trace the key elements of the most relevant soft law documents pertaining to disability in the period preceding the adoption of the CRPD.
- ✓ Understand the role of the World Health Organization in the disability rights agenda.
- ✓ Understand the relationship between the CRPD and the International Classification of Functioning, Disability and Health.
- ✓ Identify how the core human rights treaty bodies have dealt with disability.
- ✓ Comprehend why the CRPD was a necessary instrument in international human rights law.
- ✓ Trace the principal turning points that occurred in the years preceding the adoption of the CRPD.

Disability is a human rights issue! I repeat: disability is a human rights issue. Those of us who happen to have a disability are fed up being treated by society and our fellow citizens as if we did not exist [. . .] We are human beings with equal value, claiming equal rights.[1]

1 INTRODUCTION

As outlined in Chapter 1 of this textbook, the rights of persons with disabilities were not always viewed through the lens of equality. Rather, people with disabilities were perceived as objects, instead of being viewed as subjects of the law. For a long time, the focus of action remained on the impairments of disabled people and attempts to 'cure' their functional limitations through rehabilitation, welfare and other means. Slowly but surely, a human rights perspective began to emerge in the UN. A dramatic shift has taken place over the last few decades with regard to the conceptualisation of disability and the protection of disability rights. The UN has moved firmly away from a charity-based approach towards a human rights model of disability.

Disability is now viewed from the vantage point of non-discrimination, equality and human dignity. This slow but steady endorsement of a human rights perspective was best exemplified by the Standard Rules on the Equalization of Opportunities for People with Disabilities (Standard Rules). That document constituted a turning point in the history of disability rights at the UN level. This was followed by renewed calls for a binding human rights treaty addressing disability. The adoption of the CRPD in 2006 represents the high-water mark in the evolution of the protection of the rights of people with disabilities at the international level.

The aim of this chapter is to highlight the gaps that existed in the protection of the rights of persons with disabilities before the CRPD came onto the international human rights landscape and the developments made in that regard. This chapter is not intended to provide a complete overview of the work of the UN and its bodies and agencies; instead, this chapter delineates the principal disability-related developments that have occurred within the human rights division of the UN in the last few decades. In that regard, only the instruments that paved the way towards the adoption of the CRPD are analysed. Further to this introductory section, section 2 of the chapter discusses, in a chronological fashion, the role of the UN in promoting and protecting the

[1] Speech by Bengt Lindqvist, Special Rapporteur on Disability of the United Nations Commission for Social Development, at the nineteenth Congress of Rehabilitation International, Rio de Janeiro, 25–30 August 2000.

rights of persons with disabilities. Section 3 addresses the role of the International Labour Organization (ILO), while section 4 examines the role of the World Health Organization (WHO) in the international disability agenda.

2 THE ROLE OF THE UNITED NATIONS IN PROMOTING THE RIGHTS OF PERSONS WITH DISABILITIES

The UN institutions have played a pivotal role in increasing awareness of disability rights and in promoting equalisation of opportunities for disabled people. The developments that have taken place have, however, been 'slow and uneven',[2] according to Quinn and Degener.

2.1 From the Early Seventies to the Standard Rules

From 1945–1955, the UN addressed disability from a medical perspective. In the period stretching from the late 1950s to the beginning of the 1970s, the focus of the UN bodies shifted towards a welfare approach, and that was accompanied by a process of de-institutionalisation as well as calls for increased participation of disabled persons in society.[3] In spite of these developments, there was a lack of mainstreaming pertaining to disability rights before the early 1970s. As soon as a heightened consciousness of disability rights began to emerge at the global level, the UN bodies began to respond by adopting a number of soft law instruments and initiating various world conferences on disability. As a result of the instruments adopted during that period, disability slowly came to be viewed within the UN as a human rights issue rather than a welfare matter.

The rights-based approach to disability was first evidenced by the adoption of several resolutions by the UN General Assembly (UNGA). Two, in particular, are notable for the emphasis that they place on the equal rights of people with disabilities. For example, the Declaration on the Rights of Mentally Retarded Persons[4] accords the same rights to persons with psychosocial disabilities as to all other individuals, 'to the extent feasible'. A further resolution adopted by the UNGA on 9 December 1975, the Declaration on the Rights of Disabled Persons,[5] states that persons with disabilities are entitled

[2] Gerard Quinn and Theresia Degener, *Human Rights and Disability: The Current Use and Future Potential of the United Nations Human Rights Instruments in the Context of Disability* (New York/Geneva: United Nations, 2002), p. 1.

[3] Information taken from UN Enable website, 'The United Nations and Disabled People – The First Fifty Years', available at https://www.un.org/esa/socdev/enable/dis50y00.htm.

[4] UN Declaration on the Rights of Mentally Retarded Persons, 20 December 1971, UNGA Resolution 2856. See also the UN Principles for the Protection of People with Mental Health Illness and the Improvement of Health Care, 17 December 1991, UN Doc. A/RES/66/119.

[5] UN Declaration on the Rights of Disabled Persons, 9 December 1975, UNGA Resolution 3447.

to the same civil and political rights as others. It also promotes positive measures designed to enable disabled people to become as self-reliant as possible. In spite of the advances made in those documents, Stein points to the fact that these instruments possess 'vestiges of the medical model by assuming individuals are disabled due to "special" medical problems that require segregated social services and institutions as remedies'.[6] While this criticism has merit, those instruments were a predecessor to other UN instruments, which were designed to foster increased participation and inclusion of persons with disabilities in society, and ultimately they acted as a forerunner to the CRPD itself.

During the 1980s, the UNGA drafted the World Programme of Action Concerning Disabled Persons (WPA),[7] which was adopted in December 1982. The WPA proclaimed 1981 the International Year of Disabled Persons, a key theme of which was 'full participation and equality'. The WPA sought to target three key fields of action, namely prevention, rehabilitation and equalisation of opportunities. While the first two fields are related to the medical model of disability, the social model underpinned the third field of action – equalisation of opportunities in various areas, such as education and employment. The WPA also defined equalisation of opportunities as 'the process through which the general system of society, such as the physical and cultural environment, housing and transportation, social and health services, educational and work opportunities, cultural and social life, including sports and recreational facilities, are made accessible to all'.[8]

Quinn and Degener have stated that the developments outlined above, particularly the inclusion of equality of opportunities in the discourse on disability, provided evidence 'of the slow but sure shift' towards a human rights model in the UN.[9] The WPA clearly acknowledged the role played by social and environmental barriers in impeding participation and equality for people with disabilities[10] in the definition of 'handicap' outlined in Figure 2.1.

[6] Michael Ashley Stein, 'Disability Human Rights' (2007) 95 *California Law Review* 88. In particular, Stein points to para. 8 of the Declaration on the Rights of Disabled Persons to support his assertion.

[7] UN World Programme of Action Concerning Disabled Persons, adopted by the General Assembly on 3 December 1982 by its Resolution UN Doc. A/RES/37/52. The text of the WPA is included in A/RES/351/Add. 1, available at https://www.un.org/development/desa/disabilities/resources/world-programme-of-action-concerning-disabled-persons.html.

[8] Ibid. para. 12.

[9] Quinn and Degener, *Human Rights and Disability: The Current Use and Future Potential of the United Nations Human Rights Instruments in the Context of Disability*, note 2, p. 31.

[10] See note 7, para. 7.

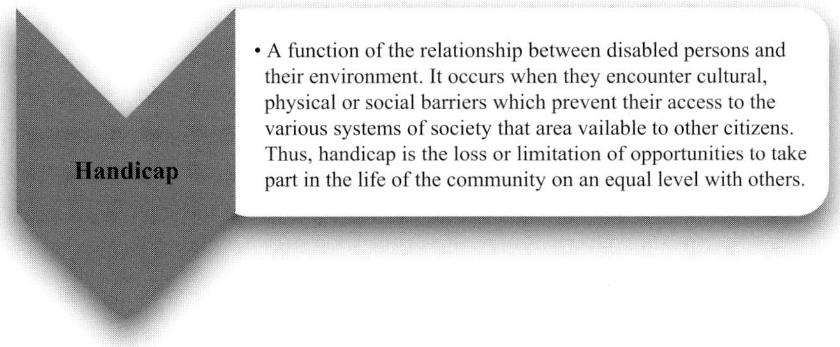

Figure 2.1 Definition of 'Handicap' in the World Programme of Action Concerning Disabled Persons

Following the WPA, the period spanning from 1983 to 1992 was proclaimed the International Decade of Disabled Persons, providing a timeline for national authorities to implement the WPA.

In 1993, the Vienna Declaration and Programme of Action, adopted by the World Conference on Human Rights on 25 June 1993, highlighted that 'special attention needs to be paid to ensuring non-discrimination, and the equal enjoyment of all human rights and fundamental freedoms by disabled persons, including their active participation in all aspects of society'.[11] The Declaration also highlighted that persons with disabilities should be guaranteed equal opportunity 'through the elimination of all socially determined barriers, be they physical, financial, social or psychological, which exclude or restrict full participation in society'.[12] In a similar vein, the Copenhagen Declaration and Programme of Action, adopted at the World Summit for Social Development in March 1995,[13] recognised that people with disabilities are often forced into poverty and unemployment. The Declaration called for the elimination of discrimination against persons with disabilities and the need to support them in educational and employment contexts. Moreover, in 1998, the UN Commission on Human Rights (UNCHR) acknowledged general responsibility for people with disabilities under its mandate, through its resolution entitled Human Rights of Persons with Disabilities.[14]

[11] UNGA, Vienna Declaration and Programme of Action, 12 July 1993, UN Doc. A/CONF.157/23, para. 22.

[12] Ibid. para. 64.

[13] United Nations, *Report of the World Summit for Social Development*, Copenhagen, 6–12 March 1995, UN Doc. A/CONF.166/9.

[14] UN Commission on Human Rights, Resolution No. 1998/31 on Human Rights of Persons with Disabilities, 17 April 1998, UN Doc. E/CN.4/RES/1998/31.

2.2 The Standard Rules

The decade beginning in 1990 has been described as a 'banner decade for disability law'.[15] Prior to the adoption of the CRPD, the Standard Rules constituted the most important non-binding instrument adopted by the UN bodies. The underlying tenets of the Standard Rules are equal access, and participation and inclusion of disabled persons in mainstream society.

DID YOU KNOW THAT ...?

The Standard Rules actually came into being after efforts to foster support for a convention on the rights of persons with disabilities failed at a global meeting of experts on disability, which was held in Stockholm, Sweden. Many representatives at that meeting believed that the existing international instruments provided sufficient protection for the rights of disabled persons, and that, instead of adopting an international treaty, it would be more appropriate to draft another soft law instrument on disability. This consensus led to the drafting of the Standard Rules, with the milestone Resolution 48/96 being adopted on 20 December 1993.

Similar to the WPA, the Standard Rules underscore the goal of equalisation of opportunities. The Rules include target areas for participation as well as implementation and monitoring mechanisms. They place a clear emphasis on discriminatory environmental factors as contributors in the process of disablement. The UN Committee on Economic, Social and Cultural Rights (CESCR) describes the Standard Rules as being 'of major importance'.[16] Moreover, Reyes asserts that they constitute 'an important change in paradigm', in the sense that they move away from 'a medical-assistance perspective towards an approach focusing on rights with an interdisciplinary focus, emphasi[s]ing the psychosocial, environmental and contextual perspective in its broadest sense'.[17]

Even though the Standard Rules preceded the CRPD, they have many elements in common with the Convention. In the first instance, they adopt

[15] Theresia Degener, 'International Disability Law – A New Legal Subject on the Rise: The Interregional Experts' Meeting in Hong Kong, December 13–17, 1999' (2000) 18 *Berkeley Journal of International Law* 184.

[16] UN Committee on Economic, Social and Cultural Rights (CESCR), General Comment No. 5, 9 December 1994, UN Doc. E/1995/22, para. 7(b).

[17] Maria S. Cisternas Reyes, 'Standard Rules on Equality of Opportunities for Persons with Disabilities: Legal View of Provisions on Support Services, Auxiliary Resources and Training/ View from Latin America', in Marcia Rioux, Lee Ann Basser and Melinda Jones (eds.), *Critical Perspectives on Human Rights and Disability Policy* (Leiden/Boston: Brill, 2011), pp. 419–50.

a strong human rights perspective by addressing issues of structural access, and they promote the inclusion of persons with disabilities in mainstream society, in a similar manner to the CRPD. The Standard Rules also address discriminatory barriers and require national governments to eradicate such barriers. They acknowledge the importance of accessibility. Rule 5, for example, relates to access to the physical environment, as well as access to information and communications, and reasonable accommodation in the context of education and employment. The Standard Rules also emphasise a participatory role for persons with disabilities and their representative organisations.

At the date of their adoption, the Standard Rules constituted a comprehensive document designed to signify 'a strong moral and political commitment on behalf of [s]tates to take action for the equali[s]ation of opportunities for persons with disabilities'.[18] Whatever their merits, the Standard Rules did not succeed in filling the existing gaps in human rights protection for disabled people, partly due to the fact that they do not constitute a binding instrument and they lack a direct enforcement mechanism. In view of this, the Declaration on the Rights of People with Disabilities in the New Century was adopted at the World NGO Summit on Disability, which took place in Beijing, China on 12 March 2000.[19] That Declaration repeated previous calls for a binding convention to promote and protect the rights of people with disabilities, and it highlighted priority areas for such a convention (Figure 2.2).

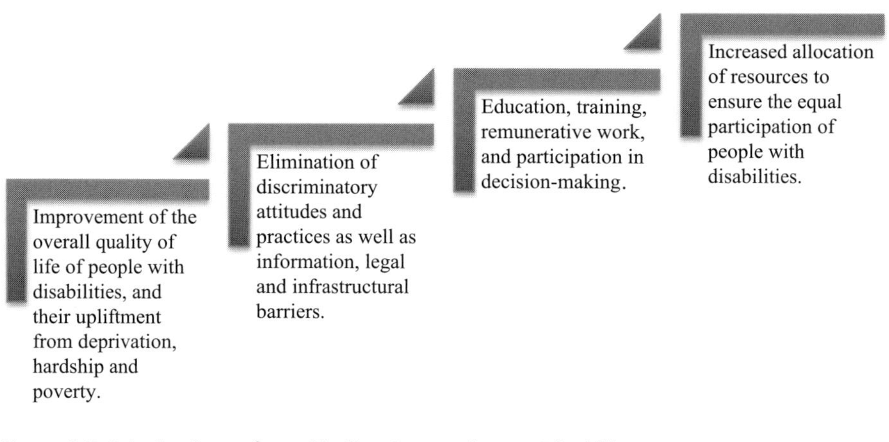

Figure 2.2 Priority Areas for a Binding Convention on Disability

18 Standard Rules on the Equalization of Opportunities for Persons with Disabilities, 20 December 1993, UN Doc. A/RES/48/96, para. 14.

19 UNGA and Economic and Social Council, Declaration on the Rights of People with Disabilities in the New Century, 5 May 2000, UN Doc. A/54/861–E/2000/47.

2.3 United Nations Committee on Economic, Social and Cultural Rights and General Comment No. 5

Before the CRPD, the treaty bodies were generally reluctant to engage with disability issues. This may have been due to the fact that the realisation of disability rights often requires the adoption of positive measures, and the treaty bodies were reluctant to delve into issues regarding resource allocation, which is a matter for States Parties themselves. The CESCR is the only one of the core human rights treaty bodies that had adopted a general comment specifically on the rights of persons with disabilities prior to the entry into force of the CRPD.[20] General Comment No. 5, issued in 1994, was a forerunner of some of the provisions that would later appear in the CRPD itself.

General Comment No. 5 details the manner in which the International Covenant on Economic, Social and Cultural Rights (ICESCR) should be interpreted in order to ensure its equal application to persons with disabilities and consequently their equal enjoyment of the rights guaranteed in the Covenant. The CESCR, in the General Comment, adopts a similar approach to disability rights as that adopted by other UN bodies around that time, informed by the social model. It acknowledges the close link between the equality and non-discrimination norms, on the one hand, and participation and inclusion in society for persons with disabilities, on the other hand. It states, at paragraph 15 thereof, that:

> [t]hrough neglect, ignorance, prejudice and false assumptions, as well as through exclusion, distinction or separation, persons with disabilities have very often been prevented from exercising their economic, social or cultural rights *on an equal basis* with persons without disabilities.

It goes on to highlight the specific areas where the effects of disability-based discrimination have been particularly severe, namely in the fields of education, employment, housing, transport, cultural life, and access to public places and services.[21] The General Comment recognises the discriminatory barriers that hinder realisation of the rights of persons with disabilities. For example, the CESCR notes that ensuring that disabled people can work will require the elimination of 'prominent and persistent' discrimination as well as

[20] UN Committee on the Elimination of Discrimination against Women (CEDAW), General Recommendation No. 24 on Article 12 of the Convention (Women and Health), 1999, UN Doc. A/54/38/Rev.1 refers specifically to women with disabilities. Paragraph 6 thereof urges States to give special attention to the health needs and rights of women belonging to vulnerable and disadvantaged groups such as women with physical or mental disabilities. The Human Rights Committee (HRC) also issued a General Comment in 1982, General Comment No. 8 on Liberty and Security of the Person, which included a reference to persons with psychosocial disabilities.

[21] CESCR, General Comment No. 5, note 16, para. 15.

'the physical barriers that society has erected in areas such as transport, housing and the workplace'.[22]

The CESCR also explains that the reason for which there was no explicit disability-related provision in the ICESCR was because of 'the lack of awareness of the importance of addressing this issue explicitly, rather than only by implication, at the time of the drafting of the Covenant over a quarter of a century ago'.[23] The Committee goes on to state that it is now 'very widely accepted that the human rights of persons with disabilities must be protected and promoted through general, as well as specially designed laws, policies and programmes'.[24]

The CESCR confirms that disability-based discrimination falls under the heading of 'other status' in the Covenant.[25]

CESCR General Comment No. 5 on Persons with Disabilities (1994)

5. Since the Covenant's provisions apply fully to all members of society, persons with disabilities are clearly entitled to the full range of rights recognized in the Covenant. In addition, insofar as special treatment is necessary, States parties are required to take appropriate measures, to the maximum extent of their available resources, to enable such persons to seek to overcome any disadvantages, in terms of the enjoyment of the rights specified in the Covenant, flowing from their disability. Moreover, the requirement contained in article 2(2) of the Covenant that the rights 'enunciated ... will be exercised without discrimination of any kind' based on certain specified grounds 'or other status' clearly applies to discrimination on the grounds of disability.

Significantly, General Comment No. 5 includes within the definition of disability-based discrimination 'a denial of reasonable accommodation', and it highlights the emphasis that the Standard Rules place on accessibility measures.[26] In fact, the General Comment refers, at several junctures, to the Standard Rules. It states that the Rules 'are of major importance and constitute a particularly valuable reference guide in identifying more precisely the relevant obligations of States parties under the [ICESCR]'.[27]

[22] Ibid. paras. 20 and 22. [23] Ibid., para. 6. [24] Ibid. [25] Ibid. para. 5.

[26] General Comment No. 5 of the CESCR recommends that States 'should promote the accessibility to and availability of places for cultural performances and services'. It also emphasises the fact that 'the right to adequate housing includes the right to accessible housing for persons with disabilities' (ibid. paras. 36 and 33, respectively.). In addition, General Comment No. 5 reiterates Rule 4 of the Standard Rules by stating that it is also necessary to ensure that support services, including assistive devices, are available for persons with disabilities, to assist them to increase their level of independence in their daily living and to exercise their rights. Ibid., citing the Standard Rules, Rule 4 (ibid., para. 33.).

[27] Ibid. para. 7.

General Comment No. 5 also underlines the importance of regulating discrimination in the private sphere in the context of persons with disabilities. In that regard, the CESCR emphasises the 'obligation to protect' the rights of disabled persons from non-state actors, and it asserts that 'it is essential that private employers, private suppliers of goods and services, and other non-public entities be subject to both non-discrimination and equality norms in relation to persons with disabilities'.[28]

The General Comment also recognises the importance of positive measures to eliminate the systemic inequalities encountered by disabled persons for too long in every aspect of life:

> The obligation in the case of such a vulnerable and disadvantaged group is to take positive action to reduce structural disadvantages and to give appropriate preferential treatment to people with disabilities in order to achieve the objectives of full participation and equality within society for all persons with disabilities.[29]

As the CESCR acknowledges, 'this almost invariably means that additional resources will need to be made available for this purpose and that a wide range of specially tailored measures will be required'.[30]

On the whole, the tenets of the General Comment align with the CRPD and show the advancement of disability rights in the international sphere pre-CRPD.

3 THE INTERNATIONAL LABOUR ORGANIZATION AND DISABILITY

One of the UN agencies that has developed a comprehensive disability rights agenda, within the realm of its mandate, is the ILO. The ILO was founded in 1919 and includes representatives of employers' and workers' organisations as well as national governments. Its primary goal is to promote opportunities for women and men to obtain decent conditions of work, equity, security and human dignity. The ILO is entrusted with elaborating labour standards, developing policies and programmes to promote the right to work, and drafting comprehensive instruments on work-related rights. It has addressed disability rights, by adopting important instruments designed to create equal opportunities for disabled people in the fields of employment and vocational rehabilitation.[31]

The first ILO instrument adopted in respect of persons with disabilities was the Recommendation concerning Vocational Rehabilitation of the Disabled,

[28] Ibid. para. 11. The CESCR observes that there is a 'need to ensure that not only the public sphere, but also the private sphere, are, within appropriate limits, subject to regulation to ensure the equitable treatment of persons with disabilities'.

[29] Ibid. para. 9. [30] Ibid. [31] See below Chapter 8.

which was adopted in 1955.[32] Two further instruments followed almost thirty years later:

i. The Vocational Rehabilitation and Employment (Disabled Persons) Convention (No. 159), adopted in 1983, which provides for vocational rehabilitation measures for all disabled people and for the promotion of employment opportunities as well as the equal treatment of disabled men and women.[33] This Convention, although still endorsing a medical approach to disability, arguably paved the way for active labour market policies, which will be elaborated on in Chapter 8.
ii. The Vocational Rehabilitation and Employment (Disabled Persons) Recommendation (No. 168)[34] was adopted in 1983 and applies to all disabled workers. That Recommendation builds on the International Year of Disabled Persons and the WPA. In its Preamble, the Recommendation notes 'that these developments have made it appropriate to adopt new international standards ... which take account, in particular, of the need to ensure equality of opportunity and treatment to all categories of disabled persons, in both rural and urban areas, for employment and integration into the community'. The Recommendation was explicitly stated as being complementary to the 1983 Convention, outlined above.

VOCATIONAL REHABILITATION AND EMPLOYMENT (DISABLED PERSONS) CONVENTION NO. 159 (1983)

Article 1

1. For the purposes of this Convention, the term *disabled person* means an individual whose prospects of securing, retaining and advancing in suitable employment are substantially reduced as a result of a duly recognised physical or mental impairment.

2. For the purposes of this Convention, each Member shall consider the purpose of vocational rehabilitation as being to enable a disabled person to secure, retain and advance in suitable employment and thereby to further such person's integration or reintegration into society.

3. The provisions of this Convention shall be applied by each Member through measures which are appropriate to national conditions and consistent with national practice.

[32] International Labour Organization, Vocational Rehabilitation (Disabled) Recommendation No. 99, Geneva, 22 June 1955.

[33] International Labour Organization, International Labour Convention No. 159 concerning Vocational Rehabilitation and Employment (Disabled Persons), Geneva, 20 June 1983.

[34] International Labour Organization, Recommendation No. 168 concerning Vocational Rehabilitation and Employment (Disabled Persons), Geneva, 20 June 1983.

4. The provisions of this Convention shall apply to all categories of disabled persons.

. . .

Article 4

The said policy shall be based on the principle of equal opportunity between disabled workers and workers generally. Equality of opportunity and treatment for disabled men and women workers shall be respected. Special positive measures aimed at effective equality of opportunity and treatment between disabled workers and other workers shall not be regarded as discriminating against other workers.

. . .

Vocational Rehabilitation and Employment (Disabled Persons) Recommendation No. 168 (1983)

7. Disabled persons should enjoy equality of opportunity and treatment in respect of access to, retention of and advancement in employment which, wherever possible, corresponds to their own choice and takes account of their individual suitability for such employment.

8. In providing vocational rehabilitation and employment assistance to disabled persons, the principle of equality of opportunity and treatment for men and women workers should be respected.

9. Special positive measures aimed at effective equality of opportunity and treatment between disabled workers and other workers should not be regarded as discriminating against other workers.

10. Measures should be taken to promote employment opportunities for disabled persons which conform to the employment and salary standards applicable to workers generally.

The CESCR states that the ILO documents constitute 'valuable and comprehensive instruments with respect to the work-related rights of persons with disabilities', and the Committee encourages States Parties to the Covenant to consider ratifying the ILO Convention.[35]

[35] CESCR, General Comment No. 5, note 16, para. 27.

4 THE WORLD HEALTH ORGANIZATION AND DISABILITY

The WHO is another specialised agency of the UN and is an important actor in the field of health care and other related issues, such as disability. The WHO has played a pivotal role in elaborating various documents prior to the adoption of the CRPD that fostered a change in the understanding of disability, from 'medicalisation' to a social approach. The sub-sections that follow elaborate on the principal disability instruments adopted by the WHO.

4.1 The International Classification of Impairments, Disabilities and Handicaps

In 1980, at a time when the UN was slowly beginning to move towards a human rights model of disability, the WHO published a document entitled 'The International Classification of Impairments, Disabilities and Handicaps' (ICIDH). That document provides a conceptual framework for the description of health and health-related conditions, such as disease, injury or congenital condition. It is designed to set out a classification system relating to the consequences of those conditions that can be used in various countries at the global level. The three dimensions of the ICIDH's conceptual framework relating to the consequences of disease are: impairment, disability and handicap (Figure 2.3).

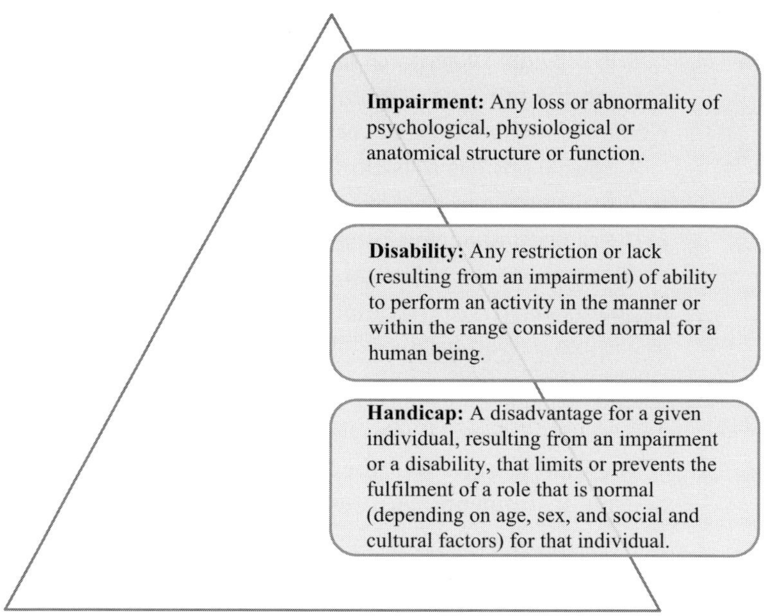

Figure 2.3 Definitions of 'Impairment', 'Disability' and 'Handicap'

As is evident from the definitions outlined in the figure above, the ICIDH does not embrace the social model of disability. It was heavily criticised on account of the fact that it sidelined the role played by social and environmental factors in contributing to disablement. In essence, the document acknowledges, but does not classify, environmental factors as contributing to the process of disablement. Due partly to the foregoing deficiencies, the WHO began revisions on the ICIDH.[36] Over a seven-year period and through a collaborative process at the international level, the successor to the ICIDH was drafted. It was entitled the International Classification of Functioning, Disability and Health (ICF).

4.2 The International Classification of Functioning, Disability and Health

In 2001, shortly before undertaking the drafting of a binding international human rights treaty, the UNGA decided that it was time to adopt a revised version of the ICIDH. The revised document, the ICF, represents a significant improvement on its predecessor and provides an authoritative framework for measuring health and disability at both individual and population levels. The ICF was endorsed by all 191 WHO Member States during the fifty-fourth World Health Assembly on 22 May 2001.[37] As a classification system, the ICF focuses on the impact of disease, disorder or injury on the functioning of an individual in society. Under the framework of the ICF, disability represents an umbrella term for impairments, activity limitations and participation restrictions. The ICF adopts the 'bio-psychosocial model' of disability, according to which disability is a product of the interaction between the characteristics of the person (impairment) and environmental factors (social, physical, attitudinal etc.). The ICF therefore recognises the fact that an individual's disease, disorder or injury is affected by contextual factors (both environmental and personal), and the document lists those factors explicitly (Figure 2.4[38]).

Notwithstanding the fact that the ICF explicitly mentions contextual factors, the document retains some of the remnants of the medical model, and some disability rights activists and scholars are of the opinion that the ICF places too much emphasis on medical factors. Kayess and French point to the

[36] See, for instance, David Pfeiffer, 'The ICIDH and the need for its Revision' (1998) 13(4) *Disability & Society* 503.

[37] UNGA, Resolution WHA 54.21, 22 May 2001.

[38] Image taken from http://icfeducation.org/what-is-icf.

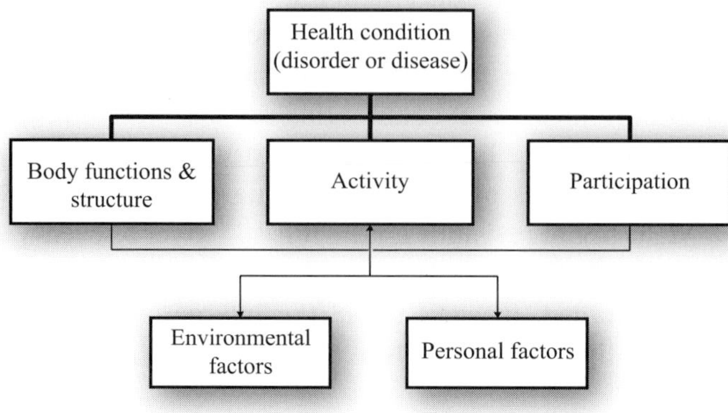

Figure 2.4 Depiction of Factors Inherent in the International Classification of Functioning, Disability and Health

fact that, in the negotiations on the CRPD, the International Disability Caucus (IDC) – which is the network of global, regional and national organisations of persons with disabilities – 'vehemently opposed reference to the ICF'. In essence, the authors argue that the IDC viewed the ICF as 'part of the human rights problem' faced by persons with disabilities, a problem which the CRPD was designed to overcome through adopting the social-contextual model of disability.[39]

In spite of the criticisms that it has attracted from certain quarters, the ICF has already been applied widely at the national and international levels in a variety of settings. The classification system inherent in the ICF has formed the basis for national health and disability reporting surveys, *inter alia*, the Multi-Country Survey Study on Health and Responsiveness (MCSS) and the World Health Survey Program, in order to measure the health status of the general population across seventy-one countries. Bickenbach argues that the ICF can serve as 'a potential bridge, not merely between indicators and data sources – which is, in practical terms, an essential facilitator of a scientifically respectable monitoring process – but also a bridge between scientific values and the political and social values expressed in the rights in the CRPD'.[40] By focusing, to quite a significant degree, on the impact of contextual factors on the functioning of a person

[39] Rosemary Kayess and Philip French, 'Out of Darkness into Light? Introducing the Convention on the Rights of Persons with Disabilities' (2008) 8(1) *Human Rights Law Review* 1, at 25.

[40] Jerome Bickenbach, 'Monitoring the United Nation's Convention on the Rights of Persons with Disabilities: Data and the International Classification of Functioning, Disability and Health' (2011) 31(11) *BMC Public Health* 1, at 7.

with a disability, the ICF has moved the focus from impairment to the environment. Once again, this signifies the overall shift in the disability rights debate – disability is no longer perceived solely as a rehabilitation and welfare issue. However, as the IDC argued during the negotiation sessions of the CRPD, the ICF remains 'a very controversial definition of disability that many disability organi[s]ations do not accept'.[41] This is one of the reasons why the negotiating states decided not to include a definition of disability in the Convention, as will be further elaborated on in Chapter 3 of this textbook.

SUMMARY

- **There were significant gaps in the protection of the rights of persons with disabilities before the CRPD came onto the international human rights landscape.**
- **In the past, the rights of people with disabilities were not always viewed through the lens of equality and human dignity at the UN level. Rather, people with disabilities were viewed as objects, not subjects of the law. For a long time, the focus was on the impairments of persons with disabilities and on attempts to 'cure' their functional limitations, through rehabilitation, welfare and other means.**
- **A dramatic shift has taken place in the UN over the last few decades with regard to the conceptualisation of disability and the protection of disability rights, and there has been an evolution from a charity-based approach to a human rights model of disability.**
- **Instruments such as the Standard Rules on the Equalization of Opportunities for Persons with Disabilities paved the way for this shift in perspective.**
- **The Standard Rules called strongly on governments to adopt appropriate measures, aimed at achieving full participation and equality of opportunities for persons with disabilities.**
- **Whatever their merits, the Standard Rules did not succeed in filling the existing gaps in human rights protection for disabled people. In particular, the Rules lacked binding enforcement mechanisms.**
- **The adoption of the CRPD in 2006 represents the high point of the evolution of disability rights protection at the level of international human rights law.**
- **Two specialised agencies, the International Labour Organization and the World Health Organization, have played an important role in advancing the disability rights agenda.**

[41] UN Ad Hoc Committee, '7th Session on Draft Article 2' (31 January 2005), available at www.un.org/esa/socdev/enable/rights/adhocmeetings.htm.

ACTIVITIES

REVIEW QUESTIONS

1. **What are the overlapping elements in the Standard Rules and General Comment No. 5 of the CESCR?**
2. **Why do the Standard Rules represent such an important instrument in the disability rights agenda?**
3. **What is the 'bio-psychosocial model' of disability?**

ESSAY QUESTIONS

1. **'The UN has progressed significantly in its conceptualisation and perception of disability in the last few decades.' *Discuss.***
2. **'The ICF was a welcome complement to its forerunner, the ICIDH, from the perspective of ensuring equality for persons with disabilities.' *Discuss.***

GROUP PROJECT

Make a timeline of the various events that took place prior to the CRPD, the most relevant instruments adopted at the UN level and the significance of those instruments in the struggle for equal rights for people with disabilities.

FURTHER READING

Cieza, A. and Stucki, G., 'The International Classification of Functioning, Disability and Health: Its Development Process and Content Validity' (2008) 44(3) *European Journal of Physical and Rehabilitation Medicine* 303–13.

Jones, M., 'Inclusion, Social Inclusion and Participation', in M. H. Rioux, L. A. Basser and M. Jones (eds.), *Critical Perspectives on Human Rights and Disability Policy* (Leiden/Boston: Brill, 2011), pp. 57–83.

Kanter, A., *The Development of Disability Rights under International Law: From Charity to Human Rights* (Abingdon: Routledge, 2015).

Kayess, R. and French, P., 'Out of Darkness into Light? Introducing the Convention on the Rights of Persons with Disabilities' (2008) 8(1) *Human Rights Law Review* 1–34.

Kostanjsek, N., 'Use of the International Classification of Functioning, Disability and Health (ICF) as a Conceptual Framework and Common Language for Disability Statistics and Health Information Systems' (2011) 11(4) *BMC Public Health* 1–6.

Masala, C. and Petretto, D. R., 'From Disablement to Enablement: Conceptual Models of Disability in the 20th Century' (2008) 30(17) *Disability Rehabilitation* 1233–44.

Quinn, G. and Degener, T., *Human Rights and Disability: The Current Use and Future Potential of the United Nations Human Rights Instruments in the Context of Disability* (New York/Geneva: United Nations, 2002).

Scheidert, M., Hurst, R., Miller, J. and Ustün, B., 'The Role of Environment in the International Classification of Functioning, Disability and

Health (ICF)' (2003) 25(11–12) *Disability Rehabilitation* 588–95.

Stein, M. A., 'Disability Human Rights' (2007) 95 *California Law Review* 75–121.

Traustadottir, R., 'Disability Studies, the Social Model and Legal Developments', in O. M. Arnardóttir and G. Quinn (eds.), *The UN Convention on the Rights of Persons with Disabilities: European and Scandinavian Perspectives* (Leiden/Boston: Brill, 2009), pp. 1–16.

3 The United Nations Convention on the Rights of Persons with Disabilities

LEARNING OUTCOMES

- ✓ Describe the process of elaboration of the CRPD.
- ✓ Identify and understand the key features of the CRPD.
- ✓ Outline and critically discuss the rationale and the structure of the CRPD.
- ✓ Critically assess the general obligations of the CRPD.
- ✓ Understand the general principles of the CRPD.
- ✓ Understand the role of the CRPD Committee in monitoring the implementation of the Convention.
- ✓ Comprehend the main tenets of Article 33 CRPD and the core features of the national monitoring system of the CRPD.
- ✓ Describe the role of other UN bodies in protecting and promoting the rights of persons with disabilities and in enhancing compliance with the CRPD globally.

The UN Convention on the Rights of Persons with Disabilities is a landmark human rights treaty. It obliges State Parties to promote, protect and ensure the full and equal enjoyment of all human rights by all persons with disabilities. Equal rights – not just charity, is the message.[1]

1 INTRODUCTION

As highlighted in Chapter 2, the CRPD is the culmination of a long process of emerging disability rights.[2] It also represents the acknowledgement that the core international human rights conventions, while undoubtedly applying to all individuals, had failed to ensure the protection of the rights of people with disabilities.[3] The CRPD is the very first international treaty that sets forth legal obligations to ensure and promote the rights of persons with disabilities,[4] and, as Harpur underlines, it has 'created a unique opportunity to drive change and provide disability scholarship and politics with a common focus'.[5]

To date, the CRPD has enhanced and stimulated a comprehensive disability rights discourse among scholars and throughout civil society, alike. This chapter builds on that wide discourse and aims to capture and summarise the main features of the Convention. To that end, this chapter is divided into eight main sections. Further to this brief introduction, section 2 examines the negotiation process of the CRPD, while section 3 addresses the scholarly debate concerning the most innovative features of the Convention. Section 4 critically discusses the structure and core provisions, as well as the general obligations and general principles of the CRPD. Section 5 provides an overview of the substantive rights enshrined in the CRPD, which will be analysed at length in subsequent chapters. Section 6 briefly highlights the role that data collection plays in respect to the human rights of persons with disabilities.

1 Thomas Hammarberg, 'Foreword', in Mental Disability Advocacy Center (MDAC), *Building the Architecture for Change: Guidelines on Article 33 of the UN Convention on the Rights of Persons with Disabilities* (2011), available at http://mdac.info/sites/mdac.info/files/Article_33_EN.pdf.

2 Maria Rita Saulle, *The Disabled Persons and the International Organizations* (New York: International Documentation Ent., 1981).

3 Gerard Quinn and Theresia Degener, *Human Rights and Disability: The Current Use and Future Potential of United Nations Human Rights Instruments in the Context of Disability* (New York/Geneva: United Nations, 2002).

4 Only the Convention on the Rights of the Child (CRC) includes a provision (Article 23) on children with disabilities.

5 Paul Harpur, 'Embracing the New Disability Rights Paradigm: The Importance of the Convention on the Rights of Persons with Disabilities' (2012) 27(1) *Disability and Society* 1.

Section 7 discusses Article 32 CRPD and the role of international cooperation. Section 8 addresses the international monitoring system of the Convention, with a particular focus on the role of the Committee on the Rights of Persons with Disabilities (CRPD Committee). Section 9 explores the national monitoring system provided for in Article 33, while section 10 focuses on the role of civil society, namely persons with disabilities, in implementing the CRPD. Finally, the role of other UN bodies in protecting and promoting the rights of persons with disabilities and in enhancing global compliance with the CRPD is explored in section 11.

2 THE NEGOTIATION OF THE UNITED NATIONS CONVENTION ON THE RIGHTS OF PERSONS WITH DISABILITIES

By the end of the 1990s, the need for a binding instrument to fully protect and promote the rights of persons with disabilities had become increasingly clear. In December 1998, a consultative Expert Group Meeting on International Norms and Standards relating to Disability, convened by the UN at Berkeley, acknowledged the need to develop 'specific instruments that refine and give detailed contextual content to those general guarantees'.[6] A similar conclusion was reached by the 1999 Interregional Seminar and Symposium, which was held in Hong Kong.[7] In 2000, the Declaration on the Rights of People with Disabilities in the New Century, adopted during a World Summit on Disability, called for a legally binding convention to ensure the rights of people with disabilities to full and equal participation in society.[8]

In 2001, Mexico successfully introduced a resolution at the UN General Assembly (UNGA), proposing that an Ad Hoc Committee should be established to draft an international treaty to protect the rights and dignity of persons with disabilities. This Ad Hoc Committee was then created through the UNGA, by means of Resolution 56/168 of 19 December 2001, with the mandate to draft a comprehensive international convention.[9]

6 The report of the meeting can be found at www.independentliving.org/docs4/disberk.pdf.

7 Marcia Rioux, Lee Ann Basser and Melinda Jones, 'Conclusion', in Marcia Rioux, Lee Ann Basser and Melinda Jones (eds.), *Critical Perspectives on Human Rights and Disability Policy* (Leiden/Boston: Brill, 2011), p. 482; for a discussion of these meetings and their outcome, see Theresia Degener, 'International Disability Law – A New Legal Subject on the Rise: The Interregional Experts' Meeting in Hong Kong, December 13–17, 1999' (2000) 18 *Berkeley Journal of International Law* 180, at 180.

8 See above Chapter 2.

9 The General Assembly renewed the mandate of the Ad Hoc Committee four times from 2002 to 2005 (Resolutions 57/229 of 18 December 2002, 58/246 of 23 December 2003, 59/198 of 20 December 2004, and 60/232 of 23 December 2005).

The Ad Hoc Committee met eight times over a period of five years.[10] During the first meeting, several states continued to express a degree of scepticism with regard to the necessity to draft a new convention specifically on disability. The former European Community (EC), now the EU, also contended that there was no obligation to adopt a legally binding instrument.[11] It was only at the second meeting of the Ad Hoc Committee, in 2003, after a series of regional meetings, and thanks to the awareness-raising activities of civil society and DPOs, that a consensus on the necessity to draft a legally binding treaty was reached. The Ad Hoc Committee then decided to establish a Working Group (WG), with the aim of formulating a draft text, which would form the basis for further negotiations. This WG consisted of twenty-seven governmental representatives, designated by regional groups; twelve representatives from non-governmental organisations (NGOs); and one representative of national human rights institutions (NHRIs). The WG draft text was the core document upon which all further proposals were based. It was reviewed extensively in the subsequent sessions of the Ad Hoc Committee.[12] The debate at the Committee's sessions was intense and often highly fraught, especially in relation to sensitive issues, such as legal capacity, sexuality and inclusion in educational settings.[13] However, the Ad Hoc Committee succeeded in striking a balance and brokering a compromise between all sides. It approved the final text of the CRPD at the beginning of December 2006 and sent it to the UNGA, where it was formally adopted by consensus a week later – on 13 December 2006. The CRPD was then opened for signature on 30 March 2007. It was signed by a large number of states on the very first day, and this constituted a record for any UN treaty.[14] In accordance with Article 45(1) CRPD, the Convention entered into force on 3 May 2008, the thirtieth day after the

[10] Theresia Degener and Andrew Begg, 'From Invisible Citizens to Agents of Change: A Short History of the Struggle for the Recognition of the Rights of Persons with Disabilities at the United Nations', in Valentina Della Fina, Rachele Cera and Giuseppe Palmisano (eds.), *The United Nations Convention on Human Rights: A Commentary* (Cham: Springer, 2017), pp. 1–38, pp. 15 et seq.

[11] Position paper by the European Union, 'Comprehensive and Integral International Convention to Promote and Protect the Rights and Dignity of Persons with Disability' (2002) A/AC.265/WP.2, available at www.un.org/esa/socdev/enable/rights/adhocmeetaac265w2e.htm.

[12] Ad Hoc Committee, Draft Comprehensive and Integral International Convention on the Protection and Promotion of the Rights and Dignity of Persons with Disabilities, UN Doc. A/AC.265/2004/WG/1, available at www.un.org/esa/socdev/enable/rights/ahcwgreportax1.htm.

[13] Arlene Kanter, 'The Promise and Challenge of the United Nations Convention on the Rights of Persons with Disabilities' (2007) 34 *Syracuse Journal International Law and Commerce* 287, at 289.

[14] Ibid. at 288. See also at www.un.org/development/desa/disabilities/convention-on-the-rights-of-persons-with-disabilities.html.

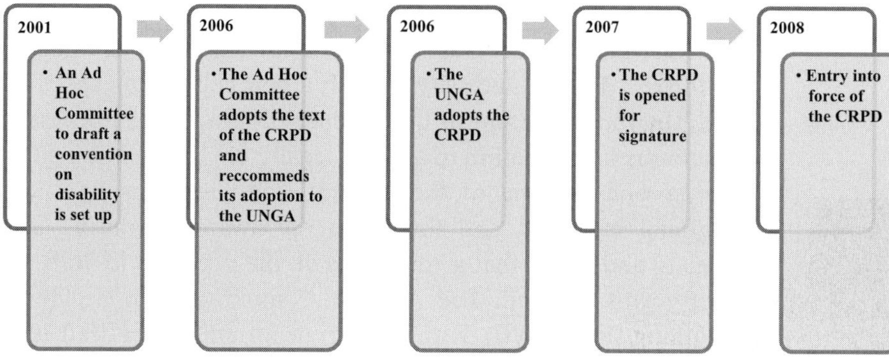

Figure 3.1 Timeline of the CRPD Negotiation Process

date of the deposit of its twentieth instrument of ratification or accession.[15] These important milestones are illustrated in Figure 3.1.

The CRPD negotiations involved the highest level of participation by representatives of DPOs, of other civil society organisations and NGOs of any human rights convention in history.[16] As a result, those actors played a vital role in developing and negotiating the final text.[17] Representatives of accredited DPOs not only participated in all public meetings held by the Ad Hoc Committee, but also in informal consultations.[18] States also included persons with disabilities and disability experts in their delegations at meetings, after having consulted with them at the national level in the preparatory process.[19] Some States incorporated people with disabilities as official heads of their delegations.

In order to promote and support the participation of DPOs from all over the world, the Ad Hoc Committee established a UN Voluntary Fund on Disability. That fund enabled the payment of the travel and accommodation costs of several people with disabilities, to facilitate their attendance at each session of the Ad Hoc Committee. In addition, in order to foster participation, the UN Secretariat made official documents immediately available in Braille and in

[15] Generally, a state first signs a treaty, before ratifying it. Ratification defines the act whereby a state indicates its consent to be bound to a treaty. By way of contrast, 'accession' is the act whereby a state later becomes a party to a treaty that has already been negotiated and signed by other states, without having signed the treaty itself. Accession has the same legal effect as ratification.

[16] Rosemary Kayess and Philip French, 'Out of Darkness into Light? Introducing the Convention on the Rights of Persons with Disabilities' (2008) 8(1) *Human Rights Law Review* 1, at 25.

[17] Gerard Quinn, 'A Short Guide to the United Nations Convention on the Rights of Persons with Disabilities', in Lisa Waddington and Gerard Quinn (eds.), *European Yearbook of Disability Law* (Antwerp/Oxford/Portland: Intersentia, 2009), pp. 89–114, p. 98.

[18] Tara Melish, 'The UN Disability Convention: Historic Process, Strong Prospects, and Why the U.S. Should Ratify' (2007) 14(2) *Human Rights Brief* 37, at 43.

[19] Ibid. at 43.

other accessible formats. This participatory approach was unparalleled and proved extremely successful. According to Degener and Begg, 'all those who participated in the process contributed to one of the richest, least politicised and most inclusive human rights debates at the United Nations for some years'.[20]

UN Secretary-General Kofi Annan's message on the adoption of the CRPD, as delivered by Mark Malloch Brown, Deputy Secretary-General (13 December 2006), available at www.un.org/press/en/2006/sgsm10797.doc.htm.

For most people in this room, today marks an important event: the day the General Assembly adopts the Convention on the Rights of Persons with Disabilities. But for 650 million persons around the world living with disabilities, today promises to be the dawn of a new era – an era in which disabled people will no longer have to endure the discriminatory practices and attitudes that have been permitted to prevail for all too long.

This Convention is a remarkable and forward-looking document.

...

While it focuses on the rights and development of people with disabilities, it also speaks about our societies as a whole – and about the need to enable every person to contribute to the best of their abilities and potential ... It was the community of the disabled themselves that worked tirelessly and insistently to promote this Convention, and the United Nations responded. In three short years, the Convention became a landmark several times over: it is the first human rights treaty to be adopted in the twenty-first century; the most rapidly negotiated human rights treaty in the history of international law; and the first to emerge from lobbying conducted extensively through the Internet ...

3 THE UNITED NATIONS CONVENTION ON THE RIGHTS OF PERSONS WITH DISABILITIES AS A HUMAN RIGHTS TREATY

As highlighted earlier in this textbook,[21] the Convention is underpinned by the social-contextual model of disability and the view that 'disability results from

[20] Theresia Degener and Andrew Begg, 'From Invisible Citizens to Agents of Change: A Short History of the Struggle for the Recognition of the Rights of Persons with Disabilities at the United Nations', note 10, p. 37. See also Theresia Degener, 'A New Human Rights Model of Disability', in Della Fina, Cera and Palmisano (eds.), *The United Nations Convention on the Rights of Persons with Disabilities: A Commentary*, note 10, pp. 42–59.

[21] See above the Introduction chapter, section 2.

the interaction between persons with impairments and attitudinal and environmental barriers that hinder their full and effective participation in society on an equal basis with others'.[22] However, the CRPD also has the merit of making disability a human rights issue (as discussed in sub-section 3.1 below) and of reformulating human rights in a disability context (as examined in sub-section 3.2 below).

3.1 Disability as a Human Rights Issue

Stein and Lord suggest that the CRPD 'seeks to recast disability as a social construction'.[23] In doing so, the Convention departs from previous documents in the area of disability by focusing on the removal of barriers to ensure the equal exercise and enjoyment of rights by persons with disabilities and their full participation in society. Hence, it marks the definitive abandonment of the medical model at the international level. The CRPD represents a paradigm shift in the way in which disability is conceptualised and strives to ensure that national disability policies reflect this shift. According to Degener, the CRPD is also innovative in that it embraces the human rights model of disability,[24] by ensuring that all disabled persons enjoy legal capacity and by including a comprehensive set of rights (civil and political rights as well as economic, social and cultural rights).[25]

It is undisputed that the CRPD has made disability a human rights issue and is, in itself, a core human rights treaty. In this respect, Seatzu posits that the Convention has been modelled on existing human rights treaties, which encompass duties and obligations that are of a special character, i.e. duties that are assumed by each contracting country in relation to individuals within their jurisdiction, as opposed to duties existing between states.[26]

3.2 New Rights or Old Rights?

It is generally stipulated that the CRPD does not establish new rights for people with disabilities. The mandate of the Ad Hoc Committee, under whose auspices the CRPD was developed, was to apply existing human rights to the particular

[22] Preamble para. (e) of the CRPD.

[23] Michael Stein and Janet Lord, 'Future Prospects for the United Nations Convention on Disability', in Gerard Quinn and Oddný Mjöll Arnardóttir (eds.), *The UN Convention on the Rights of Persons with Disabilities: European and Scandinavian Perspectives* (Leiden/Boston: Brill, 2009), pp. 17–64. See also Shivaun Quinlivan, 'The United Nations Convention on the Rights of Persons with Disabilities: An Introduction', (2012) 13(1) ERA Forum, 71–85, at 74.

[24] See above Chapter 1, sub-section 2.4.

[25] Degener, 'A New Human Rights Model of Disability', note 20.

[26] Francesco Seatzu, 'The Convention on the Rights of Persons with Disabilities and International Human Rights Law' (2018) 7 *International Human Rights Law Review* 82.

circumstances of people with disabilities.[27] In the same vein, the Handbook for Parliamentarians on the Convention on the Rights of Persons with Disabilities, released by the Office of the United Nations High Commissioner for Human Rights (OHCHR), affirms that the CRPD 'clarifies the obligations and legal duties of States to respect and ensure the equal enjoyment of all human rights by all persons with disabilities', complementing existing human rights treaties.[28] In general, all of the relevant official UN documents and explanatory notes on the Convention affirm that the CRPD does not create any new rights.

However, as already mentioned in the Introduction to this textbook, the Convention undoubtedly possesses an innovative character. According to Kayess and French, the CRPD modifies, transforms and adds to traditional human rights concepts in key respects and incorporates a disability-specific interpretation of existing human rights.[29] The Convention recognises that, in order to protect and respect some classical human rights, quite substantial interventions by States Parties are required. In doing so, the CRPD converts traditionally negative rights (i.e. rights based on non-interference by the State) into positive rights, which imply far-reaching State obligations and concrete positive actions.[30] For example, the right to freedom of expression is traditionally conceived of as protecting the individual against arbitrary interference by both the State and other individuals. Notably, Article 21 CRPD couples freedom of expression and opinion with the right to access information, and it requires States Parties to 'take all appropriate measures to ensure that persons with disabilities can exercise the right to freedom of expression and opinion', to provide information in accessible formats and to accept and facilitate the use of sign languages, Braille, augmentative and alternative communications. The CRPD also introduces new concepts, such as accessibility,[31] that are instrumental to the full realisation of the rights of people with disabilities.[32]

[27] Kayess and French, 'Out of Darkness into Light? Introducing the Convention on the Rights of Persons with Disabilities', note 16, at 20.

[28] Office of the United Nations High Commissioner for Human Rights (OHCHR), *Handbook for Parliamentarians on the Convention on the Rights of Persons with Disabilities and its Optional Protocol: From Exclusion to Equality Realizing the Rights of Persons with Disabilities* (2007), available at www.un.org/disabilities/documents/toolaction/ipuhb.pdf.

[29] Kayess and French, 'Out of Darkness into Light? Introducing the Convention on the Rights of Persons with Disabilities', note 16, at 32. In a similar vein, Celik affirms that, even though the CRPD seems to be relying on the traditional concepts in human rights law, such as human dignity, 'it certainly reinterprets these concepts' (Elif Celik, 'The Role of CRPD in Rethinking the Subject of Human Rights', (2017) 21(7) *The International Journal of Human Rights*, 933–955, at 949). See also Patricia Cuenca Gomez, *Los derechos fundamentales de las personas con discapacidad. Un análisis a la luz de la Convención de la ONU* (Madrid: Universidad de Alcalá, 2012).

[30] Ibid, at 33.

[31] See below Chapter 5.

[32] See generally, Harpur, 'Embracing the New Disability Rights Paradigm: The Importance of the Convention on the Rights of Persons with Disabilities', note 5.

Scholars have also acknowledged that the scope of the Convention is unprecedented.[33] Indeed, Mégret has asserted that the CRPD 'comes very close to either creating new rights or formulating rights in the context of disability that have never been framed as such'.[34] On the one hand, the CRPD re-formulates and amplifies existing rights. On the other hand, it creates 'incidental rights'[35] to ensure that existing rights can be enjoyed. This is true of reasonable accommodation, which represents a gateway to the exercise of other rights and constitutes a right in itself.[36] Moreover, the CRPD includes a number of provisions that are uncommon in human rights treaties, such as Article 31 on statistics and Article 32 on international cooperation, including international development programmes.

Finally, unlike traditional international human rights law, 'the Convention makes a very significant effort to highlight, sometimes with considerable detail, how the rights it proposes to protect are to be implemented and guaranteed'.[37] In that regard, MacKay, the chairman of the Ad Hoc Committee, has affirmed that '[w]hat the Convention endeavours to do is to elaborate in detail the rights of persons with disabilities and set out a code of implementation'.[38] As pointed out by Quinn, the CRPD provides a 'moral compass for changes as well as legal benchmarks against which to measure that change'.[39]

4 THE STRUCTURE OF THE UNITED NATIONS CONVENTION ON THE RIGHTS OF PERSONS WITH DISABILITIES AND ITS MAIN FEATURES

Having discussed above the innovative value of the CRPD, this section aims to identify the core features of the Convention, its foundational principles and main obligations, on which there will be further elaboration in subsequent chapters.

[33] Kanter, 'The Promise and Challenge of the United Nations Convention on the Rights of Persons with Disabilities', note 13, at 289.

[34] Fréderic Mégrét, 'The Disabilities Convention: Human Rights of Persons with Disabilities or Disability Rights?' (2008) 30(2) *Human Rights Quarterly* 494, at 510.

[35] Harpur, 'Embracing the New Disability Rights Paradigm: The Importance of the Convention on the Rights of Persons with Disabilities', note 5, at 2.

[36] See below Chapter 4.

[37] Mégret, 'The Disabilities Convention: Human Rights of Persons with Disabilities or Disability Rights?', note 34.

[38] United Nations, 'The Convention in Brief', available at www.un.org/development/desa/disabilities/convention-on-the-rights-of-persons-with-disabilities/the-convention-in-brief.html.

[39] Quinn, 'A Short Guide to the United Nations Convention on the Rights of Persons with Disabilities', note 17.

Articles 1 and 2	Provisions with an interpretive character
Articles 3–9	Provisions of general application
Articles 10–30	Substantive rights and obligations
Articles 31–40	Provisions on implementation and monitoring
Articles 40–50	Provisions on accession and entry into force

Figure 3.2 The Structure of the CRPD

4.1 The Structure of the Convention at a Glance

The CRPD includes a Preamble and fifty articles (Figure 3.2). The Preamble, which is not binding, is quite long and detailed, and it is comprised of twenty-five paragraphs. It plays an important role in the interpretation of the CRPD, as numerous themes addressed therein are then translated into substantive rights and obligations.[40] The overall structure of the CRPD corresponds roughly to other human rights treaties. However, interestingly, and in contrast with other human rights conventions, the CRPD includes an explanatory title for each article, to facilitate the reading and interpretation of the text. The Optional Protocol to the CRPD (OP-CRPD), containing eighteen articles, accompanies the Convention. It includes the individual complaints procedure, which enables any individual in a State Party to the Convention to bring a claim in respect of an alleged violation of his or her rights, through submitting an individual communication to the CRPD Committee.

Articles 1 and 2 CRPD have an interpretive character.[41] Article 1 outlines the purpose of the Convention, which is to 'promote, protect and ensure the full and equal enjoyment of all human rights and fundamental freedoms by all persons with disability, and to promote respect for their dignity'. This provision requires States Parties to promote (i.e. to foster recognition of), to protect (i.e. to prevent interference with) and to ensure (i.e. to enable the realisation of) the rights of persons with disabilities.[42] Article 2 contains the definitions of 'communication', 'language', 'discrimination on the basis of disability', 'reasonable accommodation' and 'universal design'.

Articles 3–9 CRPD are provisions of general application, to be applied across the text of the Convention as a whole. Article 3 enunciates the CRPD's general

[40] Rachele Cera, 'Preamble', in Della Fina, Cera and Palmisano (eds.), *The United Nations Convention on Human Rights: A Commentary*, note 10, pp. 77–88.

[41] Kayess and French, 'Out of Darkness into Light? Introducing the Convention on the Rights of Persons with Disabilities', note 16, at 26.

[42] Ibid.

principles, while Article 4 includes general obligations, with a view to encouraging 'national legal and policy reform and guiding domestic implementation of the Convention'.[43] As will be examined in Chapter 4, Article 5 CRPD requires States Parties to 'prohibit all discrimination on the basis of disability'. Article 6 strives to ensure that States Parties recognise the multiple and intersectional nature of discrimination that women with disabilities face,[44] while Article 7 aims to protect the rights of children with disabilities. By including the foregoing provisions, the CRPD acknowledges 'different layers of identity' of persons with disabilities.[45] Articles 6 and 7 must also be read in light of recital (p) of the Preamble, which expresses concern about the 'multiple or aggravated forms of discrimination' to which persons with disabilities are subjected. Article 8 recognises that awareness-raising is necessary to remove attitudinal barriers faced by people with disabilities and to allow for the full realisation of the paradigm shift intended by the CRPD. It requires States Parties to combat stereotypes 'through immediate, effective and appropriate measures' and to promote positive perceptions of persons with disabilities. Article 9 explicates the general principle of accessibility, which is enunciated in Article 3 CRPD. It obliges States Parties to dismantle barriers, by promoting different forms of accessibility in the public and private spheres, including physical, technological, economic and social accessibility as well as information and communications accessibility. As will be discussed in Chapter 5, accessibility is of key importance for the realisation of all of the rights enshrined in the CRPD.

Articles 10 to 30 cover a broad spectrum of both civil and political rights as well as economic, social and cultural rights. These provisions vary considerably in length and in their level of detail. Some of them, due to their broad formulation, cannot be allocated to one of the traditional categories of rights: this is, for instance, the case with regard to Article 12 on legal capacity and Article 19 on independent living. None of these provisions can be read in isolation, and they must be interpreted in light of the principles enunciated in Article 3.

Articles 31 to 40 concern, broadly speaking, the implementation and monitoring of the Convention at the national and international levels. As discussed in section 7 below, Article 31 has an instrumental nature, obliging States Parties to carry out extensive data collection, in order to effectively implement the CRPD. Article 32 focuses on international cooperation as a tool to facilitate the realisation of the rights in the CRPD, through, for

[43] Andrea Broderick, 'Article 4 CRPD: General Obligations', in Ilias Bantekas, Michael Ashley Stein, and Dimitris Anastasiou (eds.), *The UN Convention on the Rights of Persons with Disabilities: A Commentary* (Oxford: Oxford University Press, 2017), pp. 106–39, p. 107.

[44] See below Chapter 4.

[45] Degener, 'A New Human Rights Model of Disability', note 20, p. 37.

example, the transfer of knowledge on issues such as accessibility. Articles 33 to 40 set out the monitoring system of the CRPD. This includes the establishment of focal points, coordination mechanisms and independent monitoring mechanisms at the national level and the establishment of a treaty body, the CRPD Committee, to monitor the implementation of the Convention at the international level. The OP-CRPD enables the CRPD Committee to hear individual and group communications and to undertake inquiries on systematic violations of the Convention. Article 40 specifies that States Parties must meet regularly at the Conference of States Parties (COSP), 'in order to consider any matter with regard to the implementation of the present Convention'.

The final provisions of the CRPD, Articles 40 to 50, concern the accession processes to, and the entry into force of, the Convention. Article 44 allows the accession of 'regional integration organi[s]ations', which are defined as organisations 'constituted by sovereign States of a given region, to which its member States have transferred competence in respect of matters governed by the present Convention'. This provision was included specifically to allow for the accession of the EU to the CRPD. It is not unprecedented, as other multilateral treaties, for example, the United Nations Educational, Scientific and Cultural Organization (UNESCO) Convention on the Protection and Promotion of the Diversity of Cultural Expressions,[46] include similar articles that refer to 'regional integration organisations' or 'regional economic integration organisations', where it is clear that what is intended by the term is the EU. However, it is the first provision of this kind to be included in a UN human rights treaty.

4.2 The (Non-)Definition of Disability in the Convention

During the negotiations, there was considerable disagreement on whether or not to include a definition of disability in the text of the CRPD. Some States suggested not including a precise definition, in order to prioritise flexibility and the need for a dynamic interpretation over time. For instance, the European Commission, negotiating on behalf of the EU, argued that the approach adopted by the EU in its discrimination legislation, which does not contain any definition of disability, was preferable. A number of States expressed concern that a broad definition of disability would have required them to recognise, in domestic legislation, a large number of groups not traditionally considered to be persons with disabilities, such as individuals with HIV/AIDS. Many States suggested that a definition of disability would become outdated and would risk leaving certain groups outside the Convention's scope.

[46] UNESCO, Convention on the Protection and Promotion of the Diversity of Cultural Expressions, 20 December 2005.

Conversely, DPOs and NGOs argued that, in the absence of a definition of disability in the Convention itself, national definitions of disability would prevail, preventing uniform implementation of the CRPD. In the WG it was agreed that, if included in the text of the Convention, a definition of disability should reflect the social-contextual model.

As a result of a long debate, and in order to strike a compromise between these contrasting views, the final text of the CRPD provides an open-ended conceptualisation of disability, both in the non-binding Preamble and in Article 1. By contrast, Article 2, devoted to definitions, does not mention disability, nor does it refer to people with disabilities. The Preamble, at recital (e) thereof, affirms that '[d]isability is an evolving concept and that disability results from the interaction between persons with impairments and attitudinal and environmental barriers that hinders their full and effective participation in society on an equal basis with others'. Article 1(2) CRPD, which outlines the purpose of the Convention, states as follows: '[p]ersons with disabilities include those who have long-term physical, mental, intellectual or sensory impairments which in interaction with various barriers may hinder their full and effective participation in society on an equal basis with others'. This is intended to provide a minimum ground of protection to be fulfilled by States Parties to the Convention, allowing for a dynamic approach that can facilitate adaptations over time and in different socio-economic settings. The CRPD does not define disability any further than this, and it does not set forth any distinction between different categories of disability.

To date, the CRPD Committee has not had the opportunity to discuss the content and meaning of Article 1 of the Convention. It did, however, briefly elaborate on the concept of disability in *S.C.* v. *Brazil*, an individual communication that was ultimately declared inadmissible.[47] The Committee emphasised that 'persons with disabilities include, but are not limited to, those who have long-term physical, mental, intellectual or sensory impairments which, in interaction with various barriers, may hinder their full and effective participation in society'.[48] The Committee focused on the social context, and it affirmed that 'the difference between illness and disability is a difference of

> Read the decision of the Committee in *SC* v. *Brazil*, and write a short case-note.

[47] CRPD Committee, *S.C. v. Brazil*, Communication No. 10/2013, UN Doc. CRPD/C/12/D/10/2013.

[48] Ibid. para. 6.3.

degree and not a difference of kind' and that a 'health impairment which initially is conceived of as illness can develop into an impairment in the context of disability as a consequence of its duration or its chronicity'.[49] The Committee also mentioned the 'human rights-based model of disability' and the need for the diversity of persons with disabilities to be taken into account, in combination with attitudinal and environmental barriers. In a decision adopted in August 2017 in relation to a person with albinism, the Committee recalled, once again, that a 'human rights-based model of disability requires the diversity of persons with disabilities to be taken into account'.[50] In that connection, it clarified that albinism falls within the definition of 'disability' as enshrined by Article 1 CRPD.

4.3 The General Principles of the Convention

ARTICLE 3 CRPD

The principles of the present Convention shall be:

(a) Respect for inherent dignity, individual autonomy including the freedom to make one's own choices, and independence of persons;
(b) Non-discrimination;
(c) Full and effective participation and inclusion in society;
(d) Respect for difference and acceptance of persons with disabilities as part of human diversity and humanity;
(e) Equality of opportunity;
(f) Accessibility;
(g) Equality between men and women;
(h) Respect for the evolving capacities of children with disabilities and respect for the right of children with disabilities to preserve their identities.

Article 3 CRPD outlines the general, or normative, principles upon which the Convention is based. These principles are intended to guide States Parties in the implementation of the Convention and should also serve as a benchmark against which States Parties assess the conformity of domestic laws with the Convention. The identification of a set of general principles is a usual feature in international law. However, in the context of human

[49] Ibid.

[50] CRPD Committee, *X v. Tanzania*, Communication No. 22/2014, UN Doc. CRPD/C/18/D/22/2014. A similar statement is included in CRPD Committee, General Comment No. 7, 9 November 2018, UN Doc. CRPD/C/GC/7, para. 9.

rights treaties, general principles are typically drawn from the substantive provisions of the treaty, rather than being condensed into one article. In this respect, Article 3 can be considered quite 'unique among the core human rights treaties'.[51]

Respect for human dignity is a key feature of international human rights law and in several domestic constitutions (e.g. Article 1 of the German Constitution and Article 10 of the Spanish Constitution). However, the CRPD, differently from previous international treaties and domestic provisions, couples the principle of respect for human dignity with that of individual autonomy and freedom to make one's own choices. The latter principle has significant relevance for people with disabilities, who have experienced, and continue to experience, deprivations of their legal capacity.

Non-discrimination is another general principle of the Convention. It is contained in Article 3(b) CRPD and is closely intertwined with that of equality of opportunity in Article 3(e), gender equality in Article 3(f) and also with the principle of respect for difference contained in Article 3(d). In addition, it is linked to the principle of respect for the evolving capacities of children with disabilities in Article 3(h) of the Convention. The foregoing general principles, read in combination, endeavour to redress disadvantage, address stigma and stereotyping and remove the barriers that prevent the full enjoyment of fundamental rights. The CRPD also recognises multiple and intersectional discrimination in recital (p) of the Preamble and in Article 6, and adopts a multi-dimensional approach to equality by requiring States Parties to respect and accommodate the difference of people with disabilities.

The principle of full and effective participation and inclusion of people with disabilities in society features among the core objectives of the CRPD, and it is closely linked to the full enjoyment of both civil and political rights as well as economic, social and cultural rights.

Finally, Article 3(f) CRPD qualifies accessibility as a general principle. This provision builds on Rule 5 of the Standard Rules on the Equalization of Opportunities for People with Disabilities (Standard Rules), which acknowledges the essential role that accessibility plays in the context of disability. Accessibility occupies a key position in the Convention and references to this principle, fully explicated in Article 9, can be found in several other provisions (e.g. Articles 13, 21 and 30).

[51] Valentina Della Fina, 'Article 3: General Principles', in Della Fina, Cera and Palmisano (eds.), *The United Nations Convention on Human Rights: A Commentary*, note 10, pp. 120–36. On Article 3 see also Sarah Arduin, 'Article 3: General Principles', in Ilias Bantekas, Michael Ashley Stein, and Dimitris Anastasiou (eds.), *The UN Convention on the Rights of Persons with Disabilities. A Commentary* (Oxford: Oxford University Press, 2018), pp. 84–105.

4.4 The General Obligations in the Convention

Article 4 CRPD is a key provision that 'defines the scope of these obligations and their legal nature'.[52] This section focuses, in particular, on Article 4(1) and (2), while Article 4(3) is discussed in section 7.

4.4.1 *Article 4(1) CRPD*

ARTICLE 4(1) CRPD

1. States Parties undertake to ensure and promote the full realization of all human rights and fundamental freedoms for all persons with disabilities without discrimination of any kind on the basis of disability. To this end, States Parties undertake:

a) To adopt all appropriate legislative, administrative and other measures for the implementation of the rights recognized in the present Convention;
b) To take all appropriate measures, including legislation, to modify or abolish existing laws, regulations, customs and practices that constitute discrimination against persons with disabilities;
c) To take into account the protection and promotion of the human rights of persons with disabilities in all policies and programmes;
d) To refrain from engaging in any act or practice that is inconsistent with the present Convention and to ensure that public authorities and institutions act in conformity with the present Convention;
e) To take all appropriate measures to eliminate discrimination on the basis of disability by any person, organization or private enterprise;
f) To undertake or promote research and development of universally designed goods, services, equipment and facilities, as defined in article 2 of the present Convention, which should require the minimum possible adaptation and the least cost to meet the specific needs of a person with disabilities, to promote their availability and use, and to promote universal design in the development of standards and guidelines;
g) To undertake or promote research and development of, and to promote the availability and use of new technologies, including information and communications technologies, mobility aids, devices and assistive technologies, suitable for persons with disabilities, giving priority to technologies at an affordable cost;

[52] Valentina Della Fina, 'Article 4: General Obligations', in Della Fina, Cera and Palmisano (eds.), *The United Nations Convention on Human Rights: A Commentary*, note 10, pp. 137–55, p. 141.

h) To provide accessible information to persons with disabilities about mobility aids, devices and assistive technologies, including new technologies, as well as other forms of assistance, support services and facilities;
i) To promote the training of professionals and staff working with persons with disabilities in the rights recognized in the present Convention so as to better provide the assistance and services guaranteed by those rights.

The formulation of Article 4 evokes that of Article 1(1) CRPD, and both provisions must be read in conjunction. By undertaking to 'ensure and promote' the full realisation of the rights of persons with disabilities under the Convention, States Parties 'have vowed to adopt several concrete positive measures in safeguarding the full spectrum of rights contained in the Convention'.[53] States Parties are required to adopt legislative, administrative, financial, judicial and all other necessary measures to ensure the realisation of the object and purpose of the CRPD. In addition, they must review and amend national laws and policies, to ensure compliance with the CRPD.

Article 4(1)(c) requires that States Parties mainstream disability in all their policies. This provision suggests that States Parties must carry out periodic screening, to assess the compliance of policies and programmes with the CRPD. Additionally, Article 4(1)(d) requires States Parties to ensure that public authorities and institutions act in compliance with the Convention. There is no definition of 'public authorities and institutions' in the CRPD, as these will be defined and identified at the domestic level. Article 4(1)(d) can be read in conjunction with Article 4(5), which affirms that the obligations laid out in the Convention 'extend to all parts of federal States without any limitations or exceptions'. The latter provision is quite common in international treaty law, and it is designed to ensure that regional and federal bodies and authorities do not escape their implementation obligations under the Convention due to their devolved state structure.[54]

Article 4(1)(e) CRPD requires States Parties to take measures to abolish disability discrimination by persons, organisations or private enterprises. This provision is modelled on Article 2(e) of the Convention on the Elimination of All Forms of Discrimination against Women (CEDAW)[55] and must be read in conjunction with Articles 3 and 5 CRPD. Article 4(1)(e) is particularly

[53] Broderick, 'Article 4 CRPD: General Obligations', note 43, p. 116. [54] Ibid. p. 138.

[55] Convention on the Elimination of All Forms of Discrimination against Women, 18 December 1979, in force 3 September 1981, adopted and opened for signature, ratification and accession by General Assembly Resolution No. 34/180. See in particular Article 2(e) CEDAW, which

significant because it clarifies that States Parties are not only required to ensure that discrimination against persons with disabilities by the State and its organs is prohibited, but they must also ensure that the prohibition of discrimination extends to the private sphere. This illustrates that discriminatory acts against a disabled person by private employers or private service providers (transport providers, internet providers, shops, banks etc.) are forbidden by the Convention.[56]

Moreover, Article 4(1) CRPD includes several specific obligations that are linked to the realisation of the principle of accessibility. These encompass the obligation to engage in or promote the research and development of new technologies[57] and the obligation to provide accessible information about assistive technology to persons with disabilities.[58]

Finally, it is worth noting that Article 4(1)(i) CRPD requires States Parties to promote training on the rights provided for in the CRPD to those working with disabled persons. This requirement to ensure training of professionals and staff also features in Article 8(2)(d), which requires States Parties to promote training programmes on the rights of persons with disabilities within the context of awareness-raising activities. Training is also essential when it comes to the implementation of Article 9 CRPD. In its General Comment No. 2 on accessibility, which will be thoroughly discussed in Chapter 5, the CRPD Committee affirms that 'since a lack of accessibility is often the result of insufficient awareness and technical know-how, Article 9 requires that States [P]arties provide training to all stakeholders on accessibility for persons with disabilities'.[59]

4.4.2 *Article 4(2) CRPD*

ARTICLE 4(2) CRPD

With regard to economic, social and cultural rights, each State Party undertakes to take measures to the maximum of its available resources and, where needed, within the framework of international cooperation, with a view to achieving progressively the full realization of these rights, without prejudice to those obligations contained in the present Convention that are immediately applicable according to international law.

requires States to take all appropriate measures to eliminate discrimination against women by any person, organisation or enterprise.

[56] Broderick, 'Article 4 CRPD: General Obligations', note 43, p. 123. [57] Article 4(g) CRPD.

[58] Article 4(h) CRPD.

[59] CRPD Committee, General Comment No. 2, 22 May 2014, UN Doc. CRPD/C/GC/2, para. 19.

While the CRPD reaffirms 'the universality, indivisibility, interdependence and interrelatedness of all human rights and fundamental freedoms' in its Preamble, Article 4(2) CRPD sets out the traditional distinction between rights that are subject to immediate implementation (i.e. civil and political rights) and those that are to be realised progressively (i.e. economic, social and cultural rights). Progressive realisation clauses are included in many international human rights treaties, and, in this respect, the CRPD follows a well-established pattern. Article 4(2) CRPD acknowledges the fact that States Parties are allowed to realise socio-economic rights progressively, with a view to achieving their full protection and promotion over time, because the realisation of such rights is often heavily dependent on the availability of resources.

The OHCHR has stated that progressive realisation is 'a practical device that acknowledge(s) the real world challenges' and 'helps to avoid overburdening states, employers and other duty-bearers'.[60] However, the UN Committee on Economic, Social and Cultural Rights (CESCR) has affirmed that progressive realisation 'should not be misinterpreted as depriving the obligation [to give effect to rights] of all meaningful content'; rather, it imposes an obligation on States to move 'as expeditiously and effectively as possible' and devote the maximum of available resources towards the full realisation of rights.[61] So far, the CRPD Committee has not commented on the meaning of progressive realisation, but has made some cursory remarks in its General Comment No. 4 on Article 24.[62] In that General Comment, the Committee has made clear that 'progressive reali[s]ation must be read in conjunction with the overall objective of the Convention'.[63] It can be inferred that States Parties cannot invoke Article 4(2) to justify non-compliance with the Convention.

5 OVERVIEW OF THE SUBSTANTIVE RIGHTS IN THE CONVENTION

Many of the substantive rights included in the CRPD will be discussed in more detail in subsequent chapters of this textbook. However, this section aims to give an overview of the main rights contained in the Convention, highlighting trends and patterns in the text of the CRPD.

As mentioned above, the distinction between civil and political rights, on the one hand, and social, economic and cultural rights, on the other hand, is

[60] OHCHR, *From Vision to Action: The Road to Implementation of the Convention* (2007), available at www.un.org/esa/socdev/enable/documents/Stat_Conv/High%20Commissioner%20PM%20speakingnoteshrsigningpanelFINAL.doc.

[61] UN Committee on Economic, Social and Cultural Rights (CESCR), General Comment No. 3, 14 December 1990, UN Doc. E/1991/23, para. 9.

[62] CRPD Committee, General Comment No. 4, 2 September 2016, CRPD/C/GC/4. See below Chapter 8.

[63] Ibid.

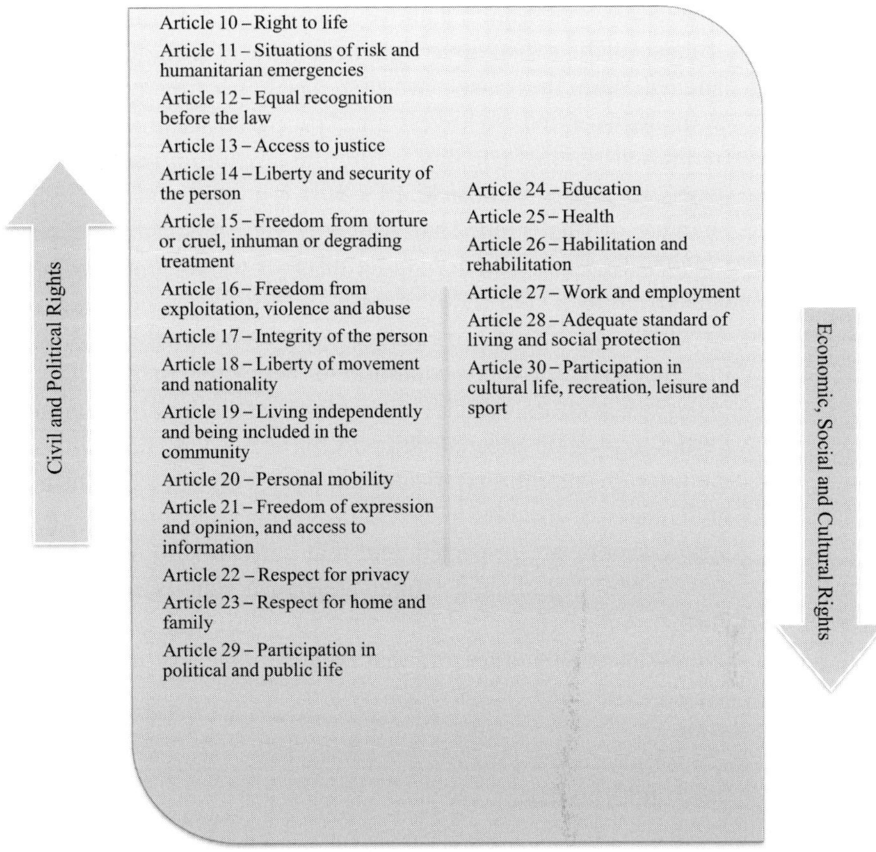

Figure 3.3 Civil and Political versus Economic, Social and Cultural Rights in the CRPD

quite blurred throughout the CRPD. However, one can argue that Articles 10 to 23 and Article 29 can be considered to fall within the ambit of civil and political rights, whereas Articles 24 to 28 and Article 30 CRPD can be qualified as economic, social and cultural rights, as depicted in Figure 3.3.

Articles 24 to 28 and Article 30 CRPD focus on the inclusion and participation of persons with disabilities in the mainstream education system, labour market, as well as in cultural and social life. Kayess and French note that the core feature of these provisions lies in requiring States Parties:

> . . . to incorporate a 'twin-track' approach to meeting the economic, social and cultural rights of persons with disability, which involves, first, incorporating disability sensitive measures into mainstream service delivery, and second, ensuring the provision of necessary specialist services and special measures in a manner that facilitates the inclusion and participation of persons with disability within the general community.[64]

[64] Kayess and French, 'Out of Darkness into Light? Introducing the Convention on the Rights of Persons with Disabilities', note 16, at 31.

In general, as highlighted above in section 3.2. of this chapter, the formulation of most of the substantive rights enunciated in the CRPD is broader and more detailed than the classic wording used in other human rights treaties. For example, as noted by Kayess and French, Article 13 'significantly extends the traditional right of equality before the law into a positive obligation to ensure access to justice'.[65] Article 19 CRPD (on independent living) is also a good example of this trend. That Article is very broad and represents a somewhat unique provision, which is quite difficult to categorise (while generally being considered as a civil right). Article 19 CRPD must be read in conjunction with Article 12 (on the right to equal recognition before the law), since the enjoyment of legal capacity is a pre-condition for being able to live an independent life and make free choices. Article 12 prohibits institutionalisation and requires States Parties to provide adequate support for people with disabilities to live within the mainstream community. In addition, States Parties must ensure that the will and preferences of disabled people, concerning their place of residence and living arrangements, are respected, and that persons with disabilities have full access to services, including personal assistance that is responsive to their needs. Furthermore, Article 19 CRPD aims to ensure that people with disabilities can live in their own homes and that they can take part in all community activities.

DID YOU KNOW THAT ...?

A study of twenty-eight European countries, published in 2007 and entitled 'Deinstitutionalisation and community living – outcomes and costs: report of a European Study' (www.kent.ac.uk/tizard/research/DECL_network/documents/DECLOC_Volume_2_Report_for_Web.pdf), estimated that at least 1.2 million people with disabilities were living in institutions in Europe.

A more recent report published in 2016 by the European Parliament, entitled 'European Structural and Investment Funds and People with Disabilities in the European Union' (www.europarl.europa.eu/RegData/etudes/STUD/2016/571386/IPOL_STU(2016)571386_EN.pdf), affirms that it is unknown how many people with disabilities live in institutional care facilities across the EU. However, there are indications that the number of people with disabilities being placed in institutional care has increased.

A similar trend has been observed in India by the Equals Centre for Promotion of Social Justice (www.ohchr.org/Documents/HRBodies/CRPD/DGD/2016/TheEqualsCentrePromotionSocialJusticeIndia.doc), which has affirmed that, between 2013 and 2016, the state's allocation of resources to institutions has doubled.

[65] Ibid. at 32.

In declaring the right to health, Article 25 CRPD places emphasis on the principle of equality and establishes that people with disabilities must be accorded the same range, quality and standard of services and health programmes that are available to others and must have access to specialist health services which are adequate to their needs. Article 25 CRPD must be read in combination with Article 26, which enshrines the right to habilitation and rehabilitation, a right that features for the first time in a human rights treaty. This latter provision is instrumental to the realisation of the principle of participation of persons with disabilities in society.

Article 28 CRPD concerns the right to an adequate standard of living and social protection. This Article joins together, in the same provision, the guarantees enshrined in Articles 9 and 11 of the International Covenant on Economic, Social and Cultural Rights (ICESCR), but it is arguably broader than the traditional right to social security. Article 28 CRPD requires States Parties to ensure housing, services and assistance for disability-related needs as well as assistance with disability-related expenses in circumstances of poverty. It also includes more generalised obligations in relation to poverty reduction, and it recognises, in line with Articles, 3, 6 and 7 CRPD, that women and girls with disabilities are in a particularly vulnerable position.

Some CRPD provisions are, by contrast, formulated in general terms, and they lack detail. This is the case, for example, with regard to Article 10 CRPD, which does not take an explicit position on pre-birth screenings, genetic testing and abortion. These issues are not touched upon in Article 25 CRPD either. The latter provisions introduce obligations for States Parties to ensure health care on a non-discriminatory basis in the area of sexual and reproductive health. In a similar vein, Article 23 CRPD, regarding respect for home and the family, requires States Parties to ensure to people with disabilities equal opportunities to experience parenthood, to marry and to found a family; to decide on the number and spacing of children; and to have access to reproductive and family planning education and means. Article 10 CRPD does not include any reference to termination of life either, while Article 25 includes only a general prohibition of 'denial of health care or health services or food and fluids on the basis of disability'.[66] The CRPD Committee has, to date, remained silent on these sensitive issues. It has, however, expressed concern about the high rate of suicide among people with disabilities[67] and has questioned the possibility for guardians to take decisions on matters pertaining to the termination or withdrawal of life-sustaining treatment.[68]

[66] Article 25 para. (f) CRPD.

[67] CRPD Committee, Concluding Observations on the Initial Report of Sweden, 11 April 2014, UN Doc. CRPD/C/SWE/CO/1, para 29.

[68] CRPD Committee, Concluding Observations on the Initial Report of Spain, 23 September 2011, UN Doc. CRPD/C/ESP/CO/1, paras. 29–30.

6 DISABILITY AND STATISTICS

Article 31 CRPD requires States Parties to collect information, including statistical and research data on people with disabilities, in order to formulate and implement disability policies, and to disseminate these statistics widely to the general public, making them fully accessible. While this is an unusual provision in the context of international human rights law, it is not entirely new. It builds upon Rule 13 of the Standard Rules, which encourages States to undertake the responsibility for the collection and dissemination of information on the living conditions of disabled people.

Pedersen affirms that Article 31 CRPD, while often overlooked by scholars, has the potential to be one of the provisions having the largest impact[69] and that it can stimulate the adoption of more effective disability policies. Statistics can support legislative developments, policy-making, and monitoring and reporting on the implementation of the Convention. The CRPD Committee has also highlighted, in almost all of its concluding observations (COs), the importance of collecting data on disability and on implementing Article 31.

To date, the availability of reliable and comparable data on the lives of people with disabilities has been both fragmentary and inconsistent. The data collected at the national, regional and international levels tend to show different interpretations of disability. Aside from the use of diverse data collection methods, until recently, disability statistics focused on impairments and on the limitations of persons with disabilities. By contrast, the CRPD requires data collection on the existence or non-existence of barriers that could hinder the individual's full and effective participation in society on an equal basis with others.

In 2001, the UN released the Guidelines and Principles for the Development of Disability Statistics.[70] These were designed to facilitate the development of statistics and indicators on the situation of persons with disabilities. Those guidelines are currently under discussion, and a revised publication is likely to

[69] Mads Pedersen, 'Article 31: Statistics and Data Collection', in Della Fina, Cera and Palmisano (eds.), *The United Nations Convention on Human Rights: A Commentary*, note 10, pp. 557–68.

[70] The Guidelines are available at https://unstats.un.org/unsd/publication/SeriesY/SeriesY_10e.pdf. In order to complement these UN Guidelines and in response to the need for more standardised disability statistics, the World Health Organization (WHO) and the United Nations Economic and Social Commission for Asia and the Pacific (ESCAP) implemented a joint project on improving disability statistics and measurement in the region. In 2008, they published a training manual, which aims to 'assist in stimulating more disability data collection in accordance with international standards and data dissemination for both national and international disability policy analysis, formulation and evaluation worldwide' (WHO-ESCAP, *Training Manual on Disability Statistics*, ST/ESCAP/2499, Bangkok, 2008, available at https://unstats.un.org/unsd/censuskb20/Attachments/2008ESCAP_TrainManDisabty-GUID7c07895389164cdab0b0b7609136f117.pdf).

be released in the future, in order to enable countries to monitor progress on the inclusion of disabled people in society and, ultimately, to ensure the full implementation of the CRPD.

7 DISABILITY AND INTERNATIONAL COOPERATION

As mentioned above, Article 32 CRPD obliges States Parties to undertake appropriate and effective measures of cooperation, also within the framework of regional and international organisations, and to promote the rights of persons with disabilities on a global scale, in conjunction with DPOs and civil society.

Kayess and French note that this provision was perhaps one of the most fiercely contested during the negotiations on the CRPD. Some States opposed the idea of creating legal obligations to undertake international cooperation, on the basis that this would contradict the usual practice at the international level.[71] In fact, within the core human rights treaties, references to international cooperation are rare and can only be found in the ICESCR and in the UN Convention on the Rights of the Child (CRC). In particular, a concern emerged among some developed countries and at EU level that Article 32 CRPD would lead to an expectation from developing states of increased financial aid.[72] By contrast, other states recognised the importance of fully integrating a disability dimension in international cooperation activities and in trade agreements.[73] In order to find a compromise between these two opposing viewpoints, Article 32 CRPD focuses on the significance of international cooperation in support of national efforts in implementing the Convention. Despite considering international cooperation to be complementary to national policies, the final text of Article 32 has a broad scope. It requires States Parties to cooperate internationally, involving people with disabilities, in order to share knowledge and good practices, and to enhance accessibility and the elimination of barriers. In doing so, Article 32 has a profoundly innovative value in international human rights law.

[71] Valentina Della Fina, 'Article 32: International Cooperation', in Della Fina, Cera and Palmisano (eds.), *The United Nations Convention on Human Rights: A Commentary*, note 10, pp. 569–89.

[72] Kayess and French, 'Out of Darkness into Light? Introducing the Convention on the Rights of Persons with Disabilities', note 16, at 32.

[73] In relation to disability, the importance of international cooperation in enhancing the rights of persons with disabilities globally had already been acknowledged in the Standard Rules.

CASE STUDY

The Italian Development Cooperation Disability Action Plan, issued by the Italian Ministry of Foreign Affairs, Directorate-General for Development Cooperation (MFA-DGCS)

Italy ratified the CRPD in 2009, after having signed it in 2007. With a view to implementing Article 32, the Directorate-General for Development Cooperation (DGCS) of the Ministry of Foreign Affairs (MFA) approved the Guidelines for the Introduction of the Disability Issue within the Policies and Activities of the Italian Cooperation in November 2010. Following the adoption of the Guidelines and through a participatory process, in 2013, the MFA produced a detailed Action Plan to create projects targeted at persons with disabilities, with dedicated funding, and to establish a fund to cover the additional costs associated with the participation of persons with disabilities. This Action Plan also provides for the effective monitoring of these actions and for a range of awareness-raising and promotional activities.

8 IMPLEMENTATION AND MONITORING OF THE CONVENTION AT THE INTERNATIONAL LEVEL: THE ROLE OF THE COMMITTEE ON THE RIGHTS OF PERSONS WITH DISABILITIES

As mentioned above, Article 34 CRPD provides for the establishment of the CRPD Committee, whose task is to examine States Parties' reports on the implementation of the Convention. The Committee also has the task of examining individual complaints and conducting inquiries on systematic breaches of the Convention (inquiry procedure) under the OP-CRPD. This section examines the composition and structure of the CRPD Committee as well as its functions.

8.1 The Committee in a Nutshell

The CRPD Committee is currently composed of eighteen independent experts. At the time of the entry into force of the Convention, the Committee had twelve members, with an increase of six members provided for after sixty ratifications or accessions had been reached (Article 34(2) CRPD). The members of the Committee serve in their individual capacity, and they do not represent States Parties. Article 35 CRPD is particularly clear in this respect – it requires members of the CRPD Committee 'to be independent and impartial and not holding any position whether in the legislative, judiciary or the executive branch that may undermine their impartiality'. The Committee members are elected from a list of persons

> Check the current composition of the Committee. Has gender and geographical balance been achieved in your opinion?

nominated by States Parties at the COSP for a four-year term, with the possibility of being re-elected once. Members are elected, taking into consideration the need for an equitable geographical distribution and gender balance. However, the composition of the Committee in 2017 included only one woman, and the Committee expressed concern about the lack of a balanced gender representation.[74] In its current composition, the geographical distribution of the members is as follows: one expert from Latin America and the Caribbean; five experts from Africa; five experts from Asia-Pacific; four experts from Eastern Europe; and three experts from Western Europe and other States. In June 2018, the election of nine new members of the Committee took place, in order to substitute those members whose mandate was due to expire at the end of December 2018.

The Committee adopted its own Rules of Procedure in 2010, and it revised them in 2016.[75] The Committee members are entitled to benefit from the general immunity of experts conducting missions for the UN.

8.2 The Committee as a Monitoring Body

As with all human rights treaty bodies, the CRPD Committee gives an authoritative interpretation of the CRPD provisions through general comments, which include recommendations on how to implement specific articles of the Convention.

The CRPD Committee is also in charge of monitoring the implementation of the Convention. Article 35 CRPD requires that States Parties submit regular reports to the Committee regarding the domestic implementation of the Convention. The first report is due within two years after the entry into force of the Convention for the State Party concerned, and subsequent reports are due at least every four years thereafter or when the CRPD Committee requests it. In 2009, the

[74] CRPD Committee, Statement on 'Achieving Gender Balance and Equitable Geographical Distribution in the Elections of Members of the Committee' (2017), available at www.ohchr.org/EN/NewsEvents/Pages/DisplayNews.aspx?NewsID=22244&LangID=E.

[75] CRPD Committee, Revised Rules of Procedure of the Committee on the Rights of Persons with Disabilities, 9 October 2016, UN Doc. CRPD/C/1/Rev.1.

CRPD Committee released a document on Reporting Guidelines, in order to advise States Parties on the form and content of their reports,[76] so as to ensure that States Parties' reports are comprehensive and are presented in a uniform manner. Article 36 CRPD enables the Committee to consider these reports and give recommendations. In particular, following a dialogue with the reporting state, the CRPD Committee adopts 'concluding observations' (COs), which are transmitted to the state concerned and which are also made public. Under the follow-up procedure, the CRPD Committee can require States Parties to focus on specific issues of concern that it has identified in its COs and provide written information on the adoption of the measures recommended by the Committee.

8.3 The Committee as a Quasi-Judicial Body

The system set forth in the CRPD with regard to the Committee is complemented by the OP-CRPD, which entrusts the Committee with the tasks of examining individual complaints regarding alleged CRPD violations and of undertaking *ex officio* inquiries on serious violations.

The individual complaints procedure permits individuals and groups of individuals in a State Party that has ratified the OP-CRPD to complain that the state has breached one of its obligations under the Convention (Article 1 OP-CRPD). The individual must be a victim of a violation of the CRPD, and the CRPD Committee, in *A. M.* v. *Australia*,[77] affirms that:

> [f]or a person to claim to be the victim of a violation of a right protected by the Convention, he or she must show either that an act or an omission of the State party concerned has already adversely affected his or her enjoyment of that right, or that such an effect is imminent, for example on the basis of existing law and/or judicial or administrative decision or practice ...

According to Article 2 OP-CRPD, an individual communication is deemed to be inadmissible if it is anonymous; or constitutes an abuse of the right of submission of such communications; or is incompatible with the provisions of the Convention; or where the same matter has already been examined by the Committee; or has been or is being examined under another procedure of international investigation or settlement. In addition, where a communication is manifestly ill-founded or not sufficiently substantiated, it is also deemed to be inadmissible, as it is when the facts that are the subject of the communication occurred prior to the entry into force of the OP-CRPD for the State Party concerned, unless those facts continued after that date. Moreover, for a communication to be admissible, all

[76] CRPD Committee, Guidelines on Treaty-specific Document to be Submitted by States Parties under Article 35, paragraph 1, of the Convention on the Rights of Persons with Disabilities, 18 November 2009, UN Doc. CRPD/C/2/3.

[77] CRPD Committee, *A. M.* v. *Australia*, Communication No. 12/2013, UN Doc. CRPD/C/13/D/12/2013.

available domestic remedies must have been exhausted, unless the application of the remedies is unreasonably prolonged or ineffective (Article 2(4) OP-CRPD).

According to Article 6 OP-CRPD, if the CRPD Committee receives reliable information indicating grave or systematic violations by a State Party of any of the Convention's provisions, the Committee can launch the inquiry procedure. The Committee invites the State Party concerned to submit observations on the information that it has collected regarding the systematic violations alleged against the State Party.

DID YOU KNOW THAT ...?

The first inquiry procedure conducted by the CRPD Committee concerned the UK. In April 2013, the Committee received a formal request from a number of DPOs, alleging serious and systematic violations of the provisions of the Convention. In particular, it was claimed that legislation, policies and measures adopted by the UK on social security schemes and on work and employment disproportionately affected people with disabilities, in particular their rights to live independently and to be included in the community (Article 19 CRPD), to an adequate standard of living and social protection (Article 28 CRPD), and to work and employment (Article 27 CRPD). In 2016, the Committee considered that there was reliable evidence that the threshold of grave or systematic violations of the rights of persons with disabilities had been met in the State Party, and it provided the UK with several recommendations in that regard.

The second inquiry procedure under Article 6 OP-CRPD concerned Spain. It was launched in response to submissions from DPOs and one of the entities of the Spanish independent monitoring framework. It alleged that, despite legal reforms at the national level, Spain's education laws and policies perpetuated the medical model of disability. In June 2018, the CRPD Committee issued a report stating that Spain's segregation and exclusion of students with disabilities from mainstream education, on grounds of their impairments, amounted to grave violations of the CRPD and recommended that Spain should enact legislative reform to align its national laws with Article 24 CRPD.

9 IMPLEMENTATION AND MONITORING AT THE NATIONAL LEVEL

Rioux affirms that 'the recognition of right[s] is a watershed but not a panacea'.[78] To ensure the effective realisation of rights, implementation and monitoring are essential. The CRPD recognises this and, in addition to a

[78] Marcia Rioux, 'Introduction', in Marcia Rioux, Paula Pinto and Gillian Parekh (eds.), *Disability, Rights Monitoring, and Social Change* (Toronto: Canadian Scholars' Press, 2015), p. 2.

Art. 33(1) CRPD	• ONE or MORE FOCAL POINT(S)
Art. 33(1) CRPD	• A COORDINATION MECHANISM
Art. 33(2) CRPD	• A FRAMEWORK
Art. 33(3) CRPD	• INVOLVEMENT OF CIVIL SOCIETY

Figure 3.4 Article 33 CRPD and Its 'Architecture for Change'

provision for international monitoring, it obliges States Parties to put in place structures at the national level to facilitate the implementation of the Convention and to monitor this implementation. In other words, the CRPD recognises that the full realisation of the rights guaranteed by the CRPD depends on appropriate governance mechanisms. As discussed above, the Convention emphasises the importance of developing structural policies to promote equality.

Article 33 CRPD sets forth the obligations to: designate one or more 'focal points' to implement the CRPD; give due consideration to the establishment of a mechanism to coordinate the implementation process; and put in place a structure to protect, promote and monitor the implementation of the Convention. This has been described as a key innovation, with the potential to transform the 'majestic generalities' of the Convention into concrete reform at the domestic level.[79] In addition, Article 33(3) CRPD requires States Parties to involve civil society, in particular DPOs, in monitoring processes (See Figure 3.4.).

This section briefly discusses the content of, and the obligations stemming from, Articles 33(1) and 33(2) CRPD. Article 33(3) CRPD, which reiterates the obligation to involve people with disabilities in monitoring and policy-making, is analysed in section 10 of this chapter, in conjunction with Article 4(3) CRPD.

[79] Gerard Quinn, 'Resisting the "Temptation of Elegance": Can the Convention on the Rights of Persons with Disabilities Socialise States to Right Behaviour?', in Quinn and Arnardóttir (eds.), *The UN Convention on the Rights of Persons with Disabilities: European and Scandinavian Perspectives*, note 23, p. 217. According to Aichele, Article 33 enjoys wide acceptance among States Parties, since no reservations were made and only two states lodged interpretive declarations (Valentin Aichele, 'Article 33: National Implementation and Monitoring', in Ilias Bantekas, Michael Ashley Stein, and Dimitris Anastasiou (eds.), *The UN Convention on the Rights of Persons with Disabilities. A Commentary* (Oxford: Oxford University Press, 2018), pp. 978–1011, p. 981). See also Meredith Raley, 'Article 33 of the CRPD: Its Potential for Realising the Human Rights of Persons with Disabilities', in Charles O'Mahony and Gerard Quinn, *Disability Law and Policy: An Analysis of the UN Convention* (Dublin: Clarus Press, 2017), pp. 477–483.

9.1 The Focal Point(s) and the Coordination Mechanism

ARTICLE 33(1) CRPD

States Parties, in accordance with their system of organi[s]ation, shall designate one or more focal points within government for matters relating to the implementation of the present Convention, and shall give due consideration to the establishment or designation of a coordination mechanism within government to facilitate related action in different sectors and at different levels.

As stated in Article 33(1) CRPD, a focal point must be set up within government for matters relating to the implementation of the Convention. The focal point must be located at the governmental level, and it must have the necessary resources to carry out its function and be accessible to persons with disabilities.[80] Article 33(1) CRPD leaves a margin of discretion to the State Party on whether to create a single focal point or multiple focal points. However, during the negotiations of the CRPD, a strong preference for multiple focal points was expressed.[81] This would also facilitate the mainstreaming of the rights of persons with disabilities across various policy fields, as required by Article 4(1)(c) CRPD. The main features of the focal point required by Article 33 CRPD are outlined in Figure 3.5.

Although the text of Article 33 is quite general, de Beco and Hoefmans argue that the focal point should produce a CRPD implementation action plan; keep constant contact with DPOs; provide technical guidance to the various sectors of the public administration on how to implement the CRPD; and also promote specific actions to support the human rights approach to disability, such as research, studies and seminars, involving experts, universities, public agencies and authorities, civil society. This would aid in realising the paradigm shift enshrined in the CRPD.[82] The tasks of the focal point are outlined in Figure 3.6.

[80] OHCHR, *Contribution to the Office of the United Nations High Commissioner for Human Rights' Thematic Study to Enhance Awareness on the Structure and Role of National Mechanisms for the Implementation and Monitoring of the Convention on the Rights of Persons with Disabilities*, available at www2.ohchr.org/english/issues/disability/submissions.htm.

[81] Luigino Manca, 'Article 33: National Implementation and Monitoring', in Della Fina, Cera and Palmisano (eds.), *The United Nations Convention on the Rights of Persons with Disabilities: A Commentary*, note 10, pp. 592–606, p. 594.

[82] Gautier De Beco and Alexander Hoefmans, 'National Structures for Implementation and Monitoring', in Gautier De Beco (ed.), *Article 33 of the UN Convention on the Rights of Persons with Disabilities* (Leiden: Martinus Nijhoff Publishers, 2013), pp. 22–3; see also, MDAC, *Building the Architecture for Change: Guidelines on Article 33 of the UN Convention on the Rights of Persons with Disabilities*, note 1.

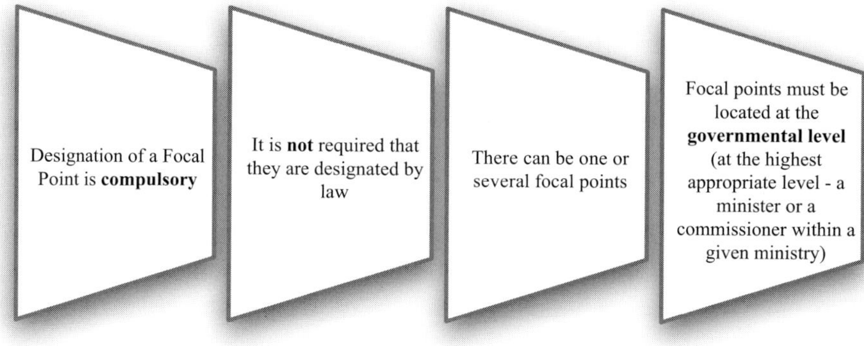

Figure 3.5 The Main Features of the Focal Point

Ensure **coherent** government activity in the area of disability	Produce a **CRPD implementation action plan**
	Establish **contact with DPOs** and proactively involve them
	Provide **technical guidance** and promote statistical data collection
	Promote specific actions to **support** the human rights approach

Figure 3.6 The Main Tasks of the Focal Point

Article 33(1) CRPD also requires States Parties to give due consideration to the establishment or designation of a coordination mechanism, to boost cooperation between different sectors of the public administration and different levels of government, in order to avoid isolated or even contradictory measures. The establishment or designation of a coordination mechanism is not a legal obligation, however. There is no clear distinction between the functions of the focal point and the coordination mechanism required by the Convention. However, in decentralised states, the establishment of the coordination mechanism will be of vital importance to ensuring the smooth implementation of the Convention across different levels of government.

9.2 The Framework under Article 33(2) CRPD

ARTICLE 33(2) CRPD

States Parties shall, in accordance with their legal and administrative systems, maintain, strengthen, designate or establish within the State Party, a framework, including one or more independent mechanisms, as appropriate, to promote, protect and monitor implementation of the present Convention. When designating or establishing such a mechanism, States Parties shall take into account the principles relating to the status and functioning of national institutions for protection and promotion of human rights.

As seen above, Article 33(2) CRPD requires the setting up of a framework to promote, protect and monitor the implementation of the Convention. In Article 33 CRPD, there is no concrete definition of what the framework should consist of. Article 33(2) CRPD provides that States Parties can designate or establish one or more bodies as part of the framework. They can also either designate existing bodies or they can establish new *ad hoc* bodies.[83] It is clear, however, that the framework should include 'one or more independent mechanisms'. In designating or establishing such a mechanism, States Parties to the Convention 'shall take into account' the 'Principles relating to the Status of National Institutions for the Promotion and Protection of Human Rights' (also known as the Paris Principles).[84] The Paris Principles sketch out the responsibilities, composition and working methods of NHRIs, placing emphasis on two fundamental principles, namely independence and pluralism. Broadly speaking, independence refers to the fact that NHRIs must not be subject to governmental control, while pluralism refers to the need for NHRIs to include and engage in dialogue with civil society.

The task of the independent mechanisms is to promote, protect and monitor the implementation of the CRPD. The first function implies awareness-raising activities to foster a human rights approach to disability also among persons with disabilities themselves. The second function entails the possibility of dealing with individual claims of violations of the rights provided for in the CRPD. The third function of monitoring requires evaluating the extent to which the CRPD has been effectively implemented and verifying where violations and breaches still persist, with the view to putting an end to them (See Figure 3.7.).

[83] De Beco and Hoefmans, 'National Structures for Implementation and Monitoring', note 82, p. 34.

[84] UN General Assembly, National Institutions for the Promotion and Protection of Human Rights, 20 December 1993, 85th plenary meeting, UN Doc. A/RES/48/134.

The framework should perform these tasks:	**Promote the implementation of the CRPD,** i.e. provide information; carry out awareness-raising activities and educational activities; promote implementation methods and tools; and inform persons with disabilities about their rights.
	Carry out the task of protection, i.e. provide a complaints mechanism; provide mediation; establish programmes of prevention; undertake 'strategic litigation' (supporting people with disabilities to file a complaint to the CRPD Committee).
	Monitor the implementation of the CRPD, i.e. assess the extent to which there has been implementation.

Figure 3.7 Functions of the Framework

10 THE ROLE OF PERSONS WITH DISABILITIES IN IMPLEMENTING AND MONITORING THE CONVENTION

Linqvist[85] argues that one of the seminal features of the CRPD is the emphasis on the participation of people with disabilities in the implementation and monitoring processes. Participation features as a general principle of the Convention and in several substantive CRPD provisions, as highlighted earlier in this chapter. Article 4(3) CRPD is a key provision in this respect.

ARTICLE 4(3) CRPD

In the development and implementation of legislation and policies to implement the ... Convention, and in other decision-making processes concerning issues relating to persons with disabilities, States Parties shall closely consult with and actively involve persons with disabilities, including children with disabilities, through their representative organi[s]ations.

Article 4(3) CRPD requires close consultation with, and active involvement of, disabled people, through their representative organisations, in the development and implementation of legislation and policies and in all decision-making

[85] Bengt Lindqvist, 'Background: Monitoring – A Key Element in Realizing Human Rights for All', in Rioux, Pinto and Parekh (eds.), *Disability, Rights Monitoring, and Social Change*, note 78, p. 21.

processes concerning issues relating to persons with disabilities. This provision is considered to be the outcome of the highly participatory process that characterised the negotiation of the CRPD, and it 'seeks to ensure that a high level of participation is maintained at the domestic level as the Convention is implemented'.[86] The final text of Article 4(3) CRPD reflects the slogan that was adopted by the disability rights movement during the negotiation process: 'Nothing About Us Without Us'. This provision is of key importance, as the successful implementation of the CRPD can only be achieved through constant dialogue with people with disabilities, in order to identify challenges and areas of concern.

Article 4(3) does not provide a definition of 'representative organisations of persons with disabilities'. However, the 'Guidelines on the Participation of Disabled Persons Organizations (DPOs) and Civil Society Organizations in the Work of the Committee', released by the CRPD Committee in April 2014, and the most recent General Comment No. 7, published in November 2018, clarify that DPOs are those in which at least half of their membership is 'comprised by a majority of persons with disabilities' and are 'governed, led and directed by persons with disabilities'.[87]

CRPD Committee, General comment No. 7 on the participation of persons with disabilities, including children with disabilities, through their representative organizations, in the implementation and monitoring of the Convention (2018)

11. ... Organizations of persons with disabilities have certain characteristic aspects, including the fact that:
    (a) They are established predominantly with the aim of collectively acting, expressing, promoting, pursuing and/or defending the rights of persons with disabilities and should be generally recognized as such;
    (b) They employ, are represented by, entrust or specifically nominate/appoint persons with disabilities themselves;
    (c) They are not affiliated, in the majority of cases, to any political party and are independent from public authorities and any other non-governmental organizations of which they might be part/members of;

[86] MDAC, *Building the Architecture for Change: Guidelines on Article 33 of the UN Convention on the Rights of Persons with Disabilities*, note 1.

[87] CRPD Committee, Guidelines on the Participation of Disabled Persons Organizations (DPOs) and Civil Society Organizations in the Work of the Committee, UN Doc. CRPD/C/11/2, para. 3, available at www.ohchr.org/en/hrbodies/crpd/pages/crpdindex.aspx See also CRPD Committee, General Comment No. 7, 9 November 2018, UN Doc. CRPD/C/GC/7, para 11.

(d) They may represent one or more constituencies based on actual or perceived impairment or can be open to membership of all persons with disabilities;
(e) They represent groups of persons with disabilities reflecting the diversity of their backgrounds (in terms of, for example, sex, gender, race, age, or migrant or refugee status). They can include constituencies based on transversal identities (for example, children, women or indigenous people with disabilities) and comprise members with various impairments;
(f) They can be local, national, regional or international in scope;
(g) They can operate as individual organizations, coalitions or cross-disability or umbrella organizations of persons with disabilities, seeking to provide a collaborative and coordinated voice for persons with disabilities in their interactions with, among others, public authorities, international organizations and private entities.

12. Among the different types of organizations of persons with disabilities that the Committee has identified are:
(a) Umbrella organizations of persons with disabilities, which are coalitions of representative organizations of persons with disabilities. Ideally, there should be only one or two umbrella organizations at each level of decision-making. To be open, democratic and represent the full and wide diversity of persons with disabilities, they should accept all organizations of persons with disabilities as members. They should be organized, led and controlled by persons with disabilities. They only speak on behalf of their member organizations and solely on matters that are of mutual interest and collectively decided upon. However, they cannot represent individual persons with disabilities because they often lack detailed knowledge of personal backgrounds. Individual organizations of persons with disabilities representing specific communities are in a better position to play such a role. However, persons with disabilities should be able to decide for themselves which organizations they want to represent them. The existence of umbrella organizations within States parties should not, under any circumstances, hinder individuals or organizations of persons with disabilities from participating in consultations or other forms of promoting the interests of persons with disabilities;
(b) Cross-disability organizations, which are composed of persons representing all or some of the wide diversity of impairments. They most frequently organize at the local and/or national levels, but can also exist at the regional and international levels;
(c) Self-advocacy organizations representing persons with disabilities in different, often loosely and/or locally formed, networks and platforms. They advocate for the rights of persons with disabilities, especially persons

with intellectual disabilities. Their establishment, with appropriate, sometimes extensive, support to enable their members to express their opinions, is of fundamental importance to political participation and participation in decision-making, monitoring and implementation processes. This is particularly relevant for persons who are prevented from exercising their legal capacity, institutionalized and/or denied the right to vote. In many countries, self-advocacy organizations are discriminated against through the refusal of a legal status because of laws and regulations that deny the legal capacity of their members;

(d) Organizations including family members and/or relatives of persons with disabilities, which are pivotal in facilitating, promoting and securing the interests and supporting the autonomy and active participation of their relatives with intellectual disabilities, dementia and/or children with disabilities, when these groups of persons with disabilities want to be supported by their families as united networks or organizations. In such cases, these organizations should be included in consultation, decision-making and monitoring processes. The role of parents, relatives and caregivers in such organizations should be to assist and empower persons with disabilities to have a voice and take full control of their own lives. Such organizations should actively work to promote and use supported decision-making processes to ensure and respect the right of persons with disabilities to be consulted and to express their own views;

(e) Organizations of women and girls with disabilities, which represent women and girls with disabilities as a heterogeneous group. The diversity of women and girls with disabilities should include all types of impairments. Ensuring the participation of women and girls with disabilities is indispensable in consultations addressing specific issues that exclusively or disproportionately affect women and girls with disabilities, and issues related to women and girls in general, such as gender equality policies;

(f) Organizations and initiatives of children and young persons with disabilities, which are fundamental for the participation of children in public and community life and for their right to be heard and their freedom of expression and association. Adults have a key and supportive role to play in promoting an environment that enables children and young persons with disabilities to establish and act, formally or informally, within their own organizations and initiatives, including through cooperation with adults and other children and young persons.

13. Organizations of persons with disabilities should be distinguished from organizations "for" persons with disabilities, which provide services and/or advocate on behalf of persons with disabilities, which, in practice, may result in a conflict of interests in which such organizations prioritize their purpose as private entities over the rights of persons with disabilities. States parties

should give particular importance to the views of persons with disabilities, through their representative organizations, support the capacity and empowerment of such organizations and ensure that priority is given to ascertaining their views in decision-making processes.

14. A distinction should also be made between organizations of persons with disabilities and civil society organizations. The term "civil society organization" comprises different kinds of organizations, including research organizations/institutes, organizations of service providers and other private stakeholders. Organizations of persons with disabilities are a specific type of civil society organization.

In line with Article 4(3), DPOs and civil society as a whole have an essential role to play in the work of the CRPD Committee, also with respect to the interpretation of the CRPD. In addition, DPOs must be involved in monitoring the implementation of the CRPD. In order to comply with Article 33(2) CRPD, States Parties must involve persons with disabilities and their representative organisations in the framework discussed above. Article 33(3) is also a provision particularly advancing the participation of disabled people in the monitoring process.

ARTICLE 33(3) CRPD

Civil society, in particular persons with disabilities and their representative organi[s]ations, shall be involved and participate fully in the monitoring process.

As highlighted in Figure 3.8, this provision requires the involvement of both DPOs and civil society through other participatory mechanisms, but States Parties are given wide room for manoeuvre in selecting participatory

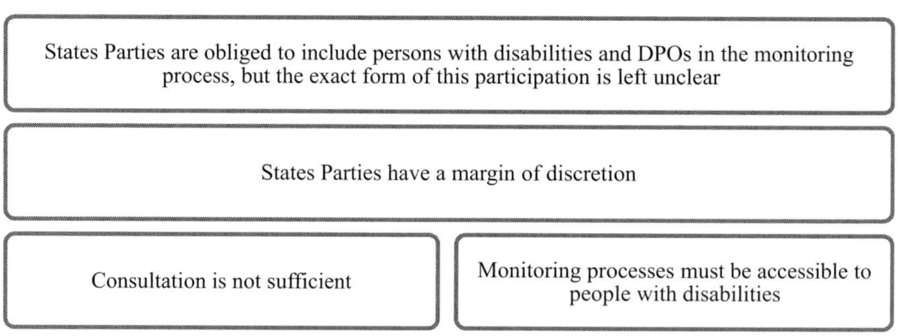

Figure 3.8 Article 33(3) CRPD and Its Requirements

techniques that fit best in their systems of governance. The CRPD Committee, in its General Comment No. 7, has noted that States Parties must support and fund the strengthening of capacity within civil society, to ensure their effective participation. It has also emphasised that organizations of persons with disabilities should have appropriate resources.

11 THE ROLE OF OTHER UNITED NATIONS BODIES IN PROMOTING THE IMPLEMENTATION OF THE CONVENTION

The CRPD provides for its own treaty body entrusted with monitoring and promoting the implementation of the CRPD. However, many other bodies within the UN system play an important role when it comes to the promotion of the rights enshrined in the CRPD.

The Human Rights Council, an inter-governmental body composed of fourty-seven states and created in 2006,[88] is responsible for the promotion and protection of all human rights in UN Member States, including the rights of disabled people. The Council adopted its first resolution on the human rights of persons with disabilities, Resolution 7/9, in 2008. Since then, the Council has endeavoured to make its work accessible to, and inclusive of, persons with disabilities. In December 2017, the Council 'Task Force for Accessibility for persons with disabilities' released a detailed Action Plan to address existing barriers preventing persons with disabilities from participating in, and accessing the work of the Council, and its mechanisms. The Plan also sets out to identify the resources needed, when possible, and the timeline as well as the responsible entity. The Council has also sought to mainstream disability in all areas of its work.

Another UN body, the OHCHR, has the task of promoting and protecting all human rights. It supports the work of the core human rights treaty bodies, including the CRPD Committee, that are mandated to monitor national-level implementation of international human rights treaties. The OHCHR also provides assistance and expertise to governments, to help in the implementation of international human rights standards on the ground. It also supports the work of special rapporteurs, including the Special Rapporteur on the rights of persons with disabilities, who holds a specific mandate to promote compliance with the CRPD.

The Special Rapporteur on the rights of persons with disabilities was set up by Human Rights Council Resolution 26/20, of 14 July 2014. In that resolution, the Council expressed concern that disabled people face barriers in their participation in society and violations of their rights. In acknowledging

[88] The Council was created by the UNGA on 15 March 2006 by Resolution No. 60/251.

> Read the most recent statements and reports of the Special Rapporteur on the rights of persons with disabilities. What issues has the Special Rapporteur raised?

that greater attention was needed to address these barriers, the Council entrusted the Special Rapporteur with the task of working together with other human rights bodies, including the CRPD Committee, towards the realisation of the rights of persons with disabilities. The Special Rapporteur is also tasked with the role of developing a regular dialogue with States and other stakeholders, in order to raise awareness and promote good practices in relation to the rights of persons with disabilities. Moreover, the Special Rapporteur has a mandate to consult with national monitoring frameworks designated under Article 33(2) CRPD, in order to identify, exchange and promote good practices in the implementation of the CRPD. The mandate of the Special Rapporteur is wide, as he or she is entrusted to do the following: to gather, request, receive and exchange information and communications from states; and to make concrete recommendations on how to promote and protect the rights of persons with disabilities. The current Rapporteur, in 2015, Ms Catalina Devandas-Aguilar, identified three priority clusters: supporting the active participation of persons with disabilities in all decision-making processes affecting their lives; combating poverty; and promoting change in social perceptions about persons with disabilities.[89] On the whole, the Rapporteur plays a special role in raising awareness of the rights of disabled individuals and in combating stereotypes.

SUMMARY

- **The CRPD is the first legally binding document that seeks to ensure the equal enjoyment of all human rights and fundamental freedoms by all persons with disabilities.**

[89] Catalina Devandas-Aguilar, *Report of the Special Rapporteur on the Rights of Persons with Disabilities* (2015) UN Doc. A/HRC/28/58.

- The CRPD embodies a paradigm shift regarding the way in which disability has been conceptualised, and it purports a human rights approach to disability.
- The CRPD negotiations involved the highest level of participation of civil society and DPOs in the history of human rights treaties. DPOs played a vital role in developing the final text of the Convention.
- The mandate of those drafting the Convention was not to create new rights; rather it was to clarify existing human rights law in the specific context of disability. Notwithstanding this, the content of the CRPD is highly innovative, in that it aims to ensure the participation of persons with disabilities in civil, political, economic, social and cultural life, by accommodating their difference.
- The CRPD includes a Preamble and fifty articles. The Preamble, which is not binding, plays an important role in the interpretation of the CRPD. The Optional Protocol to the Convention contains eighteen articles.
- Articles 3 (General Principles) and 4 (General Obligations) are core provisions of the Convention. They determine the scope of States Parties' obligations, and they represent the legal benchmarks against which to assess the compliance of domestic laws and policies with the CRPD.
- The general principles of the Convention are further elaborated on in Articles 5 to 9 CRPD. Article 5 enunciates the overarching principle of non-discrimination and equality, while Article 9 contains the principle of accessibility to the physical environment, to goods and services, and information and communications technology.
- Articles 10 to 30 CRPD enumerate specific obligations and encompass a wide range of civil, political, economic, social and cultural rights.
- Article 33(1) CRPD requires States Parties to designate at least one focal point in government to ensure the effective implementation of the Convention. That Article encourages national authorities to set up a coordination mechanism, to ensure mainstreaming and coordination of disability policies across all sectors and at all levels of government. Furthermore, Article 33(2) CRPD obliges States Parties to designate a framework that includes one or more independent bodies to promote and protect the rights of persons with disabilities and to monitor the implementation of the CRPD.
- The CRPD places a particular emphasis on the participation of civil society and people with disabilities in the implementation of the Convention. Participation of persons with disabilities is included as a general principle in Article 3. Article 4(3) imposes an obligation upon States Parties to consult and involve disabled people, including children with disabilities, through their representative organisations, in the implementation of the CRPD and in the drafting of national legislation and policies that affect them. In addition, Article 33(3) requires the involvement of both DPOs and civil society through other participatory mechanisms.
- At the international level, the Convention provides for monitoring through the creation of a committee of independent experts, the Committee on the Rights of Persons with Disabilities.
- The Optional Protocol to the CRPD accords the CRPD Committee the competence to examine individual complaints on alleged violations of the Convention by States Parties to the Protocol under the individual complaints procedure.

ACTIVITIES

REVIEW QUESTIONS

1. **Is disability defined by the CRPD?**
2. **What are the general principles of the CRPD?**
3. **Why is it important that the CRPD prescribes the involvement of persons with disabilities in law- and policy-making?**

ESSAY QUESTIONS

1. **'The CRPD does not purport to create new rights; rather, it seeks to clarify existing human rights law in the specific context of disability.' *Discuss.***
2. **'What are the main challenges in establishing national implementation and monitoring structures?' *Discuss.***

GROUP PROJECT

The State of Freedonia is a federal state that ratified the CRPD in January 2009. After ratification of the Convention, the Freedonian Government designated as its national focal point the Ministry for Health and Welfare. As of May 2017, the national focal point remains the sole focal point in the State of Freedonia. The federal entities have not yet designated any focal points, as this would be too expensive for their respective administrations. No coordination mechanism was designated, as the Freedonian Government claimed that this was unnecessary. Freedonia does not have a National Human Rights Institution. Thus, in 2010, after long discussions with two major disability organisations, the Freedonian Government established a new body, composed by experts in the field of disability, as the independent mechanism. However, the Freedonian Government did not include any representative organisations of persons with disabilities in the body. The independence of that body is guaranteed by the fact that it does not receive any instructions from the government.

Discuss the group project and assess whether Freedonia is in compliance with Article 33 CRPD.

FURTHER READING

Bickenbach, J. E., 'Disability, Culture and the UN Convention' (2009) 31(14) *Disability and Rehabilitation* 1111–24.

Cisternas Reyes, M. S., 'Reflections on the First Working Period of the United Nations Committee on the Rights of Persons with Disabilities (2009–2012)', in M. H. Rioux, P. C. Pinto and G. Parekh (eds.), *Disability, Rights Monitoring, and Social Change, Building Power out of Evidence* (Toronto: Canadian Scholars Press, 2015), pp. 55–66.

De Beco, G., *Study on the Implementation of Article 33 of the UN Convention on the Rights of Persons with Disabilities in Europe* (Study written for the Regional Office for Europe of the UN High Commissioner for Human Rights, 2014), available at http://europe.ohchr.org/Documents/Publications/Art_33_CRPD_study.pdf.

De Beco, G. and Hoefmans, A., 'National Structures for the Implementation and Monitoring of the UN Convention on the Rights of Persons with Disabilities', in G. De Beco (ed.), *Article 33 of the UN Convention on the Rights of Persons with Disabilities* (Leiden/Boston: Martinus Nijhoff, 2013), pp. 11–66.

Harnacke, C. and Graumann, S., 'Core Principles of the UN Convention on the Rights of Persons with Disabilities: An Overview', in J. Anderson and J. Philips (eds.), *Disability and Universal Human Rights: Legal, Ethical, and Conceptual Implications of the Convention on the Rights of Persons with Disabilities* (Utrecht: Netherlands Institute of Human Rights, SIM, 2012).

Harpur, P., 'Embracing the New Disability Rights Paradigm: The Importance of the Convention on the Rights of Persons with Disabilities' (2012) 27(1) *Disability and Society* 1–14.

Kanter, A. S., 'The Promise and Challenge of the United Nations Convention on the Rights of Persons with Disabilities' (2007) 34 *Syracuse Journal of International Law and Commerce* 287–321.

Lang, R. et al., 'Implementing the United Nations Convention on the Rights of Persons with Disabilities: Principles, Implications, Practice and Limitations' (2011) 5(3) *ALTER – European Journal of Disability Research* 206–20.

Quinn, G., 'Resisting the "Temptation of Elegance": Can the Convention on the Rights of Persons with Disabilities Socialise States to Right Behaviour?', in O. M. Arnardóttir and G. Quinn (eds.), *The UN Convention on the Rights of Persons with Disabilities: European and Scandinavian Perspectives* (Leiden/Boston: Brill, 2009), pp. 215–56.

Sabatello, M. and Schulze, M. (eds.), *Human Rights and Disability Advocacy* (Philadelphia: University of Pennsylvania Press, 2014).

4 Equality and Non-Discrimination for Persons with Disabilities

LEARNING OUTCOMES

- ✓ Understand the key non-discrimination norms contained in Article 5 CRPD and how each of those contributes to ensuring equality for persons with disabilities.
- ✓ Comprehend the definitions contained in Article 2 CRPD.
- ✓ Understand the importance of the reasonable accommodation duty as a facilitator of equality.
- ✓ Identify the central elements of the duty to reasonably accommodate.
- ✓ Demonstrate awareness of the difference between reasonable accommodation and positive action.
- ✓ Identify the key features of multiple and intersectional discrimination.
- ✓ Comprehend the significance of the equality and non-discrimination norms in the CRPD in the overall context of the disability rights agenda.
- ✓ Locate the non-discrimination norms within various theoretical models of equality.

> *One of the main unarticulated premises of the philosophy of 'equality of opportunity', in general and in the context of disability, is that every human being has something to contribute to humanity and that social structures should be built inclusively with human empowerment as a key goal.*[1]

1 INTRODUCTION

People with disabilities have traditionally been marginalised from society and subjected to systemic inequalities. The CRPD seeks to remedy this marginalisation and exclusion from mainstream society. The non-discrimination and equality norms, contained in Article 5 of the Convention (but with cross-cutting application), have been described as the 'leitmotif' of the CRPD.[2] The Convention endorses an inclusive approach to equality. In its General Comment No. 6 on equality, the CRPD Committee defines 'inclusive equality' as a 'new model of equality' that has been developed through the CRPD.[3] Inclusive equality seeks to ensure equal opportunities for disabled people as well as equal results. Ensuring equal opportunities requires the removal of discriminatory barriers, so that each disabled person is facilitated in developing his or her full potential and is enabled to participate in society on an equal basis with others. Equality of results, on the other hand, seeks to place individuals with disabilities in the same position as their non-disabled counterparts, regardless of individual merit or capacity.

This chapter analyses Article 5 CRPD, as a key norm in guaranteeing the exercise and enjoyment by persons with disabilities of all human rights without any discrimination. Following this brief introduction, section 2 will discuss the four paragraphs of Article 5, each dealing with a different aspect of the equality and non-discrimination norms. Section 2 also provides an analysis of the relevant constituent elements of Article 2 CRPD, which contains important definitions. Section 3 discusses the duty to reasonably accommodate persons with disabilities, while section 4 analyses the principle of equality in connection with positive action. Section 5 examines the prohibition of multiple and intersectional discrimination contained in Article 6 CRPD. Section 6 outlines the rights of children with disabilities, including the right to non-discrimination, as

[1] Gerard Quinn and Theresia Degener (eds.), *Human Rights and Disability: The Current Use and Future Potential of United Nations Human Rights Instruments in the Context of Disability* (Geneva: Office of the High Commissioner for Human Rights, United Nations, 2002), p. 18.

[2] Oddný Mjöll Arnardóttir, 'A Future of Multidimensional Disadvantage Equality', in Gerard Quinn and Oddný Mjöll Arnardóttir (eds.), *The UN Convention on the Rights of Persons with Disabilities: European and Scandinavian Perspectives* (Leiden/Boston: Brill, 2009), pp. 41–66, p. 41.

[3] CRPD Committee, General Comment No. 6, 26 April 2018, UN Doc. CRPD/C/GC/6, para. 11. In other contexts, 'inclusive equality' is a term that had previously been coined by authors such as Sally Witcher: Sally Witcher, *Inclusive Equality: A Vision for Social Justice* (Bristol: Bristol University Press, 2014).

provided for in Article 7 CRPD. Finally, section 7 analyses the model of equality contained in the CRPD from a theoretical and comparative perspective.

2 ARTICLE 5 CRPD

Article 5 CRPD has a broad and far-reaching remit. As well as encompassing a prohibition of discrimination, through guarantees of equality before and under the law, Article 5 also requires States Parties to the Convention to ensure equal protection and equal benefit of the law without discrimination. In addition, Article 5 entails positive obligations, which require States Parties to take measures such as reasonable accommodation and positive action, in order to ensure the participation and inclusion of persons with disabilities in society on an equal basis with others. The sub-sections below discuss the scope of the non-discrimination norm in the CRPD and the core obligations stemming from Article 5 CRPD.

2.1 The Definition and Scope of the Non-Discrimination Norm

The duties to prohibit discrimination and to provide reasonable accommodation contained in Article 5 CRPD span all human rights in the Convention. Thus, they must be implemented in numerous fields and by a wide variety of social actors, including in the context of employment, education, health care and the supply of services. Before considering the various elements of Article 5 CRPD, it is necessary to refer to Article 2(3) of the Convention, which contains the definition of 'discrimination on the basis of disability', as shown in Figure 4.1.

The wording of the definition of 'discrimination' contained in Article 2 CRPD partly reflects the definitions contained in other human rights treaties at the international level, notably the definitions in the Convention on the Elimination of All Forms of Discrimination against Women (CEDAW) and the International Convention on the Elimination of All Forms of Racial Discrimination (CERD).[4] However, Article 2 CRPD goes further than both of those conventions, since it classifies an unjustified denial of reasonable accommodation as a form of discrimination. In that respect, the Convention adds considerable weight to the equality norm for people with disabilities.

Other than specifying that a denial of reasonable accommodation is a form of discrimination, the CRPD does not provide further information on the forms of discrimination to be prohibited by States Parties. Nonetheless, the phrase 'on the basis of disability' in Article 2 of the CRPD has been construed by the CRPD Committee in its General Comment No. 6 on equality (at

[4] International Convention on the Elimination of All Forms of Racial Discrimination, 21 December 1965, in force 4 January 1969, UN General Assembly (UNGA) Resolution 2106.

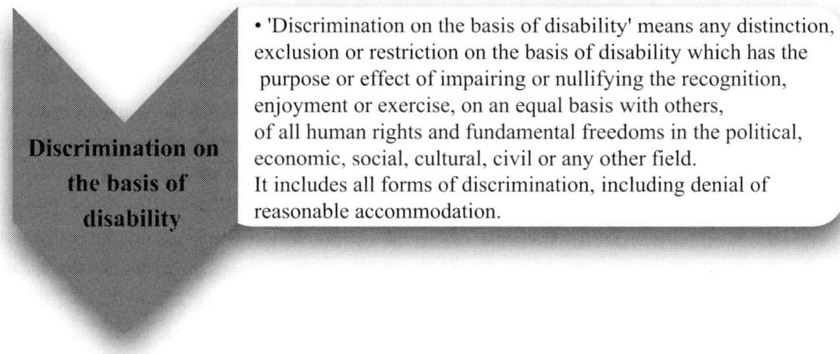

Figure 4.1 Discrimination on the Basis of Disability

paragraphs 18–20 thereof) as covering many different forms of discrimination. Article 2 clearly prohibits direct discrimination. The concept of 'indirect discrimination', whereby laws, policies or practices appear neutral *prima facie* but have a disproportionately negative impact on persons with disabilities, is also implied under Article 2. In addition, Waddington and Broderick contend that 'since the definition of discrimination under the CRPD covers "all forms of discrimination", it can be taken to mean that harassment is covered, as well as an instruction to discriminate',[5] although the latter form of discrimination has not been mentioned by the CRPD Committee in its General Comment No. 6 on equality. The Committee affirms that the prohibition of multiple discrimination in Article 6 of the Convention also covers intersectional discrimination.[6] Furthermore, the CRPD Committee confirms that the definition of 'discrimination on the basis of disability' can be construed as including not only those who have an actual impairment themselves but also those who are discriminated against on account of their association with a person with a disability, those who encounter discrimination as a result of a perceived impairment, or those who have a disposition to a disability that lies in the future.[7] The Committee further notes that discrimination on the basis of disability can arise with regard to 'persons who have a disability at present, who have had a disability in the past or who have a disposition to a disability that lies in the future'.[8] It is important to take note of the various forms of discrimination

[5] Lisa Waddington and Andrea Broderick, *Promoting Equality and Non-Discrimination for Persons with Disabilities* (Strasbourg: Council of Europe, 2017), p. 10.

[6] See below section 5.

[7] CRPD Committee, Concluding Observations on the Initial Report of Spain, 23 September 2011, UN Doc. CRPD/C/ESP/CO/1, para. 20.

[8] CRPD Committee, General Comment No. 6, note 3, para. 20. See generally Andrea Broderick and Lisa Waddington, Remarks on the outline of the draft General Comment on Article 5 (June 2017), available at http://www.ohchr.org/EN/HRBodies/CRPD/Pages/WSEqualityArt5.aspx;

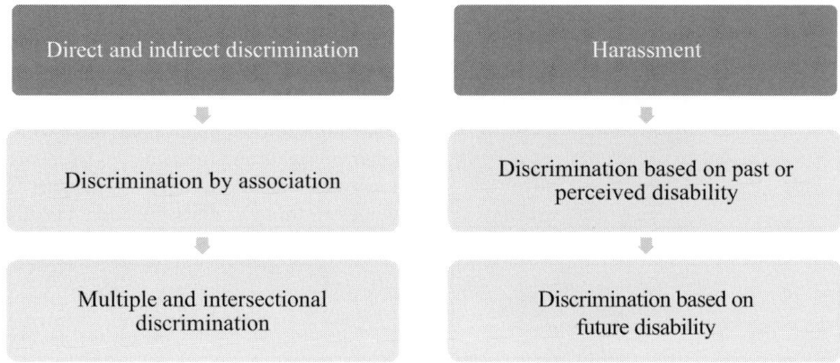

Figure 4.2 Forms of Discrimination in the CRPD

covered by the CRPD (Figure 4.2), since, as Trömel points out, this will have implications for States Parties 'when implementing the Convention and, in particular, when drafting national anti-discrimination legislation'.[9]

2.2 Article 5(1) CRPD

ARTICLE 5(1) CRPD

States Parties recogni[s]e that all persons are equal before and under the law and are entitled without any discrimination to the equal protection and equal benefit of the law.

2.2.1 *Equality before the Law*

The right to equality before the law is guaranteed by several provisions in international human rights treaties.[10] Nowak claims that the phrase 'equality before the law' does not 'give rise to a claim of whatever nature to

See also Andrea Broderick and Lisa Waddington, Remarks on the draft General Comment No. 6 on the right of persons with disabilities to equality and non-discrimination (November 2017), available at http://www.ohchr.org/EN/HRBodies/CRPD/Pages/WSPersonsDisabilitiesEqualityResponsability.aspx.

[9] Stefan Trömel, 'A Personal Perspective on the Drafting History of the United Nations Convention on the Rights of Persons with Disabilities', in Lisa Waddington and Gerard Quinn (eds.), *European Yearbook of Disability Law* (Antwerp/Portland: Intersentia, 2009), pp. 115–37, p. 124.

[10] For example, Article 14(1) and Article 26 ICCPR, Article 5(a) CERD and Article 15 CEDAW.

substantive equality but instead solely to a formal claim that existing laws be applied in the same manner to all those subject to them'.[11] The UN Committee on Economic, Social and Cultural Rights (CESCR) states, in its General Comment No. 16 on the equal rights of men and women, that 'the principle of equality before the law must be respected by administrative agencies, and courts and tribunals, and implies that those authorities must apply the law equally to men and women'.[12] This means that judges and other officials in the justice system must not act arbitrarily, and they must not discriminate on the basis of disability when applying the law or enforcing it. The CRPD Committee asserts, at paragraph 14 of its General Comment No. 6 on equality, that the requirement of 'equality before the law' describes 'the entitlement of persons to equal treatment by and in the application of the law, as a field. In order that this right may be fully reali[s]ed, the judiciary and law enforcement officers must not, in the administration of justice, discriminate against persons with disabilities'.

2.2.2 *Equality under the Law*

The guarantee of 'equality under the law' is not the same as 'equality before the law', in spite of the fact that these terms are often used interchangeably. Lacy states that the requirement of 'equality under the law' mandates that 'legal standards be general in the sense, first, that their content is the same for all to whom they apply, and second, that their range of application should be as broad as possible, normally including all citizens or all in a jurisdiction'.[13] The CRPD Committee affirms, at paragraph 14 of its General Comment No. 6, that 'equality under the law' refers to the opportunity 'to engage in legal relationships'. The Committee further asserts that 'while equality before the law refers to the right to be protected by the law, equality under the law refers to the right to use the law for personal benefit'.

2.2.3 *Equal Benefit of the Law*

The guarantee of 'equal benefit of the law' is not contained in any other international human rights treaty. However, it is enshrined in some domestic legal systems, which are useful to look at in order to fully understand the meaning of Article 5 CRPD. For example, Article 15 of the Canadian Charter of

[11] Manfred Nowak, *UN Covenant on Civil and Political Rights: CCPR Commentary*, 2nd edn (Kehl am Rhein: Engel, 2005), p. 605.

[12] UN Committee on Economic, Social and Cultural Rights (CESCR), General Comment No. 16, 13 May 2005, UN Doc. E/C.12/2005/4, para. 9.

[13] William Lacy, 'Equality Under and Before the Law' (2011) 61(3) *University of Toronto Law Journal* 411, at 415.

Rights and Freedoms[14] includes the principle of 'equal benefit of the law', and it was interpreted by the Canadian Supreme Court, for instance, in *Eldridge* v. *British Colombia (Attorney General)*.[15] The applicants in that case, who were patients with hearing impairments, claimed that they had not been afforded equal benefit of the law under Article 15 of the Canadian Charter, due to a failure to provide them with sign language interpretation. The Canadian authorities argued that the legislation in question[16] afforded free medical services to both the hearing and Deaf populations on an equal basis and, therefore, that the legislation did not discriminate against the applicants *prima facie*. However, the Supreme Court ruled that, even though the right was enshrined 'on an equal basis' in the relevant legislation, 'discrimination can accrue from a failure to take positive steps to ensure that disadvantaged groups benefit equally from services offered to the general public'.[17]

The guarantee of equal benefit of the law can be said to imply that individuals should enjoy the rights accorded to them in practice. Ensuring the equal benefit of the law to persons with disabilities will require that States Parties to the CRPD adopt positive measures in certain circumstances. For instance, ensuring the right to political participation for persons with disabilities will require measures such as accessibility measures or putting in place individualised supports.[18]

2.3 Article 5(2) CRPD

ARTICLE 5(2) CRPD

States Parties shall prohibit all 'discrimination on the basis of disability' and guarantee to persons with disabilities equal and effective legal protection against discrimination on all grounds.

[14] See Section 9(1) of the South African Constitution, which also contains the phrase 'equal benefit of the law'. It states that: 'Everyone is equal before the law and has the right to equal protection and benefit of the law'; see further, Sandra Fredman, 'Substantive Equality Revisited' (2016) 14(3) *International Journal of Constitutional Law* 712.

[15] *Eldridge* v. *British Columbia (A.G.)* [1997] 3 SCR 624.

[16] The relevant legislation was the Medical and Health Care Services Act [S.B.C. 1992, c. 76 (now the Medicare Protection Act, R.S.B.C. 1996, c. 286), ss. 1, 4(1)(c), (j), 6, 8)] and the Hospital Insurance Act [R.S.B.C. 1979, c. 180 (now R.S.B.C. 1996, c. 204), ss. 3(1), 5(1), 9, 10(1), 29(b)].

[17] *Eldridge* v. *British Columbia (A.G.)*, note 15, paras. 77 and 80.

[18] See below Chapter 9, section 4.

Nowak contends that the guarantee of equal protection of the law imposes 'a positive obligation on States Parties to take steps to protect against discrimination'.[19] The CRPD Committee emphasises, at paragraph 16 of its General Comment No. 6 on equality, that the obligation entails that 'national legislatures refrain from maintaining or establishing discrimination against persons with disabilities when enacting laws and policies'. Ensuring effective protection against discrimination in accordance with Article 5(2) CRPD will entail providing resources and adopting positive measures, such as effective redress mechanisms and sanctions (through criminal, civil or administrative processes, as appropriate) when a person with a disability has been discriminated against. Guaranteeing equal protection of the law also means ensuring the removal of all barriers hindering access to justice – environmental, legal and structural barriers as well as attitudinal barriers in the judicial system. According to the Office of the United Nations High Commissioner for Human Rights (OHCHR):

> lawyers, judges and agents of justice should be targeted in capacity-building efforts to ensure their understanding of the human rights-based approach to disability, particularly of the unconditional application of the principle of non-discrimination to persons with disabilities.[20]

3 THE DUTY TO REASONABLY ACCOMMODATE PERSONS WITH DISABILITIES

ARTICLE 5(3) CRPD

In order to promote equality and eliminate discrimination, States Parties shall take all appropriate steps to ensure that reasonable accommodation is provided.

The reasonable accommodation obligation in the CRPD forms an integral part of the social-contextual and human rights models of disability and is contained in Article 5(3). The duty to ensure the provision of reasonable accommodation is imposed on States Parties, which are the principal duty-bearers under international human rights law. In that regard, States Parties themselves undertake the responsibility to guarantee that public or private entities and individuals provide reasonable accommodation, where appropriate. The

[19] Nowak, *UN Covenant on Civil and Political Rights: CCPR Commentary*, note 11, p. 630.

[20] Office of the United Nations High Commissioner for Human Rights (OHCHR), *Equality and Non-Discrimination under Article 5 of the Convention on the Rights of Persons with Disabilities* (December 2010) UN Doc. A/HRC/34/26, para. 74.

definition, scope, objectives and limitation of the reasonable accommodation duty are explained in the sub-sections below.

3.1 Definition and Scope of the Duty to Accommodate

By way of contrast with the prohibition of direct discrimination, which requires equal treatment, the reasonable accommodation duty requires different treatment to reflect the diverse needs of persons with disabilities. Reasonable accommodation is defined in Article 2 CRPD, as shown in Figure 4.3.

The reasonable accommodation duty spans, and is implicit in, all of the substantive rights and obligations under the Convention, by virtue of the cross-cutting nature of the non-discrimination norm. There are three key features of the definition of 'reasonable accommodation' in Article 2 CRPD: the individualised character of reasonable accommodation, the effectiveness of the measures adopted and the burden on the duty-bearer.

Article 2 CRPD defines the duty as arising 'where needed in a particular case', and this emphasises the individualised nature of reasonable accommodations. Lawson points to the fact that:

> the individual-oriented nature of the reasonable accommodation obligation thus requires duty-bearers to resist making assumptions as to what might be most appropriate for a particular individual and demands that instead they engage in a dialogue with such a person about how the relevant disadvantages might most effectively be tackled.[21]

In the context of the right to education, which will be discussed in Chapter 9, the CRPD Committee affirms that 'there is no "one size fits all" formula to reasonable accommodation, as different students with the same impairment may require different accommodations'.[22] The Committee states that:

> accommodations may include changing the location of a class, providing different forms of in-class communication, enlarging print, materials and/or subjects in sign, or providing all handouts in an alternative format, providing students with a note-taker, or a language interpreter or allowing students to use assistive technology in learning and assessment situations.[23]

Reasonable accommodations can also be 'non-material' in nature, according to the Committee. This can entail measures such as 'allowing a student more time, reducing levels of background noise (sensitivity to sensory overload), using alternative evaluation methods and replacing an element of the

[21] Anna Lawson, 'Reasonable Accommodation in the Convention on the Rights of Persons with Disabilities and Non-Discrimination in Employment: Rising to the Challenges?', in Charles O'Mahony and Gerard Quinn (eds.), *Disability Law and Policy: An Analysis of the UN Convention* (Dublin: Clarus Press, 2017), pp. 359–74, at 362.

[22] CRPD Committee, General Comment No. 4, 26 August 2016, UN Doc. CRPD/C/CG/4, para. 30.

[23] Ibid.

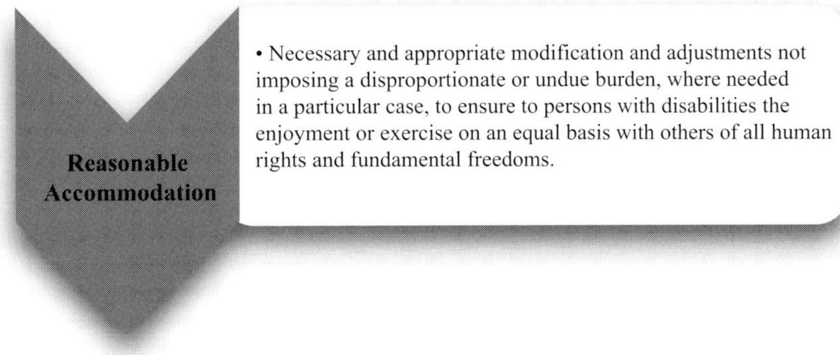

Figure 4.3 Reasonable Accommodation

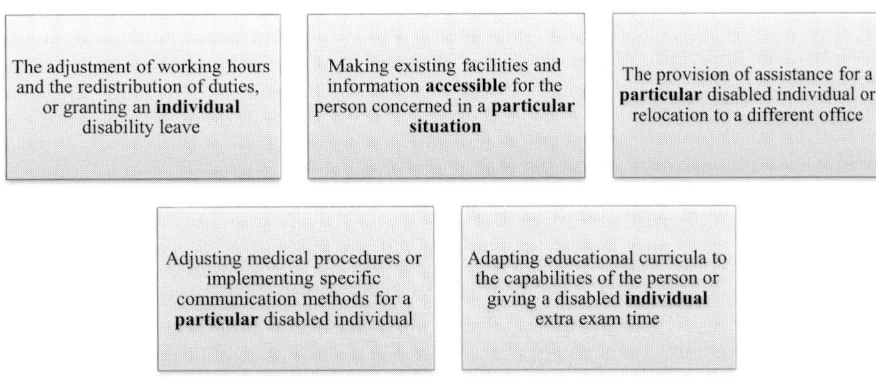

Figure 4.4 Examples of Reasonable Accommodation

curriculum with an alternative'.[24] Examples of reasonable accommodations are outlined in Figure 4.4.[25]

The second important feature of the duty to reasonably accommodate in Article 2 CRPD concerns the result that must be achieved by the measure itself, namely that any modification or adjustment adopted must be 'necessary and appropriate' to remove the disadvantage for the disabled person concerned. The use of the word 'appropriate' implies that accommodations must be effective in ensuring that persons with disabilities can exercise

[24] Ibid.

[25] These examples have been drawn partly from the OHCHR, *Equality and Non-Discrimination under Article 5 of the Convention on the Rights of Persons with Disabilities*, note 20, para. 28.

their human rights on an equal basis with others.[26] Therefore, if a disabled person requests an accommodation in an employment context, 'one must consider the extent to which the requested accommodation will contribute to ensuring participation in the workforce'.[27] This interpretation of the term 'appropriateness' also seems to be consistent with EU law.[28] In *Michael Lockrey* v. *Australia*,[29] the CRPD Committee clearly emphasises the effectiveness of reasonable accommodations in allowing participation in the activity concerned. In that individual communication, the Committee considered that the adjustments provided by the State Party for individuals with hearing impairments did not enable the author to participate in jury service on an equal basis with others.

The third feature of the definition of reasonable accommodation requires consideration of the burden of the particular adjustment on the duty-bearer concerned. According to the definition of 'reasonable accommodation' contained in Article 2 CRPD, duty-bearers should provide a reasonable accommodation that does not amount to a 'disproportionate or undue burden'. The CRPD Committee, in its General Comment No. 6, has elaborated on the concept of 'reasonable accommodation' and its limitation, which is discussed in subsection 3.3 below.

3.2 Objective of the Duty to Reasonably Accommodate

The objective of the duty to reasonably accommodate persons with disabilities is stated in Article 5(3) CRPD as being to promote equality and to eliminate discrimination, which are two different but overlapping goals, as recognised by the Committee on the Elimination of Discrimination against Women (CEDAW Committee).[30]

In combination with the general obligations of the CRPD, particularly Article 4(1)(b), the duty to eliminate discrimination requires, among other things, that States Parties 'take all appropriate measures, including legislation, to modify or abolish existing laws, regulations, customs and practices that constitute discrimination against persons with disabilities'. In order to eliminate discrimination, States Parties should include an unjustified denial of reasonable accommodation as a form of discrimination in national laws

[26] Andrea Broderick, *The Long and Winding Road to Equality and Inclusion for Persons with Disabilities: The United Nations Convention on the Rights of Persons with Disabilities* (Cambridge-Antwerp: Intersentia, 2015), p. 160.

[27] Ibid. p. 161. [28] See below Chapter 11.

[29] CRPD Committee, *Michael Lockrey* v. *Australia*, Communication No. 13/2013, UN Doc. CRPD/C/15/D/13/2016, at para. 8.5 in particular.

[30] UN Committee on the Elimination of All Forms of Discrimination against Women (CEDAW Committee), Concluding Observations on the Initial Report of Belgium, 9 October 2002, UN Doc. A/57/38 (Part II), para. 146.

and policies. States Parties must also ensure that public entities put in place legal remedies for disabled persons who have been discriminated against because of a denial of reasonable accommodation. In addition, they should ensure that private entities do not arbitrarily deny persons with disabilities measures of reasonable accommodation. This is implicit in Article 4(1)(e) CRPD, which requires States Parties 'to take all appropriate measures to eliminate discrimination on the basis of disability by any person, organi[s]ation or private enterprise'. The requirement to prohibit discrimination on the basis of disability is an immediate obligation in connection with socio-economic rights as well as civil and political rights.[31]

> Draw up a list of activities that you feel contribute to eliminating discrimination and/or promoting equality for people with disabilities.

With regard to the duty to promote equality, Hendriks affirms that the 'active promotion of equality … goes further than [the] mere prohibition of less favourable treatment of individuals or groups'.[32] Thus, the obligation to promote equality requires the adoption of positive measures by States Parties to the CRPD, including awareness-raising measures.[33] The UN Human Rights Committee (HRC), the treaty body that monitors the International Covenant on Civil and Political Rights (ICCPR), has stated that any awareness-raising on discrimination must be directed towards the population at large[34] and towards the public service[35] (law enforcement

[31] CRPD Committee, General Comment No. 6, note 3, paras. 23 and 41(b).

[32] Aart Hendriks, 'Disabled Persons and Their Right to Equal Treatment: Allowing Differentiation while Ending Discrimination' (1995) 1(2) *Health and Human Rights* 152, at 157.

[33] CRPD Committee, General Comment No. 6, note 3, para. 39.

[34] UN Human Rights Committee (HRC), Concluding Observations on the Report of Togo, 28 November 2002, UN Doc. CCPR/CO/76/TGO, para. 22; HRC, Concluding Observations on the Report of Georgia, 19 April 2002, UN Doc. CCPR/CO/74/GEO, para. 13, cited by Wouter Vandenhole, *Non-Discrimination and Equality in the View of the UN Human Rights Treaty Bodies* (Antwerp: Intersentia, 2005), p. 202.

[35] HRC, Concluding Observations on the Report of the Philippines, 01 December 2003, UN Doc. CCPR/CO/79/ PHL, para. 13; HRC, Concluding Observations on the Initial Report of the United Kingdom, 27 July 1995, UN Doc. CCPR/C/79/Add.55, para. 26, cited by Vandenhole,

officers, the legal profession and the judiciary).[36] In a similar vein, in several concluding observations (COs), the CRPD Committee recommends that States Parties should make greater efforts to raise awareness of non-discrimination among members of the legal profession, particularly the judiciary, and among persons with disabilities themselves, including through establishing training programmes on the concept of 'reasonable accommodation'.[37] These observations can be linked to Article 8 CRPD on awareness-raising.[38] Waddington and Broderick argue that the promotion of equality will also require States Parties to embed an equality perspective in their laws and policies, as well as to develop guidelines on the duty to reasonably accommodate persons with disabilities.[39]

It is also important to ensure that effective remedies are put in place, in order for persons with disabilities to obtain redress where reasonable accommodations have been unfairly denied to them. The CRPD Committee has already expressed its concerns regarding the enforcement mechanisms available to disabled people who have been discriminated against, including unjustified denials of reasonable accommodation.[40]

3.3 The Limitation of the Duty to Accommodate

As noted above, the duty to accommodate is subject to a limitation, which is contained in Article 2 CRPD. That Article states that the denial of reasonable accommodation may be justified if it constitutes a 'disproportionate' or 'undue burden'. As affirmed by the CRPD Committee in *Jungelin* v.

Non-Discrimination and Equality in the View of the UN Human Rights Treaty Bodies, note 34, p. 202.

[36] Broderick, *The Long and Winding Road to Equality and Inclusion for Persons with Disabilities: The United Nations Convention on the Rights of Persons with Disabilities*, note 26, p. 114.

[37] See e.g. CRPD Committee, Concluding Observations on the Initial Report of Tunisia, UN Doc. CRPD/C/TUN/CO/1 (2011), para. 13.

[38] Article 8(1) CRPD requires States Parties to adopt effective and appropriate measures: (a) to raise awareness throughout society, regarding persons with disabilities, and to foster respect for the rights and dignity of persons with disabilities; (b) to combat stereotypes, prejudices and harmful practices relating to persons with disabilities, including those based on sex and age, in all areas of life; and (c) to promote awareness of the capabilities and contributions of persons with disabilities.

[39] See generally Lisa Waddington and Andrea Broderick, *Promoting Equality and Non-Discrimination for Persons with Disabilities*, note 5.

[40] CRPD Committee, Concluding Observations on the Initial Report of the Czech Republic, 15 May 2015, UN Doc. CRPD/C/CZE/CO/1, para. 12.

Sweden,[41] States Parties enjoy a margin of discretion with regard to determining when a burden will be regarded as 'undue' or 'disproportionate'. The Committee appears to indicate that it will not interfere unduly with the national court's decision regarding the limitation of the accommodation duty, particularly in circumstances where the national court has thoroughly assessed the claim of denial of reasonable accommodation and where the assessment conducted by the national court is not arbitrary or does not amount to a denial of justice.[42] However, the Committee has made clear in other decisions, such as *H. M.* v. *Sweden*,[43] that it may find non-compliance with Article 5 in circumstances where the State Party has not obliged public or private entities to depart from its policy in order to accommodate the needs of a disabled individual. In *Michael Lockrey* v. *Australia*, the Committee also emphasises that, if a State Party or other duty-bearer puts forward an argument that the reasonable accommodation claimed by an individual imposes a disproportionate or undue burden, it must provide 'data or analysis to demonstrate that it would constitute a disproportionate or undue burden'.[44] The concepts of 'disproportionate' and 'undue' burden would appear to be interchangeable terms. This was confirmed by the CRPD Committee in its General Comment No. 6.

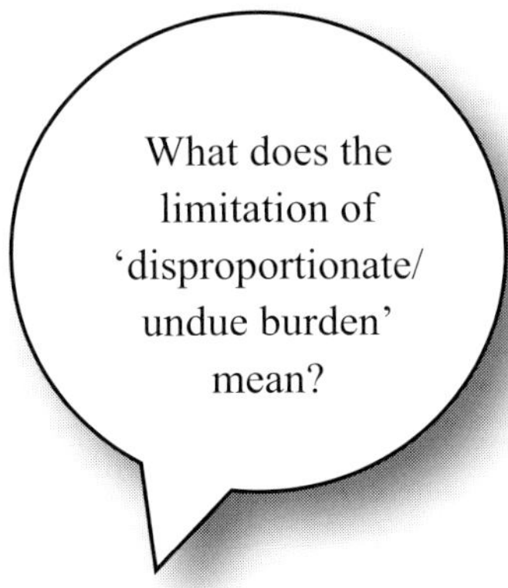

[41] CRPD Committee, *Jungelin* v. *Sweden*, Communication No. 5/2011, UN Doc. CRPD/C/12/D/5/2011. See below Chapter 5, section 5.

[42] Ibid. para. 10(6).

[43] CRPD Committee, *H. M.* v. *Sweden*, Communication No. 3/2011, UN Doc. CRPD/C/7/D/3/2011.

[44] *Michael Lockrey* v. *Australia*, note 29, para. 8(5). In the *Lockrey* communication the State Party did not provide any argument 'justifying that no adjustment, such as a special oath before a court, could be made to enable the person assisting with steno-captioning to perform his or her functions without affecting the confidentiality of the deliberations of the jury'. The CRPD Committee therefore found that the State Party had not taken the necessary steps to ensure reasonable accommodation for the author and concluded that the refusal to provide steno-captioning, without thoroughly assessing whether that would constitute a disproportionate or undue burden, amounts to disability based discrimination, in violation of the author's rights under Article 5(1) and (3) of the Convention. See further the discussion in Chapter 7, section 4 concerning the following individual communication: CRPD Committee, Gemma Beasley v. Australia, Communication No. 11/2013, 25 May 2016, CRPD/C/15/D/11/2013.

CRPD Committee, General Comment No. 6 on Equality and Non-Discrimination (2018)

25(b): 'Disproportionate or undue burden' should be understood as a single concept that sets the limit of the duty to provide reasonable accommodation. Both terms should be considered synonyms insofar as they refer to the same idea: that the request for reasonable accommodation needs to be bound by a possible excessive or unjustifiable burden on the accommodating party.

The term 'reasonable' in the duty to reasonably accommodate should not be interpreted as another limitation of the duty, as was explained by the CRPD Committee in its General Comment No. 6.

CRPD Committee, General Comment No. 6 on Equality and Non-Discrimination (2018)

25(a): 'Reasonable accommodation' is a single term, and 'reasonable' should not be misunderstood as an exception clause; the concept of 'reasonableness' should not act as a distinct qualifier or modifier to the duty. It is not a means by which the costs of accommodation or the availability of resources can be assessed – this occurs at a later stage, when the 'disproportionate or undue burden' assessment is undertaken. Rather, the reasonableness of an accommodation is a reference to its relevance, appropriateness and effectiveness for the person with a disability. An accommodation is reasonable, therefore, if it achieves the purpose (or purposes) for which it is being made, and is tailored to meet the requirements of the person with a disability.

It is noteworthy that duty-bearers are not expected to provide the 'best possible'[45] accommodation measure. If a range of different accommodations are possible, then the duty-bearer should discuss all potential measures with the disabled individual, in order to choose the most appropriate.

[45] Delia Ferri and Anna Lawson, *Reasonable Accommodation for Disabled People in Employment: A Legal Analysis of the Situation in EU Member States, Iceland, Liechtenstein and Norway* (Luxembourg: Publications Office of the European Union, 2016), p. 70.

DID YOU KNOW THAT ...?

The fact that duty-bearers are not expected to provide the 'best possible' accommodation measure has been confirmed by the Ombudsman in the Czech Republic, who, however, has emphasised the need for an accommodation to be individualised and to reflect the nature of the disability in question. The Czech Ombudsman has also stated that, when providing reasonable accommodation, a compromise between the highest effectiveness and lowest costs must be reached (Delia Ferri and Anna Lawson, *Reasonable Accommodation for Disabled People in Employment: A Legal Analysis of the Situation in EU Member States, Iceland, Liechtenstein and Norway, major thematic report written for the European Network of Legal Experts on Equality and Non-Discrimination*, Luxembourg: Publications Office of the European Union, 2016, pp. 70 and 76).

It would appear that the decision as to whether to grant an accommodation in a particular case 'will rest on an underlying proportionality test, which seeks to balance the rights of, and burdens and benefits to, all persons affected by the proposed accommodation'.[46] Although the CRPD is not explicit in this respect, the definition of what is 'proportionate' will vary according to the particular context at issue and depends on various factors, as is clear from a review of legislation, case law and academic literature.[47] The primary factors, shown in Figure 4.5, are: the cost of the accommodation, the benefit to the disabled person (and potentially to others), and other non-financial considerations.

The *travaux préparatoires* of the CRPD reveal that the disproportionate or undue burden test is associated with the 'resource implications' of the duty to accommodate – the 'type of entity, size of entity, financial capacity and the cost of the reasonable accommodation'.[48] Waddington highlights the fact that the cost of a requested accommodation is the 'primary factor' that has been taken into account in national laws and case law, in determining whether the duty can be limited.[49] In that regard, costs are not merely financial in nature but should 'extend to a consideration of the manner in which the accommodation alters the nature of the entity's business or causes excessive difficulties

[46] Broderick, *The Long and Winding Road to Equality and Inclusion for Persons with Disabilities: The United Nations Convention on the Rights of Persons with Disabilities*, note 26, p. 176.

[47] Ibid.

[48] See the comments of the European Disability Forum at the Third Session of the Ad Hoc Committee, 25 May 2004, volume 4(2), available at https://static.un.org/esa/socdev/enable/rights/ahc3sum7.htm.

[49] Lisa Waddington, 'Reasonable Accommodation', in Dagmar Schiek, Lisa Waddington and Mark Bell (eds.), *Cases, Materials and Text on National, Supranational and International Non-Discrimination Law* (Oxford/New York: Hart Publishing, 2007), p. 731.

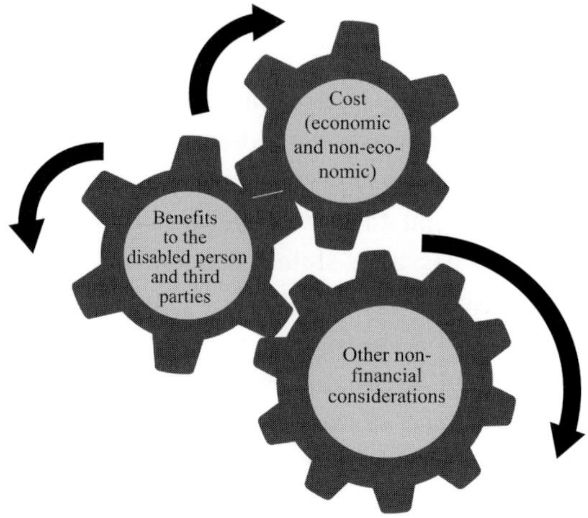

Figure 4.5 Factors Related to the Disproportionate or Undue Burden Test

for an entity'.[50] On the whole, the financial costs of providing a reasonable accommodation should be weighed in relation to other factors, such as the activities of the undertaking as well as other organisational factors (e.g. the negative impact of the requested accommodation on the entity in question). Costs will also be balanced against the availability of public subsidies or any other assistance available from the State Party to aid in the provision of a reasonable accommodation.

De Campos Velho Martel also notes that 'a serious cost-benefit analysis of reasonable accommodation includes more than just economic factors . . . It must also include the costs of stigma and the benefits of inclusion, not only to the person requesting the accommodation, but also to third parties'.[51] This means that the advantages accruing to the disabled person who benefits from a reasonable accommodation should also be considered in light of the advantages accruing to other parties. For instance, widening the entrance to a business premises to permit access by an employee in a wheelchair also offers greater ease to other employees and visitors (e.g. individuals in wheelchairs, parents with buggies or people with limited

[50] Broderick, *The Long and Winding Road to Equality and Inclusion for Persons with Disabilities: The United Nations Convention on the Rights of Persons with Disabilities*, note 26, p. 176.

[51] Leticia De Campos Velho Martel, 'Reasonable Accommodation: The New Concept From an Inclusive Constitutional Perspective' (2007) 8(14) *Sur International Journal on Human Rights* 84, citing Cass Sunstein, 'Cost-Benefit Analysis Without Analyzing Costs of Benefits: Reasonable Accommodation, Balancing, and Stigmatic Harms' (2007) *University of Chicago, Public Law Working Paper* No. 149, at 2–4, available at http://ssrn.com/abstract=959712.

mobility). In this respect, Ferri and Lawson cite Norwegian legislation, which includes factors such as the effects that the dismantling of disabling barriers will have and whether the accommodation can benefit employees other than the disabled person.[52] According to the authors, this 'seems to imply that an expensive accommodation is more likely to be required if it would lead to a significant advantage for a disabled individual, while also benefiting other people'.[53] It is interesting to note that the factor of third party benefits has been mentioned in a joint dissenting opinion by five CRPD Committee members in *Jungelin* v. *Sweden*.[54] Additionally, in a case in Belgium, the First Instance Court of Ghent[55] stated that the financial burden is only one element that must be considered in assessing the 'reasonableness' of a requested accommodation. The Court held that reasonableness is to be set against the advantages resulting from the provision of such accommodation.[56]

52 Ferri and Lawson, *Reasonable Accommodation for Disabled People in Employment: A Legal Analysis of the Situation in EU Member States, Iceland, Liechtenstein and Norway*, note 45, p. 75.

53 Ibid.

54 Joint opinion of Committee members Mr Carlos Rios Espinosa, Ms Theresia Degener, Mr Munthian Buntan, Ms Silvia Judith Quan-Chang and Ms Maria Soledad Cisternas Reyes (dissenting), para. 5.

55 Belgium, Court of First Instance of Ghent (*tribunal de première instance – Rechtbank van eerste aanleg*) (emergency proceedings), *Marie Gerday (representing her son Dylan Moens)* v. *Sint-Bavohumaniora and the Flemish Community; Ronny Van Landuyt and Carine Van De Ginste (representing their daughter Sylvie Van Landuyt)* v. *Maria Assumpta and the Flemish Community; Yalçin Batur and Sandra Roose (representing their daughter Charlotte Batur)* v. *Schoolcomité van het Sint-Franciskusinstituut and the Flemish Community*, judgment of the President, 15 July 2009.

56 Lisa Waddington and Andrea Broderick, *Disability Law and the Duty to Reasonably Accommodate Beyond Employment: A Legal Analysis of the Situation in EU Member States* (Luxembourg: Publications Office of the European Union, 2016), p. 129. In that case, the applicants (parents of three children with hearing impairments attending mainstream school) claimed that an allocation of 5–9 hours a week of interpretative assistance in the school was insufficient for their children to follow the required educational courses. As a result, they brought a case against their children's respective schools and the Flemish Community, claiming that the refusal to grant their children additional assistance hours amounted to a denial of reasonable accommodation. The judge discharged the school from its obligation, but held the Flemish community liable for a failure to provide reasonable accommodation. The Court ordered the Flemish Community to, *inter alia*, cease the above-mentioned denials of reasonable accommodation and to provide the plaintiffs with assistance hours corresponding to 70% of their school time within five months of the notification of the judgment. For further discussion of this case, see European Network of Legal Experts in the Non-discrimination Field, *Report on Measures to Combat Discrimination Directives 2000/43/ EC and 2000/78/EC*, Country Report (2011) Belgium, written by Emmanuelle Bribosia and Isabelle Rorive, pp. 49–51.

Finally, non-financial considerations have also been taken into account in certain jurisdictions. Waddington cites[57] the German Social Law Code on the rehabilitation and participation of disabled persons as taking into account, among other things, health and safety rules laid down by national law in determining whether a requested accommodation imposes a disproportionate burden on an employer.

4 EQUALITY AND POSITIVE ACTION

ARTICLE 5(4) CRPD

Specific measures which are necessary to accelerate or achieve *de facto* equality of persons with disabilities shall not be considered discrimination under the terms of the present Convention.

In addition to the duty to reasonably accommodate, other sub-sections of Article 5 CRPD oblige States Parties to take active steps to secure *de facto* equality for persons with disabilities. One such provision is that contained in Article 5(4) of the Convention, requiring the adoption of positive action. The scope and the content of that provision are explained in the sub-sections below.

4.1 Positive Action under International Human Rights Law

Positive action (or affirmative action) clauses can be found in several international human rights treaties. Article 1 CERD and Article 4 CEDAW both allow for 'special measures', a term used in international human rights law to endorse the adoption of measures designed to correct for disadvantages attributable to past or current discriminatory laws, policies and practices. In the disability context, the term 'special' has a derogatory meaning, as pointed out by the Working Group of the Ad Hoc Committee (WG).[58] Article 5(4) CRPD

[57] Waddington, 'Reasonable Accommodation', note 49, p. 730, citing the German Social Law Code, Book Nine 9 (SGB IX), Rehabilitation and Participation of Disabled Persons of 19 June 2001, Section 81(4) SGB IX.

[58] Footnote 28, Report of the Working Group to the Ad Hoc Committee, Annex I: Draft articles for a Comprehensive and Integral International Convention on the Protection and Promotion of the Rights and Dignity of Persons with Disabilities, available at www.un.org/esa/socdev/enable/rights/wgcontrib- chair1.html. As discussed in Chapter 3 of this textbook, the Ad Hoc Committee was created through the General Assembly, by means of Resolution 56/168 of 19 December 2001, with the mandate to draft a comprehensive and integral international convention. The Ad Hoc Committee decided to establish a Working Group (WG), with the aim

is a positive action clause that endorses 'specific measures', targeted at fostering equal opportunities and accelerating *de facto* equality for people with disabilities. Barmes describes positive action as any activity 'designed to improve the position, in terms of the distribution of benefits ... of a given social group ... on the basis that its members suffer systematic disadvantage in that regard'.[59] Since positive action does not target the *status quo*, dominant ideologies or entrenched stereotypes, it should be adopted as part of a broader policy initiative aimed at achieving true equality and wider structural change for people with disabilities. Positive action is usually temporary in nature,[60] with the objective of advancing 'effective equality'.[61] Cook notes that:

> generally speaking, temporary special measures are time-limited positive measures intended to enhance opportunities for historically and systematically disadvantaged groups, with a view to bringing group members into the mainstream of political, economic, social, cultural and civil life.[62]

Some authors have questioned whether positive action is *prima facie* incompatible with the non-discrimination norm, in that it favours a certain group. Others, such as de Schutter, argue that the opposite is true.[63] In paragraph 14 of its General Recommendation 25, the CEDAW Committee states that the 'application of temporary special measures in accordance with the Convention is one of the means to reali[s]e *de facto* or substantive equality for women,

of formulating a draft text, which would form the basis for further negotiations. The WG consisted of twenty-seven governmental representatives, designated by regional groups; twelve representatives from non-governmental organisations; and one representative of national human rights institutions (NHRIs). The WG Draft Text was the core document, upon which all further proposals were based. See further Chapter 3 of this textbook.

59 Lizzie Barmes, 'Equality Law and Experimentation: The Positive Action Challenge' (2009) 68 *Cambridge Law Journal* 623, at 623.

60 There are, however, some circumstances in which permanent positive action may be required under international human rights law. See below sub-section 4.2.

61 CESCR, General Recommendation No. 32, 24 September 2009, UN Doc. CERD/C/GC/32, para. 11.

62 Rebecca Cook, 'Obligations to Adopt Temporary Special Measures under the Convention on the Elimination of All Forms of Discrimination Against Women', in Ineke Boerefijn, Fons Coomans, Jenny Goldschmidt, Rikki Holtmaat and Ria Wolleswinkel (eds.), *Temporary Special Measures: Accelerating de Facto Equality of Women under Article 4(1) UN Convention on the Elimination of All Forms of Discrimination Against Women* (Antwerp: Intersentia, 2003), p. 119.

63 Olivier de Schutter, 'Positive Action', in Schiek, Waddington and Bell (eds.), *Cases, Materials and Text on National, Supranational and International Non-Discrimination Law*, note 49, p. 785.

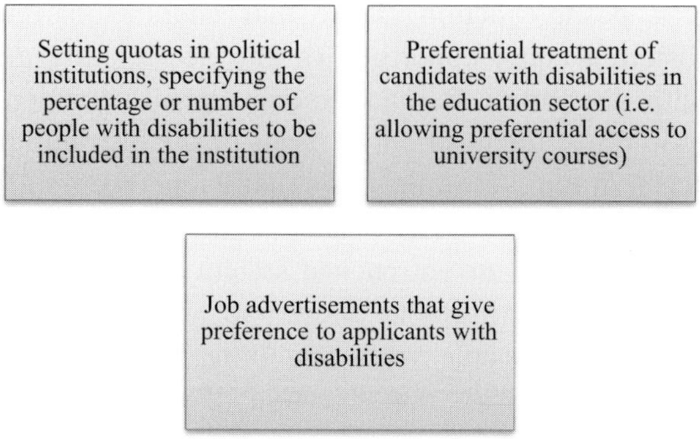

Figure 4.6 Examples of Positive Action

rather than an exception to the norms of non-discrimination and equality'.[64] Furthermore, in its General Comment No. 5 on persons with disabilities, the CESCR observes that:

> [b]ecause appropriate measures need to be taken to undo existing discrimination and to establish equitable opportunities for persons with disabilities, such actions should not be considered discriminatory in the sense of [A]rticle 2(2) of the ICESCR as long as they are based on the principle of equality and are employed only to the extent necessary to achieve that objective.[65]

Figure 4.6 sets out examples of positive action.[66]

4.2 The Difference between Positive Action and Reasonable Accommodation

The CRPD distinguishes between positive action and reasonable accommodation. The Convention simply allows for positive action in Article 5(4), whereas the provision of reasonable accommodation under Article 5(3) is mandatory. However, both types of measures have similar objectives. They are designed to increase the participation and inclusion of persons with disabilities in society. Notwithstanding this, the duty to accommodate is 'focused on current discriminatory obstacles to the enjoyment of rights by persons with disabilities, whereas positive action seeks to target the present effects of past discrimination'.[67]

[64] CEDAW Committee, General Recommendation No. 25, 2004, UN Doc. HRI/GEN/1/Rev.9 (Volume II), para. 14.

[65] CESCR, General Comment No. 5, 9 December 1994, UN Doc. E/1995/22, p. 19, para. 18.

[66] Broderick, *The Long and Winding Road to Equality and Inclusion for Persons with Disabilities: The United Nations Convention on the Rights of Persons with Disabilities*, note 26, pp. 129 et seq.

[67] Ibid. p. 120.

CRPD Committee, General Comment No. 6 on Equality and Non-Discrimination (2018)

25(c): 'Reasonable accommodation' should . . . not be confused with 'specific measures', including 'affirmative [positive] action measures'. While both concepts aim at achieving *de facto* equality, reasonable accommodation is a non-discrimination duty, whereas specific measures imply a preferential treatment of persons with disabilities over others to address historic and/or systematic/systemic exclusion from the benefits of exercising rights.

Examples of specific measures include temporary measures for countering the low numbers of women with disabilities employed in the private sector and support programmes to increase the number of students with disabilities in tertiary education. Similarly, reasonable accommodation should not be confused with the provision of support, such as personal assistants, under the right to live independently and be included in the community, or support to exercise legal capacity.

Another difference between positive action and reasonable accommodation lies in the fact that the unjustified failure to provide reasonable accommodation constitutes discrimination, and a failure to take positive action does not. A further distinguishing feature relates to the individualised nature of the reasonable accommodation duty when compared with the group dimension inherent to positive action.[68] The duty to accommodate involves 'an individual assessment and a tailored individual solution',[69] both in terms of the actual accommodation requested and the assessment as to whether the accommodation constitutes a disproportionate or undue burden on an entity. On the other hand, positive action consists of generalised measures, targeted at members of socially disadvantaged groups.[70] The reasonable accommodation duty:

> has the advantage of being tailored specifically to meet the needs of the disabled individual and, thereby, avoids (for instance) the controversial aspects of positive

[68] Ibid. p. 119.

[69] Lisa Waddington, *Implementing and Interpreting the Reasonable Accommodation Provision of the Framework Employment Directive: Learning from Experience and Achieving Best Practice* (Brussels, 2004), p. 8.

[70] See further Lisa Waddington and Mark Bell, 'Exploring the Boundaries of Positive Action under EU Law: A Search for Conceptual Clarity' (2011) 48(5) *Common Market Law Review* 1503, at 1523–4. On the issue of group-based measures and individual rights, as well as the difficulty for individuals to base a claim on CRPD obligations that relate to positive action, see Lisa Waddington, 'Positive Action Measures and the UN Convention on the Rights of Persons with Disabilities: Case Note: Communication No. 9/2012 *A.F. v. Italy*' (2016) 2 *International Labor Rights Case Law* 396.

action measures, which often hinge on stereotypes[71] and generalised assumptions regarding marginalised groups.[72]

Positive action is generally limited in time, and it will be subject to review, in order to determine whether the measures have achieved their goal. However, as Waddington and Bell affirm, 'this does not mean that positive action must be time-limited, but it is not automatically assumed to be indefinite'.[73] Notably, Article 5(4) CRPD allows for the adoption of both temporary and permanent positive action. Permanent, or ongoing, measures may be required on account of the particular nature of some impairments, such as for severe intellectual impairments. By way of contrast, reasonable accommodations 'are not generally assumed to have any preordained time-limit'.[74]

5 WOMEN WITH DISABILITIES

ARTICLE 6 CRPD

1. States Parties recognise that women and girls with disabilities are subject to multiple discrimination, and in this regard shall take measures to ensure the full and equal enjoyment by them of all human rights and fundamental freedoms.

2. States Parties shall take all appropriate measures to ensure the full development, advancement and empowerment of women, for the purpose of guaranteeing them the exercise and enjoyment of the human rights and fundamental freedoms set out in the present Convention.

Article 6 CRPD is a provision of transversal application, which prohibits discrimination on the basis of gender and disability. It is the first binding equality provision in international human rights law to address multiple discrimination explicitly. While Article 6 refers only to 'multiple discrimination', the CRPD Committee affirms that it also encompasses intersectional discrimination.[75] The two forms of discrimination are not the same, and the

[71] On this point, see, for example, Stephen Coate and Glenn Loury, 'Will Affirmative-Action Policies Eliminate Negative Stereotypes?' (1993) 83(5) *The American Economic Review* 1220.

[72] Broderick, *The Long and Winding Road to Equality and Inclusion for Persons with Disabilities: The United Nations Convention on the Rights of Persons with Disabilities*, note 26, pp. 155–156; see also, Shelagh Day and Gwen Brodsky, 'The Duty to Accommodate: Who Will Benefit?' (1996) 75 *Canadian Bar Review* 433.

[73] Waddington and Bell, 'Exploring the Boundaries of Positive Action under EU Law: A Search for Conceptual Clarity', note 70, at 1523–4.

[74] Ibid. [75] CRPD Committee, General Comment No. 6, note 3, para. 36.

Committee distinguishes between them in its General Comment No. 6 on equality. It notes that 'multiple discrimination'[76] constitutes 'a situation where a person can experience discrimination on two or several grounds, in the sense that discrimination is compounded or aggravated'. Intersectional discrimination, on the other hand, 'refers to a situation where several grounds operate and interact with each other at the same time in such a way that they are inseparable and thereby expose relevant individuals to unique types of disadvantage and discrimination'.[77]

DID YOU KNOW THAT …?

Certain laws and initiatives have been adopted across the globe, with a view to combating multiple and intersectional discrimination. For example, in Bulgaria, the Protection Against Discrimination Act, SG 86/30 (2003) imposes a duty on public authorities to give priority to positive measures for the benefit of victims of multiple discrimination. The Bulgarian authorities have also set up a Protection against Discrimination Commission, which hears cases related to multiple discrimination and sits in an extended panel for that purpose. Austrian disability non-discrimination legislation, specifically Article 9(4) of the Austrian Federal Disability Equality Act (*Bundes-Behindertengleichstellungsgesetz* (2016)), takes into account instances of multiple discrimination in the assessment of damages. In addition, in the Canadian Human Rights Act (R.S.C., 1985, c. H-6), Article 3(1) of the Act includes a prohibition of multiple discrimination.

There are also ongoing developments in other jurisdictions on the issue of multiple and intersectional discrimination. For instance, in Argentina, the report *Hacia un Plan Nacional contra la Discriminación – La Discriminación en Argentina. Diagnóstico y Propuestas* identifies the need for policies that foster inclusion and address intersectional discrimination (www.obserdiscriminacion.gob.ar/wp-content/uploads/2009/10/plannacional.pdf).

The Preamble of the CRPD emphasises the need for gender mainstreaming in all efforts by States Parties to implement the Convention, and it recognises, at recital (p), the:

[76] Fredman makes a distinction between consecutive (or sequential) multiple discrimination and additive multiple discrimination. Sandra Fredman, *Intersectional Discrimination in EU Gender Equality and Non-Discrimination Law* (Luxembourg: Publications Office of the European Union, 2016), p. 7.

[77] CRPD Committee, General Comment No. 6, note 3, para. 19.

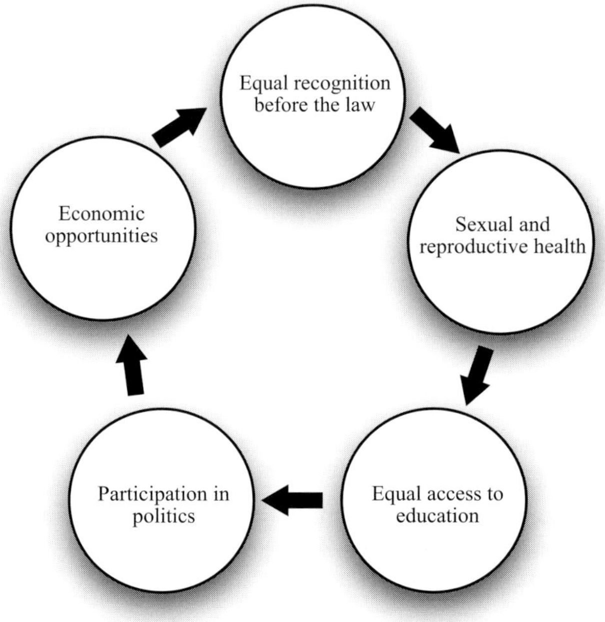

Figure 4.7 Multiple and Intersectional Discrimination against Women with Disabilities

difficult conditions faced by persons with disabilities who are subject to multiple or aggravated forms of discrimination on the basis of race, colour, sex, language, religion, political or other opinion, national, ethnic, indigenous or social origin, property, birth, age or other status.

The CRPD calls for measures to safeguard the full enjoyment by women of their rights, such as their equal rights and freedoms to services, education, employment, health care, freedom from torture, exploitation and violence. As mentioned above in Chapter 3, Article 3 CRPD also includes 'equality between men and women' as one of the underlying principles to be upheld by all States Parties.

Disabled women are especially vulnerable to discriminatory practices. This has been acknowledged by the CRPD Committee in its General Comment No. 3 on women with disabilities,[78] which highlights that multiple and intersectional discrimination against women and girls with disabilities is particularly prevalent in certain fields,[79] as shown by Figure 4.7.

[78] CRPD Committee, General Comment No. 3, 26 August 2016, UN Doc. CRPD/C/GC/3.

[79] Ibid. para. 2. See generally Mary Keogh, 'Disability, Gender and Development', in O'Mahony and Quinn (eds.), *Disability Law and Policy: An Analysis of the UN Convention*, note 21, pp. 45–54.

CRPD Committee, General Comment No. 3 on Women and Girls with Disabilities (2016)

17. Discrimination against women and girls with disabilities can take many forms: (a) direct discrimination; (b) indirect discrimination; (c) discrimination by association; (d) denial of reasonable accommodation; and (e) structural, or systemic, discrimination . . .

(a) Direct discrimination occurs when women with disabilities are treated less favourably than another person in a similar situation for a reason related to a prohibited ground. It also includes detrimental acts or omissions on the basis of prohibited grounds where there is no comparable similar situation. For example, direct discrimination occurs when the testimonies of women with intellectual or psychosocial disabilities are dismissed in court proceedings because of legal capacity, thus denying those women justice and effective remedies as victims of violence;
(b) Indirect discrimination refers to laws, policies or practices that appear neutral when taken at face value but that nonetheless have a disproportionately negative impact on women with disabilities. For example, health-care facilities may appear neutral but are discriminatory when they do not include accessible examination beds for gynaecological screenings;
(c) Discrimination by association is discrimination against persons on the basis of their association with a person with a disability. Often, women in a caregiver role experience discrimination by association. For example, the mother of a child with a disability may be discriminated against by a potential employer who fears that she may be a less engaged or available worker because of her child;
(d) Denial of reasonable accommodation is discrimination that occurs when necessary and appropriate modifications and adjustments (that do not impose a disproportionate or undue burden) are denied despite being needed to ensure that women with disabilities enjoy, on an equal basis with others, their human rights and fundamental freedoms. For example, a woman with a disability may be denied reasonable accommodation if she cannot undergo a mammogram at a health centre owing to the physical inaccessibility of the built environment;
(e) Structural, or systemic, discrimination is reflected in hidden or overt patterns of discriminatory institutional behaviour, discriminatory cultural traditions and discriminatory social norms and/or rules . . . For example, owing to stereotyping based on the intersection of gender and disability, women with disabilities may face barriers when reporting violence, such as disbelief and dismissal by the police, prosecutors and courts.

According to the CRPD Committee, States Parties should follow the tripartite typology of human rights obligations (respect, protect and fulfil) with regard to the rights of women with disabilities. In that regard, States Parties should respect (i.e. not interfere with) their rights, by abolishing 'existing laws, regulations, customs and practices that constitute discrimination against women with disabilities'.[80] In addition, States Parties must protect the rights of women with disabilities, by ensuring due diligence with respect to violations by third parties and ensuring training of professionals in the judicial sector as well as the provision of effective remedies.[81] Finally, States Parties should fulfil (i.e. ensure the realisation of) the rights of women with disabilities, by ensuring mainstreaming of their rights in all national action plans and in sectoral plans concerning, for example, gender equality, health, violence and employment.[82]

6 CHILDREN WITH DISABILITIES

ARTICLE 7 CRPD

1. States Parties shall take all necessary measures to ensure the full enjoyment by children with disabilities of all human rights and fundamental freedoms on an equal basis with other children.

2. In all actions concerning children with disabilities, the best interests of the child shall be a primary consideration.

3. States Parties shall ensure that children with disabilities have the right to express their views freely on all matters affecting them, their views being given due weight in accordance with their age and maturity, on an equal basis with other children, and to be provided with disability and age-appropriate assistance to reali[s]e that right.

Children with disabilities 'face double prejudice on account of the combined disadvantage accruing to them due to their impairment and age'.[83] They often experience discrimination at key stages of their development, including in

[80] Ibid. para. 25. [81] Ibid. para. 26. [82] Ibid. para. 27.

[83] Andrea Broderick, 'Article 7 UN CRPD: Children with Disabilities', in Valentina Della Fina, Rachele Cera and Giuseppe Palmisano (eds.), *The United Nations Convention on the Rights of Persons with Disabilities: A Commentary* (Cham: Springer, 2017), pp. 195–212, p. 196; see generally Ilias Bantekas, 'Article 7: Children with Disabilities' in Ilias Bantekas, Michael Stein and Dimitris Anastasiou, *The UN Convention on the Rights of Persons with Disabilities: A Commentary* (Oxford: Oxford University Press, 2018).

access to education[84] and health care, among other services.[85] In addition, 'the harmful effects of disability discrimination in childhood are often compounded for children experiencing multiple and intersectional forms of discrimination, in particular girls with disabilities'.[86] Article 7 CRPD seeks to combat that disadvantage through various sub-provisions, and it falls within the articles of transversal application (Articles 1–9 CRPD). This means that it applies to all rights in the Convention.

Article 7(1) CRPD requires States Parties to take all necessary measures to ensure equality for children with disabilities in the enjoyment of rights – both civil and political, as well as economic, social and cultural rights. In addition to prohibiting all forms of disability-based discrimination against children in laws and policies, States Parties to the CRPD are required to monitor the provision of reasonable accommodations to children with disabilities. An explicit obligation to provide children with 'age-appropriate accommodations'[87] is contained in Article 13(1) of the Convention (on access to justice).[88] As the CRPD Committee notes, these 'procedural accommodations' in the context of access to justice 'should not be confused with reasonable accommodation; while the latter is limited by the concept of disproportionality, procedural accommodations are not'.[89] States Parties are also obliged to take other 'necessary measures' to ensure the fulfilment of the rights of disabled children. Such measures may entail 'legislative and policy measures, educational and awareness-raising measures or cultural and political measures, among others'.[90] Children with disabilities should have 'adequate supports to satisfy the whole range of their developmental needs'.[91] These needs include 'physical, mental, social and cultural needs . . . communication needs',[92] and they can be satisfied through early childhood care.

[84] According to the World Report on Disability, children with disabilities are less likely to attend school, thus experiencing limited opportunities for human capital formation and facing reduced employment opportunities and decreased productivity in adulthood. World Health Organization and World Bank, *World Report on Disability* (2011), pp. 205 et seq.

[85] In its General Comment No. 9, the Committee on the Rights of the Child acknowledges the fact that discrimination often occurs in a wide variety of areas, including in service provision. This results, *inter alia*, in the exclusion of children with disabilities from education 'and denies them access to quality health and social services'. UN Committee on the Rights of the Child (CRC Committee), General Comment No. 9, 27 February 2007, UN Doc. CRC/C/GC/9, para. 8.

[86] Broderick, 'Article 7 UN CRPD: Children with Disabilities', note 83, p. 201.

[87] Article 13(1) CRPD.

[88] Another explicit reasonable accommodation duty is contained in Article 24(2)(c) CRPD in relation to the right to education. See below Chapter 9.

[89] CRPD Committee, General Comment No. 6, note 3, para. 25(d).

[90] Broderick, 'Article 7 UN CRPD: Children with Disabilities', note 83, p. 203.

[91] Ibid.

[92] Ibid.

Article 7(2) CRPD contains the 'best interests' principle, which requires systematic consideration of the manner in which children's rights and interests will be affected by certain decisions, including those affecting children indirectly.[93] In Article 7(2), there is no definition of what is meant by 'best interests', nor is there any information contained in the drafting history of the CRPD with regard to the factors that might be taken into account in deciding what the best interests of a particular disabled child are. This has the potential to give rise to problems of interpretation, particularly in the judicial sphere, and most notably related to children with psychosocial disabilities[94] or those with intellectual impairments. There is 'a significant risk of paternalism'[95] inherent in the principle itself, and the application of the concept of 'best interests' may result in 'the danger of an over-reliance on medical opinion and the adoption of an approach that is not rights-based'.[96]

Article 7(3) CRPD seeks to ensure the participation of children in all decisions related to their well-being and to ensure that children with disabilities have the right to express their views freely on all matters that may affect them. Unlike its counterpart in Article 12(1) of the UN Convention on the Rights of the Child (CRC), Article 7(3) CRPD does not limit the right of participation to children who are deemed to be 'capable' of expressing their views – it provides instead that all disabled children are entitled to express their views. In order to ensure the realisation of the rights contained in Article 7(3), States Parties must guarantee the provision of disability and age-appropriate assistance. The UN General Assembly (UNGA) has called on states 'to adopt measures, including providing or promoting the use of accessible means, modes and formats of communication, to facilitate the enjoyment of the right to be heard by children with disabilities'.[97] This might include the use of assistive devices, communication aids and interpreters. The CRPD Committee also emphasises the importance of supports in enabling children with disabilities to express their views.[98]

Article 7(3) CRPD provides that 'due weight' should be given to the views of children with disabilities in accordance with their age and maturity, on an equal basis with other children. An EU study has pointed out that matters relating to children with disabilities must not be considered solely on the basis of the age of the child in question, since this 'can effectively exclude them

[93] CRC Committee, General Comment No. 5, 27 November 2003, UN Doc. CRC/GC/2003/5, para. 12.

[94] Mary Donnelly, 'Decision Making for Mentally Incompetent People: The Empty Formula of Best Interests?' (2001) 20 *Medical Law Journal* 405.

[95] Broderick, 'Article 7 UN CRPD: Children with Disabilities', note 83, p. 206. [96] Ibid.

[97] UNGA, Resolution No. A/64/435 on Rights of the child, 3 March 2010, para. 33(t).

[98] See, for instance, CRPD Committee, Concluding Observations on the Initial Report of New Zealand, 31 October 2014, UN Doc. CRPD/C/NZL/CO/1, paras. 17–18; CRPD Committee, Concluding Observations on the Initial Report of Denmark, 29 October 2014, UN Doc. CRPD/C/DNK/CO/1, paras. 20–21.

from decision making processes that affect them'.[99] This is particularly so in the case of children with severe cognitive impairments, whose age may not necessarily correlate with their stage of development. Thus, all aspects of the capabilities of the child in question must be taken into account under Article 7(3) CRPD. Finally, Article 7(3) CRPD also requires States Parties to respect the evolving capacities of children. This mirrors the general principle contained in Article 3(h) of the Convention. In all areas of life, States Parties to the CRPD must, therefore, ensure to maximise the capabilities of disabled children in autonomous decision-making processes.

7 THE MODEL OF EQUALITY IN THE CRPD

This final section outlines how the understanding of the equality and non-discrimination principles contained in the CRPD fits within various theoretical models of disability[100] and the academic debate on equality in general.

7.1 The Inclusive Equality Model

The formal model of equality 'focuses exclusively on equal treatment in the application and enforcement of laws and rights. It requires that individuals are treated in the same manner, if they are situated in a similar situation, and that laws and policies are formulated in a neutral manner'.[101] Lawson points to the fact that the formal model 'would insist, for instance, that a university treat identically qualified applicants in the same way regardless of the fact that they might have different genders, racial background, or physical impairments'.[102] The formal equality model corresponds largely to the prohibition of direct discrimination. Article 5(1) CRPD seeks to ensure formal equality in its guarantees of equality before and under the law.

By way of contrast with formal equality, as the CESCR highlights, the substantive model of equality focuses on 'the effects of laws, policies and practices and with ensuring that they do not maintain, but rather alleviate, the inherent

[99] Marta Ballestreros et al., *Study on Member States' Policies for Children with Disabilities* (Luxembourg: Publications Office of the European Union, 2013), p. 13.

[100] See above Chapter 1.

[101] Broderick, *The Long and Winding Road to Equality and Inclusion for Persons with Disabilities: The United Nations Convention on the Rights of Persons with Disabilities*, note 26, p. 31. On models of equality, see generally, Maria Ventegodt Liisberg, *Disability and Employment: A Contemporary Disability Human Rights Approach Applied to Danish, Swedish and EU Law and Policy* (Cambridge-Antwerp: Intersentia, 2011).

[102] Anna Lawson (ed.), *Disability and Equality Law in Britain: The Role of Reasonable Adjustment* (Portland: Hart Publishing, 2008), p. 19.

disadvantage that particular groups experience'.[103] The substantive model of equality seeks to investigate hidden, or covert, forms of discrimination, such as indirect discrimination. It also seeks to ensure that the characteristics of individuals who are different from the 'norm' are taken into account and accommodated within non-discrimination provisions. Article 5 CRPD clearly ensures this through its guarantees of equal protection and equal benefit of the law. Moreover, the reasonable accommodation duty is an innovative addition to non-discrimination law at the international level, seeking to ensure equality of opportunities as well as *de facto* equality. The accommodation duty brings a redistributive element into the non-discrimination norm, by requiring States Parties to make available material resources to ensure that both public and private entities provide accommodations, where needed. Article 5(4) CRPD also legitimates both temporary and permanent, or ongoing, positive action, whenever the circumstances so require, in order to accelerate or achieve *de facto* equality for persons with disabilities. Positive action is closely associated with substantive equality, by seeking to target the *status quo* of inequality and historical discrimination against disabled persons.

The CRPD goes even further than substantive equality, since the Convention is based on a model of inclusive equality.[104]

CRPD Committee, General Comment No. 6 on Equality and Non-Discrimination (2018)

11. Inclusive equality is a new model of equality developed throughout the Convention. It embraces a substantive model of equality and extends and elaborates on the content of equality in: (a) a fair redistributive dimension to address socioeconomic disadvantages; (b) a recognition dimension to combat stigma, stereotyping, prejudice and violence and to recogni[s]e the dignity of human beings and their intersectionality; (c) a participative dimension to reaffirm the social nature of people as members of social groups and the full recognition of humanity through inclusion in society; and (d) an accommodating dimension to make space for difference as a matter of human dignity.
The Convention is based on inclusive equality.

Inclusive equality is reflected, among others, in the CRPD's accessibility obligations in Article 9, its endorsement of universal design in Article 2 CRPD[105] and its awareness-raising duties in Article 8. The transformative potential of the CRPD is also reflected by the fact that the non-discrimination norm, and particularly the duty to reasonably accommodate persons with disabilities, applies across the Convention's substantive socio-economic rights.

[103] CESCR, General Comment No. 16, note 12, para. 7.
[104] CRPD Committee, General Comment No. 6, note 3, para. 11.
[105] See below Chapter 5.

The inclusive model of equality is bolstered by the models of disability underpinning the Convention – the social-contextual and human rights models of disability. The combination of those models has resulted in an acknowledgement of the fact that a barrier-free society is essential to ensuring full and effective participation and inclusion of people with disabilities in society.

7.2 The Innovative Character of the Equality Norm in the CRPD

The understanding of the equality norm has evolved greatly in recent years, at the level of international human rights law generally. Before the CRPD, differential characteristics were perceived as constituting an exception to the rule of equal treatment. In that regard, Arnardóttir traces the evolution from the era of 'universal sameness' to the era of 'specific difference' and, more recently, to the era of 'multidimensional disadvantage equality'.[106] According to her, the era of 'universal sameness' is encapsulated in the provisions of the ICCPR and the ICESCR. The provisions of those treaties are open-ended non-discrimination provisions which seek to ensure that the universal equality norm applies to everyone in the same manner. The non-discrimination provisions of the ICCPR and the ICESCR do not account for differential characteristics.

The era of 'specific difference' equality is evidenced by the non-discrimination provisions in both CERD and CEDAW. Those treaties allow for maintaining a focus on differential characteristics in the form of specific identity markers, but only in certain circumstances. Both treaties enable a consideration of instances of indirect discrimination, and they also permit States Parties to endorse the adoption of special measures or positive action, wherever necessary.[107] However, the 'specific difference' equality era did not enable wider disadvantages in mainstream society to be taken into account, and this is where the CRPD differs from earlier human rights treaties. Arnardóttir defines the era surrounding the adoption of the CRPD as embracing 'multidimensional disadvantage' equality. The CRPD's model of

> Read the core human rights treaties, and identify how the CRPD differs from those treaties from the perspective of equality.

[106] Arnardóttir, 'A Future of Multidimensional Disadvantage Equality', note 2, pp. 47–64.
[107] Ibid. pp. 49–54.

inclusive equality endorses legal measures that look to differential characteristics where necessary, but rather focus on wider systems of disadvantage in mainstream society. The Convention advocates key legal tools, such as indirect discrimination, positive action, reasonable accommodation duties and accessibility obligations, as means by which to eradicate barriers that perpetuate inequalities. Furthermore, the CRPD tailors the universal equality norm to the specific needs of disabled people, and the Convention seeks to combat instances of multiple and intersectional discrimination.

Due to the significant advancements in the understanding of the non-discrimination norm embodied in Article 5 CRPD and related articles, that norm can potentially be applied in practice to advance the equal rights of persons with disabilities to participate and be included in society.

SUMMARY

- **Article 5 CRPD encompasses a prohibition of discrimination, through guarantees of equality before and under the law. Article 5 also requires States Parties to ensure equal protection and equal benefit of the law, without any discrimination.**
- **In addition, Article 5 sets forth positive obligations, such as the duty of reasonable accommodation. In addition, that Article permits the adoption of positive action. Positive action is designed to correct for disadvantages attributable to past or current discriminatory laws, policies and practices.**
- **Many forms of discrimination are covered under the CRPD, including: direct discrimination, indirect discrimination, an unjustified denial of reasonable accommodation, harassment, discrimination by association, discrimination based on perceived or past disability, and multiple and intersectional discrimination.**
- **The focus under the reasonable accommodation duty is on the specific circumstances of each case, taking into account the effectiveness of the adjustments in removing the disadvantage for the disabled person and the practicality for the duty-bearer of providing the accommodation.**
- **The duties contained in Article 5 CRPD to prohibit discrimination and to provide reasonable accommodation span all human rights in the CRPD.**
- **All barriers to the enforcement of the prohibition of discrimination and the reasonable accommodation duty should be eliminated. This entails the provision of effective disability-sensitive training of the judiciary, lawyers and all staff associated with the judicial services.**
- **On the whole, Article 5 CRPD goes far beyond the non-discrimination provisions of the other core international human rights treaties. The CRPD endorses an inclusive model of equality, by means of which it seeks to target deep-rooted structural inequalities and to guarantee the empowerment of disabled people as well as to ensure that they can participate and be included in mainstream society on an equal basis with others.**

ACTIVITIES

REVIEW QUESTIONS

1. **What are the key elements of the duty to reasonably accommodate in the CRPD?**
2. **What are the factors inherent in the disproportionate or undue burden test?**
3. **What are the key features of Article 7 CRPD?**

ESSAY QUESTIONS

1. **'The equality and non-discrimination norms contained in the CRPD fit neatly within the various theoretical models of disability and the conceptions of equality that have been elaborated by scholars to date.'** ***Discuss.***
2. **'The CRPD contains an innovative provision on multiple and intersectional discrimination.'** ***Discuss.***

GROUP PROJECT

Aisling has cerebral palsy and, as a result, she has limited muscle control and dexterity. She uses an electric wheelchair for mobility. She lives in an apartment that is located in a historical building in the city centre of Freedonia City (in the State of Freedonia). Since there are a few steps leading to the door of her apartment and since the doors are too narrow for her wheelchair, Aisling asks the City Council for permission to build a ramp and to widen the doors. She also asks the City Council for permission to install electric doors, which might facilitate her in entering and leaving the building. The City Council refuses to grant Aisling these permissions, on the grounds that these modifications will alter the historical building and that they are not permitted under the Freedonian Historical Building Law. Aisling claims that this refusal amounts to an unjustified denial of reasonable accommodation.

Discuss the group project, taking into account that Freedonia is a State Party to the CRPD.

FURTHER READING

Arnardóttir, O. M., 'A Future of Multidimensional Disadvantage Equality', in O. M. Arnardóttir and G. Quinn (eds.), *The UN Convention on the Rights of Persons with Disabilities: European and Scandinavian Perspectives* (Leiden: Martinus Nijhoff, 2009), pp. 41–66.

De Schutter, O., 'Positive Action', in D. Schiek, L. Waddington and M. Bell (eds.), *Cases, Materials and Text on National, Supranational and International Non-Discrimination Law* (Oxford: Hart Publishing, 2007), pp. 757–870.

European Parliament, *Discrimination Engendered by the Intersection of Gender and Disability* (Luxembourg: Publications Office of the European Union, 2013).

Fredman, S., 'Disability Equality and the Existing Anti-Discrimination Paradigm – European Discrimination Law', in A. Lawson and C. Gooding (eds.), *Disability Rights in Europe: From Theory to Practice* (Oxford/Portland: Hart Publishing, 2005), pp. 199–218.

Hendriks, A., 'The Significance of Equality and Non-Discrimination for the Protection of the Rights and Dignity of Disabled Persons', in T. Degener and Y. Koster-Dreese (eds.), *Human Rights and Disabled Persons: Essays and Relevant Human Rights Instruments* (Dordrecht: Martinus Nijhoff, 1995), pp. 40–62.

Lawson, A., 'The UN Convention on the Rights of Persons with Disabilities and European Disability Law: A Catalyst for Cohesion?', in O. M. Arnardóttir and G. Quinn (eds.), *The UN Convention on the Rights of Persons with Disabilities: European and Scandinavian Perspectives* (Leiden: Martinus Nijhoff, 2009), pp. 81–109.

Lord, J. E. and Brown, R., 'The Role of Reasonable Accommodation in Securing Substantive Equality for Persons with Disabilities: The UN Convention on the Rights of Persons with Disabilities', in M. H. Rioux, L. A. Basser and M. Jones (eds.), *Critical Perspectives on Human Rights and Disability Policy* (Leiden: Martinus Nijhoff, 2011), pp. 273–308.

MacKinnon, C. A., 'Substantive Equality: A Perspective' (2011) 96 *Minnesota Law Review* 1–27.

McCallum, R. and Martin, H., 'Comment: The CRPD and Children with Disabilities' (2013) 20 *Australian International Law Journal* 17–31.

Megret, F. and Msipa, D., 'Global Reasonable Accommodation: How the Convention on the Rights of Persons with Disabilities Changes the way we think about Equality' (2014) 30 *South African Journal on Human Rights* 252–274.

Office of the High Commissioner for Human Rights, *Equality and Non-discrimination under Article 5 of the Convention on the Rights of Persons with Disabilities*, UN Doc. A/HRC/34/26, pp. 1–18.

Rioux, M. H. and Riddle, C. A., 'Values in Disability Policy and Law: Equality', in M. H. Rioux, L. A. Basser and M. Jones (eds.), *Critical Perspectives on Human Rights and Disability Policy* (Boston: Martinus Nijhoff, 2011), pp. 33–56.

5 Accessibility for Persons with Disabilities

LEARNING OUTCOMES

- ✓ Understand the concepts of 'accessibility' and 'universal design'.
- ✓ Identify the accessibility norms under the CRPD.
- ✓ Comprehend the significance of accessibility in relation to equality and non-discrimination and within the overall disability rights agenda.
- ✓ Understand the main accessibility-related obligations contained in Article 9 CRPD.
- ✓ Identify the challenges inherent in implementing Article 9 CRPD.
- ✓ Demonstrate awareness of the role of accessibility in ensuring participation and inclusion in society.
- ✓ Comprehend the difference between accessibility and reasonable accommodation.
- ✓ Understand the main obligations enshrined in Article 21 CRPD on access to information.

Accessibility allows us to tap into everyone's potential.[1]

1 INTRODUCTION

The CRPD contains the innovative principle of accessibility, a principle which is not mentioned in other international treaties, even though rights of access are spelled out in several human rights conventions.[2] For example, Article 25 (c) of the International Covenant on Civil and Political Rights (ICCPR) includes the right of every citizen to have access, on an equal basis, to public services. Article 5(f) of the International Convention on the Elimination of All Forms of Racial Discrimination (CERD) stipulates 'the right of access to any place or services intended for use by the general public, such as transport, hotels, restaurants, cafes, theatres and parks'. In its General Comment No. 14, the UN Committee on Economic, Social and Cultural Rights (CESCR) emphasises that health facilities, goods and services must be accessible to everyone without discrimination.[3] In the field of disability, a provision on accessibility was already included in Rule 5 of the Standard Rules for the Equalization on Opportunities for Persons with Disabilities (Standard Rules).[4] That Rule encourages States to recognise the overall importance of accessibility in the process of the equalisation of opportunities in all spheres of society and to introduce programmes of action to make the physical environment as well as information and communication accessible.

The CRPD builds on previous human rights law and on the Standard Rules. The CRPD Committee's General Comment No. 2 suggests that 'accessibility should be viewed as a disability-specific reaffirmation of the social aspect of the right of access'[5] established by pre-existing UN human rights treaties. According to Lord, however, the CRPD 'adds considerable content to accessibility',[6] which is considered as 'a precondition for persons with disabilities to live independently and participate fully and equally in society',[7] and as a

[1] Statement by Debra Ruh, Chief Executive Officer and Founder of Ruh Global Communications, a company that focuses on Global Disability Inclusion, Digital Marketing, ICT Accessibility, Human Rights and implementation of the CRPD, 31 October 2016.

[2] Janet Lord, 'Accessibility and Human Rights Fusion in the CRPD: Assessing the Scope and Content of the Accessibility Principle and Duty under the CRPD' (7 October 2010), Paper delivered at the General Day of Discussion on Accessibility, CRPD Committee, Geneva.

[3] UN Committee on Economic, Social and Cultural Rights (CESCR), General Comment No. 14, 11 August 2000, UN Doc. E/C.12/2000/4.

[4] See above Chapter 2, sub-section 2.2.

[5] CRPD Committee, General Comment No. 2, 11 April 2014, UN Doc. CRPD/C/GC/2, para. 4.

[6] Lord, 'Accessibility and Human Rights Fusion in the CRPD: Assessing the Scope and Content of the Accessibility Principle and Duty under the CRPD', note 2.

[7] CRPD Committee, General Comment No. 2, note 5, para. 1.

gateway[8] to the enjoyment of other human rights. The significance of accessibility is best explained by McCallum, the former Chair of the CRPD Committee, who states that there is nothing 'more crucial for persons with disabilities than accessibility'.[9] The Preamble to the Convention, at recital (v) thereof, explicitly recognises:

> the importance of accessibility to the physical, social, economic and cultural environment, to health and education and to information and communication, in enabling persons with disabilities to fully enjoy all human rights and fundamental freedoms.

Accessibility is also mentioned as one of the general principles in Article 3 CRPD, and it is spelled out in Article 9 CRPD as well as in other substantive provisions of the Convention. The CRPD also includes concepts and measures that are related to accessibility: first, the concept of 'universal design', which is not mentioned in Article 9 but is spelled out in Article 4 as a general and cross-cutting obligation; and, secondly, assistive devices, which are essential to guaranteeing accessibility in particular situations and for specific groups of people.

This chapter reflects on how accessibility is understood in the CRPD and interpreted by the CRPD Committee. Further to this introduction, section 2 conducts a broad examination of the multidimensional concept of 'accessibility' and its relationship with universal design and assistive devices. Section 3 discusses the role of accessibility rights in the CRPD, while section 4 focuses on the content and scope of Article 9 of the Convention, addressing the relationship between accessibility and non-discrimination. Section 5 investigates the differences between accessibility and reasonable accommodation, in light of the CRPD Committee's jurisprudence. Finally, section 6 briefly analyses Article 21 CRPD on access to information and communications.

2 ACCESSIBILITY, UNIVERSAL DESIGN AND ASSISTIVE DEVICES: TRACING THE CONCEPTUAL BOUNDARIES

Before analysing the content and the scope of accessibility obligations in the CRPD, this section briefly discusses the concepts of 'accessibility', 'universal design' and 'assistive devices' from a technical perspective.

[8] Stefan Tromel, 'A Personal Perspective on the Drafting History of the United Nations Convention on the Rights of Persons with Disabilities', in Lisa Waddington and Gerard Quinn (eds.), *European Yearbook of Disability Law* (Antwerp/Portland: Intersentia, 2009), pp. 115–37, p. 118.

[9] Ron McCallum, *Opening Remarks at the General Day of Discussion on Accessibility of the Committee on the Rights of Persons with Disabilities* (7 October 2010), General Day of Discussion on Accessibility, CRPD Committee, Geneva.

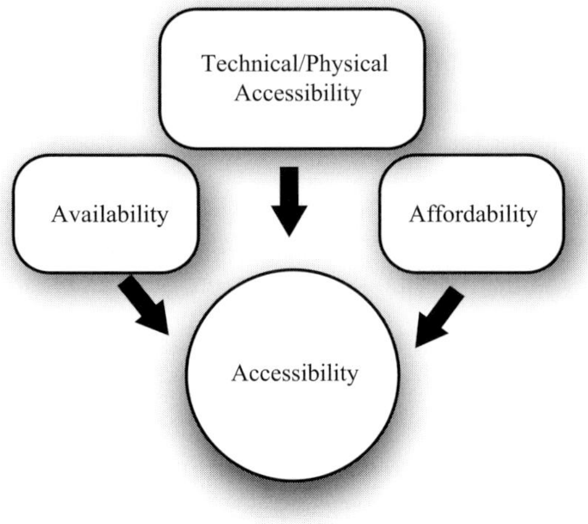

Figure 5.1 Accessibility As a Multidimensional Concept

2.1 Accessibility

The term 'accessible' is broadly considered to be synonymous with the following terms: 'approachable', 'attainable', 'available', 'close', 'convenient', 'handy', and 'within reach'.[10] 'Accessibility' is used in many different contexts, where it may mean different things. The International Organization for Standardization (ISO) and the International Electronic Commission (IEC) define the term 'accessible design' as 'design focused on principles of extending standard design to people with some type of performance limitation to maximize the number of potential customers who can readily use a product, building or service'.[11] Accessibility has various dimensions, as shown in Figure 5.1. In order for a good or a service to be fully accessible, not only must all users be able to physically interact with it, but they must also be aware of its existence and must be able to avail of it.[12] In order to meet the definition of an accessible good or service, the criterion of economical affordability must also be met.

[10] Susanne Iwarson and Agnetha Stahl, 'Accessibility, Usability and Universal Design – Positioning and Definition of Concepts Describing Person–Environment Relationships' (2003) 25(2) *Disability and Rehabilitation* 58.

[11] ISO/IEC, *Guide 71. Guidelines for Standards Developers to Address the Needs of Older Persons and Persons with Disabilities* (2001), available at www.iso.org/iso/iso_iec_guide_71_2001.pdf. In the context of standardisation, several definitions for the term accessibility exist, but, in general, the term is used with a broad understanding. Additional definitions are included in the updated Guide 71: 'Guide for Addressing Accessibility in Standards' ISO/IEC GUIDE 71:2014(E).

[12] Delia Ferri, *Analytical Framework for a Comparative Analysis of Accessible Technology Law and Policy* (DISCIT Report, 2014).

2.2 Universal Design

The concept of 'accessibility' is intertwined with that of 'universal design' (UD). Traditional design adds accessibility features to otherwise inaccessible products, building or services.[13] By contrast, UD considers the diverse needs and abilities of all individuals throughout the design process.[14]

UD is premised on the idea that the population is comprised of individuals with diverse characteristics. Mace and Lusher frame UD as a concept that benefits users regardless of medical diagnosis of disability:

> [i]nstead of responding only to the minimum demands of laws which require a few special features for disabled people, it is possible to design most manufactured items and building elements to be usable by a broad range of human beings including children, elderly people, people with disabilities, and people of different sizes. This ... is a concept that is now entirely possible and one that makes economic and social sense.[15]

Universally designed goods and services can be accessed, understood and used to the greatest extent possible by all people, regardless of their age, size, ability or disability. Grimble et al. investigated claims that universally designed environments are more usable by all consumers than non-universally designed environments.[16] Through case studies, they also evaluated the perceptions and performance of participants with varying degrees of physical and/or sensory impairments, and they discovered, through the perceived and observed behaviour of the participants, that UD did indeed benefit diverse users to a greater extent.

DID YOU KNOW THAT ...?

The origins of UD date back to the early 1950s. Ronald Mace, an American architect and product designer, coined the term UD in 1985 to describe 'a way of designing a building or facility, at little or no extra cost, so that it is both attractive and functional

[13] Iwarson and Stahl, 'Accessibility, Usability and Universal Design – Positioning and Definition of Concepts Describing Person–Environment Relationships', note 10.

[14] For discussion on the theorisation of Universal Design, see Aimi Hamraie, 'Universal Design and the Problem of "Post-Disability" Ideology' (2016) 8(3) *Design and Culture* 285.

[15] Ruth Lusher and Ronald Mace, 'Design for Physical and Mental Disabilities', in Joseph Wilkes and Robert Packard (eds.), *Encyclopedia of Architecture: Design Engineering and Construction* (New York: John Wiley and Sons, 1989), cited in https://projects.ncsu.edu/ncsu/design/cud/pubs_p/docs/ACC%20Environments.pdf, p. 10.

[16] Michael Grimble, Gary Danford and David Schoell, *The Effectiveness of Universal Design: Case Study Demonstrations* (IDeA Center, SUNY Buffalo, 2010). These authors also claim that UD is effective in lowering the perceived difficulty of activities, which are considered as requiring less effort and assistance.

for all people, disabled or not'. A more refined theorisation of UD emerged in 1997, when the group of architects led by Mace laid down its seven constituent principles:

Principle 1: Equitable Use

The design is useful and marketable to people with diverse abilities.

Principle 2: Flexibility in Use

The design accommodates a wide range of individual preferences and abilities.

Principle 3: Simple and Intuitive Use

Use of the design is easy to understand, regardless of the user's experience, knowledge, language skills, or current concentration level.

Principle 4: Perceptible Information

The design communicates necessary information effectively to the user, regardless of ambient conditions or the user's sensory abilities.

Principle 5: Tolerance for Error

The design minimises hazards and the adverse consequences of accidental or unintended actions.

Principle 6: Low Physical Effort

The design can be used efficiently and comfortably and with a minimum of fatigue.

Principle 7: Size and Space for Approach and Use

Appropriate size and space is provided for approach, reach, manipulation and use, regardless of user's body size, posture or mobility.

D'souza suggests that UD has become a new paradigm in recent years, which aims at a holistic approach, ranging in scale from product design to architecture, urban design and information technology.[17] As mentioned above, the principle of UD has been incorporated in the CRPD. However, various schools of thought have elaborated further on this concept and have coined different terms, with slightly different nuances, to refer to what essentially appears to be the same concept. In Europe, the term 'Design for All' is the term that is used most frequently. It has been defined by the European Institute for Design and Disability (EIDD),[18] a European platform composed of different organisations, as 'design for human diversity, social inclusion and equality'. In

[17] Newton D'souza, 'Chapter 1: Is Universal Design a Critical Theory?', in Simeon Keates, John Clarkson, Patrick Langdon and Peter Robinson (eds.), *Designing a More Inclusive World* (Cham: Springer, 2005), pp. 3–9.

[18] EIDD Design for all Europe, 'What is EIDD-DFA Europe', available at http://dfaeurope.eu/what-is-eidd-dfa-europe/.

2004, the EIDD adopted a declaration, the 'Stockholm Declaration', to highlight the foundational principles and the rationale for 'Design for All', and to stress that it will be an increasingly necessary element 'in pro-active strategies for sustainable development'.[19]

EIDD Stockholm Declaration

... Across Europe, human diversity in age, culture and ability is greater than ever. We now survive illness and injury and live with disability as never before. Although today's world is a complex place, it is one of our own making, one in which we therefore have the possibility – and the responsibility – to base our designs on the principle of inclusion.

Design for All is design for human diversity, social inclusion and equality. This holistic and innovative approach constitutes a creative and ethical challenge for all planners, designers, entrepreneurs, administrators and political leaders.

Design for All aims to enable all people to have equal opportunities to participate in every aspect of society. To achieve this, the built environment, everyday objects, services, culture and information – in short, everything that is designed and made by people to be used by people – must be accessible, convenient for everyone in society to use and responsive to evolving human diversity ... (http://dfaeurope.eu/wp-content/uploads/2014/05/stockholm-declaration_english.pdf)

In the UK, the term 'inclusive design' is often used as a synonym for Design for All, and it is described by the British Standard on Managing Inclusive Design[20] as:

> [t]he design of mainstream products and/or services that are accessible to, and usable by, as many people as reasonably possible on a global basis, in a wide variety of situations and to the greatest extent possible without the need for special adaptation or speciali[s]ed design.

According to Persson et al., the words 'as reasonably possible' in the definition above entail one of the main differences between UD and Design for All, as they seem 'to suggest that the inclusion of people with disabilities can be disregarded if considered too difficult to achieve or too costly' under a Design for All approach.[21]

[19] The text of the declaration is available at http://dfaeurope.eu/wp-content/uploads/2014/05/stockholm-declaration_english.pdf.

[20] BSI TBSI, *Design Management Systems, Managing Inclusive Design, Guide* (2005) vol. BS 7000-6:2005.

[21] Hans Persson, Henrik Åhman, Alexander Arvei Yngling and Jan Gullikson, 'Universal Design, Inclusive Design, Accessible Design, Design for All: Different Concepts – One Goal? On the

Most recently, however, the concept of UD (and other similar theorisations, such as Design for All) has encountered various criticisms, both in terms of its feasibility and cost. For example, a research group based in Dundee (Scotland) claims that the goals pursued through these approaches are not realistic for all products.[22] It also argues that these approaches tend to encourage designers to follow a traditional path to produce a prototype design, and only then to investigate how to modify their interfaces and systems to cope with older and/or disabled users, and this can lead to an inefficient design process and inappropriate design, which may be unusable in practice.[23] This Scottish research team, thus, proposes to pursue a 'User-Sensitive Inclusive Design (USID)',[24] where the word 'inclusive' endorses a more realistic view which enables designers to include people with disabilities within the potential user group in an effective and efficient way.

2.3 Assistive Devices

UD does not eliminate the need for assistive devices in certain situations and for particular groups. Several examples exist regarding the interaction between UD and assistive devices: for instance, in a cinema, people with hearing aids can hear the sound track if the cinema is equipped with a compatible induction loop system.[25]

> Read the ISO classification of assistive products. Is it comprehensive in your opinion?

The term 'assistive device' is commonly used interchangeably with that of 'assistive product', which is defined by the ISO as being:

> [a]ny product (including devices, equipment, instruments and software), especially produced or generally available, used by or for persons with disability: for participation; to protect, support, train, measure or substitute

Concept of Accessibility – Historical, Methodological and Philosophical Aspects' (2015) 14(4) *Universal Access in the Information Society* 505.

[22] Peter Gregor, Alan Newell and Mary Zajicek, 'Designing for Dynamic Diversity: Interfaces for Older People' (2002) *Proceedings of the Fifth International ACM Conference on Assistive Technologies* 151.

[23] Alan Newell, Peter Gregor, Margaret Morgan and Caitriona Macaulay, 'User-Sensitive Inclusive Design' (2011) 10(3) *Universal Access in the Information Society* 235.

[24] Ibid.

[25] Soren Ginnerup, *Achieving Full Participation through Universal Design* (Strasbourg: Council of Europe Publishing, 2009), p. 11.

for body functions/structures and activities; or to prevent impairments, activity limitations or participation restrictions.[26]

The ISO classification system includes a list of assistive products for personal medical treatment, orthoses and prostheses; assistive products for personal care and protection, assistive products for personal mobility; assistive products for housekeeping, furnishings and adaptations to homes and other premises; and assistive products for employment and vocational training, and assistive products for recreation.[27]

Sometimes, the term 'assistive technologies' (AT) is used instead of 'assistive devices'. This is an umbrella term to cover various types of high-tech or low-tech products. For example, the World Health Organization (WHO) Global Disability Action Plan 2014–2021 states that AT includes a wide range of tools: from low vision devices, to hearing aids; from augmentative and alternative communication to walking frames and wheelchairs.[28]

3 THE SIGNIFICANCE OF ACCESSIBILITY IN THE CRPD

This section briefly discusses the scope of accessibility obligations in the CRPD and identifies the most relevant provisions in that regard.

3.1 The Definition and Scope of the Accessibility Norm

As mentioned in the introduction to this chapter and in Chapter 3, accessibility features as a general principle of the Convention in Article 3(f) CRPD. Broad accessibility obligations are formulated in Article 9 and in other substantive provisions of the Convention.[29] Some scholars identify

[26] ISO, *Assistive Products for Persons with Disability – Classification and Terminology* (2011), vol. 9999:2011, available at www.iso.org/iso/iso_catalogue/catalogue_tc/catalogue_detail.htm?csnumber=50982.

[27] Ibid.

[28] World Health Organization (WHO), Global Disability Action Plan 2014–2021 (World Health Organization, 2015). The WHO has also launched a specific program to promote Global Cooperation on Assistive Technology (GATE). The objective of this program is to improve access to high quality and affordable assistive technology for people with disabilities. On the GATE programme see, *inter alia*, Chapal Khasnabis, Zafar Mirza, and Malcolm MacLachlan, 'Opening the GATE to Inclusion for People with Disabilities', (2015) *The Lancet* 2229; and Fleur Heleen Boot, John Dinsmore, Chapal Khasnabis, and Malcolm MacLachlan, 'Intellectual Disability and Assistive Technology: Opening the GATE Wider', (2017) 5 *Front Public Health* 10.

[29] Francesco Seatzu, 'Article 9: Accessibility', in Valentina Della Fina, Rachele Cera and Giuseppe Palmisano (eds.), *The United Nations Convention on the Rights of Persons with Disabilities: A Commentary* (Cham: Springer, 2017), pp. 225–42, p. 227. See also Anna Lawson, 'Article 9: Accessibility', in Ilias Bantekas, Michael Ashley Stein, and Dimitris

'accessibility rights' in the Convention.[30] This is intended to refer to the right to use goods, services and facilities available to the public without discrimination, and obtain an equal benefit from them. For instance, Article 12 CRPD refers to access to the necessary support to exercise legal capacity. Article 21 provides for access to information. Article 30 sets out the right of access to cultural goods and services. Article 13 provides for the right to access justice. References to accessibility are also included in Article 4 CRPD, which contains the Convention's general obligations. Article 4(g), for example, mentions accessible information. Furthermore, Article 31 requires the accessibility of statistical and research data on disability;[31] and Article 49 requires that States Parties make the text of the CRPD available in accessible formats.

The CRPD encompasses a broad understanding of accessibility, including physical accessibility, economic accessibility (i.e. affordability) and accessibility of information, and it addresses accessibility 'in all its complexity'.[32] In this respect, Lawson clarifies that 'for CRPD purposes, accessibility covers more than technical design specifications for products, information and signage or the built environment. It also covers communication and forms of live assistance'.[33]

3.2 Accessibility, Universal Design and Assistive Devices

The CRPD also introduces UD obligations. UD is defined in Article 2 CRPD as the 'design of products, environments, programmes and services to be usable by all people, to the greatest extent possible, without the need for adaptation or speciali[s]ed design'. In particular, Article 4(1)(f) CRPD requires States Parties:

> to undertake or promote research and development of universally designed goods, services, equipment and facilities, which should require the minimum possible adaptation and the least cost to meet the specific needs of a person with disabilities, to promote their availability and use, and to promote universal design in the development of standards and guidelines.

According to Cera,[34] the inclusion of UD in the CRPD reflects the human rights paradigm shift of the Convention and the principles of respect for difference and equality.

Anastasiou (eds.), *The UN Convention on the Rights of Persons with Disabilities. A Commentary* (Oxford: Oxford University Press, 2018), pp. 258–286.

[30] Ibid. See also Andrea Broderick, 'Of Rights and Obligations: The Birth of Accessibility' (2019) *The International Journal of Human Rights*.

[31] See above Chapter 3, section 6. [32] CRPD Committee, General Comment No. 2, note 5.

[33] Anna Lawson, *Maximising the Impact and Effectiveness of Accessibility Measures for Goods and Services: Learning from National Experience* (2012) Synthesis Report for the Academic Network of European Disability Experts, p. 34, available at http://www.disability-europe.net/theme/accessibility.

[34] Rachele Cera, 'Article 2: Definitions', in Della Fina, Cera and Palmisano (eds.), *The United Nations Convention on the Rights of Persons with Disabilities: A Commentary*, note 29, pp. 107–18.

DID YOU KNOW THAT ...?

The concept of UD features in few national laws. In some instances, these pre-date the CRPD. This is the case of the Canadian 'Accessibility for Ontarians with Disabilities Act (AODA)' and the Irish Disability Act 2005. In Norway, Act No. 42 of June 20, 2008 relating to a prohibition against discrimination on the basis of disability (Anti-Discrimination and Accessibility Act), which has been in force since January 2009, includes a general clause on UD.

In addition, there are several policies on UD. For example, in 2009, the Norwegian Government enacted the Action Plan for Universal Design and Improved Accessibility 2009–2013: 'Norway Universally Designed by 2025' (www.regjeringen.no/globalassets/upload/bld/nedsatt-funksjonsevne/norway-universally-designed-by-2025-web.pdf). This is designed to support the implementation of the 2008 Norwegian Act.

Entities have also been created with a view to fostering UD. For example, in France, an Interdepartmental Observatory on Accessibility and Universal Design was established in 2010, and it was entrusted with the role of evaluating and disseminating examples of good practice in accessibility and UD.

While UD minimises the need for individualised reasonable accommodations, the CRPD acknowledges that it does not completely eliminate the need for technical aids and AT. The Convention juxtaposes the promotion of UD with the provision of assistive devices, and it considers both measures to be essential in realising the principle of accessibility. Article 4(1)(h) CRPD obliges States Parties to 'provide accessible information to persons with disabilities about mobility aids, devices and assistive technologies, including new technologies, as well as other forms of assistance, support services and facilities'. Article 20 CRPD, on personal mobility, requires that States Parties facilitate access by people with disabilities 'to quality mobility aids,[35] devices, assistive technologies and forms of live assistance and intermediaries, including by making them available at affordable cost'. It also imposes a duty on States Parties to encourage producers of AT 'to take into account all aspects of mobility for persons with disabilities'. Moreover, this provision requires States Parties to promote and support the supply of auxiliary tools for persons with disabilities, and it underpins the requirement to remove any restrictions hindering the provision of technological aids for mobility. In those regards, according to Fasciglione,[36]

[35] Mobility devices are designed to facilitate or enhance users' personal mobility. Examples of these devices include crutches, walking frames, wheeled walkers, wheelchairs (manual and powered), tricycles, scooters, but also prostheses.

[36] Marco Fasciglione, 'Article 20: Personal Mobility', in Della Fina, Cera and Palmisano (eds.), *The United Nations Convention on the Rights of Persons with Disabilities: A Commentary*, note 29, pp. 375–85, p. 380.

the CRPD allows for a variety of different policy options, to ensure increased production and/or supply of mobility devices depending on the context of each country. Article 20 must be read in conjunction with Article 26 CRPD, on habilitation and rehabilitation. The latter provision, at paragraph 3, obliges States Parties to 'promote the availability, knowledge and use of assistive devices and technologies, designed for persons with disabilities, as they relate to habilitation and rehabilitation'. The CRPD Committee, in its General Comment No. 2, acknowledges the role of technological advancements in improving participation of persons with disabilities in society, including certain specific assistive devices, such as hearing enhancement systems and ambient assistive systems.[37]

4 ARTICLE 9 CRPD

Article 9 CRPD embraces the social-contextual model of disability, and, as discussed above in Chapter 4, is a core feature of the inclusive equality model that is enshrined in the CRPD. It articulates a series of accessibility obligations, which are discussed in the sub-sections below.

4.1 Article 9(1) CRPD

ARTICLE 9(1) CRPD

To enable persons with disabilities to live independently and participate fully in all aspects of life, States Parties shall take appropriate measures to ensure to persons with disabilities access, on an equal basis with others, to the physical environment, to transportation, to information and communications, including information and communications technologies and systems, and to other facilities and services open or provided to the public, both in urban and in rural areas. These measures, which shall include the identification and elimination of obstacles and barriers to accessibility, shall apply to, *inter alia*:

a) Buildings, roads, transportation and other indoor and outdoor facilities, including schools, housing, medical facilities and workplaces;
b) Information, communications and other services, including electronic services and emergency services.

[37] CRPD Committee, General Comment No. 2, note 5, para. 22.

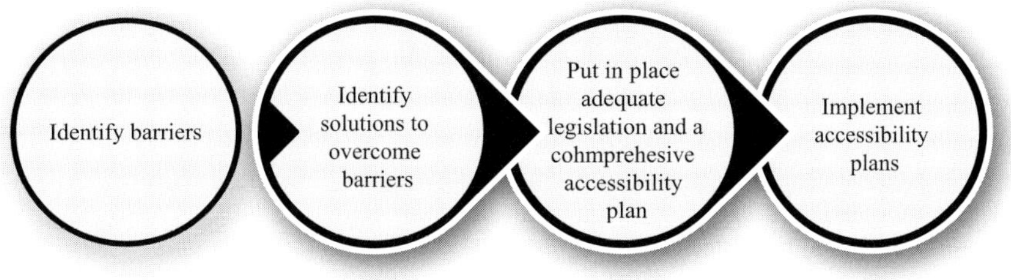

Figure 5.2 Steps Necessary to Ensure Accessibility

Article 9(1) demands the adoption of all measures that are necessary to ensure accessibility on a progressive basis.[38] Unlike the reasonable accommodation duty, which is of immediate effect, the obligation to ensure accessibility is intended to be implemented gradually by States Parties. Even though accessibility is an obligation of progressive realisation, in line with Article 4(2) CRPD States Parties must implement Article 9 to the maximum of available resources.[39]

According to Article 9(1), these measures 'shall include the identification and elimination of obstacles and barriers to accessibility'. As shown in Figure 5.2, this obligation to identify barriers to accessibility, and solutions to overcome them, implies the involvement of persons with disabilities and DPOs, in compliance with Article 4(3) CRPD. Furthermore, the CRPD Committee emphasises the need for effective domestic policies, plans and strategies in order to ensure accessibility and the need for adequate monitoring processes.[40]

4.2 Article 9(2) CRPD

ARTICLE 9(2) CRPD

States Parties shall also take appropriate measures:

a) To develop, promulgate and monitor the implementation of minimum standards and guidelines for the accessibility of facilities and services open or provided to the public;

b) To ensure that private entities that offer facilities and services which are open or provided to the public take into account all aspects of accessibility for persons with disabilities;

c) To provide training for stakeholders on accessibility issues facing persons with disabilities;

[38] See below sub-section 4.3. [39] See above Chapter 3, sub-section 4.4.2.

[40] CRPD Committee, General Comment No. 2, note 5, para. 33.

d) To provide in buildings and other facilities open to the public signage in Braille and in easy to read and understand forms;
e) To provide forms of live assistance and intermediaries, including guides, readers and professional sign language interpreters, to facilitate accessibility to buildings and other facilities open to the public;
f) To promote other appropriate forms of assistance and support to persons with disabilities to ensure their access to information;
g) To promote access for persons with disabilities to new information and communications technologies and systems, including the Internet;
h) To promote the design, development, production and distribution of accessible information and communications technologies and systems at an early stage, so that these technologies and systems become accessible at minimum cost.

Article 9(2) CRPD sets forth a wide range of detailed obligations. It does not, however, specify accessibility criteria for national law.[41] Narasimhan notes that 'the Convention defines obligations in relation to desired outcomes by application areas, rather than in specific technical terms'.[42]

Article 9(2)(a) requires States Parties to develop accessibility standards. In fulfilling that obligation, States Parties can delegate the writing of technical standards to non-state authorities. The CRPD implicitly acknowledges that technical specifications and accessibility standards have mostly been laid down in booklets, studies prepared by 'think-tanks', or in rules elaborated by Standard-Setting Organisations (SSOs), i.e. bodies that typically consist of industry representatives and other stakeholders.[43] The CRPD Committee has urged States Parties to provide for the mandatory application of accessibility standards and to ensure that those standards are 'in accordance with the standards of other States [P]arties in order to ensure interoperability with regard to free movement within the framework of liberty of movement and nationality (Article 18) of persons with disabilities'.[44]

Article 9(2)(b) and 9(2)(d) CRPD make clear that States Parties must ensure that private entities provide for accessible buildings, services and facilities. In its General Comment No. 2, the CRPD Committee confirms that, 'as long as

[41] Nadina Foggetti, 'E-Accessibility Definition in the UN Convention on the Rights of Persons with Disabilities: Current Issues and Future Perspectives' (2012) *Computer and Telecommunications Law Review* 57.

[42] Nirmita Narasimhan (ed.), *E-Accessibility Policy Handbook for Persons with Disabilities Based upon the ITU-G3ict e-Accessibility Policy Toolkit for Persons with Disabilities* (Mumbai: Hemkunt, 2010), p. 3.

[43] See below Chapter 12, section 6.

[44] CRPD Committee, General Comment No. 2, note 5, para. 18.

goods, products and services are open or provided to the public, they must be accessible to all, regardless of whether they are owned and/or provided by a public authority or a private enterprise'.[45] In a similar vein, the CRPD Committee's General Comment No. 5, on living independently and being included in the community, states that 'community services open to the public such as libraries, swimming pools, public parks/spaces, shops, post offices and cinemas must be accessible and responsive to the requirements of persons with disabilities'.[46] This interpretation of Article 9 is premised on the need to promote and fulfil the principles of non-discrimination and equality.

The CRPD Committee has also had the opportunity to discuss the responsibility of States Parties in relation to the lack of accessibility of private facilities in *Nyusti and Takács* v. *Hungary*[47] and in *Bacher* v. *Austria*.[48]

The individual communication of Szilvia Nyusti and Péter Takács, two individuals with visual impairments, concerned Hungary's failure to ensure that persons with disabilities could access banking services offered by a private financial institution. The authors of the communication argued that such a failure constituted a violation of the CRPD. When considering the communication, the CRPD Committee recalled Article 4(1)(e), which requires States Parties 'to take all appropriate measures to eliminate discrimination on the basis of disability by any person, organi[s]ation or private enterprise'. The Committee then focused on the duty of States Parties to ensure accessibility, and, in particular, referred to Article 9 (2)(b). It highlighted that the CRPD imposes obligations only on States Parties, not on private entities. Nonetheless, States Parties must guarantee that private entities offer accessible services and do not discriminate. While the Committee acknowledged that Hungary had, indeed, taken measures to

> Read the CRPD Committee's decision in *Nyusti and Takács* v. *Hungary*. Do you agree with the CRPD Committee's views in the decision?

[45] Ibid. para. 13.

[46] CRPD Committee, General Comment No. 5, 27 October 2017, UN Doc. CRPD/C/GC/5, para. 53.

[47] CRPD Committee, *Nyusti and Takács* v. *Hungary*, Communication No. 1/2010, UN Doc. CRPD/C/9/D/1/2010.

[48] CRPD Committee, *Bacher* v. *Austria*, Communication No. 26/2014, UN Doc. CRPD/C/19/D/26/2014.

enhance the accessibility of banking facilities, it ultimately held that there had been a violation of Article 9(2)(b) of the Convention.[49]

Bacher v. *Austria*[50] is even more exemplary, as it concerned a private building and a dispute between neighbours over the path granting access to the building. The author, Mr Bacher, has Down's syndrome, is on the autism spectrum and occasionally uses a wheelchair. His parents constructed wooden steps for him to gain access to the house, as well as a roof over the path to protect it from bad weather. Planning permission was granted by the local authority to build the roof, with the agreement of the neighbours having been obtained. However, the owner of one of the neighbouring houses, Mr R, had not been invited to attend the meeting to discuss the planning permission. He sued Mr Bacher and his parents, claiming that the roof had reduced the width of the path and that its height violated his right of way. The Austrian court decided in favour of Mr R and ordered that the roof be demolished. The various attempts to make Mr Bacher build an alternative path to access his house failed, and, due to the demolition of the roof, the original path was severely damaged by the weather. Mr Bacher's family brought a case against the neighbours in front of the District Court of Schwaz, requesting that they make a financial contribution to the repair of the path, arguing that, had the roof not been demolished, the path would not have fallen into disrepair and Mr Bacher could have used it safely. Having been unsuccessful in front of the national court, Mr Bacher presented a communication to the CRPD Committee. The Committee reiterated that 'States [P]arties are obliged not only to respect Convention rights and, it follows, to refrain from infringing upon them, but also to protect those rights by adopting measures to prevent the direct or indirect interference of individuals in the enjoyment of those rights'.[51] On that basis, the Committee affirmed that '[a] property right issue linked to the exercise of a contract between individuals and the conflict arising from it . . . has to be interpreted through the Convention'.[52] Since Article 9 requires States Parties to take appropriate measures to ensure that persons with disabilities have access, on an equal basis with others, to all facilities and services open or provided to the public, both in urban and in rural areas, the private or public nature of the facility is immaterial. The Committee, thus, concluded that there had been a violation of Article 9 CRPD, read in conjunction with Article 3 CRPD.

Article 9(2)(c) CRPD also obligates States Parties to ensure adequate training for stakeholders (e.g. employers, enterprises that offer goods and services to the public, landlords, etc.) on accessibility issues. The CRPD Committee clarifies that training 'should be provided not only to those designing goods, services and products, but also to those who actually produce them', and that

[49] Anna Lawson, 'Accessibility Obligations in the UN Convention on the Rights of Persons with Disabilities: *Nyusti & Takács v. Hungary*' (2014) 30(2) *South African Journal on Human Rights* 380.

[50] *Bacher* v. *Austria*, note 48. [51] Ibid. para. 9.3. [52] Ibid.

it should involve persons with disabilities to improve the understanding of existing needs and barriers.[53]

Article 9 CRPD does not mention assistive devices. Rather, Article 9(2)(e) places an emphasis on the role of intermediaries or personal assistants (including guides, readers and professional sign language interpreters) 'to facilitate accessibility to buildings and other facilities open to the public'.

Finally, Article 9(2)(f) and 9(2)(g) impose obligations on States Parties to promote access to new information and communications technologies (ICT) for persons with disabilities, while Article 9(2)(h) requires them to promote the design, development, production and distribution of accessible ICT. These provisions must be read in conjunction with the general obligation laid down in Article 4(1)(g) and with Article 21 CRPD, which provide for the right to access information (discussed below in section 6).

CASE STUDY

China's Implementation Plan for Barrier-Free Construction

The Chinese Law on the Protection of Persons with Disabilities provides that a barrier-free environment involves a variety of aspects, including barrier-free buildings, roads, transportation, and information and communications. Local governments have promulgated local laws on accessibility of buildings. The Chinese government also formulated the Implementation Plan for Barrier-Free Construction during the Eleventh Five-Year Plan (2006–2010), which sought to establish barrier-free cities in 100 cities nationwide. This was praised by the CRPD Committee in its Concluding Observations on the initial Chinese report (Initial Report of China to the CRPD Committee, 8 February 2011, para. 41; and CRPD Committee, Concluding Observations on the Initial Report of China, 15 October 2012).

4.3 Challenges in the Implementation of Article 9 CRPD

There is a debate among scholars as to whether Article 9 CRPD establishes accessibility as a right in itself,[54] or as a pre-condition for ensuring other rights of access.[55]

[53] CRPD Committee, General Comment No. 2, note 5, para. 19.

[54] Seatzu claims that Article 9 recognises that all persons with disabilities 'have a right of accessibility and have the right to exercise it on an equal basis'. Seatzu, 'Article 9: Accessibility', note 29, p. 227.

[55] Anna Lawson, 'Accessibility Obligations in the UN Convention on the Rights of Persons with Disabilities: *Nyusti & Takács v. Hungary*', note 49; see also Frederic Mégret, 'The Disabilities

Some scholars affirm that Article 9 creates a right to accessibility, which should be considered as a socio-economic right.[56] In this vein, Lord affirms that Article 9 gives rise to various obligations that 'will require resources and extensive systemic change'[57] and which should be implemented progressively. The CRPD Committee remains somewhat ambiguous on the point. It identifies accessibility as a 'precondition' for the enjoyment of other human rights and as 'a means to achieve *de facto* equality for all persons with disabilities'.[58] It affirms that accessibility should be considered 'in the context of the right to access from the specific perspective of disability'.[59] In its General Comment No. 5, the CRPD Committee also identifies, as a core element of Article 19 CRPD on independent living, the obligation:

> [t]o develop, implement, monitor and sanction non-compliance with legislation, plans and guidance on accessibility requirements for basic mainstream services to achieve societal equality, including participation by persons with disabilities within social media, and secure adequate competence in information and communications technologies to ensure that such technologies are developed, including on the basis of universal design, and protected.

The CRPD Committee seems to leave States Parties some leeway in establishing how accessibility can be implemented. It maintains that '[b]arriers to access to existing objects, facilities, goods and services aimed at or open to the public shall be removed gradually in a systematic and, more importantly, continuously monitored manner, with the aim of achieving full accessibility'.[60] It also argues that:

> States Parties are obliged to ensure that persons with disabilities have access to the existing physical environment, transportation, information and communication and services open to the general public. However, as this obligation is to be implemented gradually, States parties should establish definite time frames and allocate adequate resources for the removal of existing barriers[61]

In addition, the Committee contends that the potential cost of barrier removal may not be used as an excuse to avoid the obligations contained in Article 9 CRPD.

As mentioned above in section 3, Article 9 CRPD does not refer explicitly to UD. However, the CRPD Committee, reading Article 9 in conjunction with

Convention: Human Rights of Persons with Disabilities or Disability Rights?' (2008) 30 *Human Rights Quarterly* 494.

[56] Seatzu, 'Article 9: Accessibility', note 29, p. 232.

[57] Lord, 'Accessibility and Human Rights Fusion in the CRPD: Assessing the Scope and Content of the Accessibility Principle and Duty under the CRPD', note 2.

[58] CRPD Committee, General Comment No. 5, note 46, para. 40.

[59] CRPD Committee, General Comment No. 2, note 5, para. 22.

[60] Ibid. para. 1.

[61] Ibid. para. 24.

other principles of the Convention and in light of its purpose, affirms that States Parties should ensure the strict application of UD to all new goods and services.[62] One of the reasons mentioned by the CRPD Committee for this is the potential reduction of the costs of further adaptation. However, this statement of the Committee does not seem to reflect the challenges inherent to UD. Vanderheiden asserts that, even though there are key examples of UD projects in the electronic and communication industries, they do not represent the majority of current practice.[63] According to Gassmann and Repeyer, industry has little experience when it comes to UD, and the tasks and costs associated with it are frequently considered to be unknown.[64]

The approach adopted by the CRPD Committee seems to recognise that the implementation of Article 9 is subject to the doctrine of progressive realisation.[65] However, the Committee has not fully clarified the nature and scope of CRPD accessibility obligations, nor the relationship between accessibility and non-discrimination. In its General Comment No. 2, the Committee states that lack of accessibility should be considered discriminatory 'where the service or facility was established after relevant accessibility standards were introduced', or 'where access could have been granted to the facility or service (when it came into existence) through reasonable accommodation'.[66] Accordingly, the Committee suggests that, when reviewing their accessibility legislation, 'States Parties must consider and, where necessary, amend their laws to prohibit discrimination on the basis of disability'.[67] This means that the existence of accessibility barriers can entail discrimination on the grounds of disability only in some cases, namely when the service is inaccessible because it does not comply with already established accessibility standards or where there has been an unjustified failure to provide reasonable accommodation.[68] In that sense, Article 9 CRPD can be seen as a 'pragmatic translation of the principle of equality'.[69]

[62] Ibid.

[63] Gregg Vanderheiden and Jim Tobias, *Barriers, Incentives and Facilitators for Adoption of Universal Design Practices by Consumer Product Manufacturers* (1998), available at http://trace.wisc.edu/docs/hfes98_barriers/barriers_incentives_facilitators.htm.

[64] Oliver Gassmann et al., 'Universal Design: Innovations for All Ages', in Florian Kohlbacher and Cornelius Herstatt (eds.), *The Silver Market Phenomenon* (Cham: Springer, 2008), pp. 101–16.

[65] CRPD Committee, General Comment No. 6, 26 April 2016, UN Doc. CRPD/C/GC/6, para. 42.

[66] CRPD Committee, General Comment No. 2, note 5, para. 31.

[67] Ibid.

[68] Anna Lawson, 'Accessibility Obligations in the UN Convention on the Rights of Persons with Disabilities: *Nyusti & Takács v. Hungary*', note 49.

[69] Delia Ferri, 'The Conclusion of the UN Convention on the Rights of Persons with Disabilities by the EU/EC: A Constitutional Perspective', in Lisa Waddington and Gerard Quinn (eds.), *European Yearbook of Disability Law* (Antwerp/Portland: Intersentia, 2010), vol. 2, pp. 47–71.

5 ACCESSIBILITY AND REASONABLE ACCOMMODATION

The CRPD Committee's General Comments No. 2 and No. 6 clearly distinguish between accessibility obligations and the reasonable accommodation duty.

The main difference between accessibility and reasonable accommodation is that the former is group-related, while, as discussed in Chapter 4, the latter has an individualised nature. Consequently, accessibility obligations are anticipatory in nature. The CRPD Committee asserts that the 'duty to provide accessibility is an *ex ante* duty' and that States Parties therefore have 'the duty to provide accessibility before receiving an individual request to enter or use a place or service'.[70] The reasonable accommodation duty is, by contrast, an '*ex nunc* duty', enforceable only 'from the moment an individual with an impairment needs it in a given situation, for example, workplace or school, in order to enjoy her or his rights on an equal basis in a particular context'.[71]

Another key difference is that the reasonable accommodation duty is subject to the limitation of disproportionate or undue burden.[72] By contrast, 'accessibility must be implemented gradually but unconditionally'.[73] In particular, the CRPD Committee clarifies that 'the entity obliged to provide accessibility may not excuse the omission to do so by referring to the burden of providing access for persons with disabilities'.[74] *Jungelin* v. *Sweden*[75] is illustrative in this respect. The complaint to the CRPD Committee was raised by Ms Jungelin, a person with visual impairments. Despite the fact that she possessed the required qualifications for the job for which she had applied in the Swedish Social Insurance Agency, she was not hired because the Agency's intranet system was not accessible. It was argued by the Agency that the system could not be adjusted to her visual impairment. Her claim that this amounted to an unjustified denial of reasonable accommodation and, consequently, discrimination on the ground of disability was rejected by the domestic courts. Those courts, endorsing the defence of the employer, took the view that the cost of adjusting the computer system would have imposed a disproportionate burden on the employer. The CRPD Committee considered that States Parties enjoy a certain margin of appreciation when assessing the proportionality of accommodation measures. The Committee refused to find that Sweden fell short of its obligations under Article 5 CRPD. Article 9 was not discussed in the *Jungelin* case, and the CRPD Committee missed the opportunity to clarify the steps that governments are expected to take in order to encourage employers to make their workplaces accessible to all.

[70] CRPD Committee, General Comment No. 2, note 5, para. 25. [71] Ibid. para. 26.

[72] See above Chapter 4. [73] CRPD Committee, General Comment No. 6, note 65, para. 42.

[74] Ibid. para. 25.

[75] CRPD Committee, *Jungelin* v. *Sweden*, Communication No. 5/2011, UN Doc. CRPD/C/12/D/5/2011. See also above Chapter 4.

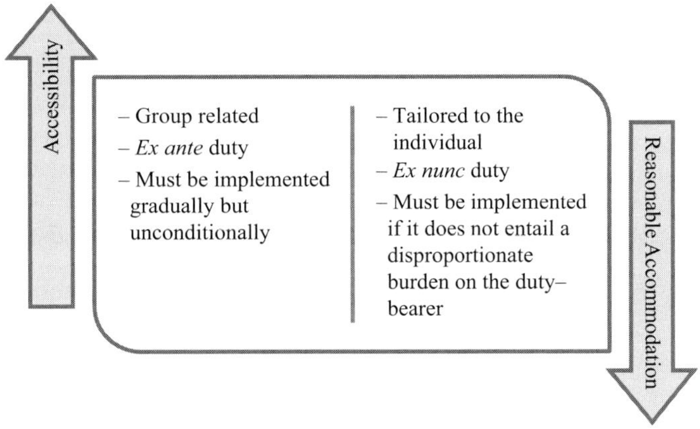

Figure 5.3 Accessibility and Reasonable Accommodation

The distinctive features of accessibility and reasonable accommodation respectively are summarised in Figure 5.3.

6 THE RIGHT TO ACCESS INFORMATION AND COMMUNICATIONS

The CRPD places particular emphasis on the right to access ICT. As the CRPD Committee notes in its General Comment No. 2, 'without access to information and communication, enjoyment of freedom of thought and expression and many other basic rights and freedoms for persons with disabilities may be seriously undermined'.[76]

'Communication' is defined broadly in Article 2 as including:

> languages, display of text, Braille, tactile communication, large print, accessible multimedia as well as written, audio, plain-language, human reader and augmentative and alternative modes, means and formats of communication, including accessible information and communication technology.

ICT is not explicitly defined in the CRPD. General Comment No. 2 affirms that '[w]hile different people and organi[s]ations understand differently what . . . ICT . . . means, it is generally acknowledged that ICT is an umbrella term that includes any information and communication device or application and its content'.[77] Hence, ICT is said to include 'a wide range of access technologies, such as radio, television, satellite, mobile phones, fixed lines, computers, network hardware and software'.[78]

[76] CRPD Committee, General Comment No. 2, note 5, para. 21. [77] Ibid. para. 5. [78] Ibid.

The right to access ICT is mentioned in Article 9, and it is spelled out in Article 21 CRPD. As highlighted above, it is also referred to in the general obligations of the Convention.[79] The following sub-sections discuss these provisions in turn.

6.1 Information and Communications in Article 9 CRPD

Article 9(1) CRPD applies to information and communications, including ICT, in the same way as it applies to the physical environment and transportation.

As discussed above, Article 9(2)(a), (b) and (c) mention general measures that must be taken in order to ensure accessibility, including ICT accessibility, such as the development and 'implementation of minimum standards and guidelines for the accessibility of facilities and services open or provided to the public' and training for stakeholders. In addition, Article 9(2)(d) provides for measures that need to be adopted in order to guarantee accessibility of information connected with the use of buildings or transportation or other services open to the public.

As mentioned above, Article 9(2)(f) and (g) concern accessibility of information. They provide that States Parties 'promote other appropriate forms of assistance and support to persons with disabilities to ensure their access to information' and 'promote access for persons with disabilities to new information and communication technologies and systems, including the Internet', respectively. In addition, Article 9(2)(h) obliges States Parties to 'promote the design, development, production and distribution of accessible information and communications technologies and systems at an early stage, so that these technologies and systems become accessible at minimum cost'. The CRPD Committee had the opportunity to interpret the scope of these obligations in *F* v. *Austria*.[80] Mr F, a blind Austrian citizen, complained that the local authorities had failed to install digital audio systems when extending their tram network and that this violated the principle of accessibility in the Convention. Since he was relying on public transportation for all of his daily activities, both private and professional in nature, he also claimed that the refusal by the Austrian authorities to install the audio system on the extended network constituted a breach of Articles 19 and 20 CRPD. According to him, the lack of an audio system on the tram prevented him from living an independent life and violated his right to personal mobility. Against this, Austria claimed, *inter alia*, that the audio system was 'by no means a prerequisite for using a public means of transport' and that the 'everyday aim' of using public means of transport could be achieved by Mr F without the audio system. The Austrian authorities also claimed that the audio system in question did not provide information that is

[79] See Article 4(1)(g), CRPD.

[80] CRPD Committee, *F* v. *Austria*, Communication No. 21/2014, CRPD/C/14/D/21/2014.

absolutely necessary for passengers. In examining the individual communication, the CRPD Committee recalled Article 9(2)(f) CRPD and affirmed that:

> the importance of information and communications technology lies in its ability to open up a wide range of services, transform existing services and create greater demand for access to information and knowledge, particularly in underserved and excluded populations, such as persons with disabilities.[81]

The CRPD Committee also noted that the local authorities had started to equip the tram stops of the city with digital audio systems, but none of the new stops of the most recently built tram lines were equipped with this system. The Committee asserted that the service providers already knew about the audio system and that it could have been installed at a limited cost at the time of construction of the new line. The Committee endorsed Mr F's argument that the audio system would have provided him and other individuals with visual impairments with immediate access to real-time information on an equal basis with others. Ultimately, the Committee found that the non-installation of the audio system by the State Party resulted in a denial of access to information and communications technologies, and to facilities and services open to the public on an equal basis with others, and amounted to a violation of the Convention.

CRPD Committee, F v. Austria, UN Doc. CRPD/C/14/D/21/2014

9. The Committee on the Rights of Persons with Disabilities ... is of the view that the State party has failed to fulfil its obligations under Articles 5(2); and 9(1) and (2)(f) and (h) of the Convention. The Committee therefore makes the following recommendations to the State party:

(a) With respect to the author, the State [P]arty is under an obligation to remedy the lack of accessibility to the information visually available for all lines of the tram network. The State [P]arty should also provide adequate compensation to the author for the legal costs incurred during domestic proceedings and the costs incurred in filing the present communication;

(b) In general, the State [P]arty is under an obligation to take measures to prevent similar violations in the future, including by:

(i) Ensuring that the existing minimum standards for the accessibility of public transport guarantee the access of all persons with visual and other types of impairments to the live information visually available to other users of the tram and of all other forms of public

[81] Ibid. para. 8(5).

transport. In this context, the Committee recommends that the State [P]arty create a legislative framework with concrete, enforceable and time-bound benchmarks for monitoring and assessing the gradual modification and adjustment necessary to enable the access by persons with visual impairment to the information that is visually available. The State [P]arty should also ensure that all newly procured tram lines and other public transport networks are fully accessible for persons with disabilities;

(ii) Ensuring that appropriate and regular training on the scope of the Convention and its Optional Protocol, including on accessibility for persons with disabilities, is provided to all service providers involved in the design, construction and equipment of public transport networks, to guarantee that future networks are built and equipped in compliance with the principle of universal design;

(iii) Ensuring that disability rights laws concerned with non-discriminatory access in areas such as transport and procurement include access to information and communications technology and the many goods and services central to modern society that are offered through such technology. The Committee recommends that the review and adoption of these laws and regulations be carried out in close consultation with persons with disabilities and their representative organizations, in accordance with [A]rticle 4 (3) of the Convention, as well as all other relevant stakeholders, including members of the academic community and expert associations of architects, urban planners, engineers and designers. Legislation should incorporate and be based on the principle of universal design and should provide for the mandatory application of accessibility standards and for sanctions for those who fail to apply them.

6.2 Article 21 CRPD

ARTICLE 21 CRPD

States Parties shall take all appropriate measures to ensure that persons with disabilities can exercise the right to freedom of expression and opinion, including the freedom to seek, receive and impart information and ideas on an equal basis with others and through all forms of communication of their choice, as defined in article 2 of the present Convention, including by:

a) Providing information intended for the general public to persons with disabilities in accessible formats and technologies appropriate to different kinds of disabilities in a timely manner and without additional cost;

b) Accepting and facilitating the use of sign languages, Braille, augmentative and alternative communication, and all other accessible means, modes and formats of communication of their choice by persons with disabilities in official interactions;
c) Urging private entities that provide services to the general public, including through the Internet, to provide information and services in accessible and usable formats for persons with disabilities;
d) Encouraging the mass media, including providers of information through the Internet, to make their services accessible to persons with disabilities;
e) Recognizing and promoting the use of sign languages.

Building on well-established human rights law provisions, such as Article 19 ICCPR, Article 21 CRPD recognises the freedom of opinion and expression. In line with other human rights instruments, Article 21 CRPD embraces both an active and a passive aspect of the freedom of information. The active element entails the right to impart or share information and articulate ideas and opinions, while the second includes the right to seek and receive information.[82] As a civil and political right, Article 21 CRPD is subject to immediate realisation. This provision is notable in that it tailors established rights to persons with disabilities. As noted by Cera, 'Article 21 does not address the parameters of the rights to freedom of expression and opinion in the same vein as other human rights treaties'. Furthermore, Cera argues that Article 21 transforms a right that was formerly based on non-interference (or a 'negative' right) into a 'positive State obligation'.[83] It provides for a clear obligation to ensure public information in accessible formats and to recognise sign languages, Braille, and augmentative and alternative communication.

An important innovation in Article 21 is the explicit reference to 'all forms of communication', a term which is defined in Article 2 of the Convention and mentioned above.

Article 21 CRPD goes on to provide a non-exhaustive list of measures that should be adopted to promote freedom of opinion and expression. It lays down three main obligations. First, it requires that States Parties ensure that information, whether provided by public or private entities, intended for the general public is available in accessible formats. It calls on States Parties to ensure that persons with disabilities may gain access to information 'in a timely manner' and 'without any additional cost'.[84] Secondly, it obliges States Parties to encourage mass media to make their services accessible to people with

[82] Rachele Cera, 'Article 21: Freedom of Expression and Opinion, and Access to Information', in Della Fina, Cera and Palmisano (eds.), *The United Nations Convention on the Rights of Persons with Disabilities: A Commentary*, note 29, pp. 387–400.

[83] Ibid. p. 363. [84] Ibid. p. 393.

disabilities. Thirdly, Article 21 calls for the recognition, acceptance and promotion of the use of sign languages, Braille, augmentative and alternative communication, and all other accessible means, modes, and formats of communication. Notably, as will be discussed further in Chapter 9, the CRPD is the first international human rights treaty that recognises sign languages,[85] and the CRPD Committee recommends that States Parties actively promote the use of sign language and calls for the adoption of laws giving official recognition to it.[86]

SUMMARY

- **The inclusion of the principle of accessibility within a human rights treaty is a novelty and reflects the paradigm shift purported by the CRPD.**
- **Accessibility is one of the general principles set out in Article 3 CRPD. Accessibility obligations are also spelled out in Article 9 CRPD and in other substantive provisions of the Convention.**
- **In the CRPD, accessibility is conceived of as a pre-condition for persons with disabilities to live independently and participate fully and equally in society, and as a gateway for the enjoyment of other human rights.**
- **The CRPD encompasses a broad understanding of accessibility, including physical accessibility, accessibility of information and economic accessibility (i.e. affordability).**
- **The CRPD does not specify accessibility criteria for domestic law, and it defines accessibility obligations in relation to desired outcomes rather than in specific technical terms.**
- **In addition to referring to accessibility, the CRPD also introduces obligations in relation to universal design, which is defined in Article 2 CRPD as the design of products, environments, programmes and services to be usable by all people, to the greatest extent possible, without the need for adaptation or specialised design.**
- **The CRPD Committee's General Comment No. 2 distinguishes between accessibility obligations and reasonable accommodation. Accessibility obligations are group-related and anticipatory in nature. The reasonable accommodation duty is, by contrast, conceived of as an '*ex nunc* duty', enforceable only from the moment a person with disabilities needs it in a given situation.**
- **Article 21 CRPD provides for the right to freedom of opinion and expression, which consists of the freedom to seek, receive, and impart information and ideas on an equal basis with others, and through all forms of communication of choice.**

[85] Before the CRPD, the UN Human Rights Committee (HRC), in its General Comment No. 34, recognised sign language as a form of expression protected under Article 19(2) ICCPR, but it did not address the exercise of the right to freedom of expression of persons with disabilities (HRC, General Comment No. 34, 12 September 2011, UN Doc. CCPR/C/GC/34, para. 12).

[86] See below Chapter 9.

ACTIVITIES

REVIEW QUESTIONS

1. **What are the key elements of Article 9 CRPD?**
2. **What are the differences between accessibility obligations and the reasonable accommodation duty?**
3. **What are the main obligations under Article 21 CRPD?**

ESSAY QUESTIONS

1. **'The main difference between accessibility and reasonable accommodation, as identified in General Comment No. 2, is that accessibility obligations are anticipatory in nature, while reasonable accommodation duties are *ex nunc* duties.' *Discuss.***
2. **'Article 9 stipulates obligations that should be implemented progressively.' *Discuss.***

GROUP PROJECT

Denise is a visually impaired person. She also has a chronic disease that renders her unable to walk for long distances and to use stairs without help. Denise decides to spend a week in a relaxing resort in Seaside City in the State of Freedonia. She books a train ticket to reach Seaside City. However, the train does not include any audio system, and Denise mistakenly gets off at the wrong station. She then takes a taxi to reach Seaside City. After her holiday, she decides to bring a claim against the local transport authorities of Freedonia. She contends that they are in breach of Article 9 CRPD.

Discuss the group project, taking into account the fact that Freedonia is a State Party to the CRPD.

FURTHER READING

Blanck, P., 'eQuality: The Right to the Web' in Blanck, P. and Flynn, E. (eds.), *Routledge Handbook of Disability Law and Human Rights* (London: Routledge), 2016 pp. 166–94.

Blanck, P., 'The Struggle for Web Equality by Persons with Cognitive Disabilities' (2014) 32(1) *Behavioral Sciences & the Law* 4–32.

Broderick, A., 'Of Rights and Obligations: The Birth of Accessibility' (2019) *The International Journal of Human Rights.*

Easton, C., 'An Examination of the Internet's Development as a Disabling Environment in the Context of the Social Model of Disability and Anti-Discrimination Legislation in the UK and USA' (2013) 12(1) *Universal Access in the Information Society* 105–14.

Easton, C., 'The Web Content Accessibility Guidelines 2.0: An Analysis of Industry Self-Regulation' (2011) 19 *International Journal of Law and Information Technology* 74–93.

Gassmann, O. et al., 'Universal Design – Innovations for All Ages', in Florian Kohlbacher and Cornelius Herstatt (eds.), *The Silver Market Phenomenon* (Cham: Springer, 2008), pp. 101–16.

Ginnerup, S., *Achieving Full Participation Through Universal Design* (Strasbourg: Council of Europe Publishing, 2009).

Jackson, M. A., 'Models of Disability and Human Rights: Informing the Improvement of Built Environment Accessibility for People with Disability at Neighborhood Scale?' (2018) 7(1) *Laws* 10, available at www.mdpi.com/2075-471X/7/1/10.

Kline, J. and Ferri, D., 'Enabling People with Disabilities through Effective Accessible Technology Policies', in R. Halvorsen, B. Hvinden, J. Bickenbach, D. Ferri and A. M. Guillén Rodriguez (eds.), *The Changing Disability Policy System: Active Citizenship and Disability in Europe* (Abingdon/New York: Routledge, 2017), vol. 1, pp. 127–43.

Lawson, A., 'Accessibility Obligations in the United Nations Convention on the Rights of Persons with Disabilities: *Nyusti and Takács v Hungary*' (2014) 30 *South African Journal on Human Rights* 380–92.

Lawson, A., 'Challenging Disabling Barriers to Information and Communication Technology in the Information Society: A United Kingdom Perspective', in G. Quinn and L. Waddington (eds.), *European Yearbook of Disability Law* (Antwerp/Portland: Intersentia, 2010), vol. 2, pp. 131–48.

Lawson, A., 'Reasonable Accommodation and Accessibility Obligations: Towards a More Unified European Approach?' (2010) *European Anti-Discrimination Law Review* 11–21.

Lazar, J. and Stein, M. (eds.), *Disability, Human Rights, and Information Technology* (Philadelphia: University of Pennsylvania Press, 2017).

Lepofsky, M. D. and Graham, R. N. M., 'Universal Design in Legislation: Eliminating Barriers for People with Disabilities' (2009) 30(2) *Statute Law Review* 97–122.

Lewis, O., 'Case Analysis: *Nyusti and Takacs v Hungary*: Decision of the UN Committee on the Rights of Persons with Disabilities' (2013) 4 *European Human Rights Law Review* 419–24.

Varney, E., *Disability and Information Technology: A Comparative Study in Media Regulation* (Cambridge/New York: Cambridge University Press, 2013).

6 Legal Capacity and Human Dignity

LEARNING OUTCOMES

- ✓ Identify the links between the right to legal capacity, and the principles of human dignity, autonomy and independence of people with disabilities.
- ✓ Comprehend the importance of ensuring the right to legal capacity in Article 12 CRPD and how its denial affects the exercise of other rights for persons with disabilities.
- ✓ Demonstrate awareness of the discrimination encountered by people with disabilities in the exercise of their legal capacity.
- ✓ Understand the essential differences between legal capacity and mental capacity.
- ✓ Demonstrate awareness of the paradigm shift that Article 12 CRPD embraces, from substitute decision-making towards supported decision-making.
- ✓ Identify the key obligations contained in Article 12 CRPD.
- ✓ Describe the supports that can be provided to facilitate the exercise of legal capacity.
- ✓ Comprehend what is meant by the 'will and preferences' of persons with disabilities.
- ✓ Describe the best practices that exist in the implementation of Article 12 CRPD.

Legal capacity is the affirmation, at both a legal and societal level, of the personhood of an individual and the existence of . . . rights and obligations which inhere in them as a result.[1]

1 INTRODUCTION

Article 12 CRPD enshrines the right to equal recognition before the law, or the right to legal capacity. This right entails the recognition of an individual as both a holder of rights and as an actor under the law, capable of creating, modifying or ending legal relationships. Legal capacity is indispensable for the exercise of civil, political, economic, social and cultural rights. The denial of legal capacity to people with disabilities has, in many instances, led to their being deprived of fundamental rights, including the right to vote, the right to marry and found a family, reproductive rights, parental rights and the right to liberty.

The right to legal capacity is intrinsically linked to the principle of human dignity, which underlies all international human rights treaties. It seeks to ensure the recognition of diversity and human difference. The principle of human dignity lies at the core of Article 12 CRPD, requiring that the inherent capabilities of persons with disabilities should be respected in all decisions that they make.

This chapter highlights the key tenets of Article 12 CRPD and describes in detail the normative content of that provision. In section 2, the links between legal capacity, human dignity, autonomy and independence of persons with disabilities are elaborated on. Section 3 addresses States Parties' obligations under Article 12. Section 4 discusses the paradigm shift from substitute decision-making to supported decision-making. Section 5 further delineates the inter-relationship between Article 12 and Article 19 CRPD (on living independently and being included in the community). Finally, section 6 outlines the connection between Article 12 and Article 23 CRPD (on family and reproductive rights).

2 SETTING THE SCENE: LEGAL CAPACITY, HUMAN DIGNITY AND AUTONOMY

The concept of 'human dignity' lies at the core of the CRPD. It features not only in the object and purpose of the Convention but also in its general principles. Article 3(a) CRPD mandates respect for the inherent dignity, individual autonomy (including the freedom to make one's own choices) and

[1] Council of Europe (CoE), *A Study on the Equal Recognition before the Law: Contribution towards the Council of Europe Strategy on the Rights of Persons with Disabilities* (Strasbourg: Council of Europe Publishing, 2017), p. 6.

independence of persons with disabilities. This focus on human dignity is carried through to Article 3(d) CRPD, which seeks to ensure 'respect for difference and acceptance of persons with disabilities as part of human diversity and humanity'.

Some authors criticise the use of 'human dignity' as a norm in the sphere of international human rights law, as they claim that it is indeterminate – in other words, that it is not clear exactly what it means as a guiding value for human rights law.[2] The principle of human dignity has been deemed to require that consideration be given to 'the equal worth of all human beings'.[3] This is similar to what Liebenberg terms 'treatment as an equal'.[4] She observes that 'the quest for equal worth or dignity is not a quest for uniformity but a quest to eliminate the disadvantages and inferior status that attach to membership of particular groups'.[5] The Preamble of the CRPD reflects this sentiment.[6]

Liebenberg remarks upon the fact that 'human dignity as a value is irrevocably linked with the protection of freedom and autonomy'.[7] She argues that dignity derives from the 'central idea that we show respect for human potential and agency by creating an environment of basic liberties and material support which enables [disadvantaged groups] to flourish'.[8] Therefore, Liebenberg argues that it can be used as a norm to tackle 'conditions of material disadvantage and its impact on different groups in our society'.[9]

The principle of human dignity lies at the heart of Article 12 CRPD, requiring that the inherent capabilities and legal capacity of persons with disabilities should be respected in all decisions that they make. The CRPD Committee implies that legal capacity is a universal attribute inherent in all persons by virtue of their humanity and that it must be upheld for persons with disabilities on an equal basis with others.[10] The manner in which the right to legal capacity has been interpreted by the CRPD Committee in its General Comment No. 1 also demonstrates that the Committee values highly the autonomy and dignity of persons with disabilities. In that regard, the Committee envisages that support measures be provided to persons with disabilities in order to facilitate the exercise of their legal capacity. According to the Committee, these measures must respect the autonomy of persons with disabilities, both in their freedom to reject offers of support or to end the support relationship at

[2] See, for example, Dennis Davis, 'Equality: The Majesty of Legoland Jurisprudence' (1999) 116 *South African Law Journal* 398.

[3] Andrea Broderick, *The Long and Winding Road to Equality and Inclusion for Persons with Disabilities: The United Nations Convention on the Rights of Persons with Disabilities* (Cambridge-Antwerp: Intersentia, 2015), p. 225.

[4] Sandra Liebenberg, 'The Value of Human Dignity in Interpreting Socio-Economic Rights' (2005) 21 *South African Journal on Human Rights* 1, at 14.

[5] Ibid. at 5. [6] Para. (h) of the Preamble of the CRPD.

[7] Liebenberg, 'The Value of Human Dignity in Interpreting Socio-Economic Rights', note 4, at 5.

[8] Ibid. at 8. [9] Ibid. at 11.

[10] See CRPD Committee, General Comment No. 1, 19 May 2014, UN Doc. CRPD/C/GC/1.

any time.[11] The Office of the United Nations High Commissioner for Human Rights (OHCHR) also highlights the importance of autonomy in its assertion that measures to fulfil the right to legal capacity are necessary to provide 'legal recognition of the right of persons with disabilities to self-determination'.[12] In summary, the right to legal capacity contained in Article 12 has been deemed to be 'one of the cardinal human rights that is indispensable to [ensure] respect [of] inherent dignity and autonomy of persons with disabilities and [to] ensure full and effective inclusion of persons with disabilities in society'.[13]

3 EQUAL RECOGNITION BEFORE THE LAW: THE RIGHT TO LEGAL CAPACITY

The right to equal recognition before the law, or equality before the law, is a foundational civil right under international human rights law. The Universal Declaration of Human Rights (UDHR) and the International Covenant on Civil and Political Rights (ICCPR) specifically guarantee the right to equality before the law.[14] That right is also reflected in other core international and regional human rights treaties.[15] The right to equal recognition before the law that appears in the instruments adopted prior to the CRPD is a narrower right than that contained in the CRPD. In previous human rights treaties, the right to equal recognition before the law was considered to guarantee only the right to equal standing before the law. In the sub-sections below, it is highlighted that Article 12 CRPD also includes the right to be viewed as a legal actor, capable of enforcing rights. This combination of equal standing before the law and the right to act under the law comprises the right to legal capacity as enshrined in Article 12.

[11] Ibid. para. 29.

[12] UN Human Rights Council, *Thematic Study by the Office of the United Nations High Commissioner for Human Rights on Enhancing Awareness and Understanding of the Convention on the Rights of Persons with Disabilities*, 26 January 2009, UN Doc. A/HRC/10/48, para. 45.

[13] Mohammad Hamza Marishet, 'Legal Capacity of Persons with Disabilities in Ethiopia: The Need to Reform Existing Legal Frameworks' (2017) 55 *International Journal of Law and Psychiatry* 8, at 8.

[14] It is notable that Article 4(2) ICCPR allows no derogation from this right, even in times of public emergency. Although there is no derogation clause in Article 12 CRPD, the prohibition on derogations contained in the ICCPR also covers the CRPD by virtue of Article 4(4) CRPD. The latter Article establishes that the provisions of the CRPD do not derogate from existing international law.

[15] For example, Article 15 of the Convention on the Elimination of All Forms of Discrimination against Women (CEDAW) guarantees the equality of women before the law on an equal basis with men with regard, *inter alia*, to concluding contracts, administering property and exercising their rights in the justice system. In addition, Article 3 of the African Charter on Human and Peoples' Rights (African Charter) provides for the right of every person to be equal before the law. Article 3 of the American Convention on Human Rights (ACHR) also enshrines the right to legal personality and the right of every individual to recognition as a person before the law.

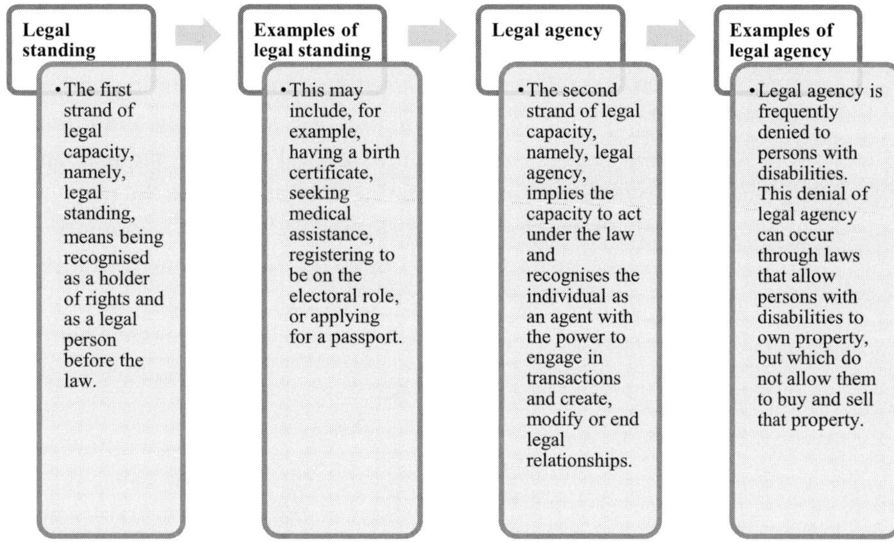

Figure 6.1 Legal Standing versus Legal Agency

3.1 The Concept of Legal Capacity

Like all other individuals, persons with disabilities need to make key life decisions – decisions concerning health care, finances, property, employment, relationships, living arrangements, and so forth. These decisions span the various rights granted to people with disabilities under the CRPD. In order to be deemed 'capable' of making these decisions, the law requires various types of capacity. Among others, the law requires one to have contractual capacity, legal capacity to make health care decisions, testimonial capacity (to be a witness) and testamentary capacity (to make a will).

Historically, persons with disabilities have been discriminated against in the exercise of their legal capacity. Being labelled 'disabled' has often led to an automatic assumption under the law that the individual in question lacks legal capacity. All persons with disabilities, including those with physical, psychosocial, intellectual or sensory impairments, can be affected by the denial of their legal capacity and the imposition of substitute decision-making. However, persons with intellectual or psychosocial disabilities are disproportionately affected by the denial of legal capacity.

The term 'legal capacity' has been interpreted by the CRPD Committee, in its General Comment No. 1, as including two strands: legal standing and legal agency.[16] In order for the right to legal capacity to be fulfilled, both strands of legal capacity (explained in Figure 6.1) must be recognised and cannot be separated.

[16] CRPD Committee, General Comment No. 1, note 10, para. 14.

By way of contrast with the term 'legal capacity', the term 'mental capacity' refers to the decision-making ability of an individual. The CRPD Committee notes that mental capacity 'is contingent on social and political contexts, as are the disciplines, professions and practices which play a dominant role in assessing mental capacity'.[17] Thus, unlike legal capacity, mental capacity depends on external conditions and internal factors inherent to the person with a disability.

There have been several criticisms of the CRPD Committee's interpretation of Article 12 in its General Comment No. 1. Some authors argued that the content of the draft General Comment on legal capacity was impractical and radical, particularly the CRPD Committee's stance in never allowing an assessment of mental capacity to lead to a denial of legal capacity; however, not all of the criticisms were taken on board in the final General Comment.[18] Following its publication, several authors have continued to assert that the binary division of capacity into mental and legal capacity, as the CRPD Committee does in the General Comment, is not an appropriate solution for the implementation of Article 12 CRPD.[19] For instance, Dawson

Should the concepts of 'legal capacity' and 'mental capacity' be completely separated in assessments of capacity?

[17] Ibid.

[18] See, for instance, the comments of the University of Cambridge, Cambridge Intellectual and Developmental Disabilities Research Group, *Submission to the CRPD Committee on the Draft General Comment on Article 12 CRPD* (31 January 2014) and the Law Society of Scotland, *Submission to the CRPD Committee on the Draft General Comment on Article 12 CRPD* (November 2013), available at www.ohchr.org/en/hrbodies/crpd/pages/dgcarticles12and9.aspx.

[19] See generally Melvyn Colin Freeman et al., 'Reversing Hard Won Victories in the Name of Human Rights: A Critique of the General Comment on Article 12 of the UN Convention on the Rights of Persons with Disabilities' (2015) 2(9) *Lancet Psychiatry* 844; see also, Michelle Browning, Christine Bigby and Jacinta Douglas, 'Supported Decision Making: Understanding How Its Conceptual Link to Legal Capacity Is Influencing the Development of Practice' (2014) 1(1) *Research and Practice in Intellectual and Developmental Disabilities* 34; see further, Piers Gooding, 'Supported Decision-Making: A Rights-Based Disability Concept and Its Implications for Mental Health Law' (2013) 20(3) *Psychiatry, Psychology and Law* 431, who argues that there are two divergent readings of Article 12, and this adds another layer of complexity to an already challenging and highly nuanced issue (at 438–39). In that regard, Gooding cites, among others: Perter Bartlett, '"The Necessity Must be Convincingly Shown to Exist": Standards for Compulsory Treatment for Mental Disorder Under the Mental Health Act 1983' (2011) 19 *Medical Law Review* 514, at 541; Michael Bach and Lana Kerzner, 'A New

claims that many aspects of the legal system require assessments of mental capacity, including the concept of 'intention' or '*mens rea*' in criminal law, and defences, such as diminished responsibility. This criticism is entirely valid. However, it is important to point out the background to the CRPD Committee's interpretation of Article 12, in order to understand why the Committee makes a distinction between mental and legal capacity. Historically, the mental capacity of individuals with disabilities has been inextricably linked to their right to legal capacity. As a result, if a person's 'decision-making ability is found to fall short of whatever "test" a court or other body applied, their legal capacity could be removed or restricted on the basis of a deficient assessment of mental capacity'.[20] This has led to substitute decision-making regimes being put in place for countless numbers of persons with disabilities. Substitute decision-making means that a legal representative of the person with a disability makes decisions for him or her.

Traditionally, there have been three approaches to legal capacity (summarised in Figure 6.2):

i. Under the status approach, being labelled 'disabled' translates to an assumption under the law that a person lacks legal capacity.
ii. The outcome approach is based on the maxim that, in circumstances where a person makes a bad decision or a number of bad decisions, that person should lose the right to continue making decisions.
iii. The functional approach entails an assessment of a person's legal capacity on an issue-specific basis. According to the CRPD Committee, the functional approach 'attempts to assess mental capacity and deny legal capacity accordingly'. It is often based on assessments as to 'whether a person can understand the nature and consequences of a decision and/or whether he or she can use or weigh the relevant information'.[21] The functional approach presumes that a person has capacity, unless the opposite is proven. The functional approach may seem 'disability-neutral' *prima facie*; however, functional assessments of capacity 'are almost invariably applied to individuals who are deemed to have a psychosocial or intellectual disability'.[22]

The modern approach to legal capacity, as embodied in Article 12 CRPD, entails a functional approach, combined with the provision of supports, where required, in order to enable each individual with a disability to make his or her own life decisions. In its General Comment No. 1, the CRPD Committee affirms that an

Paradigm for Protecting Autonomy and the Right to Legal Capacity', Report to the Law Commission of Ontario 2010, available at www.lco-cdo.org/en/disabilities- call-for-papers-bach-kerzner

[20] CoE, *A Study on the Equal Recognition before the Law: Contribution towards the Council of Europe Strategy on the Rights of Persons with Disabilities,* note 1, p. 8.

[21] CRPD Committee, General Comment No. 1, note 10, para. 15.

[22] Ibid.

individual's status 'as a person with a disability or the existence of an impairment (including a physical or sensory impairment) must never be grounds for denying legal capacity or any of the rights provided for in [A]rticle 12'.[23]

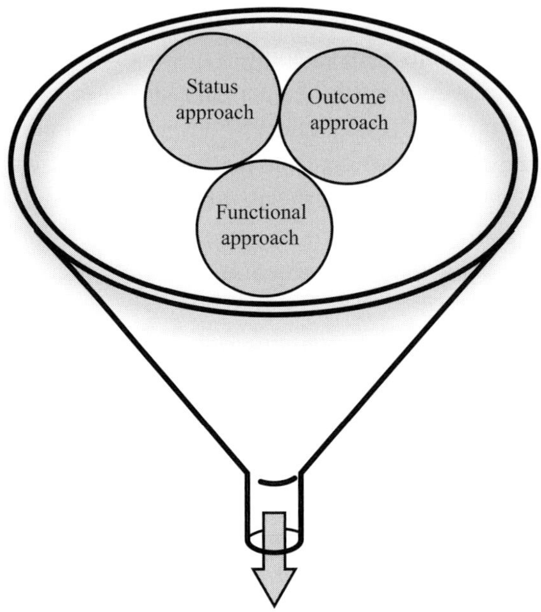

Figure 6.2 Traditional Approaches to Legal Capacity

3.2 Article 12 CRPD

While Article 12 has been deemed by academic commentators a 'controversial' legal norm,[24] it has also been perceived as laying down a set of provisions which constitute a 'true revolution' that challenges the traditional approaches to legal capacity adopted in many countries worldwide.[25] The European Union Agency for Fundamental Rights (FRA) claims that Article 12 'represents a significant departure from previous conceptions of the role and scope of legal

[23] Ibid. para 9.

[24] Alex Pearl, 'Article 12 of the United Nations Convention on the Rights of Persons with Disabilities and the Legal Capacity of Disabled People: The Way Forward?' (2013) 1(1) *Leeds Journal of Law and Criminology* 1, at 7.

[25] Patricia Cuenca Gomez et al., 'The Impact of Article 12 of the Convention on the Rights of Persons with Disabilities on Qatar's Private Law' (2017) 9(4) *The Age of Human Rights Journal* 81, at 82; see also Tina Minkowitz, 'The United Nations Convention on the Rights of Persons with Disabilities and the Right to be Free from Non-Consensual Psychiatric Interventions' (2007) 34 *Syracuse Journal of International Law and Commerce* 405, at 408.

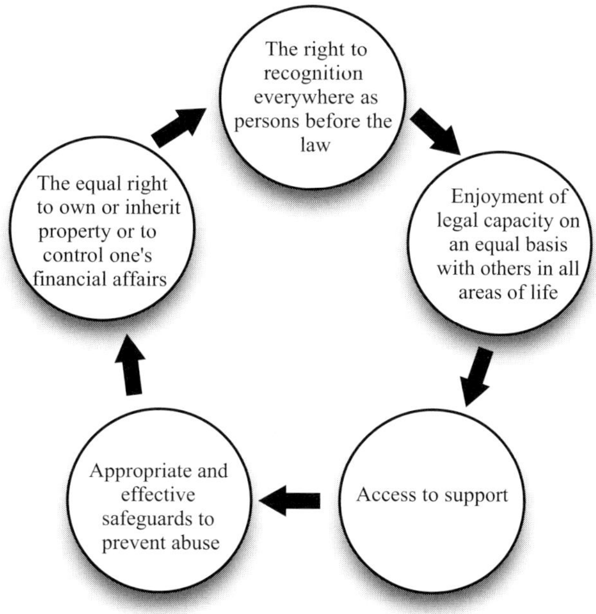

Figure 6.3 Article 12 Obligations

capacity legislation'.[26] The normative content of Article 12 CRPD, and the obligations that emanate therefrom, can be deduced from the text of the provision, in conjunction with the CRPD Committee's General Comment No. 1. Those obligations are summarised in Figure 6.3.

Article 12(1) CRPD reaffirms the right of persons with disabilities to be recognised as persons before the law. In that regard, the CRPD Committee emphasises that the recognition of every individual's legal personality is a prerequisite for the recognition of legal capacity.[27]

Article 12(2) CRPD provides that persons with disabilities must enjoy legal capacity on an equal basis with others in all areas of life. In that connection, it should be reiterated that legal capacity not only entitles an individual to the full protection of his or her rights within legal systems but also recognises the person as an agent who can perform acts with legal effect.

Article 12(3) CRPD recognises that States Parties have an obligation to provide disabled persons with access to the necessary supports in the exercise of their legal capacity, in order to enable them to make decisions that have legal effect. Support provided in the exercise of legal capacity must respect the rights, will and preferences of a person with a disability, and it should never

[26] European Union Agency for Fundamental Rights (FRA), *Legal Capacity of Persons with Intellectual Disabilities and Persons with Mental Health Problems* (Luxembourg: Publications Office of the European Union, 2013), p. 55.

[27] CRPD Committee, General Comment No. 1, note 10, para. 11.

amount to substitute decision-making.[28] While the term 'will and preferences' is not defined in the CRPD itself, nor is it defined by the CRPD Committee in General Comment No. 1, Arstein-Kerslake and Flynn note that 'an individual's "will" is used to describe the person's long-term vision of what constitutes a "good life" for them. The term "preferences", on the other hand, tends to refer to likes and dislikes, or ways in which a person prioritises different options available to them'.[29] Article 12(3) CRPD does not specify the form that support measures should take. According to the CRPD Committee, informal and formal support arrangements, of varying types and intensity, are covered under Article 12.[30]

Article 12(4) CRPD requires that States Parties must ensure that all measures relating to the exercise of legal capacity provide for appropriate and effective safeguards, to prevent abuse. According to Article 12(4), safeguards must guarantee that those measures respect the will and preferences of the disabled individual. This might include allowing a person with a disability to make his or her own mistakes. In addition, safeguards should be designed to ensure that any measures adopted relating to the exercise of legal capacity: are free of conflict of interest and undue influence; are proportional and tailored to the person's circumstances; apply for the shortest time possible; and are subject to regular review by a competent, independent and impartial authority or judicial body. Arstein-Kerslake and Flynn argue that 'informal support may not have sufficient safeguarding processes built in to protect the rights, will and preferences of the individuals using the support – but has the benefit that the providers of this support are more likely to know the person well and to be in the person's life for a long time'.[31] On the other hand, the authors note that:

> formal support structures may be subject to greater safeguards and a guarantee of "independence" but they run a serious risk of becoming over-professionalised, creating another intrusion in the lives of people with disabilities, and potentially creating an additional barrier for the individual to overcome before her decision-making is recognised.[32]

Thus, the best option may include a combination of 'both informal supports with safeguards and non-invasive formal supports'.[33]

Article 12(5) CRPD requires States Parties to the Convention to take appropriate and effective measures to ensure the equal right of persons with

[28] Ibid. para. 17.

[29] Anna Arstein-Kerslake and Eilionóir Flynn, 'The General Comment on Article 12 of the Convention on the Rights of Persons with Disabilities: A Roadmap For Equality Before the Law' (2016) 20(4) *The International Journal of Human Rights* 471, at 471. See also George Szmukler, '"Capacity", "Best Interests", "Will and Preferences" and the UN Convention on the Rights of Persons with Disabilities' (2019) 18(1) *World Psychiatry* 34–41.

[30] CRPD Committee, General Comment No. 1, note 10, para. 17.

[31] Arstein-Kerslake and Flynn, 'The General Comment on Article 12 of the Convention on the Rights of Persons with Disabilities: A Roadmap for Equality Before the Law', note 29, at 476.

[32] Ibid. [33] Ibid.

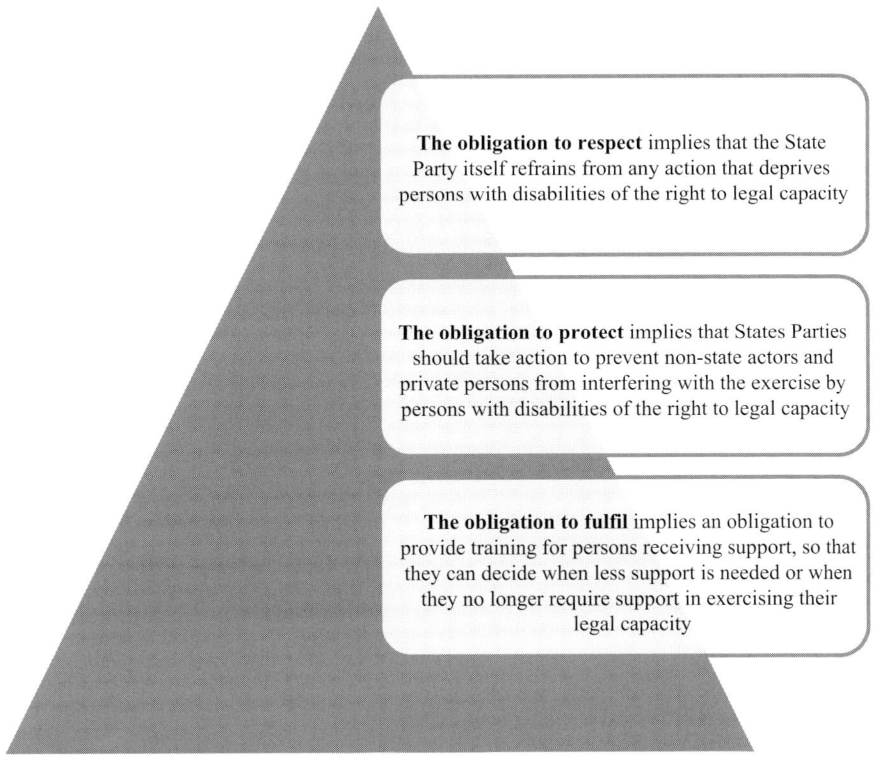

Figure 6.4 The Obligations to Respect, Protect and Fulfil the Right to Legal Capacity

disabilities to own or inherit property; to control their own financial affairs; and to have equal access to bank loans, mortgages and other forms of financial credit. States Parties must ensure that persons with disabilities are not arbitrarily deprived of their property.

As with all human rights, States Parties have an obligation to respect, protect and fulfil the right of all persons with disabilities to legal capacity.[34] These overarching obligations of States Parties to the CRPD are explained in Figure 6.4.

4 THE PARADIGM SHIFT: FROM SUBSTITUTE TO SUPPORTED DECISION-MAKING

This section traces the paradigm shift that Article 12 CRPD embodies with respect to the decision-making regimes that have traditionally been applied to persons with disabilities.

[34] CRPD Committee, General Comment No. 1, note 10, para. 24.

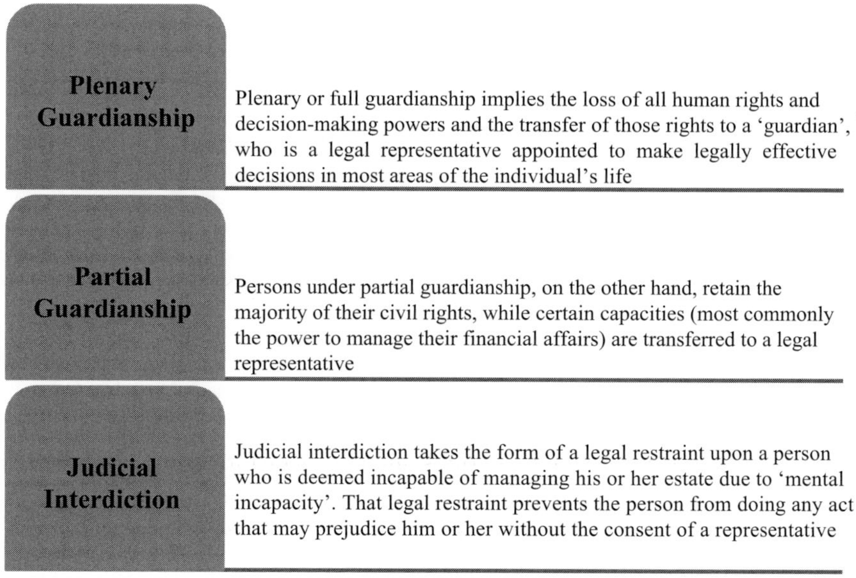

Figure 6.5 Forms of Substitute Decision-Making

4.1 Substitute Decision-Making

The term 'substitute decision-making' describes 'a mechanism by which the ability of an individual to be an actor under the law in all areas of their life is removed by the [s]tate and the decision is made for them by others'.[35] Once a substitute decision-making regime has been put in place, the individual concerned is not allowed to exercise his or her legal agency in respect of all decisions or some decisions. The extent of deprivation or restriction of legal capacity in an individual case depends on the type of substitute decision-making regime that is put in place. Substitute decision-making regimes can take many different forms, including plenary guardianship, partial guardianship or judicial interdiction (described in Figure 6.5).

The CRPD Committee recognises that, while substitute decision-making regimes that violate Article 12 can take many different forms, they share certain common characteristics, namely that:

i. Legal capacity is removed from an individual, even if this is in respect of a single decision.
ii. A substitute decision-maker can be appointed by someone other than the individual concerned, and this can be done against his or her will.

[35] CoE, *A Study on the Equal Recognition before the Law: Contribution towards the Council of Europe Strategy on the Rights of Persons with Disabilities*, note 1, p. 7.

iii. Any decision made by a substitute decision-maker is based on what is believed to be in the objective 'best interests' of the person concerned, as opposed to being based on the person's own 'will and preferences'.[36]

Often, the imposition of a substitute decision-making regime goes hand-in-hand with the placement of a person with a disability in an institutional setting, giving rise to further denials of legal capacity. Even when the imposition of a substitute decision-making regime does not result in institutionalisation, the denial of legal capacity can result in the systematic breach of that person's rights. Substitute decision-making regimes formed a central part of the individual communication brought before the CRPD Committee by Zsolt Bujdosó (and five other individuals) against Hungary.[37] The authors of that individual communication had been placed under partial or plenary guardianship, pursuant to various judicial decisions, on account of their intellectual disabilities. As an automatic consequence of their placement under guardianship, the authors' names were removed from the electoral register, in accordance with Article 70(5) of the Hungarian Constitution that was applicable at the time. That Article provided that persons placed under total or partial guardianship did not have the right to vote. Due to this restriction on their legal capacity, the authors of the individual communication were prevented from participating in the Hungarian parliamentary elections, held on 11 April 2010, and the municipal elections held on 3 October 2010. The authors remained disenfranchised up to the date of the individual communication. They claimed that the automatic deletion of their names from the electoral registers breached Article 29 CRPD (the right to participate in political and public life), read alone and in conjunction with Article 12 of the Convention. The authors claimed, more specifically, that their automatic disenfranchisement, regardless of the nature of their disability and their individual abilities, was discriminatory and unjustified.

CRPD Committee, Zsolt Bujdosó, Jánosné Ildikó Márkus, Viktória Márton, Sándor Mészáros, Gergely Polk and János Szabó v. Hungary, UN Doc. CRPD/C/10/D/4/2011

9.4 The Committee recalls that [A]rticle 29 of the Convention requires States [P]arties to ensure that persons with disabilities can effectively and fully participate in political and public life on an equal basis with others, including by

[36] CRPD Committee, General Comment No. 1, note 10, para. 27.

[37] CRPD Committee, *Zsolt Bujdosó, Jánosné Ildikó Márkus, Viktória Márton, Sándor Mészáros, Gergely Polk and János Szabó (represented by counsel, János Fiala, Disability Rights Center)* v. *Hungary*, Communication No. 4/2011, UN Doc. CRPD/C/10/D/4/2011.

guaranteeing their right to vote. Article 29 does not provide for any reasonable restriction or exception for any group of persons with disabilities. Therefore, an exclusion of the right to vote on the basis of a perceived or actual psychosocial or intellectual disability, including a restriction pursuant to an individuali[s]ed assessment, constitutes discrimination on the basis of disability, within the meaning of [A]rticle 2 of the Convention. The Committee refers to its concluding observations on Tunisia, in which it recommended 'the urgent adoption of legislative measures to ensure that persons with disabilities, *including persons who are currently under guardianship or trusteeship*, can exercise their right to vote and participate in public life, on an equal basis with others' (emphasis added) . . .

9.5 The Committee further recalls that under [A]rticle 12, paragraph 2, of the Convention, States parties must recogni[s]e and uphold the legal capacity of persons with disabilities 'on an equal basis with others in all aspects of life', including political life, which encompasses the right to vote. Under [A]rticle 12, paragraph 3, of the Convention, States [P]arties have a positive duty to take the necessary measures to guarantee to persons with disabilities the actual exercise of their legal capacity. Accordingly, the Committee is of the view that, by depriving the authors of their right to vote, based on a perceived or actual intellectual disability, the State [P]arty has failed to comply with its obligations under [A]rticle 29 of the Convention, read alone and in conjunction with [A]rticle 12 of the Convention.

4.2 Supported Decision-Making

Article 12 CRPD encapsulates, more than any other Convention provision, the 'paradigm shift' that the CRPD embraces – in other words, the move away from a paternalistic 'deficits' approach, which focuses on the functional limitations of the person, towards one based on increasing the capabilities of the individual. The human rights model of disability that underlies the CRPD has promoted a related shift away from a substitute decision-making paradigm towards one that is based on supported decision-making. States Parties to the Convention are required to recognise the 'universal legal capacity' of all individuals, regardless of disability or decision-making skills.[38] Supported-decision-making represents the new paradigm for facilitating universal legal capacity.

> How do you think that the supports envisaged under Article 12 work in practice?

[38] CRPD Committee, General Comment No. 1, note 10, para. 25.

Article 12 completely rejects the 'status' and 'outcome-based' approaches to legal capacity. As outlined above, Article 12 encapsulates the 'modern' functional approach – that is, an approach that is centred on the provision of varied supports enabling persons to exercise legal capacity.[39] For example, people with disabilities may choose one or more trusted support persons to assist them in adopting certain types of decisions, or may call on other forms of support, such as peer support, advocacy (including self-advocacy support), or assistance with communication.

Caution must be exercised with regard to informal support mechanisms. As Arstein-Kerslake and Flynn point out, many decisions made in the 'informal sphere of familial relationships and services for daily decision-making . . . do not appear to have legal consequences or give rise to . . . exertion of legal agency'.[40] However, 'for many people with cognitive disabilities, some of the most damaging decision-making denials occur within these informal spheres'.[41] Support provided to individuals with disabilities in the exercise of their legal capacity might include measures relating to accessibility. For example, requiring financial institutions to provide information in an understandable format or to provide professional sign language interpretation, would enable persons with disabilities to perform the legal acts required to open a bank account or conclude contracts. Support can also include diverse, non-conventional methods of communication, especially for those who use non-verbal forms of communication to express their will and preferences.[42]

4.3 Criticism of the Interpretation of Article 12 CRPD

As mentioned above, Article 12 CRPD itself and its interpretation by the CRPD Committee raise some controversial issues.[43] As noted above, some authors claim that mental capacity and legal capacity cannot be completely disentangled, as the CRPD Committee advocates.[44] Many other criticisms have been voiced regarding the CRPD Committee's interpretation of Article 12. Certain scholars argue that the concept of 'universal legal capacity' contained in General Comment No. 1 could hinder the exercise of other human rights. This might be the case where the informed consent of a person with a disability needs to be obtained in an emergency situation and where it is not possible to ascertain the will and

[39] Ibid. para. 17.

[40] Anna Arstein-Kerslake and Eilionóir Flynn, 'The Right to Legal Agency: Domination, Disability and the Protections of Article 12 of the Convention on the Rights of Persons with Disabilities' (2017) 13(1) *International Journal of Law in Context* 22, at 24.

[41] Ibid. [42] CRPD Committee, General Comment No. 1, note 10, para. 17.

[43] For a full elaboration on these issues, see CoE, *A Study on the Equal Recognition before the Law: Contribution Towards the Council of Europe Strategy on the Rights of Persons with Disabilities*, note 1, pp. 16–17.

[44] See above section 3.

preferences of the individual, even after all reasonable support measures have been provided. Freeman et al. argue that 'several fundamental rights, such as the enjoyment of the highest attainable standard of health, access to justice, the right to liberty and even the right to life, might instead be violated and subject to unintended consequences' as a result of the right to legal capacity found in Article 12.[45] Perlin[46] puts forward a similar argument when he contends that interpretations of the General Comment that call for the abolition of the insanity defence are incompatible with the rest of the CRPD, violating an individual's right to a fair trial and giving rise to the possibility of torture in prison. De Bhaillís and Flynn counter those arguments, by stating that they are 'ironic given that the denial of legal capacity often leads to an individual being deprived of her liberty and subject to involuntary treatment'.[47]

Other authors do not rule out the possibility of applying some form of substitute decision-making where an individual has severe disabilities, as they are of the opinion that it is not realistic for those individuals to be supported in the exercise of their legal capacity.[48] In other words, those commentators do not agree that support is a viable option for everyone or that substituted decision-making, as defined in the CRPD Committee's General Comment No. 1, should be abolished.

Arstein-Kerslake and Flynn address two so-called 'hard cases'.[49] These 'hard cases' fall into two categories, according to the authors: first, where respecting the will and preferences would result in serious harm to the person with a disability himself or herself or to others; and, secondly, where an individual's will and preferences are conflicting. With regard to the first category, the authors contend that 'a support person, or outside decision-maker, does not have to respect a person's will and preferences if to do so would implicate her in a criminal act'.[50] With respect to the second category of 'hard case' above, where an individual's will and preferences conflict, Arstein-Kerslake and Flynn note that, when the individual concerned has not set out their wishes

[45] Freeman et al., 'Reversing Hard Won Victories in the Name of Human Rights: A Critique of the General Comment on Article 12 of the UN Convention on the Rights of Persons with Disabilities', note 19.

[46] Michael Perlin, 'God Said to Abraham/Kill Me a Son: Why the Insanity Defence and the Incompetency Status Are Compatible with and Required by the Convention on the Rights of Persons with Disabilities and Basic Principles of Therapeutic Justice' (2015), available at https://papers.ssrn.com/sol3/papers.cfm?abstract_id=2683480.

[47] Clíodhna de Bhaillís and Eilionóir Flynn, 'Recognising Legal Capacity: Commentary and Analysis of Article 12 CRPD' (2017) 13(1) *International Journal of Law in Context* 6, at 15.

[48] Michelle Browning, Christine Bigby and Jacinta Douglas, 'Supported Decision Making: Understanding How Its Conceptual Link to Legal Capacity Is Influencing the Development of Practice' (2014) 1(1) *Research and Practice in Intellectual and Developmental Disabilities* 34.

[49] Arstein-Kerslake and Flynn, 'The General Comment on Article 12 of the Convention on the Rights of Persons with Disabilities: A Roadmap for Equality Before the Law', note 29, at 482.

[50] Ibid.

in advance (such as in an 'advance directive'), or has not appointed a person to support them in exercising their legal capacity, this may require the appointment of an outside decision-maker to discern what the CRPD Committee calls the 'best interpretation' of the individual's will and preferences.[51] The appointment of such an outside decision-maker should not, however, be undertaken lightly. Before any interpretation of the person's will and preferences is made, the individual with a disability should be consulted on how he or she wishes to exercise his or her legal capacity.

4.4 Good Practices on Supported Decision-Making

Certain jurisdictions adopt good practices in the area of supported decision-making. Outlined below, in the case study boxes, are a handful of examples of good practices.

CASE STUDY

Bulgarian Pilot Project on Legal Capacity

In Bulgaria, a pilot project entitled 'Empowerment of People with Disabilities' was carried out by the Bulgarian Association of Persons with Intellectual Disabilities. The project sought to test approaches for supported decision-making in respect of at least twenty people with intellectual disabilities. (Council of Europe, *A Study on the Equal Recognition before the Law: Contribution towards the Council of Europe Strategy on the Rights of Persons with Disabilities*, 2017, p. 48).

Canadian Representation Agreements

British Columbia's Representation Agreement Act 1996 facilitates individuals to decide on issues in advance, and it contains a presumption of capacity in respect of people with intellectual and psychosocial disabilities. Section 8 of the Act provides for a test of 'incapability', taking into account the following factors:

i. Whether the adult communicates a desire to have a representative;
ii. Whether the adult demonstrates choices and preferences and can express feelings of approval or disapproval of others;
iii. Whether the adult is aware that making the representation agreement or changing/revoking any of the provisions means that the representative may make, or stop making, decisions that affect the adult;
iv. Whether the adult has a relationship of trust with the representative.

[51] Ibid. citing CRPD Committee, General Comment No. 1, note 10, para. 21; on this point, see Adrian Ward, 'Abolition of Guardianship? "Best Interests" Versus "Best Interpretation"' (2015) 32 *Scots Law Times* 150.

(A. Arstein-Kerslake, *Restoring Voice to People with Cognitive Disabilities: Realizing the Right to Equal Recognition before the Law*, Cambridge University Press, 2017, p. 204).

Swedish Personal Ombudsmen

Sweden established a nationwide system of Personal Ombudsmen (PO) in 2000. This system provides support in decision-making for individuals with severe psychosocial disabilities. POs assist individuals in taking control of their own affairs and identifying care needs; drawing up action plans. The national scheme grew out of ten pilot projects which the Swedish government had funded between 1995 and 1998. Of particular note is the PO-Skåne project, which was created by an organisation of individuals who had previously used institutional and psychiatric care (Zero Project website: https://zeroproject.org/policy/sweden-2/).

5 LEGAL CAPACITY AND INDEPENDENT LIVING

ARTICLE 19 CRPD

States Parties to this Convention recogni[s]e the equal right of all persons with disabilities to live in the community, with choices equal to others, and shall take effective and appropriate measures to facilitate full enjoyment by persons with disabilities of this right and their full inclusion and participation in the community, including by ensuring that:

(a) Persons with disabilities have the opportunity to choose their place of residence and where and with whom they live on an equal basis with others and are not obliged to live in a particular living arrangement;
(b) Persons with disabilities have access to a range of in-home, residential and other community support services, including personal assistance necessary to support living and inclusion in the community, and to prevent isolation or segregation from the community;
(c) Community services and facilities for the general population are available on an equal basis to persons with disabilities and are responsive to their needs.

Article 19 contains the right to live independently and be included in the community. That Article bears a close relationship with Article 12 CRPD. The CRPD Committee has recognised this close relationship in its General

Comment No. 1. In that connection, the Committee has stated that, in order to ensure the full realisation of the rights provided for in Article 12, 'persons with disabilities must have the opportunity to live independently in the community and to make choices and to have control over their everyday lives, on an equal basis with others, as provided for in [A]rticle 19'.[52]

The CRPD Committee links the obligation to provide support in Article 12(3) with the right to live in the community contained in Article 19. According to the Committee, this means that support in the exercise of legal capacity should be provided 'through a community-based approach'.[53] In other words, States Parties must recognise that 'communities are assets and partners in the process of learning what types of support are needed in the exercise of legal capacity, including raising awareness about different support options'.[54] The Committee believes that, in seeking support models for individuals with disabilities who wish to exercise their legal capacity, States Parties must acknowledge 'the social networks and naturally occurring community support (including friends, family and schools) of persons with disabilities as key to supported decision-making'.[55] This is consistent with the emphasis placed in Article 19 on ensuring the full inclusion and participation of persons with disabilities in the community.

Both the right to exercise legal capacity and the right to community living are hindered by the continued segregation of persons with disabilities in institutions in many countries on a global scale. In particular, the denial of legal capacity to those with psychosocial and intellectual disabilities, through guardianship or similar regimes, enables substitute decision-makers to consent to their placement in institutional settings. The CRPD Committee acknowledges the extent of this problem, and it has stated in both its General Comment No. 1 (on legal capacity) and in its General Comment No. 5 (on living independently and being included in the community) that deinstitutionalisation 'must be achieved, and legal capacity must be restored to all persons with disabilities, who must be able to choose where and with whom to live', in accordance with Article 19 CRPD.[56] In its General Comment No. 5, the CRPD Committee reaffirms the link between Articles 12 and 19 of the Convention and reiterates the thrust of its General Comment No. 1.

[52] CRPD Committee, General Comment No. 1, note 10, para. 44. [53] Ibid. para. 45.

[54] Ibid. [55] Ibid.

[56] Ibid. para. 46; see also, CRPD Committee, General Comment No. 5, 27 October 2017, UN Doc. CRPD/C/GC/5, para. 38(a).

CRPD Committee, General Comment No. 5 on Living Independently and Being Included in the Community (2018)

27. Legal personality and legal agency are the bases for the reali[s]ation of independent living within the community for persons with disabilities. Article 19 is, therefore, linked to the recognition and exercise of legal personality and legal capacity as enshrined in [A]rticle 12 of the Convention and further explained in the Committee's [G]eneral [C]omment No. 1 (2014) on equal recognition before the law.

. . .

80. Equal recognition before the law [(Article 12)] ensures that all persons with disabilities have the right to exercise their full legal capacity and therefore have the equal right to exercise choice and control over their own lives by choosing where, with whom and how they want to live and to receive support in accordance with their will and preferences. To fully reali[s]e the transition to supported decision-making and implement the rights enshrined in [A]rticle 12, it is imperative that persons with disabilities have the opportunity to develop and express their wishes and preferences in order to exercise their legal capacity on an equal basis with others. To achieve this, they have to be a part of the community. Furthermore, support in the exercise of legal capacity should be provided using a community-based approach which respects the wishes and preferences of individuals with disabilities . . .

6 LEGAL CAPACITY AND FAMILY LIFE

ARTICLE 23 CRPD

States Parties shall take effective and appropriate measures to eliminate discrimination against persons with disabilities in all matters relating to marriage, family, parenthood and relationships, on an equal basis with others, so as to ensure that:

(a) The right of all persons with disabilities who are of marriageable age to marry and to found a family on the basis of free and full consent of the intending spouses is recognized;
(b) The rights of persons with disabilities to decide freely and responsibly on the number and spacing of their children and to have access to age-appropriate information, reproductive and family planning education are recognized, and the means necessary to enable them to exercise these rights are provided;
(c) Persons with disabilities, including children, retain their fertility on an equal basis with others.

2. States Parties shall ensure the rights and responsibilities of persons with disabilities, with regard to guardianship, wardship, trusteeship, adoption of children or similar institutions, where these concepts exist in national legislation; in all cases the best interests of the child shall be paramount. States Parties shall render appropriate assistance to persons with disabilities in the performance of their child-rearing responsibilities.

3. States Parties shall ensure that children with disabilities have equal rights with respect to family life. With a view to realizing these rights, and to prevent concealment, abandonment, neglect and segregation of children with disabilities, States Parties shall undertake to provide early and comprehensive information, services and support to children with disabilities and their families.

4. States Parties shall ensure that a child shall not be separated from his or her parents against their will, except when competent authorities subject to judicial review determine, in accordance with applicable law and procedures, that such separation is necessary for the best interests of the child. In no case shall a child be separated from parents on the basis of a disability of either the child or one or both of the parents.

5. States Parties shall, where the immediate family is unable to care for a child with disabilities, undertake every effort to provide alternative care within the wider family, and failing that, within the community in a family setting.

Article 23 CRPD requires States Parties to take effective and appropriate measures to eliminate discrimination against people with disabilities in all matters relating to marriage, family, parenthood and relationships. As with all areas of life covered by the right to legal capacity, individuals with disabilities have the right to direct their lives and make their own choices with regard to family relationships, marriage, having children and in connection with other equally important decisions in the domain of family life.

In practice, however, systemic discrimination, especially against women and girls with disabilities, continues to result in the widespread denial of their right to marry, to have sexual relationships and to found families. The CRPD Committee acknowledges the fact that 'the choices made by women with disabilities, especially women with psychosocial or intellectual disabilities, are often ignored and their decisions are often substituted by those of third parties'.[57] Those third parties include legal representatives, service providers, guardians and family members. Such substitute decision-making regimes are in violation of their rights under Article 12 of the Convention.[58]

[57] CRPD Committee, General Comment No. 3, 26 August 2016, UN Doc. CRPD/C/GC/3, para. 44.

[58] Office of the United Nations High Commissioner for Human Rights (OHCHR) et al., *Eliminating Forced, Coercive and Otherwise Involuntary Sterilization: An Interagency Statement* (Geneva: World Health Organization Publications, 2014).

The CRPD Committee has referred to legal capacity in its interpretation of various Convention provisions that are related to family life. In its Concluding Observations (COs) to Spain, for example, the Committee expresses concern that 'persons with disabilities whose legal capacity is not recognised may be subjected to sterili[s]ation without their free and informed consent'[59] in violation of Article 17 (on integrity of the person). In addition, in its COs to Argentina, the Committee affirms the importance of the right to legal capacity, noting that 'the right to form a family is denied to some persons with disabilities', especially those declared 'insane' or 'lacking legal capacity', in violation of Article 23.[60]

The Committee observes that, under Article 23, 'the exercise of legal capacity must be facilitated with regard to medical and/or therapeutic treatment'.[61] This entails 'ensuring that persons with disabilities can take their own decisions on retaining their fertility and reproductive autonomy'.[62] The Committee notes that:

> restricting or removing legal capacity can facilitate forced interventions, such as sterili[s]ation, abortion, contraception, female genital mutilation, surgery or treatment performed on intersex children without their informed consent and forced detention in institutions.[63]

The UN Special Rapporteur on torture emphasises that the forced sterilisation of women with disabilities may constitute torture or cruel or inhuman treatment, and that forced sterilisation constitutes a crime against humanity when committed as part of a widespread or systematic attack directed against any civilian population.[64]

The CRPD Committee highlights the multiple and intersectional discrimination faced by women with disabilities.[65] In that regard, the Committee remarks that 'wrongful stereotyping related to disability and gender is a form of discrimination that has a particularly serious impact on the enjoyment of sexual and reproductive health and rights, and the right to a found a family'.[66] The Committee states that:

> like all women, women with disabilities have the right to choose the number and spacing of their children, as well as the right to have control over and decide freely and

[59] CRPD Committee, Concluding Observations on the Initial Report of Spain, 23 September 2011, UN Doc. CRPD/C/ESP/CO/1.

[60] CRPD Committee, Concluding Observations on the Initial Report of Argentina, 8 October 2012, UN Doc. CRPD/C/ARG/CO/1.

[61] Ibid. para. 44. [62] Ibid. [63] Ibid. paras. 35 and 44.

[64] UN Human Rights Council, Promotion and Protection of All Human Rights, Civil, Political, Economic, Social and Cultural Rights, Including the Right to Development: Report of the Special Rapporteur on Torture and Other Cruel, Inhuman or Degrading Treatment or Punishment, Manfred Nowak, 15 January 2008, UN Doc. A/HRC/7/3, paras. 38–9.

[65] Ibid. para. 39.

[66] Programme of Action of the International Conference on Population and Development and the Beijing Platform for Action and the outcome documents of their review conferences.

responsibly on matters related to their sexuality, including sexual and reproductive health, free of coercion, discrimination and violence.[67]

Women with disabilities may also face harmful eugenic stereotypes. These types of stereotypes assume that they will give birth to children with disabilities and thus lead women with disabilities to being discouraged or prevented from becoming mothers.[68] In addition, harmful stereotypes have meant that women with disabilities may be denied access to information and communications, including education regarding their sexuality and on sexual relations. It is often wrongly presumed that persons with disabilities are asexual, particularly those with intellectual disabilities or deaf and blind women, and do not, therefore, require such information.[69] This lack of access to information can increase the risk of individuals with disabilities being subjected to sexual violence.[70] This is in direct violation of Article 16 CRPD, which requires that States Parties take all appropriate legislative, administrative, social, educational and other measures to protect persons with disabilities from all forms of exploitation, violence and abuse, including their gender-based aspects.

SUMMARY

- **Legal capacity entails the recognition of an individual as both a holder of rights and as an actor under the law, capable of creating, modifying or ending legal relationships.**
- **By way of contrast with the term 'legal capacity', the term 'mental capacity' refers to the decision-making ability of an individual.**
- **Legal capacity is indispensable for the exercise of civil, political, economic, social and cultural rights. It acquires a special significance for persons with disabilities when they have to make fundamental decisions regarding the right to health, education and work, among many other rights.**
- **The principle of human dignity lies at the heart of Article 12 CRPD, requiring that the inherent capabilities and legal capacity of persons with disabilities should be respected in all decisions that they make.**
- **Article 12 CRPD requires States Parties to move away from substitute decision-making regimes to supported decision-making, whereby a range of measures are provided to facilitate the exercise of legal capacity by all persons with disabilities.**
- **According to Article 12 CRPD, support provided in the exercise of legal capacity must respect the will and preferences of persons with disabilities, and it should never amount to substitute decision-making.**
- **Safeguards for the exercise of legal capacity must include protection against undue influence, but that protection must also respect the will and preferences of the person, including allowing him or her to take risks and make mistakes.**

[67] Ibid.

[68] *Report of the Special Rapporteur on Violence Against Women, Its Causes and Consequences*, 3 August 2012, UN Doc. A/67/227, para. 36.

[69] Ibid. para. 40.

[70] Ibid. para. 41; see, for example, CRPD Committee, Concluding Observations on the Initial Report of Mexico, 27 October 2014, UN Doc. CRPD/C/MEX/CO/1, para. 50(b).

- The obligation to provide support in Article 12(3) CRPD is closely connected to the right to live in the community contained in Article 19. According to the Committee, this means, among other things, that support in the exercise of legal capacity should be provided through a community-based approach.
- The denial of legal capacity has unduly hindered the right of women with disabilities to found a family and be provided with appropriate assistance to raise their children.

ACTIVITIES

REVIEW QUESTIONS

1. What are the key differences between legal capacity and mental capacity?
2. What are the key elements of the status, outcome and functional approaches to legal capacity?
3. Can you elaborate on the inter-relationship between legal capacity and independent living?

ESSAY QUESTIONS

1. 'The denial of legal capacity to persons with disabilities has, in many instances, led to their being deprived of fundamental rights, including the right to vote, the right to marry and found a family, reproductive rights, parental rights and the right to liberty.' *Discuss.*
2. 'Safeguards for the exercise of legal capacity should include protection against undue influence and should also respect the will and preferences of the person.' *Discuss.*

GROUP PROJECT

In June 2015, Mr Red was diagnosed with a form of bipolar disorder. This manifests itself in occasional symptoms, such as sudden dizziness, anger, reckless behaviour, claustrophobia and insomnia. In spite of this, Mr Red is able to live independently and works as a janitor in a local office building in Freedonia City in the state of Freedonia. In general, he is well able to take care of himself and has been having treatment since his diagnosis, which is keeping his symptoms at bay. However, Mr Red has a tendency to be irresponsible with money and to buy expensive goods and luxury accessories.

In December 2015, Mr Red decided to purchase a Ferrari car, and he used all his savings to pay the deposit. When his parents learned about the purchase, they decided to apply to the District Court of Freedonia to place him under full guardianship, without saying anything to him. The Court ruled that Mr Red should be placed under full guardianship. Mr Red was not invited to take part in the Court hearing, and the Court officials did not engage with him throughout the proceedings.

Discuss the group project, taking into account the fact that Freedonia is a State Party to the CRPD.

FURTHER READING

Arstein-Kerslake, A., 'An Empowering Dependency: Exploring Support for the Exercise of Legal Capacity' (2016) 18(1) *Scandinavian Journal of Disability Research* 77–92.

Arstein-Kerslake, A., 'Legal Capacity and Supported Decision-Making: Respecting Rights and Empowering People', in C. O'Mahony and G. Quinn (eds.), *Disability Law and Policy: An Analysis of the UN Convention* (Dublin: Clarus Press, 2017), pp. 69–78.

Bilchitz, D., 'Dignity, Fundamental Rights and Legal Capacity: Moving Beyond the Paradigm Set by the General Comment on Article 12 of the Convention on the Rights of Persons with Disabilities' (2016) 3 *South African Journal on Human Rights* 410–37.

Browning, M., Bigby, C. and Douglas, J., 'Supported Decision Making: Understanding How Its Conceptual Link to Legal Capacity Is Influencing the Development of Practice' (2014) 1(1) *Research and Practice in Intellectual and Developmental Disabilities* 34–45.

Dawson, J., 'A Realistic Approach to Assessing Mental Health Law Compliance with the UNCRPD' (2015) 40 *International Journal of Law and Psychiatry* 70–9.

De Bhaillís, C. and Flynn, E., 'Recognising Legal Capacity: Commentary and Analysis of Article 12 CRPD' (2017) 13(1) *International Journal of Law in Context* 6–21.

Dhanda, A., 'Legal Capacity in the Disability Convention: Stranglehold of the Past or Lodestar for the Future' (2006–2007) 34(2) *Syracuse Journal of International Law and Commerce* 429–62.

Dinerstein, R. D., 'Implementing Legal Capacity Under Article 12 of the UN Convention on the Rights of Persons with Disabilities: The Difficult Road from Guardianship to Supported Decision-Making' (2012) 19(2) *Human Rights Brief* 8–12.

Flynn, E. and Arstein-Kerslake, A., 'The Support Model of Capacity: Fact, Fiction or Fantasy?' (2014) 32(1) *Berkeley Journal of International Law* 124–43.

Freeman, M. C. et al., 'Reversing Hard Won Victories in the Name of Human Rights: A Critique of the General Comment on Article 12 of the UN Convention on the Rights of Persons with Disabilities' (2015) 2(9) *Lancet Psychiatry* 844–50.

Gooding, P., 'Supported Decision-Making: A Rights-Based Disability Concept and Its Implications for Mental Health Law' (2013) 20(3) *Psychiatry, Psychology and Law* 431–51.

Gooding, P., *A New Era for Mental Health Law and Policy. Supported Decision-Making and the UN Convention on the Rights of Persons with Disabilities* (Cambridge/New York: Cambridge University Press, 2017).

Keys, M., 'Article 12: Equal Recognition Before the Law', in V. Della Fina, R. Cera and G. Palmisano (eds.), *The United Nations Convention on the Rights of Persons with Disabilities: A Commentary* (Cham: Springer, 2017), pp. 263–79.

Keys, M., 'Article 12 of the UN Convention on the Rights of Persons with Disabilities and the European Convention on Human Rights', in C. O'Mahony and G. Quinn (eds.), *Disability Law and Policy: An Analysis of the UN Convention* (Dublin: Clarus Press, 2017), pp. 81–98.

Keys, M., 'Legal Capacity Reform in Europe: An Urgent Challenge', in G. Quinn and L. Waddington (eds.), *European Yearbook of Disability Law* (Antwerp/Portland: Intersentia, 2009), vol. 1, pp. 59–88.

McSherry, B. and Maker, Y., 'International Human Rights and Mental Health: Challenges for Law and Practice', (2018) 25(2) *Journal of Law and Medicine*, 315–319.

Minkowitz, T., 'Legal Capacity: Alternatives to Functional Capacity', in C. O'Mahony and G. Quinn (eds.), *Disability Law and Policy: An Analysis of the UN Convention* (Dublin: Clarus Press, 2017), pp. 101–10.

Shogren, K.A., Wehmeyer, M., Martinis, J. and Blanck, P., *Supported Decision-Making. Theory, Research, and Practice to Enhance Self-Determination and Quality of Life* (Cambridge/New York: Cambridge University Press, 2018).

Weller, P., 'Supported Decision-Making and the Achievement of Non-discrimination: The Promise and Paradox of the Disabilities Convention', (2008) 26(2) *Law in Context*, 85–110.

7 Persons with Disabilities and the Justice System

LEARNING OUTCOMES

- ✓ Understand the concept of access to justice and its role in the international human rights system.
- ✓ Identify and comprehend the main barriers faced by persons with disabilities in the justice system.
- ✓ Understand the key norms concerning access to justice included in the CRPD.
- ✓ Assess the significance of access to justice in relation to the protection of the rights of people with disabilities.
- ✓ Understand the obligations stemming from Article 13 CRPD.
- ✓ Demonstrate awareness of the inter-relationship between legal capacity and access to justice.
- ✓ Understand how the rights of people with disabilities are safeguarded by the CRPD when they come into contact with the criminal justice system.
- ✓ Demonstrate awareness of the good practices exhibited by certain States Parties to the CRPD in overcoming the barriers that hinder access to justice when persons with disabilities are victims of crimes, are offenders themselves or are working as legal professionals.

Achieving meaningfully equal rights for persons with disabilities will require removing the barriers that hinder persons with disabilities from accessing courts to claim their human rights, and fighting against their isolation in institutions or in the back-rooms of family homes. Failure to ensure that vulnerable persons have effective access to justice will allow the abuses committed against them to continue.[1]

1 INTRODUCTION

The term 'access to justice' usually refers to access to the legal system.[2] It encompasses the right to a fair trial and legal representation, and it is related to the concept of the 'rule of law'. However, recent scholarship,[3] including disability law doctrine,[4] has advanced a broader understanding of 'access to justice', which 'covers different stages of the process of obtaining a solution to justice problems'[5] and embraces effective access for people with disabilities to the legal system, to procedures, to buildings used in the administration of justice, and to legal information. This wider definition of 'access to justice' is characterised by procedural and substantive dimensions. Flynn, recalling Bahdi,[6] contends that procedural justice is linked to the legal process itself and to the ways in which claims are adjudicated upon.[7] Substantive justice, on the other hand, is linked to the very idea of equality and to the need to redress the disadvantage experienced by persons with disabilities as a marginalised

[1] Council of Europe Commissioner for Human Rights, *Third Party Intervention by the Council of Europe Commissioner for Human Rights under Article 36, paragraph 3, of the European Convention on Human Rights – Application No. 47848/08* (2011), p. 8, available at https://rm.coe.int/16806da650.

[2] Eilionóir Flynn, *Disabled Justice? Access to Justice and UN Convention on the Rights of Persons with Disabilities* (London/New York: Routledge, 2016), p. 11.

[3] Julinda Beqiraj and Lawrence McNamara, *Children and Access to Justice: National Practices, International Challenges* (Bingham Centre for the Rule of Law Report, 2016), p. 5 and literature cited in the report.

[4] Ibid. p. 11; in the same vein, see Stefanie Ortoleva, 'Inaccessible Justice: Human Rights, Persons with Disabilities and the Legal System' (2011) *ILSA Journal of International and Comparative Law* 282, at 284; see also, Anna Lawson and Eilionóir Flynn, 'Disability and Access to Justice in the European Union: Implications of the UN Convention on the Rights of Persons with Disabilities', in Gerard Quinn, Eilionóir Flynn and Lisa Waddington (eds.), *European Yearbook of Disability Law* (Antwerp/Portland: Intersentia, 2013), vol. 4, pp. 7–44.

[5] Julinda Beqiraj, Lawrence McNamara and Victoria Wicks, *Access to Justice for Persons with Disabilities: From International Principles to Practice* (London: International Bar Association, 2017), p. 14.

[6] Reem Bahdi, 'Women's Access to Justice in the MENA (Middle East and North Africa) Region' (31 October 2007), available at https://papers.ssrn.com/sol3/papers.cfm?abstract_id=1716864.

[7] Ibid. cited in Flynn, *Disabled Justice? Access to Justice and UN Convention on the Rights of Persons with Disabilities*, note 2, p. 15.

group.[8] Substantive justice 'concerns itself with an assessment of the rights claims that are available to those who seek a remedy'.[9] Access to justice is an indispensable factor in promoting empowerment and in securing access to equal human dignity. Access to justice is not only a fundamental right in itself, but it is also a pre-condition for the enjoyment of all other rights. It provides a unique legal tool that can be used to counter discrimination, stigma and the exclusion faced by persons with disabilities.[10] Flynn also suggests that a 'participatory element of access to justice' emerges from Article 13 CRPD, which 'is closely linked to conceptions of equal citizenship'.[11]

Access to justice is also deeply interrelated with the exercise of other human rights, and difficulties for people with disabilities in accessing justice are linked to broader challenges. For example, if a person is unable to travel to a police station, to an ombudsman's office or to a courtroom because of a lack of accessible transportation, then he or she will be unable to make a claim. In a similar vein, if a person is deprived of legal capacity, he or she will not be able to bring a case before a court. Forced institutionalisation might also prevent people with disabilities from reporting abuses.

Against this background, the present chapter reflects on the scope of the right to access justice in the CRPD, taking into account the CRPD Committee's decisions. Section 2 analyses the right to access justice in international human rights law. Section 3 turns to an examination of the barriers that people with disabilities face when they interact with the justice system. Section 4 discusses the CRPD norms that aim to ensure equal access to the judicial system and protection from inhuman treatment in the event of a conviction, with a particular focus on the scope and content of Article 13 CRPD. Section 5 addresses the challenges associated with the participation of people with disabilities in the criminal justice system. Section 5 does not endeavour to discuss in detail the question of criminal responsibility, nor does it delve into an analysis of the insanity defence, unfitness to plead and incompetence to stand trial; rather, it presents an overview of how the rights of people with disabilities are safeguarded by the CRPD when they come into contact with the criminal justice system, either as offenders or as victims.

[8] Access to justice is especially crucial for vulnerable persons and marginalised groups, such as persons with disabilities. A working paper released by the OECD in 2016, available at www.oecd.org/gov/Understanding-effective-access-justice-workshop-paper-final.pdf notes that '[t]here is increasing (although limited) evidence that disadvantaged groups are typically those that are most vulnerable to legal problems, resulting from uneven exposure to the circumstances that can give rise to legal and social problems and/or their lower ability to avoid or mitigate problems'.

[9] Flynn, *Disabled Justice? Access to Justice and UN Convention on the Rights of Persons with Disabilities*, note 2, p. 13.

[10] Ibid. p. 17. [11] Ibid. p. 18.

2 SETTING THE SCENE: ACCESS TO JUSTICE AS A HUMAN RIGHT

Prior to the entry into force of the CRPD, there was no specific articulation of a general right to access justice. Nevertheless, that right can be traced back to Article 8 of the Universal Declaration of Human Rights (UDHR), which states that '[e]veryone has the right to an effective remedy by the competent national tribunals for acts violating the fundamental rights guaranteed to him by the constitution or by law'. The right to access justice can also be traced back to Article 10 UDHR, which establishes the right to a fair hearing. In addition, Article 14(1) of the International Covenant on Civil and Political Rights (ICCPR) articulates the right to equality before the law and the right to a fair trial in a more detailed fashion, while Article 10 ICCPR sets forth the presumption of innocence and rights related to participation in a criminal procedure as well as the principle of *ne bis in idem*.[12]

The other core UN human rights treaties include, to various extents, provisions on equality of persons before the law and the rights to an effective remedy and a fair trial.[13] Those might be considered as constituting the origins of a broader right to access justice. In elaborating on these provisions, some of the UN human rights treaty bodies have mentioned a general right of access to justice that must be ensured for all persons on a non-discriminatory basis. Notable in this respect is General Comment No. 3 of the UN Committee Against Torture,[14] on Article 14 of the Convention against Torture and Other Cruel, Inhuman or Degrading Treatment or Punishment (CAT), which contains the right to a remedy for victims of torture.[15] It affirms that:

[12] This means that 'no one shall be liable to be tried or punished again for an offence for which he has already been finally convicted or acquitted in accordance with the law and penal procedure of each country' (Article 14(5) ICCPR).

[13] See e.g. the International Convention on the Elimination of All Forms of Racial Discrimination (CERD) and the Convention on the Elimination of All Forms of Discrimination against Women (CEDAW). For example, the CERD guarantees the right of everyone 'to equal treatment before the tribunals and all other organs administering justice'. Article 15 CEDAW requires that States treat women 'equally in all stages of procedure in courts and tribunals'; for a more detailed discussion, see Flynn, *Disabled Justice? Access to Justice and UN Convention on the Rights of Persons with Disabilities*, note 2, pp. 22 et seq.; see also, Eilionóir Flynn, 'Article 13: Access to Justice', in Valentina Della Fina, Rachele Cera and Guiseppe Palmisano (eds.), *The United Nations Convention on the Rights of Persons with Disabilities: A Commentary* (Cham: Springer, 2017), pp. 281–94. For a general discussion on access to justice in international human rights law, see, among others, Francesco Francioni et al., *Accesso alla giustizia dell'individuo nel diritto internazionale e dell'Unione Europea* (Milano: Giuffre' Editore, 2008).

[14] UN Committee Against Torture (CAT), General Comment No. 3, 13 December 2012, UN Doc. CAT/C/GC/3.

[15] Article 14 CAT reads as follows: '(1) Each State Party shall ensure in its legal system that the victim of an act of torture obtains redress and has an enforceable right to fair and adequate compensation, including the means for as full rehabilitation as possible. In the event of the death of the victim as a result of an act of torture, his dependants shall be entitled to

> States [P]arties shall ensure that access to justice and to mechanisms for seeking and obtaining redress are readily available and that positive measures ensure that redress is equally accessible to all persons regardless of race, colour, ethnicity, age, religious belief or affiliation, political or other opinion, national or social origin, gender, sexual orientation, gender identity, mental or other disability, health status, economic or indigenous status, reason for which the person is detained, including persons accused of political offences or terrorist acts, asylum-seekers, refugees or others under international protection, or any other status or adverse distinction, and including those marginali[s]ed or made vulnerable on bases such as those above.[16]

In the European human rights system,[17] Article 13 of the European Convention on Human Rights (ECHR)[18] establishes the right to an effective remedy at the domestic level, which must be guaranteed to everyone without discrimination. In the EU, the right to access justice stems from the Charter of Fundamental Rights of the European Union (EU CFR),[19] mainly Articles 47 (the rights to an effective remedy and to a fair trial) and 48 (the presumption of innocence and right of defence). These Articles set out the right to a hearing within a reasonable time; the opportunity to receive legal advice, defence and representation; and a restatement of the presumption of innocence. Similar provisions, albeit with slightly diverse formulations, are included in the African Charter on the Human and Peoples' Rights (African Charter)[20] and in the American Convention on Human Rights (ACHR).[21]

Each of the foregoing provisions contains rights and protection with regard to the relationship between the individual and the justice system, applicable to all human beings in a wide range of scenarios, but they do not contextualise and protect the specific needs of people with disabilities.

3 PERSONS WITH DISABILITIES AND THE JUSTICE SYSTEM: BARRIERS AND CHALLENGES TO ACCESS

Before focusing on the normative content of the CRPD, it is useful to contextualise the right to access justice for people with disabilities, by giving an overview of the specific barriers and challenges that they face when

compensation. (2) Nothing in this article shall affect any right of the victim or other persons to compensation which may exist under national law.'

[16] CAT, General Comment No. 3, note 14, para. 32. [17] See below Chapter 13.

[18] Convention for the Protection of Human Rights and Fundamental Freedoms, 4 November 1950, entered into force 3 September 1953, ETS 5.

[19] OJ 2012 No. C326/1.

[20] African Charter on Human and Peoples' Rights, adopted on 27 June 1981, OAU Doc. CAB/LEG/67/3 rev. 5, 21 I.L.M. 58 (1982), entered into force 21 October 1986.

[21] American Convention on Human Rights, 22 November 1969, entered into force 18 July 1978.

confronted with the justice system, as claimants, victims or offenders, or in their capacity as legal professionals. This allows one to understand the relevance of, and the rationale for, the CRPD's provisions on access to justice. Additional remarks on the barriers that persons with disabilities face as victims of crimes or offenders are discussed in the final part of this chapter.

3.1 Persons with Disabilities as Claimants or Victims

Several types of barriers can make it impossible for people with disabilities to claim and to vindicate their rights.[22]

When it comes to normative barriers, the most obvious are those laws which limit or remove legal capacity.[23] Such laws have a direct impact on legal standing and on the recognition of the individual before the law (i.e. legal personality).[24] However, disabled persons who are not deprived of their legal capacity may still face barriers linked to discriminatory provisions that prevent them from vindicating their rights. Negative attitudes and stigma on the part of the police, lawyers or judges 'may result in persons with disabilities being considered and treated as less credible at all stages of legal processes – including when reporting a crime'.[25]

Moreover, people with disabilities encounter physical barriers, in terms of access to legal information, which is a crucial aspect when seeking a judicial remedy. Among other documents, the United Nations Development Programme (UNDP)[26] has recognised that '[le]gal awareness is the foundation for fighting injustice' and that, often, 'disadvantaged people cannot seek remedies for injustice when they do not know what their rights and entitlements are under the law'.[27] People with disabilities can be unaware of their rights (and unable to access information on those rights) because no accessible formats are available. Even when such information is available, disabled individuals might experience difficulties because they cannot physically access the buildings used by judicial institutions.

[22] UN Department of Economic and Social Affairs, Division for Social Policy Development, 'Toolkit on Disability for Africa. Access to Justice for Persons with Disabilities' (2016), available at www.un.org/development/desa/technical-cooperation/2016/11/18/toolkit-on-disability-for-africa/.

[23] See above Chapter 6.

[24] Flynn, *Disabled Justice? Access to Justice and UN Convention on the Rights of Persons with Disabilities*, note 2, p. 67; on legal capacity see above Chapter 6.

[25] UN Department of Economic and Social Affairs, Division for Social Policy Development 'Toolkit on Disability for Africa. Access to Justice for Persons with Disabilities', note 22, p. 6.

[26] See above Chapter 1, sub-section 3.4.

[27] United Nations Development Programme (UNDP), *Access to Justice Practice Note* (2004), p. 10, available at www.undp.org/content/dam/aplaws/publication/en/publications/democratic-governance/dg-publications-for-website/access-to-justice-practice-note/Justice_PN_En.pdf.

In many countries, people with disabilities are still placed in institutional settings (such as full-time residential services, group homes, or other types of congregated settings, like social care homes). Institutional settings might pose an additional barrier in accessing information, because people with disabilities often have contact only with paid carers or staff, family members and other people with disabilities.

Another quite typical barrier is the difficulty in finding legal professionals who have knowledge of disability issues and awareness of the rights of people with disabilities.[28] Even if experienced legal professionals are available, economic barriers might prevent people with disabilities from being able to hire a lawyer or seek specialised legal support.[29] In fact, people with disabilities constitute a disproportionate number 'among the world's poor', and a lack of economic resources can affect not only 'the ability to engage and pay for quality legal counsel', where it is not free, but also the ability 'to engage in litigation, which can be expensive and lengthy'.[30]

People with intellectual disabilities rarely have direct contact with a lawyer, which hinders the possibility for them to seek legal advice. Family members are usually required to take legal advice on behalf of the individual with an intellectual disability (or together with them). This is linked to the lack of independence that people with intellectual disabilities traditionally experience, and it is most likely to occur in cases of deprivation of legal capacity.

When a court proceeding is commenced, people with disabilities might face procedural barriers, being denied the possibility to communicate with the court, officers of the court, and with everyone else who has a role in the justice system.[31] This often occurs in the case of those with sensory

[28] Stefanie Ortoleva, 'Inaccessible Justice: Human Rights, Persons with Disabilities and the Legal System', note 4, at 300–2; Flynn, *Disabled Justice? Access to Justice and UN Convention on the Rights of Persons with Disabilities*, note 2, pp. 58–60 and 74; UN Department of Economic and Social Affairs, Division for Social Policy Development, 'Toolkit on Disability for Africa. Access to Justice for Persons with Disabilities', note 22; Claire Edwards, Gillian Harolds and Shane Kilcommins, *Access to Justice for People with Disabilities as Victims of Crime in Ireland* (School of Applied Social Studies and Centre for Criminal Justice and Human Rights, Faculty of Law, University College Cork, 2012), available at http://nda.ie/Publications/Justice-and-Safeguarding/Access-to-Justice/. The latter report highlights that '[a] number of authors have pointed to a failure on the part of legal professionals to understand the capabilities of people with learning disabilities, or adapt their questioning of this group in court to facilitate "best evidence"', p. 73.

[29] Beqiraj, McNamara and Wicks, *Access to Justice for Persons with Disabilities: From International Principles to Practice*, note 5, p. 14.

[30] UN Department of Economic and Social Affairs, Division for Social Policy Development, 'Toolkit on Disability for Africa. Access to Justice for Persons with Disabilities', note 22, p. 6.

[31] In some countries there are, however, legal provisions that ensure accessibility of courtrooms. For example, in Ireland, court buildings are subject to measures set out in the Disability Act 2005. This includes the provision that public buildings are made accessible to people with

disabilities, when, for example, sign interpretation or translation of documents in Braille, alternative and augmented communication (AAC) is needed but is not provided.[32]

When people with disabilities take the stand as witnesses, they might face stigmatisation, since they are frequently not considered to be credible witnesses. Domestic legislation usually treats them as 'vulnerable' witnesses and sets out measures to accommodate their giving testimony. Such measures include the use of intermediaries in court and the use of videolink for giving evidence (as an exception to the *viva voce* examination in an open court). However, these measures might not prove sufficient to counteract negative attitudes by judicial staff.

Finally, children with disabilities might experience amplified difficulties in accessing justice from both a procedural and a substantive point of view. A report released by the Mental Disability Advocacy Centre (MDAC) reveals that children with intellectual or psychosocial disabilities experience a variety of human rights violations, including denial of education and placement in institutions that segregate them from mainstream community life. Children with disabilities are at a higher risk of becoming victims of ill-treatment, exploitation and other forms of abuse.[33] They are also overrepresented in the criminal justice system as alleged offenders, often undeservedly so, and as victims. This can result in denial of access to justice. Since these children may not be able to communicate in ways in which people can easily understand, '[b]arriers exist where adjustments and supports are not provided to accommodate these characteristics'.[34] The MDAC report finds that, in many countries, children with intellectual disabilities 'were excluded from judicial proceedings, or were made to endure processes that were formal, inflexible and ultimately denied them the right to be heard'.[35] The main barriers to access to justice are depicted in Figure 7.1.

disabilities, and that information for people with visual and hearing impairments is made as accessible as possible, where it is requested. Published information affecting people with intellectual disability should also be produced in an easy-read format.

32 The term 'AAC' covers a wide range of communication techniques which are alternatives to spoken communication, such as gestures, sign languages, communication boards and web-based applications that permit the user to communicate. These tools are used to help people with particular disabilities, which affect their communication abilities, including, for instance, intellectual disability, cerebral palsy or motor neuron disease. Flynn, *Disabled Justice? Access to Justice and UN Convention on the Rights of Persons with Disabilities*, note 2, pp. 90–1.

33 MDAC, *Access to Justice for Children with Mental Disabilities: International Standards and Findings from Ten EU Member States* (2015), available at www.mdac.org/sites/mdac.info/files/access_to_justice_children_ws2_standards_and_findings_english.pdf.

34 Ibid. p. 11. 35 Ibid. p. 5.

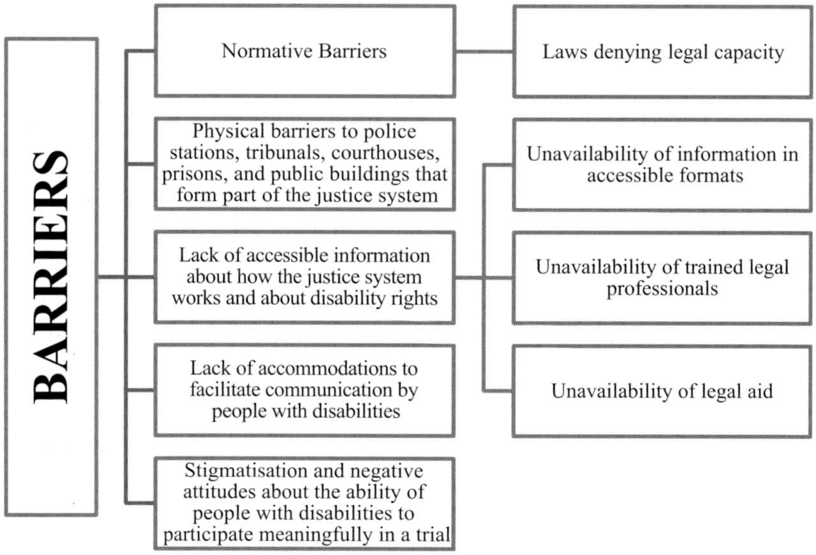

Figure 7.1 Main Barriers to Access to Justice

3.2 Persons with Disabilities as Legal Professionals or Jurors

The possibility for people with disabilities to engage in employment as legal professionals (as lawyers, judges or simply as employees within the justice system) is currently limited by many factors. Persons with disabilities face difficulties in accessing legal education and training. This is not only due to lack of accessibility and reasonable accommodation in legal education, as well as the inaccessibility of exams for admittance to the bar, but it is also attributable to attitudinal barriers (i.e. stigmatisation) that prevent people with disabilities from acquiring a legal qualification. Historically, law schools did not admit applicants with disabilities (this may still happen today in some countries) and, despite a few notable exceptions,[36] the adaptation of teaching and evaluation strategies to facilitate students with disabilities is perceived as problematic.[37] The fear is that it might compromise the quality of legal education or have a negative impact on the qualifications of law school graduates. Additionally, postgraduate legal training often does not take account of the accessibility challenges faced by disabled students.[38] When

[36] David Larson, 'Access to Justice for Persons with Disabilities: An Emerging Strategy' (2014) *Laws* 220, at 229.

[37] Ortoleva, 'Inaccessible Justice: Human Rights, Persons with Disabilities and the Legal System', note 4, at 303.

[38] Donald Stone, 'The Disabled Lawyers Have Arrived; Have They Been Welcomed with Open Arms into the Profession – An Empirical Study of the Disabled Lawyers' (2009) *Law and Inequality: A Journal of Theory and Practice* 93; Ortoleva, 'Inaccessible Justice: Human Rights, Persons with Disabilities and the Legal System', note 4, at 303–4; Flynn, *Disabled*

persons with disabilities succeed in achieving a legal qualification, they might face difficulties in actually working as legal professionals, due to the unavailability of reasonable accommodation in the workplace as well as the general lack of accessibility of courtrooms.[39]

In some contexts, people with disabilities are clearly excluded from taking up positions in the justice system, as it is believed that they may not be able to carry out the functions that these roles require. In countries where juries are an element of the judicial system, people with disabilities are often denied the right to be on those juries, because they are considered to be unable to understand the trial, to deliberate, or to render fair judgments.[40] However, even if no formal rules exist preventing people with disabilities from taking roles as adjudicators or jurors, they might face certain prejudices in attempting to do so. Bequiraj et al. report that Philip French (an Australian advocate) has denounced the 'enormous cultural resistance to the idea that people with disabilit[ies] can adjudicate cases'. They note that, in *Finney* v. *The Hills Grammar School*, members of the public wrote letters to the *Sydney Morning Herald* questioning the 'suitability of the disabled adjudicator' (a blind person) to adjudicate on a case involving discrimination in education.[41]

4 ACCESS TO JUSTICE IN THE CRPD

Article 13 CRPD articulates the right to access justice. That provision, which is deeply interconnected with other norms of the Convention, addresses the challenges that people with disabilities face when they are confronted with judicial bodies and procedures or when they want to seek a remedy. The subsections below discuss the obligations stemming from Article 13 and succinctly examine other related provisions.

4.1 Article 13 CRPD

Article 13 CRPD is a largely unprecedented provision, as no similar right had been articulated in previous international human rights treaties. The Standard

Justice? Access to Justice and UN Convention on the Rights of Persons with Disabilities, note 2, pp. 117–40.

39 Ortoleva, 'Inaccessible Justice: Human Rights, Persons with Disabilities and the Legal System', note 4.

40 Kristi Bleyer, Kathryn McCarty and Erica Wood, 'Access to Jury for Persons with Disabilities' (1995) 19(2) *Mental and Physical Disability Law Reporter* 249; Ortoleva, 'Inaccessible Justice: Human Rights, Persons with Disabilities and the Legal System', note 4, at 305.

41 Beqiraj, McNamara and Wicks, *Access to Justice for Persons with Disabilities: From International Principles to Practice*, note 5, p. 21.

Rules on the Equalization of Opportunities for Persons with Disabilities (Standard Rules) did not expressly address the concept of 'access to justice'.

Article 13 CRPD (similar to all of the rights spelled out in the Convention) cannot be read in isolation – it must be interpreted in light of the general principles listed in Article 3. Primarily, it must be read in conjunction with the principles of equality and non-discrimination (which, *inter alia*, require States Parties to recognise that all persons with disabilities are equal before and under the law, and are entitled without any discrimination to equal protection and equal benefit of the law).[42] According to Bequiraj et al.:

> when applied to legal proceedings, non-discrimination provisions constitute an important pillar of access to justice for persons with disabilities; that is, in order to enjoy effective access to justice, persons with disabilities must be treated equally before the law and have equal opportunities to participate in the justice system.[43]

The CRPD Committee, in its General Comment No. 6, clarifies that '[t]he rights and obligations with respect to equality and non-discrimination outlined in Article 5 raise particular considerations with respect to Article 13'.[44]

Article 13 is also directly connected to the principle of accessibility. General Comment No. 2 of the CRPD Committee makes clear that '[t]here can be no effective access to justice if buildings of law-enforcement organs and [the] judiciary are [not] physically accessible', nor can there be effective access to justice if the services they provide and information and communications are not accessible.[45] In this respect, the general accessibility obligations laid down in Article 9 CRPD and the requirements of Article 21 CRPD to make information and communications accessible reinforce the obligations provided for in Article 13. The CRPD Committee also affirms that 'in order to provide transparency, a [State Party's] action must ensure that all relevant information is accessible and available and that there is adequate recording and reporting of all relevant claims, cases and court orders'.[46]

Article 31 CRPD is also highly relevant in the context of access to justice. The absence of reliable information, including statistical data, on claimants, victims and offenders with disabilities, as well as on the accessibility of legal procedures, has an adverse impact on access to justice. By contrast, the

[42] Anna Lawson and Eilionóir Flynn, 'Disability and Access to Justice in the European Union: Implications of the UN Convention on the Rights of Persons with Disabilities', in Lisa Waddington, Eilionóir Flynn and Gerard Quinn (eds.), *European Yearbook of Disability Law* (Antwerp/Portland: Intersentia, 2013), vol. 4, pp. 7–44; on the principle of equality see above Chapter 4.

[43] Beqiraj, McNamara and Wicks, *Access to Justice for Persons with Disabilities: From International Principles to Practice*, note 5, p. 15.

[44] CRPD Committee, General Comment No. 6, 26 April 2018, UN Doc. CRPD/C/GC/6, para. 51.

[45] CRPD Committee, General Comment No. 2, 11 April 2014, UN Doc. CRPD/C/GC/2, para. 33.

[46] CRPD Committee, General Comment No. 6, note 44, para. 54.

collection of data prescribed by Article 31 CRPD[47] would enable States Parties to implement justice policies, with a view to giving effect to the obligations laid down in Article 13 CRPD.

4.1.1 *Article 13(1) CRPD*

ARTICLE 13(1) CRPD

1. States Parties shall ensure effective access to justice for persons with disabilities on an equal basis with others, including through the provision of procedural and age-appropriate accommodations, in order to facilitate their effective role as direct and indirect participants, including as witnesses, in all legal proceedings, including at investigative and other preliminary stages.

As noted by Flynn, Article 13(1) is primarily focused on the participation of persons with disabilities in the legal system, including in 'all investigative and preliminary stages'.[48] Article 13 CRPD refers to persons with disabilities as 'direct and indirect' participants in the justice system. Although this phrase is not defined in the text of the Article itself, it seems to enlarge the scope *ratione personae* of the provision to all persons with disabilities who are, to some extent, involved in a particular legal proceeding or have been in contact with the judicial system in some manner. To date, the CRPD Committee has not discussed the personal scope of Article 13 in detail. However, in *Gemma Beasley* v. *Australia*,[49] the Committee clarifies that 'the performance of jury duty is an integral part of the Australian judicial system and, as such, it constitutes "participation" in legal proceedings', thus falling within the realm of Article 13 CRPD.

The obligations laid down in Article 13(1) CRPD are both negative and positive. States Parties must ensure that domestic judicial bodies and private actors (e.g. legal professionals) do not interfere with, or prevent the enjoyment of, access to justice by persons with disabilities. In addition, States Parties are placed under a positive obligation to take action to guarantee that people with disabilities are able to exercise that same right. Figure 7.2 sets out the obligations of States Parties under Article 13(1) CRPD.

The CRPD Committee, in its General Comment No. 6,[50] identifies the main obligations that must be fulfilled in order to ensure effective access to justice and processes for people with disabilities (outlined in Figure 7.3): first, the delivery of accessible information must be ensured; secondly, the recognition

[47] See above Chapter 3. [48] Flynn, 'Article 13: Access to Justice', note 13, p. 285.

[49] CRPD Committee, *Gemma Beasley* v. *Australia*, Communication No. 11/2013, UN Doc. CRPD/C/15/D/11/2013.

[50] CRPD Committee, General Comment No. 6, note 44, para. 51 et seq.

Article 13(1) CRPD	To guarantee effective access to justice on an equal basis with others
	To ensure effective access to justice in all phases of the administration of justice, including at preliminary stages, such as initial investigations
	To ensure that people with disabilities are both direct and indirect participants, including being witnesses
	To provide procedural and age-appropriate accommodations

Figure 7.2 Article 13(1) CRPD and Its Obligations

Delivery of information in an understandable and accessible manner	Recognition and accommodation of diverse forms of communication
Physical accessibility throughout all stages of the process	Financial assistance in the form of legal aid, where applicable

Figure 7.3 Access to Justice According to the CRPD Committee

and accommodation of diverse forms of communication is vital; thirdly, physical accessibility and financial assistance must be provided, where appropriate. According to the CRPD Committee, suitable measures that can protect persons who are unable to defend themselves against discrimination, even when provided with support, are actions in the public interest (*actio popularis*).

Article 13(1) CRPD does not refer explicitly to reasonable accommodation. However, it is clear that the obligation to provide necessary and appropriate adjustments also applies in the context of access to justice. This emerges from the CRPD Committee's decision in *Makarov* v. *Lithuania*.[51] Boris Makarov submitted his communication to the CRPD Committee on behalf of his deceased wife, who suffered multiple disabilities as a consequence of a road accident caused by a third party (V. M.). Mr Makarov claimed, *inter alia*, that

[51] CRPD Committee, *Makarov* v. *Lithuania*, Communication No. 30/2015, UN Doc. CRPD/C/18/D/30/2015.

Ms Makarova was not duly informed about the court proceeding against V. M. and that she was unable to participate in the trial due to the lack of adjustments for her impairments. The CRPD Committee considered the alleged violation of Articles 12 and 13(1) of the Convention. With regard to the latter Article, the CRPD Committee stated that, whilst it was evident that Ms Makarova wanted her position to be heard during the court hearings, 'she was not provided with any form of accommodation to enable her to do so',[52] in violation, *inter alia*, of Article 13(1) CRPD.

Article 13 CRPD refers to procedural and age-appropriate accommodations, which, according to Flynn, might be considered more generic and general (i.e. less individualised) measures than reasonable accommodation. Procedural accommodations must be adopted by States Parties in order to enable the participation of people with disabilities in the justice system.[53] In its General Comment No. 6, the CRPD Committee clarifies that the accommodations mentioned in Article 13 CRPD 'are distinguishable from reasonable accommodation in that procedural accommodations are not limited by disproportionality'[54] (in other words, by the disproportionate/undue burden defence inherent in the reasonable accommodation duty). An illustration of a procedural accommodation, according to the CRPD Committee, 'is the recognition of diverse communication methods of persons with disabilities standing in courts and tribunals'.[55] Age-appropriate accommodations, according to the Committee, 'may consist of disseminating information about available mechanisms to bring complaints forward and access to justice using age-appropriate and plain language'.[56] In the Concluding Observations (COs) on the Latvian initial report, the Committee recommends that Latvia:

> ensure the provision of judicial procedural accommodation, including by means of the Easy Read format, professional sign language interpretation and the use of Braille easy-read format, for all persons with disabilities and establish related safeguards to enable the participation of persons with disabilities in all legal proceedings on an equal basis with others.[57]

In the COs on the initial report of Canada, the Committee urges Canada to 'introduce additional criteria to the provision of accessibility in the justice sector, ensuring that the options available comprise Braille, sign language interpretation, alternative modes of communication and easy-read versions of documents'.[58] Similar statements were included in other COs and, in some

[52] Ibid., para. 7.6.

[53] Flynn, *Disabled Justice? Access to Justice and UN Convention on the Rights of Persons with Disabilities*, note 2, p. 36; on legal capacity see above Chapter 6.

[54] CRPD Committee, General Comment No. 6, note 44, para. 51. [55] Ibid. [56] Ibid.

[57] CRPD Committee, Concluding Observations on the Initial Report of Latvia, 10 October 2017, UN Doc. CRPD/C/LVA/CO/1.

[58] CRPD Committee, Concluding Observations on the Initial Report of Canada, 8 May 2017, UN Doc. CRPD/C/CAN/CO/1.

instances, the Committee mentions the need to ensure the 'availability of non-discriminatory access to assistive technologies'[59] within judicial proceedings.

Despite the Committee's clarification that 'reasonable accommodations' and the 'procedural accommodations' mentioned in Article 13 are distinct concepts, they seem to overlap and are often dealt with together in the Committee's decisions. This is evident in the jurisprudence related to jurors, namely *Gemma Beasley* v. *Australia*[60] and *Michael Lockrey* v. *Australia*[61] (already discussed in Chapter 4).[62] In both individual communications, the authors were Deaf persons who had been summoned to serve as jurors. Gemma Beasley required Australian Sign Language (Auslan) in order to communicate with others and to perform her jury duties, but the public officer advised her that such support could not be provided. Mr Lockrey required real-time steno-captioning, and, due to the fact that this was not available, he was excused from jury service. In summary, both authors claimed violations of various provisions of the CRPD, including Articles 5 and 13 CRPD, on account of being excluded from a jury, *de facto* on the grounds of disability. In both cases, the Committee considered that Australia had violated Article 13 CRPD. In particular, in *Gemma Beasley* v. *Australia*, the decision of the public official not to provide Auslan interpretation was considered to amount to a violation of Article 13(1), read alone and in conjunction with Articles 3, 5(1) and 29(b) of the Convention. In this decision, the Committee states that Auslan interpretation amounts to a reasonable accommodation and that the Australian authorities did not provide adequate justifications as to why it would entail a disproportionate burden. In doing so, the Committee seems not to be fully consistent in the way in which it classifies interpretation in court, which, in the COs mentioned above, is considered as a procedural accommodation that is not subject to the disproportionality test.[63]

DID YOU KNOW THAT ...?

In 2016, the Scottish Courts and Tribunals Service (SCTS), established by the Judiciary and Courts (Scotland) Act 2008, published a consultation paper on how to make jury service more accessible for individuals with sight and/or hearing impairments. It recommended, *inter alia*, that:

[59] CRPD Committee, Concluding Observations on the Initial Report of Bosnia and Herzegovina, 2 May 2017, UN Doc. CRPD/C/BIH/CO/1.

[60] *Gemma Beasley* v. *Australia*, note 45.

[61] CRPD Committee, *Michael Lockrey* v. *Australia*, Communication No. 13/2013, CRPD/C/15/D/13/2016.

[62] Another case concerned the same issue but was declared inadmissible, CRPD Committee, *A. M.* v. *Australia*, Communication No. 12/2013, CRPD/C/13/D/12/2013.

[63] *Gemma Beasley* v. *Australia*, note 45, para 8.5 et seq.

– Jury citation documents be amended to invite potential jurors, including those who have visual or hearing impairments, to contact the court at an early stage, in order to explore accommodations.
– A central point of contact (Juror Liaison Officer) be appointed at each court, who can coordinate juror requests for reasonable accommodations.
– Consideration be given to the use of technologies, e.g. laptops, electronic tablets or iPads, for the purposes of enhancing the presentation of evidence.

(J. Beqiraj, L. McNamara and V. Wicks, *Access to Justice for Persons with Disabilities: From International Principles to Practice*, London: International Bar Association, 2017, p. 28).

The requirement of age-appropriate accommodations in Article 13(1) reflects an intersectional approach to equality and access to justice, and it must be read in conjunction with Article 7 on children with disabilities. It is evident that the Convention attempts to address the increased difficulties encountered by children with disabilities in accessing justice, which were briefly discussed above in section 3.

It has also been argued that Article 13 CRPD should be interpreted as providing for a general right to legal aid.[64] In several COs, the CRPD Committee highlights the need to allocate the necessary human and financial resources to legal aid centres and to provide legal aid to persons with disabilities who live in poverty or in institutions.[65] In general, the Committee seems to acknowledge that a lack of financial resources can pose significant barriers to accessing legal advice and representation, and to ultimately seeking access to justice.

4.1.2 *Article 13(2) CRPD*

ARTICLE 13(2) CRPD

2. In order to help to ensure effective access to justice for persons with disabilities, States Parties shall promote appropriate training for those working in the field of administration of justice, including police and prison staff.

[64] Frances Gibson, 'Article 13 of the Convention on the Rights of Persons with Disabilities – A Right to Legal Aid?' (2010) 15(2) *Australian Journal of Human Rights* 123.

[65] CRPD Committee, Concluding Observations on the Initial Report of Mexico, 26 October 2014, UN Doc. CRPD/C/MEX/CO/1.

Article 13(2) CRPD imposes a positive obligation on States Parties to promote appropriate training for those working in the field of the administration of justice. In its General Comment No. 6, the CRPD Committee adopts a broad interpretation of the term 'administration of justice' in its requirement to ensure training of police and prison staff.

CRPD Committee, General Comment No. 6 on Equality and Non-Discrimination (2018)

55. In order to encourage appropriate respect for and fulfilment of rights and obligations, it is necessary to train law enforcement officers, raise awareness among rights holders and build the capacity of duty bearers. Appropriate training should include:

(a) The complexities of intersectionality and the fact that persons should not be identified purely on the basis of impairment. Awareness-raising on intersectionality issues should be relevant to particular forms of discrimination and oppression;
(b) The diversity among persons with disabilities and their individual requirements in order to gain effective access to all aspects of the justice system on an equal basis with others;
(c) The individual autonomy of persons with disabilities and the importance of legal capacity for all;
(d) The centrality of effective and meaningful communications to successful inclusion; and
(e) Measures adopted to ensure the effective training of personnel, including lawyers, magistrates, judges.

4.2 Article 13 CRPD and Other Provisions: Relationship and Interdependence

Article 13 is intrinsically linked with all of the other rights that are enshrined in the CRPD. However, one of the provisions that is most directly relevant to the relationship between persons with disabilities and the justice system is Article 12 CRPD, which was already discussed in Chapter 6. It is worth noting that the CRPD Committee, in its General Comment No. 1, makes the relationship between Articles 12 and 13 CRPD clear, by stating that:

Article 12 of the Convention guarantees support in the exercise of legal capacity, including the capacity to testify in judicial, administrative and other adjudicative proceedings. Such support could take various forms, including recognition of diverse communication

> Read the text of the CRPD, and identify all of the provisions that are relevant to ensuring effective access to justice for people with disabilities.

methods, allowing video testimony in certain situations, procedural accommodation, the provision of professional sign language interpretation and other assistive methods. The judiciary must also be trained and made aware of their obligation to respect the legal capacity of persons with disabilities, including legal agency and standing.[66]

Articles 14 (on liberty and security), 15 (regarding freedom from torture or cruel, inhuman or degrading treatment or punishment), 16 (concerning freedom from exploitation, violence and abuse) and 17 (protecting the integrity of the person) CRPD are also very relevant, and they must be read in conjunction with Article 13.

Article 14, which is further discussed in section 5 of this chapter, requires States Parties to ensure that persons with disabilities are not deprived of their liberty unlawfully or arbitrarily; that any deprivation of liberty is in conformity with the law; and that the existence of a disability shall in no case justify a deprivation of liberty. The implementation of Article 14 is crucial in ensuring that people with disabilities are not subjected to human rights violations while detained or while residing in institutions. In 2015, the CRPD Committee released guidelines on this provision[67] and affirmed that it is contrary to Article 14 to allow for the involuntary detention of individuals with disabilities based on the perceived danger that such individuals pose to themselves or to others. In those guidelines, the CRPD Committee also clearly established the link between Articles 14 and 19 CRPD (which enshrines the right to independent living).[68] Beqiraj et al. affirm that Articles 14 and 19 CRPD 'codify this changed attitude towards institutionalisation'.[69] In other words, there must be robust procedural safeguards against involuntary placement in an institution, and an effective possibility for judicial review of such placements must exist in the event that they do occur.

[66] CRPD Committee, General Comment No. 1, April 2014, UN Doc. CRPD/C/GC/1, para. 35.

[67] CRPD Committee, Guidelines on Article 14 of the Convention on the Rights of Persons with Disabilities. The Right to Liberty and Security of Persons with Disabilities, adopted during the Committee's 14th session, held in September 2015.

[68] Ibid.

[69] Beqiraj, McNamara and Wicks, *Access to Justice for Persons with Disabilities: From International Principles to Practice*, note 5, p. 24.

Article 15(1) CRPD reaffirms the prohibition of torture and cruel, inhuman, or degrading treatment or punishment, which is already well established in international human rights law, as well as the prohibition of medical or scientific experimentation.[70] Article 15(2) requires that States Parties 'take all effective legislative, administrative, judicial or other measures to prevent persons with disabilities, on an equal basis with others, from being subjected to torture or cruel, inhuman or degrading treatment or punishment'. This implies that, when a violation occurs, States Parties should guarantee that individuals with disabilities have access to adequate redress.

Article 16 directs States Parties to put in place effective legislation and policies, to ensure that exploitation, violence and abuse against people with disabilities are identified, investigated and, where appropriate, prosecuted. It also provides for positive obligations to put an end to and prevent exploitation and abuse through appropriate measures, including judicial remedies.[71]

Article 17 sets out the right of each disabled individual to have his or her physical and mental integrity respected on an equal basis with others. As noted by Keys, this is 'a single-sentence statement and is the only provision in the CRPD that does not include further guidance or elaboration on its meaning'.[72] A comparable provision is contained in Article 3 EU CFR, but there are no similar provisions in the other core UN human rights treaties. The CRPD Committee, when dealing with Article 17, has mainly focused on non-consensual treatment in mental health care and non-consensual sterilisation.[73] Nonetheless, this provision (as well as the prohibition of non-consensual health treatment contained in Article 25 CRPD) is extremely relevant in relation to detention and criminal conviction, as will be discussed below in section 5.

[70] Its formulation is identical to that of Article 7 ICCPR; Antonio Marchesi, 'Article 15: Freedom from Torture or Cruel, Inhuman or Degrading Treatment or Punishment', in Della Fina, Cera and Palmisano (eds.), *The United Nations Convention on Human Rights: A Commentary,* note 13, pp. 307–16.

[71] Antonio Marchesi, 'Article 16: Freedom from Exploitation, Violence and Abuse', in Della Fina, Cera and Palmisano (eds.), *The United Nations Convention on Human Rights: A Commentary,* note 13, pp. 317–25, p. 322. Article 16(3) CRPD imposes an obligation on States Parties to 'ensure that all facilities and programmes designed to serve persons with disabilities are effectively monitored by independent authorities'. According to Laing, effective independent monitoring is a key mechanism to help safeguard people with disabilities from violence, exploitation and abuse. However, Laing suggests that, since the scope of Article 16 extremely wide, States Parties may encounter challenges in achieving effecting monitoring (Judy Laing, 'Preventing Violence, Exploitation and Abuse of Persons with Mental Disabilities: Exploring the Monitoring Implications of Article 16 of the United Nations Convention on the Rights of Persons with Disabilities' (2017) 53 *International Journal of Law and Psychiatry* 27).

[72] Mary Keys, 'Article 17: Protecting the Integrity of the Person', in Della Fina, Cera and Palmisano (eds.), *The United Nations Convention on Human Rights: A Commentary,* note 13, pp. 327–37.

[73] See above Chapter 6.

5 THE CRPD AND THE CRIMINAL JUSTICE SYSTEM

Individuals with disabilities may become involved in criminal proceedings, whether as victims, witnesses or suspects and defendants. There are, however, a number of specific challenges (which the CRPD attempts to confront) associated with the participation of people with disabilities in the criminal justice system.[74] The Convention does not include a specific provision on victims and offenders with disabilities or on the criminal trial itself. Nevertheless, Articles 13, 14, 15 and 16 CRPD include obligations that are relevant to the participation of people with disabilities in the criminal justice system. This section, building on the previous sections, presents these obligations, without discussing in detail each of the provisions (which have been briefly outlined above).

5.1 Victims with Disabilities

The scholarly literature in this area consistently suggests that people with disabilities are more likely to be victims of crimes than non-disabled individuals.[75] The data available confirm this, even though it has been shown that people with disabilities face major difficulties in reporting crimes. Beqiraj et al. affirm that '[t]here is some evidence regarding a disjuncture between victimisation of persons with disabilities and crime reporting rates, which reiterates the invisibility of persons with disabilities at the policy level'.[76] In fact, police stations are often inaccessible, and police officers do not know how to deal with victims with disabilities.[77]

?

DID YOU KNOW THAT ...?

In 2012, the Canadian Human Rights Commission (CHRC) released a Report on Equality Rights of People with Disabilities (www.chrc-ccdp.gc.ca/sites/default/files/rerpd_rdepad-eng.pdf). That report claims that both men and women with disabilities are more likely to be victims of crimes. In particular, it highlights the fact that people with disabilities experience greater emotional or financial abuse by a spouse or partner during their lifetime than people without disabilities. Women with

[74] Tammy Smith et al., 'Individual with Intellectual and Developmental Disabilities in the Criminal Justice System and Implications for Transition Planning' (2008) 43(4) *Education and Training in Developmental Disabilities* 421, at 424.

[75] Edwards, Harold and Kilcommins, *Access to Justice for People with Disabilities as Victims of Crime in Ireland*, note 28, p. 12.

[76] Beqiraj, McNamara and Wicks, *Access to Justice for Persons with Disabilities: From International Principles to Practice*, note 5, p. 45.

[77] Ibid. pp. 30 et seq.

disabilities were significantly more at risk than men with disabilities, and they were also more at risk than men or women without disabilities. There were more hate crimes reported by adults with disabilities compared to adults without disabilities. Women with disabilities reported experiencing proportionally greater levels of violent assault. Individuals with disabilities also reported feeling more vulnerable to crime.

The United States National Crime Victimization Survey (NCVS, www.bjs.gov/index.cfm?ty=pbdetail&iid=5986) highlights that, between 2011 and 2015, the rate of violent victimisation of people with disabilities was at least 2.5 times the unadjusted rate for those without disabilities. The rate of violent victimisation of males with disabilities was 31.8 per 1,000, compared to 14.1 per 1,000 in the case of males without disabilities. For females with disabilities, the rate of violent victimisation was 32.8 per 1,000, compared to 11.4 per 1,000 in the case of females without disabilities.

Article 13 is the core provision of the CRPD with respect to ensuring that victims with disabilities have access to justice. The obligations placed on States Parties aim to tackle barriers in reporting a crime. In that connection, Article 13(2) explicitly mentions training for the police.

CASE STUDY

Singapore's Appropriate Adult Scheme

The Appropriate Adult Scheme was introduced with the aim of assisting people with intellectual disabilities who come into contact with the police. The scheme recognises that persons with disabilities may be especially vulnerable to experiencing distress during police investigations and may, in particular, have difficulties communicating facts. Under the scheme, trained volunteers, otherwise known as 'appropriate adults', are present during the police interview to provide support to persons with disabilities, including bridging communication gaps and providing emotional support. Since January 2015, the scheme has been implemented in all police divisions across Singapore. (Initial Report of Singapore to the CRPD Committee, 30 June 2016, UN Doc. CRPD/C/SGP/1, para. 172).

Articles 15 and 16 CRPD are also relevant with respect to ensuring that victims with disabilities can access justice. As clarified by the CRPD Committee in several COs, both Articles oblige States Parties, to varying extents, to put in place adequate measures to ensure that people with disabilities who are victims of violence or ill-treatment have access to services and information (e.g. hotlines, shelters, victim support services, consultation and counselling), and to effective complaint mechanisms that have a mandate to provide compensation and impose sanctions on perpetrators.[78]

When it comes to the actual criminal process, it has been noted that, in addition to the general barriers already highlighted in section 2 of this chapter, there might be specific procedural barriers associated with the criminal procedure. For example, the common law justice system, in countries such as Ireland, the United Kingdom, the United States, Australia and New Zealand, is based on an adversarial process, in which the principle of orality is key. This, in itself, can disadvantage people with disabilities, who might experience difficulties in communicating in a clear and persuasive manner (especially if the appropriate accommodations are not adopted).[79] As mentioned above, Article 13 CRPD makes clear that procedural accommodations need to be made to allow people with disabilities to testify.

5.2 Offenders with Disabilities

5.2.1 *The CRPD and Criminal Responsibility*

As discussed in Chapter 6 of this textbook, the CRPD does not permit the denial of legal capacity. This poses challenges when it comes to people with disabilities who commit crimes and results in declarations of 'unfitness to stand trial' and/or assessments of criminal non-responsibility. These can give rise to custodial orders or the deprivation of liberty in the form of institutionalisation, for indefinite periods in some instances, which have been deemed contrary to the CRPD. Minkowitz contends that '[i]f persons with disabilities have the legal capacity to act on an equal basis with others, this . . . implies as a corollary the legal responsibility for those consequences on an equal basis with others'. She also relies on the CRPD Committee and asserts that:

> [a]n obligation to eliminate the practice of deeming a person unfit to plead or to stand trial has been found under both Article 13 and Article 14, being derived from the right to have equal substantive and procedural guarantees in a proceeding related to the deprivation of liberty.[80]

The UN Office of the High Commissioner for Human Rights (OHCHR) considers it discriminatory and unlawful to automatically exempt persons with

[78] See e.g. CRPD Committee, Concluding Observations on the Initial Report of Morocco, 25 September 2017, UN Doc. CRPD/C/MAR/CO/1.

[79] Edwards, Harolds and Kilcommins, *Access to Justice for People with Disabilities as Victims of Crime in Ireland*, note 28.

[80] Tina Minkowitz, 'Rethinking Criminal Responsibility From a Critical Disability Perspective: the Abolition of Insanity/Incapacity Acquittals and Unfitness to Plead, and Beyond' (2014) 23 (3) *Griffith Law Review*, 434, at 445 and 447.

disabilities from criminal liability on the basis of disability.[81] The OHCHR affirms that:

> in the area of criminal law, recognition of the legal capacity of persons with disabilities requires abolishing a defence based on the negation of criminal responsibility because of the existence of a mental or intellectual disability. Instead disability-neutral doctrines on the subjective element of the crime should be applied, which take into consideration the situation of the individual defendant.[82]

In the same vein, the CRPD Committee states that:

> ... declarations of unfitness to stand trial or incapacity to be found criminally responsible in criminal justice systems and the detention of persons based on those declarations are contrary to [A]rticle 14 of the Convention ...[83]

Under the CRPD, disability (in particular, psychosocial or intellectual disability) should be deemed immaterial when establishing laws concerning criminal responsibility. However, this position is controversial and other authors claim that, in light of the current overrepresentation of those with psychosocial and intellectual disabilities in our prison population, 'to reduce the scope of our mental condition defences will exacerbate rather than ameliorate the problem'.[84] According to Peay, both the negation of criminal responsibility and a finding of incapability to stand trial expose the individual concerned to a 'highly stigmatic finding' and can place the 'accused person in limbo with respect to the potential non-resolution of their criminal culpability whilst exposing them to compulsory treatment for mental disorder'.[85]

Finally, it must be noted that diversion from the penal system and from penal detention[86] is not considered in breach of the Convention, as such, and the

[81] UN Human Rights Council, *Thematic Study by the Office of the United Nations High Commissioner for Human Rights on Enhancing Awareness and Understanding of the Convention on the Rights of Persons with Disabilities*, 26 January 2009, UN Doc. A/HRC/10/48.

[82] Ibid. para. 47.

[83] CRPD Committee, Guidelines on Article 14 of the Convention on the Rights of Persons with Disabilities, note 67, para. 16.

[84] Jill Peay, 'Mental Incapacity and Criminal Liability: Redrawing the Fault Lines?' (2015) *International Journal of Law and Psychiatry* 25–35, at 26 and literature cited in it.

[85] Ibid. at 26.

[86] O'Mahony defines diversion as 'provisions, processes and initiatives that have a statutory or non-statutory basis that seek to divert defendants and offenders with [mental health problems] and [intellectual disability] from the criminal justice system at all points of contact'. See Charles O'Mahony, 'Diversion: A Comparative Study of Law and Policy Relating to Defendants and Offenders with Mental Health Problems and Intellectual Disability' (2013) PhD thesis, NUI Galway, available at https://aran.library.nuigalway.ie/xmlui/bitstream/handle/10379/4481/Ph.D%20Final%20May%202014%20Charles%20O'Mahony.pdf?sequence=1. See also Charles O'Mahony, 'The Implications of the United Nations Convention on the Rights of Persons with Disabilities on Criminal Responsibility', in Charles O'Mahony and Gerard Quinn (eds.), *Disability Law and Policy: An Analysis of the UN Convention* (Dublin: Clarus Press, 2017), pp. 221–235.

Committee makes it clear that criminal detention should be a last resort, when other programmes, such as restorative justice programmes, are insufficient to deter future crime.[87]

5.2.2 *The CRPD and Involuntary Placement*

The institutionalisation of a person with a disability in a psychiatric institution often arises as a consequence of a declaration of unfitness to stand trial. In some countries, the involuntary placement in institutions of persons with disabilities is carried out when the person is considered to be 'socially dangerous'.[88] These practices are in breach of Article 14 CRPD.

Article 14(1) is very clear in this respect, and, in that regard, it diverges from the 1997 Oviedo Convention, or the Convention on Human Rights and Biomedicine, which openly refers to the possibility of involuntary placement in its Article 7 on the protection of persons who have a mental disorder.

ARTICLE 14(1) CRPD

1. States Parties shall ensure that persons with disabilities, on an equal basis with others:

(a) Enjoy the right to liberty and security of person;
(b) Are not deprived of their liberty unlawfully or arbitrarily, and that any deprivation of liberty is in conformity with the law, and that the existence of a disability shall in no case justify a deprivation of liberty.

The CRPD Committee has clearly affirmed that this provision:

> does not permit any exceptions whereby persons may be detained on the grounds of their actual or perceived impairment. However, legislation of several States [P]arties, including mental health laws, still provide instances in which persons may be detained on the grounds of their actual or perceived impairment, provided there are other reasons for their detention, including that they are deemed dangerous to themselves or others. This practice is incompatible with [A]rticle 14; it is discriminatory in nature and amounts to arbitrary deprivation of liberty.[89]

The Committee has also clarified that involuntary placement of persons with disabilities in psychiatric institutions on health care grounds 'contradicts the

[87] CRPD Committee, Guidelines on Article 14 of the Convention on the Rights of Persons with Disabilities, note 67, para. 21.

[88] See above Chapter 6.

[89] CRPD Committee, Guidelines on article 14 of the Convention on the Rights of Persons with Disabilities, note 67, para. 6.

absolute ban on deprivation of liberty on the basis of impairments' under Article 14(1)(b) as well as the principle of free and informed consent of the person concerned with respect to health care, laid out in Article 25.[90] In the same vein, the Committee has established that the 'involuntary detention of persons with disabilities based on risk or dangerousness . . . is contrary to the right to liberty, and amounts to arbitrary deprivation of liberty'.[91] Despite this absolute ban, several States Parties to the CRPD continue to be in breach of Article 14 and still deprive persons with disabilities of their liberty.[92]

The OHCHR generally endorses the stance adopted by the CRPD Committee with regard to Article 14 CRPD and, on multiple occasions, has reaffirmed that it does not permit any exceptions whereby persons may be detained on the grounds of their actual or perceived disability.[93]

CASE STUDY

Hospitals for Persons with Psychosocial Disabilities in Oman

Under Oman's Basic Law, a citizen's personal liberty is safeguarded and may not be infringed, and no citizen may be detained without the authorisation or decision of a competent court. Illegal detention and illegal deprivation or restriction of a citizen's personal liberty by other means are prohibited, as is the illegal searching of a citizen's person. No individual may use violence, threats or methods involving the restriction of personal liberty to coerce a person with a disability to do labour.

As highlighted by a World Health Organization (WHO) report (www.who.int/mental_health/who_aims_oman_report.pdf), government agencies, NGOs, professional associations and international agencies have promoted public education and awareness-raising campaigns on mental health, and there is a permanent psychiatrist working in Omani prisons.

However, the CRPD Committee, in its COs on the Initial Report of Oman expresses concern about detentions based on impairment as well as the forced institutionalisation of persons with disabilities, especially those with psychosocial and/or intellectual disabilities, and about the condition of 'mental hospitals' currently operating in Oman. The Committee also expresses

[90] Ibid. para. 10. [91] Ibid.

[92] In its COs on the Initial Report of Australia, the CRPD Committee urged the State Party to 'review its laws that allow for the deprivation of liberty on the basis of disability, including psychosocial or intellectual disabilities, and repeal provisions that authori[s]e involuntary internment linked to an apparent or diagnosed disability'. See CRPD Committee, Concluding Observations on the Initial Report of Australia, 24 October 2013, UN Doc. CRPD/C/AUS/CO/1, para. 32(c).

[93] United Nations Office of the High Commissioner of Human Rights (OHCHR), *Statement on Article 14 of the Convention on the Rights of Persons with Disabilities* (2014), available at www.ohchr.org/EN/NewsEvents/Pages/DisplayNews.aspx?NewsID=15183.

concern about the number of patients admitted to the Ibn Sina Hospital without their free and informed consent (CRPD Committee, COs on the Initial Report of Oman, 17 April 2018, UN Doc. CRPD/C/OMN/CO/1, para. 29).

Some scholars advance a less restrictive interpretation of Article 14 CRPD than that advanced by the OHCHR and the CRPD Committee, highlighted above. For example, Seatzu contends that 'an involuntary placement of a person with disabilities could be deemed compatible with Article 14 [CRPD] if it is reali[s]ed in a disability-neutral situation, for instance, if the involuntary [placement] is linked *in concreto* to the defen[c]e of public order'.[94] These interpretations, however, seem to fall short of the standard set out in the authoritative interpretation of the Committee, which has been quite clear on the absolute ban on involuntary placement and on detention based on presumptions of risk or dangerousness.

5.3 Persons with Disabilities in Detention

If people with disabilities are considered responsible for crimes and held in detention, they must be guaranteed adequate conditions and reasonable accommodation. The key provision in this respect is Article 14(2) CRPD.

ARTICLE 14(2) CRPD

States Parties shall ensure that if persons with disabilities are deprived of their liberty through any process, they are, on an equal basis with others, entitled to guarantees in accordance with international human rights law and shall be treated in compliance with the objectives and principles of this Convention, including by provision of reasonable accommodation.

Failure to provide reasonable accommodation for persons in detention arguably amounts to ill-treatment and, ultimately, to a breach of the CRPD. Lawson recalls that the link between reasonable accommodation and ill-treatment in prison was recognised in 2008 by the UN Special Rapporteur on Torture and Other Cruel, Inhuman or Degrading Treatment or Punishment,

[94] Francesco Seatzu, 'Article 14: Liberty and Security of the Person', in Della Fina, Cera and Palmisano (eds.), *The United Nations Convention on Human Rights: A Commentary*, note 13, pp. 295–306, p. 299.

who observed that 'the lack of reasonable accommodation in detention facilities may increase the risk of exposure to neglect, violence, abuse, torture and ill-treatment'.[95]

In April 2014, in *X* v. *Argentina*, the CRPD Committee considered whether Argentina had violated its obligations under the Convention in respect of a person with a disability serving a custodial sentence.[96] The author of the individual communication, Mr X, was held in pre-trial detention in connection with an allegation against him before the Federal Criminal Court. During his detention he suffered a stroke, which caused various impairments. He was authorised to start an in-patient rehabilitation programme, but he was refused house arrest several times. He was then transferred to an inaccessible prison hospital, unsuitable for a disabled person. The accommodations made by the prison authorities were, in fact, insufficient, because the bathroom was too small and could not be accessed using a wheelchair. The author also alleged that there was a lack of assistance and substandard conditions of detention. The CRPD Committee upheld the claims of the applicant, and it ruled that Argentina had failed to fulfil its obligations under Article 14(2) CRPD (and Article 9). In addition, the Committee made it clear that:

> in light of the lack of accessibility and a sufficient degree of reasonable accommodation, the author has been placed in substandard conditions of detention that are incompatible with the right set forth in [A]rticle 17 of the Convention.[97]

Article 14(2) is a core CRPD provision that seeks to protect people with disabilities from ill-treatment in detention,[98] which is also prohibited by other international treaties. For example, besides Article 14 CRPD, Article 3 ECHR had provided an early ground for the judicial development of the concept of reasonable accommodation in prisons. As will be discussed in Chapter 13, various judgments of the European Court of Human Rights (ECtHR or Strasbourg Court) classify the inadequate conditions of detention of prisoners with disabilities as being in violation of Article 3 ECHR. In those cases, the Strasbourg Court recognises the general duty of Contracting States to the ECHR to provide accessible prison settings, alongside the obligation to take all

95 Anna Lawson, 'Disability Equality, Reasonable Accommodation and the Avoidance of Ill-Treatment in Places of Detention: The Role of Supranational Monitoring and Inspection Bodies' (2012) 16(6) *The International Journal of Human Rights* 845, at 851.

96 CRPD Committee, *X* v. *Argentina*, Communication No. 8/2012, UN Doc. CRPD/C/11/D/8/2012.

97 Ibid. para. 8(6).

98 Article 14(2) CRPD must be accompanied by monitoring and review mechanisms in relation to persons with disabilities who have been deprived of their liberty. This has been clearly affirmed by the CRPD Committee, which has also referred to Article 16(3) CRPD. The latter provision explicitly involves monitoring all facilities and programmes that serve persons with disabilities in order to prevent all forms of exploitation, violence and abuse. See CRPD Committee, Guidelines on Article 14 of the Convention on the Rights of Persons with Disabilities, note 67, para. 19.

'reasonable steps' to address the needs of disabled detainees. The most relevant decision is *Price* v. *United Kingdom*[99] in which, for the first time, the ECtHR acknowledged that reasonable accommodation is an essential element in protecting human dignity and preventing inhuman treatment.[100] The facts of the case concern the inadequate conditions of detention of Ms Price, a severely disabled woman who also suffered from a serious kidney condition. During her stay in prison, she had to sleep in her wheelchair, and she had serious difficulties in using the toilet facilities, which substantially aggravated her physical situation. The ECtHR held that the conditions in which Ms Price was detained amounted to degrading treatment, notwithstanding any evidence of an intention to humiliate her.[101] The Strasbourg Court, thus, addressed the failure to accommodate her needs in a prison setting. This approach is similar to the one adopted by the CRPD Committee in *X* v. *Argentina*,[102] and it sits well with the interpretation given to Article 14(2) CRPD. However, while the ECtHR, in *Price*, identified reasonable accommodation as a component of the prohibition of ill-treatment, the CRPD Committee, in line with the wording of Article 14 CRPD, considers reasonable accommodation as an autonomous obligation with a cross-cutting nature. The concept of 'reasonable accommodation' in places of detention has also been recalled by the ECtHR in many other cases, which will be analysed in Chapter 13.

SUMMARY

- **The concept of 'access to justice' is characterised by procedural and substantive dimensions. The former is linked to the processes through which claims are adjudicated. The latter is linked to the very idea of equality and to the need to redress the disadvantage experienced by persons with disabilities.**
- **Prior to the entry into force of the CRPD, there was no specific articulation of the right to access justice. This right can, nevertheless, be traced back to Article 8 UDHR, which states that '[e]veryone has the right to an effective remedy by the competent national tribunals for acts violating the fundamental rights guaranteed**

[99] European Court of Human Rights (ECtHR), *Price* v. *United Kingdom*, Application No. 33394/96, 10 July 2001.

[100] Lawson, 'Disability Equality, Reasonable Accommodation and the Avoidance of Ill-Treatment in Places of Detention: The Role of Supranational Monitoring and Inspection Bodies', note 95. On involuntary detention in the ECHR and on the interpretation of Article 5 ECHR in light of Article 14 CRPD, see Suzanne Doyle, 'Article 14 of the UN Convention on the Rights of Persons with Disabilities in light of Article 5 of the European Convention on Human Rights: The Challenge for Council of Europe Member States regarding the Involuntary Detention of Persons with Mental Disabilities', in Charles O'Mahony and Gerard Quinn, Disability Law and Policy: An Analysis of the UN Convention (Dublin: Clarus Press, 2017), pp. 161–163.

[101] *Price* v. *United Kingdom*, note 99, para. 30.

[102] *X* v. *Argentina*, note 96.

to him by the constitution or by law', and to Article 10 UDHR, which establishes the right to a fair hearing.

- Several types of barriers make it impossible for people with disabilities to claim and to vindicate their rights. When it comes to normative barriers, the most obvious ones take the form of laws that limit or remove legal capacity. There are also physical barriers in terms of access to legal information, which is a crucial aspect when seeking a judicial remedy. Another quite typical barrier is the difficulty of finding legal professionals who have knowledge of disability issues and awareness of disability rights.
- When a court proceeding is commenced, people with disabilities might face procedural barriers, being denied the possibility to communicate with the court, officers of the court, and with everyone else who has a role in the justice system.
- Article 13 CRPD requires that States Parties ensure that domestic judicial bodies and private actors (e.g. legal professionals) do not interfere with or prevent the enjoyment of access to justice by persons with disabilities.
- Article 13 CRPD does not explicitly refer to the duty to reasonably accommodate. However, it is clear that the general obligation to provide necessary and appropriate adjustments also applies in the context of access to justice. Article 13(1) CRPD refers, instead, to procedural and age-appropriate accommodations, which might be considered more generic and general (i.e. less individualised) measures to be adopted by States Parties, in order to enable the participation of people with disabilities in the justice system.
- Articles 14 (on liberty and security), 15 (regarding freedom from torture or cruel, inhuman or degrading treatment or punishment), 16 (concerning freedom from exploitation, violence and abuse), and 17 (protecting the integrity of the person) CRPD are also very relevant, and they must be read in conjunction with Article 13.
- Article 14 CRPD requires States Parties to ensure that people with disabilities are not deprived of their liberty unlawfully or arbitrarily, and that any deprivation of liberty is in conformity with the law. It also mandates that the existence of a disability shall in no case justify a deprivation of liberty. The implementation of Article 14 is crucial in ensuring that persons with disabilities are not subjected to human rights violations while detained or while residing in institutions.
- If people with disabilities are considered responsible for crimes and held in detention, they must be guaranteed adequate conditions and reasonable accommodation.

ACTIVITIES

QUESTIONS

1. What barriers do people with disabilities experience in accessing justice?
2. What obligations are included in Article 13 CRPD, and what is the role of reasonable accommodation in ensuring access to justice?
3. Why is the implementation of Article 14 CRPD important in the context of detention of persons with disabilities?

ESSAY QUESTIONS

1. **Discuss the consequences of people with disabilities being excluded from participation in the justice system, and reflect on how Article 13 CRPD can be used to advance access to justice in domestic policy frameworks.**
2. **'Article 14 CRPD does not permit any exceptions whereby individuals may be detained on the grounds of their actual or perceived impairment.' *Discuss.***

GROUP PROJECT

Francis is deaf and, while visiting a friend in Beautiful Town in Freedonia, she witnesses a car being stolen. She clearly sees a man tampering with the car and breaking the glass. She goes to the police of Beautiful Town to report the incident. She is told that, because she is deaf, they cannot take her statement. She offers to write her statement down, but she is then told that her written statement holds no legal value.

Discuss the group project, taking into account the fact that Freedonia is a State Party to the CRPD.

FURTHER READING

Arstein-Kerslake, A. et al., 'Human Rights and Unfitness to Plead: The Demands of the Convention on the Rights of Persons with Disabilities' (2017) 17(3) *Human Rights Law Review* 399–419.

Beqiraj, J., McNamara, L. and Wicks, V., *Access to Justice for Persons with Disabilities: From International Principles to Practice* (London: International Bar Association, 2017).

Chandler, K., White, B. and Willmott, L., 'Safeguarding Rights to Liberty and Security where People with Disability are Subject to Detention and Restraint: A Rights-based Approach (Part One)' (2018) 25(3) *Psychiatry, Psychology and Law* 465–84.

Flynn, E., 'Making Human Rights Meaningful for People with Disabilities: Advocacy, Access to Justice and Equality before the Law' (2013) 4 *International Journal of Human Rights* 491–510.

Gooding, P. et al., 'Unfitness to Stand Trial and the Indefinite Detention of Persons with Cognitive Disabilities in Australia: Human Rights Challenges and Proposals for Change' (2017) 40 *Melbourne University Law Review* 816–65.

Gooding, P. and Bennet, T., 'The Abolition of the Insanity Defense in Sweden and the United Nations Convention on the Rights of Persons with Disabilities: Human Rights Brinksmanship or Evidence It Won't Work?' (2018) 21(1) *New Criminal Law Review: An International and Interdisciplinary Journal* 141–69.

Hepner, I., Woodward, M. N. and Stewart, J., 'Giving the Vulnerable a Voice in the Criminal Justice System: The Use of Intermediaries with Individuals with Intellectual Disability' (2015) 22 *Psychiatry, Psychology and Law* 453–64.

Hyun, E., Lyndsey, H. and McConnell, D., 'Experiences of People with Learning Disabilities in the Criminal Justice System' (2014) 4 *British Journal of Learning Disabilities* 308–14.

Keilty, J. and Connelly, G., 'Making a Statement: An Exploratory Study of Barriers Facing Women with an Intellectual Disability when Making a Statement about Sexual Assault to Police' (2010) 16(2) *Disability and Society* 273–91.

Lawson, A., 'Disability Equality, Reasonable Accommodation and the Avoidance of Ill-Treatment in Places of Detention: the Role of Supranational Monitoring and Inspection Bodies' (2012) 16(6) *The International Journal of Human Rights* 845–64.

Lawson, A. and Flynn, E., 'Disability and Access to Justice in the European Union: Implications of the UN Convention on the Rights of Persons with Disabilities', in L. Waddington, G. Quinn and E. Flynn (eds.), *European Yearbook of Disability Law* (Antwerp/Portland: Intersentia, 2013), vol. 4, pp. 7–44.

MDAC, Access to Justice for Children with Mental Disabilities: International Standards and Findings from Ten EU Member States (2015), available at www.mdac.org/sites/mdac.info/files/access_to_justice_children_ws2_standards_and_findings_english.pdf.

Ortoleva, S., 'Inaccessible Justice: Human Rights, Persons with Disabilities and the Legal System' (2011) 17 *ILSA Journal of International and Comparative Law* 281–320.

8 The Right to Work of Persons with Disabilities

LEARNING OUTCOMES

- ✓ Understand the importance of the right to work in ensuring full and effective participation in society for persons with disabilities.
- ✓ Comprehend the challenges and the barriers faced by people with disabilities in the workplace.
- ✓ Delineate the key obligations set out in Article 27 CRPD.
- ✓ Understand the importance of the reasonable accommodation duty in the employment context.
- ✓ Demonstrate awareness of the importance of positive action in the employment context.
- ✓ Identify the characteristics of and the challenges inherent to sheltered employment.
- ✓ Comprehend the significance of Article 27 CRPD in the overall disability rights agenda.
- ✓ Demonstrate awareness of the good practices exhibited by States Parties in overcoming barriers that hinder access to employment for people with disabilities.

Including persons with disabilities as employees, customers and business partner is clearly the smart thing to do from a business point of view. Yet, while companies increasingly recognize the benefits of building and retaining diverse workforces, they often neglect disability in their inclusion practices.[1]

1 INTRODUCTION

Across the globe, unemployment rates for people with disabilities of working age are higher than those for people who have no disability.[2] In 2010, the Organisation for Economic Co-operation and Development (OECD) issued a report,[3] which affirmed that people with disabilities are under-represented in the workforce in all OECD countries. The Thematic Study on Work and Employment of Persons with Disabilities,[4] published by the Office of the United Nations High Commissioner for Human Rights (OHCHR) in 2012, confirmed that people with disabilities are far less likely to be in work than non-disabled individuals and that, when they are employed, they are more likely to be in low paying jobs, at lower levels of the workforce and working under poor conditions. The OECD indicates that slightly less than half of working-age individuals with disabilities are economically inactive. Access to the labour market remains one of the main challenges for people with disabilities, and the recent economic crisis has only aggravated their employment situation. This trend is also visible in the EU, where the 2011 EU Labour force survey (LFS-AHM) shows that the employment rate of people with basic activity difficulties in the EU-28 was 47.3 per cent, almost 20 percentage points below that of people without such difficulties.[5] In turn, the low employment rates experienced by people with disabilities contribute to the high rate

[1] Work in Progress, 'Embracing Disability as a Diversity Factor in the 21st Century's World of Work' (4 December 2017), available at https://iloblog.org/2017/12/04/embracing-disability-as-a-diversity-factor-in-the-21st-centurys-world-of-work/.

[2] See data reported at www.un.org/development/desa/disabilities/resources/factsheet-on-persons-with-disabilities/disability-and-employment.html.

[3] Organisation for Economic Co-operation and Development (OECD), 'Sickness, Disability and Work: Breaking the Barriers: A Synthesis of Findings across OECD Countries – Key Trends and Outcomes in Sickness and Disability' (2010) available at www.oecd.org/els/soc/46488022.pdf.

[4] Office of the United Nations High Commissioner for Human Rights (OHCHR), *Thematic Study on the Work and Employment of Persons with Disabilities. Report of the Office of the United Nations High Commissioner for Human Rights* (17 December 2012), available at www.ohchr.org/Documents/Issues/Disability/A-HRC-22-25_en.pdf.

[5] Eurostat, 'Disability Statistics – Labour Market Access' (July 2014), available at http://ec.europa.eu/eurostat/statistics-explained/index.php?title=Disability_statistics_-_labour_market_access.

of poverty of households headed by disabled individuals.[6] Sainsbury and Coleman-Fountain note that '[t]he marginali[s]ation of disabled people in employment has become a concern because it creates structural and social costs including high benefit levels and health and social inequalities, a major expenditure for state budgets in a period of economic decline'.[7]

It is widely acknowledged that people with disabilities face multiple barriers in accessing and retaining employment, in the form of: stigma and prejudices related to a fear of lack of productivity of disabled employees, lack of accessible workplaces and/or lack of reasonable accommodation. To counteract these negative factors and to promote the right to work of persons with disabilities, an 'enterprise culture', which improves workforce inclusion and enhances accessibility in the workplace, is essential. Public policies, including active labour market policies, can encourage companies to foster new ideas and solutions on accessibility and universal design (UD), which are designed to benefit workers with disabilities but which actually have potential benefits for all workers.

The CRPD has played a vital role in prompting public policies aimed at ensuring the right to work of people with disabilities and at urging public and private entities to develop accessibility and reasonable accommodation practices. Article 27 CRPD is central in this respect, as it enshrines the right to work and employment without any discrimination, and it contributes to the enjoyment of other substantive rights in the CRPD, including the right to live independently and be included in the community.

This chapter focuses on Article 27 CRPD. Further to this introduction, section 2 briefly discusses the right to work in international human rights law. Section 3 provides an overview of the obligations imposed on States Parties to the Convention under Article 27. Section 4 analyses the role of reasonable accommodation and accessibility in employment settings, building, in particular, upon the discussion on reasonable accommodations in Chapter 4 of this textbook. Section 5 reflects on sheltered and supported employment, and their compatibility with the CRPD, while section 6 examines active labour market policies, including quota systems and other positive measures.

6 IDA contribution to the OHCHR, *Thematic Study on the Work and Employment of Persons with Disabilities. Report of the Office of the United Nations High Commissioner for Human Rights*, note 4, available at www.ohchr.org/EN/Issues/Disability/Pages/WorkAndEmployment.aspx.

7 Roy Sainsbury and Edmund Coleman-Fountain, 'Diversity and Change of the Employment Prospects of Persons with Disabilities: The Impact of Redistributive and Regulatory Provisions in a Multilevel Framework' (2014), available at http://discit.eu/publications; see also Roy Sainsbury and Edmund Coleman-Fountain, 'How to Enhance Active Citizenship for Persons with Disabilities in Europe through Labour Market Participation?' (2015), available at http://discit.eu/publications.

2 SETTING THE SCENE: THE RIGHT TO WORK IN INTERNATIONAL HUMAN RIGHTS LAW

The right to work is a long-established right in international human rights law. Article 23 of the Universal Declaration of Human Rights (UDHR) affirms that:

> [e]veryone has the right to work, to free choice of employment, to just and favourable conditions of work and to protection against unemployment. Everyone, without discrimination, has the right to equal pay for equal work. Everyone who works has the right to just and favourable remuneration ensuring for himself and his family an existence worthy of human dignity, and supplemented, if necessary, by other means of social protection. Everyone has the right to form and to join trade unions for the protection of his interests.

In a similar manner to Article 23 UDHR, the International Covenant on Economic, Social and Cultural Rights (ICESCR) includes a number of important provisions relating to the right to work and equal employment opportunities. Articles 6, 7 and 8 ICESCR address the rights to gain a living, to just and favourable conditions and to form trade unions, respectively. In relation to the application of these rights to people with disabilities, General Comment No. 5 of the UN Committee on Economic, Social and Cultural Rights (CESCR) addresses some of the barriers faced by people with disabilities, such as disability-based discrimination in the field of employment and the limited work opportunities available to disabled individuals. That General Comment also highlights the need for States Parties to the ICESCR to ensure that people with disabilities can consult regularly with representative organisations of persons with disabilities on employment and other matters.

Other international human rights treaties and regional instruments, such as the European Social Charter (ESC),[8] include provisions protecting the right to work. The Standard Rules for the Equalization on Opportunities for Persons with Disabilities[9] (Standard Rules) cover the right to work in Rule No. 7, which requires UN Member States to recognise 'the principle that persons with disabilities must be empowered to exercise their human rights, particularly in the field of employment'. Rule No. 7 further provides that, in both rural and urban areas, people with disabilities 'must have equal opportunities for productive and gainful employment in the labour market'.

In addition, as discussed above in Chapter 2, the right to work has also been elaborated on by the International Labour Organization (ILO), the UN agency that sets labour standards and develops policies and programmes promoting the right to work. The ILO has drafted comprehensive instruments regarding

[8] European Social Charter of 18 October 1961, in force 26 February 1965, ETS No. 35. For further discussion, see Chapter 13.

[9] See above Chapter 2.

the work-related rights of people with disabilities. The Vocational Rehabilitation (Disabled) Recommendation No. 99 of 1955[10] provides guidance for national legislation concerning vocational training and placement of persons with disabilities. The Social Security (Minimum Standards) Convention No. 102[11] requires the authorities of States Parties that are tasked with administering medical care to cooperate with general vocational rehabilitation services, to allow persons with disabilities to return to suitable work.[12] The most prominent ILO documents are Convention No. 159[13] Concerning Vocational Rehabilitation and Employment (Disabled Persons) (1983), and Recommendation No. 168 concerning Vocational Rehabilitation and Employment (Disabled Persons) (1983).[14] As highlighted in Chapter 2, Convention No. 159 requires States Parties to formulate, implement and periodically review policies on vocational rehabilitation and employment of disabled persons. The types of measures that are called for under those instruments include government support in order to eliminate the potential exploitation of disabled people in the context of vocational training and sheltered employment. Recommendation No. 168 is informed by the principle of equality, and it establishes, *inter alia*, that people with disabilities shall enjoy equality of opportunity and treatment in respect of access to, retention of and advancement in employment.

The ILO has also released a series of studies aimed at providing guidance on inclusive practices in employment contexts. Particularly relevant in this respect is the ILO Code of Practice on Managing Disability in the Workplace, published in 2002.[15] That code aims 'to guide employers – be they large, medium-sized or small enterprises, in the private or public sector, in developing or highly industriali[s]ed countries – to adopt a positive strategy in managing disability related issues in the workplace'.[16] While addressed to employers, the Code of Practice is an essential instrument for public authorities, which provide the legislative framework for promoting equal opportunities and equal treatment in the workplace.[17]

[10] International Labour Organization, Vocational Rehabilitation (Disabled) Recommendation No. 99, Geneva, 22 June 1955.

[11] International Labour Convention No. 102 concerning Minimum Standards of Social Security, 28 June 1952, in force 27 April 1955.

[12] Ibid. Article 35.

[13] International Labour Organization, International Labour Convention No. 159 concerning Vocational Rehabilitation and Employment (Disabled Persons), Geneva, 20 June 1983.

[14] International Labour Organization, Recommendation No. 168 concerning Vocational Rehabilitation and Employment (Disabled Persons), Geneva, 20 June 1983.

[15] International Labour Organization, 'ILO Code of Practice: Managing Disability in the Workplace' (13 February 2002), available at https://www.ilo.org/skills/pubs/WCMS_103324/lang-en/index.htm.

[16] Ibid. p. 6.

[17] Arthur O'Reilly, *The Right to Decent Work of Persons with Disabilities* (Geneva: ILO Publications, 2007), p. 109.

DID YOU KNOW THAT ...?

There are also networks and international initiatives that involve companies. The ILO Global Business and Disability Network (http://www.businessanddisability.org/) is a network of multinational enterprises, employers' organisations business networks and disabled persons' organisations that share knowledge and identify good practices. The ILO Global Business and Disability Network also helps companies to build their technical expertise on disability issues. It has several key objectives:

i. **Promoting and respecting the rights of persons with disabilities by raising awareness and combating stigma and stereotypes faced by persons with disabilities.**
ii. **Developing policies and practices that protect persons with disabilities from all types of discrimination.**
iii. **Promoting equal treatment and equal opportunities for persons with disabilities, by providing reasonable accommodation in the recruitment process, on-the-job, during apprenticeships, during training, during job retention, throughout career development and with regard to other relevant terms and conditions of employment.**
iv. **Progressively making companies' premises and communications to staff accessible for all employees with disabilities.**
v. **Undertaking appropriate measures to enable current employees who acquire a disability to retain or return to their employment.**

3 ARTICLE 27 CRPD

This section briefly discusses how the right to work is guaranteed in the CRPD and identifies the most relevant obligations set out in Article 27 of the Convention.

3.1 The Scope of the Right to Work in the CRPD

ARTICLE 27 CRPD

1. States Parties recogni[s]e the right of persons with disabilities to work, on an equal basis with others; this includes the right to the opportunity to gain a living by work freely chosen or accepted in a labour market and work environment that is open, inclusive and accessible to persons with disabilities.

States Parties shall safeguard and promote the reali[s]ation of the right to work, including for those who acquire a disability during the course of employment, by taking appropriate steps, including through legislation, to, *inter alia*:

(a) Prohibit discrimination on the basis of disability with regard to all matters concerning all forms of employment, including conditions of recruitment, hiring and employment, continuance of employment, career advancement and safe and healthy working conditions;
(b) Protect the rights of persons with disabilities, on an equal basis with others, to just and favourable conditions of work, including equal opportunities and equal remuneration for work of equal value, safe and healthy working conditions, including protection from harassment, and the redress of grievances;
(c) Ensure that persons with disabilities are able to exercise their labour and trade union rights on an equal basis with others;
(d) Enable persons with disabilities to have effective access to general technical and vocational guidance programmes, placement services and vocational and continuing training;
(e) Promote employment opportunities and career advancement for persons with disabilities in the labour market, as well as assistance in finding, obtaining, maintaining and returning to employment;
(f) Promote opportunities for self-employment, entrepreneurship, the development of cooperatives and starting one's own business;
(g) Employ persons with disabilities in the public sector;
(h) Promote the employment of persons with disabilities in the private sector through appropriate policies and measures, which may include affirmative action programmes, incentives and other measures;
(i) Ensure that reasonable accommodation is provided to persons with disabilities in the workplace;
(j) Promote the acquisition by persons with disabilities of work experience in the open labour market;
(k) Promote vocational and professional rehabilitation, job retention and return-to-work programmes for persons with disabilities.

2. States Parties shall ensure that persons with disabilities are not held in slavery or in servitude, and are protected, on an equal basis with others, from forced or compulsory labour.

Article 27 CRPD establishes the legal framework containing States Parties' obligations in relation to work and employment of persons with disabilities. It aims to guarantee the right to work and employment of persons with disabilities in the open labour market on an equal basis with others, and it details the types of measures that are necessary to ensure access without discrimination for persons with disabilities to the open labour market and to ensure their equal participation. Ferri and Lawson comment on the 'breadth of coverage' of Article 27.[18] They point to the fact that the scope of Article 27 is 'wide', extending to 'general technical and vocational guidance programmes, placement services and vocational and continuing training' and 'labour and trade union rights'. It also extends to 'self-employment, entrepreneurship, ... cooperatives and ... one's own business'.[19] In addition, Article 27 extends to all stages of employment, including conditions of recruitment, continuance of employment, career advancement and safe and healthy working conditions. Notably, as pointed out in previous chapters of this textbook, the Convention imposes obligations on States Parties, who are the duty-bearers under international law. This means that private employers are not direct duty-bearers under the Convention. Notwithstanding this, States Parties must ensure that the actions of the private sector are in compliance with the CRPD. This implies that both public and private employers are required to take positive measures to ensure inclusion of persons with disabilities in the workforce.

Ferraina claims that Article 27 'cross-[references] the prescriptions of the ICESCR, though not in an exhaustive way, as it intends by no means to replace the ICESCR', but, according to her, Article 27 stresses 'the importance of applying a disability lens in the field of work'.[20] That Article goes far beyond the prescriptions of pre-existing international human rights provisions that enshrine the right to work.

3.2 Key Obligations under Article 27 CRPD

Pursuant to Article 27 CRPD, States Parties recognise the right of persons with disabilities to work on an equal basis with others. The key underlying premise of Article 27 is that States Parties must ensure that disabled persons have the opportunity to gain a living by work freely chosen or accepted in a labour market and work environment that is 'open, inclusive and accessible' to people with disabilities. This entails several key obligations.

Article 27(1)(a) requires States Parties to prohibit discrimination on the basis of disability with regard to all matters in employment. Notably, Article 27(1)(a)

[18] Delia Ferri and Anna Lawson, *Reasonable Accommodation for Disabled People in Employment: A Legal Analysis of the Situation in EU Member States, Iceland, Liechtenstein and Norway* (Luxembourg: Publications Office of the European Union, 2016), p. 43.

[19] Ibid.

[20] Sabrina Ferraina, 'Analysis of the Legal Meaning of Article 27 of the UN CRPD: Key Challenges for Adapted Work Settings' (2012) *Cornell University ILR School Gladnet Collection*, p. 10, available at https://digitalcommons.ilr.cornell.edu/cgi/viewcontent.cgi?referer=https://www.google.de/&httpsredir=1&article=1559&context=gladnetcollect.

covers all forms of employment. Broad language was chosen specifically by the drafters of the Convention in order to indicate that Article 27 covers the public and private sectors, the non-profit sector, sheltered workshops and other alternative types of employment. Thus, the prohibition of discrimination applies to all of these sectors. The situations in which discrimination can occur are wide-ranging, as envisaged by Article 27(1)(a) – discrimination can arise when disabled people are being recruited or hired but also in the course or continuance of employment, during career advancement/promotion, and so forth. Discrimination is, therefore, prohibited at all stages of the employment relationship. In this respect, Fasciglione notes that the prohibition of discrimination covers:

> recruitment processes such as advertising, interviewing and other selection processes; review of hiring standards to remove indirect discrimination that places persons with disabilities at a disadvantage; recruitment decisions; terms and conditions of employment such as remuneration rates, work hours and leave; promotion, transfer, training or other benefits associated with employment, or dismissal or any other detriment, such as demotion or retrenchment; [and] benefits related to the (non-discriminatory) termination of employment.[21]

Notably, while the full realisation of economic, social and cultural rights, including the right to work, is to be realised progressively under Article 4(2) CRPD (subject to the maximum of a State Party's available resources), the prohibition of discrimination on the basis of disability is an obligation having immediate effect. This includes the duty to provide a reasonable accommodation.

Article 27(1)(b) requires States Parties to ensure that conditions of work for persons with disabilities are just and favourable. This means that States Parties must provide equal opportunities and equal remuneration for work of equal value, as well as safe and healthy working conditions, including protection from harassment, and the redress of grievances.[22] Notably, the CRPD Committee requires States Parties to 'ensure that persons with disabilities are paid no less than the minimum wage and do not lose the benefit of disability allowances when they start work'.[23] States Parties are also 'obliged to ensure equal and effective access to benefits and entitlements, such as retirement or unemployment benefits. Such entitlements must not be

[21] Marco Fasciglione, 'Article 27 of the CRPD and the Right of Inclusive Employment of People with Autism', in Valentina Della Fina and Rachele Cera (eds.), *Protecting the Rights of People with Autism in the Fields of Education and Employment* (Cham: Springer, 2015), pp. 145–70, p. 147. See also Marco Fasciglione, 'Article 27: The Right to Work', in Valentina Della Fina, Rachele Cera and Giuseppe Palmisano (eds.), *The United Nations Convention on the Rights of Persons with Disabilities: A Commentary* (Cham: Springer, 2017), pp. 496–508.

[22] Ibid.

[23] CRPD Committee, General Comment No. 6, 26 April 2018, UN Doc. CRPD/C/GC/6, para. 67(c).

infringed upon by exclusion from employment, thereby further exacerbating the situation of exclusion'.[24]

According to Article 27(1)(c), States Parties are required to ensure that people with disabilities are able to exercise their labour and trade union rights on an equal basis with others. This provision is linked to the principle of participation in society and must be read in conjunction with Article 4(3) of the Convention.

Article 27(1)(d) obliges States Parties to enable persons with disabilities to have effective access to general technical and vocational guidance programmes, placement services and vocational and continuing training. Ensuring access implies the adoption of accessibility measures as well as ensuring non-discrimination on the basis of disability, in particular in the entrance requirements that apply to training programmes.

Article 27(1)(e) requires States Parties to promote employment opportunities and career advancement for persons with disabilities in the labour market. Frequently, employers assume a lack of capability on the part of the disabled individual, and this results in stigmatisation that hinders the participation of persons with disabilities in the workforce. States Parties must address these prejudices through awareness-raising campaigns and other initiatives. In this respect, Article 27(1)(e) is intrinsically connected to Article 8 CRPD. In addition to that, States Parties must assist disabled individuals in returning to employment. This obligation is linked to the implementation of Article 26 (on rehabilitation), which requires States Parties to promote 'comprehensive habilitation and rehabilitation services and programmes, particularly in the areas of health, employment, education and social services'. The obligations in Article 27(1)(e) are reiterated in Article 27(1)(k), which obliges States Parties to ensure the promotion of vocational and professional rehabilitation, job retention and return-to-work programmes for persons with disabilities.

Article 27(1)(f) requires States Parties to undertake the promotion of opportunities for self-employment, entrepreneurship, the development of cooperatives and starting one's own business; while Article 27(1)(g) and (1)(h) require States Parties to ensure, respectively, the employment of persons with disabilities in the public sector and in the private sector, through appropriate policies, which may include affirmative action programmes, incentives and other measures. These active labour market policies are dealt with below in section 6.

Article 27(1)(i) obliges States Parties to ensure that reasonable accommodation is provided to persons with disabilities in the workplace. This obligation, discussed in further detail in section 4 below, does not simply entail the material accommodation itself; it also requires States Parties to raise

[24] Ibid. para. 67(e).

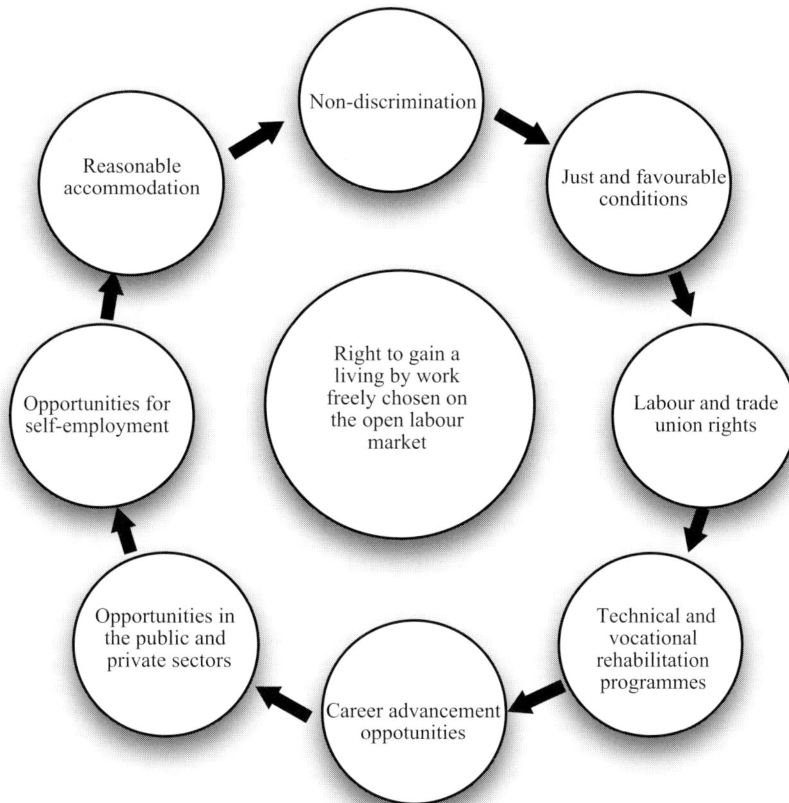

Figure 8.1 Key Obligations under Article 27 CRPD

awareness and 'provide training on the employment of persons with disabilities and reasonable accommodation for employers, representative organi[s]ations of employees and employers, unions and competent authorities'.[25]

Article 27(1)(j) obliges States Parties to promote the acquisition by persons with disabilities of work experience in the open labour market. This provision seeks to ensure that States Parties move away from sheltered employment, where people with disabilities are segregated from the mainstream workforce, towards supported employment initiatives that promote inclusion.

Finally, Article 27(2) mandates States Parties to ensure that persons with disabilities are not held in slavery or in servitude, and are protected, on an equal basis with others, from forced or compulsory labour.

The key obligations outlined above are depicted in Figure 8.1.

[25] CRPD Committee, General Comment No. 6, note 23, para. 67(h).

Fasciglione links Article 27 to the Convention's general obligations. In that regard, he cites[26] Article 4(1)(a) and (b) of the Convention, which imposes two general obligations on States Parties; namely: (a) to adopt all appropriate legislative, administrative and other measures for the implementation of the rights recognised in the Convention related to work and employment; and (b) to take all appropriate measures, including legislation, to modify or abolish laws, regulations, customs and practices that constitute discrimination against persons with disabilities in the areas of work and employment.[27] He also points to the fact that Article 27 CRPD imposes different levels of substantive obligations on States: on the one hand, States Parties to the Convention 'are obliged to abstain from infringing rights of persons with disabilities', and, on the other hand, 'the Convention requires them to adopt positive measures to promote employment opportunities for persons with disabilities … especially with regard to private-sector employers'.[28] This includes positive action, such as quotas, which specify the percentage of people with disabilities who should occupy a particular employment position.

Article 27 undoubtedly confers individual rights to reasonable accommodation and to be free from discrimination. However, Waddington argues that it is unclear whether individuals can base claims directly on Article 27 when they relate to positive action more generally.[29] This emerges clearly from the CRPD Committee's decision in *A. F.* v. *Italy*.[30] The author of the individual communication, who was a person with a registered disability, claimed, *inter alia*, a breach of Article 27 CRPD on the ground that he was subjected to discrimination on the basis of his disability. The complainant sat a competitive recruitment examination at the University of Modena and Reggio Emilia. Italian Law No. 68/1999, of 12 March 1999, required that employers with a workforce of more than fifty employees ensure that at least 7 per cent of their workforce are people who are registered as disabled. To that end, the law required that public employers reserve a quota of 50 per cent of the positions to be filled through competitive exams for registered persons with disabilities. A. F. obtained the third highest mark in the exam; however, he was not appointed to the post that he had applied for, and this was not the first time that he had been unsuccessful in the exam. He argued that Law No. 68/1999 had been breached and, furthermore, that the 50 per cent quota for public exams had not been respected. He argued that he should be awarded the position that he had applied for. Following his unsuccessful claim before the domestic courts,

[26] Marco Fasciglione, 'Article 27 of the CRPD and the Right of Inclusive Employment of People with Autism', note 21, p. 147.

[27] Ibid. [28] Ibid.

[29] Lisa Waddington, 'Positive Action Measures and the UN Convention on the Rights of Persons with Disabilities: Case Note: Communication No. 9/2012 A. F. v. Italy, UN Committee on the Rights of Persons with Disabilities, 19 May 2015' (2016) 2 *International Labor Rights Case Law* 396.

[30] CRPD Committee, *A. F.* v. *Italy*, Communication No. 9/2012, UN Doc. CRPD/C/13/D/9/2012.

A. F. submitted an individual communication to the CRPD Committee, in which he claimed that Italy was in violation of Article 27 CRPD. In finding that the complainant's rights had not been violated, the Committee rendered a brief decision on the merits of the communication, of which the essential points are outlined in the text below.

CRPD Committee, A. F. v. Italy, UN Doc. CRPD/C/13/D/9/2012

8.3. The Committee recalls that, in accordance with [A]rticle 27 (a), (e), (g) and (i) of the Convention, States [P]arties have the responsibility to prohibit discrimination on the basis of disability with regard to all matters concerning all forms of employment, including conditions of recruitment, hiring and employment, continuance of employment, career advancement and safe and healthy working conditions; to promote employment opportunities and career advancement for persons with disabilities in the labour market, as well as assistance in finding, obtaining, maintaining and returning to employment; to employ persons with disabilities in the public sector; and to ensure that reasonable accommodation is provided to persons with disabilities in the workplace.

8.4. The Committee also recalls that it is generally for the courts of States [P]arties to the Convention to evaluate facts and evidence in a particular case, unless it is found that the evaluation was clearly arbitrary or amounted to a denial of justice.

8.5. In the present case, the Committee considers that the author did not provide any element which would enable the Committee to conclude that the provisions of the national legislation and its application amounted to a violation of his individual rights under the Convention. The Committee also considers that the Council of State thoroughly and objectively assessed all the elements submitted by the author and the University of Modena and Reggio Emilia before reaching the conclusion that the non-selection of the author for the position for which he had applied was not discriminatory. The Committee considers that the author did not provide any evidence which would enable it to conclude that the decision of the Council of State was manifestly arbitrary or amounted to a denial of justice. In the circumstances, the Committee concludes that the decision made was based on objective and reasonable considerations. Consequently, the Committee is of the view that it cannot establish a violation of [A]rticle 27 of the Convention.

Reflecting on the facts and context of the case, Waddington[31] claims that the CRPD Committee failed to 'reflect on the role of structural discrimination',

[31] Waddington, 'Positive Action Measures and the UN Convention on the Rights of Persons with Disabilities: Case Note: Communication No. 9/2012 A. F. v. Italy', note 29.

which, according to Waddington, 'can have an accumulative effect and is often difficult to identify'.[32] She points out that 'disabled people are often exposed to ongoing exclusion and disadvantage which reduces their opportunities on the labor market' and that quota systems 'can be met by employing disabled people in poorly paid low status jobs, without giving [them] access to positions commanding higher salaries and higher status'.[33] In that vein, she highlights the difficulty in realising the objectives of Article 27 CRPD.

4 REASONABLE ACCOMMODATION AND ACCESSIBILITY IN EMPLOYMENT SETTINGS

Reasonable accommodation has been discussed extensively in Chapter 4. However, this section briefly addresses the duty to accommodate persons with disabilities in the workplace. Building on the general analysis conducted in Chapter 5 of this textbook, this section also discusses the need for accessible workplaces, to ensure inclusion and participation of disabled workers.

4.1 Reasonable Accommodation

Fasciglione remarks that States Parties to the CRPD are required to construct 'enabling and conducive' working environments for people with disabilities.[34] One vital element in creating such environments is the duty to provide reasonable accommodation, according to Article 27(1)(i). The material scope of this obligation is wide, and accommodations should be provided to disabled people when they work as an employee in the public or private sector company; when they participate in general technical and vocational guidance programmes; when they exercise labour and trade union rights; and when they engage in self-employment.

In employment contexts, reasonable accommodation is concerned with the removal of the disadvantage to which a person with a disability would otherwise be subjected by an employer's standard working practices or systems, usually designed to suit non-disabled people.[35] The CRPD does not include any example of reasonable accommodation. However, the CRPD Committee's General Comment No. 6 on equality and non-discrimination gives the following examples of

[32] Ibid.

[33] See Lisa Waddington, 'Legislating to Employ People with Disabilities: The European and American Way' (1994) 1(4) *Maastricht Journal of European and Comparative Law* 377.

[34] Fasciglione, 'Article 27 of the CRPD and the Right of Inclusive Employment of People with Autism', note 21, p. 147.

[35] Ferri and Lawson, *Reasonable Accommodation for Disabled People in Employment Contexts*, note 18.

> Can you think of examples of reasonable accommodations in employment settings for people with specific types of disabilities?

reasonable accommodation in the workplace: 'making existing facilities and information accessible to the individual with a disability; modifying equipment; reorgani[s]ing activities; rescheduling work … or enabling access to support personnel without disproportionate or undue burden'.[36] Other examples of reasonable accommodations can be found in the EU Employment Equality Directive, which will be discussed in Part II of this textbook, and in studies or documents published by other UN bodies or agencies, such as the OHCHR and the World Health Organization (WHO). In 2016, the ILO also compiled a list of good practices in relation to reasonable accommodations in the employment context.[37]

In general, reasonable accommodation in an employment setting entails technical solutions and physical adjustments (i.e. modification of the workplace, also through the use of assistive devices) and organisational accommodations, which include a reduction in working time, or different organisational patterns. This is demonstrated by Figure 8.2.

Since the beginning of its mandate, the CRPD Committee has urged States Parties to ensure that they define the denial of reasonable accommodation as a form of discrimination in national legislation. In its first Concluding Observations (COs) issued to Tunisia, the Committee instructed the State Party to 'act with urgency to include an explicit prohibition of disability-based discrimination in an anti-discrimination law, particularly those governing elections, labour, education and health, among others'.[38]

The implementation of the duty of reasonable accommodation in national disability-related legislation 'has been slow in many countries'.[39] According to Fasciglione, this is due to several factors. First, 'the notion of reasonable

[36] CRPD Committee, General Comment No. 6, note 23, para. 26.

[37] The study is available at www.ilo.org/global/topics/equality-and-discrimination/WCMS_536630/lang–en/index.htm.

[38] CRPD Committee, Concluding Observations on the Initial Report of Tunisia, 13 May 2011, UN Doc. CRPD/C/TUN/CO/1, paras. 12–13.

[39] Fasciglione, 'Article 27 of the CRPD and the Right of Inclusive Employment of People with Autism', note 21, p. 151.

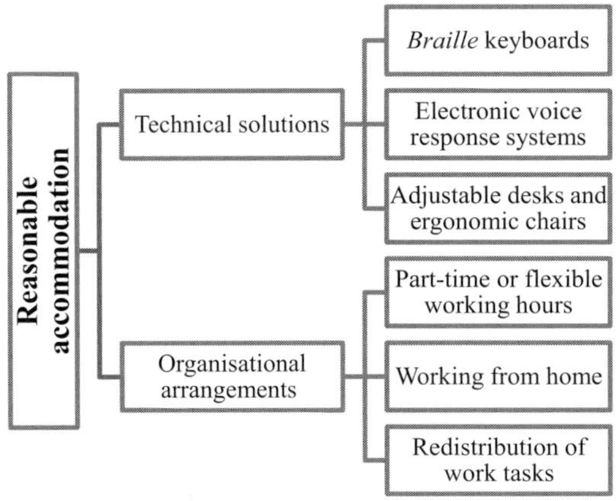

Figure 8.2 Reasonable Accommodation in Employment Settings

accommodation (an individual requirement) is often confused with accessibility measures (a general requirement) or with positive [action]'.[40] Thus, a clear distinction must be maintained in national legal and policy systems between the various types of measures being adopted in order to secure suitable workplaces for individuals with disabilities. In the second place, Fasciglione argues that the poor implementation of accommodation measures 'may be due to the reluctance of employers to recruit persons with disabilities determined by the fear of having to make expensive workplace adjustments'.[41] This is a misconception, as the provision of reasonable accommodation is often low cost or cost-free. An example of this is allowing a person with a visual impairment to bring a guide dog into work,[42] which does not entail an undue or disproportionate burden on the employer.

The individual communication heard by the Committee in *Jungelin* v. *Sweden*,[43] already discussed in Chapters 4 and 5 of this textbook, sheds light on the proportionality test to be applied in order to ascertain whether the reasonable accommodation entails a disproportionate burden. While the Committee ultimately concluded that the author's rights had not been violated,[44] the opinion of the dissenting Committee members was that the requested

40 Ibid. 41 Ibid.

42 Andrea Broderick, *The Long and Winding Road to Equality and Inclusion for Persons with Disabilities: The United Nations Convention on the Rights of Persons with Disabilities* (Cambridge-Antwerp: Intersentia, 2015), p. 169.

43 CRPD Committee, *Marie-Louise Jungelin (represented by the Swedish Association of Visually Impaired Youth (US) and the Swedish Association of the Visually Impaired (SRF)* v. *Sweden*, Communication No. 5/2011, UN Doc. CRPD/C/12/D/5/2011.

44 Referring to the State's margin of appreciation, the Committee concluded that the author's rights had not been violated because it found that the domestic court had thoroughly and objectively assessed the alternatives.

accommodation should be considered in light of the context. They remarked that:

> the test of reasonableness and proportionality should therefore ensure, *inter alia*, that … the measures of accommodation were requested to promote the employment of a person with disability, with the professional capacity and experience to perform the functions corresponding to the position [for which] he or she applied.[45]

CASE STUDY

Belgian Brochure on Reasonable Accommodation

The Belgian Federal Government has published an accessible brochure on reasonable accommodation in the field of employment in the French and Flemish languages, in order to raise awareness among employers regarding the CRPD's obligations (Cel Publicaties van de Federale Overheidsdienst Werkgelegenheid, Arbeid en Sociaal Overleg, *Weigwijs in de Redelijke Aanpassingen ten Behoeve van Personen met een Handicap op het Werk* (2005), available at: https://www.werk.be/sites/default/files/Diversiteit_Redelijkeaanpassingen_federaalvademecum_versie0907.pdf).

4.2 Accessibility of Workplaces

According to the CRPD Committee, people with disabilities cannot effectively enjoy their work and employment rights, as described in Article 27 of the Convention, if the workplace itself is not accessible.[46] As discussed in Chapters 3 and 5, accessibility is recognised as a general principle of the CRPD, and broad accessibility obligations are formulated in Article 9 and in other substantive provisions of the Convention.[47] Workplaces are mentioned in Article 9(1)(a) as an example of the facilities that must be made accessible. As already mentioned in Chapter 5, Article 9(2)(b) CRPD makes it clear that States Parties

[45] Joint opinion of Committee members Mr Carlos Rios Espinosa, Ms Theresia Degener, Mr Munthian Buntan, Ms Silvia Judith Quan-Chang and Ms Maria Soledad Cisternas Reyes (dissenting), para. 4.

[46] CRPD Committee, General Comment No. 2, 22 May 2014, UN Doc. CRPD/C/GC/2, para. 41.

[47] Francesco Seatzu, 'Article 9: Accessibility', in Valentina Della Fina, Rachele Cera and Giuseppe Palmisano (eds.), *The United Nations Convention on the Rights of Persons with Disabilities: A Commentary* (Cham: Springer, 2017), pp. 225–42, p. 227.

must ensure that private entities (including employers) provide for accessible services and facilities. The CRPD Committee confirms that, 'as long as goods, products and services are open or provided to the public, they must be accessible to all, regardless of whether they are owned and/or provided by a public authority or a private enterprise'.[48]

As *Jungelin* v. *Sweden* demonstrates, a work environment must be physically and technologically accessible. Many other aspects of accessibility are of vital importance in ensuring the participation of individuals with disabilities in the workplace. In fact, the submissions made to the Thematic Study on the Work and Employment of Persons with Disabilities, produced by the OHCHR,[49] points to the fact that many states globally have adopted measures to ensure accessibility of workplaces in all respects, including ensuring accessible transport to reach the workplace.

DID YOU KNOW THAT ...?

The submissions made by Andorra and Egypt to the Thematic Study on the Work and Employment of Persons with Disabilities demonstrate the types of accessibility measures that have been adopted in the field of transport, in order to enable people with disabilities to travel to the workplace. In addition, the submission made by Paraguay shows that sign language interpretation is provided for Deaf workers. Moreover, Germany and Mexico have put in place legislation seeking to ensure that accessibility is realised in public and private sector workplaces with more than a certain number of employees (Thematic Study by the Office of the United Nations High Commissioner for Human Rights on Enhancing Awareness and Understanding of the Convention on the Rights of Persons with Disabilities, 26 January 2009, available at www.un.org/disabilities/documents/reports/ohchr/A.HRC.10.48AEV.pdf).

In 2015, the then Attorney-General, the Honorable George Brandis QC, asked the Australian Human Rights Commission to conduct the first National Inquiry into Employment Discrimination against Older Australians and Australians with Disability, entitled Willing to Work. The report was released in 2016 and sets out recommendations to businesses, examples of existing good practice and a list of strategies to address discrimination in employment. The report recommends that businesses should seek to engage with flexible work systems, by making job design, work location and hours flexible for all, as far as the demands of the role allow. Among the best practices

[48] CRPD Committee, General Comment No. 2, note 46, para. 13.

[49] UN Human Rights Council, *Thematic Study by the Office of the United Nations High Commissioner for Human Rights on Enhancing Awareness and Understanding of the Convention on the Rights of Persons with Disabilities*, 26 January 2009, UN Doc. A/HRC/10/48.

surveyed were Accessibility and Inclusion Plans (www.humanrights.gov.au/our-work/disability-rights/publications/willing-work-good-practice-examples-employers-2016).

In the United States, the Equal Employment Opportunity Commission (EEOC) has also produced an Enforcement Guidance (www.eeoc.gov/policy/docs/accommodation.html), in order to clarify the rights and responsibilities of employers and persons with disabilities regarding reasonable accommodation. It identifies three categories of accommodations: accommodations that are required to ensure equal opportunity in the application process; accommodations that enable employees with disabilities to perform the essential functions of the position held or desired; and accommodations that enable employees with disabilities to enjoy equal employment benefits to those enjoyed by employees without disabilities.

It is also important for States Parties to raise awareness on the benefits that accessibility can bring, since, as the CRPD Committee notes, a lack of accessibility is often the result of insufficient awareness and technical know-how.[50] This awareness-raising obligation is in line with Article 8 CRPD and Article 9 (2)(c), which requires States Parties to the Convention to provide training to all stakeholders on accessibility for persons with disabilities.

CASE STUDY

South African Toolkit for the Private Sector

The South African Human Rights Commission has created a toolkit for employers of all sizes across various sectors of employment, in order to foster the right to work of people with disabilities and to present a strong business case for employing individuals with disabilities in South Africa (www.sahrc.org.za/home/21/files/SAHRC%20Disability%20toolkit%20FOR%20CD.pdf).

The guidelines set out in the Toolkit are general, so that they can easily be adapted by employers, and they highlight, among many other items, the importance of accessibility of workplaces. The Toolkit identifies practical steps for private employers, in order to make the workplace accessible:

i. Start with assembling a team of individuals, to dedicate time assessing, planning and implementing accessibility modifications at your workplace;
ii. Seek experts in accessibility to act as consultants for your business;
iii. Identify local disabled people's organisations that may be able to assist and play an advisory role for your business;

[50] CRPD Committee, General Comment No. 2, note 46, para. 19.

iv. Assess the needs of individuals with disabilities in your workplace and include them in the assessment, planning and implementation of accessibility modifications in the workplace; and
v. Assess existing conditions in your workplace and determine what changes, if any, need to be made.

CASE STUDY

Italy Project on Diversity at Work

A project entitled 'Diversity at work' (www.forumsolidarieta.it/servizi_3/bandi_finanziamenti_4/diversitalavoro.aspx) was launched in Italy in 2008. The project had the objective of searching for talented individuals and offering equal opportunities to all in the workplace. The project was initiated by the Italian equality body *Ufficio Nazionale Antidiscriminazioni Razziali* (National Anti-Racial Discrimination Office), Sodalitas, Synesis and the Adecco Foundation for equal opportunities. The project was designed to create an opportunity for businesses to meet people with disabilities and foreign nationals, thus allowing for contact between employers and individuals who often experience discrimination.

5 THE RIGHT TO WORK, SHELTERED EMPLOYMENT AND SUPPORTED EMPLOYMENT

As outlined above in section 3, Article 27 CRPD requires States Parties to ensure opportunities for employment for persons with disabilities in the open labour market. This reference to the 'open' labour market stems from a desire to fight against the long history of segregation of individuals with disabilities in controlled working environments. These environments are generally called 'sheltered workshops', and they are most often associated with individuals with psychosocial or intellectual disabilities, since these individuals were, and still are, often deemed 'incapable' of working in the mainstream workplace. The sub-sections below discuss sheltered employment and compare and contrast that with supported employment.

5.1 Sheltered Employment

There is no common definition of what a 'sheltered workshop' is. In Europe, 'sheltered employment' is defined by the European Commission as employment in an undertaking where 'at least 30% of workers are workers with disabilities'.[51] However, at the global level, the definitions of sheltered employment vary. The Council of Europe (CoE) uses a broad definition of sheltered employment, stating that:

> it can cover a number of diversified situations, amongst which are sheltered workshops and work centres. Sheltered work should have a double purpose: to make it possible for people with disabilities to carry out a worthwhile activity and to prepare them as far as possible, for work in normal employment.[52]

In theory, through sheltered workshops, disabled individuals should be provided with training and employment services that are designed to assist them in moving towards an optimum level of social and vocational functioning. Thus, in principle, sheltered workshops have the objective of enabling individuals to work according to their own productive capacity and to be paid fairly for that work, as well as to facilitate the entry of disabled individuals to the open labour market. However, more often, disabled individuals who are employed in sheltered workshops are confined to that segregated working environment for long periods of time.

During the negotiation sessions on Article 27 CRPD, there was fierce debate surrounding the inclusion of any reference to sheltered workshops in the text of Article 27. For instance, the International Disability Caucus (IDC) sought to exclude references to alternative forms of employment, such as sheltered workshops. In the opinion of the IDC, 'it is not appropriate to separate out people who are in a particular work situation that, historically and today, continues to be exploitative because it is segregated and separate standards apply'.[53] People with Disability Australia (PWDA) also took a strong position against sheltered workshops. PWDA called for the drafters of the Convention not to 'create rights to segregated employment settings that might permanently warehouse persons with disability'.[54] Mental Disability Rights International (MDRI) remarked that 'sheltered workshops represent an outdated concept that

[51] Commission Regulation (EU) No. 651/2014 of 17 June 2014 declaring certain categories of aid compatible with the internal market in application of Articles 107 and 108 of the Treaty (General block exemption Regulation), OJ 2014 No. L187.

[52] Council of Europe, Recommendation No. R (92)(6) concerning a coherent policy for the rehabilitation of people with disabilities, adopted by the Committee of Ministers on 9 April 1992 at the 474th meeting of the Ministers' Deputies.

[53] Ad Hoc Committee, '6th Session' (10 August 2005), available at www.un.org/esa/socdev/enable/rights/adhocmeetings.htm.

[54] Ibid.

creates barriers and even represent a form of institutionalisation'.[55] The EU also expressed its concern about the possibility that disabled individuals who avail themselves of alternative forms of work, such as sheltered employment, might be dealt with less favourably in those alternative forms of employment than in the general labour market.[56]

Scholarly writings on sheltered workshops also question the validity of these forms of working environments. For example, Visier notes that questions of the employment status and fundamental rights of the workers involved commonly arise where sheltered workshops are concerned.[57] According to Ferraina, the negotiation process leading to the adoption of Article 27 CRPD highlighted several concerns with regard to the continued maintenance and role of sheltered workplaces, taking into account the underlying premises of the CRPD as a whole. These concerns included the economic exploitation of disabled workers as well as the disadvantageous treatment of persons with disabilities regarding working conditions (for instance, discrimination with regard to employment, salary, and promotion, on the sole ground of disability).[58] Whitehead reiterates some of these concerns, and he also states that most disabled people who enter sheltered workshops 'stay for an extended period of time, some because there are no other job opportunities in the community, others because they cannot function in competitive employment, but others remain in the workshop because the shop is dependent on their productivity (to generate operating income)'.[59] O'Reilly maintains that sometimes people with disabilities receive only 'pocket money' in addition to their normal disability benefit and 'employment and occupational safety and health laws often do not apply'.[60]

Notwithstanding the foregoing concerns, it remains the case that sheltered workshops still exist on a global level, and they continue to provide employment to countless numbers of disabled individuals. Whatever their merits or the disadvantages associated with them, Ferraina points to the fact that the status of existing sheltered workshops under the CRPD is problematic,

[55] Ad Hoc Committee, '7th Session', vol. 8(1) (16 January 2006), available at www.un.org/esa/socdev/enable/rights/adhocmeetings.htm.

[56] Ad Hoc Committee, '3rd Session' (2 June 2004), available at www.un.org/esa/socdev/enable/rights/adhocmeetings.htm.

[57] Laurent Visier, 'Sheltered Employment for Persons with Disabilities' (1998) 137(3) *International Labour Review* 347, at 348.

[58] Ferraina, 'Analysis of the Legal Meaning of Article 27 of the UN CRPD: Key Challenges for Adapted Work Settings', note 20, p. 26.

[59] Claude Whitehead, 'Effective Accommodation or Exploitation' (1978) *National Center for Law and the Handicapped*, available at https://mn.gov/mnddc/parallels2/pdf/70s/78/78-SWS-DOL-D.pdf.

[60] O'Reilly, 'The Right to Decent Work of Persons with Disabilities', note 17, p. 71.

> Do sheltered workshops exist in your country? How are they regulated?

since these workshops are not mentioned in the Convention and, therefore, there are no 'hints on how to (re)define the facilities they provide and how to make sure the services they provide are correctly understood by authorities and society as a whole'.[61]

In light of the foregoing debate, questions remain about what is actually meant by 'inclusive, open and accessible' working environments in Article 27, and whether, as Ferraina states, this would automatically exclude protected forms of employment that take care of 'vulnerable people in need of extra support, or whether this would include them provided they meet the requirements [set out in Article 27 CRPD]'.[62] Whatever the answer to that question is, there is no doubt that, rather than actively promoting sheltered workshops, States Parties to the Convention must work towards setting up adapted mainstream working environments, wherever possible, with all the challenges that this entails.

5.2 Supported Employment

Supported employment originated in the United States as an alternative to sheltered workshops and rehabilitation programmes for people with severe disabilities. Although the term is not used consistently in the literature or in national policies, and is sometimes used interchangeably with sheltered employment, nonetheless, it constitutes a different form of employment. Supported employment is usually defined as 'paid work in integrated work settings, with ongoing support services, for persons with severe disabilities'.[63] It is most commonly observed in the context of individuals with intellectual or psychosocial disabilities. Even though there are a variety of ways in which supported employment may be provided, its main feature is that the individual with a disability has a 'real job' as well as the benefits and the dignity that arise from gainful employment.[64] Various forms of supported employment include individual placement,

[61] Ferraina, 'Analysis of the Legal Meaning of Article 27 of the UN CRPD: Key Challenges for Adapted Work Settings', note 20, at 26.

[62] Ibid. [63] Ibid. at 42.

[64] Paul Wehman, 'Supported Employment: What is it?' (2012) 37 *Journal of Vocational Rehabilitation* 139.

enclaves, mobile work crews and small business arrangements.[65] O'Reilly explains that:

an enclave is a group of individuals, usually three to eight, who work in a special training group within a host company . . . A mobile work crew may be a similar-sized group, with one or more supervisors, which travels through a community offering speciali[s]ed contract services, such as gardening or grounds-keeping. The small business option could be a manufacturing service or a subcontract operation, with a small number of workers with disabilities and non-disabled workers.[66]

Bellamy et al. point to the fact that 'there is a nearly infinite array of supported employment strategies and structures, each of which combines a particular kind of work opportunity with a particular method of ongoing support', and that each form of supported employment 'has advantages and drawbacks in terms of generating real employment outcomes while overcoming barriers to employment experienced by the individuals with disabilities'.[67]

Rule 7(7) of the Standard Rules affirms that, while the aim should always be for persons with disabilities to obtain employment in the open labour market, 'for persons with disabilities whose needs cannot be met in open employment, small units of sheltered or supported employment may be an alternative'. Notably, the drafting history of the CRPD does not refer to supported employment specifically, but, as pointed out in the preceding sub-section, alternative models of employment (those not available in the open labour market) were not favoured by the delegations taking part in the negotiations to the CRPD. This is reflected in the fact that the final text of the CRPD does not refer to supported employment; rather, it requires States Parties to provide individuals with disabilities with equal opportunities to take part in an open, inclusive and accessible labour market. This raises questions as to whether supported employment can be considered fully compatible with the CRPD.

6 ACTIVE LABOUR MARKET POLICIES

As discussed above, Article 27 CRPD requires States Parties to adopt positive measures to foster employment opportunities for people with disabilities. According to Waddington et al., active labour market policies:

[65] Sherril Moon and Susan Griffin, 'Supported Employment Service Delivery Models', in Paul Wehman and Sherril Moon (eds.), *Vocational Rehabilitation and Supported Employment* (Baltimore: Paul H. Brooks Publishing Company, 1988).

[66] O'Reilly, 'The Right to Decent Work of Persons with Disabilities', note 17, pp. 71 and 72.

[67] Ibid. citing Thomas Bellamy, Larry Rhodes and Joyce Albin, 'Supported Employment', in William Kieran and Jack Stark (eds.), *Pathways to Employment for Adults with Developmental Disabilities* (Baltimore: Brooks, 1986), pp. 129–38.

assume that the market will not deliver optimum employment or social outcomes and often target disabled people, older and younger workers, and people who are long-term unemployed although they can potentially be directed at any (group of) individuals who are out of work.[68]

The use of active labour market policies to advance employment opportunities for individuals with disabilities is, according to Waddington et al. 'linked to a historic shift from "compensatory" approaches towards those based on equal rights, greater accessibility and support in the workplace'.[69] Active labour market policies constitute a key tool to foster inclusion of persons with disabilities in the workplace in several regions of the world. For instance, in the EU, they have been addressed in the 2015 Guidelines for the Employment Policies of the Member States adopted by the Council in October 2015.[70] The most prominent types of active labour market policies directed at people with disabilities consist of subsidised employment, vocational rehabilitation and training, and quota schemes.[71] The current section focuses on quota systems and other types of positive measures that serve to facilitate the employment of individuals with disabilities.

6.1 Quota Systems

Quota systems generally require employers to hire a minimum percentage of workers with disabilities. There are, however, variations between systems, particularly in relation to the obligatory or voluntary nature of quotas, the material and personal scope of quotas, as well as the effectiveness of sanctions in circumstances where an employer fails to meet the quota. Quota systems can be divided into two main categories: strict quotas and flexible quotas.[72] The first type of quota system represents an obligation-based approach

[68] Lisa Waddington, Mads Peresen and Maria Ventegodt Liisberg, 'Get a Job! Active Labour Market Policies and Persons with Disabilities in Danish and European Union Policy' (2016) 39(1) *Dublin University Law Journal* 1, at 2.

[69] Ibid. at 7.

[70] Council Decision (EU) 2015/1848 of 5 October 2015 on guidelines for the employment policies of the Member States for 2015, OJ 2015 No. L268/28.

[71] See generally Lisa Waddington, Mark Priestley and Betul Yalcin, 'Equality of Opportunity in Employment? Disability Rights and Active Labour Market Policies', in Peter Blanck and Eilinoir Flynn (eds.), *Routledge Handbook of Disability Law and Human Rights* (Oxon/New York: Routledge, 2016), pp. 72–87.

[72] See generally Oliver de Schutter, 'Positive Action', in Dagmar Schiek, Lisa Waddington and Mark Bell (eds.), *Cases, Materials and Text on National, Supranational and International Non-Discrimination Law* (Oxford: Hart Publishing, 2007), pp. 757–870.

(a mandatory quota), and the second type represents an incentive-based approach to promoting employment.[73]

Quotas are allowed under Article 5(4) of the Convention, and they are specifically mentioned by the CRPD Committee in its General Comment No. 6 on equality.[74] Notwithstanding the fact that quotas are permissible under the CRPD, doubts persist about their suitability as a form of inclusive policy. In that regard, Waddington highlights that quotas are, in general, premised on the idea that people with disabilities would not be hired unless employers are forced to do so and that individuals with severe disabilities are unable to compete for jobs.[75] For this reason, quotas might serve to reinforce stigmatisation of people with disabilities.

However, in spite of the criticism surrounding them, they are still the most frequent type of active labour market policy used at a global level. For those States Parties to the CRPD which adopt, or are intending to adopt, quota systems to promote employment for disabled people, it is vital to ensure that any measure adopted under Article 5(4) 'must be consistent with all the principles and provisions of the Convention'.[76] This would appear to signal that quotas cannot be used to promote sheltered forms of employment.

6.2 Positive Measures

In the context of individuals with disabilities, there are a range of other positive measures that can be adopted by States Parties to the Convention in fulfilment of the obligations contained in Article 27 CRPD. Such measures might include subsidies for the costs of adaptations, tax breaks for employers or preference in public procurement procedures. Positive measures can be divided into three main categories, as outlined in the sub-sections below: financial, legislative and awareness-raising measures.

[73] Irmgard Borghouts-Van de Pas, 'Labour Market Participation of the Disabled: Policies and Practices in Europe' (2010) 2 *European Journal of Social Security* 121.

[74] CRPD Committee, General Comment No. 6, note 23, para. 28.

[75] Lisa Waddington, 'Reassessing the Employment of People with Disabilities in Europe: From Quotas to Anti-Discrimination Laws' (1996) 18(62) *Comparative Labour Law Journal* 62, at 71. In addition, doubts arise with regard to the effectiveness of quotas. In countries such as the United Kingdom, quotas have generally been deemed to be ineffective and are not used as an active labour market policy. See in that regard, among many others, Patricia Thornton, *Employment Quotas, Levies and National Rehabilitation Funds for Persons with Disabilities: Pointers for Policy and Practice*, report prepared on behalf of the International Labour Office (1998), available at https://digitalcommons.ilr.cornell.edu/cgi/viewcontent.cgi?article=1083&context=gladnetcollect.

[76] Office of the United Nations High Commissioner for Human Rights (OHCHR), *Equality and non-discrimination under Article 5 of the Convention on the Rights of Persons with Disabilities* (December 2010), UN Doc. A/HRC/34/26, para. 20.

6.2.1 *Financial Measures*

Financial measures in the field of employment can serve to promote equality, by compensating employers for any additional costs related to the employment of persons with disabilities. While, in many cases, no such costs arise, at times employers may need to provide specialised equipment and additional training or adapt the workplace. These are all reasonable accommodations, and the availability of public funding to compensate employers for such costs means that it is highly unlikely that providing such a reasonable accommodation will amount to a disproportionate financial burden for the employer.

CASE STUDY

Estonian Law on Support for Employers

In Estonia, support is granted to employers on the basis of a contract between the Unemployment Insurance Fund and the employer. That fund compensates the employer for between 50 and 100 per cent of the cost of making the necessary adaptation. The fund can also provide the disabled individual with free use of technical equipment, whenever this is required to carry out employment. Two other services which are provided are communication support at a job interview and the assistance of a support person. These services are granted to individuals if they are necessary to overcome disability-related obstacles to employment and if other employment services are deemed not to be effective (L. Waddington and A. Broderick, *Promoting Equality and Non-Discrimination for Persons with Disabilities*, Strasbourg: Council of Europe, 2017, p. 33).

6.2.2 *Legislative Measures*

Legislative measures have long been recognised as a means by which the employment of persons with disabilities can be promoted. Such measures continue to form the primary means by which disability equality is promoted in the field of employment, notwithstanding the fact that several authors recognise that 'the adoption of non-discrimination law in EU Member States has not made any significant indent in their employment rates'.[77]

[77] Waddington, Peresen and Ventegodt Liisberg, 'Get a Job! Active Labour Market Policies and Persons with Disabilities in Danish and European Union Policy', note 68, at 7.

DID YOU KNOW THAT ...?

Several countries have equality laws in place in the field of employment. For instance, the Finnish Non-Discrimination Act (1325/2014) obliges all employers who employ more than thirty people to take steps to foster equality. This equality duty not only requires that discrimination is prohibited but that active steps are taken to promote equality. Section 7(1) of the Act provides that the employer must assess the realisation of equality in the workplace and, taking into account the needs of the workplace, develop the working conditions as well as the methods complied with in the selection of personnel and in making decisions concerning the personnel. Section 7(2) of the Act requires employers to draft an inclusive plan on the necessary measures for the promotion of equality. These measures and their effectiveness must be discussed with disabled personnel or their representatives.

Many countries include reasonable accommodation duties in their laws. Others even prevent employers (with some exceptions) from asking potential recruits questions about their health status before a job offer is made. This is the case, for instance, in the UK, where section 60 of the Equality Act 2010 (c. 15) makes it an offence to ask questions about an applicant's health or disability status.

6.2.3 *Awareness-Raising Measures*

As mentioned above, awareness-raising measures are intrinsically linked to the obligations of States Parties under Article 27 CRPD. These types of measures often serve to reinforce the other types of positive measures outlined above. In particular, they can also be utilised to boost the effectiveness of quotas, in the sense that they seek to eliminate prejudicial attitudes of employers.

CASE STUDY

The United Kingdom's Business Disability Forum

The UK's Business Disability Forum is a not-for-profit member organisation, which brings together business people, persons with disabilities and government agents to discuss the reforms that are necessary to achieve workplace equality so that people with disabilities can contribute to business success, to society and to economic growth. The forum provides support by sharing expertise, giving advice, providing training and facilitating networking opportunities (L. Waddington and A. Broderick, *Promoting Equality and Non-Discrimination for Persons with Disabilities*, Strasbourg: Council of Europe, 2017, p. 34).

SUMMARY

- The enjoyment of the right to work is a key factor in promoting equality for disabled individuals.
- Without the opportunity to engage in employment in the open labour market, individuals with disabilities remain marginalised and their contribution to society is undervalued.
- The key elements of Article 27 CRPD are: the right to gain a living by work freely chosen in the open labour market; non-discrimination; the provision of just and favourable conditions; labour and trade union rights; the establishment of technical and vocational rehabilitation programmes; the provision of career advancement opportunities; opportunities for self-employment; opportunities for employment in the public and private sector; and the provision of reasonable accommodation.
- The mandate of 'open' labour market employment for persons with disabilities stems from a desire to fight against the long history of segregation of individuals with disabilities in controlled and segregated working environments.
- Article 27 CRPD requires States Parties to ensure that reasonable accommodation is provided in the workplace to persons with disabilities. The material scope of this obligation is wide, and accommodations should be accorded to persons with disabilities when they work as an employee in the public or private sector company; when they participate in general technical and vocational guidance programmes; when they exercise labour and trade union rights; and when they engage in self-employment.
- For many people with disabilities across the world, a common barrier to participating in employment is the lack of accessible buildings or accessible information and communications. Many other aspects of accessibility are of vital importance in ensuring the participation of individuals with disabilities in the workplace, including accessibility of interviews and the accessibility of transport, in order to get to the workplace.
- Article 27 CRPD requires States Parties to adopt other positive measures to foster employment opportunities for people with disabilities. In that regard, active labour market policies are required, including but not limited to quotas.

ACTIVITIES

REVIEW QUESTIONS

1. What are the key obligations laid down in Article 27 CRPD?
2. What are the concerns related to sheltered employment?
3. What is the role of reasonable accommodation in the context of employment?

ESSAY QUESTIONS

1. 'Greater efforts are required to ensure that reasonable accommodation is fully understood as a legal requirement, to facilitate the full participation of persons with disabilities in employment.' *Discuss.*

2. **'Identifying the business reasons for employing people with disabilities and the challenges that such employment may pose is vital to determining the most effective policies that can fully implement Article 27 CRPD.'** ***Discuss.***

GROUP PROJECT

Alison has just graduated from Freedonia University with a degree in 'business and fashion'. When she sees an opening for a business specialist in the ABC Company, a manufacturer of beauty products located in Freedonia, she decides to apply. In her application, she states that she is a wheelchair user and that she has a hearing impairment. ABC Company calls her for an interview in the main building of the company, located in the historical centre of Freedonia City. When she arrives, Alison discovers that the building is accessible only by means of the stairs and no ramp is available. After having asked the concierge for help to get up the stairs, she discovers that the interview will be conducted in a very small room on the first floor. The old elevator in the building is broken, and Alison has to ask the members of the interview panel if the interview can be conducted in a different room. The panel moves the interview to the ground floor, albeit unwillingly. However, the new room chosen for the interview is extremely big and has a very bad set of acoustics. For this reason, Alison struggles to hear and to comprehend the questions posed to her by the interview panel. She asks to be sat nearer to the panel, but her request is refused. A couple of days later, Alison receives an email in which she is told that she has not been selected for the post. After a request for feedback, Alison receives an email stating that despite her high qualifications, she is not fit for the post.

Discuss the group project, taking into account the fact that Freedonia is a State Party to the CRPD.

FURTHER READING

Einat, A., 'Universalizing the Right to Work of Persons with Disabilities: An Equality and Dignity Based Approach' (2015) *Hebrew University of Jerusalem Legal Research Paper* No. 15–09.

Fasciglione, M., 'Article 27 of the CRPD and the Right of Inclusive Employment of People with Autism', in V. Della Fina and R. Cera (eds.), *Protecting the Rights of People with Autism in the Fields of Education and Employment* (Cham: Springer, 2015), pp. 497–507.

Fasciglione, M., 'Article 27: The Right to Work', in V. Della Fina, R. Cera and G. Palmisano (eds.), *The United Nations Convention on the Rights of Persons with Disabilities: A Commentary* (Cham: Springer, 2017), pp. 496–508.

Flores, N., Jenaro, C., Orgaz, M. B. and Martín, M. V., 'Understanding Quality of Life of Workers with Intellectual Disabilities' (2011) 24 *Journal of Applied Research in Intellectual Disabilities* 133–44.

International Labour Organization, 'Promoting Diversity and Inclusion through workplace Adjustments: A Practical Guide' (2016), available at www.ilo.org/global/topics/equality-and-discrimination/WCMS_536630/lang–en/index.htm.

Kuznetsova, Y., Yalcin, B. and Priestley, M., 'Labour Market Integration and Equality for Disabled People: A Comparative Analysis of Nordic and Baltic Countries' (2017) 51(4) *Social Policy and Administration* 577–97.

Lodovici et al., *Discrimination and Access to Employment for Female Workers with Disabilities* (Luxembourg: Publications Office of the European Union, 2017).

Mantouvalou, V. (ed.), *The Right to Work*: Legal and Philosophical Perspectives (Oxford: Hart Publishing, 2015).

May-Simera, C., 'Reconsidering Sheltered Workshops in Light of the United Nations Convention on the Rights of Persons with Disabilities' (2018) 7 *Laws* 6–17.

Nardodkar, R., Pathare, S., Ventriglio, A., Castaldelli-Maia, J., Javate, K. R., Torales, J. and Bhugra, D., 'Legal Protection of the Right to Work and Employment for Persons with Mental Health Problems: A Review of Legislation Across the World' (2016) 28(4) *International Review of Psychiatry* 375–84.

Waddington, L., Priestly, M. and Yalcin, B., 'Equality of Opportunity in Employment: Disability Rights and Active Labour Market Policies', in P. Blanck and E. Flynn (eds.), *Routledge Handbook of Disability Law and Human Rights* (Oxon/New York: Routledge, 2017), pp. 72–87.

Welti, F., Wansing, G. and Schäfers, M. (eds.), *The Right to Work for Persons with Disabilities. International Perspectives* (Baden Baden: Nomos, 2018).

9 Disability Rights, Social Inclusion and Core Policy Issues

LEARNING OUTCOMES

- ✓ Understand the core policy issues that affect several substantive CRPD rights, including the right to education, the right to access culture and the right to take part in political and public life.
- ✓ Comprehend the importance of those rights in achieving social inclusion of people with disabilities.
- ✓ Identify the key obligations enshrined in Article 24 CRPD on the right to education.
- ✓ Comprehend why the right to education is so pivotal in the lives of persons with disabilities and in ensuring their enjoyment of other substantive CRPD rights, including the rights to work and live independently.
- ✓ Describe the key obligations contained in Article 30 CRPD on the right to access culture.
- ✓ Comprehend the role that access to culture plays in ensuring inclusion in society for persons with disabilities.
- ✓ Describe the key obligations contained in Article 29 CRPD on the right to participate in political and public life.
- ✓ Demonstrate awareness of the key role that the right to vote plays in ensuring participation in political and public life for people with disabilities.

[I]t has been demonstrated that people who were deemed too "disabled" to benefit from community inclusion thrive in an environment where they are valued, where they partake in the everyday life of their surrounding community ...[1]

1 INTRODUCTION

As briefly discussed in Chapter 6, the right to live independently and to be included in the community, set out in Article 19 CRPD, is premised on the recognition of legal capacity for people with disabilities on an equal basis with others. However, the realisation of Article 19 is also inextricably linked to the possibility for people with disabilities to participate in community and social life. As noted by the former Council of Europe Commissioner for Human Rights (CoE CoHR), the right to live in the community is related to 'how health, education, social support systems and the labour market are shaped', and it is contingent 'on the accessibility of public spaces and services'.[2] Living in the community and being included in society also entails being able to contribute actively to social and political choices, through effective participation in elections. Moreover, enjoyment of the right to live independently depends on the opportunities that are available to an individual to access and participate in the cultural life of a country on an equal basis with others.

Building on the analysis conducted in previous chapters, this chapter addresses selected substantive CRPD rights, namely the right to education, the right to access culture and the right to participate in political and public life. The reason for dealing with those rights in one chapter is that they all engender core policy issues that arise in the context of disability, and they are particularly relevant within the discourse on equality and inclusion of people with disabilities in society as well as being complementary to the right to live independently. The Office of the United Nations High Commissioner for Human Rights (OHCHR) notes that the right to inclusive education is one of the key factors in promoting equality for persons with disabilities.[3] Likewise, the right to access culture contributes to facilitating full and equal participation of individuals with disabilities in mainstream society. The lack of enjoyment of the right to participate in political and public life leaves people with disabilities at the margins of society in terms of the adoption of key decisions

[1] Thomas Hammarberg, *The Right of People with Disabilities to Live Independently and Be Included in the Community. Issue Paper Published by the Council of Europe Commissioner for Human Rights* (Strasbourg: Council of Europe Publishing, 2012), p. 9.

[2] Ibid. p. 11.

[3] Office of the United Nations High Commissioner for Human Rights, *Equality and Non-Discrimination under Article 5 of the Convention on the Rights of Persons with Disabilities*, December 2010, UN Doc. A/HRC/34/26, para. 14.

that affect their everyday lives. The rights to education, access to culture and political participation also deserve particular attention, since they underlie the enjoyment of other substantive rights in the CRPD. For instance, without an education, people with disabilities cannot develop the necessary life and social skills to work or live independently. Likewise, when disabled people are denied access to culture or political participation, their quality of life and their ability to contribute to decision-making is seriously hindered.

As previously outlined in Chapter 3, human rights have traditionally been divided into two categories, namely civil and political rights, on the one hand, and economic, social and cultural rights, on the other hand. The rights to education and access to culture fall within the category of social and cultural rights, while the right to vote and participate in political and public life falls within the category of civil and political rights. While acknowledging this difference in categorisation, the present chapter aims to highlight the interdependence of these two sets of rights.

Against this background and following this brief introduction, section 2 discusses the right to education for persons with disabilities as enshrined in Article 24 CRPD. That section contains an overview of the evolution of the right to inclusive education and the meaning of the concept. It then outlines the goals of inclusive education and the measures to be adopted by States Parties under Article 24 CRPD, and addresses access to higher education. The rest of that section discusses the key challenges encountered in implementation of Article 24 CRPD as well as good practices in the field. Section 3 of the chapter turns to an examination of the right to access culture and the obligations stemming from that right. The right to access (and participate in) cultural life has often been considered to be less relevant than the right to education or the right to work, and little attention has traditionally been paid to it. However, in recent years, access to cultural goods and services for people with disabilities has emerged as a topic of scholarly enquiry and policy debate, and it currently forms one of the priority areas, *inter alia*, of the Council of Europe (CoE).[4] Finally, section 4 of the chapter is devoted to the right to political participation, which is an essential component in achieving active citizenship. That section discusses the normative content of Article 29 CRPD, which 'goes beyond the basic right to vote and be elected to public office in order to address the right of persons with disabilities to take part in other aspects of public life and civil society'.[5]

[4] In 2015, the Council of Europe (CoE) published a report, claiming the need for urgent 'political and practical responses pertaining to one of the essential dimensions of life . . .: participation in culture, sports, tourism and leisure activities' (Damjan Tatic, *Access for People with Disabilities to Culture, Tourism, Sports and Leisure Activities: Towards Meaningful and Enriching Participation* (Strasbourg: Council of Europe Publishing, 2015)).

[5] Rachele Cera, 'Article 29: Political Participation', in Valentina Della Fina, Rachele Cera and Giuseppe Palmisano (eds.), *The United Nations Convention on Human Rights: A Commentary* (Cham: Springer, 2017), pp. 525–9.

2 THE RIGHT TO EDUCATION

This section outlines the contours of the right to education in international human rights law, paying particular attention to the right to inclusive education under the CRPD and the key norms contained in Article 24 of the Convention. The focus of this section is, among other issues, on the distinction between exclusionary, segregated, integrated and inclusive education.

2.1 Setting the Scene: The Right to Education in International Human Rights Law

The right to education is a fundamental human right, contained, among others, in the Universal Declaration on Human Rights (UDHR),[6] the International Covenant on Economic, Social and Cultural Rights (ICESCR)[7] and the UN Convention on the Rights of the Child (CRC).[8] Under international human rights law, the right to education is 'both an end in itself as well as a means towards attaining all other human rights'.[9] Former UN Special Rapporteur on the Right to Education, Katarina Tomasevski, has described education as 'a bridge to all human rights'.[10]

The enjoyment of the right to education is indispensable for people with disabilities, in order to unlock the exercise of other substantive human rights and to ensure their full and equal participation in mainstream society. The Committee on the Rights of the Child (CRC Committee) recognises this in its General Comment No. 9, in which it notes that 'the lack of appropriate education and vocational training discriminates against [children with disabilities] by denying them job opportunities in the future'.[11] During the negotiation sessions leading to the adoption of the CRPD, education was described as 'the vector for all human development' and 'a predicate to the full enjoyment of a wide range of civil, political, economic, social and cultural rights, including political participation, freedom of expression, and access to employment'.[12]

[6] Article 26 UDHR. [7] Article 13 ICESCR. [8] Article 23 CRC.

[9] Andrea Broderick, *The Long and Winding Road to Equality and Inclusion for Persons with Disabilities: The United Nations Convention on the Rights of Persons with Disabilities* (Cambridge-Antwerp: Intersentia, 2015), p. 293.

[10] Katerina Tomasevski, *Education Denied: Costs and Remedies* (London: Zed Books Ltd, 2003), p. 172.

[11] UN Committee on the Rights of the Child (CRC Committee), General Comment No. 9, 27 February 2007, UN Doc. CRC/C/GC/9, para. 8.

[12] *Statement by the United States Delegation: at Round Table 2: CRPD Article 24 – Inclusion and the Right to Education Third Conference of States Parties* (New York, United Nations, 2 September 2010).

2.2 The Right to Inclusive Education

The CRPD contains a mandate of inclusive education.[13] Prior to the adoption of the CRPD, the right to inclusive education was not contained in a binding human rights treaty. However, there were certain milestones at the international level that shaped the development of the right to inclusive education. Several soft law human rights documents guarantee the right to education based on the principles of non-discrimination and universality, recognising that education should be available to all individuals on an equal basis. In 1960, the United Nations Educational, Scientific and Cultural Organization (UNESCO) Convention against Discrimination in Education was adopted,[14] and in the last decade of the twentieth century, three soft law documents emanated from international conferences on education. In 1990, the World Conference on Education for All took place in Thailand. At that conference, the World Declaration on Education (WDE) was published, in conjunction with the Framework for Action to Meet Basic Learning Needs. Those policy documents served to renew the commitment of the international community to providing Education for All (EFA). The Preamble of the WDE reiterated that the provision of education at that particular time was seriously deficient and that it must be qualitatively improved and must also be made universally available.[15] Importantly, the WDE acknowledged that 'steps need to be taken to provide equal access to education to every category of disabled persons as an integral part of the education system'.[16] Shortly after the adoption of the WDE, the Standard Rules on the Equalization of Opportunities for Persons with Disabilities (Standard Rules) sought to ensure equal educational opportunities for children, youth and adults with disabilities in integrated settings.[17] Finally, in 1994, the UNESCO World Conference on Special Needs Education: Access and Equality was held in Salamanca, Spain. This led to the adoption of the Salamanca Statement and Framework for Action on Special Needs Education.[18] The significance of that document lies in the fact that 'it marked

[13] See generally Gauthier de Beco, 'Transition to Inclusive Education Systems According to the Convention on the Rights of Persons with Disabilities' (2016) 34 *Nordic Journal of Human Rights* 40, at 40.

[14] United Nations Educational, Scientific and Cultural Organization (UNESCO) Convention against Discrimination in Education, adopted at the UNESCO General Conference, 14 November to 15 December 1960.

[15] Preamble of the UNESCO Declaration 'The World Declaration on Education for All: Meeting Basic Learning Needs' (1990) adopted by the UNESCO World Conference on Education for All on 9 March 1990, available at www.unesco.org/education/wef/en-conf/jomtien%20declaration%20eng.shtm.

[16] Ibid. [17] Rule 6 of the Standard Rules.

[18] The Salamanca Statement and Framework for Action on Special Needs Education, adopted at the World Conference on Special Needs Education: Access and Quality, Salamanca, Spain, 7–10 June 1994.

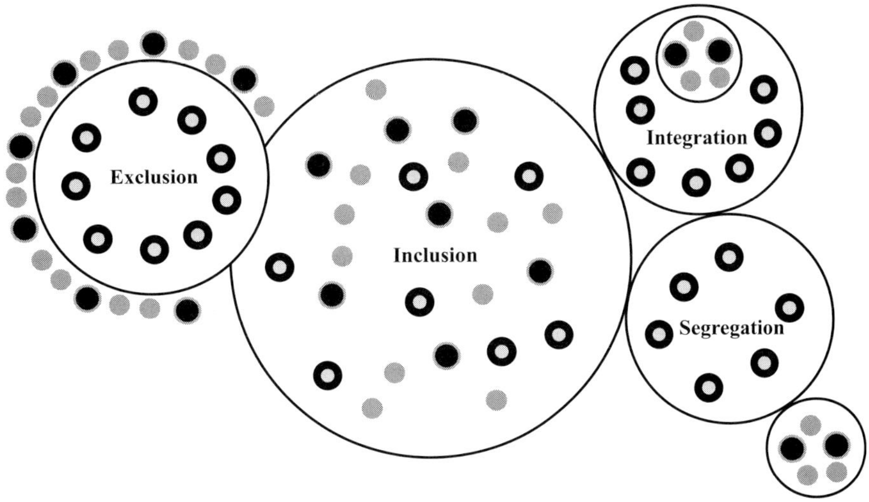

Figure 9.1 The Evolving Nature of the Right to Education for Persons with Disabilities

the beginnings of the acknowledgment at the international level of the importance of educating children in inclusive learning environments'.[19]

The right to education for persons with disabilities has evolved in four different stages: exclusion, segregation, integration and inclusion. Those four stages are highlighted in Figure 9.1.[20]

Historically, people with disabilities were excluded from educational settings, often having been deemed 'uneducable', in particular (but not only) individuals with severe intellectual disabilities. This has led to their being denied access to education. According to the CRPD Committee, 'exclusion occurs when students are directly or indirectly prevented from or denied access to education in any form'.[21]

Over time, education was gradually provided for people with disabilities in segregated settings, whereby disabled children were placed in designated 'special' schools, on account of the fact that they were deemed to be unable to cope with mainstream educational structures. Segregation is defined by the CRPD Committee as occurring 'when the education of students with disabilities is provided in separate environments designed or used to respond to a particular or various impairments, in isolation from students without disabilities'.[22]

[19] Ibid.

[20] The picture is taken from Think Inclusive, 'Inclusion, Exclusion, Segregation and Integration: How are they different?', available at www.thinkinclusive.us/inclusion-exclusion-segregation-integration-different/.

[21] CRPD Committee, General Comment No. 4, 2 September 2016, UN Doc. CRPD/C/GC/4, para. 11.

[22] Ibid.

The trend towards segregation of children with disabilities in special schools was followed by a move towards integrated education, whereby disabled individuals were placed in mainstream educational institutions. Integrated education systems seek to ensure that the disabled learner fits in with the 'norm'. Integrated education does not necessarily endeavour to remove existing barriers to learning for a particular individual. As a result, the former UN Special Rapporteur on the Right to Education (who succeeded Ms Tomasevski), Mr Vernor Muñoz Villalobos, has outlined the fact that 'the "integration" of learners with disabilities without full inclusion can lead to isolation of the learner and ultimately, [can be] an obstacle to meeting the education needs of all learners'.[23] Within integrated education, learners are generally divided into distinct categories according to their particular disability, and they are often provided with education in 'special classes'.

Both segregated and integrated education systems reflect, to different degrees, the outdated medical model of disability, in the sense that they focus on the functional limitations of the child in question, and they require the disabled learner to adapt to inaccessible educational institutions.[24]

An inclusive learning system is designed to ensure that people with disabilities can participate fully and access the right to education on an equal basis with others. This entails the elimination of barriers that restrict the participation of disabled learners in mainstream educational settings. These barriers might include physical barriers in the environment, such as inaccessible school buildings; communication and language barriers, such as inaccessible curricula; or attitudinal barriers, such as the resistance of teachers to instruct disabled learners or the unsupportive attitudes of other students. The elimination of such barriers necessarily

Does your university provide an inclusive educational system?

[23] Report of the Special Rapporteur on the Right to Education, Vernor Muñoz Villalobos, *The Right to Education of Persons with Disabilities*, 19 February 2007, UN Doc. A/HRC/4/29, para. 40.

[24] Andrea Broderick, 'The Right to Inclusive Education: Article 24 of the UN Convention on the Rights of Persons with Disabilities and the Irish Experience' (2018) 1 *The Irish Yearbook of International Law* 29.

involves the provision of material support to students with disabilities, where necessary.

As will be discussed further below, Article 24 CRPD does not define what is meant by the concept of 'inclusive education'. However, according to the CRPD Committee, inclusion:

> involves a process of systemic reform embodying changes and modifications in content, teaching methods, approaches, structures and strategies in education to overcome barriers with a vision serving to provide all students of the relevant age range with an equitable and participatory learning experience and [an] environment that best corresponds to their requirements and preferences.[25]

The former UN Special Rapporteur on the Right to Education elaborates on this child-centred focus in his third annual report on education:

> inclusive education is based on the principle that all children should learn together, wherever possible, regardless of difference. Inclusive education acknowledges that every child has unique characteristics, interests, abilities and learning needs and that those learners with special education needs must have access to and be accommodated in the general education system through a child-centred pedagogy.[26]

2.3 Article 24 CRPD

ARTICLE 24 CRPD

1. States Parties recogni[s]e the right of persons with disabilities to education. With a view to reali[s]ing this right without discrimination and on the basis of equal opportunity, States Parties shall ensure an inclusive education system at all levels and life long learning directed to:

(a) The full development of human potential and sense of dignity and self-worth, and the strengthening of respect for human rights, fundamental freedoms and human diversity;
(b) The development by persons with disabilities of their personality, talents and creativity, as well as their mental and physical abilities, to their fullest potential;

[25] CRPD Committee, General Comment No. 4, note 21, para. 11.

[26] Report of the Special Rapporteur on the Right to Education, Vernor Muñoz Villalobos, note 23.

(c) Enabling persons with disabilities to participate effectively in a free society.

2. In reali[s]ing this right, States Parties shall ensure that:

(a) Persons with disabilities are not excluded from the general education system on the basis of disability, and that children with disabilities are not excluded from free and compulsory primary education, or from secondary education, on the basis of disability;
(b) Persons with disabilities can access an inclusive, quality and free primary education and secondary education on an equal basis with others in the communities in which they live;
(c) Reasonable accommodation of the individual's requirements is provided;
(d) Persons with disabilities receive the support required, within the general education system, to facilitate their effective education;
(e) Effective individuali[s]ed support measures are provided in environments that maximi[s]e academic and social development, consistent with the goal of full inclusion.

3. States Parties shall enable persons with disabilities to learn life and social development skills to facilitate their full and equal participation in education and as members of the community. To this end, States Parties shall take appropriate measures, including:

(a) Facilitating the learning of Braille, alternative script, augmentative and alternative modes, means and formats of communication and orientation and mobility skills, and facilitating peer support and mentoring;
(b) Facilitating the learning of sign language and the promotion of the linguistic identity of the deaf community;
(c) Ensuring that the education of persons, and in particular children, who are blind, deaf or deafblind, is delivered in the most appropriate languages and modes and means of communication for the individual, and in environments which maximi[s]e academic and social development.

4. In order to help ensure the reali[s]ation of this right, States Parties shall take appropriate measures to employ teachers, including teachers with disabilities, who are qualified in sign language and/or Braille, and to train professionals and staff who work at all levels of education. Such training shall incorporate disability awareness and the use of appropriate augmentative and alternative modes, means and formats of communication, educational techniques and materials to support persons with disabilities.

5. States Parties shall ensure that persons with disabilities are able to access general tertiary education, vocational training, adult education and lifelong learning without discrimination and on an equal basis with others. To this end, States Parties shall ensure that reasonable accommodation is provided to persons with disabilities.

Article 24 CRPD constitutes the first binding legal enunciation of the right to inclusive education. The key obligation contained in Article 24 is the realisation of 'an inclusive education system at all levels and lifelong learning'. Article 24 does not provide a normative definition of 'inclusive education'; however, it sets out a range of measures to be adopted by States Parties to the CRPD. The sub-sections that follow elaborate on the goals of inclusive education and the measures that are required of States Parties in order to achieve inclusion in educational settings.[27]

2.3.1 *The Goals of Inclusive Education*

The overarching theme of Article 24 is that education must be effective. Article 24(2)(d) provides that States Parties must ensure that 'persons with disabilities receive the support required, within the general education system, to facilitate their effective education'. According to the text of Article 24(1)(a), inclusive education systems should ensure 'the full development of human potential and sense of dignity and self-worth' and 'the strengthening of respect for ... human diversity'. Furthermore, according to Article 24(1)(b), education systems must enable persons with disabilities to develop 'their personality, talents and creativity, as well as their mental and physical abilities, to their fullest potential'.

The third goal to be achieved by inclusive education, as laid down in Article 24(1)(c), is to enable 'persons with disabilities to participate effectively in a free society'. States Parties are, therefore, required to create real opportunities for individuals with disabilities to foster their capabilities, in order to enable them to take an active role in society, wherever possible.

2.3.2 *The Measures Required to Achieve Inclusion*

In order to achieve the goals listed above, Article 24 CRPD sets down a comprehensive list of obligations to be complied with by States Parties to

[27] Some parts of sub-section 2.3.2 are drawn from Andrea Broderick, 'Equality of What? The Capability Approach and the Right to Education for Persons with Disabilities' (2018) 6(1) *Social Inclusion* 29.

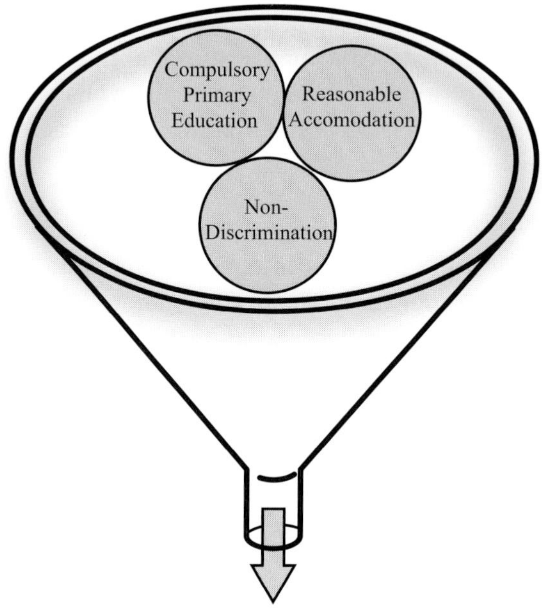

Figure 9.2 Minimum Core Obligations Related to the Right to Education

the Convention. The measures required under Article 24 are based on the social-contextual model of disability, which targets disadvantages arising from the interaction between learners' impairments and external factors, caused by environmental or attitudinal barriers to learning. Article 24 is also built on the human rights model of disability. Both models are discussed extensively in Chapter 2 of this textbook.

Article 24 seeks to ensure equality of access to all levels of education (primary, secondary and tertiary education as well as vocational training, adult education and lifelong learning) and the provision of equal opportunities. Since the right to education is a socio-economic right, most elements of the right are progressively realisable. Notwithstanding this, certain elements of the right have immediate effect. Drawing on the work of the UN Committee on Economic, Social and Cultural Rights (CESCR), States Parties to the CRPD are deemed to have 'a minimum core obligation to ensure the satisfaction of, at the very least, minimum essential levels' of each of the elements of the right to education.[28] The core obligations, depicted in Figure 9.2, have to be realised immediately by States Parties and are not subject to progressive realisation.[29]

The CRPD Committee urges States Parties to ensure at least twelve years of free, publicly funded, inclusive and equitable quality primary and secondary

[28] UN Committee on Economic, Social and Cultural Rights (CESCR), General Comment No. 3, 14 December 1990, UN Doc. E/1991/23, para. 10.

[29] CRPD Committee, General Comment No. 4, note 21, paras. 33 and 40.

education, of which at least nine years are compulsory.[30] Compulsory, quality, free and accessible primary education is an immediate obligation, according to the Committee.[31] The prohibition of non-discrimination is also an immediate and core obligation of States Parties to the CRPD.[32] According to the CRPD Committee, States Parties must ensure non-discrimination and non-exclusion from education for individuals with disabilities.[33] This is in line with Article 24 (2)(a) of the Convention itself, which requires States Parties to ensure that 'persons with disabilities are not excluded from the general education system on the basis of disability, and that children with disabilities are not excluded from free and compulsory primary education, or from secondary education, on the basis of disability'.

Pursuant to Article 24(2)(b) CRPD, States Parties must ensure that persons with disabilities can access an inclusive, quality and free primary education and secondary education on an equal basis with others in the communities in which they live. The Committee recommends that States Parties take urgent steps to remove all legal, administrative and other forms of discrimination impeding the right of access to inclusive education.[34]

The measures required under Article 24 seek to address the wide diversity of needs of individual learners. In that respect, Article 24(2)(c) requires States Parties to ensure that reasonable accommodation of the individual learner's requirements is provided, and that duty has been deemed to be a core obligation by the CRPD Committee.[35] According to the Committee, reasonable accommodation measures may include: changing the location of a class; certain modifications in learning materials or providing all handouts in an alternative format; providing a note-taker or a language interpreter to students; or allowing them to use assistive technologies (AT).[36] Moreover, the Committee also encourages States Parties to provide non-material accommodations, such as: allowing more time for studying; alternative evaluation methods; or replacing an element of curriculum by an alternative element.[37]

As well as satisfying the minimum core of the right to education, States Parties have several other obligations under Article 24 CRPD. In order to ensure inclusive education, effective individualised support measures are envisaged under Article 24(2)(d) and (e). Individualised support measures aim to alter education systems in a general fashion, to ensure inclusion over a longer period of time.[38] This does not mean that these measures do not have to be tailored to cater for the individual needs of each learner.[39] According to the CRPD Committee, individualised supports entail 'the provision of sufficient

[30] Ibid. para. 41(c). [31] Ibid. para. 24. [32] Ibid. [33] Ibid. [34] Ibid. para. 40.

[35] Ibid. On reasonable accommodation see above Chapter 4. [36] Ibid. para. 29. [37] Ibid.

[38] Gauthier De Beco, 'The Right to Inclusive Education According to Article 24 of the UN Convention on the Rights of Persons with Disabilities: Background, Requirements and (Remaining) Questions' (2014) 32(3) *Netherlands Quarterly of Human Rights* 263, at 281.

[39] Ibid.

trained and supported teaching staff, school counsellors, psychologists, and other relevant health and social service professionals, as well as access to scholarships and financial resources'.[40] The difference between Article 24(2)(d) and Article 24(2)(e) is that the former envisages supports within the mainstream system, while the latter outlines that supports must be provided in environments that maximise academic and social development, consistent with the goal of full inclusion. During the negotiation sessions leading to the adoption of the CRPD, the World Federation of the Deaf (WFD) advocated for the option of separate schooling for students who are deaf, blind or deaf-blind. The WFD expressed its concern that inclusion might become 'a simple placement in a regular school without meaningful interaction with classmates and professionals . . . [which is] . . . tantamount to exclusion of the deaf learner from education and society'.[41] Article 24(2)(e) CRPD seeks to ensure that the types of concerns expressed by the WFD were taken into account in the final text of the Convention. According to some authors,[42] that Article arguably maintains the option for disabled individuals, particularly those who are blind, deaf or deaf-blind, to attend specialised schools, as long as those schools provide an environment that 'maximi[s]es academic and social development'.

Importantly, Article 24(2)(e) and Article 24(3) acknowledge the fact that education is not merely an academic tool. Rather, education should 'enable persons with disabilities to learn life and social development skills to facilitate their full and equal participation in education and as members of the community'. To that end, States Parties are required to facilitate the learning of Braille, alternative script, augmentative and alternative modes, means and formats of communication and orientation and mobility skills, and facilitating peer support and mentoring.[43] In addition, States Parties are required to facilitate the learning of sign language and the promotion of the linguistic identity of the Deaf community.[44]

The training of professionals and staff working with persons with disabilities is one of the explicitly enumerated general obligations of States Parties contained in Article 4 CRPD, and it is reaffirmed in Article 24(4). In its Concluding Observations (COs), the CRPD Committee acknowledges the fact that teacher training is indispensable in order to ensure that existing education

[40] CRPD Committee, General Comment No. 4, note 21, para. 63.

[41] World Federation of the Deaf, *Education Rights for Deaf Children: A Policy Statement of the World Federation of the Deaf* (2007), available at www.wfdeaf.org/databank/policies.

[42] De Beco, 'The Right to Inclusive Education According to Article 24 of the UN Convention on the Rights of Persons with Disabilities: Background, Requirements and (Remaining) Questions', note 38, at 282. See also Oddny M. Arnardóttir, 'The Right to Inclusive Education for Children with Disabilities – Innovations in the CRPD', in Asbjørn Eide, Jakob Th. Möller and Ineta Ziemele, *Making Peoples Heard: Essays on Human Rights in Honour of Gudmundur Alfredsson* (Leiden-Boston: Martinus Nijhoff, 2011), pp. 197–228.

[43] Article 24(3)(a) CRPD. [44] Article 24(3)(b) CRPD.

systems are transformed into fully inclusive ones and that existing barriers are eradicated.[45] According to the Committee, it is necessary to conduct pre-service training for new teachers and in-service training[46] of both teaching and non-teaching school staff.[47] De Boer et al. confirm that teachers who gained proper training 'hold more positive attitudes towards inclusive education than teachers who have less experience and received less training'.[48]

Finally, Article 24(5) CRPD seeks to ensure that persons with disabilities are able to access general tertiary education, vocational training, adult education and lifelong learning without discrimination and on an equal basis with others. Access to higher education is discussed in the sub-section that follows.

2.4 Access to Higher Education

At the global level, people with disabilities are under-represented in higher education. For example, according to the European Commission, access to inclusive, quality education remains 'elusive' for many people with disabilities across Europe.[49]

DID YOU KNOW THAT ...?

Only about 29.5 per cent of persons with disabilities in the age group 30–34 have completed higher (tertiary) education or equivalent, compared with 42.5 per cent for persons without disabilities. Achieving increased levels of participation in tertiary education is a core European policy goal. The Europe 2020 Strategy aims to ensure that at least 40 per cent of 30–34-year-olds complete third level education by 2020. Moreover, the Education and Training 2020 Strategy clearly emphasises the need to promote equity in access to, and participation in, tertiary education, as well as social cohesion and active citizenship. The active engagement of disabled people in higher education is also supported by the European Disability Strategy 2010–2020 (European Commission, Staff Working Document, *Progress report on the implementation of the European Disability Strategy* 2010–2020, p. 4).

[45] CRPD Committee, Concluding Observations on the Initial Report of Costa Rica, 11 May 2014, UN Doc. CRPD/C/CRI/CO/1, para. 46; CRPD Committee, Concluding Observations on the Initial Report of Azerbaijan, 11 May 2014, UN Doc. CRPD/C/AZE/CO/1, para. 41(c).

[46] UN General Assembly, *Thematic Study on the Right of Persons with Disabilities to Education – Report of the Office of the United Nations High Commissioner for Human Rights*, 18 December 2013, UN Doc. A/HRC/25/29, para. 53.

[47] CRPD Committee, General Comment No. 4, note 21, para. 35.

[48] Anke de Boer, Sip Jan Pijl and Alexander Minnaert, 'Regular Primary Schoolteachers' Attitudes Towards Inclusive Education: A Review of the Literature' (2011) 15(3) *International Journal of Inclusive Education* 347.

[49] European Commission, *Staff Working Document, Progress report on the implementation of the European Disability Strategy* (2010–2020), p. 4.

According to the European Network on Independent Living (ENIL), there are a number of challenges inherent in increasing the participation of people with disabilities in higher education, one of which is 'how to achieve excellence in higher education, while at the same time making it more inclusive'.[50] Other challenges include the diversity of entry procedures to third level education. In that regard, ENIL notes that 'many educational institutions acknowledge that students with disabilities who have studied in special schools have a very small, if any, chance to transit to third level education'.[51] In particular, 'some fields of study may ... be closed to people with certain impairments, such as teaching, medicine, nursing, or engineering'.[52]

Guaranteeing the active engagement of people with disabilities in higher education is a key objective of Article 24(5) CRPD. To give effect to that Article, States Parties are required to ensure that persons with disabilities are able to access general tertiary education, vocational training, adult education and lifelong learning, without discrimination and on an equal basis with others, and they are required to ensure the provision of reasonable accommodation to that end. As highlighted above, primary education is a core immediate obligation of States Parties. By way of contrast, access to higher education is to be achieved progressively. Nonetheless, States Parties are required to take steps towards that goal immediately after ratification of the Convention, including ensuring that people with disabilities are able to access education in both public and private academic institutions on an equal basis with others, providing reasonable accommodation and the adoption of positive action in favour of learners with disabilities in higher educational institutions.[53]

2.5 Key Challenges in Implementation of the Right to Inclusive Education

In many developing countries, an overwhelming majority of disabled children are excluded from mainstream education at every level. In a 2007 report, former UN Special Rapporteur on the Right to Education noted that, while the net enrolment rate in primary education in the developing world had increased to 86 per cent over all regions,[54] 'estimates of the number of children

[50] ENIL's written contribution to the Day of General Discussion on the right to education for persons with disabilities, available at www.ohchr.org/Documents/HRBodies/CRPD/DGD/2015/ENIL.doc.

[51] Ibid. [52] Ibid. [53] CRPD Committee, General Comment No. 4, note 21, para. 38.

[54] Report of the Special Rapporteur on the Right to Education, Vernor Muñoz Villalobos, note 23, para. 8. See also the United Nations, *The Millennium Goals Development Report* (2006), p. 6, available at http//mdgs.un.org/unsd/mdg/Resources/Static/Products/Progress2006/MDGReport2006.pdf. For more recent data see Division for Inclusive Social Development (DISD) of the United Nations Department for Economic and Social Affairs, *UN 2018 Flagship Report on Disability and Development*, available at https://www.ohchr.org/Documents/HRBodies/CRPD/UN2018FlagshipReportDisability.pdf, particularly at p.100.

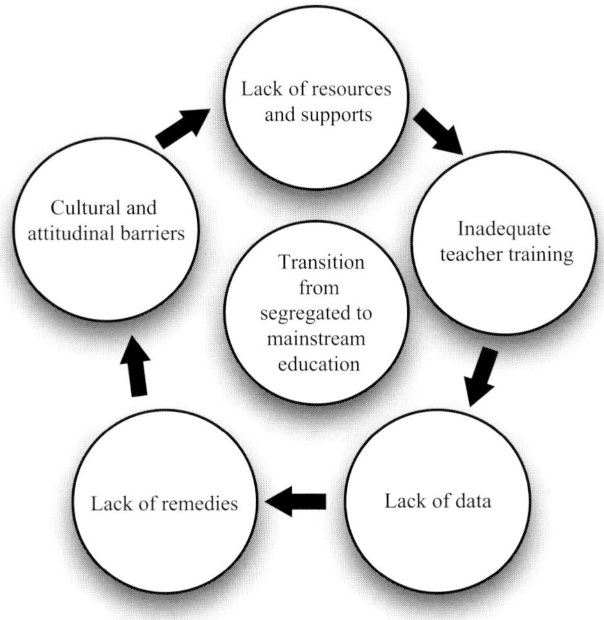

Figure 9.3 Key Challenges in Implementation of Article 24 CRPD

with disabilities attending school in developing countries range from less than 1% to 5%'.[55] Developed countries also struggle to fulfil the right to education. Figure 9.3 illustrates a non-exhaustive list of the challenges that are experienced in the provision of inclusive education.

2.5.1 *Transition from Segregated Educational Settings to Inclusive Education*

In both European and African countries, as well as across the continents of Asia, the Americas and Australia, access to mainstream education for children, young people and adults with disabilities remains a great challenge. While many laws and policies have been put in place in States Parties to the CRPD seeking to ensure inclusion, there remains a high number of children with disabilities with either no access to education or only access to segregated education.[56] Certain groups of disabled individuals are at high risk of being forced into segregated educational provision. These include children with

[55] Ibid. citing Susan Peters, *Inclusive Education: An EFA Strategy for All Children* (World Bank, November 2004), available at www.worldbank.org/; see also, UNESCO, *Guidelines for Inclusion: Ensuring Access to Education for All* (Paris: UNESCO Publishing, 2005), p. 11.

[56] Joint statement by Inclusion International, Inclusion Europe and Mental Disability Advocacy Centre, *Challenging Discrimination at the Expense of Promoting Equality,* 14 February 2013,

intellectual disabilities, those with severe psychosocial impairments and associated challenging behaviour as well as those with multiple impairments.[57] Deaf children also face significant barriers in accessing mainstream education and are still commonly placed in special schools.

A report published by the European Association of Service Providers (EASPD) reveals that 'the general increase of inclusive education has not caused a general decrease of persons with [special educational needs] in special schools or other segregating facilities'.[58] On the contrary, the report draws attention to the fact that 'especially in countries with a traditional special education system the number of children and youngsters in special schools has also been increasing [and as a consequence] persons with more severe educational needs [are still] mostly excluded from inclusive education'.[59]

DID YOU KNOW THAT ...?

The negative trends outlined above are also evident in the COs of the CRPD Committee. In its COs on the Initial Report of Tunisia, for instance, the Committee notes 'with deep concern' the fact that, in practice, the national authorities' inclusion strategy has not been equally implemented in all schools (CRPD Committee, COs on the Initial Report of Tunisia, 13 May 2011, UN Doc. CRPD/C/TUN/CO/1, para. 30). In addition, the Committee's COs to Australia express concern regarding the fact that 'students with disabilities continue to be placed in special schools and many of those who are in regular schools are largely confined to special classes or units' (CRPD Committee, COs on the Initial Report of Australia, 24 October 2013, UN Doc. CRPD/C/AUS/CO/1, para. 45). Additionally, in its COs to Thailand, the Committee observes 'that the right to inclusive education remains unfulfilled for many persons with disabilities; that some schools refuse to admit students with disabilities; and that staff and educational establishments, particularly in rural and remote areas, have limited capacity, skills and resources' (CRPD Committee, COs on the Initial Report of Thailand, 12 May 2016, UN Doc. CRPD/C/THA/CO/1, para. 45). Moreover, the Committee draws attention to the fact that, in Korea, despite the existence of an inclusive education policy, some students with disabilities who have been enrolled in regular schools return to special schools (CRPD Committee, COs on the Initial Report of Korea, 29 October 2014, UN Doc. CRPD/C/KOR/CO/1, para. 45).

---

available at http://inclusion-international.org/challenging-discrimination-at-the-expense-of-promoting-equality/.

[57] Ibid.

[58] European Association of Service Providers (EASPD), *Barometer of Inclusive Education in Selected European Countries* (ZPE-Schriftenreihe Nr. 31), p. 38, available at www.investt.eu/sites/default/files/barometerreport.pdf.

[59] Ibid.

2.5.2 *Lack of Resources and Supports*

Research suggests that, even where education is provided in mainstream environments, learners with disabilities remain isolated and excluded in the educational systems of many European countries.[60] Despite the lack of data on the cost of special schools when compared with inclusive education, the World Report on Disability highlights the fact that inclusive settings are generally perceived to be more cost-effective than segregated settings, at least in the long term.[61] Nonetheless, in the short-to-medium term, limited or inadequate financial resources continue to act as a barrier to inclusive education. This problem often stems from a lack of resources in States Parties to the CRPD, combined with a lack of willingness to attribute whatever resources do exist to inclusive education, an issue which is obviously aggravated in developing countries.

CASE STUDY

Education in Uganda

In Uganda, despite a relatively strong regulatory framework on education, funding of inclusive education remains an issue. A report, published in 2013 by the Civil Society Budget Advocacy Group, highlighted that only 0.33 per cent of the educational budget had been allocated to financing education for persons with disabilities in the periods 2010/11 and 2012/13, even though the Persons with Disabilities Act (2006) stipulates that not less than 10 per cent of all educational expenditure should be allocated to the needs of disabled people. According to the National Development Plan (NDP), 10 per cent of children in school have special needs, and their access to adequate education is hampered by limited technical, human, financial and physical public resources (Civil Society Budget Advocacy Group and Democratic Government Facility, *Financing Special Needs Education in Uganda*, 2013, p. 7).

In addition, within mainstream environments, there are major anomalies in the provision of sufficient and effective supports for individuals with disabilities. The EASPD report, mentioned above, highlights the fact that, in many countries, legislation has not been accompanied by the 'necessary resources to

[60] NESSE Network of experts for the European Commission, Education and Disabilities/Special Needs, *Policies and practices in education, training and employment for students with disabilities and special needs in the EU* (2012), available at www.nesse.fr/nesse/activities/reports/activities/reports/disability-special-needs-1.

[61] World Health Organization, *World Report on Disability* (2011), available at www.who.int/disabilities/world_report/2011/report.pdf.

provide inclusive arrangements for all persons with [special educational needs] in regular schools or other educational facilities'.[62] In its COs to Australia, the CRPD Committee points to the fact that 'students with disabilities enrolled in regular schools receive a substandard education due to a lack of reasonable accommodation'.[63]

2.5.3 *Inadequate Teacher Training*

In addition to a lack of material resources and supports, challenges in the implementation of Article 24 CRPD also arise with regard to human resources. The EASPD report points to the fact that, in certain countries, there is a 'strong tendency' among teachers to resist 'individual curricula, didactical adaptations and teaching methods'.[64] Moreover, there are 'huge regional variations'[65] in terms of teacher training. The CRPD Committee has also commented on the fact that there is a distinct lack of teacher training on disability in mainstream education.[66] As a result, the Committee has urged States Parties to 'ensure that inclusive education is an integral part of core teacher-training in universities'.[67]

2.5.4 *Lack of Data*

In many countries, disaggregated statistics on disability do not exist in the realm of education. Those countries that do collect data on education often neglect to collect systematic data on lifelong learning or the participation of people with disabilities in higher education. ENIL observes that 'there is also a lack of disaggregated data around the intersections of disability and gender, and disability and ethnicity'.[68] As a result, 'there seems to be little attention paid to the experience of females in terms of access to education and educational outcomes'.[69]

Several challenges exist when it comes to collecting data on the implementation of Article 24, and it is difficult to ascertain how inclusive education systems really are. This arises, in part, due to a lack of consistency in the terminology surrounding inclusive education. According to ENIL, each European country has its own definition of 'disability' and 'special educational needs', and 'this means that it can be difficult to establish who is included or excluded in the figures, making comparisons between different countries

[62] EASPD, *Barometer of Inclusive Education in Selected European Countries*, note 58.

[63] CRPD Committee, Concluding Observations on the Initial Report of Australia, 24 October 2013, UN Doc. CRPD/C/AUS/CO/1, para. 45.

[64] EASPD, *Barometer of Inclusive Education in Selected European Countries*, note 58.

[65] Ibid.

[66] See, for instance, CRPD Committee, Concluding Observations on the Initial Report of Tunisia, 13 May 2011, UN Doc. CRPD/C/TUN/CO/1, para. 31.

[67] Ibid.

[68] ENIL's written contribution to the Day of General Discussion on the right to education for persons with disabilities, note 50.

[69] Ibid.

and monitoring of progress cumbersome'.[70] The use of differing definitions of 'special educational needs' also makes it 'difficult to track inclusion efforts', according to ENIL.[71] De Beco points to the usefulness of indicators in measuring inclusion.[72] Both the OHCHR and the CRPD Committee require States Parties to create monitoring frameworks that contain 'structural, process and outcome indicators, and specific benchmarks and targets for each indicator'.[73] These types of indicators can be used to measure the existing barriers in inclusive education, the progress achieved in ensuring inclusion as well as the percentage of students with disabilities in mainstream schools who obtained their final certification.[74]

2.5.5 *Lack of Legal Remedies*

The CRPD Committee has remarked on the 'lack of legal remedies and mechanisms to claim redress for violations'.[75] The Committee puts forth the view that States Parties must introduce independent, effective, accessible, transparent, safe and enforceable complaints mechanisms and legal remedies in cases of violations of the right to education.[76] Individuals with disabilities must also have access to justice systems that are responsive to their particular needs. Those systems must provide accommodation measures and be capable of addressing disability-based claims.[77] States Parties must also ensure that information about the right to education itself is widely disseminated, in collaboration with DPOs.[78]

Can you think of any cultural or attitudinal barriers to inclusive education in your country?

2.5.6 *Cultural and Attitudinal Barriers to Inclusion*

In countries that still adopt a medicalised perspective on disability, cultural and attitudinal barriers often hinder the inclusion of persons with

[70] Ibid. [71] Ibid.

[72] Gauthier de Beco, 'Transition to Inclusive Education Systems According to the Convention on the Rights of Persons with Disabilities', note 13.

[73] CRPD Committee, General Comment No. 4, note 21, para. 73; UN General Assembly, *Thematic Study on the Right of Persons with Disabilities to Education – Report of the Office of the United Nations High Commissioner for Human Rights*, note 46, para. 62.

[74] Ibid. [75] CRPD Committee, General Comment No. 4, note 21. [76] Ibid. [77] Ibid.

[78] Ibid. para. 63.

disabilities in educational settings. This is due, in part, to prejudicial attitudes regarding the capabilities of persons with disabilities and also concerning their ability to contribute to the economic life of a country.

CASE STUDY

Education of Children with Disabilities in India

Disability has been deemed to be a major limitation on progress towards the realisation of universal primary education in India. While statistics at the domestic level are inconsistent, estimates suggest that school participation among children with disabilities never rises above 70 per cent, far below the national average of around 90 per cent.

The disaggregated data set highlights important variations. Almost three-quarters of children with severe impairments remain out of school, compared with about 35 to 40 per cent of children with mild or moderate impairments. The most likely children to be excluded are those with psychosocial disabilities (two-thirds of whom never enrol in school) or children who are blind (over half of whom never enrol in school).

Prejudicial attitudes among members of the public remain one of the greatest barriers to equal education for people with disabilities in India, and it is reported that children with psychosocial disabilities face the most deeply entrenched prejudice. In a public attitude survey carried out in Uttar Pradesh and Tamil Nadu, almost half of the respondents were of the opinion that such children could not attend regular or special schools. Another commonly held view in India is that individuals with psychosocial disabilities would not find decent employment (R. Reiser, *Implementing Inclusive Education: A Commonwealth Guide to Implementing Article 24 of the UN Convention on the Rights of Persons with Disabilities*, 2nd edn, Commonwealth Secretariat, 2012, p. 22).

2.6 Good Practices in the Field of Inclusive Education

In spite of the significant gaps in the implementation of Article 24 CRPD, several States Parties to the CRPD demonstrate good practices in the field. The good practices highlighted below are not intended to provide an exhaustive account of all good practices adopted in States Parties to the Convention.

As well as commenting on the gaps in States Parties' education systems, the CRPD Committee has acknowledged the significant efforts being made in implementation of the Convention. The Committee has, for instance, commended Sweden for its inclusive education system, in which only 1.5 per cent of children are instructed outside mainstream schools.[79]

CASE STUDY

The Inclusive Education System in Italy

Italy abandoned segregated educational practices many decades ago and, since then, has implemented wide-ranging laws and policies on inclusive education. There appears to be a general consensus among legal scholars that, even prior to the ratification of the CRPD in 2009, the Italian legal and policy framework was characterised by a relatively high standard of protection of the right to education of pupils with disabilities. In September 2014, the Italian Government initiated a process of modernisation of the whole educational system. In 2015, the Government enacted Law 107/2015, whose aim is to improve the functionality of the Italian educational system and to empower the Government to adopt specific provisions that aim to ensure the full enjoyment of the right to education for people with disabilities. Law 107/2015 appears to demonstrate a commitment towards the realisation of a truly inclusive educational system in Italy, one which is to be achieved through redefining the training to be undertaken by prospective support teachers. The teacher training system is set out in legislative decrees, together with specific norms aimed at ensuring the continuity in service of support teachers in order to guarantee an effective right to education. Despite this strong regulatory framework, practical challenges have been highlighted, including the lack of resources (Delia Ferri, 'The Past, Present and Future of the Right to Inclusive Education in Italy', in Gauthier De Beco, Shivaun Quinlivan and Janet Lord (eds.), *The Right to Inclusive Education in International Human Rights Law* (Cambridge: Cambridge University Press, 2019); Delia Ferri, 'Inclusive Education in Italy: A Legal Appraisal 10 Year[s] after the Signature of the UN Convention on the Rights of Persons with Disabilities' (2017) 12(2) *Journal of Theories and Research in Education* 1).

Several countries have implemented programmes and policies, calling for the active participation of parents in decisions concerning their children's right to education.[80] In Finland, for example, parents' participation in

[79] CRPD Committee, Concluding Observations on the Initial Report of Sweden, 11 May 2014, UN Doc. CRPD/C/SWE/CO/1, para. 4.

[80] Ibid.

special education is obligatory.[81] A Danish project, entitled 'Children's Voice', consults with parents and children to elicit their views on the well-being and experiences of each learner. Finland has also implemented various programmes seeking to ensure greater accessibility in its education system.[82]

3 PERSONS WITH DISABILITIES AND ACCESS TO CULTURE

This section examines the right to access culture and participate in cultural life. In particular, it analyses the obligations that stem from Article 30 CRPD.

3.1 Setting the Scene: Access to Culture and Participation in Cultural Life in International Human Rights Law

The right to access cultural goods and services and to participate in the creation of culture is deeply rooted in international human rights law. Article 27 UDHR affirms that 'everyone has the right to freely participate in the cultural life of the community, to enjoy the arts and to share in scientific advancement and its benefits'. In the same vein, Article 15(1)(a) ICESCR recognises 'the right of everyone to take part in cultural life', and other international conventions provide for the right to access and participate in cultural life.[83]

The UDHR and the ICESCR do not contain a definition of 'culture' or 'cultural life'. However, in its General Comment No. 21 on Article 15 ICESCR, the CESCR adopts a wide definition of culture, encompassing:

> ways of life, language, oral and written literature, music and song, non-verbal communication, religion or belief systems, rites and ceremonies, sport and games, methods of production or technology, natural and man-made environments, food, clothing and shelter and the arts, customs and traditions through which individuals, groups of individuals and communities express their humanity.[84]

That General Comment also specifies that the right to take part in cultural life must not be read in isolation – it needs to be considered in conjunction with the right to enjoy the benefits of scientific progress; the right of everyone to

[81] Report of the Special Rapporteur on the Right to Education, Vernor Muñoz Villalobos, note 23, para. 79.

[82] On the Danish project see further UNESCO, *A Guide for Ensuring Inclusion and Equity in Education* (2017), p. 28, available at http://unesdoc.unesco.org/images/0024/002482/248254e.pdf. On the Finnish programmes see Lisa Waddington and Andrea Broderick, *Promoting Equality and Non-Discrimination for Persons with Disabilities* (Strasbourg: Council of Europe Publishing, 2017), p. 42.

[83] Elsa Stamatopoulou, *Cultural Rights in International Law. Article 27 of the Universal Declaration of Human Rights and Beyond* (Leiden/Boston: Martinus Nijhoff, 2007).

[84] CESCR, General Comment No. 21, 21 December 2009, UN Doc. E/C.12/GC/21, para. 13.

benefit from the protection of moral and material interests resulting from any scientific, literary or artistic production of which they are the author; and the freedom indispensable for scientific research and creative activity. The foregoing rights are also included in Article 15 ICESCR.[85] The right of everyone to take part in cultural life is also intrinsically linked to the right to education, and it is interdependent on other rights enshrined in the Covenant.[86]

Article 10 of the European Convention on Human Rights (ECHR) affirms the right to freedom of expression. Article 15 of the European Social Charter (ESC) provides for the right of persons with disabilities to independence, social integration and participation in the life of the community. At the same time, it establishes the duty of States Parties to the Charter to promote the full inclusion of people with disabilities and their 'participation in the life of the community, in particular through measures, including technical aids, aiming to overcome barriers to communication and mobility and enabling access to transport, housing, cultural activities and leisure'. As will be discussed in Part II of this textbook, the Charter of Fundamental Rights of the European Union (EU CFR) affirms the right of persons with disabilities 'to benefit from measures designed to ensure their independence, social and occupational integration and participation in the life of the community'. The EU CFR also recognises the rights to freedom of expression and information (in Article 11) and freedom of arts and science (in Article 13). Those provisions are formulated in a general fashion, and neither of them includes an explicit reference to people with disabilities or to their specific needs.

The first document to include a specific provision on disability and culture was the Standard Rules, in Rule 10. That rule was aimed at encouraging UN Member States to ensure 'that persons with disabilities are integrated into and can participate in cultural activities on an equal basis', and that 'persons with disabilities have the opportunity to utili[s]e their creative, artistic and intellectual potential'. It also provided that States should 'promote the accessibility to and availability of places for cultural performances and services', and 'initiate the development and use of special technical arrangements to make literature, films and theatre accessible to persons with disabilities'. However, only with the adoption of the CRPD did a binding international human rights law provision explicitly affirm the right of disabled individuals to access cultural goods and services.

Article 30 CRPD has put an end to the seemingly marginal relevance of arts and culture for people with disabilities. It has also fostered a debate within other international treaty bodies on the need to ensure access to cultural goods and services for people with disabilities. It is notable that General Comment

[85] Ibid. para. 2. [86] Ibid.

No. 21[87] of the CESCR, published in 2009, refers to Article 30 CRPD, and it explicitly mentions accessibility of cultural goods and services. In the same vein, the CRC Committee, in its General Comment No. 17 (on the right of the child to rest, leisure, play, recreational activities, cultural life and the arts), 'welcomes' Article 30 CRPD,[88] recognising its ground-breaking value.[89] The new CoE Disability Strategy 2017–2023, which will be discussed further in Chapter 13, identifies, among its priority areas, the duty to ensure the 'participation, involvement and inclusion of persons with disabilities in the media, entertainment and cultural life as both active actors and users'.[90]

DID YOU KNOW THAT ...?

Even though several good practices exist in terms of fostering the accessibility of cultural goods and services, these are generally limited to a small set of specific public strategies, to single cultural institutions (such as international museums), to renewed archaeological sites or selected public libraries. A wide range of cultural goods and services remain mostly inaccessible to people with disabilities. The International Telecommunication Union (ITU) Report of 2011, Making Television Accessible (available at www.itu.int/en/ITU-D/Digital-Inclusion/Persons-with-Disabilities/Documents/Making_TV_Accessible-English.pdf), observes that, at the global level, many of the 1 billion or more people with disabilities are unable to enjoy the audiovisual services that are broadcast in their homes. The 2015/2016 report of the Arts Council of England (ACE) affirms that, in terms of people enjoying the arts and museums, disabled audiences continue to be under-represented. In addition, the high costs of cultural performances are often an obstacle for individuals with disabilities when it comes to performing arts. With regard to disabled performers, the UNESCO signals that some national support schemes targeted at artists with disabilities are in place. However, the limited national statistics that are available across the EU show that representation of disabled workers in the arts remains very disappointing (ACE, *Annual Report and Accounts* 2015/2016, available at www.artscouncil.org.uk/our-organisation/annual-reports).

[87] Ibid. paras. 3 and 16.

[88] CRC, General Comment No. 17, 17 April 2013, UN Doc. CRC/C/GC/17.

[89] Additionally, the European Disability Strategy 2010–2020 (EDS) of the European Union emphasises the need for the participation of people with disabilities in society and acknowledges that the 'EU action will support national activities to make sports, leisure, cultural and recreational organisations and activities accessible'.

[90] CoE Strategy on the Rights of Persons with Disabilities 2017–2023, available at https://www.coe.int/en/web/disability/strategy-2017-2023. See further Chapter 13.

3.2 Article 30 CRPD

ARTICLE 30 CRPD

1. States Parties recogni[s]e the right of persons with disabilities to take part on an equal basis with others in cultural life, and shall take all appropriate measures to ensure that persons with disabilities:

(a) Enjoy access to cultural materials in accessible formats;
(b) Enjoy access to television programmes, films, theatre and other cultural activities, in accessible formats;
(c) Enjoy access to places for cultural performances or services, such as theatres, museums, cinemas, libraries and tourism services, and, as far as possible, enjoy access to monuments and sites of national cultural importance.

2. States Parties shall take appropriate measures to enable persons with disabilities to have the opportunity to develop and utili[s]e their creative, artistic and intellectual potential, not only for their own benefit, but also for the enrichment of society.

3. States Parties shall take all appropriate steps, in accordance with international law, to ensure that laws protecting intellectual property rights do not constitute an unreasonable or discriminatory barrier to access by persons with disabilities to cultural materials.

4. Persons with disabilities shall be entitled, on an equal basis with others, to recognition and support of their specific cultural and linguistic identity, including sign languages and deaf culture.

5. With a view to enabling persons with disabilities to participate on an equal basis with others in recreational, leisure and sporting activities, States Parties shall take appropriate measures:

(a) To encourage and promote the participation, to the fullest extent possible, of persons with disabilities in mainstream sporting activities at all levels;
(b) To ensure that persons with disabilities have an opportunity to organi[s]e, develop and participate in disability-specific sporting and recreational activities and, to this end, encourage the provision, on an equal basis with others, of appropriate instruction, training and resources;
(c) To ensure that persons with disabilities have access to sporting, recreational and tourism venues;
(d) To ensure that children with disabilities have equal access with other children to participation in play, recreation and leisure and sporting activities, including those activities in the school system;

(e) To ensure that persons with disabilities have access to services from those involved in the organi[s]ation of recreational, tourism, leisure and sporting activities.

Article 30(1) CRPD provides for the right of persons with disabilities to participate in cultural life. The wording of the first paragraph of the provision closely follows the UDHR and does not set out any definition of 'cultural life'. However, Article 30 seems to encompass a broad understanding of 'culture', and it should be interpreted in line with the meaning given to Article 15 ICESCR by the CESCR in its General Comment No. 21. The rest of Article 30 CRPD details States Parties' obligations. In particular, it requires States Parties to take all appropriate measures to ensure that persons with disabilities have access to cultural materials, television programmes, films, theatre and other cultural activities as well as to places where cultural performances are held or services are provided, and to monuments and sites.

Ensuring accessibility of cultural goods and services is, thus, the main overall obligation stemming from Article 30(1) CRPD. That provision, echoing Article 9 CRPD, recognises that accessibility is a pre-condition to realising the right to participate in culture. This was also highlighted by the CRPD Committee in its General Comment No. 2.[91]

CRPD Committee, General Comment No. 2 on Accessibility (2014)

Everyone has the right to enjoy the arts, take part in sports and go to hotels, restaurants and bars. However, wheelchair users cannot go to a concert if there are only stairs in the concert hall. Blind persons cannot enjoy a painting if there is no description of it they can hear in the gallery. Hard of hearing persons cannot enjoy a film if there are no subtitles. Deaf persons cannot enjoy a theatrical play if there is no sign language interpretation. Persons with intellectual disabilities cannot enjoy a book if there is no easy-to-read version or a version in augmentative and alternative modes. Article 30 of the Convention requires that States parties recogni[s]e the right of persons with disabilities to take part in cultural life on an equal basis with others. States parties are required to take all appropriate measures to ensure that persons with disabilities:

(a) Enjoy access to cultural materials in accessible formats;

[91] CRPD Committee, General Comment No. 2, 22 May 2014, UN Doc. CRPD/C/GC/2, para. 44.

(b) Enjoy access to television programmes, films, theatre and other cultural activities, in accessible formats;
(c) Enjoy access to places for cultural performances or services, such as theatres, museums, cinemas, libraries and tourism services, and, as far as possible, enjoy access to monuments and sites of national cultural importance.

The provision of access to cultural and historical monuments that are part of national heritage may indeed be a challenge in some circumstances. However, States parties are obliged to strive to provide access to these sites. Many monuments and sites of national cultural importance have been made accessible in a way that preserves their cultural and historical identity and uniqueness.

The key role played by accessibility in facilitating access to culture is also emphasised by the CESCR's General Comment No. 21,[92] which states that:

> effective and concrete opportunities for individuals and communities to enjoy culture fully, within physical and financial reach for all in both urban and rural areas, without discrimination. It is essential, in this regard, that access for older persons and persons with disabilities, as well as for those who live in poverty, is provided and facilitated. Accessibility also includes the right of everyone to seek, receive and share information on all manifestations of culture in the language of the person's choice, and the access of communities to means of expressions and dissemination.

Articles 30(2) and (3) CRPD have the clear aim of increasing the low participation rate of people with disabilities in culture generally, both as artists and end users of cultural goods and services. To that end, those provisions establish that States Parties must take all appropriate measures to enable persons with disabilities to develop their creative, artistic and intellectual potential, and ensure that laws protecting intellectual property rights do not constitute an unreasonable or discriminatory barrier to the access of people with disabilities to cultural materials. The latter obligation relates primarily to copyright,[93] which might act as a barrier that prevents cultural materials being made available to disabled users in accessible formats. In that respect, the CRPD is now complemented by a new international treaty aimed specifically at ensuring access to printed materials for persons with disabilities – the Marrakesh Treaty to Facilitate Access to Published Works for Persons Who Are Blind,

[92] CESCR, General Comment No. 21, note 84, paras. 3 and 16.
[93] Copyright (and related rights) provides an incentive for the creation of new works and other protected matter (music, films, print media, software, performances, broadcasts, etc.) and their exploitation. It is intended to protect literary and artistic works against copying and to reward ability and/or skill, which will enhance the cultural life of the community.

Visually Impaired, or Otherwise Print Disabled (Marrakesh Treaty).[94] That Treaty was adopted on 27 June 2013 in Marrakesh by the World Intellectual Property Organization (WIPO), and it entered into force on 30 September 2016. Broadly speaking, the Marrakesh Treaty requires States Parties to introduce limitations and exceptions to copyright rules, in order to allow the reproduction and distribution of published works in formats designed to be accessible, and to permit the exchange of those works across borders by non-profit organisations that support people with disabilities.[95] The obligations included in the Marrakesh Treaty have a more limited scope *ratione personae* and *materiae* than Article 30 CRPD. Those covered by the Treaty are individuals who are blind, visually impaired, print-disabled or individuals with a physical disability that prevents them from holding a book. The Treaty concerns only works 'in the form of text, notation and/or related illustrations, whether published or otherwise made publicly available in any media', including audio books. The CRPD Committee has emphasised the importance of the Marrakesh Treaty in several of its COs, expressing its concern when States Parties to the CRPD have not ratified it.[96] In some instances, the CRPD Committee urges States Parties that have ratified the Marrakesh Treaty to fully implement its obligations. In the case of Guatemala, for example, the Committee noted that national legislation on copyright and related rights had not yet been brought into line with the Marrakesh Treaty and expressed its concern for the absence of entities authorised to produce published material in accessible formats.[97]

Article 30(4) CRPD provides for the recognition and support of the specific cultural and linguistic identity of people with disabilities, including various sign languages and Deaf culture, which will be discussed below.

Finally, Article 30(5) CRPD focuses on the participation of people with disabilities in recreational, leisure and sporting activities, which must be ensured 'on an equal basis with others'.

[94] The text of this treaty is available at www.wipo.int/treaties/en/ip/marrakesh/.

[95] States Parties are free to implement the Treaty taking into account their own legal systems and practices, and the limitations to copyright must comply with a 'three-step test' (which is laid down in the Berne Convention). In particular, any exception or limitation: (1) shall cover only certain special cases; (2) shall not conflict with the normal exploitation of the work; and (3) shall not unreasonably prejudice the legitimate interests of the rightholder.

[96] CRPD Committee, Concluding Observations on the Initial Report of the UK, 3 October 2017, UN Doc. CRPD/C/GBR/CO/1, para. 62; CRPD Committee, Concluding Observations on the Initial Report of Luxembourg, 10 October 2017, UN Doc. CRPD/C/LUX/CO/1, para. 52; CRPD Committee, Concluding Observations on the Initial Report of Cyprus, 8 May 2017, UN Doc. CRPD/C/CYP/CO/1, para. 59.

[97] CRPD Committee, Concluding Observations on the Initial Report of Guatemala, 30 September 2016, UN Doc. CRPD/C/GTM/CO/1, para. 71.

3.3 Sign Language and Deaf Culture

An area in which the CRPD is opening up new perspectives is that of sign language, which is explicitly mentioned in several parts of the Convention. As noted by Batterbury,[98] the CRPD 'has the potential to be an effective tool to achieve language policy which promotes greater social justice' for people using sign languages.[99]

It is worth recalling that sign languages are conveyed by means of hand movements and the use of facial expressions and lip patterns. They take the form of visual-gestural actions, composed of four basic hand forms: hand shape (e.g. open or closed); hand location (e.g. on the middle of the forehead or in front of the chest); hand movement (e.g. upward or downward); and hand orientation (e.g. palm facing up or out). There is no universal sign language, but each country has its own national sign language.[100] The importance of sign language lies in the fact that it is a tool that can be used to guarantee full accessibility for Deaf persons, and it is also a feature of cultural identity. On the one hand, Article 2 CRPD explicitly states that the term 'language' includes 'spoken and signed languages and other forms of non spoken languages'. As mentioned in Chapter 5, Article 9(2)(e) CRPD obliges States Parties 'to provide forms of live assistance and intermediaries, including ... professional sign language interpreters, to facilitate accessibility to buildings and other facilities open to the public'. In a similar vein, Article 21(b) CRPD requires States Parties to accept and facilitate 'the use of sign languages, Braille, augmentative and alternative communication, and all other accessible means'. Article 21(e) CRPD requires States Parties to recognise and promote the use of sign languages, while Article 24(3)(b) obliges them to facilitate 'the learning of sign language and the promotion of the linguistic identity of the [D]eaf community'. Similarly, Article 30(4) CRPD affirms that '[p]ersons with disabilities shall be entitled, on an equal basis with others, to recognition and support of their specific cultural and linguistic identity, including sign languages and [D]eaf culture'.

98 Sarah Batterbury, 'Language Justice for Sign Language Peoples: The UN Convention on the Rights of Persons with Disabilities' (2012) 11 *Language Policy* 253.

99 Ibid. at 254. In particular, Batterbury argues that 'despite its disability locus, the CRPD opens a pathway to eventual sign language policy in the minority language policy arena'.

100 Mark Wheathly and Annika Pabsh, *Sign Language Legislation in the European Union* (Brussels: EUD, 2012), pp. 12 et seq. There is a significant amount of scholarly works on the features of sign languages and on their history. For example, the journal *Sign Language Studies* publishes a wide range of original scholarly articles relevant to signed languages and signing communities. It provides a forum for the dissemination of important ideas and opinions concerning these languages and the communities who use them.

DID YOU KNOW THAT ...?

In November 2017, the UN General Assembly declared 23 September as the International Day of Sign Languages (UNGA Resolution, UN Doc. A/C.3/72/L.36/Rev.1). By marking the importance of sign languages, the UN acknowledges that early access to quality education available in sign language is vital to Deaf persons. It also recognises the importance of preserving sign languages as part of linguistic and cultural diversity. The resolution was initially advanced by the Permanent Mission of Antigua and Barbuda to the UN, following a request by the World Federation of the Deaf (WFD). The choice of 23 September commemorates the date that the WFD was established in 1951. This day marks the birth of the organisation that has advocated globally the preservation of sign languages and Deaf culture. The first International Day of Sign Languages was celebrated on 23 September 2018 as part of the International Week of the Deaf.

The CRPD does not conceptualise Deaf people as a linguistic minority.[101] However, it acknowledges the existence of Deaf culture. As noted in Chapter 5, the CRPD is the first international human rights treaty that recognises sign language,[102] and the COs of the CRPD Committee to date recommend that States Parties actively promote the use of sign language and call for the adoption of laws giving official recognition to it. Nevertheless, as noted by Ball, the Convention goes beyond a mere minority language approach. By focusing on individual rights and on the specific circumstances of each individual sign language user, the Convention obliges States Parties to tailor solutions that ensure accessibility for each Deaf individual, regardless of

[101] Some authors argue that Deaf people possess their own distinct language(s), each with a unique vocabulary and grammar, have a shared set of experiences, relating to the consequences of deafness in a hearing culture, a shared history and distinct set of institutions. For this reason, they can be qualified as a linguistic group, rather than as persons with disabilities. See Harlan Lane, 'Do Deaf People Have a Disability?' (2002) *Sign Language Studies* 356, available at http://gallyprotest.org/do_deaf_people_have_a_disability.pdf; see also, Joseph Murray, 'Linguistic Human Rights Discourse in Deaf Community Activism' (2015) 15(4) *Sign Language Studies* 379; for a critical discussion, see Maya Sabatello, 'Disability, Cultural Minorities, and International Law: Reconsidering the Case of the Deaf Community' (2005) *Whittier Law Review* 1025. In accordance with what appears to be commonly accepted, in this textbook, a capital "D" is used when referring to the culture and community of Deaf people. A lowercase "d" is used to refer to the audiological status of an individual.

[102] As noted in Chapter 5 (note 85), before the CRPD, the UN Human Rights Committee (HRC), in its General Comment No. 34, recognised sign language as a form of expression protected under Article 19(2) ICCPR.

whether the particular sign language is recognised as a minority language at the national level.[103]

CASE STUDY

The Deaf Community in Australia

Auslan is the language used in the Australian Deaf community. It dates back approximately 200 years, when British, Irish and Scottish immigrants brought sign language to Australia (www.ndp.org.au/images/factsheets/NDP_Factsheet04.pdf). Gradually, Auslan developed its own unique features, and it continues to evolve. It is not the same as English, in that it has its own distinct grammar and syntax. It cannot be spoken and has no written form. It is conveyed by signs that are made using precise hand shapes, facial expressions and body movements. Additionally, 'finger spelling' is used where no sign exists, for example to spell the name of a place (https://metrosouth.health.qld.gov.au/sites/default/files/content/deafness-mental-health-culture-auslan.pdf). In 1991, the Australian Government recognised Auslan as a community language. Despite that official recognition, Deaf people have not been automatically granted the right to use Auslan when communicating with public authorities. In 2013, the CRPD Committee expressed concern about Australia's failure to provide all information in accessible formats and to effectively promote and facilitate the use of Auslan when persons with disabilities are engaged in official interactions (CRPD Committee, COs on the Initial Report of Australia, 21 October 2013, UN Doc. CRPD/C/AUS/CO/1).

3.4 Participation in Sport and Leisure

Article 30(5) CRPD requires States Parties to enable persons with disabilities to participate in recreational, leisure and sporting activities on an equal basis with others. As noted by Manca, the right enshrined in Article 30(5) is not an innovation introduced by the CRPD.[104] Article 24 UDHR proclaims that 'everyone has the right to rest and leisure', and a similar provision is included

[103] Andrea Ball, 'Equal Accessibility for Sign Language under the Convention on the Rights of Persons with Disabilities' (2011) *Case Western Reserve Journal of International Law* 759, at 784.

[104] Luigino Manca, 'Article 30: Participation in Cultural Life, Recreation, Leisure and Sport', in Della Fina, Cera and Palmisano (eds.), *The United Nations Convention on Human Rights: A Commentary*, note 5, pp. 541–55, p. 547. See also Rafael F. de Asís Roig, 'Reflexiones sobre discapacidad, deporte e inclusión' (2018) 27 *Universitas: Revista de filosofía, derecho y política*, pp. 8–20.

Read the text of the CRPD, and identify other provisions that can be relevant to ensuring effective access to sport and leisure activities.

in Article 7 ICESCR. Rule 11 of the Standard Rules also called on States to 'take measures to ensure that persons with disabilities have equal opportunities for recreation and sports'. The content of the latter provision has, largely, been incorporated into the CRPD.[105]

Recognising the importance of leisure and sports for people with disabilities as a means to ensure their participation in society, the CRPD places specific obligations on States Parties in that regard. Article 30(5)(a) and (b) oblige States Parties to ensure the 'participation, to the fullest extent possible, of persons with disabilities in mainstream sporting activities', and require the involvement of people with disabilities in the development of sporting activities as well as their active participation therein. Article 30(5)(a) and (b) are premised on the idea that sport can help to 'reduce the stigma and discrimination associated with disability', because it can transform 'community attitudes about persons with disabilities by highlighting their skills and reducing the tendency to see the disability instead of the person'.[106]

Article 30(5)(c) and (e), respectively, mandate the accessibility of sport and recreational activities and access to services, highlighting, once again, that accessibility is essential in enabling the full enjoyment of the right to participation in society generally for persons with disabilities. The foregoing provisions must be read in conjunction with Article 9, which prescribes that all venues open to the public must be accessible.

Finally, Article 30(5)(d) is devoted to children with disabilities. It requires States Parties to ensure equal 'participation in play, recreation and leisure and sporting activities' of all children with disabilities. That provision must be read in light of Article 7 CRPD, which recognises children as autonomous holders of rights.[107]

[105] Ibid. p. 548.

[106] Department of Economic and Social Affairs, Division for Inclusive Social Development, 'Disability and Sports', available at www.un.org/development/desa/disabilities/issues/disability-and-sports.html.

[107] Luigino Manca, 'Article 30: Participation in Cultural Life, Recreation, Leisure and Sport', note 104, p. 548.

3.5 The Committee on the Rights of Persons with Disabilities and the Right to Access Culture

The CRPD Committee has not yet had the opportunity to discuss Article 30 CRPD. As mentioned above, it only examined the accessibility of cultural goods and services cursorily in its General Comment No. 2.[108] The Committee acknowledges that 'the provision of access to cultural and historical monuments that are part of national heritage may indeed be a challenge in some circumstances'.[109] However, it stresses that States Parties 'are obliged to strive to provide access to these sites', and that several monuments and sites of national cultural importance have been already made accessible 'in a way that preserves their cultural and historical identity and uniqueness'.[110] In its General Comment No. 5 on Independent Living, the CRPD Committee states that the realisation of Article 19 'must be effective in different economic, social, cultural and political contexts'.[111] It also reiterates that independent living is linked to ensuring:

> access to transport, information, communication and personal assistance, place of residence, daily routine, habits, decent employment, personal relationships, clothing, nutrition, hygiene and health care, religious, *cultural* and sexual and reproductive rights.[112]

The Committee emphasises that these activities (including cultural activities) 'are linked to the development of a person's identity and personality'.[113]

General Comment No. 5 also makes it clear that the right to be included in the community, set out in Article 19 CRPD, includes the right to have:

> access to all measures and events of political and cultural life in the community, among others public meetings, sports events, cultural and religious festivals and any other activity in which the person with disability wishes to participate.[114]

The Committee makes clear the connection between Articles 19 and 30 CRPD, the latter being a complement to the obligation already set forth in Article 19. In fact, the Committee maintains that '[c]ultural life, recreation, leisure and sports [Article 30] are important dimensions of life in the community in which inclusion can be pursued and achieved, for example by ensuring that events, activities and facilities are accessible to persons with disabilities and inclusive'.[115] It provides examples of what can help inclusivity. In that regard, the Committee mentions 'personal assistants, guides, readers, professional sign language and tactile interpreters' and specifies that 'assistants necessary for participating in cultural and leisure activities should be free of paying entrance'.[116]

[108] CRPD Committee, General Comment No. 2, note 91. [109] Ibid. para. 44. [110] Ibid.

[111] CRPD Committee, General Comment No. 5, 27 September 2017, UN Doc. CRPD/C/GC/5, para. 8.

[112] Ibid. para. 16. [113] Ibid. [114] Ibid. [115] Ibid. para. 94. [116] Ibid.

3.6 Good Practices on the Right to Culture

Several countries are trying to improve the accessibility of their cultural goods and services. Outlined below is a small selection of good practice examples (drawn from States Parties to the CRPD) with regard to the right to participate in cultural life.[117]

CASE STUDY

Cultural Initiatives in Norway and France

Seven Norwegian orchestras have installed audio induction loops or other equipment, to help hearing-impaired individuals, and they have installed lifts or other arrangements for wheelchair users and others with mobility difficulties. Some music institutions have also entered into a cooperation with the Norwegian Association of the Blind and Partially Sighted regarding special facilities for those with visual impairments. In the sphere of stage productions, seventeen national/regional institutions have made adaptations for wheelchair users and others with mobility difficulties, and most of those institutions have also installed aids, such as audio induction loops. In addition, the Norwegian Library of Talking Books and Braille (NLB) produces and lends out public library literature, including newspapers and study literature to persons with disabilities (Initial Report of Norway to the CRPD Committee, 7 December 2015, UN Doc. CRPD/C/NOR/1).

In France, the *Association Musique et situations de handicap* runs a national resource centre, aimed at adapting music classes to the needs of pupils with disabilities and developing projects that enable music-making by people with disabilities. The *Centre de Ressources Théâtre et Handicap* includes a specialist resource centre, a drama school and a centre offering emerging young performers, who are linked with disability in one way or another, support in implementing their projects. Another organisation, *Accès Culture*, offers free technical assistance to people with impaired hearing or eyesight or those with psychosocial disabilities, so that they can attend theatres and dance or opera performances in an autonomous manner. Its activity, involving coordination between the specialist departments of forty-nine national theatres or opera houses in seventeen regions, consists in adapting certain performances, by using a range of technical resources: audio description, supertitling and adaptation in French sign language (Damian Tatic, *Access for People with Disabilities to Culture, Tourism, Sports and Leisure Activities: Towards Meaningful and Enriching Participation*, Strasbourg: Council of Europe Publishing, 2015, p. 50).

[117] These examples are merely representative, and they are not intended to provide an exhaustive overview of all good practices engaged in by States Parties' governments.

4 PERSONS WITH DISABILITIES AND PARTICIPATION IN POLITICAL AND PUBLIC LIFE

This section discusses participation in political and public life of persons with disabilities. The first sub-section briefly examines the protection of the right to political participation in international human rights law. The second sub-section turns to the examination of the obligations set out in Article 29 CRPD, while the final sub-section provides some examples of good practices.

4.1 Setting the Scene: The Right to Political Participation in International Human Rights Law

The right to political participation is well established in international human rights law. The UDHR provides that '[e]veryone has the right to take part in the government of his country . . .' and that the 'will [of the people] shall be expressed in periodic and genuine elections which shall be by universal and equal suffrage and shall be held by secret vote or by equivalent free voting procedures'. Article 25 ICCPR sets forth, in a comprehensive fashion, the right to political participation. However, the ICCPR makes no specific mention of voting issues for people with disabilities, nor does it recognise their differential characteristics in exercising their political rights.[118] At the regional level, several provisions of human rights treaties establish the right to vote, under the overall heading of the right to political participation. For example, Article 3 of Protocol No. 1 obliges Contracting States to the ECHR 'to hold free elections at reasonable intervals by secret ballot, under conditions which will ensure the free expression of the opinion of the people in the choice of the legislature'.

The Standard Rules did not include a specific rule on the right to vote. However, they emphasised that States were 'under an obligation to enable persons with disabilities to exercise their rights, including their human, civil and political rights, on an equal basis with other citizens', and they placed great emphasis on participation in society generally.

Notwithstanding the foregoing human rights provisions, people with disabilities have been excluded from the political arena for too long because of legislation depriving them of legal capacity (and, with that, the right to vote and stand for elections) and also because of inaccessible procedures and facilities. Discriminatory laws that restrict or prohibit the right to vote for individuals with psychosocial or intellectual disabilities who are under

[118] Michael Waterstone, 'Political Participation for People with Disabilities', in Marcia Rioux, Lee Ann Basser and Melinda Jones, *Critical Perspectives on Human Rights and Disability Law* (Leiden/Boston: Brill, 2011), p. 374.

guardianship are still a reality in several countries.[119] Even where there are no discriminatory laws in place, political participation of people with disabilities has traditionally been low. Studies of voter turnout conducted in the US have shown that people with disabilities have a turnout rate that is far lower than that of the general population (depending on the election and the type of disability concerned)[120] and that the number of people with disabilities being registered to vote is lower than that of individuals without a disability. Other studies conducted in Europe have highlighted the multiple barriers that prevent people with disabilities from participating in political and public life, including a lack of accessible voting stations and information as well as stigmatisation.[121] As will be discussed below, Article 29 CRPD aims to counteract and put an end to these barriers, by specifying how States Parties must guarantee to persons with disabilities the same voting rights as those enjoyed by the general population.

4.2 Article 29 CRPD

ARTICLE 29 CRPD

States Parties shall guarantee to persons with disabilities political rights and the opportunity to enjoy them on an equal basis with others, and shall undertake:

(a) To ensure that persons with disabilities can effectively and fully participate in political and public life on an equal basis with others, directly or through freely chosen representatives, including the right and opportunity for persons with disabilities to vote and be elected, *inter alia*, by:

i. Ensuring that voting procedures, facilities and materials are appropriate, accessible and easy to understand and use;

[119] Data on European countries can be found at http://fra.europa.eu/en/publication/2014/right-political-participation-persons-disabilities-human-rights-indicators; see also, Mark Priestley et al., 'The Political Participation of Disabled People in Europe: Rights, Accessibility and Representation' (2016) 42 *Electoral Studies* 1.

[120] Thad Hall and Michael Alvarez, 'Defining the Barriers to Political Participation for Individuals with Disabilities. The Information Technology and Innovation Foundation: Accessible Voting Technology Initiative' (2012) *Working Paper* No. 001, available at http://elections.itif.org/reports/AVTI-001-Hall-Alvarez-2012.pdf.

[121] Priestley et al., 'The Political Participation of Disabled People in Europe: Rights, Accessibility and Representation', note 119. See also the recent papers published by the Fundamental Rights Agency (FRA) and by the European Economic and Social Committee (EESC): FRA, Who Will (not) Get to Vote in the 2019 European Parliament Elections?, available at https://fra.europa.eu/sites/default/files/fra_uploads/fra-2019-right-vote-ep-elections-legal-capacity_en.pdf; EESC, The Real Right of Persons with Disabilities to Vote in EP Elections, SOC/554-EESC-2017, available at https://www.eesc.europa.eu/en/our-work/opinions-information-reports/information-reports/real-right-persons-disabilities-vote-ep-elections.

ii. Protecting the right of persons with disabilities to vote by secret ballot in elections and public referendums without intimidation, and to stand for elections, to effectively hold office and perform all public functions at all levels of government, facilitating the use of assistive and new technologies where appropriate;
iii. Guaranteeing the free expression of the will of persons with disabilities as electors and to this end, where necessary, at their request, allowing assistance in voting by a person of their own choice;

(b) To promote actively an environment in which persons with disabilities can effectively and fully participate in the conduct of public affairs, without discrimination and on an equal basis with others, and encourage their participation in public affairs, including:

i. Participation in non-governmental organi[s]ations and associations concerned with the public and political life of the country, and in the activities and administration of political parties;
ii. Forming and joining organi[s]ations of persons with disabilities to represent persons with disabilities at international, national, regional and local levels.

The opening paragraph of Article 29 CRPD 'clearly establishes the principle of equality in the enjoyment of political rights'.[122] The whole provision has a very wide scope, which goes 'beyond the realm of voting', and 'beyond the basic right to vote and be elected to public office'.[123] Article 29 obliges States Parties to ensure equal rights for people with disabilities to participate in public and political life, including enabling them to engage in non-governmental organisations and political parties; ensuring free and accessible voting procedures, facilities and materials; and facilitating equal standing for elections and the holding of public office at all levels of government. As with all of the other rights provided for in the Convention, Article 29 must be read in light of the general principles as well as other provisions of the Convention. Articles 8, 21 and 30 CRPD are particularly relevant in this connection. Indeed, political participation requires that awareness is raised, among all relevant stakeholders, of the needs and the contributions of people with disabilities in the political process. Furthermore, to enable meaningful participation, it is essential that people with disabilities have access to relevant information and communication as well as mass media (see Figure 9.4.).

Article 29(a) focuses on the electoral rights of individuals with disabilities, namely the right to vote, to stand for election and to hold office without

[122] Cera, 'Article 29: Political Participation', note 5. [123] Ibid. p. 526.

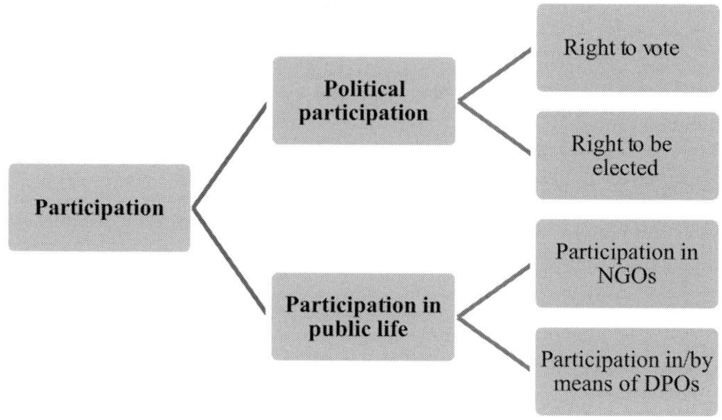

Figure 9.4 Article 29 CRPD

discrimination on an equal basis with others. As highlighted above in Chapter 6, in *Bujdosó* v. *Hungary*,[124] the CRPD Committee affirmed that any exclusion from the right to vote on the basis of a psychosocial or intellectual disability, including a restriction pursuant to an individualised assessment, constitutes discrimination on the ground of disability. In a similar vein, in *Kiss* v. *Hungary*,[125] the European Court of Human Rights (ECtHR) held that the automatic and generalised restriction on the right to vote of individuals placed under protective measures (provided for in the Hungarian Constitution) constituted a violation of Article 3 of Protocol No. 1 to the ECHR. However, the approach of the ECtHR is more nuanced than that of the CRPD Committee. The Strasbourg Court accepted that the withdrawal of the right to vote pursued a legitimate aim, namely to ensure that only citizens capable of assessing the consequences of their decisions could take part in public affairs. However, it held that a blanket ban on the right to vote affecting all persons under protection, regardless of their actual mental abilities, was in breach of the ECHR.

Article 29(a) CRPD makes clear that extending formal political rights to persons with disabilities is not sufficient and obliges States Parties to adopt positive measures, to ensure that these rights are fully enjoyed by people with disabilities. The CRPD Committee, in its General Comment No. 2, highlights

[124] CRPD Committee, *Zsolt Bujdosó, Jánosné Ildikó Márkus, Viktória Márton, Sándor Mészáros, Gergely Polk and János Szabó (represented by counsel, János Fiala, Disability Rights Center)* v. *Hungary*, Communication No. 4/2011, CRPD/C/10/D/4/2011.

[125] ECtHR, *Kiss* v. *Hungary*, Application No. 38832/06, 20 May 2010.

the importance of accessibility in the realisation of the right to political participation.[126] It emphasises that:

> [p]ersons with disabilities would be unable to exercise those rights equally and effectively if States parties failed to ensure that voting procedures, facilities and materials were appropriate, accessible and easy to understand and use. It is also important that political meetings and materials used and produced by political parties or individual candidates participating in public elections are accessible. If not, persons with disabilities are deprived of their right to participate in the political process in an equal manner.[127]

Article 29 CRPD requires States Parties to make use of assistive and new technologies, to enable people with disabilities to effectively hold office and carry out public functions. In a similar vein, Article 29(a)(iii) obliges States Parties to ensure that people with disabilities can vote freely but that they can also be assisted, if necessary, by a person of their own choice. The latter provision is to be read in light of Article 12 CRPD,[128] which requires States Parties to adopt appropriate measures to support individuals in exercising their legal capacity. The requirement to provide assistance in voting raises several risks in relation to preserving the secrecy of the vote, and it exposes people with disabilities to the possibility of manipulation. Those risks are not completely mitigated by the fact that the voting assistant, allowed under Article 29(a)(iii), must be chosen by the person with a disability.

Article 29(b) focuses on the participation of people with disabilities in public administration and public affairs. In the first instance, it requires States Parties to encourage the participation of people with disabilities in NGOs and associations, and 'in the activities and administration of political parties'. According to Cera, Article 29(b) 'is intended to facilitate the mainstreaming of disability issues and contribute with a disability perspective to public policy making'.[129] In the second instance, it establishes the right to join and form representative organisations of persons with disabilities (DPOs), and it obliges States Parties to make it possible for people with disabilities to do so. The emphasis on DPOs, together with the

Read *Fiona Given* v *Australia*. What are the main findings of the CRPD Committee?

[126] CRPD Committee, General Comment No. 2, note 91, para. 43. See also CRPD *Committee*, *Fiona Given* v *Australia*, Communication No. 19/2014, CRPD/C/19/D/19/2014.

[127] Ibid. para. 43.

[128] See above Chapter 6.

[129] Cera, 'Article 29: Political Participation', note 5, p. 536.

reference to 'organisations of persons with disabilities' in Article 33(3) CRPD,[130] is essential in facilitating not only meaningful participation but also the empowerment of people with disabilities.

4.3 Good Practices on the Right to Political Participation

In accessible environments, people with disabilities can be active citizens, who are engaged in the political life of their communities,[131] through voting in elections, by being members of political parties, attending political meetings and contacting elected officials. There are still challenges to the realisation of the right to political participation for persons with disabilities, but some good practices can be identified. A small selection of good practice examples are provided below.[132]

CASE STUDY

Venezuelan Electoral Law

In Venezuela, Articles 189 and 190 of the Electoral Process Act establish the obligation of governing bodies to ensure that voting tools are designed to be accessible to voters with disabilities and that voters with disabilities are able to exercise their right to vote without intermediaries. Those provisions also establish that information and educational campaigns should be accessible to voters with disabilities. Consequently, all audiovisual messages must include simultaneous interpretation into sign language, and informational material on ballot choices must be provided in Braille. In 2011, the Venezuelan National Council for Persons with Disabilities and the National Electoral Council established a facilitation mechanism for voting for persons with disabilities. That mechanism provides for dedicated polling facilities for disabled individuals, which are located on the ground floor of all voting centres. In addition, a special mechanism that will enable persons with a visual impairment to cast their ballots using a special Braille-based device is currently being implemented (Initial Report of the Bolivarian Republic of Venezuela to the CRPD Committee, 6 October 2017, UN Doc. CRPD/C/VEN/1, paras. 166 et seq.).

[130] See above Chapter 3.

[131] FRA report, *The Right to Political Participation of Persons with Disabilities – Summary*, available at http://fra.europa.eu/en/publication/2014/right-political-participation-persons-disabilities-human-rights-indicators.

[132] These examples are merely representative, and they are not intended to provide an exhaustive overview of all good practice engaged in by States Parties' governments.

CASE STUDY

The 'Vote Smart' Campaign in Romania and the 'Get My Vote' Initiative in the UK

The 'Vote Smart' campaign was organised by the Pentru Voi Foundation (an organisation member of Inclusion Europe) and the Institute for Public Policies and Inclusion Romania. It aimed to create a communication network between voters and candidates for county council elections and administrative sectors in Bucharest, which aimed to enable people to vote in an informed way. The campaign took place in 2008 and offered the opportunity for political candidates from five counties in Romania (Timis, Giurgiu, Hunedoara, Mures and Sibiu), and six candidates from Bucharest to present ways in which they would promote the social inclusion of people with intellectual disabilities to voters. Their answers were made public in the central and local press and through the organisations involved in the campaign to inform the electorate.

In the UK, for the general election in 2010, the 'Get My Vote' campaign was launched to ensure that people with an intellectual disability could participate in the election process. The campaign achieved a high level of engagement with parliamentary candidates. All three of the main political parties (and smaller parties) produced their manifestos in easy-to-read versions to reach voters with intellectual disabilities. As a result of the campaign, the number of people with an intellectual disability who voted doubled from 16 per cent to 31 per cent (shown by a survey of over 1,100 people with a learning disability) compared with previous elections (Inclusion Europe, *Good Practices for Accessible Elections in Europ*e, available at http://inclusion-europe.eu/wp-content/uploads/2015/04/Good_Practices_EN.pdf).

SUMMARY

- **The rights to education and access to culture fall within the category of economic, social and cultural rights. Those rights are subject to progressive realisation, but they also contain certain elements that are deemed to be capable of having immediate effect.**
- **The right to participate in political and public life is a civil and political right, which is capable of immediate effect.**
- **Article 24 CRPD enshrines the right to inclusive education–a process of ensuring systemic reform of educational systems and embodying modifications in educational content, teaching methods as well as educational structures and strategies.**
- **Article 24 CRPD seeks to eradicate environmental, attitudinal and learning barriers, with a view to ensuring that all students of the relevant age range can engage in an equitable and participatory learning environment that corresponds to their needs.**

- While many laws and policies have been put in place in States Parties to the CRPD seeking to ensure inclusion in education, there remains a high number of disabled individuals with either no access to education or only access to segregated education.
- Article 30 CRPD encompasses a broad understanding of culture and details States Parties' obligations in that regard. In particular, it requires States Parties to take all appropriate measures to ensure that people with disabilities have access to cultural materials, television programmes, films, theatre and other cultural activities as well as to places where cultural performances are held or services are provided, and to monuments and sites.
- People with disabilities have been excluded from the political arena for too long because of legislation depriving them of legal capacity (and, with that, the right to vote and stand for elections) and also because of inaccessible procedures and facilities.
- Article 29 CRPD aims to counteract these barriers by specifying how persons with disabilities are entitled to the same voting rights as the general population.

ACTIVITIES

REVIEW QUESTIONS

1. What are the core and immediate obligations inherent in the right to education?
2. How is the accessibility obligation in Article 9 CRPD linked to the right to access culture?
3. What are the core obligations enshrined in Article 29 CRPD?

ESSAY QUESTIONS

1. Assess the key challenges that arise in inclusive educational settings and how these might be solved.
2. 'Legal restrictions on the right to vote of some persons with disabilities, particularly those with intellectual impairments, are in breach of Article 29 CRPD.' *Discuss*.

GROUP PROJECT

Francis, who is deaf, and his friend Anthony, who uses a wheelchair, want to go to the cinema to watch the acclaimed Oscar-winning movie 'Fifty Shades of Fantasy'. Anthony calls various cinemas to ensure that the screening is captioned, but he discovers that only the Freedonia Film Institute in Freedonia City (the capital city of Freedonia), which is quite far away from their homes, displays captioned movies. He also discovers that there are only two captioned screenings per week, on weekdays (not at the weekend), and only in the early afternoons. Since they really want to watch the movie, Francis and Anthony decide to take a day off, to go to the screening together on a particular Wednesday afternoon. When they arrive at the cinema, they discover that the places allocated to

wheelchair users are only in the first row, in a specially allocated area, and that, for security reasons, people with mobility impairments cannot sit elsewhere. Francis cannot view the captioning well from the front row, as it is too close to the screen. They ask the personnel of the cinema to allow them to move, but the cinema employees suggest that the only solution is for Anthony to stay in the front row in the allocated area and for Francis to sit in a different row. Despite their disappointment, Francis and Anthony sit in different rows to watch the movie. They decide to consult a lawyer the following day, as they intend to bring a claim against the cinema.

Discuss the group project, taking into account the fact that Freedonia is a State Party to the CRPD.

FURTHER READING

Atkinson, V. et al., 'Disability Rights and Election Observation: Increasing Access to the Political Process' (2017) 35(4) *Nordic Journal of Human Rights* 375–91.

Broderick, A., 'Equality of What? The Capability Approach and the Right to Education for Persons with Disabilities' (2018) 6(1) *Social Inclusion* 29–39.

De Beco, G., 'The Right to Inclusive Education According to Article 24 of the UN Convention on the Rights of Persons with Disabilities: Background, Requirements and (Remaining) Questions' (2014) 32(3) *Netherlands Quarterly of Human Rights* 263–87.

De Beco, G., 'Transition to Inclusive Education Systems According to the Convention on the Rights of Persons with Disabilities' (2016) 34(1) *Nordic Journal of Human Rights* 40–59.

Della Fina, V., 'Article 24 CRPD: Education', in V. Della Fina, R. Cera and G. Palmisano (eds.), *The United Nations Convention on the Rights of Persons with Disabilities: A Commentary* (Cham: Springer Publications, 2017), pp. 439–70.

Kauppinen, L. and Jokinen, M., 'Including Deaf Culture And Linguistic Rights' in Sabatello, M. and Schulze, M. (eds.), *Human Rights and Disability Advocacy* (Philadelphia: University of Pennsylvania Press, 2014), pp. 131–145.

Mattila, M. and Achillefs, P., 'Disability, Perceived Discrimination and Political Participation' (2017) 38(5) *International Political Science Review* 505–19.

Phasha, N., Mahlo, D. and Sefa Dei, G. J., *Inclusive Education in African Contexts: A Critical Reader* (Sense Publishers, 2017).

Priestley, M., Stickings, M., Loja, E. et al., 'The Political Participation of Disabled People in Europe: Rights, Accessibility and Representation' (2016) 43 *Electoral Studies* 1–9.

Reiser, R., *Implementing Inclusive Education: A Commonwealth Guide to Implementing Article 24 of the UN Convention on the Rights of Persons with Disabilities*, 2nd edn (London: Commonwealth Secretariat, 2012).

Sganga, C., 'Disability, Right to Culture and Copyright: Which Regulatory Option?' (2015) 29 (2–3) *International Journal of Law, Computers and Technology* 88–115.

Terzi, L., 'Reframing Inclusive Education: Educational Equality as Capability Equality' (2014) 44(4) *Cambridge Journal of Education* 479–93.

Waterstone, M., 'Political Participation for People with Disabilities', in M. H. Rioux, L. A. Basser and M. Jones (eds.), *Critical Perspectives on Human Rights and Disability Law* (Leiden/Boston: Brill, 2011), pp. 371–95.

Wilson, J., 'Reimagining Disability and Inclusive Education through Universal Design for Learning' (2017) 37(2) *Disability Studies Quarterly*.

Part II

The European Union Framework

10 Disability Law and Policy in the European Union

LEARNING OUTCOMES

- ✓ Identify the main turning points in the development of EU disability law and policy.
- ✓ Understand the key EU competences that are relevant to the protection and promotion of the rights of persons with disabilities.
- ✓ Demonstrate awareness of the most relevant provisions concerning disability in the Charter of Fundamental Rights of the EU.
- ✓ Comprehend the role of the EU in advancing the rights of persons with disabilities.
- ✓ Critically assess the strengths and weaknesses of the European Disability Strategy 2010–2020.
- ✓ Describe the role of the EU in negotiating the CRPD.
- ✓ Identify the main challenges related to the implementation of the CRPD within the EU.
- ✓ Understand the effects of the CRPD in the EU legal order.

A modern disability policy is one that focuses on enabling and empowering people. People who are capable of claiming their fundamental rights and of making decisions for their own lives as active members of our society and Social Market Economy. Indeed, what we're interested in is how to give every single person the opportunity to make the most out of his or her Abilities.[1]

1 INTRODUCTION

The European Union (EU) – formerly the European Economic Community (EEC) and, later, the European Community (EC) – is a supranational organisation, or, as the Court of Justice of the European Union (CJEU) terms it, a '*sui generis* organisation',[2] which, at the time of writing this textbook, is composed of twenty-eight Member States. However, in a referendum held on 23 June 2016, the United Kingdom (UK) voted to leave the EU and is currently in the process of withdrawing from the Union. On 29 March 2017, the British government invoked Article 50 of the Treaty on European Union (TEU) and was expected to leave the EU on 29 March 2019. However, at the moment of writing this textbook, the future contours of this UK exit remain quite uncertain. In March 2019, the Withdrawal Agreement, negotiated by the then UK Prime Minister, Theresa May, with the EU, was rejected by the House of Commons (the lower house of the UK Parliament). On 10 April 2019, the European Council agreed to grant the UK a flexible extension of the Article 50 TEU period, until 31 October 2019. Thus, the UK's exit from the EU (termed 'Brexit') is only addressed briefly in this chapter.

At the beginning of its history, the EU focused on economic integration and was built on the idea of a 'common market' (now the 'internal market'), i.e. a territory without any internal borders or other regulatory obstacles to the free movement of goods, capital, services and workers.[3] The idea underpinning the original Treaty establishing the EEC was that of eliminating economic barriers by facilitating free trade between states, in order to ensure the economic and

[1] Marianne Thyssen, *Towards Barrier-free Europe. European Disability Card,* Keynote speech at conference, 2 June 2015, available at https://ec.europa.eu/commission/commissioners/2014–2019/thyssen/announcements/keynote-speech-conference-towards-barrier-free-europe-european-disability-card_en.

[2] Case 26/62, *Van Gend en Loos* v. *Nederlandse Administratie der Belastingen*, ECLI:EU:C:1963:1.

[3] Article 2 EC (now repealed) stated that the Community had as its task the establishment of a common market, and one of the activities of the Community listed in Article 3 EC (now repealed) was the creation of 'an internal market characteri[s]ed by the abolition, as between Member States, of obstacles to the free movement of goods, persons, services and capital' (now Article 26 of the Treaty on the Functioning of the European Union – TFEU).

social progress of Europe. However, the material scope of EU action has progressively widened to cover non-economic objectives.

As mentioned in the introduction to this textbook, the EU has developed a significant (and constantly evolving) body of disability law and policy in the last thirty years, which reflects its overall constitutional development and the widening of its sphere of action. The most recent milestone in this process of development is the ratification of the CRPD by the EU. This chapter highlights the key turning points in the history of disability policy in the EU and discusses the main tenets of the current EU legislative and policy action designed to protect, promote and ensure the rights of persons with disabilities. Following this introductory section, section 2 sketches out the institutional structure and the competences of the EU. It is not, by any means, devoted to explaining the nature of the EU and its constitutional framework; it is merely intended to recall general EU concepts and principles in order to support the reader's understanding of the information presented in subsequent chapters. Section 3 examines the evolution of EU disability law and policy in a chronological fashion. Section 4 discusses the current legal and policy framework regarding EU action on disability, while section 5 focuses on the EU's ratification of the CRPD and on the effects that the Convention has in the EU legal order. Section 6 briefly examines the CRPD Committee's Concluding Observations (COs) on the EU's initial report on the implementation of the Convention. Finally, section 7 briefly discusses Brexit and its consequences with regard to the rights of people with disabilities, taking into account the developments that have occurred up until 1 December 2018. This chapter is necessarily succinct, as subsequent chapters will delve into distinct issues of EU disability law.

2 THE EUROPEAN UNION AT A GLANCE

This section traces the main constitutional features of the EU. It first sketches out the main values and objectives of the EU, before concisely explaining the institutional set-up and the competences of the Union.

2.1 EU Values and Objectives

The values and objectives of the EU, the principles governing its actions, EU competences and its institutional structure are all set out in the TEU and in the Treaty on the Functioning of the European Union (TFEU),[4] which can be considered as the 'constitutional charter'[5] of the Union. Both Treaties have the

[4] For an overview, see, among others, Damian Chalmers, Gareth Davies and Giorgio Monti, *European Union Law* (Cambridge: Cambridge University Press, 2014).

[5] Case 294/83, *Les Verts* v. *European Parliament*, ECLI:EU:C:1986:166.

same legal value. In 2000, the EU also adopted the Charter of Fundamental Rights of the European Union (EU CFR), which, in 2009, acquired the same legal status as the Treaties, by virtue of Article 6 TEU.[6]

As stated in Article 2 TEU:

> [t]he Union is founded on the values of respect for human dignity, freedom, democracy, equality, the rule of law and respect for human rights, including the rights of persons belonging to minorities. These values are common to the Member States in a society in which pluralism, non-discrimination, tolerance, justice, solidarity and equality between women and men prevail.

Article 3(1) TEU affirms that the EU's aim is 'to promote peace, its values and the well-being of its peoples'. In addition, it lists a number of goals that the EU must pursue. One of those goals is the establishment of the internal market, which was the original tenet of the EEC and remains at the core of the EU project. Within the internal market, goods, services, capital and people can travel freely throughout the EU. All EU citizens have the right to study, work or retire in a Member State other than their home state (i.e. the Member State from which they come).

Article 6 TEU sets forth the parameters of the protection of fundamental rights in the EU context. The EU recognises the rights, freedoms and principles set out in the Charter of Fundamental Rights. Article 6(3) TEU affirms that:

> [f]undamental rights, as guaranteed by the European Convention for the Protection of Human Rights and Fundamental Freedoms and as they result from the constitutional traditions common to the Member States, shall constitute general principles of the Union's law.

Article 6(2) mandates the EU's accession to the ECHR, which will be discussed further in Chapter 13.

Finally, it must be recalled that Article 47 TEU explicitly recognises that the EU has legal personality. This means that the EU can conclude and negotiate international agreements, such as the CRPD, and become a member of international organisations.

2.2 The Institutional Set-Up of the EU

The EU institutions are listed in Article 13 TEU, and their tasks are laid down in the Treaties. As stated in Article 10 TEU, the EU is based on the principle of

[6] The Charter was initially proclaimed on 7 December 2000 and was proclaimed again, after amendments, on 12 December 2007. It was incorporated into the draft 2004 Constitutional Treaty, which was rejected by 'No' votes in referenda in France and the Netherlands in 2005. It has become primary law by virtue of the Lisbon Treaty, which entered into force in 2009. Even prior to the Lisbon Treaty, the Charter was an influential form of soft law. On the Charter of Fundamental Rights of the European Union (EU CFR), see, among many others, Robert Schütze, *European Constitutional Law* (Cambridge: Cambridge University Press, 2012), pp. 422–8.

representative democracy, and EU citizens are directly represented at Union level in the European Parliament. Member States are represented in the European Council and the Council of the European Union (Council). The European Commission embodies the interests of the Union as a whole.

The European Council sets the EU's overall political agenda, but it has no legislative powers. Led by its President and comprising national Heads of State or Government and the President of the Commission, the European Council meets at least twice every six months. By contrast, the Council is formed by government ministers from each Member State and meets in ten different configurations, corresponding to different policy areas. Depending on the topic being discussed, each Member State sends the minister who is responsible for that particular policy area. Together with the European Parliament, the Council is the main decision-making body of the EU. The Council adopts EU laws together with the European Parliament; coordinates EU policies on the basis of European Council guidelines; concludes agreements between the EU and third countries or international organisations; and adopts the annual EU budget (jointly with the European Parliament). The Commission is the EU's executive arm and has the power to initiate legislation and implement it once it has been adopted. It also has the power to execute the EU budget. It oversees the application of Union law under the control of the CJEU. The CJEU,[7] which is the judicial institution of the EU, is responsible for the interpretation of EU law and for reviewing the legality of EU acts. Any national court can request the CJEU to interpret a provision of EU law or to rule on the validity of such a provision, through bringing a reference for a preliminary ruling.

The EU has a number of other institutions and bodies that play specialised roles. Among them, the European Economic and Social Committee represents civil society (including representatives of persons with disabilities), employers and employees, while the European Committee of the Regions represents regional and local authorities. The European Ombudsman investigates complaints about maladministration by EU institutions and bodies. Finally, a host of specialised agencies handle a range of technical, scientific and management tasks. Among them, the European Union Agency for Fundamental Rights (FRA), which was established in 2007, has the specific task of providing independent, evidence-based advice on fundamental rights.

2.3 EU Competences

EU action is underpinned by the principle of conferral, meaning that the EU can only exercise the competences conferred upon it by the Treaties, in order

[7] The CJEU consists of the Court of Justice, the General Court and the Civil Service Tribunal.

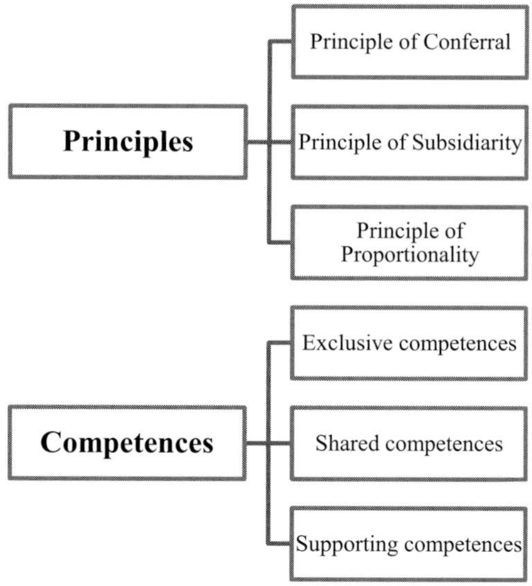

Figure 10.1 EU Principles and Competences

to attain the objectives set out therein. Article 4 TEU clearly provides that competences that are not conferred upon the EU in the Treaties remain with the Member States. The TFEU clarifies the division of competences between the EU and its Member States and distinguishes between three types of competences: exclusive, shared and supporting competences. In areas of exclusive competence, the EU alone is able to legislate and to adopt binding acts. In areas of shared competence, both the EU and its Member States are able to legislate, but Member States can exercise their own competence where the EU does not act or has decided not to exercise its competence. Where the EU has supporting competences, it can only intervene to support, coordinate or complement the action of its Member States, and EU legislation must not entail the harmonisation of national laws. The principles of subsidiarity and proportionality govern the exercise of EU competences. In areas in which the EU does not have exclusive competences, the principle of subsidiarity allows EU intervention only when the objectives of an action cannot be sufficiently achieved by the Member States alone but can be achieved more effectively at Union level.[8] The principle of proportionality requires that the actions of the EU must be limited to what is necessary to achieve the objectives set out in the Treaties. The key EU principles and competences are outlined in Figure 10.1.

[8] Article 5(3) of the Treaty on European Union (TEU) and Protocol No. 2 on the application of the principles of subsidiarity and proportionality.

The EU can adopt secondary legislation (i.e. directives, regulations and decisions) in the areas of its own competence. EU directives must be transposed into national law by the Member States. Article 288 TFEU states that a directive is binding as to the result to be achieved, but it leaves the discretion to Member States' authorities to decide on the form and means of transposition of the directive. Regulations are immediately applicable in EU Member States, and they do not require implementation into national law. Decisions are binding on those individuals to whom they are addressed.

There are three main institutions involved in the EU legislative process: the European Commission, which is the sole EU institution that can table legislative proposals; the European Parliament; and the Council.

3 THE EMERGENCE OF THE EUROPEAN UNION DISABILITY LAW AND POLICY

This section examines, in a chronological fashion, the emergence of EU disability law and policy. The first sub-section briefly analyses the early policy framework, while the second and third sub-sections focus on the legal and policy developments brought about by the entry into force of the Treaty of Amsterdam.

3.1 The Early Policy Framework

The earliest EU actions on disability date back to the 1970s. They were primarily aimed at granting assistance to EU Member States in providing services to persons with disabilities.[9] These initiatives mainly took the form of non-binding (soft law) instruments or action programmes to enhance the exchange of information between EU Member States, and they were confined to the areas of employment and vocational training.[10] In the 1980s, under the

[9] Lisa Waddington and Matthew Diller, 'Tensions and Coherence in Disability Policy: The Uneasy Relationship between Social Welfare and Civil Rights Models of Disability in American, European and International Employment Law', in Mary Lou Breslin and Silvia Yee (eds.), *Disability Rights Law and Policy* (Ardsley/New York: Transnational Publishers, 2002), pp. 241–80.

[10] See, e.g., Council Resolution of 27 June 1974 establishing the Initial Community Action Programme for the Vocational Rehabilitation of Handicapped Persons (1974–1979), OJ 1974 No. C80/30; First Community Action Programme on the Social Integration of Handicapped People (1983–1988), OJ 1981 No. C347/1, 21 December 1981; HELIOS I Community Action Programme for Disabled People (1988–1991), OJ 1988 No. L104/38; Council Decision 93/136/EEC of 25 February 1993 on HELIOS II Community Action Programme to Assist Disabled People (1993–1996), OJ 1993 No. L56/30.

influence of the UN disability declarations on persons with disabilities (highlighted in Chapter 2), the European disability agenda gradually started to extend beyond its initial, narrow, scope. The 1986 Recommendation on the Employment of Disabled People in the European Community is exemplary in this respect.[11] It was based on the principle of 'fair opportunities' for people with disabilities within a European labour market, to be achieved *via* non-discrimination measures. In that period, however, EU action was still focused on stimulating a policy debate rather than on laying down concrete actions on disability.[12]

In the course of the 1990s, the Standard Rules for the Equalization on Opportunities for Persons with Disabilities (Standard Rules), which, for the first time, contextualised disability within the frame of human rights, inspired the first comprehensive EU policy plan: the New Community Disability Strategy 1996 (1996 Strategy).[13] The 1996 Strategy was inspired by the social model and referred to human diversity and equality of opportunities. However, the EU's role was, once again, confined to supporting cooperation among its Member States, mostly through the identification and exchange of good practices.[14] In fact, the 1996 Strategy recognised that the Member States had the primary responsibility for actions aimed at eliminating exclusion and discrimination based on disability and that policies would vary within national, regional or local contexts.

Read the 1996 Strategy and compare and contrast it with the Standard Rules. What are the main similarities?

[11] Council Recommendation 86/379/EEC of 24 July 1986 on the Employment of Disabled People in the Community, OJ 1986 No. L 225/43.

[12] Commission Communication of 30 July 1996, Equality of Opportunity for People with Disabilities: A New European Community Disability Strategy, COM (96) 406 final. See also Daniel Kelemen and Lisa Vanhala, 'The Shift to the Rights Model of Disability in the EU and Canada' (2010) *Regional and Federal Studies* 1, at 1.

[13] Gerard Quinn and Eilionóir Flynn, 'Transatlantic Borrowings: The Past and Future of EU Non-Discrimination Law and Policy on the Ground of Disability' (2012) 60 *American Journal of Comparative Law* 23.

[14] Mark Priestley, 'In Search of European Disability Policy: Between National and Global' (2007) 1 *ALTER – Revue Européenne de recherche sur l'handicap* 61.

Communication from the Commission of 30 July 1996 Equality of Opportunity for People with Disabilities: A New European Community Disability Strategy COM (96) 406 final

...

15. The historical policy response to disability has been largely one of social compensation through charity, separate provision outside the mainstream of society and the development of specialist caring services. However needed and well intentioned, these policy responses have arguably compounded the problem of exclusion and under-participation.

16. One of the greatest challenges facing our societies today is that of valuing and making space for human diversity. Traditional economic and social processes have tended, however, to be constructed on the basis of assumptions about normality that have not included people with disabilities. A classic example is the design of transport systems and public buildings based on assumptions about the 'average' person that fail to take account of people with reduced mobility. Consequently, such persons have either been excluded from mainstream processes or have had their opportunities for participation considerably diminished.

17. The very absence, or virtual invisibility, of people with disabilities in the mainstream has tended only to contribute to popular stereotypes. This, in turn, has contributed to a self-perpetuating cycle of exclusion. It is in this way that prejudicial attitudes, the lack of equal opportunities, and discrimination can be seen to reinforce each other.

18. There is a growing recognition that this situation should not continue ... The driving force behind this evolution has been a realisation that human difference can best be valued by the creation of social and economic processes that are built inclusively with all persons equally in mind. The core value of equality – rendered here as equal opportunities – is now seen as the central benchmark against which economic and social structures must be assessed. It forms the essence of the rights-based approach to disability. The equal opportunities ideal is of course broader than, but nevertheless subsumes the principle of non-discrimination.

19. The overall task can best be summed up in the term 'mainstreaming'. This entails the formulation of policy to facilitate the full participation and involvement of people with disabilities in economic, social and other processes, while respecting personal choice. It also means that the relevant issues should no longer be considered separately from the mainstream policy-making apparatus, but should be clearly seen as an integral element. This approach applies to – and has benefits for – all people with disabilities regardless of the kind or degree of severity of disability in question.

...

24. The Commission considers that it is essential for the European Community to clarify and confirm its overall disability strategy, the core of which should be a shared commitment by all Member States to promote equal opportunities, to eliminate discrimination in this field and to recognise the rights of people with disabilities.

25. Any consideration of the role of the European Community in this field must commence with the acknowledgement that our societies, and the Member State governments which represent them, bear the primary responsibility for actions to eliminate exclusion and discrimination based on disability. As policies to assist people with disabilities have their own cultural and social framework in each Member State, it follows that the form of responses to the objective of equal opportunities will vary with the national, regional or local context.

3.2 The Entry into Force of the Treaty of Amsterdam and the Emergence of EU Disability Law

The major change in EU disability policy dates back to 1999, with the entry into force of the Treaty of Amsterdam, which conferred a sound competence on the EU (i.e. the former EC) to combat disability discrimination, by virtue of Article 13 EC (now Article 19 TFEU). The Treaty of Amsterdam also included a Declaration stating that EU institutions must take account of the needs of persons with disabilities in drawing up measures under the former Article 95 EC (now Article 114 TFEU). Further to these constitutional changes, Directive 2000/78/EC of 27 November 2000 establishing a general framework for equal treatment in employment and occupation (Employment Equality Directive)[15] marked the first legislative intervention designed to address discrimination on the ground of disability. As will be discussed further in Chapter 11, that Directive still forms the cornerstone of EU disability law. The EU CFR, proclaimed in 2000, gave a renewed focus to the rights of people with disabilities. In fact, the Charter contains different provisions related directly or indirectly to disability. The most notable among them are: Article 20, which provides for equality before the law; Article 21(1), which provides for an all-embracing prohibition on discrimination; and Article 26 on the integration of persons with disabilities.

The gradual emergence of EU disability law, as described above, is depicted in Figure 10.2.

[15] Council Directive 2000/78/EC of 27 November 2000 establishing a general framework for equal treatment in employment and occupation, OJ 2000 No. L303/16.

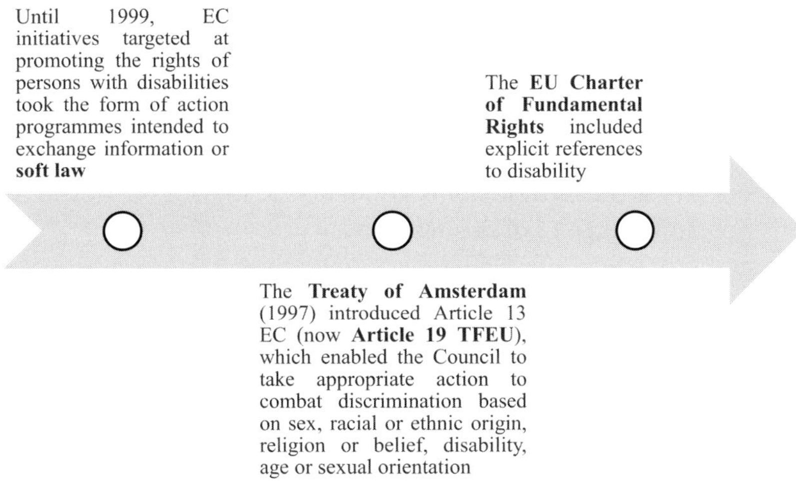

Figure 10.2 The Emergence of EU Disability Law

3.3 The EU Disability Action Plan 2003–2010

The constitutional developments brought about by the Treaty of Amsterdam and the proclamation of the EU CFR provoked a major shift at the EU policy level. In 2003, the EU Disability Action Plan 2003–2010 (EU DAP) was adopted to carry forward the 1996 Strategy, outlined above.[16] The EU DAP was an ambitious long-term policy plan, whose ultimate objective was to 'boost equal opportunities for people with disabilities' so as to create a 'sustainable dynamic for the full inclusion of people with disabilities into society', fostering implementation of the Employment Equality Directive. In a similar vein to the 1996 Strategy, the EU DAP was informed by the social model of disability and by the Standard Rules, and it aimed at mainstreaming disability issues across all EU policies. However, unlike its predecessor, it was characterised by a clear structure and identified specific areas for EU action. In addition, in order to achieve effective results and to improve the existing situation of people with disabilities, every two years, the Commission identified specific priority areas for intervention within the realm of the EU DAP. In 2006–2007, the following were identified as priority areas: inclusion of people with disabilities in the labour market; quality support and care services; accessibility of mainstream goods and services; and increasing the EU's analytical capacity in order to promote independent living.[17] Notably, these are still core areas of EU action under the current European Disability Strategy 2010–2020 (EDS). The final

[16] Commission Communication of 30 October 2003, Equal Opportunities for People with Disabilities: A European Action Plan, COM (2003) 650 final.

[17] Commission Communication of 28 November 2005, Situation of Disabled People in the Enlarged European Union: The European Action Plan 2006–2007, COM (2005) 604 final.

phase of the EU DAP (2008–2009) identified accessibility as the most pressing priority.[18] It acknowledged that accessible goods, services and infrastructures are essential in sustaining non-discriminatory and inclusive forms of participation in many aspects of everyday life in an ageing society, along with the elimination of barriers to education and to the labour market. This special focus on accessibility is also reflected in the EDS, as will be discussed further in Chapter 12 of this textbook.

4 THE CURRENT FRAMEWORK OF EUROPEAN UNION DISABILITY LAW AND POLICY

The developments that occurred in the 1990s and in the 2000s led to the mainstreaming of disability in EU law and policy and to the emergence of disability law and policy as a distinct field of EU action. Against this background, this section discusses the constitutional framework of the EU and the main legal principles pertaining to EU action on the whole.

4.1 The Constitutional Framework

4.1.1 *The EU Treaties*

The principles of equality and non-discrimination are firmly embedded in the EU Treaties. Article 2 TEU includes among the values upon which the Union is founded the principle of equality. Article 3 TEU states that the EU 'shall combat social exclusion and discrimination'. Article 9 TEU mandates the EU institutions to afford all citizens equal attention. Furthermore, Article 21 TEU sets forth the requirement that the EU be guided by the principle of equality in any external action adopted. Although the foregoing provisions do not create any legal rights, their prominent position in the TEU shows that the EU is committed to ensuring equality of opportunity and developing an even more substantive form of protection of fundamental rights in the future.[19] Article 19 TFEU (former Article 13 EC) remains the main provision that confers legislative competence on the EU in relation to combating discrimination on the ground, *inter alia*, of disability. In addition, Article 10 TFEU requires that, 'in defining and implementing its policies and activities, the Union shall aim to combat discrimination based on ... disability'. That horizontal clause allows the EU to integrate the fight against discrimination into all EU actions. The latter two Articles are highlighted in further detail in Figure 10.3.

[18] Commission Communication of 26 November 2007, Situation of Disabled People in the European Union: The European Action Plan 2008–2009, COM (2007) 738 final.

[19] Erica Howard, 'EU Equality Law: Three Recent Developments' (2011) 17 *European Law Journal* 785; Evelyn Ellis and Philippa Watson, *EU Anti-Discrimination Law* (Oxford: Oxford University Press, 2012).

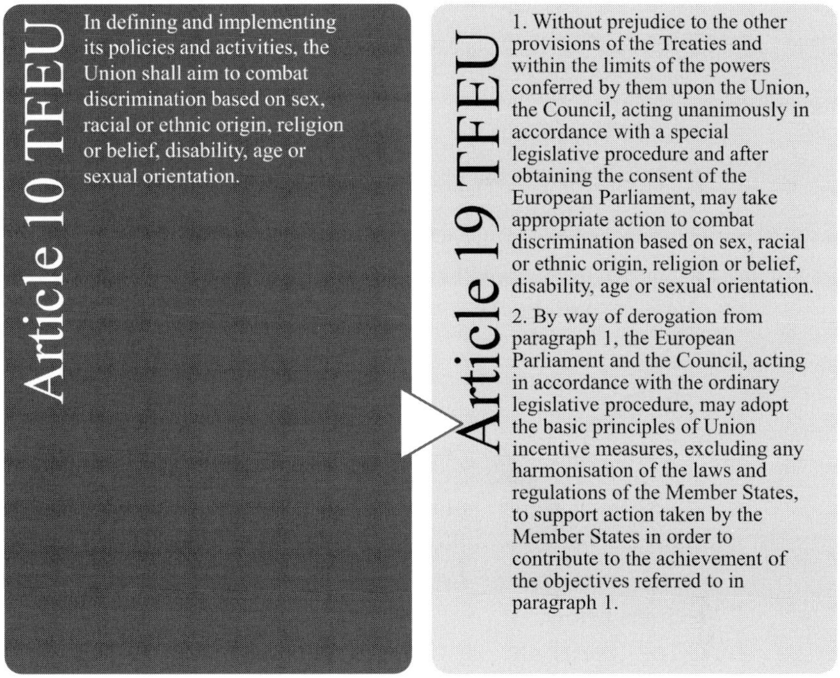

Figure 10.3 The Constitutional Provisions that Empower the EU to Combat Discrimination

4.1.2 *The EU Charter of Fundamental Rights*

As mentioned above, the EU CFR, which has the same legal value as the Treaties, includes relevant provisions on disability, but it does not expand the existing EU competences, which are laid down in the Treaties.[20] Hence, the power of the EU institutions to promote and protect fundamental rights (including the rights of persons with disabilities) is limited to the competences attributed to those institutions in the Treaties.

As stated in its Preamble, the Charter aims to 'strengthen the protection of fundamental rights in the light of changes in society, social progress and scientific and technological developments'. It consists of seven chapters and fifty-four Articles. The six substantive chapters of the EU CFR are as follows: Dignity (Articles 1–5), Freedoms (Articles 6–19), Equality (Articles 20–26), Solidarity (Articles 27–38), Citizens' Rights (Articles 39–46) and Justice (Articles 47–50). The last chapter deals with the interpretation and application of the Charter.

[20] Article 6 TEU. Similarly, Article 51 EU CFR states that the 'Charter does not establish any new power or task for the Community or the Union, or modify powers and tasks defined by the Treaties'. See also Case C-354/13, *Kaltoft* v. *Municipality of Billund*, ECLI:EU:C:2014:2463, paras. 36–9.

Read the Charter, and identify the provisions that are most relevant to people with disabilities (besides Articles 21 and 26).

The Charter reflects rights guaranteed in the European Convention on Human Rights (ECHR), the European Social Charter (ESC) and the case law of the CJEU. Moreover, the Charter reflects the constitutional traditions common to all Member States. All of the provisions of the Charter (outlined in Figure 10.4)[21] are of potential relevance to persons with disabilities, who must enjoy all of the rights enshrined in it without discrimination. However, the most relevant provisions for the purposes of the analysis conducted in this section are Articles 21 and 26, which are examined in the subsections below.

The Charter sets out two different kinds of provisions: rights and principles. Article 51(1) EU CFR specifies that, while rights should be respected, principles should be observed, and the application of both should be promoted. To determine whether a provision is a right or a principle, it is necessary to refer to the Explanations Relating to the Charter of Fundamental Rights[22] and also to the case law of the CJEU.

Article 52(3) EU CFR establishes that:

> [i]nsofar as this Charter contains rights which correspond to rights guaranteed by the Convention for the Protection of Human Rights and Fundamental Freedoms [the ECHR], the meaning and scope of those rights shall be the same as those laid down by the said Convention. This provision shall not prevent Union law providing more extensive protection.

The CJEU has also held, in *J. McB.* v. *L. E.*, that the meaning of EU CFR rights should be established not only on the basis of provisions of the ECHR but also on clear and consistent case law of the European Court of Human Rights (ECtHR).[23] The Charter sets out only a minimum ground of protection. Article 53 EU CFR stipulates that no provision in the Charter may be interpreted as restricting fundamental rights protected by other mechanisms which the EU or its Member States are a party to, including the ECHR.

[21] Figure 10.4 draws on Lukasz Bojarski, *The Charter of Fundamental Rights as a Living Instrument* (2014), pp. 18–19, available at http://bim.lbg.ac.at/sites/files/bim/attachments/cfreu_manual_0.pdf.

[22] Explanations Relating to the Charter of Fundamental Rights of 14 December 2007, OJ 2007 No. C303/02.

[23] Case C-400/10, *J. McB.* v. *L. E.*, ECLI:EU:C:2010:582.

Dignity

Right to:
- Life
- Dignity
- Respect for one's physical and mental integrity
- Free and informed consent

Prohibition of:
- Killings/the death penalty
- Torture
- Degrading and inhumane treatment
- Organ trafficking
- Cloning
- Eugenic practices
- Slavery/forced labour
- Human trafficking

Freedoms

Freedom of:
- Expression and information
- Thought, conscience, religion
- Art and science
- Association and assembly
- Conducting a business

Right to:
- Liberty and protection from arbitrary detention
- Marry
- Found a family
- Respect for private and family life
- Education
- Protection of personal data
- Choose an occupation and engage in work
- Property and bequeath
- Protection of intellectual property
- Asylum for refugees
- Protection against collective expulsion/ extradition to a state that violates fundamental human rights

Equality

Equality:
- Before the law
- Equality of women and men
- Cultural, religious and language diversity

Rules of respect of the rights of:
- Children
- Elderly
- Persons with disabilities

Prohibition of discrimination based on:
- Sex
- Race and colour
- Ethnic or social origin
- Genetic features
- Language
- Religion or belief
- Political or any other opinion
- Membership of a national minority
- Property
- Birth
- Disability
- Age
- Sexual orientation

Figure 10.4 The Rights Guaranteed in the EU Charter of Fundamental Rights

Solidarity

Right of workers to:
- Information
- Consultation
- Collective bargaining
- Access to placement services
- Fair and just working conditions
- Protection in the event of unjustified dismissal
- Protection of young people at work

Prohibition of:
- Child labour

Rules of:
- Reconciliation of family and professional life
- Protection of family – legal, economic and social

Right to:
- Protection during maternity
- Maternal and paternal leave
- Social security benefits
- Social and housing assistance
- Access to services of general economic interest

Rules of protection of:
- Health
- Consumers
- Environment

Citizens' Rights

Right to:
- Vote and to stand as a candidate in elections to the European Parliament
- Vote and to stand as a candidate in municipal elections
- Consular protection
- Petition
- Refer to the European Ombudsman
- Access to documents
- Good administration

Freedom of:
- Movement and residence

Justice

Right to:
- An effective remedy before the court
- An independent and impartial tribunal previously established by law
- Have one's case fairly and publicly heard, within a reasonable time
- Be advised and have legal aid
- Defend oneself
- The presumption of innocence

Prohibition of:
- Being held guilty of any criminal offence not prescribed by law at the time when it was committed
- Disproportionate penalties
- Being tried or punished twice for the same criminal offence

Figure 10.4 (*cont.*)

The Charter applies to all EU institutions and bodies, offices and agencies. In October 2010, the European Commission adopted a specific Strategy for the effective implementation of the Charter of Fundamental Rights by the European Union,[24] in order to ensure the compatibility with the Charter of all EU acts throughout the legislative process. Since all legislative proposals at the EU level have to be in conformity with the Charter, each proposal for a new legislative act is scrutinised by the Commission against a checklist of possible violations of fundamental rights. The Charter also applies at the national level when Member States implement or apply EU law. This means that the Charter must be respected by Member States when transposing EU directives into national legislation, when applying EU law (e.g. an EU regulation) and when provisions of EU law are at stake in judicial proceedings before a national court.

4.1.3 *Article 21(1) EU CFR*

ARTICLE 21(1) EU CFR

Any discrimination based on any ground such as sex, race, colour, ethnic or social origin, genetic features, language, religion or belief, political or any other opinion, membership of a national minority, property, birth, disability, age or sexual orientation shall be prohibited.

Article 21(1) EU CFR lists disability as one of the grounds on which discrimination must be prohibited. That provision draws on the former Article 13 EC (Article 19 TFEU) as well as on Article 14 ECHR and on Article 11 of the Convention on Human Rights and Biomedicine as regards genetic heritage.[25] It must be noted that Article 14 ECHR does not explicitly mention disability.[26] However, as will be discussed in Chapter 13, the ECtHR held, for the first time in *Glor* v. *Switzerland*, that Article 14 ECHR, which prohibits 'discrimination on any ground such as sex, race, colour, language, religion, political or other

[24] Commission Communication of 19 October 2010, Strategy for the Effective Implementation of the Charter of Fundamental Rights by the European Union, COM (2010) 573 final. See also Commission Staff Working Paper of 6 May 2011, Operational Guidance on taking account of Fundamental Rights in Commission Impact Assessments, SEC(2011) 567 final.

[25] Explanations relating to the Charter of Fundamental Rights, note 22.

[26] Article 14 ECHR prohibits discrimination on a range of grounds and reads as follows: 'The enjoyment of the rights and freedoms set forth in this Convention shall be secured without discrimination on any ground such as sex, race, colour, language, religion, political or other opinion, national or social origin, association with a national minority, property, birth or other status'. See below Chapter 13.

opinion, national or social origin, association with a national minority, property, birth or other status', has to be interpreted as covering disabilities and various health conditions under the 'other status' clause.[27] Finally, it is important to point out that the sphere of operation of Article 21(1) EU CFR is not restricted either to a particular context or to the enjoyment of the rights conferred by the Charter itself, but it extends to all EU actions.

4.1.4 *Article 26 EU CFR*

ARTICLE 26 EU CFR

The Union recognises and respects the right of persons with disabilities to benefit from measures designed to ensure their independence, social and occupational integration and participation in the life of the community.

Article 26 EU CFR on integration of persons with disabilities is based on Article 15 of the ESC, and it draws on point 26 of the Community Charter of the Fundamental Social Rights of Workers. It entails a specific recognition of the rights of persons with disabilities, and it supplements the principle of non-discrimination articulated in Article 21 EU CFR. Article 26 EU CFR is reflective of the social model, focusing on inclusion and participation in society and the need to ensure the independence of persons with disabilities. However, Article 26 is classified as a principle rather than a right (in accordance with Article 51 and Article 52(5) of the Charter).[28] This means that it is intended to guide the EU institutions when they legislate but that it does not oblige them to act and is not directly enforceable, as highlighted by the CJEU in *Glatzel*.[29]

[27] European Court on Human Rights (ECtHR), *Glor* v. *Switzerland*, Application No. 13444/04, 30 April 2009.

[28] Article 51(1) provides that: 'The provisions of this Charter are addressed to the institutions, bodies, offices and agencies of the Union with due regard for the principle of subsidiarity and to the Member States only when they are implementing Union law. They shall therefore respect the rights, observe the principles and promote the application thereof in accordance with their respective powers and respecting the limits of the powers of the Union as conferred on it in the Treaties'. Article 52(5) stipulates that: 'The provisions of this Charter which contain principles may be implemented by legislative and executive acts taken by institutions, bodies, offices and agencies of the Union, and by acts of Member States when they are implementing Union law, in the exercise of their respective powers. They shall be judicially cognisable only in the interpretation of such acts and in the ruling on their legality'.

[29] Case C-356/12, *Wolfgang Glatzel* v. *Freistaat Bayern*, ECLI:EU:C:2014:350.

Case C-356/12, *Glatzel*

78. . . . although Article 26 of the Charter requires the European Union to respect and recognise the right of persons with disabilities to benefit from integration measures, the principle enshrined by that article does not require the EU legislature to adopt any specific measure. In order for that article to be fully effective, it must be given more specific expression in European Union or national law. Accordingly, that article cannot by itself confer on individuals a subjective right which they may invoke as such . . .

4.2 EU Disability Legislation in a Nutshell

In December 2010, the EU ratified (i.e. formally concluded) the CRPD, thereby becoming a Party to a UN human rights treaty for the first time.[30] As shown in Figure 10.5, the CRPD is now part of the EU's legal framework, and it has acquired a sub-constitutional status: it is situated below the Treaties (and the Charter) and above EU secondary law (i.e. EU legislation).[31]

With regard to EU secondary law, the Employment Equality Directive remains the main piece of legislation that protects and promotes the rights of people with disabilities, as mentioned above. A proposal for a new non-discrimination directive[32] to tackle discrimination outside the labour market is also under discussion at the EU level, but its approval and entry into force should not be expected too soon.[33] However, the EU legal framework currently includes disability-related provisions in various areas, such as transport, lifts, public procurement, and electronic communications networks and services.[34] These will be examined in subsequent chapters of this textbook.

[30] Council Decision 2010/48/EC of 26 November 2009 concerning the conclusion, by the European Community, of the United Nations Convention on the Rights of Persons with Disabilities, OJ 2010 No. L23/35. That concluding decision was formally adopted on 26 November 2009 under the EC Treaty.

[31] See below section 5.

[32] Proposal for a Council Directive on implementing the principle of equal treatment between persons irrespective of religion or belief, disability, age or sexual orientation, COM (2008) 426 def.

[33] See further Chapter 11.

[34] Janina Arsenjeva, *Annotated Review of European Union Law and Policy with Reference to Disability* (prepared under the direction of Professor Lisa Waddington, on behalf of the Academic Network of European Disability Experts – ANED) (2017), available at www.disability-europe.net/theme/eu-law-and-policy.

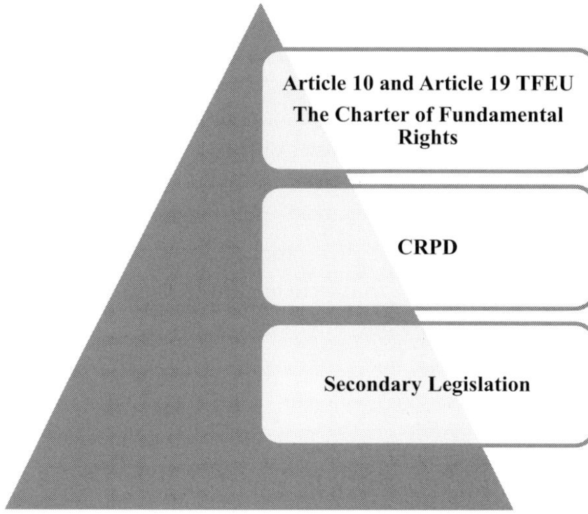

Figure 10.5 The Legal Framework

DID YOU KNOW THAT ...?

Statistical data show that EU citizens with disabilities are consistently disadvantaged in terms of employment, education and social inclusion, as discrimination is still a major barrier to their participation in society. At only 48.7 per cent, the employment rate of people with disabilities remains much lower than that of people without disabilities (72.5 per cent). Moreover, 30 per cent of people with a disability are at risk of poverty or social exclusion in the EU, compared to 21.5 per cent of people without disabilities. People with disabilities across the EU have also been hit hard by the most recent economic crisis (Commission Staff Working Document, Progress Report on the Implementation of the European Disability Strategy (2010–2020) (2 February 2017) SWD (2017) 29 final).

4.3 The Policy Framework

The European Disability Strategy 2010–2020 (EDS),[35] which proposes comprehensive and mainstream policy action, complements the legal framework in force at EU level. It lays down the current disability policy agenda, and it has the 'overall aim' of 'empower[ing] people with disabilities so that they can enjoy their full rights, and benefit fully from participating in society and in the European economy'.

[35] Commission Communication of 15 November 2010, European Disability Strategy 2010–2020: A Renewed Commitment to a Barrier-Free Europe, COM (2010) 636 final.

Communication from the Commission of 15 November 2010 European Disability Strategy 2010–2020: A Renewed Commitment to a Barrier-Free Europe COM (2010) 636 final

2. Objectives and actions

The overall aim of this Strategy is to empower people with disabilities so that they can enjoy their full rights, and benefit fully from participating in society and in the European economy, notably through the Single market. Achieving this and ensuring effective implementation of the UN Convention across the EU calls for consistency. This Strategy identifies actions at EU level to supplement national ones, and it determines the mechanisms needed to implement the UN Convention at EU level, including inside the EU institutions. It also identifies the support needed for funding, research, awareness-raising, statistics and data collection. This Strategy focuses on eliminating barriers. The Commission has identified eight main areas for action: Accessibility, Participation, Equality, Employment, Education and training, Social protection, Health, and External Action. For each area, key actions are identified, with the overarching EU-level objective highlighted in a box. These areas were selected on the basis of their potential to contribute to the overall objectives of the Strategy and of the UN Convention, the related policy documents from EU institutions and the Council of Europe, as well as the results of the EU Disability Action Plan 2003–2010, and a consultation of the Member States, stakeholders and the general public. The references to national actions are intended to supplement action at EU level, rather than to cover all national obligations under the UN Convention. The Commission will also tackle the situation of people with disabilities through the Europe 2020 strategy, its flagship initiatives and the relaunch of the single market.

> Read the Charter, and identify the provisions that are most relevant to people with disabilities (besides Articles 21 and 26).

The EDS sets out eight interconnected key areas of action: accessibility, participation, equality, employment, education and training, social protection, health and external action. For each of these areas, it identifies EU-level actions, which, alongside national measures, are designed to 'ensure effective implementation of the UN Convention across the EU'. For example, in relation to employment, the key objective of the European Commission is to '[e]nable many more people with

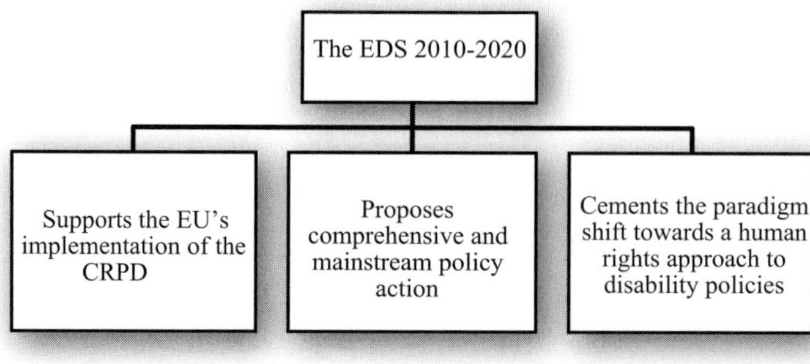

Figure 10.6 The EDS

disabilities to earn their living on the open labour market'. As will be discussed at length in Chapter 12, the EDS recognises that accessibility is a 'precondition for participation in society and in the economy'. In that connection, the EDS indicates that the Commission will use legislative and other instruments, such as standardisation, to optimise accessibility of the built environment, transport and ICT.

The underlying aims of the EDS are set out in Figure 10.6.

Although the EDS is comprehensive, it falls short of the far-reaching obligations laid down in the CRPD. In 2015, the CRPD Committee, in its COs on the initial report of the EU, recommended 'the adoption of a strategy on the implementation of the Convention, with the allocation of a budget, a time frame for implementation and a monitoring mechanism'.[36] This echoes the words of the European Disability Forum (EDF) – the major European umbrella organisation representing people with disabilities – which, in its shadow report to the CRPD Committee, had claimed that the EDS 'is limited in scope, [and] lacks funding for its implementation'.[37] The European Parliament has not expressed harsh criticism towards the EDS as such, but it has shared the concerns of the CRPD Committee in relation to the EU's lack of a clear strategy for implementing the UN Convention.[38] Those criticisms did not, however,

[36] CRPD Committee, Concluding Observations on the Initial Report of the European Union, 2 October 2015, UN Doc. CRPD/C/EU/CO/1.

[37] EDF also called for the development of a new 'European Disability Pact', to be included in the Europe 2020 Strategy as a horizontal flagship and supported by a sufficient financial allocation. The criticisms of the EDS 2010–2020 was not shared by all NGOs. ENIL–ECCL, for instance, welcomed the range of initiatives taken by the EU since its ratification of the CRPD and praised the EDS.

[38] European Parliament, *Report on the Implementation of the UN Convention on the Rights of Persons with Disabilities, with Special Regard to the Concluding Observations of the UN CRPD Committee (2015/2258(INI))*, 9 June 2016, available at http://www.europarl.europa.eu/doceo/document/A-8-2016-0203_EN.html. That report was compiled in a participatory fashion, in that several NGOs and DPOs were consulted.

lead to any substantial modification of the EDS. In 2015, the European Commission launched a public consultation to collect views from a broad range of stakeholders on the impact of the EDS, and a mid-term revision was carried out. The results of that consultation were divulged in a progress report in February 2017 and showed that the situation of people with disabilities is challenging in terms of accessibility, discrimination, participation in employment and their mobility within the EU.[39] In spite of those findings, the Commission affirmed that the EDS remains a valid instrument and an important tool to advance the protection and promotion of the rights of persons with disabilities.

DID YOU KNOW THAT ...?

The European Parliament of Persons with Disabilities (EPPD) is one of the multiple initiatives undertaken by the EU institutions to raise awareness on the rights of persons with disabilities and to ensure that decisions concerning persons with disabilities in the EU are taken together with them. To date, the EPPD has been convened three times – in 1993, 2003 and 2012. The first EPPD was organised under the initiative of the Commission, to mark the adoption of the Standard Rules. The second EPPD, organised by EDF, marked the end of the European Year of Persons with Disabilities 2003 and the 10th anniversary of the Standard Rules. The third EPPD focused on the implementation of the CRPD in the EU in a time of economic crisis. The fourth EPPD was convened in December 2017 and focused on the right of persons with disabilities to vote and participate in political and public life. It also addressed the need for a renewed disability strategy for the period 2020–2030, to follow up on the current EDS. During the EPPD, a Manifesto on European Elections 2019 was adopted by the delegates calling on EU leaders to ensure that electoral processes are fully accessible to persons with disabilities. Furthermore, participants discussed the Sustainable Development Goals (SDGs) and the importance of taking the views of people with disabilities on board in their implementation (www.edf-feph.org/newsroom/news/4th-european-parliament-persons-disabilities-disability-rights-heart-european-union).

4.4 The European Pillar of Social Rights

In November 2017, the European Pillar of Social Rights (Pillar) was solemnly proclaimed, with the aim of boosting the social dimension of Europe.[40] It is a

[39] Commission Staff Working Document, Progress Report on the Implementation of the European Disability Strategy (2010–2020) (2 February 2017), SWD (2017) 29 final.

[40] European Pillar of Social Rights, available at https://ec.europa.eu/commission/priorities/deeper-and-fairer-economic-and-monetary-union/european-pillar-social-rights_en.

soft law document that lays down twenty principles 'essential for fair and well-functioning labour markets and welfare systems in 21st century Europe'.[41] It reaffirms some of the rights already present in the EU CFR and in the Treaties, and it is intended to stimulate the debate on the social dimension of Europe. It responds to a period of harsh economic crisis and demographic change, in terms of both an ageing population and increasing migration, and it provides 'a framework of reference for policy monitoring in a number of key areas'.[42] Its three overarching themes – equal opportunities and access to the labour market, fair working conditions, and social protection and inclusion – are very relevant to people with disabilities.[43] In particular, chapter I of the Pillar, on equal opportunities and access to the labour market, reaffirms the right to equal treatment and non-discrimination, *inter alia*, on the ground of disability in the labour market, and also in access to services (principle 3). That principle 'can be assumed to underline the need for disability mainstreaming throughout the Pillar, along with gender mainstreaming and other grounds'.[44] Chapter III, on social protection and inclusion, contains a provision (principle 17) on the inclusion of people with disabilities, stating that '[p]eople with disabilities have the right to income support that ensures living in dignity, services that enable them to participate in the labour market and in society, and a work environment adapted to their needs'. Due to its non-binding legal nature, the effects of the Pillar are quite uncertain. In particular, at the time of writing this textbook, it is not clear whether it will influence EU disability policies. The Pillar certainly does not modify or alter the extent of EU competences on social policies. However, it has the potential to boost the debate on the protection of the rights of persons with disabilities within the EU legal framework.

5 THE EUROPEAN UNION RATIFICATION OF THE UNITED NATIONS CONVENTION ON THE RIGHTS OF PERSONS WITH DISABILITIES

A major milestone in the development of EU disability law and policy was the ratification of the CRPD by the EU, alongside its ratification by all EU Member States. The process leading to that ratification and the effects of the Convention in the EU legal order are examined in this section.

[41] Ibid.

[42] ANED, *Mainstreaming Disability Rights in the European Pillar of Social Rights – A Compendium* (2018), available at www.disability-europe.net/, p. 11.

[43] Ibid. p. 8. [44] Ibid. p. 12.

5.1 The Negotiation and Ratification of the CRPD

As noted by Lawson, the EU played an active part in the work of the Ad-Hoc Committee that drafted the CRPD.[45] De Burca affirms, however, that 'the initial approach of the EU to the drafting of the Convention was somewhat ambivalent'.[46] Initially, the EU was not in favour of a binding instrument, which could duplicate other international human rights treaties, rules or standards.[47] Nevertheless, once a clear consensus emerged in favour of a binding international treaty on the rights of persons with disabilities, the EU decided to support the elaboration of a legal instrument grounded on the principle of equality. On the basis of negotiating directives adopted by the Council on 24 May 2004, the Commission conducted the negotiation of the Convention on behalf of the EU, by virtue of the competence derived from Articles 13 and 95 EC (now Articles 19 and 114 TFEU), which address (disability) discrimination and the internal market, respectively.[48] The Commission then signed the UN Convention on 30 March 2007. The decision on the conclusion of the CRPD was adopted by the Council in November 2009 (Council Decision 2010/48/EC).[49] Notably, that decision contains a reservation with respect to Article 27(1) CRPD,[50] and it is accompanied by a declaration of competence. The

[45] Anna Lawson, 'The European Union and CRPD: Complexities, Challenges and Opportunities', in Valentina Della Fina, Giuseppe Palmisano and Rachele Cera, *The UNCRPD: A Commentary* (Cham: Springer, 2017), pp. 61–6.

[46] Grainne De Burca, 'The EU in the Negotiation of the UN Disability Convention' (2010) 35 *European Law Review* 2.

[47] Ibid.

[48] Proposal for a Council Decision on the signing, on behalf of the European Community, of the United Nations Convention on the Rights of Persons with Disabilities and its Optional Protocol, COM (2007) 77 final. The Council Decision ST07404/07 of 27 March 2007, authorised the former Community to sign the UN Convention on the Rights of Persons with Disabilities and issued a declaration on the Optional Protocol (Annex II of the Decision). The declaration stated that the Council of the European Union would reconsider the question of the signing of the Optional Protocol to the United Nations Convention on the Rights of Persons with Disabilities by the European Community as soon as possible; see Lisa Waddington, 'A New Era in Human Rights Protection in the European Community: The Implications of the United Nations' Convention on the Rights of Persons with Disabilities for the European Community' (2007) *Maastricht Faculty of Law Working Paper 2007/4*, available at http://digitalarchive.maastrichtuniversity.nl/fedora/get/guid:9d6d479e-fb73-4e64-81a5-f4b45c00854f/ASSET1.

[49] Council Decision 2010/48/EC, note 30. Under the Decision, the Council authorised the deposit of the instrument of formal confirmation with the Secretary General of the United Nations, which occurred in December 2010.

[50] The reservation reads as follows: 'The European Community states that pursuant to Community law (notably Council Directive 2000/78/EC of 27 November 2000 establishing a general framework for equal treatment in employment and occupation), the Member States may, if appropriate, enter their own reservations to Article 27(1) of the Disabilities Convention to the extent that Article 3(4) of the said Council Directive provides them with the right to exclude non-discrimination on the grounds of disability with respect to employment in the

declaration lists EU legislation that addresses, to varying degrees, the rights of persons with disabilities, and the scope of EU competence with regard to the CRPD ensues from these legislative acts. Indeed, the declaration (like the declarations of competences included in other decisions of the Council) is only intended to specify to third countries the distribution of competences, indicating the competences that the Member States have transferred to the EU under the Treaties in matters governed by the CRPD.

The conclusion of the CRPD was made possible under Article 44 CRPD, which allows regional integration organisations to accede to the Convention. The EU is the first and only regional organisation to have ratified the CRPD, and the CRPD is the first (and still the only) human rights treaty concluded by the EU. Since 2011, the ratification of the Convention has been welcomed by a number of non-governmental organisations (NGOs) and disabled persons' organisations (DPOs), such as EDF and the Mental Disability Advocacy Centre (MDAC).[51] Human Rights Watch (HRW) praised the EU for 'sending a clear message that disability rights are a priority in the region and worldwide'.[52] In the same vein, the CRPD Committee, in its COs on the EU's initial report,[53] commended the EU for having ratified the Convention and for having engaged in a fruitful dialogue with the Committee itself.

The EU has not yet ratified the Optional Protocol to the Convention (OP-CRPD). The CRPD Committee expressed concerns in this respect, and the European Parliament has also called on the EU to ratify the OP-CRPD, most recently in 2016.[54] The difficulties encountered in the process of ratification are due to the fact that the EU's accession to the OP-CRPD requires unanimous agreement of its Member States in the Council (and the consent of the Parliament), which has not yet been reached.

5.2 The Effects of the CRPD in the EU Legal Order

The CRPD is qualified as a mixed agreement in the EU legal order. It is well known that 'mixity' refers to the fact that part of an international agreement

armed forces from the scope of the Directive. Therefore, the Community states that it concludes the Convention without prejudice to the above right, conferred on its Member States by virtue of Community law'.

[51] MDAC, 'MDAC Welcomes European Union Ratification of UN Convention on the Rights of Persons with Disabilities' (10 January 2011), available at http://mdac.info/en/content/mdac-welcomes-european-union-ratification-un-convention-rights-persons-disabilities.

[52] Human Rights Watch, 'EU: A Commitment to Disability Rights' (30 December 2010), available at www.hrw.org/news/2010/12/30/eu-commitment-disability-rights.

[53] CRPD Committee, Concluding Observation on the Initial Report of the European Union, note 36.

[54] European Parliament, *Report on the Implementation of the UN Convention on the Rights of Persons*, note 38.

falls within the scope of the competences of the EU and part falls within the scope of the powers of the Member States.[55]

The Treaties do not address in detail the relationship between EU law and international law. Article 216(2) TFEU merely stipulates that international agreements concluded by the Union are binding upon the institutions and its Member States. The CJEU has played a vital role in interpreting these provisions and in elaborating on the legal consequences of the EU's accession to international treaties, and more generally on the relationship between EU law and international treaty law. Beginning in the early 1970s, international treaties were considered to form 'an integral part of [EU] law'[56] once they entered into force. With regard to the status of international agreements within the hierarchy of sources of law, the CJEU has argued that international treaties are formally situated below the provisions of the Treaties.[57] The Court has also stated that mixed agreements 'have the same status of purely [EU] agreements, in so far as the provisions fall within the scope of [EU] competence'.[58] Hence, the CRPD has become part of the EU legal framework, and, as highlighted above, it is inferior to the provisions of the Treaties in hierarchical terms but superior to secondary EU law.[59] The latter point implies that provisions of EU secondary law must, as far as possible, be interpreted in a manner that is consistent with the CRPD. Hence, if the wording of secondary EU legislation is open to more than one interpretation, preference should be given, as far as practicable, to the interpretation which renders the EU law provision consistent with the Convention. As will be discussed in Chapter 11, the CJEU has, up until now, attempted to interpret EU law (and in particular the Employment Equality Directive) in line with the Convention. The first case in which the Court interpreted the Employment Equality Directive in light of the CRPD was *Ring and Werge.*[60] The Court held that '[i]t follows from Decision 2010/48 that the European Union has approved the UN Convention. The provisions of that convention are thus, from the time of its entry into force, an integral part of the European Union legal order'. In line with established case law, the Court went on to affirm that the

[55] Commission Staff Working Document, Report on the Implementation of the UN Convention on the Rights of Persons with Disabilities (CRPD) by the European Union, 5 June 2014, SWD (2014) 182 final.

[56] Case 181/73, *R. and V. Haegeman* v. *Belgian State*, ECLI:EU:C:1974:41. In this decision, the Court used the notion of 'incorporation' as meaning provisions of international agreements which are not transposed and do not need further validation. They become part of the EU legal order after the conclusion of the agreement, simply by entering into force.

[57] Case C-61/94, *Commission* v. *Germany*, ECLI:EU:C:1996:313.

[58] *Ex multis*, Case C-239/03 *Commission* v. *France (Etang de Berre)*, ECLI:EU:C:2004:598.

[59] *Commission* v. *Germany*, note 57.

[60] Joined cases C-335/11 and C-337/11, *HK Danmark, acting on behalf of Jette Ring* v. *Dansk almennyttigt Boligselskab* (C-335/11) and *HK Danmark, acting on behalf of Lone Skouboe Werge* v. *Dansk Arbejdsgiverforening, acting on behalf of Pro Display A/S*, in liquidation (C-337/11), ECLI:EU:C:2013:222, paras. 30–32.

Employment Equality Directive must, as far as possible, be interpreted in a manner consistent with the CRPD.[61] Similar statements were included in *Z.* v. *A Government Department*,[62] in *Kaltoft*,[63] in *Glatzel*[64] and in subsequent cases.[65]

Even though the CRPD is superior to secondary legislation within the hierarchy of EU law sources, this does not automatically mean that EU legislation can be declared invalid if it breaches the CRPD. The validity of EU secondary law can only be assessed *vis-à-vis* an international provision if the latter is capable of displaying direct effect. Even if international agreements form an integral part of the EU legal order, the principle of direct effect – which implies the enforceability of rights for individuals *vis-à-vis* the EU and its Member States – cannot automatically be extended to those agreements. In general, to determine whether a provision displays direct effect, the Court has examined whether the Parties to the agreement have established the effect of its provisions in their internal legal order.[66] If not, the CJEU has considered whether an agreement is capable of stipulating directly effective provisions by examining 'the purpose, the spirit, the general scheme and the terms' of the agreement.[67] Thereafter, it has examined whether the relevant provision contains a clear and sufficiently precise obligation, which is not subject, in its implementation or effect, to the adoption of any subsequent measure.[68] In *Z.* v. *A Government Department*, the Court found that:

> without there being any need to examine the nature and broad logic of the UN Convention, it must be held that the provisions of the Convention are not, as regards their content, provisions that are unconditional and sufficiently precise … and that they therefore do not have direct effect in European Union law.[69]

This finding was reiterated by the Court in *Glatzel.*[70]

The CJEU has also firmly asserted its competence to interpret international agreements, including mixed agreements.[71] In *Hermès*,[72] the Court affirmed

[61] Ibid.

[62] Case C-363/12, *Z.* v. *A Government Department and The Board of management of a community school* ECLI:EU:C:2014:159.

[63] *Kaltoft*, note 20.

[64] *Glatzel*, note 29.

[65] See, in particular, Case C-406/15, *Milkova*, ECLI: EU:C:2017:198; Case C-395/15, *Mohamed Daouidi* v. *Bootes Plus SL, Fondo de Garantía Salarial, Ministerio Fiscal*, ECLI:EU: C:2016:917; Case C-270/16, *Carlos Enrique Ruiz Conejero* v. *Ferroser Servicios Auxiliares SA and Ministerio Fiscal*, ECLI:EU:C:2017:788.

[66] Joined Cases C-120/06 P and C-121/06 P, *Fabbrica italiana accumulatori motocarri Montecchio SpA (FIAMM) and Others* v. *Council of the European Union and Commission of the European Communities* ECLI:EU:C:2008:476, para. 108.

[67] Case C-280/93, *Germany* v. *Council*, ECLI:EU:C:1994:367.

[68] *FIAMM*, note 66.

[69] *Z.* v. *A Government Department*, note 62, para 90.

[70] *Glatzel*, note 29, para. 69.

[71] Case 12/86, *Meryem Demirel* v. *Stadt Schwäbisch Gmünd*, ECLI:EU:C:1987:400.

[72] Case C-53/96, *Hermès International* v. *FHT Marketing*, ECLI:EU:C:1998:292.

its jurisdiction to interpret Article 50 of the Agreement on Trade-Related Aspects of Intellectual Property Rights (the TRIPs Agreement) in very broad terms and stated that:

> where a provision can apply both to situations falling within the scope of national law and to situations falling within the scope of [EU] law, it is clearly in the [EU] interest that, in order to forestall future differences of interpretation, that provision should be interpreted uniformly, whatever the circumstances in which it is to apply.[73]

It seems that, in principle, the Court is not precluded from interpreting the CRPD, from establishing the sphere of EU and national competence and from defining the EU's obligations. However, to date, the CJEU has made no attempt in its judgments to interpret specific CRPD provisions.

DID YOU KNOW THAT ...?

In order to implement the Convention and give it full effect, in compliance with Article 33(1) CRPD, the EU has identified the Commission as its focal point. Moreover, in accordance with Article 33(2) CRPD, a framework to promote, protect and monitor the implementation of the Convention was set up in 2013. The EU framework became operational in 2013, on the basis of a proposal of the Commission, and included: the European Parliament's Petitions Committee, the European Ombudsman, the European Commission, and the EU Agency for Fundamental Rights (FRA). However, following the publication of the COs on the EU by the CRPD Committee and upon the CRPD Committees's recommendation, in 2015, the European Commission withdrew from the EU framework. The EU framework complements the national monitoring frameworks in EU Member States, which are responsible for promoting the implementation of the CRPD at the national level (https://fra.europa.eu/en/theme/people-disabilities/eu-crpd-framework).

6 THE EUROPEAN UNION UNDER THE SCRUTINY OF THE COMMITTEE ON THE RIGHTS OF PERSONS WITH DISABILITIES

Having ratified the CRPD, the EU has been subject to the scrutiny of the CRPD Committee. Like other Parties to the Convention, the EU has compiled and submitted a report to the Committee on its implementation of the CRPD. The EU's initial report was submitted in June 2014 and was examined by the CRPD

[73] Ibid. para. 23.

Committee in 2015. The Committee then adopted a list of issues concerning the information contained in the EU's report in April 2015, and the EU responded to those issues on 22 June. COs were issued by the Committee in October 2015.[74]

Similarly to the COs directed to other Parties, the COs directed to the EU include only a couple of paragraphs highlighting strengths and good practices. In particular, the Committee identified only two positive trends in the field of EU external action. The first one is the EU's practice of 'including the rights of persons with disabilities in the financing of its external actions',[75] and the embedding of disability in priority areas of the EU's communication[76] on the post-2015 Sustainable Development Goals (SDGs).[77] Secondly, the Committee praised the EU's commitment to the Sendai Framework for Disaster Risk Reduction 2015–2030.[78]

Virtually the entire document reflects the Committee's concerns and recommendations. In total, the Committee identified a series of gaps in EU policy and provided forty-two recommendations. It urged the EU to adopt a more comprehensive policy agenda and to allocate a budget to the realisation of EU policy measures. The Committee recommended, *inter alia*, the implementation of the European Mobility Card, to ensure the mobility of people with disabilities in compliance with Article 20 CRPD. The card was originally envisaged as a facilitator of the rights of people with disabilities travelling to other Member States, allowing them to receive benefits and price reductions in the areas of culture, leisure, sport and transport. To date, however, it has not been fully implemented. A pilot project on what is now called the 'EU Disability Card' was launched in February 2016, but it

[74] Lawson, 'The European Union and CRPD: Complexities, Challenges and Opportunities', note 45, p. 66. In its COs, the Committee requested the European Union to submit, within 12 months and in accordance with Article 35(2) CRPD, information on the measures taken to implement some recommendations, namely those concerning the update of the declaration of competence, the proposal for a European Accessibility Act, and the setting up of an EU monitoring framework. In January 2017, the EU submitted this information, which was then published as an addendum to the COs in November 2017 (CRPD Committee, Addendum - Information received from the European Union on follow-up to the concluding observations, 23 November 2017, UN Doc. CRPD/C/EU/CO/1/Add.1).

[75] CRPD Committee, Concluding Observations on the Initial Report of the European Union, note 36, para 4.

[76] Commission Communication of 5 February 2015, A Global Partnership for Poverty Eradication and Sustainable Development after 2015, COM (2015) 44 final.

[77] CRPD Committee, Concluding Observations on the Initial Report of the European Union, note 36, para 4.

[78] European Commission, 'Sendai Framework for Disaster Risk Reduction', available at http://ec.europa.eu/echo/partnerships/relations/european-and-international-cooperation/sendai-framework-disaster-risk-reduction_en; the Commission adopted the Communication of 8 April 2014, Post 2015 Hyogo Framework for Action: Managing risks to achieve resilience, COM (2014) 215 final.

Read the CRPD Committee COs, and identify the action that the EU has taken to date to address those concerns.

tested the card in only eight EU countries (i.e. Belgium, Cyprus, Estonia, Finland, Italy, Malta, Slovenia and Romania).[79]

The CRPD Committee expressed concern with regard to the austerity measures adopted in the EU, which deeply affect people with disabilities, because the adoption of such measures has resulted in cuts in social services and in support to families.[80] The Committee also highlighted the lack of access to justice for people with disabilities in European courts and asked for the EU to guarantee 'full access to justice and eliminate all barriers, including physical and procedural barriers'.[81] It is, however, unclear how this recommendation will be followed up. Among other provisions of the Convention, the Committee expressed various concerns with regard to the implementation of Article 14 CRPD, on liberty and security of the person. It recommended that the EU should take action to end involuntary detention or practices that are in breach of the rights of persons with disabilities. However, this is an area in which the EU still has limited competences.

7 BREXIT AND THE RIGHTS OF PERSONS WITH DISABILITIES

At the time of writing this textbook, the debate on Brexit is dynamic, and the impending withdrawal is still quite uncertain in its character. For this reason, the following sub-sections only highlight the main features of Brexit from a disability perspective, taking into account that the UK leaving the EU is a reality, but one whose concrete legal outcomes are not defined at present. Indeed, amid the discussions on the withdrawal treaty, there have been renewed calls for a second referendum, and the Irish border issue remains unresolved. Hence, this section merely draws the reader's attention to the

[79] See at http://ec.europa.eu/social/main.jsp?catId=1139.

[80] CRPD Committee, Concluding Observations on the Initial Report of the European Union, note 36, para. 56.

[81] Ibid. para. 81.

debate that currently surrounds Brexit, but it does not engage with it in any great depth due to the obvious uncertainties.

7.1 Brexit in a Nutshell

As mentioned above, Brexit is the outcome of a popular vote. In a referendum held on 23 June 2016, 51.9 per cent of the UK electorate voted to leave the EU.[82] The turnout was relatively low (72.2 per cent) considering the extremely significant nature of the decision at stake. The pattern of voting also revealed blatant differences between regions and generations within the UK. London voted overwhelmingly to remain in the EU. Scotland and Northern Ireland voted, by a large majority, to remain, while a large majority of provincial districts in England voted to leave. To date, several contributions have been published,[83] seeking to explain the reasons behind Britain's vote to leave the EU.[84] Put simply, the globalisation of recent decades has promoted de-industrialisation in the midlands and north of England, while favouring the growth of business and financial services in London. This created increased concerns about economic insecurity and inequality in several parts of England where the population voted to leave. A fear of immigration has also prompted several voters to want to leave the EU, driven by anxiety about their own economic security.[85]

On 29 March 2017, the UK Government invoked Article 50 TEU and formally indicated its willingness to withdraw from the EU.[86] Following agreement by both Houses of Government, the European Union (Withdrawal) Act 2018 received Royal Assent on 26 June 2018.[87] That has three main consequences. It repeals the European Community Act 1972 (which gave supremacy to EU law in circumstances where it conflicted with UK law); it

[82] European Union Referendum Act 2015 (c. 36).

[83] Among others, Kenneth Armstrong, *Brexit Time: Leaving the EU - Why, How and When?* (Cambridge: Cambridge University Press, 2017).

[84] Catharine Barnard, '(B)Remains of the Day: Brexit and EU Social Policy', in Frank Vandenbrouke, Catherine Barnard and Geert De Baere (eds.), *A European Social Union after the Crisis* (Cambridge: Cambridge University Press, 2017), pp. 459–76.

[85] Agust Arnorsson and Gylfi Zoega, 'On the Causes of Brexit' (2018) *European Journal of Political Economy* 24.

[86] Article 50, TEU reads as follows: 'Any Member State may decide to withdraw from the Union in accordance with its own constitutional requirements'. A Member State which decides to withdraw shall notify the European Council of its intention. In the light of the guidelines provided by the European Council, the Union shall negotiate and conclude an agreement with that state, setting out the arrangements for its withdrawal, taking account of the framework for its future relationship with the Union. That agreement shall be negotiated in accordance with Article 218(3), TFEU. It shall be concluded on behalf of the Union by the Council, acting by a qualified majority, after obtaining the consent of the European Parliament.

[87] European Union (Withdrawal) Act 2018 (c. 16).

allows for the conversion of EU law into national law; and it amends UK law to make it self-sufficient. The conversion of EU law into UK law is intended to maintain legal continuity upon the UK's exit from the EU, so that the same laws apply on the day after the UK leaves the EU as applied beforehand. The body of law that is converted and preserved under the Act is known as 'retained EU law'. The meaning and effect of retained EU law will be interpreted by domestic courts in accordance with relevant pre-exit CJEU case law and any retained general principles of EU law. That case law will have the same binding or precedent status as that of the UK Supreme Court or the High Court of Justiciary (Scotland).[88] It is important to point out that retained EU law does not include the EU CFR. Moreover, the 2018 Act has conferred on the UK Government wide powers to change the retained EU law, to be exercised up to two years after exit day.

Future UK relations with the EU are still quite uncertain. There is an ongoing discussion on what is currently termed 'hard Brexit' and 'soft Brexit'. The former alludes to the UK being outside the EU Customs Union and becoming a trading partner of the EU, just like any other non-EU country under World Trade Organization rules. The latter might involve allowing the UK to retain membership of the Customs Union and permitting the UK to retain certain freedoms of movement for goods and services and a certain level of free movement of people. Birkinshaw maintains, however, that a 'soft Brexit' is anathema to the Brexiteers in the Conservative party, who are dedicated to a hard Brexit,[89] and the debate is ultimately leading to political instability.

7.2 Brexit and the Rights of Persons with Disabilities: Challenges and Perspectives

Brexit presents several challenges in relation to the rights of persons with disabilities. In the first instance, the disability policy of the EU and the EDS 2010–2020 (and future strategies) will not apply to the UK, which will still have to implement the CRPD. Similarly, future EU legislation, such as the European Accessibility Act (EAA),[90] will not apply to the UK, which will not be obliged to implement the Act. It is not yet clear whether other pieces of EU legislation, which have directly impacted on disabled people's rights, for example, the Air Passenger Rights Regulations and other transport regulations, will be translated into UK legislation. Secondly, when it comes to disability discrimination, despite the existence of the UK's Human Rights Act

[88] Department for Exiting European Union, 'Factsheet 2: Converting and preserving law', available at https://assets.publishing.service.gov.uk/government/uploads/system/uploads/attachment_data/file/714373/2.pdf.

[89] Patrick Birlinshaw, 'Brexit Editorial' (2018) 24(1) *European Public Law* 1, at 2.

[90] See further Chapter 12.

1988[91] and the Equality Act (which implements the Employment Equality Directive and protects people with disabilities against discrimination),[92] the fact that the Charter has not been retained in UK legislation is particularly problematic. In fact, UK citizens will lose the Charter's freestanding right to equality, among other rights, as this provision is not fully replicated elsewhere in UK domestic law. A solution would be to embed more disability rights in future UK legislation, by implementing the CRPD. The European Network on Independent Living (ENIL) suggests that there is a need to inject the UK's equality strategy with strong disability dimensions and adequate funding to support its implementation.[93] Thirdly, and more generally, there are several problems and concerns associated with the fact that free movement, and the rights associated with that, will no longer be guaranteed to UK citizens. For example, people with disabilities will not enjoy citizens' rights concerning the portability (even limited) of disability allowances. The position of personal assistants and carers from EU countries in the UK will be precarious, and this may potentially endanger the right to independent living of persons with disabilities.

Overall, the UK's exit from the EU will potentially bring many serious consequences. However, the extent of those consequences cannot be fully forecast at present.

SUMMARY

- **The EU has developed a significant body of disability law and policy, which has been informed by the social model.**
- **Article 19 TFEU is the most relevant provision that confers legislative competence on the EU in relation to combating discrimination on the ground of disability (and other grounds).**
- **The EU CFR provides for the prohibition of discrimination on the ground, *inter alia*, of disability (Article 21(1) EU CFR) and includes a specific provision on the 'integration of persons with disabilities in society' (Article 26 EU CFR).**
- **The EDS proposes comprehensive and mainstream policy action, complementing the legal framework in force at EU level. It has the aim of empowering people with disabilities, so that they can enjoy their full rights and benefit from participating in society and in the European economy.**
- **The EU has been relatively successful in mainstreaming disability, and disability-related provisions have been included in several areas of EU legislation, such as transport, lifts, public procurement, and electronic communications networks and services.**

[91] Human Rights Act 1998 (c. 42). [92] Equality Act 2010 (c. 15).

[93] ENIL, 'ENIL Briefing on the Impact of Brexit on the Rights of Disabled People in the UK and Action Points', available at http://enil.eu/news/enil-briefing-on-the-impact-of-brexit-on-the-rights-of-disabled-people-in-the-uk-and-action-points/.

- The EU concluded the CRPD, through Council Decision 2010/48/EC, as a regional integration organisation within the meaning of Article 44 CRPD.
- The CRPD is an integral part of EU law, and it enjoys a quasi-constitutional status in the EU legal system, beneath the Treaties but above secondary law. As a consequence, EU secondary law must be interpreted in light of the CRPD: if the wording of secondary EU legislation is open to more than one interpretation, preference should be given, as far as possible, to the interpretation which renders the EU law provision consistent with the Convention.
- Up until now, the CJEU has attempted to interpret EU law (and, in particular, the Employment Equality Directive) in line with the Convention. The first case in which the Court interpreted the Employment Equality Directive in light of the CRPD was *Ring and Werge*.
- Having ratified the CRPD, the EU has been subject to the scrutiny of the CRPD Committee. Like other Parties to the Convention, the EU has compiled and submitted a report to the Committee on the implementation of the CRPD. The COs directed to the EU include only a couple of paragraphs highlighting strengths and good practices. Virtually the entire document reflects the CRPD Committee's concerns and recommendations on EU action or inaction.

ACTIVITIES

REVIEW QUESTIONS

1. How have EU disability laws and policies evolved over time?
2. What is the main EU policy document on disability?
3. What are the effects of the CRPD in the EU legal order?

ESSAY QUESTIONS

1. Discuss the strengths and weaknesses of the European Disability Strategy 2010–2020.
2. 'The CRPD has become an integral part of the EU legal system.' *Discuss*.

GROUP PROJECTS

The Court of Freedonia, an EU Member State, is currently deciding a case related to alleged discrimination against an individual with a disability. The Court must apply national legislation that implements the Employment Equality Directive. However, the Court thinks that the Directive (and, therefore, the national provision transposing it) is in breach of the CRPD. The Court of Freedonia is uncertain whether it can submit a preliminary ruling to the CJEU.

Discuss the group project.

FURTHER READING

Arsenjeva, J., *Annotated Review of European Union Law and Policy with Reference to Disability* (prepared under the direction of Professor Lisa Waddington, on behalf of the Academic Network of European Disability Experts – ANED) (2017), available at www.disability-europe.net/theme/eu-law-and-policy.

Ferri, D., 'The Conclusion of the UN Convention on the Rights of Persons with Disabilities by the EC/ EU: A Constitutional Perspective', in L. Waddington and G. Quinn (eds.), *European Yearbook of Disability Law* (Antwerp/Portland: Intersentia, 2010), vol. 2, pp. 47–71.

Hosking, D. L., 'Staying the Course: The European Disability Strategy 2010–2020', in L. Waddington, G. Quinn and E. Flynn (eds.), *European Yearbook of Disability Law* (Antwerp/Portland: Intersentia, 2013), vol. 4, pp. 73–97.

Lawson, A., 'The EU Rights Based Approach to Disability: Strategies for Shaping an Inclusive Society' (2005) 4 *International Journal of Discrimination and the Law* 269–87.

Lawson, A., 'The European Union and CRPD: Complexities, Challenges and Opportunities', in V. Della Fina, G. Palmisano and R. Cera, *The UNCRPD: A Commentary* (Cham: Springer, 2017), pp. 61–76.

Lawson, A., 'The UN Convention on the Rights of Persons with Disabilities and European Disability Law: A Catalyst for Cohesion?', in O. M. Arnardóttir and G. Quinn (eds.), *The UN Convention on the Rights of Persons with Disabilities: European and Scandinavian Perspectives* (Leiden/Boston: Brill, 2009), pp. 81–130.

Miller, J., 'The European Disability Rights Revolution' (2019) 44(1) *European Law Review* 66–87.

O'Brien, C., 'Article 26 – Integration of Persons with Disabilities', in S. Peers, T. Hervey, J. Kenner and A. Ward (eds.), *The EU Charter of Fundamental Rights: A Commentary* (Oxford/Portland: Hart Publishing, 2014), pp. 709–48.

Quinn, G., 'The European Social Charter and EU Anti-Discrimination Law in the Field of Disability: Two Gravitational Fields with One Common Purpose', in G. de Búrca, B. de Witte and L. Ogertschnig, *Social Rights in Europe* (Oxford/ New York: Oxford University Press, 2005), pp. 278–304.

Waddington, L., 'The Influence of the UN Convention on the Rights of Persons with Disabilities on EU Anti-Discrimination Law', in U. Belavusau and K. Henrard, *About EU Anti-Discrimination Law beyond Gender* (Oxford/Portland: Hart Publishing, 2018), pp. 339–61.

Waddington, L., 'The European Union', in L. Waddington and A. Lawson, *The United Nations Convention on the Rights of Persons with Disabilities in Practice: A Comparative Analysis of the Role of Courts* (Oxford/New York: Oxford University Press, 2018), pp. 131–52.

Waddington, L. and Lawson, A., 'The Unfinished Story of EU Disability Non-Discrimination Law', in A. Bogg, C. Costello and A. C. L. Davies (eds.), *Research Handbook on EU Labour Law* (Cheltenham: Edward Elgar, 2016), pp. 474–94.

11 Disability Discrimination in European Union Law

LEARNING OUTCOMES

- ✓ Understand the general framework of EU non-discrimination law.
- ✓ Identify the sources of EU non-discrimination law.
- ✓ Understand the key concepts in EU non-discrimination law, including 'direct discrimination' and 'indirect discrimination', and how they apply to the field of disability.
- ✓ Comprehend the key features and scope of the Employment Equality Directive with regard to discrimination on the ground of disability.
- ✓ Understand the scope of the duty to accommodate in the Employment Equality Directive.
- ✓ Identify the essential elements and the turning points of the case law of the Court of Justice of the European Union pre- and post-CRPD ratification.
- ✓ Delineate the main features of the proposed horizontal non-discrimination directive.
- ✓ Gain awareness of the differences between the scope of the non-discrimination norms in the CRPD and in EU law.

> *The principle of non-discrimination [on the basis of disability] has an established history in Europe and multiple practical results . . . although the application on the ground is diverse.*[1]

1 INTRODUCTION

As Tymowski remarks, 'equality is one of the fundamental values' on which the Union is founded, and 'it is duly reflected in the Treaties, as well as in national laws of the Member States'.[2] Hence, the promotion of equality and the fight against discrimination can be considered to be core elements of EU law.

EU non-discrimination law denotes the collective body of rules seeking to prohibit discrimination on various grounds at the EU level. Although EU non-discrimination law had a humble beginning, initially covering only discrimination on the ground of sex, it has undergone an evolution over the last few decades, both in terms of its scope and content. The original Treaty establishing the European Economic Community (EEC) – the Treaty of Rome of 1957 – contained a prohibition of discrimination on the ground of sex, applicable in the context of employment. It required equal pay between men and women, and it set out the competence to develop the first equality directives: the Equal Pay Directive of 1975[3] and the Equal Treatment Directive of 1976,[4] which prohibited discrimination on the ground of gender in access to employment, vocational training and promotion, and working conditions. As mentioned in Chapter 10, it was not until the Treaty of Amsterdam that the EU introduced a specific competence to combat discrimination on a wide range of additional grounds, namely the grounds of racial or ethnic origin, religion or belief, disability, age or sexual orientation. The aforementioned competence has led to the introduction of a series of new equality directives as well as to the revision of the gender equality directives adopted in the 1970s. In 2000, two further directives were adopted:

i. The Employment Equality Directive, prohibiting discrimination on the basis of sexual orientation, religion or belief, age and disability in the area of employment.[5]

[1] Jan Tymowski, *The Employment Equality Directive: European Implementation Assessment, European Parliamentary Research Service* (February 2016), p. 35, available at www.europarl.europa.eu/RegData/etudes/STUD/2016/536346/EPRS_STU(2016)536346_EN.pdf.

[2] Ibid. p. 5.

[3] Council Directive 75/117/EEC of 10 February 1975 on the approximation of the laws of the Member States relating to the application of the principle of equal pay for men and women, OJ 1975 No. L45/19.

[4] Council Directive 76/207/EEC of 9 February 1976 on the implementation of the principle of equal treatment for men and women as regards access to employment, vocational training and promotion, and working conditions OJ 1976 No. L39/40.

[5] Council Directive 2000/78/EC of 27 November 2000 establishing a general framework for equal treatment in employment and occupation, OJ 2000 No. L303/16. See above Chapter 10.

ii. The Racial Equality Directive, prohibiting discrimination on the basis of racial or ethnic origin, not only in the context of employment and vocational training but also in accessing the welfare system and social security as well as in the field of goods and services, among others.[6]

Although the foregoing directives lay down minimum requirements and give Member States the option to introduce or maintain more favourable provisions in domestic law, they constituted a significant expansion of the scope of EU non-discrimination law.[7] Ellis maintains that:

> this later generation of anti-discrimination law is every bit as significant as its predecessors in human, moral, political, and economic terms. The aspirations which lie behind it are justice and an improved quality of life for literally millions of people within the European Union.[8]

The Court of Justice of the European Union (CJEU) is responsible for the interpretation of the provisions of the directives, and has handed down a series of judgments regarding the manner in which one directive in particular, the Employment Equality Directive, applies in the field of disability, particularly with regard to the understanding of disability embodied in the directive.[9]

Existing EU non-discrimination law designates disability as a protected ground only in the context of employment and vocational training. A proposal has been tabled to extend protection on the ground of disability (and the other grounds listed above, namely, sexual orientation, religious belief and age) to the fields of social protection, including social security, health care and social housing; education; and access to, and supply of, goods and services, including housing (2008 proposal).[10] According to Waddington

[6] Council Directive 2000/43/EC of 29 June 2000 implementing the principle of equal treatment between persons irrespective of racial or ethnic origin, OJ 2000 No. L180/22. Moreover, in 2004, the Gender Goods and Services Directive expanded the scope of sex discrimination to the field of goods and services (Council Directive 2004/113/EC of 13 December 2004 implementing the principle of equal treatment between men and women in the access to and supply of goods and services, OJ 2004 L373/37).

[7] For more information on the historical background leading up to the entry into force of the Directives, see Mark Bell and Lisa Waddington, 'The 1996 Intergovernmental Conference and the Prospects of a Non-Discrimination Treaty Article' (1996) 25(4) *Industrial Law Journal* 320; see also, Mark Bell, 'The New Article 13 EC Treaty: A Sound Basis for European Anti-Discrimination Law?' (1999) 6(1) *Maastricht Journal of European Law* 5.

[8] Evelyn Ellis and Philippa Watson, *EU Anti-Discrimination Law* (Oxford: Oxford University Press, 2012), pp. 1–2.

[9] See below sub-sections 3.3.1 and 3.3.2.

[10] Article 3 of the Proposal for a Council Directive on implementing the principle of equal treatment between persons irrespective of religion or belief, disability, age or sexual orientation, COM (2008) 426 def. For the purpose of this chapter, the most recent publicly available version of the proposal, which differs in several respects from the original 2008 proposal, is taken as the point of reference. See the latest publicly available version of the proposed directive, dated 26 June 2019, 10740/19 (available at https://eur-lex.europa.eu/legal-content/EN/TXT/PDF/?uri=CONSIL:ST_10740_2019_INIT&from=EN). and the progress

and Broderick, the 2008 proposal 'complements pre-existing EU non-discrimination legislation'.[11] Its adoption would serve to bring the content of EU non-discrimination law somewhat closer to the requirements set out in the CRPD. However, as noted by Favalli and Ferri, 'its approval and entry into force should not be expected too soon'.[12]

The competence and functions of the EU relating to equality and other human rights were enhanced by the Lisbon Treaty, which entered into force on 1 December 2009 and made noteworthy alterations to the constitutional framework of the EU. As noted in Chapter 10, Article 19 of the Treaty on the Functioning of the European Union (TFEU) 'remains the main relevant provision which confers legislative competence on the EU in relation to combatting discrimination on disability (and other) grounds'.[13] The foregoing competence is buttressed by the horizontal clause on non-discrimination (one which cuts across various sectors) contained in Article 10 TFEU. That provision states that: 'in defining and implementing its policies and activities, the Union shall aim to combat discrimination based on . . . disability . . .'.

A significant development that has implications for EU disability non-discrimination law took the form of the accession of the EU to the CRPD.[14] The CRPD has greatly influenced the interpretation of the Employment Equality Directive. As mentioned in Chapter 10, this is on account of the fact that the CRPD forms an 'integral part of EU Law',[15] and the CRPD enjoys a quasi-constitutional status in the EU legal system, beneath the Treaties but above secondary law. Therefore, the CJEU must take the UN Convention into account when interpreting EU secondary legislation. More generally, Favalli and Ferri state that 'the [CRPD] has become the benchmark against which EU disability initiatives must be measured'.[16] Since the EU is a Party to the CRPD, the EU is bound by the Convention to the extent of its competences, and this also applies

report dated November 2018 (available at http://data.consilium.europa.eu/doc/document/ST-14253-2018-INIT/en/pdf).

[11] Lisa Waddington and Andrea Broderick, *Disability Law and the Duty to Reasonably Accommodate Beyond Employment: A Legal Analysis of the Situation in EU Member States* (Luxembourg: Publications Office of the EU, 2016), p. 7.

[12] Silvia Favalli and Delia Ferri, 'Defining Disability in the European Union Non-Discrimination Legislation: Judicial Activism and Legislative Restraints' (2016) 22(3) *European Public Law* 537, at 548.

[13] Ibid. [14] See above Chapter 10.

[15] Joined cases C-335/11 and C-337/11, *HK Danmark, acting on behalf of Jette Ring* v. *Dansk almennyttigt Boligselskab (C-335/11) and HK Danmark, acting on behalf of Lone Skouboe Werge* v. *Dansk Arbejdsgiverforening, acting on behalf of Pro Display A/S, in liquidation* (C-337/11), ECLI:EU:C:2013:222. See Lisa Waddington, 'HK Danmark (Ring and Skouboe Werge): Interpreting EU Equality Law of the UN Convention on the Rights of Persons with Disabilities' (2013) 21 *European Anti-Discrimination Law Review* 11.

[16] Favalli and Ferri, 'Defining Disability in the European Union Non-Discrimination Legislation: Judicial Activism and Legislative Restraints', note 12, at 549.

to the field of non-discrimination. However, the competence to combat disability discrimination is a competence that is shared by both the EU and its Member States.[17] Therefore, as Waddington and Broderick note, the EU is not bound to implement in full all Convention provisions relating to discrimination: 'instead the EU and its Member States which have ratified the CRPD are, in combination, bound to take such implementation measures'.[18] However, 'neither EU law nor the CRPD specifies which level is mandated to act, but where the EU does decide to act, it is bound to ensure that any action is fully compliant with the CRPD'.[19]

Following the background overview provided above, the sections that follow delve into the essential requirements of EU non-discrimination law as it applies in the field of disability. In section 2, the sources of EU non-discrimination law are discussed as well as the key concepts inherent to EU non-discrimination law, *inter alia*, 'direct discrimination', 'indirect discrimination', the 'burden of proof' and 'causation'. An overview of the key legislative enactment regulating disability discrimination in the EU is provided in section 3. In that context, the key features of the Employment Equality Directive are discussed as well as its scope. Thereafter, the case law of the CJEU relating to disability pre- and post-CRPD ratification is analysed. Finally, in section 4, the Commission's proposal for a new non-discrimination directive is examined.

2 GENERAL FEATURES OF EUROPEAN UNION NON-DISCRIMINATION LAW

This section examines in turn the core sources of EU non-discrimination law, and the main concepts underlying that body of law.

2.1 Sources of EU Non-Discrimination Law in the Context of Disability

EU non-discrimination law, including disability non-discrimination law, derives from diverse sources.

The CJEU consistently holds that the principle of equality is one of the general principles of EU law.[20] The Court also affirms that the fundamental rights of the Union 'include the general principle of equality and non-discrimination'.[21] However, in that regard, McCrudden and Prechal note that equality

[17] Lisa Waddington, 'The European Union and the United Nations Convention on the Rights of Persons with Disabilities: A Story of Exclusive and Shared Competences' (2011) 18(4) *Maastricht Journal of European and Comparative Law* 431.

[18] Waddington and Broderick, *Disability Law and the Duty to Reasonably Accommodate Beyond Employment: A Legal Analysis of the Situation in EU Member States*, note 11, p. 44.

[19] Ibid.

[20] See, among many others, Case 292/97, *Karlsson and Others*, ECLI:EU:C:2000:202.

[21] Case C-442/00, *Caballero* v. *Fondo de Garantia Salarial (Fogasa)*, ECLI:EU:C:2002:752, para. 32.

as an element of fundamental rights has an 'autonomous, if uncertain, role' in EU law.[22] According to the authors, the significance of recognising equality as a general principle is perhaps best illustrated by the *Mangold* case, where the Court stated explicitly that:

> it is the responsibility of the national court, hearing a dispute involving the principle of non-discrimination, to provide the legal protection which individuals derive from the rules of [EU] law and to ensure that those rules are fully effective, setting aside any provision of national law that may conflict with that law.[23]

McCrudden and Prechal also remark that:

> even if the parties to the case may not rely on the provisions of the directives before national courts, the national court is still obliged to respect the primacy of the general principle of equality in [EU] law, thus appearing to create the possibility of the evolution of a body of EC non-discrimination law through direct application of the general principle.[24]

The EU Treaties encapsulate specific enumerations of the equality norm, which are outlined in Figure 11.1.

Article 2 TEU	• sets out the values on which the Union is founded, *inter alia*, the principle of equality.
Article 3 TEU	• states that the EU 'shall combat social exclusion and discrimination'.
Article 20 TFEU	• prohibits discrimination on the ground of nationality.
Article 45 TFEU	• proscribes discrimination between workers who are nationals of the host Member State and those who are nationals of another Member State.
Article 157 TFEU	• provides for the right to equality between men and women in the context of pay.

Figure 11.1 Equality in the Treaties

Moreover, as mentioned in Chapter 10 and in the introduction to this chapter, Article 10 TFEU contains the horizontal non-discrimination clause, while Article 19 TFEU enacts a general legislative power to tackle several types of discrimination, including discrimination on the ground of disability.

A further important source of EU equality law is the Charter of Fundamental Rights of the European Union (EU CFR), and specifically Article 21 EU CFR, which enshrines the right to non-discrimination, including on the ground of disability

[22] Christopher McCrudden and Sacha Prechal, *The Concept of Equality and Non-Discrimination in Europe: A Practical Approach* (European Network of Legal Experts in the Field of Gender Equality, 2009), p. 4.

[23] Case C-144/04, *Mangold* v. *Rudiger Helm*, ECLI:EU:C:2005:709, para. 77.

[24] McCrudden and Prechal, *The Concept of Equality and Non-Discrimination in Europe: A Practical Approach*, note 22, p. 5.

In addition, Article 26 EU CFR articulates the right of persons with disabilities to benefit from measures designed to ensure their independence, social and occupational integration and participation in the life of the community.

Finally, as noted in the introduction to this chapter, the EU has enacted several pieces of secondary legislation with the goal of protecting against discrimination on several grounds. The enabling power contained in Article 19 TFEU has been used as the legal basis for the subsequent adoption of the 'equality directives',[25] of which the Employment Equality Directive is the most relevant in the context of disability.

2.2 Key Concepts in EU Non-Discrimination Law

2.2.1 *Symmetrical Versus Asymmetrical Protection*

Waddington notes that non-discrimination law is generally symmetrical, meaning that 'it protects from discrimination both the majority or advantaged group and the minority or disadvantaged group'.[26] For instance, EU gender equality law protects both men and women from discrimination, whilst EU racial equality law protects all individuals from discrimination on the ground of ethnic origin.[27] As Waddington points out, 'disability non-discrimination law is generally asymmetrical in nature, meaning that it only protects persons with disabilities and persons who experience discrimination on the ground of disability from discrimination'.[28]

[25] See Council Directive 2004/113/EC of 13 December 2004 on implementing the principle of equal treatment between men and women in the access to and supply of goods and services, OJ 2004 No. L373; See also Council Directive 2006/54/EC of 5 July 2006 on the implementation of the principle of equal opportunities and equal treatment of men and women in matters of employment and occupation (recast), OJ 2006 No. L204/23.

[26] Lisa Waddington, 'Fine-Tuning Non-Discrimination Law: Exceptions and Justifications Allowing for Differential Treatment on the Ground of Disability' (2015) 15(1–2) *International Journal of Discrimination and the Law* 11, at 13.

[27] Naomi Schoenbaum, 'The Case for Symmetry in Antidiscrimination Law' (2017) *GWU Law School Public Law Research Paper* No. 2016–56.

[28] Waddington, 'Fine-Tuning Non-Discrimination Law: Exceptions and Justifications Allowing for Differential Treatment on the Ground of Disability', note 26, at 13.

2.2.2 *Direct Discrimination*

The Treaty on European Union (TEU) and the TFEU do not differentiate explicitly between various forms of discrimination. The Treaties refer simply to 'discrimination' as a stand-alone concept, defining it as '[t]he application of different rules to comparable situations or the application of the same rule to different situations'.[29] This can be contrasted with secondary EU law, which provides for direct and indirect discrimination, which are two manifestations or forms of discrimination. According to the provisions of the equality directives, direct discrimination occurs where one person is treated less favourably on the grounds of a prohibited criterion (e.g. racial or ethnic origin, religion or belief, disability, age, sexual orientation or sex) than another is, has been or would be treated in a comparable situation. This entails three elements, which are detailed in Figure 11.2.

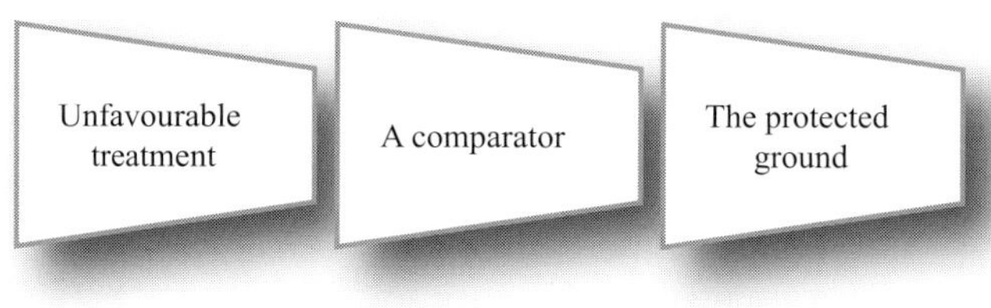

Figure 11.2 The Main Elements of Direct Discrimination

As the European Union Agency for Fundamental Rights (FRA) points out, 'at the heart of direct discrimination is the difference of treatment that an individual is subject to'. Consequently, the first element of direct discrimination is evidence of unfavourable treatment.[30] Unfavourable, or less favourable, treatment is established by means of a comparison between the alleged victim of discrimination and another individual who is situated in a similar situation who does not possess the protected characteristic. Thus, in order to invoke a claim of direct discrimination, it is necessary to demonstrate the existence of both a comparator (e.g. a male worker or a non-disabled person) as well as a situation that is comparable (either a past, present, or even a hypothetical situation).

The requirement of a comparator is sometimes 'problematic' in the disability context, as 'it is not always self-evident who the appropriate comparator might be'.[31] The comparator will generally be a non-disabled person (although, of course, the comparator can sometimes be a person with a

[29] Case C-279/93, *Finanzampt Koln-Altstadt* v. *Schumacker*, ECLI:EU:C:1995:31.

[30] European Union Agency for Fundamental Rights (FRA), *Handbook on European Non-Discrimination Law* (Luxembourg: Publications Office of the European Union, 2011), p. 44.

[31] Andrea Broderick, *The Long and Winding Road to Equality and Inclusion for Persons with Disabilities: The United Nations Convention on the Rights of Persons with Disabilities* (Cambridge-Antwerp: Intersentia, 2015), p. 32.

different impairment, depending on the circumstances of the case). In the event that the comparator is a non-disabled person, 'this often does not serve to redress the acute disadvantage already experienced by disabled people',[32] since the non-disabled individual represents the dominant 'norm'.

DID YOU KNOW THAT …?

The only justifications or exceptions that can be put forward in respect of direct discrimination are those based on the EU Treaties themselves or on EU secondary legislation. In Article 4 of the Racial Equality Directive and Article 4(1) of the Employment Equality Directive, Member States are allowed to justify differential treatment based on a characteristic related either to racial or ethnic origin or to religion, belief, disability, age and sexual discrimination on the ground of a 'genuine and determining occupational requirement', provided that the objective is legitimate and the requirement is proportionate. Additionally, the Employment Equality Directive provides for other general exceptions to the prohibition of discrimination based on religion or belief, disability, age or sexual discrimination, namely measures which, in a democratic society, are necessary for public security, for the maintenance of public order and the prevention of criminal offences, for the protection of health and for the protection of the rights and freedoms of others.

Article 3(4) of the Employment Equality Directive contains a specific exception relating to the armed forces, which can be advanced in a claim based on discrimination on grounds of disability and age. It allows Member States to provide that the provisions prohibiting discrimination on the basis of these two criteria do not apply to the armed forces.

2.2.3 *Indirect Discrimination*

According to the EU equality directives, indirect discrimination occurs in circumstances where an apparently neutral provision, criterion or practice would put persons at a particular disadvantage. The full definition of 'indirect discrimination' is contained in Article 2(2)(b) of the Employment Equality Directive and is set out in Figure 11.3.

Three key elements are encompassed under the definition of 'indirect discrimination':

i. A rule that appears to be neutral but is significantly more negative in its effects on a protected group (the notion of 'disparate impact'),
ii. A comparator, and
iii. The protected ground.[33]

[32] Ibid. [33] FRA, *Handbook on European Non-Discrimination Law*, note 30, pp. 53–59.

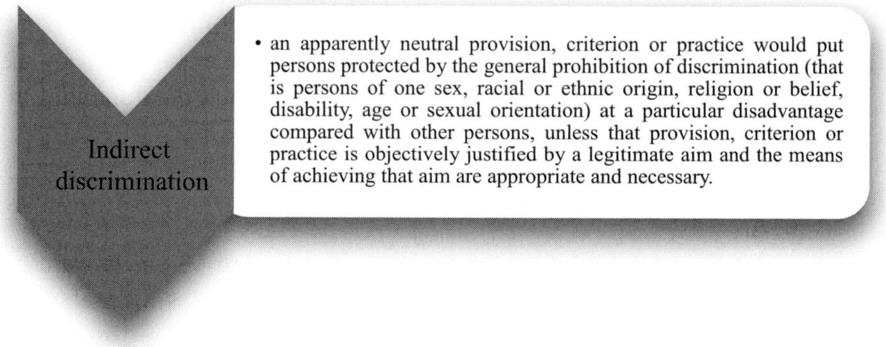

Figure 11.3 Definition of 'Indirect Discrimination'

In order to establish that indirect discrimination has occurred, the complainant must be able to identify a comparator group of persons who have received more advantageous treatment.[34] As noted by Tobler and Waaldijk, typically, the disadvantaged group consists 'not exclusively, but . . . disproportionately of persons that are protected by the discrimination ground in question'.[35] Indirect discrimination is 'an effect-related concept',[36] when compared with direct discrimination, where 'causation is a decisive element'.[37] In the context of disability, indirect discrimination has been identified as 'something that is vital in uncovering covert forms of discrimination'[38]. However, the application of the concept of 'indirect discrimination' cannot be limited to covert discrimination, as sometimes indirect discrimination has an overt character.[39] Where indirect discrimination is of a covert nature, statistical evidence is often adduced to satisfy the burden of proof.

By contrast with the justifications permitted for instances of direct discrimination, the possible justifications for indirect discrimination are framed in very general terms. Indirect discrimination will be permitted where it is objectively justified by a legitimate aim. The list of such legitimate aims is not explicitly set out in the EU equality directives, and the justifications have an open-ended

[34] Ellis and Watson, *EU Anti-Discrimination Law*, note 8, p. 152.

[35] Christa Tobler and Kees Waaldijk, 'Case C-267/06, *Tadao Maruko v. Versorgungsanstalt der deutschen Bühnen*, Judgment of the Grand Chamber of the Court of Justice of 1 April 2008' (2009) 46(2) *Common Market Law Review* 723, at 737.

[36] Justyna Maliszewska-Nienartowicz, 'Direct and Indirect Discrimination in European Union Law: How To Draw a Dividing Line?' (2014) 3(1) *International Journal of Social Sciences* 41, at 43.

[37] Ibid.

[38] Broderick, *The Long and Winding Road to Equality and Inclusion for Persons with Disabilities: The United Nations Convention on the Rights of Persons with Disabilities*, note 31, p. 35.

[39] Ellis and Watson, *EU Anti-Discrimination Law*, note 8, p. 151.

nature.[40] The case law of the CJEU elaborates on different justifications that have been accepted in various claims of indirect discrimination.[41]

2.2.4 *Instruction to Discriminate and Harassment*

Besides the more common claims of direct or indirect discrimination, two other forms of discrimination that may arise under EU law are discrimination by means of an instruction to discriminate and harassment.

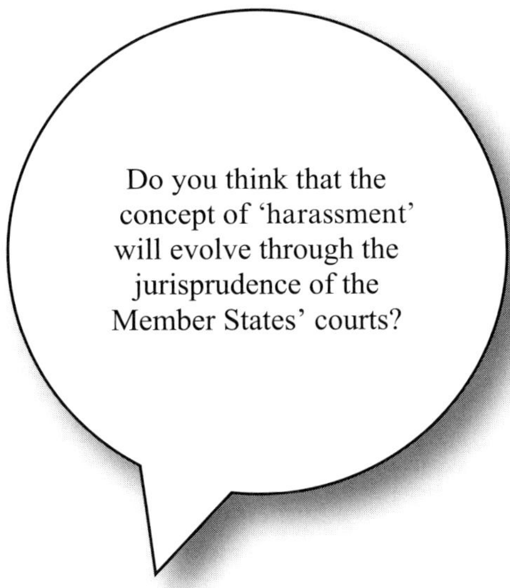

The Employment Equality Directive prohibits the giving of an instruction to discriminate, but it does not define what is meant by the concept itself. According to the FRA, the prohibition should cover situations where there is an expressed preference or an encouragement to treat individuals less favourably due to one of the protected grounds.[42]

Harassment features as a specific type of discrimination under the EU equality directives, having previously been addressed under the umbrella heading of direct discrimination. The FRA report maintains that 'its separation into a specific head under the directives is based more on the importance of singling out this particularly harmful form of discriminatory treatment, rather than a shift in conceptual thinking'.[43] Taking the specific instance of disability discrimination, Article 2(3) of the Employment Equality Directive defines harassment as 'unwanted conduct related to [disability]', which takes place 'with the purpose or effect of violating the dignity of a person and of creating an intimidating, hostile, degrading, humiliating or offensive environment'. That Article also specifies that 'in this context, the concept of harassment may be defined in accordance with the national laws and practice of the Member States'. In *Coleman* v. *Attridge*

[40] Christa Tobler, *Limits and Potential of the Concept of Indirect Discrimination* (European Commission, 2008).

[41] According to the case law of the CJEU, the concept of 'objective justification' allows the taking into account (subject to the principle of proportionality) of aims, such as: ensuring coherence of the tax system; protection of ethnic and cultural minorities living in a particular region; and encouragement of employment and recruitment by the Member States.

[42] FRA, *Handbook on European Non-Discrimination Law*, note 30, p. 67.

[43] Ibid. p. 64.

Law,[44] the CJEU held that the prohibition of harassment contained in the Employment Equality Directive is not limited to those who are disabled themselves but that it also extends to the detrimental treatment of a mother on the ground of her son's disability.

2.2.5 *The Burden of Proof*

European Union non-discrimination law allows the burden of proof to be (partially) reversed once the claimant can show sufficient evidence from which it can be adduced that discriminatory treatment may have occurred. This will raise a presumption of discrimination, which the alleged perpetrator then has to rebut. Recital 31 of the Preamble to the Employment Equality Directive provides that:

> the rules on the burden of proof must be adapted when there is a *prima facie* case of discrimination and, for the principle of equal treatment to be applied effectively, the burden of proof must shift back to the respondent when evidence of such discrimination is brought. However, it is not for the respondent to prove that the plaintiff adheres to a particular religion or belief, has a particular disability, is of a particular age or has a particular sexual orientation.

This principle of the partial reversal of the burden of proof is contained in the Racial Equality Directive[45] and the Employment Equality Directive,[46] among others. The provisions concerning the burden of proof in the aforementioned directives are framed in identical terms. Article 10(1) of the Employment Equality Directive provides for a partial reversal of the burden of proof with regard to direct and indirect discrimination.

ARTICLE 10(1) OF THE EMPLOYMENT EQUALITY DIRECTIVE

Member States shall take such measures as are necessary, in accordance with their national judicial systems, to ensure that, when persons who consider themselves wronged because the principle of equal treatment has not been applied to them establish, before a court or other competent authority, facts from which it may be presumed that there has been direct or indirect discrimination, it shall be for the respondent to prove that there has been no breach of the principle of equal treatment.

[44] Case C-303/06, *Coleman* v. *Attridge Law and Steve Law*, ECLI:EU:C:2008:415; see, further, Lisa Waddington, 'Case C-303/06, *S. Coleman v. Attridge Law and Steve Law*, Judgment of the Grand Chamber of the Court of Justice of 17 July 2008' (2009) 46 *Common Market Law Review* 2, at 665.

[45] Article 8 and Recital 21, Preamble to the Race Directive.

[46] Article 10 and Recital 31, Preamble to the Employment Equality Directive.

2.2.6 *Causation*

A further vital concept that is essential in proving discrimination under EU law is that of 'causation', a concept which has been elaborated on with regard to the Court's case law relating to sex discrimination.[47] As Ellis and Watson point out, in proving discrimination, no intention or subjective motivation needs to be shown; rather, it is sufficient to prove that the adverse treatment received by the victim is grounded upon, or caused by, a prohibited classification.[48] In other words:

> whether the alleged discrimination is direct or indirect, all that is required to establish causation is that 'but for' belonging to the protected category, the victim would not have sustained the disadvantage alleged. For this purpose, it is unnecessary to prove any particular motive or intention on the part of the respondent.[49]

3 THE EMPLOYMENT EQUALITY DIRECTIVE

The Employment Equality Directive is the principal piece of EU secondary law applying to disability. The Directive is a so-called 'Framework Directive'. This means that 'whilst some provisions, such as those defining the various forms of prohibited discrimination, are relatively elaborate and clear, other provisions are not accompanied by a detailed definition and guidance'.[50] This also means that EU Member States and, often, the CJEU 'are left to interpret, apply and develop such provisions within the general framework set by the Directive'.[51] As highlighted above, four grounds are covered under the Employment Equality Directive – religion and belief, age, disability and sexual orientation. In comparison with other grounds covered by the Directive, disability is deemed to have had 'a significant record of attention given to it at various levels, including the European one'.[52] In the sub-sections that follow, the key features and scope of the Directive are discussed. A focus is maintained on the prohibition of discrimination and the duty to reasonably accommodate. Thereafter, the disability provisions of the Employment Equality Directive are examined with regard to the interpretation given to those provisions, and in particular to the concept of 'disability', by the CJEU pre- and post-CRPD.

[47] On the issue of causation, see generally Ellis and Watson, *EU Anti-Discrimination Law*, note 8, pp. 163–169.

[48] Ibid. [49] Ibid.

[50] Lisa Waddington, 'Saying all the Right Things and Still Getting it Wrong: The Court of Justice's Definition of Disability and Non-Discrimination Law' (2015) 22(4) *Maastricht Journal of European and Comparative Law* 576, at 577.

[51] Ibid.

[52] Tymowski, *The Employment Equality Directive: European Implementation Assessment, European Parliamentary Research Service*, note 1, p. 27.

3.1 Key Features and Scope of the Employment Equality Directive

The Employment Equality Directive is founded on the general principle of equal treatment, which requires that individuals in the same situation are treated in the same manner. As highlighted in the introduction to this chapter, the Directive's legal basis is Article 19 TFEU, which permits the Council of the European Union (Council) to take appropriate action by unanimity, with the consent of the European Parliament. The first ten recitals of the Preamble to the Directive describe the emergence of a non-discrimination framework in EU law, particularly in the field of employment. Chapter I lays out the scope of the Directive across all four discrimination grounds outlined above, and it contains provisions relating to those grounds, while Chapter II of the Directive (entitled 'remedies and enforcement') regulates procedural matters that are essential for the application of the Directive. Chapter III contains specific provisions related to Northern Ireland, while Chapter IV contains miscellaneous provisions, *inter alia*, on compliance, sanctions and reporting.

In terms of its personal scope, the Directive aims to protect individuals who have certain characteristics – those who are disabled or of a certain age; those who adhere to a particular religion or hold certain beliefs; and/or those who manifest a particular sexual orientation – from discrimination. All four grounds covered under the material scope of the Directive, as listed in Article 1 thereof, reflect those listed in Article 10 TFEU. Tymowski maintains that:

> by explicitly obliging the Member States to prohibit discrimination in employment on the aforementioned grounds, the general principles set out in the Treaties – as well as international law – become more effective, and some minimum standards are now common throughout Europe.[53]

In terms of its material scope, the Employment Equality Directive covers the broad field of employment and occupation.[54] Four separate areas of employment are covered under Article 3(1) of the Directive, as indicated by Figure 11.4.

Notably, the Employment Equality Directive is considerably narrower in scope than the CRPD. As Waddington and Broderick point out, the Directive does not meet the obligations set out in the CRPD concerning the prohibition of discrimination beyond the fields of employment and occupation. This is because:

> the CRPD creates a broad and far-reaching duty to prohibit discrimination and to provide reasonable accommodations, which spans all human rights. Under the CRPD, it falls on [S]tates [P]arties to ensure that a wide array of social actors, including

[53] Ibid. p. 1.

[54] The Directive does not cover social security and social protection schemes, nor any kind of payment by the Member States that is aimed at providing access to employment or maintaining employment.

Article 3(1) of the Employment Equality Directive	Conditions for access to employment, to self-employment or to occupation, including selection criteria and recruitment conditions, including promotion;
	Access to all types and levels of vocational guidance, vocational training, advanced vocational training/retraining, including practical work experience;
	Employment and working conditions, including dismissals and pay;
	Membership of, and involvement in, an organisation of workers or employers, or any organisation whose members carry on a particular profession.

Figure 11.4 The Material Scope of the Employment Equality Directive

employers, schools, healthcare providers and suppliers of services, accommodate persons with disabilities.[55]

However, due to the fact that the Directive provides for minimum harmonisation only, several EU Member States have extended the scope of the Directive to other areas beyond the field of employment. Nonetheless, those EU Member States which have not expanded their legal provisions relating to non-discrimination and reasonable accommodation for people with disabilities to cover areas outside employment and occupation, will be required to do so.[56]

3.2 The Prohibition of Discrimination and the Duty to Reasonably Accommodate

The Employment Equality Directive prohibits direct and indirect discrimination and discrimination in the form of harassment or an instruction to discriminate. As highlighted above in section 2, the CJEU, in *Coleman* v. *Attridge Law*, interpreted the meaning of the prohibition of direct discrimination and harassment in employment and occupation to include discrimination by association with someone who is disabled. The Court ruled that, limiting the Directive's scope only to people who are themselves disabled, is liable to reduce the protection that the Directive is intended to guarantee.[57] The Court has not yet clarified whether discrimination on the basis of perceived disability falls within the ambit of discrimination on the

[55] Waddington and Broderick, *Disability Law and the Duty to Reasonably Accommodate Beyond Employment: A Legal Analysis of the Situation in EU Member States*, note 11, p. 48.

[56] Broderick, *The Long and Winding Road to Equality and Inclusion for Persons with Disabilities: The United Nations Convention on the Rights of Persons with Disabilities*, note 31, p. 106.

[57] *Coleman* v. *Attridge Law*, note 44, para. 51.

basis of disability, a form of discrimination which is deemed to be covered under the CRPD itself.[58]

As outlined in section 2 above, indirect discrimination is taken to occur under the Directive where an apparently neutral provision, criterion or practice would put persons having a particular religion or belief, disability, sexual orientation or those of a particular age at a disadvantage compared with other individuals unless:

i. that provision, criterion or practice is objectively justified by a legitimate aim and the means of achieving that aim are appropriate and necessary, or
ii. as regards persons with a particular disability, the employer or any person or organisation to whom this Directive applies, is obliged, under national legislation, to take appropriate measures in line with the principles contained in Article 5 in order to eliminate disadvantages entailed by such provision, criterion or practice.

The second point above relates to the reasonable accommodation obligation in the Employment Equality Directive, which is contained in Article 5 of the Directive.

ARTICLE 5 OF THE EMPLOYMENT EQUALITY DIRECTIVE

In order to guarantee compliance with the principle of equal treatment in relation to persons with disabilities, reasonable accommodation shall be provided. This means that employers shall take appropriate measures, where needed in a particular case, to enable a person with a disability to have access to, participate in, or advance in employment, or to undergo training, unless such measures would impose a disproportionate burden on the employer. This burden shall not be disproportionate when it is sufficiently remedied by measures existing within the framework of the disability policy of the Member State concerned.

The Directive, therefore, requires employers to provide reasonable accommodation to meet the needs of disabled individuals, unless this would result in a disproportionate burden being imposed on the employer. Some guidance is provided on the meaning of the concepts 'reasonable accommodation' and 'disproportionate burden' in the Preamble to the Directive. In that regard, recital 20 of the Preamble provides that 'appropriate measures' means 'effective and

[58] Delia Ferri and Aisling De Paor, 'Regulating Genetic Discrimination in the European Union: Pushing the EU into Unchartered Territory or Ushering in A New Genomic Era?' (2015) 17(1) *European Journal of Law Reform* 30.

practical measures to adapt the workplace to the disability'. Specific examples are provided in that paragraph, such as 'adapting premises and equipment, patterns of working time, the distribution of tasks or the provision of training or integration resources'. Reasonable accommodation can, therefore, take the form of either material or organisational measures. Notably, the Directive 'links the notion of "appropriateness" to the effectiveness of measures taken in increasing participation and inclusion in employment'.[59]

To determine whether the measures in question give rise to a disproportionate burden, recital 21 of the Preamble requires that account should be taken, in particular, of the financial and other costs entailed, the scale and financial resources of the organisation or undertaking and the possibility of obtaining public funding or any other assistance. Significantly, recital 17 of the Preamble provides that the Directive does not require an employer to recruit, promote or maintain in employment or training an individual 'who is not competent, capable and available to perform the essential functions of the post concerned or to undergo the relevant training'. However, this is 'without prejudice to the obligation to provide reasonable accommodation for people with disabilities'.

Interestingly, while the Employment Equality Directive requires that all EU Member States must introduce an obligation to provide reasonable accommodation in favour of persons with disabilities in the context of employment and vocational training, the failure to meet the reasonable accommodation duty has not been explicitly defined as a form of discrimination in the Directive. This contrasts with Article 2 CRPD, which explicitly classifies the unjustified failure to provide reasonable accommodation as a form of discrimination.

In addition to an explicit duty to provide reasonable accommodation, the Directive also permits positive action. In this respect, Article 7 of the Directive stipulates that the principle of equal treatment 'shall not prevent any Member State from maintaining or adopting specific measures to prevent or compensate for disadvantages linked to any of the grounds covered'.

3.3 Disability Provisions in the Directive and Their Interpretation

In accordance with the principle of supremacy of EU law, EU Member States are obliged to ensure that their domestic legislation conforms to the requirements of the Employment Equality Directive. In addition, in circumstances where a domestic provision conflicts with the provisions of the Directive which are directly effective (i.e. sufficiently precise and unconditional), domestic courts are required to set aside conflicting national law. The CJEU is charged with interpreting the provisions of the Directive. Notably, the

[59] Broderick, *The Long and Winding Road to Equality and Inclusion for Persons with Disabilities: The United Nations Convention on the Rights of Persons with Disabilities*, note 31, p. 160.

Directive does not contain any definition of 'disability'. This has created a large measure of uncertainty with respect to the personal scope of the Directive and the extent of protection provided by the term 'disability' itself. It is natural, therefore, that the majority of the preliminary references that have reached the CJEU concerning disability and the Employment Equality Directive have related, in some way, to the concept of 'disability' itself and, more specifically, the question of who falls within the protected category. The Court has clearly stated that the concept of 'disability' must be 'given an autonomous and uniform interpretation', and that it is not possible to refer to the laws of the Member States in order to define that concept.[60] Since 2006, the CJEU has attempted to provide such an interpretation in a series of lengthy judgments, which are considered in the sub-sections that follow.

3.3.1 *The Case Law of the CJEU Pre-CRPD Ratification*

The first case to reach the CJEU in 2006 concerning the definition of 'disability' was the case of *Chacón Navas*.[61] That case concerned a woman, Ms Chacón Navas, who, as a result of illness, had not been able to work for her employer for a considerable length of time and who was dismissed from her employment after a period of absence. The applicant challenged the decision to dismiss her, *inter alia*, on the basis that it was incompatible with the Employment Equality Directive. The national court stayed the proceedings at the national level and referred two questions to the CJEU. The national court asked whether the Employment Equality Directive, in so far as Article 1 thereof lays down a general framework for combating discrimination on the ground of disability, includes within its protective scope a worker who has been dismissed by her employer solely because she is sick. It then asked whether, in the alternative, sickness could be regarded as an 'identifying attribute' in addition to the ones listed in the Employment Equality Directive as being prohibited grounds of discrimination.

These questions concerned the personal scope (scope *ratione personae*) of the Directive. In response, the CJEU reiterated that the Employment Equality Directive was designed to combat employment discrimination. The Court defined disability in that context as 'a limitation which results in particular from physical, mental or psychological impairments and which hinders the

[60] Case C-13/05, *Sonia Chacón Navas* v. *Eurest Colectividades SA*, ECLI:EU:C:2006:456, para. 42. For an extensive overview of the Court's case law on the concept of 'disability', see generally Lisa Waddington and Andrea Broderick, *Combatting Disability Discrimination and Realising Equality: A Comparison of the UN CRPD and EU Equality and Non-discrimination Law* (Luxembourg: European Commission, 2018). See also the very comprehensive analysis provided by Lisa Waddington: Lisa Waddington, 'The Influence of the UN Convention on the Rights of Persons with Disabilities on EU Anti-Discrimination Law' in Uladzislau Belavusau and Kristin Henrard, *EU Anti-Discrimination Law Beyond Gender*, (Oxford: Hart Publishing, 2018).

[61] *Chacón Navas v. Eurest Colectividades* SA, note 60.

participation of the person concerned in professional life'.[62] The Court adopted a narrow interpretation of disability that was based on the medical model rather than the social model of disability.[63] In addition, the Court held that, for the purposes of the Directive, 'disability' is different from 'sickness', and that there was nothing in the Directive 'to suggest that workers are protected by the prohibition of discrimination on grounds of disability as soon as they develop any type of sickness'.[64] The CJEU concluded that the Directive was intended to cover situations in which it was probable that participation in working life would be hindered over a 'long period of time'.[65] In essence, the Court clarified that, although fundamental rights form an integral part of the general principles of EU law, and include the principle of non-discrimination, 'it does not follow from this that the scope of [the Employment Equality Directive] should be extended by analogy beyond the discrimination based on the grounds listed exhaustively in Article 1 thereof'.[66] In light of the fact that *Chacón Navas* came before the Court in the period immediately preceding the adoption of the CRPD, the decision of the CJEU in that case received much attention, since it seemed not to have been influenced by any of the debates taking place in the European sphere regarding the evolving definition of 'disability' itself and the EU's general disability policy.

3.3.2 *The Case Law of the CJEU Post-CRPD Ratification*

Coleman v. *Attridge Law* was the first ruling rendered by the CJEU after the adoption of the CRPD by the UN, but before the ratification of the Convention by the EU in December 2010. As stated above,[67] in the *Coleman* case, the Court held that the Employment Equality Directive protects an individual against discrimination that he or she experiences on the ground that he or she associates with a person with a disability. In the *Coleman* case itself, the CJEU ruled that discrimination against a woman who, although not herself disabled, was subjected to detrimental treatment by her employer because she had to care for her son who was disabled, constituted discrimination 'by association'.[68] The Court held that this form of discrimination is prohibited under the Directive and employed a teleological approach to interpretation of the

[62] Ibid. para. 43.

[63] Lisa Waddington, 'Equal to the Task? Re-examining EU Equality Law in Light of the United Nations Convention on the Rights of Persons with Disabilities', in Lisa Waddington, Gerard Quinn and Eilionóir Flynn (eds.), *European Yearbook of Disability Law* (Antwerp/Portland: Intersentia, 2013), vol. 4, pp. 169–200. See also Lisa Waddington, 'Case C-13/05, *Chacón Navas* v. *Eurest Colectividades SA*, judgment of the Grand Chamber of 11 July 2006' (2007) 44 *Common Market Law Review* 487–499.

[64] *Sonia Chacón Navas* v. *Eurest Colectividades SA*, note 60, para. 46.

[65] Ibid. paras. 45–6.

[66] Ibid. para. 56.

[67] See above sub-section 3.2.

[68] Constantina Karagiorgi, 'The Concept of Discrimination by Association and its Application in the EU Member States' (2014) 18 *European Anti-Discrimination Law Review* 25.

Directive, invoking its purpose. The Court stated that it does not follow from the provisions of the Directive:

> that the principle of equal treatment which it is designed to safeguard is limited to people who themselves have a disability within the meaning of the directive. On the contrary, the purpose of the directive, as regards employment and occupation, is to combat all forms of discrimination on grounds of disability. The principle of equal treatment enshrined in the directive in that area applies not to a particular category of person but by reference to the grounds mentioned in Article 1.[69]

Waddington remarks that the Court's judgment 'is to be welcomed for extending protection from direct discrimination and harassment to an individual in a particularly vulnerable situation'.[70] However, she also notes that 'it may be premature to conclude from the judgment that discrimination by association is prohibited in all situations, on all grounds, and for all forms of discrimination'.[71] On that note, Ellis and Watson remark that the Court's emphasis on grounds of discrimination 'clearly suggests that the inclusion within the legislative aim of discrimination by association applies to all the types of discrimination proscribed by EU law, but this has yet to be confirmed by the CJEU'.[72] Whatever the merits of the *Coleman* case in terms of broadening the definition of 'discrimination on the basis of disability', the Court in *Coleman* recalled the strict definition of 'disability' that it had set out in *Chacón Navas*. In both *Chacón Navas* and *Coleman*, the Court assumed that it is the impairment itself, rather than external barriers, that hinders participation in professional life.[73]

In some of its more recent case law, decided since the coming into force of the CRPD, the Court has distanced itself from its earlier jurisprudence. In fact, the CJEU has adopted a clear shift in approach by abandoning the medical model of disability and, thereby, essentially overruling *Chacón Navas*. As Ferri and Favalli argue, 'the Court based its decision to deviate from *Chacón Navas* on the principle of consistent interpretation governing the relationship between international treaty law and EU law'.[74] The CJEU's case law 'has been largely boosted' by the EU's accession to the CRPD, which 'has become a clear point of reference in the reasoning of the European judges'[75] in individual cases. As discussed in Chapter 3 of this textbook, while the CRPD does not contain a definition of 'disability' *per se*, it provides an open-ended conceptualisation of it in the non-binding Preamble and in Article 1. In particular, recital (e) of the Preamble affirms that:

[69] *Coleman* v. *Attridge Law*, note 44, para. 38.

[70] Waddington, 'Case C-303/06, *S. Coleman v. Attridge Law and Steve Law*', note 44, at 671 and 672.

[71] Ibid. [72] Ellis and Watson, *EU Anti-Discrimination Law*, note 8, p. 147.

[73] *Coleman* v. *Attridge Law and Steve Law*, note 44, paras. 45–6; *Sonia Chacón Navas* v. *Eurest Colectividades SA*, note 60.

[74] Delia Ferri and Silvia Favalli, 'Tracing the Boundaries between Disability and Sickness in the European Union: Squaring the Circle?' (2016) 23 *European Journal of Health Law* 5, at 27.

[75] Ibid. at 8.

> [d]isability is an evolving concept and that disability results from the interaction between persons with impairments and attitudinal and environmental barriers that hinders their full and effective participation in society on an equal basis with others.

The CJEU's stance on the concept of 'disability' changed significantly in the case of *Ring and Werge*,[76] in which the Court noted that the provisions of the CRPD are 'an integral part of the [EU] legal order'[77] and that secondary legislation, including the Employment Equality Directive, must be interpreted in a manner that is consistent with the CRPD, as far as possible.[78] The applicants in the case, Mrs Ring and Mrs Werge, had been dismissed by their respective employers at very short notice under Danish labour law, which allowed the dismissal of an employee at short notice where such an employee has taken 120 days of paid sickness leave during a twelve-month period. The applicants argued that they may have been able to continue in their employment if they had been provided with reasonable accommodations in the form of special office furniture and a reduction in their working time. In light of the fact that the relevant Danish legislation implements the Employment Equality Directive, the national court referred three preliminary questions to the CJEU in order to seek clarity on Member States' obligations under the Directive, two of which are of relevance for present purposes. The first question concerned the definition of 'disability' and, in particular, whether it covers an individual who, because of physical, mental or psychological injuries, cannot (or can only to a limited extent) carry out his work. The second question concerned the definition of 'reasonable accommodation' and, specifically, whether a reduction in working hours was among the measures covered by Article 5 of the Directive.

In *Ring and Werge*,[79] the CJEU defined disability for the purposes of the Directive as 'a limitation which results in particular from physical, mental or psychological impairments which in interaction with various barriers may hinder the full and effective participation of the person concerned in professional life on an equal basis with others'.[80] While the CJEU appeared to apply the social model of disability, the Court focused on the ability to participate in professional life as an essential element of protection under the Directive's provisions. Notably, the Court also observed that a reduction in working hours may be deemed to be an appropriate accommodation in a case in which the reduction makes it possible for the worker to continue in his employment. The Court held, however, that it was for the national court to assess whether a reduction in working hours represents a disproportionate burden on employers.[81]

[76] *Ring and Werge*, note 15. [77] Ibid. para. 30. [78] Ibid. para. 32.

[79] See Janneke Gerards, 'CJEU 11 April 2013, HK Danmark, EHRC 2013/133' (2013) 7 *European Human Rights Cases* 1426.

[80] *Ring and Werge*, note 15, para. 36. [81] Ibid.

Joined cases C-335/11 and C-337/11, Ring and Werge

34. By its first and second questions, which should be considered together, the referring court asks essentially whether the concept of 'disability' in [the Employment Equality Directive] must be interpreted as including the state of health of a person who, because of physical, mental or psychological impairments, cannot or can only to a limited extent carry out his work, for a period that will probably last for a long time, or permanently. It further asks whether that concept must be interpreted as meaning that a condition caused by a medically diagnosed incurable illness may be covered by that concept, that a condition caused by a medically diagnosed curable illness may also be covered by that concept, and that the nature of the measures to be taken by the employer is decisive for considering that a person's state of health is covered by that concept.

. . .

36. The concept of 'disability' is not defined by [the Employment Equality Directive] itself. The Court therefore held, in paragraph 43 of its judgment in *Chacón Navas*, that the concept must be understood as referring to a limitation which results in particular from physical, mental or psychological impairments and which hinders the participation of the person concerned in professional life.

37. The UN Convention, which was ratified by the European Union by decision of 26 November 2009, in other words after the judgment in *Chacón Navas* had been delivered, acknowledges in recital (e) that 'disability is an evolving concept and that disability results from the interaction between persons with impairments and attitudinal and environmental barriers that hinders their full and effective participation in society on an equal basis with others'. Thus the second paragraph of Article 1 of the convention states that persons with disabilities include 'those who have long-term physical, mental, intellectual or sensory impairments which in interaction with various barriers may hinder their full and effective participation in society on an equal basis with others'.

38. . . . the concept of 'disability' must be understood as referring to a limitation which results in particular from physical, mental or psychological impairments which in interaction with various barriers may hinder the full and effective participation of the person concerned in professional life on an equal basis with other workers.

39. In addition, it follows from the second paragraph of Article 1 of the UN Convention that the physical, mental or psychological impairments must be 'long-term'.

40. It may be added that, as the Advocate General observes in point 32 of her Opinion, it does not appear that [the Employment Equality Directive] is intended

to cover only disabilities that are congenital or result from accidents, to the exclusion of those caused by illness. It would run counter to the very aim of the directive, which is to implement equal treatment, to define its scope by reference to the origin of the disability.

41. It must therefore be concluded that if a curable or incurable illness entails a limitation which results in particular from physical, mental or psychological impairments which in interaction with various barriers may hinder the full and effective participation of the person concerned in professional life on an equal basis with other workers, and the limitation is a long-term one, such an illness can be covered by the concept of 'disability' within the meaning of [the Employment Equality Directive].

42. On the other hand, an illness not entailing such a limitation is not covered by the concept of 'discrimination' within the meaning of [the Employment Equality Directive]. Illness as such cannot be regarded as a ground in addition to those in relation to which [the Employment Equality Directive] prohibits discrimination (see *Chacón Navas*, paragraph 57).

43. The circumstance that the person concerned can work only to a limited extent is not an obstacle to that person's state of health being covered by the concept of 'disability'. Contrary to the submissions of DAB and Pro Display, a disability does not necessarily imply complete exclusion from work or professional life.

44. The concept of 'disability' as defined in paragraph 38 above must be understood as referring to a hindrance to the exercise of a professional activity, not, as DAB and Pro Display submit, to the impossibility of exercising such an activity. The state of health of a person with a disability who is fit to work, albeit only part-time, is thus capable of being covered by the concept of 'disability'. An interpretation such as that suggested by DAB and Pro Display would, moreover, be incompatible with the objective of [the Employment Equality Directive], which aims in particular to enable a person with a disability to have access to or participate in employment.

45. In addition, a finding that there is a disability does not depend on the nature of the accommodation measures such as the use of special equipment. It should be noted here that the definition of the concept of 'disability' within the meaning of Article 1 of [the Employment Equality Directive] comes before the determination and assessment of the appropriate accommodation measures referred to in Article 5 of the directive.

46. According to recital 16 in the preamble to [the Employment Equality Directive], such measures are intended to accommodate the needs of disabled persons. They are therefore the consequence, not the constituent element, of the concept of 'disability'. Similarly, the measures or adaptations referred to in recital 20 in the preamble make it possible to comply with the obligation under Article 5 of the directive, but do not apply unless there is a disability.

47. It follows from the above considerations that the answer to Questions 1 and 2 is that the concept of 'disability' [in the Employment Equality Directive] must be interpreted as including a condition caused by an illness medically diagnosed as curable or incurable where that illness entails a limitation which results in particular from physical, mental or psychological impairments which in interaction with various barriers may hinder the full and effective participation of the person concerned in professional life on an equal basis with other workers, and the limitation is a long-term one. The nature of the measures to be taken by the employer is not decisive for considering that a person's state of health is covered by that concept.

The Court's focus, in *Ring and Werge*, on the ability to participate in professional life is maintained in another recent case, that of *Z* v. *A Government Department.*[82] The applicant in that case, Ms Z, had a rare condition, rendering her unable to support a pregnancy. Ms Z and her husband had a child via a surrogate mother. Subsequently, Ms Z applied for paid leave, equivalent to maternity leave or adoption leave. The application was refused on the grounds that Ms Z had never been pregnant and that the child could not be adopted by her. The CJEU acknowledged the fact that the woman in question had a long-term impairment that caused her great suffering (namely, her inability to conceive naturally). In spite of that, the Court held that 'the inability to have a child by conventional means does not in itself, in principle, prevent the commissioning mother from having access to, participating in or advancing in employment'.[83] Despite the applicant's recognised disability, it is somewhat ironic that the Court ruled that it was not apparent that her condition, by itself, 'made it impossible for her to carry out her work or constituted a hindrance to the exercise of her professional activity'.[84] It also appears to be incompatible with the CRPD's broad understanding of disability discrimination. Favalli and Ferri assert that the Court made a clearer and sharper distinction between the conceptualisation of disability in the CRPD and the one adopted in the EU legal framework: '[w]hereas the UN Convention refers broadly to participation in society, the Court's definition covers only

[82] Case C-363/12, Z v. *A Government Department and The Board of Management of a Community School*, ECLI:EU:C:2014:159; see Geert de Baere, 'Shall I Be Mother? The Prohibition on Sex Discrimination, the UN Disability Convention and the Right to Surrogacy Leave under EU Law' (2015) 74(1) *Cambridge Law Journal* 44.

[83] *Z* v. *A Government Department*, note 82, para. 81.

[84] Ibid. As Waddington and Broderick point out, the Court held that there was no hindrance to the exercise of the applicant's professional activity, 'in spite of the fact that the benefits at stake in this case – namely a period of paid leave to bond with and care for a new baby – were clearly employment-related'. Waddington and Broderick, *Combatting Disability Discrimination and Realising Equality*, note 60, p. 60.

participation in professional life'.[85] As the authors point out, 'the Court relied on the limited scope of the directive *ratione materiae*, as the directive only targets disabilities that make a worker's involvement in professional life more burdensome. In doing so, it also explicitly narrowed down the definition of disability'.[86] Moreover, in *Glatzel*,[87] while examining the definition of 'disability' in relation to Article 21 EU CFR, outside the employment context,[88] the Court repeated the narrow definition of 'disability' that was applied to the applicant's detriment in *Z* v. *A Government Department*.

The outcome of the foregoing cases is that the Court effectively requires evidence that the impairment in question has an impact on the full and effective participation in professional life of the particular applicant concerned. The definition of 'disability' adopted by the Court in the cases outlined above was repeated in the Court's decision in *Kaltoft*.[89] In that case, the Court addressed the issue as to whether obesity discrimination can amount to disability discrimination and, in doing so, 'created quite a stir in the press'.[90] The case revolved around the following facts: Mr Kaltoft was employed as a child-minder in the Municipality of Billund, Denmark, until his dismissal from his employment in November 2010. Although the local authority disputed whether his obesity formed part of the reasons leading to his dismissal, the applicant claimed that he was a victim of disability discrimination, contending that obesity was a disability and that he had been dismissed by reason of being too obese to carry

[85] Favalli and Ferri, 'Defining Disability in the EU Non-Discrimination Legislation: Judicial Activism and Legislative Restraints', note 12, p. 555.

[86] Ibid.

[87] Case C-356/12, *Wolfgang Glatzel* v. *Freistaat Bayern*, ECLI:EU:C:2014:350. See Charlotte O'Brien, 'Driving Down Disability Equality? Case C-356/12 Wolfgang Glatzel v. Freistaat Bayern, Judgment of 2 May 2014' (2014) 21(4) *Maastricht Journal of European and Comparative Law* 723–738.

[88] This case did not concern the Employment Equality Directive, but rather EU Directives setting down rules for the issuing of driving licences which excluded people with certain visual impairments from acquiring certain types of driving licences.

[89] Case C-354/13, *Kaltoft* v. *Municipality of Billund*, ECLI:EU:C:2014:2463; see also Lisa Waddington, 'Case note on Case C-354/13 CJEU 18 December 2014 (*Kaltoft*), Dec 18, 2014' (2015) *European Human Rights Cases* No. 222537; see further Sara Bendi Lahuerta, 'Case C-354/13, *Kaltoft* v *Municipality of Billund* – Can Obesity be a Disability under EU Equality Law?' (European Law Blog, 9 April 2015), available at http://europeanlawblog.eu/tag/crpd/; and Iyiola Solanke, '*Kaltoft* – A Step (in the Wrong Direction?) towards Protection from Weight Discrimination under EU Law' (Eutopia Law, 22 December 2015), available at http://eutopialaw.com/2014/12/22/kaltoft-a-step-in-thewrong-direction-towards-protection-from-weight-discrimination-under-eu-law/.

[90] Mark Butler, 'Obesity as a Disability: The Implications or Non-Implications of *Kaltoft*' (2014) 20(3) *European Journal of Current Legal Issues*, available at http://webjcli.org/article/view/358/466. The very same approach to obesity can be found in Case C-270/16, *Carlos Enrique Ruiz Conejero* v. *Ferroser Servicios Auxiliares SA and Ministerio Fiscal*, ECLI:EU:C:2017:788, para. 30. See generally Andrea Broderick, 'Ruiz Conejero: (Re-)Conceptualizing Disability-based Discrimination and Sickness Absence at Work' *International Labour Law Journal* (forthcoming, 2019).

out his employment obligations. The Danish court which heard the case brought a preliminary reference to the CJEU, seeking guidance on four questions. The first three questions essentially asked whether obesity itself can be deemed to be a protected ground of discrimination. The fourth question was whether obesity is a disability covered by the protection provided for in the Employment Equality Directive, and, if so, which criteria would be decisive for assessing whether a person's obesity provides protection for that person under the prohibition of discrimination on the ground of disability under the Directive.

The Court held that obesity itself could not be deemed to be a protected ground of discrimination, since no provision of the EU Treaties covers discrimination on the ground of obesity.[91] The Court also ruled that the Directive itself does not refer to obesity[92] and that the EU CFR was not applicable.[93] With regard to whether obesity can be deemed to fall under the disability ground for the purposes of the Directive, both the Advocate General in the case and the Court itself acknowledged that, even though obesity does not, in itself, constitute a disability within the meaning of the Employment Equality Directive:

> in the event that, under given circumstances, the obesity of the worker concerned entails a limitation which results in particular from long-term physical, mental or psychological impairments that in interaction with various barriers may hinder the full and effective participation of that person in professional life on an equal basis with other workers, obesity can be deemed to be covered by the concept of 'disability' within the meaning of the Directive.[94]

However, the CJEU took a cautious approach and left it to the national court to decide whether in the present case obesity constituted a disability. Butler argues that the relevance of the *Kaltoft* case 'lies in the recognition, for the first time in EU law, that differential treatment on the basis of obesity can, depending on its effects on a person's ability to work, fall within the scope of disability discrimination'.[95] The Court said this would be the case, for example, if an obese worker was affected by reduced mobility or medical conditions related to his obesity which prevented him from carrying out his work or caused him discomfort when working.[96] However, as Butler points out, 'this conclusion simply results from the application of prior CJEU case law to the present case. As such, the *Kaltoft* ruling does not really change or extend the prior concept of disability discrimination'. Nevertheless, he claims that 'it is a remarkable judgment because it reduces legal uncertainty in this area' and 'marks another step forward towards clarifying the scope of EU equality law and bringing about a consistent application at national level'.[97]

[91] *Kaltoft* v. *Municipality of Billund,* note 89, paras. 33–4. [92] Ibid. paras. 35–6.
[93] Ibid. para. 39. [94] Ibid. para. 53.
[95] Butler, 'Obesity as a Disability: The Implications or Non-Implications of *Kaltoft*', note 90.
[96] *Kaltoft* v. *Municipality of Billund,* note 89, para. 60.
[97] Butler, 'Obesity as a Disability: The Implications or Non-Implications of *Kaltoft*', note 90.

Lisa Waddington and Andrea Broderick, *Combatting Disability Discrimination and Realising Equality: A Comparison of the UN CRPD and EU Equality and Non-discrimination Law* (Luxembourg: European Commission, 2018), pp. 57–58

The CJEU's definition of disability [in *HK Danmark* and in *Kaltoft*] refers to a limitation resulting from an impairment which, in interaction with other barriers, hinders professional participation. In Kaltoft, the Court gave some examples of relevant limitations applicable in the context of obesity. These examples all concerned physical limitations directly caused by obesity. In this respect the Court referred to: 'reduced mobility or the onset, in that person, of medical conditions preventing him from carrying out his work or causing discomfort when carrying out his professional activity' [Case C-354/13, *Kaltoft*, para. 60]. Mr Kaltoft claimed that he had no such limitations and was capable of doing his job. However, if this is true, and he was nevertheless dismissed because of his obesity, then he clearly did face a barrier – in the form of negative attitudes and prejudices on the part of his employer. Many disabled people face such barriers – in essence, discrimination resulting from false assumptions and prejudices about an individual's ability – and it is clear that the CRPD is designed to address this.

. . .

In this respect, it should be noted that the CRPD refers to two elements which contribute to disability: 'impairment' and 'various barriers' which, in combination, hinder a person's 'effective participation in society on an equal basis with others'.

. . .

[T]he CRPD does not require that the relevant impairment actually leads to a limitation, such as a reduced ability or inability to walk, read or understand.

Whilst such a limitation will usually result from an impairment, it is possible to envisage impairments which do not have this kind of effect, such as visible scars or injuries, asymptomatic HIV and other conditions. People of particularly low or high stature may also be regarded in this light – they may not experience limitations directly related to their height, but they do experience limitations when interacting with an inaccessible physical environment.

Daouidi v. *Bootes Plus SL*[98] is one of the most recent decisions in which the CJEU has been confronted directly with the concept of 'disability'. As

[98] Case C-395/15, *Mohamed Daouidi* v. *Bootes Plus SL, Fondo de Garantía Salarial, Ministerio Fiscal*, ECLI:EU:C:2016:917. Delia Ferri, 'Daouidi v Bootes Plus SL and the Concept of "Disability" in EU Anti-Discrimination Law', (2018) 10(1) *European Labour Law Journal*, 69–84.

> Read *Daouidi* v. *Bootes Plus SL* and write a short case-note.

Waddington notes,[99] the Court had the possibility to focus on 'another dimension' of its own definition of 'disability': the meaning of 'long-term' limitation. In *Daouidi,* the Court observed that the CRPD does not specify what long-term means, nor can such a definition be found in EU law, and that the concept of 'long-term' limitation of a person's capacity must be given an autonomous and uniform interpretation within EU law.[100] The Court stressed that the assessment of whether the limitation of one's capacity is 'long-term' is objective and 'factual in nature', as well as based on current medical and scientific knowledge and data.[101] In an attempt to give the national court (which will ultimately be responsible for that assessment) some guidance, the CJEU affirmed (at para. 56) that a limitation can be considered long term if 'the incapacity of the person concerned does not display a clearly defined prognosis as regards short-term progress', or, is likely to be significantly lengthy. The Court treads carefully but attempts to further elucidate the definition of 'disability' in EU non-discrimination law that has been laid down in *Ring and Werge.* It also, rather implicitly, tries to carve out the distinction between sickness and disability. However, the CJEU appears, once again, quite reticent in its approach to assessing the role of social, environmental and attitudinal barriers in disabling an individual.[102]

[99] Lisa Waddington, 'Non-discriminatie, handicap, definitie van de grond handicap, begrip langdurige beperkingen (Mohamed Daouidi v. Bootes Plus SL e.a.)' (2017) *European Human Rights Cases.*

[100] *Daouidi* v. *Bootes Plus SL,* note 98, para. 51.

[101] Ibid. paras. 55–57.

[102] While not related to the concept of 'disability', it is notable that the CJEU has recently provided some guidance on the meaning and scope of positive action in the context of persons with disabilities under Article 7(2) of the Employment Equality Directive in the case of *Milkova*: Case C-406/15, *Milkova* ECLI:EU:C:2017:198. The case concerned a specific protection granted to employees with disabilities in case of dismissal. In that case, the Court held that the purpose of Article 7(2) of Directive 2000/78 is to authorise positive action that is aimed at effectively eliminating or reducing actual instances of inequality affecting people with disabilities, which may exist in their social lives and, in particular, their professional lives, and to achieve substantive, rather than formal, equality by reducing those inequalities (para. 47). The Court affirmed that this interpretation is supported by the CRPD (para. 48). The Court further remarked that, under Article 7(2) of the Directive, Member States are 'not

On the whole, it seems that the ratification of the CRPD by the EU has marked a significant turning point in the Court's case law. The Court has made efforts to define the concept of 'disability' in the Employment Equality Directive in line with the (non-) definition of disability contained in the CRPD. However, some authors point to difficulties in the Court's reasoning in the series of judgments in which it addressed the definition of 'disability' under the Directive. As Favalli and Ferri point out:

> on the one hand, as it appears in [*Ring and Werge*] and in *Kaltoft*, disability is used as an 'umbrella-term', encompassing a large variety of different health situations. This has inevitably had the result of implicitly enlarging the scope of the Employment Equality Directive *ratione personae*. On the other hand, the restricted scope *ratione materiae* of the directive falls short of the wide social-model oriented notion of disability purported by the [CRPD]. Thus, the Court inevitably narrows down the definition of disability to make it fit within the scope of the directive, as it appears in *Z. v. A Government Department*.[103]

Waddington also points to the fact that the CJEU's definition of disability:

> places an emphasis on the need for limitations resulting from impairments (which in interaction with various barriers hinder participation in professional life), and the examples given of such limitations in the context of obesity are clearly physical, and directly connected to obesity or a related medical condition.[104]

This reflects the approach adopted by the Court in several cases that have been highlighted throughout this section of the chapter.[105] Waddington argues that in spite of the Court 'paying lip service to the social-contextual model of disability reflected in the CRPD in its definition of disability, it seems the Court is struggling to recognise and apply the model in practice'.[106]

4 THE PROPOSED NON-DISCRIMINATION DIRECTIVE

In 2008, the European Commission proposed a horizontal directive that was designed to protect individuals from discrimination on the ground of disability as well as discrimination on the other grounds protected under the Employment Equality Directive, in fields other than employment. The horizontal nature of the 2008 proposal stems from its desire to equalise levels of protection across equality grounds. The proposed non-discrimination directive is

required to maintain or adopt measures such as those provided for under that provision, but have discretion in that regard' (para. 52).

[103] Favalli and Ferri, 'Defining Disability in the European Union Non-Discrimination Legislation: Judicial Activism and Legislative Restraints', note 12, pp. 557–8.

[104] Waddington, 'Case note on Case C-354/13 CJEU 18 December 2014 (*Kaltoft*), Dec 18, 2014', note 89, para. 11.

[105] Ibid. [106] Ibid.

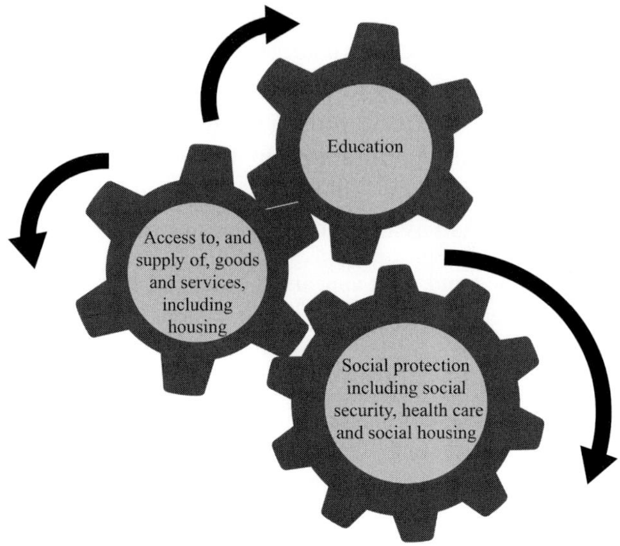

Figure 11.5 Fields Covered by the 2008 Proposal for a Horizontal Non-Discrimination Directive

intended to act as a complementary legislative mechanism to the pre-existing EU legislative framework on non-discrimination, principally the Employment Equality Directive, but it would not replace that Directive with regard to employment matters. The 2008 proposal addresses quite a wide range of fields, as illustrated by Figure 11.5.[107]

The 2008 proposal seeks to prohibit the following forms of discrimination: direct discrimination, indirect discrimination, harassment, discrimination by association, discrimination by assumption, denial of reasonable accommodation for persons with disabilities, instruction to discriminate and discrimination on multiple grounds.[108] Ferri Favalli maintain that the proposed Directive 'shows a more ambitious approach with regard to the prohibition of disability discrimination, and includes a number of additional provisions to strengthen disability discrimination law'; however, according to the authors, there is 'evident' restraint with regard to defining disability.[109]

[107] Article 3 of the 2008 proposal, note 10. For the purpose of this chapter, the most recent publicly available version of the proposal, which differs in several respects from the original 2008 proposal, is taken as the point of reference. See the latest publicly available version of the proposed directive, dated 26 June 2019, 10740/19 (available at https://eur-lex.europa.eu/legal-content/EN/TXT/PDF/?uri=CONSIL:ST_10740_2019_INIT&from=EN). and the progress report dated November 2018 (available at http://data.consilium.europa.eu/doc/document/ST-14253-2018-INIT/en/pdf).

[108] Article 2, 2008 proposal, note 107.

[109] Favalli and Ferri, 'Defining Disability in the European Union Non-Discrimination Legislation: Judicial Activism and Legislative Restraints', note 12, p. 560.

The 2008 proposal covers several of the fields that are covered by the CRPD and seeks to prohibit discrimination in those areas. However, as Waddington and Broderick point out, the material scope of the CRPD remains 'much broader' than the scope of the 2008 proposal[110] and the Employment Equality Directive taken together[111] meaning that the EU Member States which have ratified the CRPD will be obliged to prohibit disability discrimination in areas beyond those covered by EU equality law.[112] Examples of fields where discrimination should be prohibited under the CRPD, but which are not addressed by current and proposed EU law, include access to justice (Article 13) and participation in political and public life (Article 29 CRPD).[113] The 2008 proposal also does not cover:

> the organisation of the Member States' social protection systems, including decisions on the setting up, financing and management of such systems and related institutions as well as the substance, the amount, the calculation and the duration of benefits and services, and the conditions of eligibility for these benefits and services, such as, for example, age limits for certain benefits.[114]

The Commission's 2008 proposal goes further than the Employment Equality Directive in relation to the duty to provide reasonable accommodation. Article 4a(2) of the 2008 proposal sets out the following definition of 'reasonable accommodation':

> necessary and appropriate modification and adjustments not imposing a disproportionate burden, where needed in a particular case, to accommodate the specific needs of a person with a disability so as to allow that person access on an equal basis with others to the specific social protection measure, educational activity, good or service concerned.

Under the proposed directive, an unjustified failure to provide reasonable accommodation to a person with a disability is defined as a specific form of discrimination. Waddington and Broderick argue that, on the whole, the definition of reasonable accommodation in the 2008 proposal 'seems to be in line with the definition of reasonable accommodation found in Article 2 of the CRPD. Indeed, part of the definition in the 2008 proposal has been taken word for word from Article 2 of the CRPD'.[115] Notwithstanding its apparent compliance with the CRPD, the scope of the definition of reasonable accommodation contained in the 2008 proposal 'relating as it does,

[110] It is interesting to note that the original 2008 proposal, which was published prior to the EU becoming a party to the Convention, has been amended in certain aspects to bring it more fully into line with the CRPD.

[111] Waddington and Broderick, *Disability Law and the Duty to Reasonably Accommodate Beyond Employment: A Legal Analysis of the Situation in EU Member States*, note 11, p. 8.

[112] Ibid. [113] Ibid. p. 9, footnote 13.

[114] Article 3(2)(b) of the Proposal for a Council Directive on implementing the principle of equal treatment between persons irrespective of religion or belief, disability, age or sexual orientation, note 107.

[115] Waddington and Broderick, *Disability Law and the Duty to Reasonably Accommodate Beyond Employment: A Legal Analysis of the Situation in EU Member States*, note 11, p. 50.

only to access to social protection measures, educational activities, and goods and services' is naturally narrower than the scope found in the CRPD, which relates to the 'enjoyment or exercise of all human rights and fundamental freedoms'.[116]

Notably, the issue of disproportionate burden is addressed in Article 4b of the 2008 proposal, which contains a list of factors which are to be taken into account in determining the existence of a disproportionate burden, and in that regard differs from the CRPD, which does not contain any such list. The relevant factors are as follows:

i. the size, resources, net turnover and nature of the organisation or enterprise;
ii. the negative impact on the person with a disability of not providing the measure;
iii. the estimated cost;
iv. the estimated benefit for persons with disabilities generally, taking into account the frequency and duration of use of the relevant goods and services and the frequency and the duration of the relationship with the seller or provider;
v. the life span of infrastructure and objects which are used to provide a service;
vi. the historical, cultural, artistic or architectural value of the movable or immovable property in question; and
vii. the safety and practicability of the measures in question.

The current status of the 2008 proposal is uncertain, and it is still the subject of ongoing discussions at EU level, both in the Council and in the Parliament. The minutes from the meeting of the High-Level Group on Non-Discrimination, Equality and Diversity (chaired by the European Commission) in May 2015 stated that the 'Anti-Discrimination Directive is a priority for this Commission' and that 'good progress has been made' towards achieving that unanimity.[117] In June 2017, the European Commissioner for Employment, Social Affairs, Skills and Labour Mobility, Marianne Thyssen, reaffirmed that the directive remains a priority for the Commission.[118] In its 2018 report, the European Union Agency for Fundamental Rights (FRA) recommended that the EU legislator should continue its efforts for the adoption of this horizontal directive.[119] However, it would be premature to expect its entry into force in the near future.

[116] Ibid.

[117] European Commission, 'Tackling Discrimination', available at http://ec.europa.eu/justice/discrimination/files/hlg1_2015summary_en.pdf.

[118] See at www.europarl.europa.eu/legislative-train/theme-area-of-justice-and-fundamental-rights/file-anti-discrimination-directive.

[119] European Union Agency for Fundamental Rights, *Fundamental Rights Report 2018*, at p. 3, available at http://fra.europa.eu/en/publication/2018/fundamental-rights-report-2018.

SUMMARY

- The promotion of equality and the fight against discrimination is a core element of the body of primary and secondary legislation in the EU.
- Although EU non-discrimination law had a humble beginning, initially covering only discrimination on the ground of sex, it has undergone an evolution over the last few decades, both in terms of its scope and content.
- Disability non-discrimination law has received significant attention at the EU level in recent years.
- An important development which had implications for EU disability non-discrimination law took the form of the accession of the EU to the CRPD, through Council Decision 2010/48/EC.
- Under the influence of the CRPD, the CJEU's case law has witnessed a clear shift from the medical model to the social-model of disability.
- The CJEU defines disability for the purposes of the Employment Equality Directive as 'a limitation which results in particular from physical, mental or psychological impairments which in interaction with various barriers may hinder the full and effective participation of the person concerned in professional life on an equal basis with others'.
- The Court's case law on disability as a whole encompasses a mixed approach with regard to the CRPD's social-contextual model. The Court appears to have narrowed the conceptualisation of 'disability' in the CRPD to make it fit within the scope of the Employment Equality Directive.
- The Commission's proposed horizontal directive of 2008 complements the Employment Equality Directive in terms of its material scope. Under the proposed directive, the unjustified failure to provide reasonable accommodation is defined as a form of discrimination. However, the current status of the directive is highly uncertain, and it is still the subject of ongoing discussions. Thus, its entry into force is not foreseen in the near future.

ACTIVITIES

REVIEW QUESTIONS

1. What is the legal basis of the EU's specific competence to combat discrimination on the ground of disability?
2. What are the main differences between direct and indirect discrimination (in the context of disability)?
3. What is the scope (material and personal) of the Employment Equality Directive?

ESSAY QUESTIONS

1. In what ways does the Commission's proposed horizontal directive of 2008 go further than the Employment Equality Directive?

2. **'The CJEU has endeavoured to interpret the concept of "disability" in compliance with the CRPD.'** ***Discuss.***

GROUP PROJECT

Mrs Green has epilepsy, but her condition is well controlled by medication. In January 2017, she was hired by Banana Ltd, a computer manufacturing company of the State of Freedonia. She was initially employed on a six-month contract. At the time of her employment, she informed Banana Ltd of her medical condition. After four months, Mrs Green's supervisor informed her that her work performance was more than satisfactory and that Banana Ltd would like her to apply for a permanent position. At that point, Mrs Green completed an application form, where she, once again, informed her employers of her epilepsy. After submitting her application form, she was asked to undergo a medical examination by a doctor nominated by Banana Ltd. Following the medical examination, the Human Resources Department of Banana Ltd decided not to offer Mrs Green a permanent post, and they decided to terminate her contract with immediate effect, on the basis that she was not fit to operate heavy machinery.

Discuss the group project, taking into account the fact that Freedonia is a Member State of the EU.

FURTHER READING

Bailleux, A. and Hachez, I., 'Another Look at Glatzel (ECJ): Of Principles and Discriminations', in E. Brems and E. Desmet, *Integrated Human Rights in Practice: Rewriting Human Rights Decisions* (Cheltenham: Edward Elgar, 2017), pp. 351–78.

Bell, M., 'Advancing EU Anti-Discrimination Law: The European Commission's 2008 Proposal for a New Directive' (2009) 3 *The Equal Rights Review* 7–18.

Ellis, E. and Watson, P., *EU Anti-Discrimination Law* (Oxford: Oxford University Press, 2012).

Hendrickx, F., 'Disability and Reintegration in Work: Interplay between EU Non-Discrimination Law and Labour Law', in F. Hendrickx (ed.), *Reasonable Accommodation in the Modern Workplace. Potential and Limits of the Integrative Logics of Labour Law – Bulletin of Comparative Labour Relations* (Alpen aan den Rijn: Wolters Kluwer, 2016), pp. 61–72.

Hosking, D., 'European Developments. A High Bar for EU Disability Rights. Case C-13/05, *Chacon Navas v Eurest Colectividades SA*' (2007) 36(2) *Industrial Law Journal* 228–37.

Lourenço, L. and Pohjankoski, P., 'Breaking Down Barriers? The Judicial Interpretation of "Disability" and "Reasonable Accommodation" in EU Anti-Discrimination Law', in U. Belavusau and K. Henrard, *About EU Anti-Discrimination Law beyond Gender* (Oxford/Portland: Hart Publishing, 2018), pp. 321–37.

O'Brien, C., 'Driving Down Disability Equality? Case C-356/12 Wolfgang Glatzel v. Freistaat Bayern, Judgment of 2 May 2014' (2014) 21(4) *Maastricht Journal of European and Comparative Law* 723–38.

O'Brien, C., 'Union Citizenship and Disability: Restricted Access to Equality Rights and the Attitudinal Model of Disability', in D. Kochenov, *EU Citizenship and Federalism* (Cambridge: Cambridge University Press, 2017), pp. 509–39.

Perjul, V., 'Impairment, Discrimination, and the Legal Construction of Disability in the European Union and the United States' (2011) 44 *Cornell International Law Journal* 279–348.

Quinn, G. and Flynn, E., 'Transatlantic Borrowings: The Past and Future of EU Non-Discrimination Law and Policy on the Ground of Disability' (2012) 1 *American Journal of Comparative Law* 23–48.

Waddington, L., 'Breaking New Ground: The Implications of the UN Convention on the Rights of Persons with Disabilities for the European Community', in O. M. Arnardóttir and G. Quinn (eds.), *The UN Convention on the Rights of Persons with Disabilities: European and Scandinavian Perspectives* (Leiden/Boston: Brill, 2009), pp. 111–40.

Waddington, L., 'Equal to the Task? Re-Examining EU Equality Law in Light of the United Nations Convention on the Rights of Persons with Disabilities', in L. Waddington, G. Quinn and E. Flynn (eds.), *European Yearbook of Disability Law* (Antwerp/Portland: Intersentia, 2013), vol. 4, pp. 169–200.

Waddington, L., 'Future Prospects for EU Equality Law. Lessons to Be Learnt from the Proposed Equal Treatment Directive' (2011) 2 *European Law Review* 163–84.

Waddington, L., 'Not Disabled Enough: How European Courts Filter Non-Discrimination Claims Through a Narrow View of Disability' (2015) 15(1) *European Journal of Human Rights* 11–35.

Waddington, L., and Lawson, A.'The UN Convention on the Rights of Persons with Disabilities in Practice: A Comparative Analysis of the Role of Courts' (Oxford: Oxford University Press, 2018).

Whittle, R., 'The Framework Directive for Equal Treatment in Employment and Occupation: An Analysis from a Disability Rights Perspective' (2002) 27(3) *European Law Review* 303–26.

12 Accessibility in European Union Law

LEARNING OUTCOMES

- ✓ Identify the main EU legislative and policy actions aimed at fostering accessibility.
- ✓ Understand the key areas of EU competence that are relevant to accessibility.
- ✓ Demonstrate awareness of the main legislative provisions seeking to enhance accessibility in buildings, transportation and ICT.
- ✓ Comprehend the role of the European Disability Strategy 2010–2020 in promoting accessibility across Europe.
- ✓ Identify the main challenges in the implementation of the CRPD's accessibility obligations within the EU.
- ✓ Critically assess the strengths and weaknesses of the European Accessibility Act.
- ✓ Describe the role of standardisation in enhancing accessibility.
- ✓ Outline the role of EU state aid law and policy in promoting accessibility.

Accessibility in all aspects of everyday life cannot remain an option. It is a necessary investment and we have the solutions to make it happen.[1]

1 INTRODUCTION

The adoption of the European Disability Strategy 2010–2020 (EDS),[2] as discussed in Chapter 10, signalled a turning point in the ongoing process of creating a coherent and comprehensive EU policy framework on disability. It did so by identifying cross-cutting EU-level actions which, combined with national measures, are designed to empower people with disabilities and to ensure their inclusion in mainstream society. In compliance with the CRPD, which is now an integral part of EU law,[3] the EDS places heavy emphasis on accessibility,[4] which is one of the eight interconnected areas for EU action (the others being participation, equality, employment, education and training, social protection, health and external action). The EDS, in the same vein as the CRPD, recognises that accessibility is a 'precondition for participation in society and in the economy'.[5] It defines accessibility in a manner consistent with the CRPD and affirms that people with disabilities must 'have access, on an equal basis with others, to the physical environment, transportation, information and communications technologies and systems (ICT), and other facilities and services'.[6] The EDS also specifies a number of necessary actions, including the enhancement of standards and the creation of new legislation, to 'prevent, identify and eliminate obstacles and barriers to accessibility'.[7] These measures do not exist within a vacuum, however. While no provisions within the EU Treaties refer explicitly to accessibility in the context of disability, accessibility requirements for some goods and services exist in EU secondary legislation,[8] and they are relatively widespread in the area of transport – including air, rail, road and water transport.

1 Marianne Thyssen, *Speech at the European Commission Workshop on Accessibility of Products and Services* (Brussels, 3 February 2017), available at https://ec.europa.eu/commission/commissioners/2014-2019/thyssen/announcements/speech-european-commission-workshop-accessibility-products-and-services-brussels_en.

2 Commission Communication of 15 November 2010, European Disability Strategy 2010–2020: A Renewed Commitment to a Barrier-Free Europe, COM (2010) 636 final.

3 See above Chapter 10.

4 Delia Ferri, '"Subsidising Accessibility". Using EU State Aid Law and Policy to Foster Development and Production of Accessible Technology' (2015) *European State Aid Law Quarterly* 51.

5 Commission Communication of 15 November 2010, European Disability Strategy 2010–2020, note 2.

6 Ibid. 7 Ibid.

8 Lisa Waddington, 'A Disabled Market: Free Movement of Goods and Services in the EU and Disability Accessibility' (2009) 5 *European Law Journal* 575. See also Janina Arsenjeva, *Annotated Review of European Union Law and Policy with Reference to Disability* (prepared under the direction of Professor Lisa Waddington, on behalf of the Academic Network of

Against the backdrop highlighted above, this chapter examines the main tenets of the current EU action on accessibility for persons with disabilities and to identify the most relevant provisions in the EU legal framework. This chapter builds on the discussion already conducted in Chapters 10 and 11, and it includes several references to the CRPD, discussed in Part I of this textbook, which has been the major driver of the development of accessibility policies in the EU in the last decade. Further to these introductory remarks, section 2 frames the discussion by recalling the context of EU action and its legal basis. Section 3 examines the scope and content of provisions on accessibility in various domains of EU law. It analyses relevant legislation that pre-dates the conclusion of the CRPD as well as more recent regulations and directives in the fields of the physical environment, transportation, information and communication. It also briefly discusses accessibility of cultural goods and services. Section 4 provides an overview of the European Accessibility Act (EAA), while section 5 examines accessibility requirements in public procurement legislation, referring to legislation designed to regulate the purchase by governments and state-owned enterprises of goods, services and works. Section 6 succinctly addresses the role of standardisation in guaranteeing accessibility. Finally, section 7 goes on to discuss the role of EU state aid law and policy in fostering accessibility.

2 SETTING THE SCENE: ACCESSIBILITY IN THE EUROPEAN UNION

This section provides an overview of the barriers encountered by European citizens with disabilities, before succinctly explaining the EU's competence to legislate on accessibility and the relevance of accessibility in the EU policy framework.

2.1 Facts and Figures

The EDS recognises that barriers to accessibility persist in the physical environment, transportation, information and communications technologies (ICT). For example, the EDS states that 'on average in the EU-27, only 5% of public websites comply fully with web accessibility standards'.[9] Scholz et al. report that '[d]espite advances in Internet technologies, stronger non-discrimination legislation and a widening knowledge of web accessibility standards, much of the Internet remains inaccessible for many disabled people'. In 2012, the Flash Eurobarometer survey on accessibility found that, according to 93 per cent of the respondents, 'barriers to accessibility make it more difficult for people with a disability to attend

European Disability Experts – ANED) (2017), available at www.disability-europe.net/theme/eu-law-and-policy.

[9] Frederike Scholz, Betul Yalcin, and Mark Priestley, 'Internet Access for Disabled People: Understanding Socio-Relational Factors in Europe' (2014) 11(1) *Cyberpsychology: Journal of Psychosocial Research on Cyberspace*, available at http://dx.doi.org/10.5817/CP2017-1-4.

> Are there any statistics on accessibility in your own country? What do they reveal?

schools, to have a job, to vote and/or to freely move around and go on holiday'.[10] It also highlighted that seven in ten Europeans believe that more accessible goods and services would improve the lives of people with disabilities.[11] Eurostat statistics[12] also illustrate that barriers can be intersectional or compound in nature, as disabled women are more likely than disabled men to report lack of access to transport and buildings as well as mobility issues.

Lack of accessibility prevents people with disabilities from accessing education, the labour market and also from travelling for leisure purposes.[13] For example, it has been estimated that over 25 per cent of EU citizens do not take holidays due to perceived accessibility barriers.[14] In a similar vein, a 2012 report by the UK Royal National Institute of Blind People reveals that 43 per cent of persons with visual impairments would like to leave their home more often, but that travelling independently through indoor built environments, such as public offices and transport terminals, can be a difficult experience.[15]

2.2 The Competence of the EU to Act on Accessibility

The 2012 Flash Eurobarometer survey, mentioned above, suggests that 86 per cent of Europeans agree that having similar accessibility solutions across Europe would enable people with disabilities to travel, study and work in another EU country, supporting the case for

[10] European Commission, *Flash Eurobarometer Accessibility Report* (December 2012), available at http://ec.europa.eu/commfrontoffice/publicopinion/flash/fl_345_en.pdf.

[11] Ibid.

[12] Eurostat, *Disability Statistics – Barriers to Social Integration* (November 2015), available at http://ec.europa.eu/eurostat/statistics-explained/index.php?title=Disability_statistics_-_barriers_to_social_integration.

[13] Ibid.

[14] James Botwell, 'Assessing the Value and Market Attractiveness of the Accessible Tourism Industry in Europe: A Focus on Major Travel and Leisure Companies' (2015) 2(3) *Journal of Tourism Futures* 203.

[15] RNIB Report, *Sight loss UK 2012. The latest evidence* (May 2012), available at www.rnib.org.uk/sites/default/files/Sight_loss_UK_2012.pdf.

advancing EU-wide legislation on the issue.[16] In addition, as Priestley notes,[17] accessibility requirements can alter the ways in which a product or a service is designed, and they may limit the sale of certain products and services. Thus, the EU can regulate and, in some instances, harmonise accessibility requirements to prevent national differences in accessibility requirements or technical specifications from becoming barriers to the free circulation of goods, services and people. In fact, most of the existing pieces of EU legislation on accessibility are based on Article 114 TFEU, which empowers the EU to adopt legislation concerning the establishment and smooth functioning of the internal market. It must be recalled that Declaration No. 22 to the Treaty of Amsterdam stipulates that, in drawing up internal market measures under what is now Article 114 of the Treaty on the Functioning of the European Union (TFEU), EU institutions 'shall take account of the needs of persons with a disability'. Articles 53 and 62 TFEU (on the free movement of services) have also provided a legal basis for relevant instruments in certain fields, in combination with Article 114 TFEU. Moreover, Title VI TFEU (on transport) has provided a legal basis for legislation addressing accessibility for people with disabilities in different modes of transport (road, rail, water and air transport). The EU has also included accessibility requirements within legislation on the right to access EU documentation, based on Article 15 TFEU.

L. Waddington, 'Accessible goods and services and the internal market', in EDF, Paving the way towards free movement for persons with disabilities (Brussels: EDF Publications, 2011)

The availability of accessible goods and services is important for ensuring the economic and social integration of people with disabilities. Moreover, accessibility is a right that has been recognised in the United Nations Convention on the Rights of Persons with Disabilities, thereby underlining its importance. The Convention requires States Parties to take appropriate measures to ensure to persons with disabilities access, on an equal basis with others. However, accessibility is not only important for people with disabilities and their friends and families, but also from the point of view of achieving an internal market for goods and services in the European Union. Moreover, there are significant economic benefits to be gained from addressing accessibility within the framework of the internal market.

...

[16] European Commission, *Flash Eurobarometer Accessibility Report*, note 10.

[17] Mark Priestley, *National Accessibility Requirements and Standards for Products and Services in the European Single Market: Overview and Examples* (compiled on behalf of ANED) (2013), available at www.disability-europe.net/theme/accessibility.

The achievement of the internal market, in which there are no obstacles to the Free movement of goods, persons, services and capital, is a fundamental objective of the European Union. Obstacles to the internal market can come from many sources and, where such obstacles make Free movement more difficult, or distort competition, the EU can intervene. One kind of obstacle to Free movement arises when Member States set national standards that must be met when goods and services are sold in that Member State. For example, a Member State may require that a product is designed in a certain way or incorporates certain features, is packaged in a particular way, that specific goods or services meet certain quality standards, or that specific information be given to consumers about a good or service. These requirements must be met whenever a good or service is sold in that Member State, including by manufacturers or providers that are based in other Member States. Now, imagine that each Member State has its own set of national rules that must be complied with – that means that manufacturers and suppliers will have to adapt their goods and services according to the rules of each Member State, with up to 27 different sets of rules to be met. That will be both highly expensive and challenging. Manufacturers and suppliers will find it much more difficult to sell their goods and services throughout the EU, and consumers will be faced with less choice (as some suppliers withdraw from the market) and higher prices. In this situation, it is easy to see that obstacles to the internal market exist. This is the case even if the different national rules pursue an important aim, such as the health and safety of consumers.

...

In short, common EU-wide accessibility standards can help both people with disabilities, who gain greater access to accessible goods and services, and industry, which finds their market expand at no extra cost.

3 ACCESSIBILITY IN EUROPEAN UNION LEGISLATION

As mentioned in the introduction to this chapter, the EU has adopted several legislative provisions addressing different aspects of accessibility for people with disabilities. These are briefly discussed below, in conjunction with relevant EU policy documents, under three main headings which reflect the obligations laid down in Article 9 CRPD:[18] accessibility to the physical environment, to transportation, and to information and communications. This section also examines the accessibility of cultural goods and services, including audiovisual services.

[18] See above Chapter 5.

3.1 Accessibility of the Built Environment

In almost all EU Member States, national legislation provides for a general obligation to make public buildings accessible and lays down specific requirements for certain categories of buildings (e.g. schools), extending this obligation to both public and private providers.[19] These accessibility obligations are often 'grounded in national non-discrimination legislation with subsidiary national building regulations and codes'.[20]

DID YOU KNOW THAT ...?

Almost all EU Member States have specific national requirements for accessibility of public buildings. Some EU Member States also require accessibility to be ensured in private buildings. For example, in Estonia, the Building Act (adopted in 2002 and amended in 2011) includes accessibility requirements and prescribes that buildings intended for public use have to be accessible to and usable by persons with reduced mobility and by visually impaired and hearing impaired persons. In Greece, Law 4067/2012 (New Urban Planning Regulations) requires that all new buildings comply with the Design Guidelines for the Autonomous Movement and Living of People with Disabilities (Disability Office, Ministry of Environment 1986–1990), which cover technical specifications for accessible indoor and outdoor facilities. Buildings which are older than 2012 and which host public sector services, local authority services, public spaces for culture, sports, leisure and entertainment, temporary accommodation, education, health and social welfare, justice services, as well as banks, industry, trade and offices, are required to be accessible by 2020. In a similar vein, the Dutch Building Code 2012 (*Bouwbesluit*) contains compulsory accessibility requirements for every new building with a floor space of more than 400 square metres which is open to the public, including workplaces. In Bulgaria, a building with more than 30 dwellings is required to have at least one apartment adjusted for disabled people; however, due to the lack of control and enforcement, accessibility requirements are often ignored (www.disability-europe.net/dotcom).

---

[19] Priestley, *National Accessibility Requirements and Standards for Products and Services in the European Single Market: Overview and Examples*, note 17, p. 4.

[20] Ibid. p. 5. An overview of legislation on built environment accessibility is available for all EU countries from the DOTCOM database of the ANED at www.disability-europe.net/dotcom.

Even though accessibility related to the physical environment is primarily regulated at the national level, the EU has adopted directives covering certain accessibility requirements for specific physical structures: namely cableway installations[21] and lifts.[22]

The new Regulation on Cableway Installations,[23] applicable as of 21 April 2018, reproduces Annex II ('essential requirements') of the former Directive 2000/9/EC relating to cableway installations designed to carry persons,[24] which set standards for the construction of cableway installations. Paragraph 6 of that Annex on 'equipment for users' provides that '[i]t must be possible for children and persons with reduced mobility to use the installation safely if the installation is designed for the transport of such persons'. It is worth noting that the new instrument takes the form of a regulation. Given the intended scope of the measure, essential requirements and conformity assessment procedures had to be identical in all EU Member States. Thus, the EU legislator opted for a regulation (instead of a directive), which is directly applicable and 'imposes clear and detailed rules which do not give room for divergent transposition by Member'.[25] This means that cableways and components of cable cars must comply with the requirements of the regulation. Member States cannot impose additional standards with regard to disability accessibility.[26]

The Lifts Directive[27] governs the design, manufacture and installation of lifts. It is relevant for lift installers, manufacturers, owners and users of lifts, and its aim is to permit the free circulation of lifts and safety components for lifts within the internal market and to ensure a high level of safety for lift users and maintenance staff. Paragraph 1.2 of Annex I of that Directive establishes that:

> [w]here the lift is intended for the transport of persons, and where its dimensions permit, the car must be designed and constructed in such a way that its structural

[21] According to Article 3 of Council Regulation (EU) 2016/424 of 9 March 2016 on cableway installations and repealing Directive 2000/9/EC, OJ 2016 No. L81/1, 'cableway installation' means a whole on-site system, consisting of infrastructure and subsystems, which is designed, constructed, assembled and put into service with the objective of transporting persons, where the traction is provided by cables positioned along the line of travel'.

[22] Physical infrastructures related to transport are discussed in sub-section 3.2.

[23] Council Regulation (EU) 2016/424, note 21.

[24] Council Directive 2000/9/EC of 20 March 2000 relating to cableway installations designed to carry persons, OJ 2000 No. L106/21.

[25] Ibid. para. 4 of the Preamble.

[26] Like its predecessor, the Regulation only sets out the essential requirements applying to cableway installations, whereas technical details are adopted by the European Committee for Standardization (CEN) and the European Committee for Electrotechnical Standardization (CENELEC) in accordance with Council Regulation (EU) No. 1025/2012 on standards, which are examined further in section 6.

[27] Council Directive 2014/33/EU of 26 February 2014 on the harmonisation of the laws of the Member States relating to lifts and safety components for lifts, OJ 2014 No. L96/251.

features do not obstruct or impede access and use by disabled persons and so as to allow any appropriate adjustments intended to facilitate its use by them.[28]

The Directive is linked to a specific standard that indicates minimum requirements for the safe and independent use of and access to lifts: 'EN 81-70:2003 – Safety rules for the construction and installations of lifts'. Significantly, the Preamble to the Directive includes a reference to the CRPD and makes it clear that '[t]he harmonised standards relevant to this Directive should also take into account the United Nations Convention on the Rights of Persons with Disabilities'.[29]

EU law also addresses the accessibility of physical environments under Directive 89/654/EEC, concerning the minimum safety and health requirements for the workplace,[30] which refers to 'doors, passageways, staircases, washbasins, lavatories and workstations used or occupied directly by handicapped persons'. Other pieces of EU health and safety legislation focus on the prevention of diseases and on diminishing risks linked to work;[31] however, they only refer indirectly to accessible spaces.

The 2014 European Directives on Public Procurement, which replace and strengthen previous texts, also have a great potential to impact on the accessibility of the physical environment in general.[32]

Furthermore, the most recent Regulations on Structural Funds[33] are very relevant in relation to the accessibility of physical infrastructures as well as with regard to broader accessibility considerations. The Structural Funds, which include the European Regional Development Fund (ERDF), the European Social Fund (ESF), the Cohesion Fund, the European Agricultural Fund for

[28] Ibid. In addition, para. 1(6) of Annex I also establishes that '[t]he controls of lifts intended for use by unaccompanied disabled persons must be designed and located accordingly'.

[29] Ibid. A Declaration by the European Parliament, the Council and the Commission on the approximation of the laws of the Member States relating to lifts' released in conjunction with the original Directive (Council Declaration 95/357/EC of 7 September 1995 on the approximation of the laws of the Member States relating to lifts, OJ 1995 No. L213/32) complements the legislative text. It encourages Member States 'to take any national measures necessary to ensure that all levels of existing buildings, as well as those under construction are accessible to disabled people, particularly those who use wheelchairs', and it recommends that at least one lift that is accessible to people in wheelchairs be provided in all new buildings.

[30] Council Directive 89/654/EEC of 30 November 1989 concerning the minimum safety and health requirements for the workplace (first individual directive within the meaning of Article 16(1) of Directive 89/391/EEC), OJ 1989 No. L393/1.

[31] E.g. Council Directive 90/270/EEC of 29 May 1990 on the minimum safety and health requirements for work with display screen equipment (fifth individual Directive within the meaning of Article 16(1) of Directive 87/391/EEC), OJ 1990 No. L156/14.

[32] See below section 5.

[33] The regulations can be found at http://ec.europa.eu/regional_policy/en/information/legislation/regulations/.

Rural Development (EAFRD) and the European Maritime and Fisheries Fund (EMFF), support economic development across the EU. Accessibility for people with disabilities is one of the horizontal principles of the Common Provisions Regulation (CPR),[34] which also includes several references to the CRPD. Moreover, it provides *ex ante* conditionalities, obliging the Member States to make sure that the initiatives financed under the Structural Funds respect the CRPD, and it prohibits discrimination on the basis of disability in the preparation and implementation of the programmes.

ARTICLE 7 OF THE COMMON PROVISIONS REGULATION

The Member States and the Commission shall ensure that equality between men and women and the integration of gender perspective are taken into account and promoted throughout the preparation and implementation of programmes, including in relation to monitoring, reporting and evaluation.

The Member States and the Commission shall take appropriate steps to prevent any discrimination based on sex, racial or ethnic origin, religion or belief, disability, age or sexual orientation during the preparation and implementation of programmes. In particular, accessibility for persons with disabilities shall be taken into account throughout the preparation and implementation of programmes.

3.2 Accessibility of Transport

Transport is one of the EU's primary and most long-standing policy areas. Since the entry into force of the Treaty establishing the European Economic Community – the Treaty of Rome of 1957 – transport policy has been focused on eliminating borders between Member States in order to enable the free movement of individuals and goods. Aside from the primary aim of completing the internal market in the transport sector, the EU's transport policy has progressively incorporated other objectives, such as: to ensure sustainable development; to extend transport networks throughout Europe; and to ensure

[34] Council Regulation (EU) No. 1303/2013 of 17 December 2013 laying down common provisions on the European Regional Development Fund, the European Social Fund, the Cohesion Fund, the European Agricultural Fund for Rural Development and the European Maritime and Fisheries Fund and laying down general provisions on the European Regional Development Fund, the European Social Fund, the Cohesion Fund and the European Maritime and Fisheries Fund and repealing Council Regulation (EC) No. 1083/2006, OJ 2013 No. L347/320.

the safety of both infrastructure and means of transport. Thus far, the EU has adopted a wide range of regulations and directives covering rail, bus and coach, aeroplane and water transport.

Despite the fact that accessibility for people with disabilities was already relatively mainstreamed in EU transport regulations and directives prior to the entry into force of the CRPD, the Union currently aspires to further align its own legislation with the Convention. In that regard, the EDS includes a number of important commitments in the area of transport accessibility. Aside from EU legislation, the majority of EU Member States provide for specific accessibility requirements in relation to transport, infrastructure, equipment and information. In many cases, those requirements transpose those of EU directives or specify (where possible) requirements laid down in EU regulations.[35]

Currently, EU transport legislation includes various provisions on accessibility of the physical transport infrastructure. For instance, the recent Regulation on Union Guidelines for the Development of the Trans-European Transport Network (TEN-T)[36] qualifies accessibility for elderly people, persons with reduced mobility and disabled passengers as one of its objectives. Other legislative enactments guarantee equal access to modes of transport for persons with disabilities, include technical prescriptions for accessible vehicles and/or provide for accessible information for travellers with disabilities. Those laws are analysed in the sub-sections below, where various modes of transport are discussed in turn, taking into account the broader realm of EU transport policies.

3.2.1 *Rail Transport*

In relation to rail transport, existing legislation is stratified. Between 2001 and 2016, four legislative packages were adopted, to support the development of a single European railway area and to make national railway systems interoperable. The most recent, '4th Railway Package',[37] is a set of six legislative texts

[35] Priestley, *National Accessibility Requirements and Standards for Products and Services in the European Single Market: Overview and Examples*, note 17, p. 25.

[36] Council Regulation (EU) No. 1315/2013 of 11 December 2013 on Union guidelines for the development of the trans-European transport network and repealing Decision No. 661/2010/EU, OJ 2013 No. L348/1.

[37] The first railway package dates back to 2001. It aimed to enable rail operators to have access to the trans-European network on a non-discriminatory basis. The assessment of the implementation of this package conducted by the European Commission in 2006 showed positive effects. The relative position of railways towards other transport modes had stabilised, and the high level of rail transport safety had been improved. After a second package adopted in 2004, the 'third rail package' containing measures to revitalise the railways in Europe was adopted in October 2007.

Technical Pillar	Market Pillar
• Regulation (EU) 2016/796 on the European Union Agency for Railways and repealing Regulation (EC) No. 881/2004 • Directive (EU) 2016/797 on the interoperability of the rail system within the European Union (Recast of Directive 2008/57/EC) • Directive (EU) 2016/798 on railway safety (Recast of Directive 2004/49/EC)	• Regulation (EU) 2016/2338 amending Regulation (EU) 1370/2007, which deals with the award of public service contracts for domestic passenger transport services by rail ('PSO Regulation') • Directive 2016/2370/EU amending Directive 2012/34/EU, which deals with the opening of the market of domestic passenger transport services by rail and the governance of the railway infrastructure ('Governance Directive') • Regulation (EU) 2016/2337 repealing Regulation (EEC) 1192/69 on the normalisation of the accounts of railway undertakings

Figure 12.1 The 4th Railway Package

designed to create a truly internal market for rail services and a Single European Railway Area. Those legislative texts partially amend or recast existing legislative provisions or complement legislation that remains in force. The overall goal of the '4th Railway Package' is to make the European rail sector more competitive, whilst increasing safety and the interoperability of services. As shown in Figure 12.1, it comprises two pillars: the 'technical pillar' and the 'market pillar'. The 'technical pillar' is designed to reduce costs and the administrative burden for railway undertakings that operate across the EU. The 'market pillar' sets out the general right for railway undertakings established in one Member State to operate all types of passenger services everywhere in the EU.

The Directive on the interoperability of the rail system[38] establishes the conditions to be met in order to achieve greater convergence and conformity within the EU's rail system, to facilitate, improve and develop rail transport services within the Union, and 'to contribute to the completion of the single European railway area and the progressive achievement of the internal market'. Paragraph 29 of the Preamble to the Directive recalls that the CRPD:

[38] Council Directive (EU) 2016/797 of 11 May 2016 on the interoperability of the rail system within the European Union, OJ 2016 No. L138, 26 May 2016, pp. 44–101. It recasts former Council Directive 2008/57/EC of 17 June 2008 on the interoperability of the rail system within the Community, OJ 2001 No. L191/1.

establishes accessibility as one of its general principles and requires State Parties to take appropriate measures in order to ensure access for persons with disabilities on an equal basis with others, including by developing, promulgating and monitoring the implementation of minimum standards and guidelines for accessibility.

The Preamble of the Directive goes on to state that accessibility for persons with disabilities and persons with reduced mobility is 'an essential requirement for the interoperability of the Union rail system'. Since both direct and indirect discrimination on the ground of disability is prohibited, the Directive requires that Member States promote a railway system that is accessible to all (paragraph 30 of the Preamble). It then goes on to establish that, since 'technical specifications for interoperability' (TSI) have an impact on the conditions of use of rail transport by users, those users, 'including organisations of persons with disabilities', must be consulted about them (paragraph 32 of the Preamble). Accessibility features are then mentioned several times in the annexes to the Directive.

Directive (EU) 2016/797 on the Interoperability of the Rail System

Annex III – Essential Requirements

1.6. *Accessibility*

1.6.1. The 'infrastructure' and 'rolling stock' subsystems must be accessible to persons with disabilities and persons with reduced mobility in order to ensure access on an equal basis with others by way of the prevention or removal of barriers, and by way of other appropriate measures. This shall include the design, construction, renewal, upgrade, maintenance and operation of the relevant parts of the subsystems to which the public has access.

1.6.2. The 'operations' and 'telematics applications for passengers' subsystems must provide for the necessary functionality required to facilitate access for persons with disabilities and persons with reduced mobility on an equal basis with others by way of the prevention or removal of barriers, and by way of other appropriate measures.

The Rail Passengers' Rights Regulation[39] lays down various provisions with regard to the information to be provided by railway undertakings; the conclusion of transport contracts; the issuance of tickets; the liability of railway undertakings and their insurance obligations for passengers and their luggage. It also sets out the obligations of railway undertakings to

[39] Council Regulation (EC) No. 1371/2007 of 23 October 2007 on rail passengers' rights and obligations, OJ 2007 No. L315/14.

passengers in cases of delay; it contains provisions in relation to 'the protection of, and assistance to, disabled persons and persons with reduced mobility travelling by rail'; and it provides for the definition and monitoring of quality and security standards. When it comes to persons with disabilities, the Regulation aims to ensure that they can travel by rail on an equal basis with others and are provided with adequate information on accessibility and assistance in the case of delay. Several references to persons with disabilities are included in the Preamble to this Regulation.

Recitals (10) and (11) – Preamble to the Rail Passengers' Rights Regulation

(10) Rail passenger services should benefit citizens in general. Consequently, disabled persons and persons with reduced mobility, whether caused by disability, age or any other factor, should have opportunities for rail travel comparable to those of other citizens. Disabled persons and persons with reduced mobility have the same right as all other citizens to free movement, freedom of choice and to non-discrimination. *Inter alia*, special attention should be given to the provision of information to disabled persons and persons with reduced mobility concerning the accessibility of rail services, access conditions of rolling stock and the facilities on board. In order to provide passengers with sensory impairment with the best information on delays, visual and audible systems should be used, as appropriate. Disabled persons and persons with reduced mobility should be enabled to buy tickets on board a train without extra charges.

(11) Railway undertakings and station managers should take into account the needs of disabled persons and persons with reduced mobility, through compliance with the TSI for persons with reduced mobility, so as to ensure that, in accordance with Community public procurement rules, all buildings and rolling stock are made accessible through the progressive elimination of physical obstacles and functional hindrances when acquiring new material or carrying out construction or major renovation work.

The Rail Passengers' Rights Regulation includes a chapter on the specific rights of persons with reduced mobility, guaranteeing rights similar to those provided for within the Air Passengers' Rights Regulation, which is discussed in sub-section 3.2.4 below. Article 19 (on the right to transport) requires railways to establish, 'with the active involvement of representative organisations of disabled persons and persons with reduced mobility', non-discriminatory access rules for the transport of disabled persons and persons with reduced mobility. It also provides that reservations and tickets shall be offered to persons with disabilities at no additional cost. Article 20 (on information to disabled persons and persons with reduced mobility) obliges railway undertakings and ticket vendors to provide information on the accessibility of rail services, on the access conditions of rolling stock and about facilities on board. Article 21 (on accessibility) requires railway undertakings and station managers to 'ensure that the station, platforms, rolling stock and other facilities are accessible to disabled persons and persons with reduced mobility' and to 'make all reasonable efforts to enable disabled persons or persons with reduced mobility to have access to travel by rail'. Articles 22–24 concern specific support to be provided to people with disabilities. It is worth noting that Article 22 provides for assistance free of charge for boarding and disembarking from the train, while Article 23 requires assistance on board to enable persons with disabilities to have access to the same services as other passengers. Finally, Article 25 provides that, if the railway undertaking is liable for the total or partial loss of, or damage to, mobility equipment or other equipment used by persons with disabilities, the undertaking must compensate them.

3.2.2 *Road Transport*

The general aim of the EU's land transport policy is to promote efficient and safe mobility. The existing legislation that applies in the context of road transport services establishes minimum standards for working time, driving time and rest periods for professional road transport, minimum annual vehicle taxes and vehicles standards. It also sets common rules on access to the market vehicles' manufacturers and service providers. Some of the relevant legislative enactments include accessibility requirements. For example, Directive 2007/46/EC establishing a framework for the approval of motor vehicles and their trailers, and of systems, components and separate technical units intended for such vehicles[40] requires EU approval to be obtained for access to the internal market for commercial vehicles (vans, lorries, semi-trailers, trailers), buses and coaches. Manufacturers must issue a certificate

> Read the Bus and Coach Passengers Regulation and identify the provisions that ensure accessibility.

[40] Council Directive 2007/47/EC of 5 September 2007 establishing a framework for the approval of motor vehicles and their trailers, and of systems, components and separate technical units intended for such vehicles (Framework Directive), OJ 2007 No. L263/1.

of conformity for each vehicle manufactured, attesting that it conforms to the approved type. The Directive sets specific requirements for buses and coaches, including providing for greater ease of access for persons who use wheelchairs. Regulation (EC) No. 661/2009,[41] which concerns the safety of motor vehicles, includes a provision designed to ensure the accessibility of vehicles for people with disabilities and people with reduced mobility.

In a similar vein to the Rail Passengers' Rights Regulation, the Bus and Coach Passengers Regulation[42] provides, *inter alia*, for the protection of, and assistance to, persons with disabilities and persons with reduced mobility travelling by bus or coach. Notably, the Preamble to this Regulation refers explicitly to Article 9 CRPD.

3.2.3 *Water Transport*

Both legislation on inland waterway transport and on maritime transport include accessibility requirements. This is the case with Directive 2006/87/EC,[43] which harmonises the conditions for the issuance of navigation certificates by Member States. It specifies that passenger vessels have to provide for areas for use by persons with reduced mobility. Additional technical requirements are included in relation to parts of the vessel (e.g. door and corridor widths, location of handrails, accessible toilets). The Directive also requires that safety measures for persons with reduced mobility are taken into account. Directive 2009/45/EC on safety rules and standards for passenger ships (recast)[44] addresses safety requirements for persons with reduced mobility, whilst Annex III contains Guidelines for Safety Requirements for Passenger Ships and High-Speed Passenger Craft for Persons with Reduced Mobility. Furthermore, in the field of water transport, the Regulation on passenger rights[45] provides for non-discrimination and assistance to disabled persons and persons with reduced mobility travelling by sea and inland waterway. The provisions included in the regulation are similar to those examined above in relation to the Rail Passengers'

[41] Council Regulation (EC) No. 661/2009 of 13 July 2009 concerning type-approval requirements for the general safety of motor vehicles, their trailers and systems, components and separate technical units intended therefor, OJ 2009 No. L200/1.

[42] Council Regulation (EU) No. 181/2011 of 16 February 2011 concerning the rights of passengers in bus and coach transport and amending Regulation (EC) No. 2006/2004, OJ 2011 No. L55/1.

[43] Council Directive 2006/87/EC of 12 December 2006 laying down technical requirements for inland waterway vessels and repealing Council Directive 82/714/EEC, OJ 2006 No. L389, 30 December 2006, pp. 1–260.

[44] Council Directive 2009/45/EC of 6 May 2009 on safety rules and standards for passenger ships (Recast), OJ 2009 No. L163/1.

[45] Council Regulation (EU) No. 1177/2010 of 24 November 2010 concerning the rights of passengers when travelling by sea and inland waterway and amending Regulation (EC) No. 2006/2004 (1), OJ 2010 No. L334/1.

Rights Regulation. Interestingly, in a similar vein to the Bus and Coaches' Passengers Regulation, the Regulation on passenger rights refers explicitly to Article 9 CRPD in its Preamble.

3.2.4 *Air Transport*

The common EU aviation policy aims to make Europe a competitive and safe air space. Several EU regulatory measures have gradually created a competitive single market for air transport: a series of regulations removed all commercial restrictions for European airlines operating within the EU, setting up the 'European Single Aviation Market' (which has been extended to Norway, Iceland and Switzerland). In order to protect air passengers, common safety rules have been progressively extended to the entire air transport chain, and common rules for the protection of air passengers' rights (providing a minimum level of assistance in the event of serious delays or cancellation) have been adopted. Amongst those, Regulation (EC) No. 261/2004 establishes rules on compensation and assistance to passengers in the event of denied boarding and of cancellation or long delay of flights,[46] and provides, *inter alia*, that air carriers operating a flight shall give priority to persons with reduced mobility and any persons or certified service dogs accompanying them. In instances where boarding is denied, or where cancellation and delays of any length occur, persons with reduced mobility and any persons accompanying them have the right to receive care, as soon as possible, in accordance with the provisions of the Regulation.

> Read Regulation (EC) No. 1107/2006, and identify the most important non-discrimination provisions contained in that Regulation.

Regulation (EC) No. 1107/2006 complements this framework by protecting the rights of disabled persons and persons with reduced mobility when travelling by air.[47] This is one of the most relevant disability-specific

[46] Council Regulation (EC) No. 261/2004 of 11 February 2004 establishing common rules on compensation and assistance to passengers in the event of denied boarding and of cancellation or long delay of flights, and repealing Regulation (EEC) No. 295/91, OJ 2004 No. L46, 17 February 2004, pp. 1–8.

[47] Council Regulation (EC) No. 1107/2006 of 5 July 2006 concerning the rights of disabled persons and persons with reduced mobility when travelling by air, OJ 2006 No. L204/1, 26 July 2006.

instruments in the field of transportation. It establishes rules for the provision of assistance to persons with disabilities and those with reduced mobility when travelling by air. The Regulation includes non-discrimination measures. In particular, Article 3 of the Regulation affirms that an air carrier or its agent or a tour operator shall not refuse to accept a reservation for a flight or to embark on the grounds of disability. Article 7 and subsequent provisions require that persons with disabilities are provided with assistance when travelling by air.

ARTICLE 7 OF REGULATION (EC) NO. 1107/2006

1. When a disabled person or person with reduced mobility arrives at an airport for travel by air, the managing body of the airport shall be responsible for ensuring the provision of the assistance specified in Annex I in such a way that the person is able to take the flight for which he or she holds a reservation, provided that the notification of the person's particular needs for such assistance has been made to the air carrier or its agent or the tour operator concerned at least 48 hours before the published time of departure of the flight. This notification shall also cover a return flight, if the outward flight and the return flight have been contracted with the same air carrier.

2. Where use of a recognised assistance dog is required, this shall be accommodated provided that notification of the same is made to the air carrier or its agent or the tour operator in accordance with applicable national rules covering the carriage of assistance dogs on board aircraft, where such rules exist.

3. If no notification is made in accordance with paragraph 1, the managing body shall make all reasonable efforts to provide the assistance specified in Annex I in such a way that the person concerned is able to take the flight for which he or she holds a reservation.

4. The provisions of paragraph 1 shall apply on condition that:

(a) the person presents himself or herself for check-in:
  (i) at the time stipulated in advance and in writing (including by electronic means) by the air carrier or its agent or the tour operator, or
  (ii) if no time is stipulated, not later than one hour before the published departure time, or
(b) the person arrives at a point within the airport boundary designated in accordance with Article 5:

(i) at the time stipulated in advance and in writing (including by electronic means) by the air carrier or its agent or the tour operator, or

(ii) if no time is stipulated, not later than two hours before the published departure time.

5. When a disabled person or person with reduced mobility transits through an airport to which this Regulation applies, or is transferred by an air carrier or a tour operator from the flight for which he or she holds a reservation to another flight, the managing body shall be responsible for ensuring the provision of the assistance specified in Annex I in such a way that the person is able to take the flight for which he or she holds a reservation.

6. On the arrival by air of a disabled person or person with reduced mobility at an airport to which this Regulation applies, the managing body of the airport shall be responsible for ensuring the provision of the assistance specified in Annex I in such a way that the person is able to reach his or her point of departure from the airport as referred to in Article 5.

7. The assistance provided shall, as far as possible, be appropriate to the particular needs of the individual passenger.

Finally, Regulation (EC) No. 1899/2006,[48] which harmonises technical requirements and administrative procedures in the field of civil aviation, includes several provisions relating to passengers with disabilities and passengers with reduced mobility. It requires that senior cabin crew members have received training with regard to passengers with disabilities, and establishes certain requirements regarding the carriage of persons with reduced mobility.

DID YOU KNOW THAT ...?

Despite the relatively advanced laws adopted by the EU, in several Member States, means of transport are often inaccessible. A number of cases have arisen in connection with transport services, and often public authorities have been considered in breach of the non-discrimination norm because of a lack of accessibility. For example, in Italy, the Municipality of Turin was found liable for discriminating against disabled passengers and

[48] Council Regulation (EC) No. 1899/2006 of 12 December 2006 amending Council Regulation (EEC) No. 3922/91 on the harmonisation of technical requirements and administrative procedures in the field of civil aviation, OJ 2006 No. L377/1.

was ordered to promote transportation for disabled people (as well as to provide compensation to the disabled claimants). The accessibility of parking meters and ticketing machines has also been challenged. The Hungarian Equal Treatment Authority held that the car park authorities were guilty of discrimination by violating the principle of equal treatment, because their system required people to walk some 100m to reach a parking meter and did not make provision for disabled visitors. No penalty was imposed, however, because the car park agreed to amend its procedures. The inaccessibility of the physical infrastructure of a train station was held, by the Court of Appeal of England and Wales, to be unlawful discrimination in *Roads* v. *Central Trains*. (A. Lawson, *Maximising the Impact and Effectiveness of Accessibility Measures for Goods and Services: Learning from National Experience* – Synthesis Report for the Academic Network of European Disability Experts (2012), available at www.disability-europe.net/.)

3.3 Accessibility of Information and Communication

Compared to the general trend evidenced in respect of transport, EU law includes fewer obligations in relation to the accessibility of information and communication. The most relevant provisions in that regard are discussed below.

3.3.1 *Access to EU Documents*

Article 15(3) TFEU confers on EU citizens the right to access documents of the EU institutions, bodies, offices and agencies, subject to certain principles and conditions established in Regulation (EC) No. 1049/2001.[49] This right of access is also enshrined in Article 42 of the Charter of Fundamental Rights of the European Union (EU CFR), which (similarly to the Regulation) does not refer explicitly to accessibility within a disability context. However, Article 10(3) of the Regulation mentions accessible formats. It states that '[d]ocuments shall be supplied in an existing version and format (including electronically or in an alternative format such as Braille, large print or tape) with full regard to the applicant's preference)'. Regulation (EU) No. 216/2013 on the electronic publication of the EU Official Journal recalls the EU's obligations under the CRPD concerning the accessibility of information to users with disabilities.[50]

[49] Council Regulation (EC) No. 1049/2001 of 30 May 2001 regarding public access to European Parliament, Council and Commission documents, OJ 2001 No. L145/43.

[50] Council Regulation (EU) No. 216/2013 of 7 March 2013 on the electronic publication of the Official Journal of the European Union, OJ 2013 No. L69/1.

3.3.2 *Access to Information and Consumer Rights*

Several pieces of legislation include specific provisions on the release of information in accessible formats. As mentioned above, requirements regarding accessible signs and information for travellers with disabilities are included within transport legislation. Moreover, the 2016 Regulation on a European network of employment services (EURES) establishes that the information provided on the EURES portal and support services must be made accessible for persons with disabilities.[51] The Cross-Border Healthcare Directive,[52] which aims to clarify and promote the rights of patients to access healthcare in another EU Member State, stipulates that information about cross-border healthcare is to be provided in accessible formats. Significantly, the Directive also provides that patients with disabilities who need to be accompanied by a personal assistant may also apply for the reimbursement of any additional associated costs incurred, but the decision as to whether or not to refund those costs remains within the discretion of the Member States. Other acts include accessibility requirements related to certain goods and services. For example, Directive 2004/27/EC[53] prescribes that the packaging of medicinal products must include a label in Braille and that an information leaflet related to the product must be available, on request, in formats accessible to visually impaired users.

Provisions on accessibility of information within business-to-consumers (B2C) transactions have not been included explicitly within EU consumer legislation, which regulates rights that facilitate the economic participation of EU citizens in the internal market. However, Directive 2005/29/EC concerning unfair B2C practices (Unfair Commercial Practices Directive)[54] includes provisions about 'particularly vulnerable' consumers.[55] In order to determine the 'unfairness' of commercial practices, the Directive refers to the average consumer, who is reasonably well informed and reasonably observant and circumspect, and aims to protect 'particularly vulnerable' consumers. Vulnerability for the purpose of the Directive is linked to the consumers' 'mental or physical infirmity, age or credulity'. The concept of 'mental or physical

[51] Council Regulation (EU) 2016/589 of 13 April 2016 on a European network of employment services (EURES), workers' access to mobility services and the further integration of labour markets, and amending Regulations (EU) No. 492/2011 and (EU) No. 1296/2013, OJ 2016 No. L107/1.

[52] Council Directive 2011/24/EU of 9 March 2011 on the application of patients' rights in cross-border healthcare, OJ 2011 No. L88/45.

[53] Council Directive 2004/27/EC of 31 March 2004 amending Directive 2001/83/EC on the Community code relating to medicinal products for human use, OJ 2004 No. L136/34.

[54] Council Directive 2005/29/EC of 11 May 2005 concerning unfair business-to-consumer commercial practices in the internal market and amending Council Directive 84/450/EEC, Directives 97/7/EC, 98/27/EC and 2002/65/EC and Regulation (EC) No. 2006/2004 ('Unfair Commercial Practices Directive'), OJ 2005 No. L149/22.

[55] Lisa Waddington, 'Vulnerable and Confused: The Protection of "Vulnerable" Consumers under EU Law' (2013) 38(6) *European Law Review* 757.

infirmity' would appear to cover disability, but the protection that the Directive actually provides is limited. Other legislative instruments (for example, Directive 2011/83/EU on consumer rights)[56] include similar references to vulnerable consumers. However, as Waddington observes, EU instruments make little effort to identify the different causes of 'vulnerability' and they do not provide for targeted responses to remove it.[57] This author argues that, to date (at least until the EAA is approved), the EU has failed to adopt measures 'such as requiring that consumer (credit) information be provided in formats which are accessible to people with visual impairments'.[58] More recent directives seem to provide better protection for consumers with disabilities. For instance, the 2015 Directive on payment services in the internal market[59] obliges service providers to inform consumers of their rights in alternative formats that are accessible to persons with disabilities.

3.3.3 *Access to Information and Communication Technologies*

The importance of accessible ICTs has been recognised by the EU in several distinct pieces of legislation.

The Directive on harmonisation of the laws of the Member States relating to the making available on the market of radio equipment[60] addresses accessibility of telecommunications terminals for persons with disabilities. In addition, the so-called 'Telecoms Package' includes provisions on accessibility of other equipment.[61] In 2016, the Commission adopted a proposal for a European electronic communications code,[62] with the intention of modernising the current EU telecoms rules, stimulating competition and strengthening consumer rights. In June

[56] Council Directive 2011/83/EU of 25 October 2011 on consumer rights, amending Council Directive 93/13/EEC and Directive 1999/44/EC and repealing Council Directive 85/577/EEC and Directive 97/7/EC, OJ 2011 No. L304/64.

[57] Waddington, 'Vulnerable and Confused: The Protection of "Vulnerable" Consumers under EU Law', note 55.

[58] Ibid.

[59] Council Directive 2015/2366/EU of 25 November 2015 on payment services in the internal market, amending Directives 2002/65/EC, 2009/110/EC and 2013/36/EU and Regulation (EU) No. 1093/2010, and repealing Directive 2007/64/EC, OJ 2015 No. L337/35.

[60] Council Directive 2014/53/EU of 16 April 2014 on the harmonisation of the laws of the Member States relating to the making available on the market of radio equipment and repealing Directive 1999/5/EC, OJ 2014 No. L153/62.

[61] In the package, one of the most relevant instruments is Council Directive 2009/140/EC which establishes a harmonised framework for the regulation of electronic communications services, electronic communications networks, associated facilities and associated services, and certain aspects of terminal equipment to facilitate access for disabled users. Council Directive 2009/136/EC makes numerous references to the right to 'equivalent access' of disabled end-users to services available to other end-users.

[62] Proposal for a Council Directive on establishing the European electronic communications code, COM (2016) 590 final. The final text of the Directive was published in the official journal in December 2018: Directive (EU) 2018/1972 of the European Parliament and of the Council of

2018, the Council approved an amended draft of the code, which was then adopted by the Parliament and by the Council in November 2018. The final text of the Directive includes a reference to the CRPD, and several articles highlight the need to improve access for disabled end-users to electronic communications. Member States will have until 21 December 2020 to transpose this new directive into their national legislation.

To date, the most important legislative enactment in this field is Directive 2016/2102/EU on the accessibility of the websites and mobile applications of public sector bodies (Web Accessibility Directive). It aims to make the websites and mobile applications of public sector bodies more accessible to users, in particular to persons with disabilities. It addresses four principles of accessibility: perceivability (i.e. information must be presented in ways that the user can readily perceive), operability (i.e. the user interface and navigation must be operable), understandability (i.e. information and operability must be comprehensible to the user), and robustness (i.e. the content must be sufficiently robust to be interpreted by a wide variety of user groups).[63] It only sets out minimum requirements that have to be met by public sector bodies. In particular, the Web Accessibility Directive requires Member States to ensure that public sector bodies take all necessary measures to make their websites and mobile applications accessible 'by making them perceivable, operable, understandable and robust'. However, it includes a provision placing a limitation on this accessibility obligation, namely Article 5 of the Directive, which affirms that 'Member States shall ensure that public sector bodies apply the accessibility requirements … to the extent that those requirements do not impose a disproportionate burden on the public sector bodies'. Public sector bodies should carry out an initial assessment to decide whether complying with the accessibility requirements in the

> Is the 'disproportionate burden' limitation included in Article 5 of the Web Accessibility Directive compatible with Article 9 CRPD?

11 December 2018 establishing the European Electronic Communications Code (Recast), OJ 2018 No. L 321/36.

[63] Zero Project, 'Minimum Standards of Websites and Mobile Applications by the Public Sector in All 28 EU Countries' (2018), available at https://zeroproject.org/policy/pol183098bel-factsheet/.

Directive imposes a 'disproportionate burden', and, if so, they need to provide accessible alternatives. The Directive makes ample reference to standards designed to make websites and mobile apps more accessible. Those standards will be updated by an implementing act of the Commission. Although the Web Accessibility Directive represents an important step towards ensuring accessible websites across the EU, it has a limited material scope, as it covers only websites and mobile apps of public sector bodies, and it excludes private and commercial websites (which should be covered by the EAA).

3.4 Accessibility of Cultural Goods and Services

3.4.1 *Access to Audiovisual Services*

The Audiovisual Media Services Directive (AVMS)[64] encourages (but does not oblige) Member States to impose accessibility requirements on providers of audiovisual media services. The limited prescriptiveness of the AVMS in this respect has led all Member States to introduce general rules to improve the accessibility of these services for persons with visual or hearing impairments. However, the requirements laid out in Member States' laws usually have a very limited scope and are quite vague.[65] A legislative proposal to amend the Directive was published in 2016 and was then adopted by the European legislators in November 2018.[66] The Preamble to the revised Directive recalls that 'ensuring the accessibility of audiovisual content is an essential requirement in the context of the commitments taken under the [CRPD]' (paragraph 22). Moreover, Article 7 of the revised Directive provides that 'Member States shall ensure, without undue delay, that services provided by media service providers under their jurisdiction are made continuously and progressively more accessible to persons with disabilities through proportionate measures'.

[64] Council Directive 2010/13/EU of 10 March 2010 on the coordination of certain provisions laid down by law, regulation or administrative action in Member States concerning the provision of audiovisual media services (Audiovisual Media Services Directive), OJ 2010 No. L95/1.

[65] See European Parliamentary Research Service, 'The Audiovisual Media Services Directive' (2018), available at www.europarl.europa.eu/RegData/etudes/BRIE/2016/583859/EPRS_BRI%282016%29583859_EN.pdf.

[66] Proposal for a Directive of the European Parliament and of the Council amending Directive 2010/13/EU on the coordination of certain provisions laid down by law, regulation or administrative action in Member States concerning the provision of audiovisual media services in view of changing market realities, COM/2016/0287 final. The new directive, adopted on the basis of that proposal, is Directive (EU) 2018/1808 of 14 November 2018, amending Directive 2010/13/EU on the coordination of certain provisions laid down by law, regulation or administrative action in Member States concerning the provision of audiovisual media services (Audiovisual Media Services Directive) in view of changing market realities, OJ 2018 No. L 303/69). That directive modifies the existing directive on the provision of audiovisual media services from 2010 (note 64).

3.4.2 *Access to Printed Material*

Access to printed material for people with disabilities and, in particular for people with visual impairments, has been a persistent issue globally. As Sganga outlines,[67] statistics show that only 5 per cent of published works are available in accessible formats, and the number falls to 1 per cent in developing countries. In addition to the high costs of production and distribution, and the full reliance on public funds and intervention of public or non-profit organisations, copyright has traditionally represented an obstacle to the broader availability of accessible works.[68]

In Europe, copyright has been heavily regulated by the EU. From 1991 until 2017, ten harmonisation Directives, two Regulations and two recast Directives have been passed.[69] Most of the EU's copyright legislation was approved before the entry into force of the Lisbon Treaty as well as prior to the ratification of the CRPD. In terms of accessibility for people with disabilities, one of the most relevant pieces of legislation is Directive 2001/29/EC (InfoSoc Directive),[70] which sets out a harmonised legal framework on copyright and related rights. The Directive allows Member States to make exceptions to copyright regulations in respect of reproductions for the benefit of people with disabilities. In particular, recital 43 of the Preamble underlines the need for Member States to adopt all necessary measures to facilitate access to protected works 'by persons suffering from a disability which constitutes an obstacle to the use of the works themselves' and to devote specific attention to accessible formats. In its original formulation, Article 5(3)(b) provided an optional exception for the 'uses, for the benefit of people with a disability, which are directly related to the disability and of a non-commercial nature, to the extent required by the specific disability'. However, in 2008, the EU Commission published the Green Paper on Copyright in the Knowledge Economy,[71] which, *inter alia*, inquired into the opportunity to widen the exception provided for in Article 5(3)(b) and to extend it to all forms of disabilities; to oblige publishers to make available accessible copies of their

[67] Caterina Sganga, 'Disability, Right to Culture and Copyright: Which Regulatory Option?', in Delia Ferri and Anthony Giannoumis (eds.), *Fostering Accessible Technology through Regulation* (Abingdon: Routledge, 2016), p. 10.

[68] Ibid.

[69] European Commission, 'Digital Single Market: The EU Copyright Legislation', available at https://ec.europa.eu/digital-single-market/en/eu-copyright-legislation. The European Commission proposed a copyright reform on 14 September 2016. The proposed Directive updates the existing set of rules on copyright to make them suitable for a well-functioning Digital Single Market. At the time of writing this book, the reform is under discussion in the EU legislative institutions.

[70] Council Directive 2001/29/EC of 22 June 2001 on the harmonisation of certain aspects of copyright and related rights in the information society, OJ 2001 No. L167/10.

[71] European Commission, *Green Paper – Copyright in the Knowledge Economy*, COM (2008) 466 final, 16 July 2008.

protected works; and to facilitate licensing schemes with publishers to increase the availability of accessible materials. In the follow-up Communication,[72] building on the responses received to the Green Paper, the Commission emphasised the need for the Union and its Member States to respect Articles 4, 9, 21 and 30 CRPD. The Commission also recommended the creation of a stakeholder group to propose new policy responses that are compliant with the CRPD. The main result of the stakeholder dialogue group was the Memorandum of Understanding (MoU), signed on 14 September 2010 by the European Blind Union and the Federation of European Publishers, with the aim of increasing the number of accessible works and facilitating their cross-border circulation by relying on a standardised licence agreement.[73] Article 5(3)(b) was then amended in 2017 by virtue of Article 8 of the Directive 2017/1564/EU.[74] That provision[75] establishes a mandatory and harmonised exception to copyright protection that will enable copies of works made available in accessible formats (e.g. Braille, large print or audiobooks) in one Member State to be disseminated and accessed throughout the EU, without prior permission from the rights-holders.

The Directive is complemented by Regulation (EU) No. 2017/1563,[76] which allows the cross-border exchange of accessible format copies between the EU and third countries that are Party to the Marrakesh Treaty.[77]

[72] Commission Communication of 19 October 2009, Copyright in the Knowledge Economy, COM (2009) 532 final.

[73] Dan Pescod and Alicia Wise, 'EU Stakeholders Dialogue Memorandum of Understanding (MOU) On Access to Works by People with Print Disabilities' (2010), available at http://ec.europa.eu/internal_market/copyright/docs/copyright-infso/2010/20100914_mou_en.pdf.

[74] Council Directive (EU) 2017/1564 of 13 September 2017 on certain permitted uses of certain works and other subject matter protected by copyright and related rights for the benefit of persons who are blind, visually impaired or otherwise print-disabled and amending Directive 2001/29/EC on the harmonisation of certain aspects of copyright and related rights in the information society, OJ 2017 No. L242/6.

[75] This provision implements the Marrakesh Treaty to Facilitate Access to Published Works for Persons Who Are Blind, Visually Impaired or Otherwise Print Disabled, which was adopted in 2013, and currently forms part of the body of international copyright treaties administered by the World Intellectual Property Organization (WIPO). As previously mentioned in Chapter 9, the Marrakesh Treaty requires contracting parties to create exceptions or limitations to copyright and related rights for the making and dissemination of copies, in accessible formats, of certain works and other protected subject matter, and for the cross-border exchange of those copies. See above Chapter 9.

[76] Council Regulation (EU) 2017/1563 of 13 September 2017 on the cross-border exchange between the Union and third countries of accessible format copies of certain works and other subject matter protected by copyright and related rights for the benefit of persons who are blind, visually impaired or otherwise print disabled, OJ 2007 No. L242/1, 20 September 2017 (Marrakesh Regulation).

[77] The EU also signed the Marrakesh Treaty on 30 April 2014. It was only in February 2018, however, after having obtained the European Parliament's consent, that the Council of the EU finally adopted a decision approving the conclusion of the Marrakesh Treaty. The conclusion of this treaty took much longer than the ratification of the CRPD because of the

4 THE EUROPEAN ACCESSIBILITY ACT

A proposal for the EAA should have been released by the Commission in 2012. However, the work on the proposed text took far longer than initially envisaged. The proposal for the EAA was only published in December 2015.[78] After a long process (as shown in Figure 12.2), in December 2017, an agreement on the text of the EEA was reached in the Council, after the European Parliament had already adopted its position in September 2017. The final text of the EAA was approved by the European Parliament in March 2019. The Council officially adopted the EAA in April 2019.

The EAA is based on Article 114 TFEU and is considered to be a business-friendly proposal that should improve the proper functioning of the internal market for accessible goods and services. It aims to harmonise accessibility requirements for a specified list of products and services. The EAA does not intend to impose detailed technical solutions to make a product or service accessible. Rather, it seeks to establish 'accessibility principles' to be complemented by supplementary standards.

The EAA states that accessibility:

> should be achieved by the systematic removal and prevention of barriers, preferably through a universal design or 'design for all' approach, which contributes to ensuring access for persons with disabilities on an equal basis with others.

In compliance with the CRPD, the EAA affirms that universal design (UD) should not exclude assistive devices or reasonable accommodation when required.

initial disagreement between the Commission and the Council regarding the nature of the EU's competence in that regard (namely, whether it was an exclusive or shared competence). The Commission had taken the view that the EU had an exclusive competence, and no ratification of the Member States was necessary. By contrast, several Member States considered that their participation was necessary. To overcome the impasse, the Commission asked the CJEU to give its opinion on the matter, and the Court, in February 2017, confirmed the exclusive competence of the EU to conclude the Marrakesh Treaty (*Opinion 3/2015*, ECLI:EU:C:2017:114). On the CJEU Opinion, see Amedeo Arena, 'The ERTA Pre-Emption Effects of Minimum and Partial Harmonisation Directives: Insights from Opinion 3/15 on the Competence to Conclude the Marrakesh Treaty', (2018) 43(5) *European Law Review* 770.

[78] Proposal for a Directive of the European Parliament and of the Council on the approximation of the laws, regulations and administrative provisions of the Member States as regards the accessibility requirements for products and services, COM/2015/0615 final. The final text was published in the Official Journal in June 2019: (Directive (EU) 2019/882 of the European Parliament and of the Council of 17 April 2019 on the accessibility requirements for products and services, OJ 2019 L 151/70).

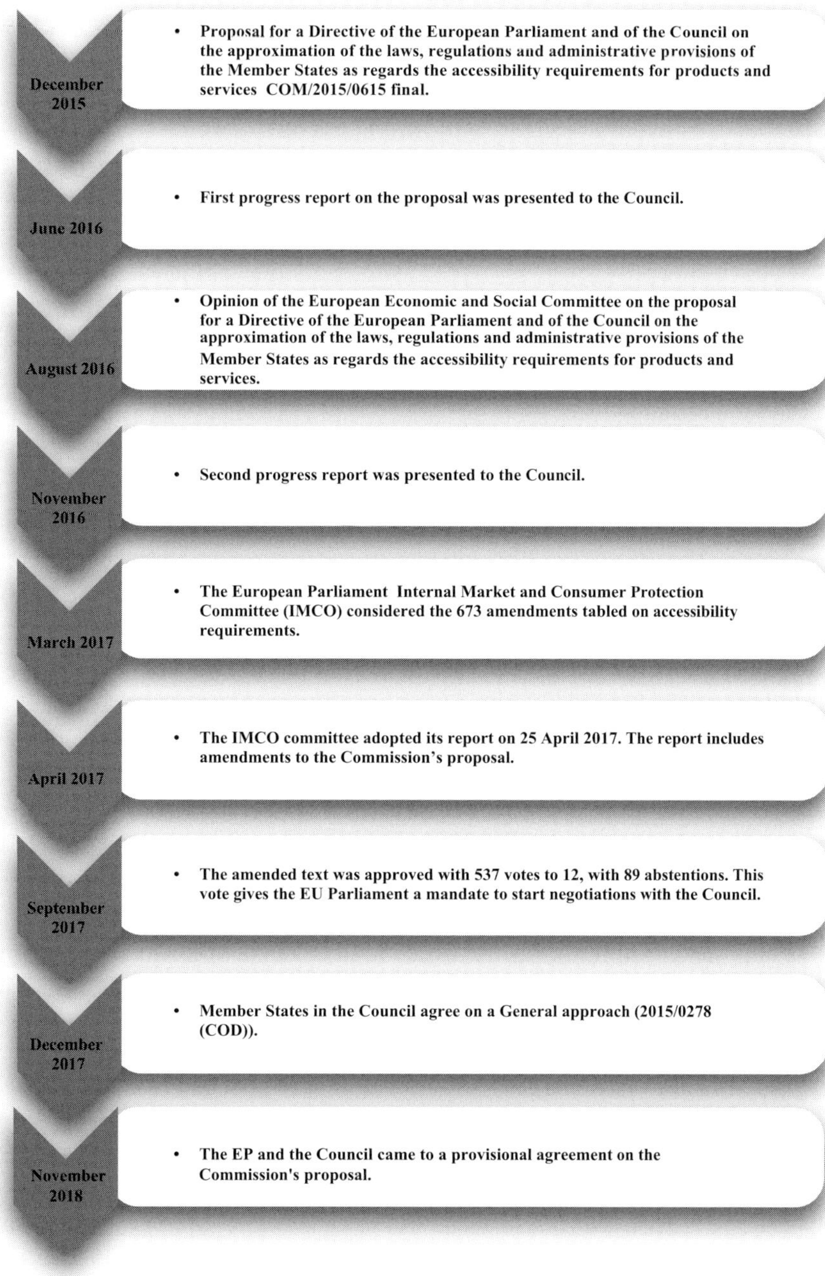

Figure 12.2 The 'Long Road' towards the European Accessibility Act

The material scope of the EAA is quite wide. The EAA applies to: computer hardware systems and operating systems; consumer terminal equipment; e-readers; Automated Teller Machines; payment terminals; ticketing machines; check-in machines used to check passengers in for passenger transport services; and interactive self-service terminals providing information (excluding machines installed as integrated parts of vehicles, aircrafts, ships or rolling stock). Moreover, it applies to a range of services: electronic communications services (with the exception of services used for the provision of machine-to-machine services); services providing access to audiovisual media services; e-books and dedicated software; e-commerce; consumer banking services; and certain elements of bus, rail and waterborne passenger transport services. With regard to the latter, the EAA should complement sectoral legislation, by ensuring that transport companies' websites, mobile applications, including ticket services, and information on transport services are fully accessible across the EU. The EAA also applies to all businesses, except microenterprises providing services within the scope of the Directive. The latter are distinguished from all other undertakings by their limited human resources and annual turnover or annual balance sheet and are exempt from complying with the accessibility requirements referred to in the Act.[79]

In the text of the EAA accessibility obligations are imposed on manufacturers, distributors, importers and service providers. However, these obligations should apply to the extent that they do not introduce a significant change in a product or service that alters the basic nature of the product or service, or to the extent that they do not impose a disproportionate burden on the economic operators concerned. In a similar vein to what is provided for in the Employment Equality Directive with regard to reasonable accommodation duties, if funding has been specifically allocated by public or private supports in order to ensure accessibility, the economic operator cannot claim that applying the accessibility requirements would impose a disproportionate burden.

[79] While Article 4 of the EAA exempts microenterprises providing services within the scope of the Directive from complying with the accessibility requirements referred to in the Directive, para. 71 of the Preamble states that '[f]or microenterprises dealing with products falling within the scope of this Directive the requirements and obligations of this Directive should be lighter in order to reduce the administrative burden'. Moreover, para. 72 of the Preamble encourages microenterprises 'to manufacture, import or distribute products and to provide services that comply with the accessibility requirements of this Directive, in order to increase their competitiveness as well as their growth potential in the internal market'. A precise definition of microenterprise is included in Article 3 of the EAA.

5 ACCESSIBILITY REQUIREMENTS IN EUROPEAN UNION PUBLIC PROCUREMENT LAW

Read the extracts from Directive 2014/25/EU in the boxes below, and discuss their content *vis-à-vis* Article 27 CRPD.

According to the European Commission, every year, over 250,000 public authorities in the EU spend approximately 14 per cent of their Gross Domestic Product (GDP) on the purchase of goods and services.[80] Public procurement refers to the process by which public authorities (for example, government departments, agencies, regional or local authorities) purchase those goods or services from private enterprises.

In the last few years, public procurement legislation has become a key 'instrument to achieve smart, sustainable and inclusive growth' and a tool to foster cross-border trade.[81] The 2014 European Directives on Public Procurement,[82] replacing similar instruments from 2004, provide that, rather than only awarding a contract on the basis of the best price, authorities are encouraged to seek and demand innovative, energy-saving solutions or insist on sustainable and socially inclusive approaches. In this context, public authorities are allowed to implement various measures to advance the rights of persons with disabilities. Notably, both 2014 Directives allow Member States to reserve the right to participate in public procurement to operators who employ persons with disabilities and/or whose main aim is their social integration.

ARTICLE 38 OF DIRECTIVE 2014/25/EU

1. Member States may reserve the right to participate in procurement procedures to sheltered workshops and economic operators whose main aim is

[80] Data retrieved from https://ec.europa.eu/growth/single-market/public-procurement_it.

[81] Commission Communication of 28 October 2015, Upgrading the Single Market: more opportunities for people and business, COM (2015) 550.

[82] Council Directive 2014/24/EU of 26 February 2014 on public procurement and repealing Directive 2004/18/EC, OJ 2014 No. L94/65; Council Directive 2014/25/EU of 26 February 2014 on procurement by entities operating in the water, energy, transport and postal services sectors and repealing Directive 2004/17/EC, OJ 2014 No. L94/243.

the social and professional integration of disabled or disadvantaged persons or may provide for such contracts to be performed in the context of sheltered employment programmes, provided that at least 30% of the employees of those workshops, economic operators or programmes are disabled or disadvantaged workers.

2. The call for competition shall make reference to this Article.

Secondly, and perhaps more importantly for the purpose of this chapter, the 2014 Directives also include several provisions that exploit the potential for public procurement to advance the accessibility of good and services, substantially strengthening the provisions set forth in the 2004 directives.[83] Both Directives set out that technical specifications in all public tenders 'shall, except in duly justified cases, be drawn up so as to take into account accessibility criteria for persons with disabilities or design for all users' (Article 60 of Directive 2014/25/EU and Article 42 of Directive 2014/24/EU). This means that public authorities can only purchase accessible goods and services.

ARTICLE 42(1) OF DIRECTIVE 2014/24/EU

1. The technical specifications as defined in point 1 of Annex VII shall be set out in the procurement documents. The technical specification shall lay down the characteristics required of a works, service or supply.

Those characteristics may also refer to the specific process or method of production or provision of the requested works, supplies or services or to a specific process for another stage of its life cycle even where such factors do not form part of their material substance provided that they are linked to the subject-matter of the contract and proportionate to its value and its objectives.

The technical specifications may also specify whether the transfer of intellectual property rights will be required.

For all procurement which is intended for use by natural persons, whether general public or staff of the contracting authority, the technical specifications shall, except in duly justified cases, be drawn up so as to take into account accessibility criteria for persons with disabilities or design for all users.

Where mandatory accessibility requirements are adopted by a legal act of the Union, technical specifications shall, as far as accessibility criteria for persons with disabilities or design for all users are concerned, be defined by reference thereto.

[83] Rosemary Boyle, 'Disability Issues in Public Procurement', in Sue Arrowsmith and Peter Kunzlik (eds.), *Social and Environmental Policies in EC Procurement Law: New Directives and New Directions* (Cambridge: Cambridge University Press, 2009), pp. 310–44.

On the whole, the 2014 Directives enable Member States to make more disability-oriented usage of public procurement and, furthermore, usage that is compliant with the CRPD.

6 ACCESSIBILITY AND STANDARDISATION

EU policy on standardisation is an important tool to eliminate barriers to trade and enhance the internal market. This section explains what constitutes a 'standard' and discusses EU standardisation policy and legislation. It then examines the most relevant standardisation mandates issued by the European Commission as well as the standards adopted on accessibility to date.

6.1 Standardisation Bodies and Standards

Lemley defines a standard as 'any set of technical specifications that either provides or is intended to provide a common design for a product or process'.[84] According to the International Organization for Standardization (ISO), a standard is a 'document, established by consensus, and approved by a recognised body, that provides for common and repeated use, rules, guidelines, or characteristics for activities or their results, aimed at the achievement of the optimum degree of order in a given context'.[85] Standards are usually issued by Standard-Setting Organisations (SSOs),[86] i.e. bodies that typically consist of industry representatives and other stakeholders. They may relate to the built environment, the goods and services which are offered on the market, transportation, or ICTs. Hosking notes that 'the most extensive and longest collaboration among industry, disabled people and regulators is in the ICT field'.[87] Standards are generally voluntary, and their regulative force is

[84] Mark Lemley, 'Intellectual Property Rights and Standard-Setting Organizations' (2002) *California Law Review*, available at https://scholarship.law.berkeley.edu/californialawreview/vol90/iss6/3/.

[85] International Organization for Standardization, *Rules for Structure and Drafting of International Standards*, 4th edn (Geneva: ISO/IEC, 2001), p. 9.

[86] These are generally termed 'co-operative or committee standards'. For a succinct overview of European Standard-Setting Organisations (SSOs), see Kevin Coates, *Competition and Regulation of Technology Markets* (Oxford: Oxford University Press, 2011), pp. 185–6. Not all standards are created by SSOs. A standard may arise from the operation of the market, as consumers gravitate towards a single product or protocol and reject its competitors. For example, the Microsoft operating systems are *de facto* standards; see Maureen O'Rourke, 'Striking a Delicate Balance: Intellectual Property, Antitrust, Contract, and Standardization in the Computer Industry' (1998) *Harvard Journal of Law and Technology*, available at http://jolt.law.harvard.edu/articles/pdf/v12/12HarvJLTech001.pdf.

[87] David Hosking, 'Promoting Accessibility for Disabled People Using EU Standardisation Policy' (2017) 42(2) *European Law Review* 145.

grounded in their perceived legitimacy. However, they can be implemented or incorporated within domestic legal frameworks by way of legislative provisions.

Within the EU, standards 'may facilitate market integration and allow companies to market their goods and services in all Member States, leading to increased consumer choice and decreasing prices'.[88]

6.2 EU Standardisation Policy in a Nutshell

A regulatory approach towards standardisation and a proper EU standardisation policy dates back to 1983 when, in order to prevent barriers to trade, the Mutual Information Directive[89] was adopted. That Directive required Member States to inform the Commission and the European Standardisation Organisations (ESOs) – the European Committee for Standardization (CEN) and the European Committee for Electrotechnical Standardization (CENELEC) – of their plans to put standards in place. In addition, Member States were to ensure that national standards would not conflict with those set by the CEN and CENELEC.[90] In 1985, the EU launched a 'New Approach' to standardisation,[91] which was then realised by means of Directive 98/34/EC[92] and other subsequent pieces of legislation. This 'New Approach' was based on four principles, which remain in place to this day. First, legislative harmonisation is limited to the adoption of directives detailing the essential safety, health, environmental or other requirements with which products must conform in order to enjoy free movement throughout the Union. Secondly, the task of

[88] Directorate for Financial and Enterprise Affairs Competition Committee, *Working Party No. 2 on Competition and Regulation-Standard Setting* (2010) DAF/COMP/WP2/WD 29, available at http://ec.europa.eu/competition/international/multilateral/2010_standardsetting.pdf; the Preamble to Council Regulation (EU) No. 1025/2012 of 25 October 2012 on European standardisation, amending Council Directives 89/686/EEC and 93/15/EEC and Directives 94/9/EC, 94/25/EC, 95/16/EC, 97/23/EC, 98/34/EC, 2004/22/EC, 2007/23/EC, 2009/23/EC and 2009/105/EC and repealing Council Decision 87/95/EEC and Decision No. 1673/2006/EC, OJ 2010 No. L316/12, states: 'Standards thus normally increase competition and lower output and sales costs, benefiting economies as a whole and consumers in particular. Standards may maintain and enhance quality, provide information and ensure interoperability and compatibility, thereby increasing safety and value for consumers' (Recital 3).

[89] Council Directive 83/189/EEC of 28 March 1983 laying down a procedure for the provision of information in the field of technical standards and regulations, OJ 1983 No. L109/8.

[90] On the early standardisation policy, see Barend Van Leeuwen, *European Standardisation of Services and its Impact on Private Law: Paradoxes of Convergence* (Oxford/Portland: Hart Publishing, 2017), ch. 3.

[91] Council Resolution 85/C 136/01 of 7 May 1985 on a new approach to technical harmonization and standards, OJ 1985 No. C136/1.

[92] Council Directive 98/34/EC of 22 June 1998 laying down a procedure for the provision of information in the field of technical standards and regulations, OJ 1998 No. L204/37.

drawing up technical production specifications is given to standardisation bodies. Thirdly, technical specifications are not mandatory and maintain their status of voluntary standards. Fourthly, national authorities are obliged to recognise that products manufactured in conformity with harmonised standards are presumed to conform to the essential requirements established by Directive 98/34/EC. The Directive also formally identified the CEN, the CENELEC and the European Telecommunications Standards Institute (ETSI) as European standardisation bodies.

In 2012, Regulation (EU) No. 1025/2012 reformed and streamlined the European standardisation system and repealed previous legislation.[93] Its main goal was 'to cover new aspects of standardisation to reflect those latest developments and future challenges in European standardisation'. The Regulation sets out rules for the establishment of European standards, the identification of ICT technical specifications as well as the financing of European standardisation and stakeholder participation. It establishes that an annual work programme is to be adopted by the Commission to identify the strategic priorities for European standardisation. The regulation also endeavours to highlight the link between standards and other Union policies, including disability policy. In particular, recital 19 of the Preamble states that:

> [s]tandards can contribute to helping Union policy address the major societal challenges such as climate change, sustainable resource use, innovation, ageing population, integration of people with disabilities, consumer protection, workers' safety and working conditions.

In addition, recital 24 of the Regulation affirms that European standardisation systems should take into account the CRPD, and it refers to the participation of persons with disabilities in the standard-setting process.

6.3 Accessibility Standards

As noted by Hosking, the 'Commission has used standardisation policy to promote its disability policy agenda for many years'.[94] Mandate 273, issued by the Commission in 1998, called for standards for disabled and elderly people's access to information and communications with a view to promoting their integration and independence and improve their quality of life.[95] In 1999,

[93] Council Regulation (EU) No. 1025/2012 of 25 October 2012 on European standardisation, amending Council Directives 89/686/EEC and 93/15/EEC and Directives 94/9/EC, 94/25/EC, 95/16/EC, 97/23/EC, 98/34/EC, 2004/22/EC, 2007/23/EC, 2009/23/EC and 2009/105/EC and repealing Council Decision 87/95/EEC and Decision No. 1673/2006/EC, OJ 2012 No. L316/12.

[94] Hosking, 'Promoting Accessibility for Disabled People Using EU Standardisation Policy', note 87, at 158.

[95] European Commission, 'M/273 Mandate to the European Standards Bodies for Standardization in the field of information and communications technologies (ICT) for

the Commission issued Mandate 283, to develop a 'guidance document' for the creation of safe and usable products for 'people with special needs'. This guidance was then published in 2001, in cooperation with the ISO and the International Electrotechnical Commission (IEC), in the form of CEN/CENELEC Guide 6 and ISO/IEC Guide 71, which were then amended and reissued in 2014.[96]

In 2005, the Commission also identified as a core priority the development of accessibility standards in the field of ICT for use in public procurement in the context of Mandate 376 – 'Accessibility requirements suitable for public procurement of ICT products and services in Europe'. This is probably the most notable and successful Mandate adopted thus far. It was meant to complement the 2004 Directives on Public Procurement, and its objective was to identify a set of functional European accessibility requirements and to provide an electronic toolkit so that public authorities could use the relevant requirements in their calls for tender. After the preparation of 'an inventory of European and international functional accessibility requirements and of gaps in existing requirements',[97] a user-friendly list of functional accessibility requirements for ICT products and services was developed. That standard – European Standard EN 301 549 – was adopted in 2014. It is a voluntary standard, clarifying the functional accessibility requirements applicable to ICT products and services. Moreover, it forms 'the basis for an accessible ICT procurement toolkit' and aims to be a useful tool with which public procurers can identify the requirements for their purchases, and one which manufacturers can employ within their design, building and quality control procedures. According to the Commission, the aforementioned standard achieves significant harmonisation with the standards set in the US.

In 2007, the Commission issued Mandate 420 to develop standards in support of accessibility requirements for public procurement in the built environment and to complement the Public Procurement Directive's requirement that technical specifications set out in contracting documents should take into account accessibility criteria for people with disabilities. Additionally, in 2010, the Commission issued Mandate 473[98] with the objective of including UD principles in all relevant standardisation initiatives. The work to elaborate those standards is currently ongoing.

disabled and elderly people' (1998), available at http://ec.europa.eu/growth/tools-databases/mandates/index.cfm?fuseaction=search.detail&id=183#.

[96] Hosking, 'Promoting Accessibility for Disabled People Using EU Standardisation Policy', note 87, at 158. See above Chapter 5.

[97] Ibid. at 159.

[98] European Commission, 'Standardisation Mandates', available at http://ec.europa.eu/growth/tools-databases/mandates/index.cfm?fuseaction=search.detail&id=461.

7 THE ROLE OF STATE AID LAW IN ENHANCING ACCESSIBILITY AND DISABILITY RIGHTS

Alongside EU regulations and directives, EU state aid policy represents an important tool that can be employed in enhancing the rights of persons with disabilities. After introducing EU state aid policy, this section discusses the most relevant EU law provisions that allow Member States to use public funding to improve accessibility and promote the rights of disabled people.

7.1 Overview of EU State Aid Law

State aid control is a distinctive feature of EU competition law[99] and was originally inserted in the Treaties, with the intention of maintaining a level playing field for undertakings and avoiding a 'subsidy race' between Member States that would undermine the creation and functioning of the internal market.[100] Article 107(1) TFEU provides that any aid granted by a Member State or through state resources, which distorts, or threatens to distort, competition by favouring certain undertakings or the production of certain goods, is incompatible with the internal market, in so far as it affects trade between the Member States. State measures are prohibited if the cumulative criteria listed in Article 107(1) TFEU (namely, transfer of state resources, conferral of economic advantage, selectivity, distortion of competition, and effect on trade between Member States) are satisfied. The concept of state aid is more general than that of a subsidy, and encompasses positive benefits, but also measures which, in various forms, mitigate the charges imposed on an undertaking. It is also an objective concept,[101] and the Commission has 'no margin of discretion' in its application.[102] In addition, under well-established case law, Article 107 (1) TFEU 'does not distinguish between the measures of [s]tate intervention concerned by reference to their causes or aims but defines them in relation to their effects'.[103] Article 107(1) TFEU is addressed to Member States and regulates the conduct of governments,[104] imposing strict limits on their ability

[99] Kelyn Bacon (ed.), *European Union Law of State Aid*, 3rd edn (Oxford: Oxford University Press, 2017), p. 4.

[100] Buendía Serra, through an interesting metaphor, affirmed that state aid control has indeed the chromosomes of an internal market policy, being premised on the understanding that aid can function as a trade barrier. Jose Luis Buendía Sierra, 'Not Like this: Some Skeptical Remarks on the "Refined Economic Approach" in State Aid' (2006) *Proceedings of 4th EStALI Expert's Forum on New Developments in European State aid Law.*

[101] Case C-83/98 P, *France* v. *Ladbroke Racing and Commission* ECLI:EU:C:1997:531, para. 25.

[102] European Commission, *Report on the implementation of the Commission Notice on the application of the state aid rules to measures* (9 February 2004), C(2004) 434, p. 6.

[103] Case 173/73, *Italy* v. *Commission* ECLI:EU:C:1974:71, para. 13.

[104] Bacon (ed.), *European Union Law of State Aid*, note 99, p. 4.

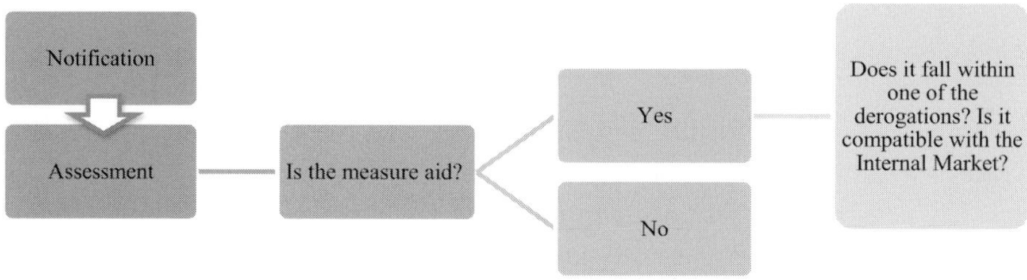

Figure 12.3 State Aid Control

to pursue their own policy objectives. The blanket prohibition on state aid is, however, accompanied by a set of exceptions laid down in Articles 107(2) and (3) TFEU. Those exceptions are premised on the assumption that markets are not entirely self-regulating. Consequently, some intervention from the state may be needed for markets to work more effectively or to respond to social constraints.

EU state aid control is based on a system of *ex ante* authorisation by the Commission under Article 108(3) TFEU. This means that state aid measures are prohibited unless the Commission has been notified of the aid, has assessed it under Article 107(2) or (3) TFEU and has approved it, as shown in Figure 12.3.

These Treaty rules on state aid are complemented by a composite system of regulations, guidelines and soft law documents issued by the Commission. Article 109 TFEU, in fact, allows for the adoption of secondary legislation in the field of state aid. Under that provision, the Council adopted Regulation 994/98,[105] i.e. the Enabling Regulation, which has empowered the Commission to adopt individual regulations in which it declares certain types of aid to be lawful and exempts them from the obligation of prior notification under Article 108(3) TFEU. Further to the Enabling Regulation, the Commission has issued a series of exemption regulations,[106] consolidated in the 2008 General Block Exemption Regulation (GBER),[107] which was subsequently replaced by a

[105] Council Regulation (EC) No. 994/98 of 7 May 1998 on the application of Articles 92 and 93 EC Treaty [now Articles 107 and 108 TFEU respectively] to certain categories of horizontal State aid, OJ 1998 No. L142/1.

[106] Commission Regulations (EC) No. 68/2001 of 12 January 2001 on the application of Articles 87 and 88 of the EC Treaty to training aid, OJ 2001 No. L10/20, 70/2001 of 12 January 2001 on the application of Articles 87 and 88 of the EC Treaty to State aid to small and medium-sized enterprises, OJ 2001 No. L10/33, 2204/2001, OJ 2001 No. L337/3 and 1628/2006, OJ 2006 No. L32/29.

[107] Commission Regulation (EC) No. 800/2008 of 6 August 2008 declaring certain categories of aid compatible with the common market in application of Articles 87 and 88 of the Treaty – General Block Exemption Regulation, OJ 2008 No. L214/3, amended by Commission Regulation (EU) No. 1224/2013 of 29 November 2013 amending Regulation (EC) No. 800/2008 as regards its period of application, OJ 2013 No. L320/2.

new GBER in 2014.[108] The GBER lays down the conditions under which aid can be considered compatible with the internal market and exempted from prior notification.

7.2 Treaty Derogations and Disability

As mentioned above, state aid is prohibited unless the Commission has been notified of the aid, has assessed it under Article 107(2) or (3) TFEU and has approved it. The former provision, Article 107(2) specifies a number of cases in which national support measures are permissible. In other words, it provides for so-called automatic justifications or derogations. In particular, social aid under Article 107(2)(a) TFEU[109] allows Member States to adopt measures having 'a social character' granted to individual consumers, without discrimination in terms of the origin of the products. This derogation not only allows and justifies a state intervention to protect certain disadvantaged segments of the population but also allows intervention by the state which is designed to protect and promote certain social rights. In the past, the Commission had argued that the term 'social character' should be interpreted narrowly and had consistently referred to aid 'addressing the needs of underprivileged population groups'.[110] This strict interpretation was in line with the general principle that 'the exceptions to the general rule of incompatibility of the aid with the [internal] market must be interpreted narrowly'.[111] The concept of 'aid having a social character' was interpreted as aid solely and directly targeted at disadvantaged sections of the population and had primarily been applied in the air transport sector. In several decisions, the Commission allowed for reduced airline fares for the benefit of people with disabilities or allowed for broadband incentives for people with disabilities. Although Article 107(2) has not been directly used to foster accessibility, it has been an important tool in enhancing the rights of persons with disabilities in respect of transportation. In addition, besides allowing for reduced transport fares, it has allowed

[108] Commission Regulation (EU) No. 651/2014 of 17 June 2014 declaring certain categories of aid compatible with the internal market in application of Articles 107 and 108 of the Treaty Text with EEA relevance, OJ 2014 No. L187/1.

[109] Article 107(2)(b) TFEU lists aid that 'makes good the damage caused by natural disasters or exceptional occurrences'. This provision also mentions at letter (c): 'aid granted to the economy of certain areas of the Federal Republic of Germany affected by the division of Germany, in so far as such aid is required in order to compensate for the economic disadvantages caused by that division'. This exemption is of limited practical relevance, and is now *ex lege* repealed.

[110] Commission Decision 2007/374/EC of 24 January 2007 on State aid C 52/2005 (ex NN 88/2005, ex CP 101/2004) implemented by the Italian Republic for the subsidised purchase of digital decoders (notified under document number C(2006) 6634), OJ 2007 No. L147/1.

[111] Ibid.

Read the 2009 Criteria for the compatibility analysis of state aid to disadvantaged and disabled workers subject to individual notification. Can you connect them to specific obligations laid down in the CRPD?

Member States to subsidise digital decoders for persons with disabilities,[112] enhancing their right to information (provided for in Article 21 CRPD).

Article 107(3) TFEU affirms that some forms of aid may be considered compatible with the internal market. In other words, it provides for discretionary justifications or derogations. While well-established case law has repeatedly stated that Article 107(3) must be interpreted strictly,[113] the Commission, when comparing and balancing the positive effects of the aid against the distortion of competition that it causes, enjoys a significant discretion in carrying out an assessment of economic, technical and policy considerations. Among these discretionary derogations, Article 107(3)(c) TFEU, concerning aid to facilitate the development of certain economic activities or of certain economic areas, where such aid does not adversely affect trading conditions to an extent contrary to the common interest, is probably the most relevant in a disability context. Under this provision, the Commission has, to date, allowed aid measures indirectly related to the social inclusion of vulnerable groups, including people with disabilities. Moreover, a series of soft law documents have clarified the way in which the Commission carries out its assessment and have identified specific social goals. For example, in 2009, the Commission set out the criteria relating to the manner in which the compatibility of notified aid measures for disadvantaged and disabled workers were assessed (i.e. individual aid targeted to combat unemployment of persons with disabilities, granted either *ad hoc* or as a part of a scheme where the grant exceeds 10 million euros).[114]

[112] State Aid No. 31982/2010 – Spain Digital decoders for persons with visual disabilities in Spain; see also, State Aid No. 36124/2013/N – Poland Prolongation of the scheme 'Compensation of costs incurred for the provision of services which are statutorily exempted from postage fees'.

[113] Among many others, Case 730/79, *Philip Morris* v. *Commission*, ECLI:EU:C:1980:209.

[114] Commission Communication of 11 August 2009, Criteria for the compatibility analysis of state aid to disadvantaged and disabled workers subject to individual notification, OJ 2009 No. C188/6.

7.3 The General Block Exemption Regulation

Commission Regulation (EU) No. 651/2014 declaring certain categories of aid compatible with the internal market in application of Articles 107 and 108 of the Treaty, better known as the GBER,[115] was adopted within the frame of the State Aid Modernisation (SAM) package.[116] This GBER replaced, and deeply revised, the former regulation, which had been passed in 2008.[117] Like its predecessor, it sets out the categories of aid and the conditions under which aid measures can receive the benefit of an exemption from notification, defines the eligible beneficiaries, the maximum proportion of the eligible costs and eligible expenses. Notably, the GBER significantly extends the possibilities for Member States to grant aid, without prior notification and approval by the Commission.

The GBER includes several disability-related provisions. It also makes express reference to the EDS and to the CRPD. Recognising that 'certain categories of disadvantaged workers and workers with disabilities still experience particular difficulties in entering and remaining in the labour market',[118] the GBER, as its predecessor did, includes specific rules on aid for the employment of workers with disabilities and aid compensating for the additional costs of employing workers with disabilities in the form of wage subsidies. Article 34 GBER lays down the criteria for aid designed to compensate for the additional costs of employing workers with disabilities to be exempted from notification. Those costs encompass the costs of adapting premises and of employing staff solely to assist the worker with a disability, of adapting or acquiring and/or validating specific equipment and software. In addition, the 2014 GBER includes the costs of training staff to assist workers with disabilities, the costs directly linked to transport of workers with disabilities to the workplace and for work-related activities, and wage costs for the hours spent by a worker with disabilities on rehabilitation. Article 53 (on culture and heritage conservation) and Article 54 (on aid for audiovisuals) are also very relevant. The rationale for these rules is to allow (and possibly to encourage) public funding designed to guarantee the

[115] Commission Regulation (EU) No. 651/2014 of 17 June 2014 declaring certain categories of aid compatible with the internal market in application of Articles 107 and 108 of the Treaty, OJ 2014 No. L187/1.

[116] Commission Communication of 8 May 2012, EU State Aid Modernisation (SAM), COM (2012) 0209 final, paras. 20–1.

[117] Commission Regulation (EC) No. 800/2008 of 6 August 2008 declaring certain categories of aid compatible with the common market in application of Articles 87 and 88 of the Treaty – General Block Exemption Regulation, OJ 2008 No. L214/3 (amended by Commission Regulation (EU) No. 1224/2013 of 29 November 2013 amending Regulation (EC) No. 800/2008 as regards its period of application, OJ 2013 No. L320/2).

[118] Recital 54 of the Preamble. This recital echoes the former text, namely Recital 64 of the 2008 GBER.

protection of cultural and linguistic identities across the EU and the multiplicity of artistic expressions. However, remarkably, both Articles 53 and 54 contain references to accessibility for persons with disabilities. Article 53(4)(d) GBER provides that aid can cover:

> costs for improving the accessibility of cultural heritage to the public, including costs for digitisation and other new technologies, costs to improve accessibility for persons with special needs (in particular, ramps and lifts for disabled persons, braille indications and hands-on exhibits in museums).

Article 53(5)(c) GBER provides that the eligible costs include, *inter alia*, the 'costs of the improvement of public access to the cultural institution or heritage sites and activities including costs of digitisation and of use of new technologies as well as costs of improving accessibility for persons with disabilities'.

On the whole, the GBER allows Member States to avail of state aid in order to boost the right of people with disabilities to work. In addition, it allows Member States to make cultural goods and services more accessible to people with disabilities, in compliance with Article 30 CRPD.

SUMMARY

- **According to the 2012 Flash Eurobarometer, 86 per cent of Europeans agree that having similar accessibility solutions across Europe would enable people with disabilities to travel, study and work in another EU country, supporting the case for advancing EU-wide legislation on the issue.**
- **Most of the existing pieces of EU legislation on accessibility are based on Article 114 TFEU, which empowers the EU to adopt legislation that supports the establishment and smooth functioning of the internal market.**
- **Title VI TFEU on transport has provided a legal basis for legislation addressing accessibility for people with disabilities in different modes of transport (road, rail, water and air transport).**
- **Even though accessibility related to the physical environment is primarily regulated at the national level, the EU has adopted directives covering certain accessibility requirements of specific physical structures, namely cableway installations and lifts.**
- **Accessibility for people with disabilities is relatively mainstreamed in EU transport regulations and directives.**
- **In a similar vein to the Air Passengers' Rights Regulation, the Rail Passengers' Rights Regulation includes a chapter on the rights of persons with reduced mobility. Regulation (EC) No. 1107/2006 is one of the most relevant disability-specific instruments in the field of transportation. It establishes rules for the protection of, and provision of assistance to, persons with disabilities and those with reduced mobility when travelling by air.**

- Several pieces of legislation include provisions on the publication of information in accessible formats.
- The Web Accessibility Directive aims to make the websites and mobile applications of public sector bodies more accessible to users, in particular to persons with disabilities. However, it only sets out minimum requirements that have to be met by public sector bodies and does not apply to private sector websites.
- The AVMSD encourages EU Member States to impose accessibility requirements on providers of audiovisual media services in the disability context.
- The EAA intends to harmonise accessibility requirements for a specified list of products and services. It does not aim to impose detailed technical solutions to make a product or service accessible. Rather, it seeks to establish 'accessibility principles' to be complemented by supplementary standards.
- The 2014 Directives on Public Procurement allow Member States to reserve the right to participate in public procurement to operators who employ persons with disabilities and/or whose main aim is their social integration. They also include several provisions that exploit the potential for public procurement to advance accessibility of good and services.
- EU standardisation policy is an important tool in eliminating barriers to trade and enhancing the internal market. On foot of Mandate 376, the European Standard EN 301 549 was adopted by ESOs. That is a voluntary standard, clarifying the functional accessibility requirements applicable to ICT products and services. Further mandates and work to develop other accessibility standards is currently undergoing.
- The GBER includes several disability-related provisions. It also makes express reference to the EDS and to the CRPD.

ACTIVITIES

REVIEW QUESTIONS

1. To what extent has the EU mainstreamed accessibility requirements in its legislation?
2. In which field has the EU been most successful in including accessibility provisions?
3. What is the role of standardisation in fostering accessibility?

ESSAY QUESTIONS

1. Discuss the strengths and weaknesses of the European Accessibility Act.
2. 'EU state aid law is a powerful tool to enhance accessibility.' *Discuss.*

GROUP PROJECT

Maria is a visually impaired person and lives in Freedonia, an EU Member State. On 30 September 2017, she turned 30 and decided to celebrate her birthday in Paris with her friend Aisling and her beloved guide dog Aurora. She booked the flight from Freedonia City

to Paris and arranged a taxi to the airport. On the day of their departure, the taxi-driver refuses to carry her dog to the airport and mentions that the dog is not allowed in the taxi for safety and hygiene reasons. The taxi-driver also states that the taxi company has a policy prohibiting its drivers from transporting animals. For this reason, Maria and Aisling ask Maria's mother to bring them to the airport. When they arrive at the airport, just in time for boarding, the desk steward of Freedonia Airlines Company refuses to allow Maria to board. He argues that persons with disabilities are not allowed to travel on the airplane. After some discussions, Maria and Aisling decide to go home. They are very angry and disappointed. They decide to contact a lawyer, as they want to lodge a complaint against the taxi company and the airline. They want to be refunded for their expenses and also want to receive compensation for the damages they have incurred.

Discuss the group project.

FURTHER READING

Adam, A. and Kreps, D., 'Disability and Discourses of Web Accessibility' (2009) 12 *Information, Communication and Society* 1041–58.

Charitakis, S., *Access Denied: The Role of the European Union in Ensuring Accessibility under the United Nations Convention on the Rights of Persons with Disabilities* (Cambridge-Antwerp: Intersentia, 2018).

Easton, C., 'Website Accessibility and the European Union: Citizenship, Procurement and the Proposed Accessibility Act' (2013) 27(1–2) *International Review of Law, Computers and Technology* 187–99.

European Disability Forum, *Alternative Report on the Implementation of the UN Convention on the Rights of Persons with Disabilities* (November 2014), pp. 23–5, available at www.icps.org.uk/images/pdf/2015%2003%2004%20EDF%20Alternative%20report%20final%20ACCESSIBLE.pdf.

Ferri, D., 'Does Accessible Technology Need an "Entrepreneurial State"? The Creation of an EU Market of Universally Designed and Assistive Technology through State Aid' (2015) 29(2–3) *International Review of Law, Computers and Technology* 137–61.

Ferri, D., 'The New General Block Exemption Regulation and the Rights of Persons with Disabilities: Smoke without Fire?' (2015) *ESTAL – European State Aid Law Quarterly*, 465–78.

Ferri, D. and Giannoumis, G. A., 'A Revaluation of the Cultural Dimension of Disability Policy in the European Union: The Impact of Digitization and Web Accessibility (2014) 32(1) *Behavioral Sciences & the Law* 33–51.

Hosking, D. L., 'Promoting Accessibility for Disabled People using EU Standardisation Policy' (2017) *European Law Review* 145–65.

Rice, D., 'Public Procurement as a Means to Achieving Social Gains – Progress and Challenges in European Legislation and Standards for Accessible Information and Communication Technology' (2015) 29(2–3) *International Review of Law, Computers and Technology* 162–82.

Sganga, C., 'Disability, Right to Culture and Copyright: Which Regulatory Option?' (2015) 29 (2–3) *International Journal of Law, Computers and Technology* 88–115.

Waddington, L., 'A Disabled Market: Free Movement of Goods and Services in the EU and Disability Accessibility' (2009) 15 *European Law Journal* 575–98.

Waddington, L., 'Vulnerable and Confused: The Protection of "Vulnerable" Consumers under EU Law' (2013) 38(6) *European Law Review* 757–83.

Part III

The Regional Frameworks

13 Disability Law and Policy in the Council of Europe

LEARNING OUTCOMES

- ✓ Identify the main turning points in the development of the disability policy of the Council of Europe.
- ✓ Understand the main tenets of the Council of Europe Strategy on the Rights of Persons with Disabilities 2017–2023.
- ✓ Understand the relevance of the CRPD in the Council of Europe.
- ✓ Identify and comprehend the provisions in the European Convention on Human Rights that are most relevant to the protection and promotion of the rights of persons with disabilities.
- ✓ Demonstrate awareness of the most significant decisions of the European Court of Human Rights regarding disability.
- ✓ Comprehend the role of the European Court of Human Rights in advancing the rights of persons with disabilities.
- ✓ Describe the role of the European Committee of Social Rights in protecting and promoting the rights of persons with disabilities.
- ✓ Identify the potential future evolution of disability rights in the Council of Europe.

> *For far too long policies concerning persons with disabilities have focused exclusively on institutional care, medical rehabilitation and welfare benefits . . . The result has been that men, women and children with disabilities have had their civil, cultural, economic, political and social rights violated. However, a gradual shift in thinking has started as a result of pressure from the disability movements and other civil society groups . . . These groups played an important and active role in the development of the UN convention and the Council of Europe Disability Action Plan.*[1]

1 INTRODUCTION

Within Europe, the Council of Europe (CoE) is the main regional organisation for the protection of human rights. The judicial and other mechanisms of the CoE constitute a regional branch of international law. The CoE has developed a significant disability policy through various initiatives and soft law documents. While it has not yet adopted any specific binding instrument on the rights of persons with disabilities, those rights are protected, to varying degrees, by the European Convention on Human Rights (ECHR),[2] the European Social Charter (ESC)[3] and the Revised European Social Charter (Revised ESC or Revised Charter).[4]

This chapter highlights the key turning points in the history of the CoE's disability policy, and it aims to discuss the main tenets of the current CoE Disability Strategy 2017–2023, which is designed to promote the rights of persons with disabilities. This chapter also aims to unveil the role played by the European Court of Human Rights (ECtHR or the 'Strasbourg Court'), which is the judicial body that monitors the implementation of the ECHR, and the European Committee of Social Rights (ECSR), which monitors the rights contained in the Revised ESC, in protecting the rights of persons with disabilities within the scope of their respective mandates. In addition, this chapter highlights the influence that the CRPD has had on the aforementioned CoE judicial and quasi-judicial mechanisms. Since the adoption of the CRPD, the relevance of the CoE as a source of international law has taken on greater importance in the framework of the debate on fragmentation *versus* systemic integration in international law. Fragmentation means 'the rise of speciali[s]ed rules and rule-systems that have no clear relationship to each other'.[5] Systemic integration, on the other hand, refers to the 'strong presumption [in international law]

[1] Thomas Hammarberg, *Human Rights in Europe: No Grounds for Complacency* (Strasbourg: Council of Europe Publishing, April 2011), p. 128.

[2] Convention for the Protection of Human Rights and Fundamental Freedoms, 4 November 1950, in force 3 September 1953.

[3] European Social Charter of 18 October 1961, in force 26 February 1965, ETS No. 35.

[4] European Social Charter (Revised) of 3 May 1996, in force 1 July 1999, ETS No. 196 of 1996.

[5] UN General Assembly (UNGA), *Fragmentation of International Law: Difficulties arising from the Diversification and Expansion of International Law. Report of the Study Group of the International Law Commission*, 13 April 2006, UN Doc. A/CN.4/L.682, p. 245.

against normative conflict'.[6] While this textbook does not focus on this debate, it does address the extent to which the CRPD's vision of interdependent human rights influences regional international law, such as the ECHR. Further to this introduction, section 2 briefly describes the structure and functions of the CoE. Section 3 examines the evolution of the CoE's disability policy in a chronological fashion. Particular attention is paid to the current Disability Strategy of the CoE. Section 4 discusses the ECHR and the most relevant disability case law of the Strasbourg Court, while section 5 focuses on the ESC and the Revised ESC as well as the most relevant decisions of the ECSR related to disability.

2 THE COUNCIL OF EUROPE AT A GLANCE

This section briefly describes the functions of the CoE and traces its main features as a regional organisation of international law.

2.1 The Institutional Set-Up of the CoE

The CoE was established on 5 May 1949, in the aftermath of the Second World War, by means of the Treaty of London, which laid down the Statute of the CoE.[7] It is the leading regional human rights organisation in Europe, and Article 4 of the Statute specifies that membership is open to any European State. The CoE is located in Strasbourg, and it currently has forty-seven Member States. Nearly all European states (including all EU Member States) have acceded to the CoE, with the exception of Belarus, Kazakhstan and the Holy See. The latter has an observer status within the organisation, together with the United States of America, Canada, Japan and Mexico.[8]

The CoE seeks to promote harmony between European countries in the fields of human rights, legal standards and democratic development. Article 1(a) of the Statute of the CoE states that the aim of the CoE is to achieve 'greater unity between its members for the purpose of safeguarding and realising the ideals and principles which are their common heritage and facilitating their economic and social progress'. The CoE drafts treaties, which set out common legal standards for its Member States on different matters, and soft law documents, which promote compliance with these standards at the policy level. The most important instrument for the protection of human rights is the ECHR, which will be discussed further in section 4 below. The ECHR protects the traditional canon of civil and political rights. Another significant instrument within the CoE is the

6 Ibid. This refers to the assumption that systems will broadly be in harmony and that they will provide for consistent principles and rules.

7 The Statute of the Council of Europe (CoE) was opened for signature in London on 5 May 1949, and it reached the seven ratifications needed to enter into force on the 3 August 1949.

8 The Observer status is governed by Statutory Resolution (93)26, adopted by the Committee of Ministers of the CoE on 14 May 1993.

ESC, which is a treaty guaranteeing social and economic rights and is, thus, 'complementary' to the ECHR. The ESC was adopted in 1961 and revised in 1996, as discussed further in section 5 below. Besides the foregoing instruments, the protection of human rights in the CoE is ensured through a range of thematic conventions, *inter alia*, the Convention on Action against Trafficking in Human Beings,[9] the European Charter for Regional or Minority Languages,[10] and the Framework Convention for the Protection of National Minorities.[11]

The CoE's structure revolves around two main organs: the Committee of Ministers (CoM) and the Parliamentary Assembly (PA). The former is the CoE's main decision-making body, which decides on core CoE policy, approves its budget and activities. It is formed by the ministers of foreign affairs of each CoE Member State or their permanent diplomatic representatives. The PA is the deliberative organ of the CoE.[12] It debates various matters within the scope of the organisation and presents conclusions, mainly in the form of recommendations, to the CoM. Both of those organs are supported by a Secretariat, directed by the Secretary General, who is elected by the PA for a five-year term and acts as the head of the CoE. A Congress of Local and Regional Authorities was set up in 1994,[13] to foster consultation and political dialogue between national governments and local and regional authorities of the Member States. Furthermore, the office of the Council of Europe Commissioner for Human Rights (CoE CoHR) was established in 1999, to promote greater awareness of human rights within CoE Member States. The tasks of the Commissioner are laid out in Resolution (99)50 and include: fostering the observance of human rights and assisting Member States in the implementation of CoE human rights standards; promoting awareness of human rights and identifying challenges and shortcomings in the domestic law and practice of the CoE Member States; and providing advice on the protection of human rights.[14]

The primary judicial body within the CoE is the ECtHR, which monitors the compliance of CoE Member States with the ECHR. The Strasbourg Court hears applications alleging that a Contracting State to the ECHR has breached one or more of the human rights provisions laid out in the ECHR and in its various protocols. An important quasi-judicial body of the CoE is the ECSR, which is

[9] Convention on Action against Trafficking in Human Beings, 16 May 2005, in force 1 February 2008, CETS No. 197.

[10] The European Charter for Regional or Minority Languages, 5 November 1992, in force 1 March 1998, ETS No. 148.

[11] Framework Convention for the Protection of National Minorities, 10 November 1994, in force 1 February 1998, ETS No. 157.

[12] It currently consists of 324 members from the 47 Member States, who are elected or appointed by national parliaments, according to Article 26 of the Statute of the CoE.

[13] In 1953, a Consultative Assembly was created and subsequently became the 'Conference of Local and Regional Authorities of Europe'.

[14] Lauri Sivonen, 'The Commissioner for Human Rights', in Gauthier De Beco, *Human Rights Monitoring Mechanisms of the Council of Europe* (London/New York: Routledge, 2013). See below section 3.4.

charged with ruling on the conformity of CoE Member States' actions with the ESC Charter, the 1988 Additional Protocol[15] and the Revised ESC.

The CoE also collaborates with various civil society organisations and NGOs. More than four hundred NGOs form the Conference of International Non-Governmental Organisations (INGOs), which collaborates with the CoM, the PA and the Congress of Local and Regional Authorities.

2.2 The CoE and the UN

The beginning of cooperation between the CoE and the UN began shortly after the inception of the CoE. On 17 October 1989, the UN General Assembly (UNGA) approved a resolution that granted observer status to the CoE in the UNGA. In November 2016, the UNGA adopted the Resolution on Cooperation between the United Nations and the Council of Europe,[16] in which it acknowledged the contribution of the CoE to the protection and strengthening of human rights and fundamental freedoms, democracy and the rule of law. That resolution also welcomed the ongoing collaboration between the two organisations across numerous fields of action.

2.3 The CoE and the EU

The CoE should not be confused with the EU nor with the EU institutions that have similar names, in particular the Council of the European Union and the European Council. However, there are important links and a long-standing collaboration between the CoE and the EU, which dates back to 1985, when Resolution No. (85)5 first laid down the basis for a strengthened cooperation between the two organisations.[17] Currently, the CoE and the EU collaborate at both the political and technical levels across all sectors of CoE activities. This collaboration is governed by a Memorandum of Understanding (MoU) that was signed in 2007.[18] The MoU confirms that the CoE is the 'benchmark for human rights, the rule of law and democracy in Europe',[19] and it identifies shared priorities between the EU and the CoE. At the EU level, these priorities are then specified and elaborated on each year by the Council of the EU.[20]

[15] Additional Protocol of 1988 extending the social and economic rights of the 1961 Charter, 5 May 1988, in force 4 September 1992, CETS No. 128.

[16] UNGA, Resolution on Cooperation between the United Nations and the Council of Europe, 21 November 2016, UN Doc. No. A/Res/71/17.

[17] CoE CoM, Resolution (85)5 on Cooperation between the Council of Europe and the European Community, 25 April 1985.

[18] CoE, Memorandum of Understanding between the Council of Europe and the European Union (2007), available at https://eeas.europa.eu/delegations/council-europe/6983/memorandum-understanding-between-council-europe-and-european-union_en.

[19] Ibid. para. 10.

[20] For 2018 and 2019, see Council of the European Union, 'EU Priorities for Cooperation with the Council of Europe in 2018–2019' (Brussels, 22 January 2018) 5293/18 COSCE 2 CFSP/PESC 38 COHOM 6.

To date, numerous joint programmes[21] have been adopted, to promote respect for human rights, the rule of law and democratic stability. These joint programmes consist of a series of awareness-raising and educational activities (i.e. conferences, workshops, etc.), which are designed by the European Commission and the CoE in consultation with national governments and aim at facilitating and supporting institutional reform.

Notably, the EU is expected to accede to the ECHR, as established by Article 6 (2) of the Treaty on European Union (TEU).[22] Protocol No. 14 to the ECHR is designed to allow this accession, the purpose of which is to achieve a coherent and consistent framework of human rights protection across Europe. In addition, this accession would serve to strengthen the role of the ECHR as a source of general principles of EU law, drawn on by the Court of Justice of the European Union (CJEU) when it hears cases that touch on matters of fundamental rights. The draft Accession Agreement of the EU to the ECHR, an agreement between the CoE Member States and the EU itself, was finalised on 5 April 2013. However, the CJEU identified a lack of compatibility of this draft agreement with EU law and gave a negative opinion regarding the proposed accession in its Opinion 2/2013 of 18 December 2014.[23] In particular, the CJEU concluded that the accession could undermine the autonomy of EU law. At the time of writing this textbook, alternative solutions (including a renegotiation of the agreement) are under consideration. In June 2018, in a staff working document, the Commission stated that, in its capacity as 'EU negotiator', it 'continues to consult with the relevant Council working party on solutions to address the objections raised by the Court and is making good progress'.[24]

[21] CoE, Joint Programmes between the Council of Europe and the European Union, available at www.jp.coe.int/default.asp.

[22] The accession of the EU to the ECHR has been discussed since the 1970s. While the CJEU considered it unfeasible in 1994 (CJEU, *Opinion 2/1994*, 28 March 1996, ECLI:EU:C:1996:140), it became a legal obligation under Article 6(2) TEU with the entry into force of the Treaty of Lisbon.

[23] CJEU, *Opinion 2/2013*, 18 December 2014, ECLI:EU:C:2014:2454. The literature on the EU accession to the ECHR and on Opinion 2/2013 is copious: see, among many others, Christina Eckes, 'EU Accession to the ECHR: Between Autonomy and Adaptation: EU Accession to the ECHR' (2013) 76(2) *The Modern Law Review* 254; Bruno de Witte and Šejla Imamović, 'Opinion 2/13 on Accession to the ECHR. Defending the EU Legal Order Against a Foreign Human Rights Court' (2015) 40 *European Law Review* 683; Tobias Lock, 'The Future of the European Union's Accession to the European Convention on Human Rights after Opinion 2/13: Is it Still Possible and is it Still Desirable?' (2015) 11(2) *European Constitutional Law Review* 239.

[24] See European Commission, Commission Staff Working Document on the Application of the EU Charter of Fundamental Rights in 2017 Accompanying the document Report from the Commission to the European Parliament, the Council, the European Economic and Social Committee and the Committee of the Regions 2017 Report on the Application of the EU Charter of Fundamental Rights, Brussels, 4 June 2018, SWD/2018/304 final. In October 2018, the Council reiterated its commitment to the EU accession to the ECHR and again invited the Commission to swiftly complete its analysis of legal issues raised by the CJEU. In February 2019, the European Parliament asked the Commission to present a new draft agreement for the accession of the Union to the ECHR providing positive solutions to the objections raised by the CJEU in Opinion 2/13 (European Parliament, Resolution of 12 February 2019 on the

3 THE EMERGENCE OF THE DISABILITY POLICY OF THE COUNCIL OF EUROPE

The CoE began to focus on disability issues in the early 1990s, when Recommendation No. R(92)(6) on a Coherent Policy for Persons with Disabilities[25] was adopted by the CoM. In that period, disability policy had started to evolve on a global scale, as explained in Chapter 2 of this textbook, and the CoE attempted to align its own policies to the fast-paced changes that were taking place worldwide, in particular at the UN level. In the sub-sections that follow, these key developments are outlined.

3.1 The Disability Action Plan 2006–2015

In the last few decades, the Committee of Ministers has adopted many disability-specific recommendations.[26] However, the first comprehensive action plan was published in April 2006, eight months before the adoption of the CRPD. The CoE Disability Action Plan 2006–2015[27] (Action Plan) sought to 'replace the piecemeal approach to disability issues that had been prevalent in the CoE up until that point', and it was intended to serve as a point of reference for all future policies and actions carried out within the CoE in the field of disability.[28] In its own words, the Action Plan sought 'to translate the aims of the Council of Europe with regard to human rights, non-discrimination, equal opportunities, full citizenship and participation of people with disabilities into a European policy framework on disability . . .'.[29] One of the key objectives of the Action Plan was 'to serve as a practical tool to develop and implement viable strategies to bring about full participation of people with disabilities in society and ultimately mainstreaming disability' throughout all the policy areas of the

implementation of the Charter of Fundamental Rights of the European Union in the EU institutional framework, 2017/2089(INI)).

[25] CoE CoM, Recommendation No. R 92(6) on a Coherent Policy for Persons with Disabilities, 9 April 1992.

[26] See, for instance, CoE Parliamentary Assembly (PA), Recommendation No. 818 on the Situation of the Mentally Ill, 8 October 1977; CoE PA, Recommendation No. 1188 on Rehabilitation Policies for the Disabled, 7 May 1992; CoE PA, Recommendation No. 1592 towards Full Social Inclusion of People with Disabilities, 29 January 2003; CoE PA, Recommendation No. 1560 towards Concerted Efforts for Treating and Curing Spinal Cord Injury, 26 April 2002.

[27] The CoE Disability Action Plan was adopted pursuant to Committee of Ministers, Recommendation No. (2006)(5) on the Council of Europe Disability Action Plan to Promote the Rights and Full Participation of People with Disabilities in Society: Improving the Quality of Life of People with Disabilities in Europe 2006–2015, 5 April 2006.

[28] Andrea Broderick, *The Long and Winding Road to Equality and Inclusion for Persons with Disabilities: The United Nations Convention on the Rights of Persons with Disabilities* (Cambridge-Antwerp: Intersentia, 2015), pp. 357–58.

[29] CoE Action Plan to Promote the Rights and Full Participation of People with Disabilities in Society: Improving the Quality of Life of People with Disabilities in Europe 2006–2015, p. 4.

Member States.[30] The fundamental principles on which the Action Plan was based include the principles of non-discrimination; equality of opportunities; full participation in society of all persons with disabilities; respect for difference and acceptance of disability as part of human diversity; dignity and individual autonomy; and the freedom to make one's own choices.[31] The Action Plan recommended specific actions in fifteen key action lines, covering nearly all areas of life of people with disabilities.[32] Those action lines corresponded largely with the substantive rights and obligations contained in the CRPD, and they are listed in Figure 13.1.

Action line No. 1: Participation in political and public life

Action line No. 2: Participation in cultural life

Action line No. 3: Information and communication

Action line No. 4: Education

Action line No. 5: Employment, vocational guidance and training

Action line No. 6: The built environment

Action line No. 7: Transport

Action line No. 8: Community living

Action line No. 9: Health care

Action line No. 10: Rehabilitation

Action line No. 11: Social protection

Action line No. 12: Legal protection

Action line No. 13: Protection against violence and abuse

Action line No. 14: Research and development

Action line No. 15: Awareness-raising

Figure 13.1 Action Lines of the CoE Disability Action Plan 2006–2015

30 Ibid. p. 5. 31 Ibid. p. 11. 32 Ibid. p. 12.

Notwithstanding the fact that the CRPD and the Action Plan differ in their legal nature and geographical scope, many of the premises and key focus areas of both instruments overlap. The Action Plan took 'due account'[33] of 'relevant existing European and international instruments, treaties and plans', particularly the developments in relation to the draft CRPD (as it was at that time).[34] The Action Plan mirrored the paradigm shift to the human rights model of disability. It recognised that:

> we have moved from seeing the disabled person as a patient in need of care who does not contribute to society to seeing him/her as a person who needs the present barriers removed in order to take a rightful place as a fully participative member of society.[35]

In a similar vein to the CRPD, the Action Plan acknowledged the cross-cutting aspects of disability discrimination, in its recognition that there are people with disabilities who face specific barriers or multiple discrimination, for example, women, children, elderly persons, and migrants with disabilities or persons with disabilities in need of a high level of support. Despite predating the CRPD, the Action Plan can be said to serve as a regional framework for the implementation of the CRPD obligations undertaken by CoE Member States.

3.2 The Disability Policy of the CoE Post-CRPD

3.2.1 *The Committee of Ministers' Recommendations*

Since the entry into force of the CRPD, the CoM has adopted many non-binding recommendations and issue papers related to disability. The influence of the CRPD can be seen quite clearly in the content of many of these recommendations.

The first recommendation that was adopted after the entry into force of the CRPD was Recommendation CM/Rec(2009)6 on Ageing and Disability in the 21st Century: Sustainable Frameworks to enable Greater Quality of Life in an Inclusive Society.[36] The fundamental principles on which that recommendation is based are drawn from both the Action Plan and the CRPD. In line with Article 4(3) CRPD, the recommendation reiterates the need to involve ageing people with disabilities and older people with disabilities in decisions affecting their lives.[37] It notes that such individuals should be

[33] Ibid. p. 4. [34] Ibid. [35] Ibid. p. 8.

[36] CoE CoM, Recommendation CM/Rec(2009)6 on Ageing and Disability in the 21st Century: Sustainable Frameworks to enable Greater Quality of Life in an Inclusive Society, 8 July 2009.

[37] Ibid. According to the recommendation, the expressions 'ageing people with disabilities' and 'older people with disabilities' refer to two distinct but related groups of people. The first group refers to people who grow old having experienced a disability for much of their lives, sometimes from birth, while the second group refers to those individuals who first experience disability at a relatively advanced age.

involved fully and directly throughout the process of designing, implementing and evaluating services.[38]

Read the recommendation and identify the fundamental principles listed in it. Can you link them to specific CRPD provisions?

In its Recommendation CM/Rec(2009)9 to Member States on the Education and Social Inclusion of Children and Young People with Autism Spectrum Disorders,[39] the CoM once again draws on the CRPD, among other international instruments. It states that:

> in line with the instruments of the Council of Europe and the United Nations Convention on the Rights of Persons with Disabilities, member states should ensure not only that education, social welfare and other public policies do not discriminate against people with disabilities, including people with autism spectrum disorder, but that equality of opportunity and appropriate educational interventions are provided.[40]

Moreover, in its Recommendation CM/Rec(2009)8 on Achieving Full Participation through Universal Design,[41] the CoM encourages governments to accept universal design (UD) 'as a philosophy and strategy supporting implementation of full citizenship and independent living of all people, including people with disabilities'.[42] It mentions the CRPD in the context of relevant international documents, but it does not draw specifically on any of the CRPD's provisions. That recommendation mirrors previous soft law documents that featured the concept of UD: Resolution ResAP(2001)1 on the Introduction of the Principles of Universal Design into the Curricula of All Occupations Working on the Built Environment[43] and Resolution ResAP(2001)3 Towards Full Citizenship of

[38] Ibid. p. 5.

[39] CoE CoM, Recommendation CM/Rec(2009)9 on the Education and Social Inclusion of Children and Young People with Autism Spectrum Disorders, 21 October 2009.

[40] Ibid. p. 2. For a discussion of UD see above Chapter 5, in particular section 2.

[41] CoE CoM, Recommendation CM/Rec(2009)8 on Achieving Full participation through Universal Design, 21 October 2009.

[42] Ibid. p. 3.

[43] CoE, Resolution ResAP(2001)1 on the Introduction of the Principles of Universal Design into the Curricula of All Occupations Working on the Built Environment, 15 February 2001 (Tomar Resolution).

Persons with Disabilities through Inclusive New Technologies.[44] It also reinforces what had been established in the action lines of the Disability Action Plan 2006–2015,[45] outlined above.

In 2010, the CoM adopted Recommendation CM/Rec(2010)2 on Deinstitutionalisation and Community Living of Children with Disabilities.[46] That recommendation, which also refers to the CRPD, stresses the right of children with disabilities to be treated on an equal basis with other children, including the right to express themselves on matters of concern to them and the essential need to have fully accessible services. The recommendation focuses primarily on the deinstitutionalisation of children with disabilities and the involvement of children with disabilities and their families as stakeholders in the process of service development.

Furthermore, Recommendation CM/Rec(2011)14 of the CoM to Member States on the Participation of Persons with Disabilities in Political and Public Life[47] demonstrates the clearest influence of the CRPD on the CoE's disability policy. In that recommendation, the CoM builds on the approach taken in the CRPD to increasing participation of persons with disabilities in political and public life, and it draws explicitly on several provisions of the Convention. The Committee refers to Article 29 CRPD, which highlights the obligation to secure for persons with disabilities the enjoyment of political rights on an equal basis with others; and Article 2 CRPD, which includes the denial of reasonable accommodation in the definition of discrimination on the basis of disability. The Committee also draws on Article 12 CRPD (on equal recognition before the law) in its assertion that CoE Member States should 'make support available to persons who may need assistance in exercising their legal capacity in various aspects of life, in particular when exercising their right to vote'[48] and that they 'should ensure that their legislation is devoid, at all levels, of provisions depriving persons with disabilities of the right to vote or stand for election'.[49] The CoM focuses, among other things, on the accessibility of political processes, and it draws on the provisions of the CRPD in that regard, stating that 'participatory democracy for persons with disabilities involves accessibility of premises, services and goods, procedures, rules, information and communications'.[50]

[44] CoE, Resolution ResAP(2001)3 towards Full Citizenship of Persons with Disabilities through Inclusive New Technologies, 24 October 2001.

[45] See, for instance, Action Line 6 of the Disability Action Plan 2006–2015.

[46] CoE CoM, Recommendation CM/Rec(2010)2 on Deinstitutionalisation and Community Living of Children with Disabilities, 3 February 2010.

[47] CoE CoM, Recommendation CM/Rec(2011)14 on the Participation of Persons with Disabilities in Political and Public Life, 16 November 2011.

[48] Ibid. [49] Ibid. [50] Ibid.

3.2.2 *The Strategy on the Rights of Persons with Disabilities 2017–2023*

In 2014–2015, the CoE carried out an evaluation of the implementation of the Action Plan in its Member States, in order to draw lessons from the ten-year period during which it had been implemented and to define a way forward in a new disability strategy.[51] Building on this evaluation process, and prompted by a recommendation of the Conference of INGOs,[52] the CoE adopted its new Strategy on the Rights of Persons with Disabilities 2017–2023 (Strategy 2017–2023) on 30 November 2016.[53] The overall goal of that Strategy is to achieve equality, dignity and equal opportunities for persons with disabilities in all areas of the CoE's field of action. The Strategy 2017–2023 identifies five priority areas (indicated in Figure 13.2) that echo the CRPD's general principles. Those priority areas also mirror, to a certain extent, the European Disability Strategy 2010–2020, adopted by the European Commission within the EU context.[54]

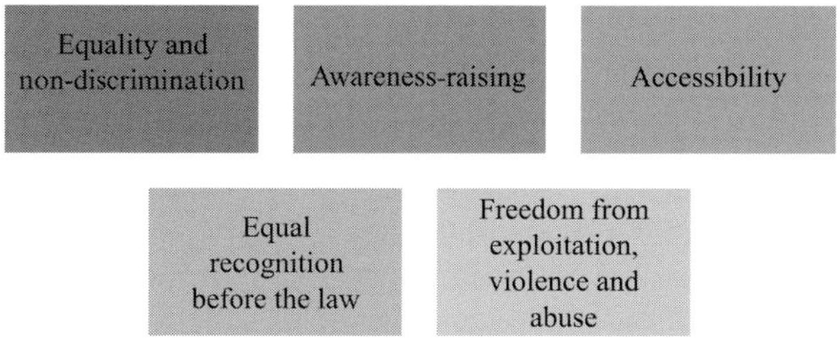

Figure 13.2 Priority Areas of the CoE Strategy on the Rights of Persons with Disabilities 2017–2023

In addition to the priority areas outlined above, the Strategy 2017–2023 identifies five cross-cutting themes: participation, cooperation and coordination; UD and reasonable accommodation; a gender equality perspective; multiple discrimination; and education and training. In a similar vein to the priority areas, those cross-cutting themes are also anchored in the CRPD, thus placing strong emphasis on the implementation of existing human rights standards. On the whole, the Strategy is intended to provide a flexible policy instrument and framework for domestic policies and can be tailored to the specific national and local contexts.

[51] See also, CoE PA, Recommendation No. 2064 on Equality and Inclusion for People with Disabilities, 30 January 2015.

[52] Conference of International Non-Governmental Organisations, Recommendation CONF/PLE (2015)REC2 on the New Disability Strategy, 25 June 2015.

[53] CoE, Human Rights: A Reality for All – Council of Europe Disability Strategy 2017–2023, available at www.coe.int/en/web/disability/strategy-2017-2023.

[54] See above Chapter 11.

Human Rights: A Reality For All Council of Europe Disability Strategy 2017–2023

3. This Strategy seeks to encompass all civil, political, economic, social and cultural rights. It sets out the commitment of the Council of Europe and its member States to make the rights a reality for all persons with disabilities, regardless of their impairments. This includes children and young persons with disabilities, wherever they are placed and without discrimination, in line with the Council of Europe Strategy for the Rights of the Child 2016–2021 and the UN Convention on the Rights of the Child. This also includes older persons, in line with the Council of Europe recommendation on the promotion of human rights of older persons.

4. In constantly changing societies new situations emerge. The ongoing economic challenges and the increasing amount of refugees and persons seeking asylum within the member States has changed priorities and has had an impact on persons with disabilities and their support services. In order to mitigate the challenges, continuous attention to and action on the rights of persons with disabilities by the decision makers, persons with disabilities, their organisations and their family members, service providers, and the population in general is required.

5. Close consultation and active involvement of persons with disabilities of all ages through their representative organisations in the work of member State governments is obligatory, as stipulated in the UNCRPD. Participation and contribution of National Human Rights Institutions, Equality Bodies and Ombudsman Institutions and their regional and international networks is of high importance. This will improve mainstreaming and implementation of strategy priorities and the UNCRPD principles. The Council of Europe will seek to increase this co-operation in all fields of its activities.

3.3 The Role of the Ad-Hoc Committee of Experts on the Rights of Persons with Disabilities

The Ad-Hoc Committee of Experts on the Rights of Persons with Disabilities (*Comité Ad Hoc sur les droits des personnes handicapées* – CAHDPH) is an intergovernmental group of experts whose main activity is 'to support the implementation of the Disability Strategy, advise and involve the various stakeholders as well as liaise with relevant intergovernmental bodies, providing expertise and a forum for the exchange of good practices and issues of concern'.[55] The CAHDPH includes representatives of Member States of the

[55] Council of Europe Disability Strategy 2017–2023, note 53, para. 77.

CAHDPH's Specific Tasks	To facilitate the exchange of good practices, in order to support CoE Member States in introducing policy reform
	To promote and support action and policies across the five priority areas and the cross-cutting themes identified by the Disability Strategy, in order to achieve equality, dignity and equal opportunities for persons with disabilities
	To facilitate dialogue with civil society and DPOs and to promote research on the cross-cutting themes of the Disability Strategy
	To review the implementation of relevant recommendations of the CoM

Figure 13.3 Specific Tasks of the CAHDPH in the Context of the Disability Strategy 2017–2023

CoE and representatives of various organs of the CoE (e.g. the PA, the Congress of Local and Regional Authorities, the ECtHR and the CoE CoHR). The latter representatives do not have any voting rights in the Committee. In addition, other international and regional organisations, such as the International Labour Organization (ILO), the EU and National Human Rights Institutions (NHRIs) may appoint representatives to sit in the CAHDPH. Disabled Peoples' Organisations (DPOs) and civil society organisations also serve as observers on the Committee.[56] Under the authority of the CoM, the CAHDPH oversees and promotes the implementation of the Disability Strategy 2017–2023. The specific tasks of the CAHDPH are outlined in Figure 13.3.

The CAHDPH is also entrusted with various tasks: to raise awareness of disability rights, to provide expertise to CoE Member States on the development of disability legislation, policies and practices and to support them in the implementation of relevant international standards, in particular the CRPD. It also advises the CoM and the Secretary General on appropriate action to be taken, and it provides advice, whenever requested, on disability-related issues that arise. Notably, the CAHDPH ensures close cooperation with other international organisations and bodies, in particular the CRPD Committee, as well as the Office of the United Nations High Commissioner for Human Rights (OHCHR) and the World Health Organization (WHO). Moreover, the CAHDPH engages in coordination and joint planning with the EU and the UN.

[56] For example, the European Association of Service Providers for Persons with Disabilities (EASPD), the European Disability Forum (EDF), and Rehabilitation International (RI).

3.4 The Role of the Commissioner for Human Rights

As mentioned above in section 2, the office of the CoE CoHR was established in 1999. It is an independent body, entrusted with promoting awareness of and respect for human rights in CoE Member States. The Commissioner encourages the adoption of policy measures, designed to achieve the effective promotion and protection of human rights. The Commissioner does not have a judicial role and, therefore, cannot receive individual complaints, but can take initiatives on the basis of reliable information concerning human rights violations. In addition, the Commissioner can intervene as a third party in ECtHR proceedings, presenting *amicus curiae.*[57]

The promotion and protection of the rights of persons with disabilities has been a key area of action for the office of the CoE CoHR since its inception. In their work, the various Commissioners[58] have also made reference to the CRPD as the international benchmark in all matters pertaining to disability. Among them, Mr Thomas Hammarberg, who acted as Commissioner from 2006 until 2012, published two progressive issue papers: one on legal capacity and one on independent living. Those papers were published with a view to contributing to law and policy reform on disability, and they include recommendations for CoE Member States. The first paper was published in 2012, and it was entitled 'Who Gets to Decide? Right to Legal Capacity for Persons with Intellectual and Psychosocial Disabilities'.[59] It acknowledges that the paradigm shift embodied by the CRPD (from the medical model to the human rights model of disability) and the CRPD's equality and non-discrimination norms 'call for a new approach to legal capacity'.[60] The issue paper notes that 'the demand for equality compels us to develop alternatives to accommodate and enable all persons with disabilities to be in charge of their lives'.[61] The Commissioner then draws, *inter alia,* on Article 12 CRPD, which can be deemed 'to be the beating heart of the [CRPD]',[62] as 'it is closely related to social inclusion, autonomy and equality, all core values of the instrument'.[63] The Commissioner urges Member States to ratify the CRPD and the Optional Protocol to the Convention and goes on to outline several recommendations to Member States. Those recommendations can be aligned very clearly with the fundamental values enshrined in the CRPD, not least the principle of equality. In the same year, Mr Hammarberg also published an issue paper on independent living, which exhibits the clear influence of the CRPD on the direction of the CoE's disability policy related to equality and inclusion in

[57] Article 36(3) of the European Convention on Human Rights.

[58] The current CoE CoHR is Dunja Mijatović, having succeeded Nils Muižnieks (2012–18), Thomas Hammarberg (2006–12) and Alvaro Gil-Robles (1999–2006).

[59] CoE CoHR, Issue Paper: 'Who Gets to Decide? Right to Legal Capacity for Persons with Intellectual and Psychosocial Disabilities', 20 February 2012.

[60] Ibid. p. 13. [61] Ibid. p. 11. [62] Ibid. p. 14. [63] Ibid.

Read the *amicus curiae* in the case of *María del Mar Caamaño Valle* v. *Spain*, and identify the most important arguments raised by the Commissioner for Human Rights.

society for individuals with disabilities. That issue paper, entitled 'The Right of People with Disabilities to Live Independently and be Included in the Community',[64] aims 'to draw out the guidance contained in international standards, and in particular Article 19 of the CRPD',[65] in order to promote an understanding of what the right to independent living looks like when implemented and when violated.[66]

In July 2018, Dunja Mijatović, who was elected as Commissioner by the PA and took up her position on 1 April 2018, intervened as a third party[67] before the ECtHR in *María del Mar Caamaño Valle* v. *Spain*,[68] which concerns the deprivation of the right to vote of a person with intellectual disabilities. The Commissioner, in her *amicus curiae* intervention, stressed that preventing people with disabilities from exercising their right to vote based on an assessment made by a judge of the person's cognitive capacity or mental health status is contrary to the CRPD and international human rights standards generally. The Commissioner also highlighted that Article 3 of Protocol 1 to the ECHR (the right to free elections) should be interpreted in light of Article 29 CRPD (the right to participate in political and public life).

4 THE EUROPEAN CONVENTION ON HUMAN RIGHTS

This section addresses how the ECHR deals with disability, before discussing the most significant decisions of the Strasbourg Court. This section also sets out the

[64] CoE CoHR, Issue Paper: 'The Right of People with Disabilities to Live Independently and be Included in the Community', 12 March 2012.

[65] Ibid. p. 9. [66] Ibid.

[67] CoE CoHR, Third Party intervention by the Council of Europe Commissioner for Human Rights under Article 36, para. 3 of the European Convention on Human Rights, available at https://rm.coe.int/third-party-intervention-before-the-european-court-of-human-rights-cas/16808c3253.

[68] ECtHR, *María del Mar Caamaño Valle* v. *Spain*, Application No. 43564/17, 17 July 2018.

relevance of the CRPD to the Court in its interpretation of ECHR provisions, in spite of the fact that, unlike the EU, the CoE is not a party to the UN Convention.

4.1 The Evolving Interpretation of the ECHR and Disability

As stated earlier in this chapter, the ECHR can be considered the primary legal instrument in the CoE. It was adopted during a period that was characterised by a welfare and paternalistic approach to disability,[69] and, for that reason, it does not address the rights of persons with disabilities, nor does its contain any express reference to disability itself. Only Article 5(1)(e) ECHR, concerning the lawful detention of 'persons of unsound mind' ('*aliéné*' in the official French version of the Convention), constitutes an indirect reference to psychosocial disability.[70]

ARTICLE 5(1)(E) ECHR

1. Everyone has the right to liberty and security of person. No one shall be deprived of his liberty save in the following cases and in accordance with a procedure prescribed by law:

...

(e) the lawful detention of persons for the prevention of the spreading of infectious diseases, of persons of unsound mind, alcoholics or drug addicts or vagrants.

In *Winterwerp* v. *Netherlands*,[71] the Court affirmed that the term 'persons of unsound mind' is 'not one that can be given a definitive interpretation'.[72] Rather, the Court stated that:

> it is a term whose meaning is continually evolving as research in psychiatry progresses, an increasing flexibility in treatment is developing and society's attitude to mental illness changes, in particular so that a greater understanding of the problems of mental patients is becoming more wide-spread.[73]

[69] Frederic Mégrét, 'The Disabilities Convention: Towards a Holistic Concept of Rights' (2008) 12 (2) *The International Journal of Human Rights* 261; Davio Björgvinsson, 'The Protection of the Rights of Persons with Disabilities in the Case Law of the European Court of Human Rights', in Oddný Mjöll Arnardóttir and Gerard Quinn (eds.), *The UN Convention on the Rights of Persons with Disabilities, European and Scandinavian Perspectives* (Leiden-Boston: Brill, 2009), p. 141.

[70] See further section 4.3.7.

[71] ECtHR, *Winterwerp* v. *Netherlands*, Application No. 6301/72, 24 October 1979.

[72] Ibid. para. 37. [73] Ibid.

DID YOU KNOW THAT ...?

Despite the absence of an explicit reference to the rights of people with disabilities in the ECHR, the Strasbourg Court has advanced disability rights by interpreting various provisions of the Convention in a wide and evolving manner, going beyond the letter of those provisions. That approach is consistent with the understanding that the ECHR is a 'living instrument', which must be interpreted in accordance with present-day conditions – a so-called 'evolutive approach'. The evolutive approach to interpretation has featured heavily in the case law of the Strasbourg Court since its early days. It was first emphasised in the case of *Tyrer* v. *United Kingdom*, wherein the Court stated that 'the Convention is a living instrument', and it 'must be interpreted in the light of present-day conditions'.

In recent years, the Strasbourg Court has shown an increased willingness to draw on international instruments as an interpretive aid for several ECHR provisions.[74] For example, in *Demir and Baykara* v. *Turkey*,[75] the ECtHR noted that 'the relevant international instruments denote a continuous evolution in the norms and principles applied in international law and show, in a precise area, that there is common ground in modern societies'.[76] Moreover, the ECtHR observed that 'the consensus emerging from specialised international instruments and from the practice of [C]ontracting States may constitute a relevant consideration for the Court when it interprets the provisions of the Convention in specific cases'.[77] Waddington contends that 'the Court's interpretation of ECHR provisions is . . . influenced by emerging international consensuses',[78] expressed, *inter alia*, through treaty law. She further argues that the CRPD 'reflects such an emerging consensus'[79] due to the high number of signatures and ratifications that the UN Convention attracted within a short period of time, both within the CoE and at a global level. In fact, as will be discussed below, since the coming into force of the

[74] On the issue of the ECHR as a 'living instrument', see Valentina Zambrano, 'Il favor dei giudici di Strasburgo verso la protezione dei diritti delle persone con disabilità nel quadro dell'interpretazione evolutiva della CEDU' (2014) *Studi in memoria di Maria Rita Saulle* 1657.

[75] ECtHR, *Demir and Baykara* v. *Turkey*, Application No. 34503/97, 12 November 2008.

[76] Ibid. para. 86. [77] Ibid. para. 85.

[78] Lisa Waddington, 'Europees Hof voor de Rechten van de Mens, 21 december 2010, nr. 45744/08, Jasinskis tegen Letland' (2011) *European Human Rights Cases* No. 222537, at 566.

[79] Ibid.

CRPD in May 2008, the Strasbourg Court has cited[80] the UN Convention on numerous occasions.[81]

4.2 The Development of Positive Obligations under the ECHR

4.2.1 *The Scope of Application of the ECHR and the CRPD*

The CRPD and the ECHR have different scopes of application, both *ratione materiae* and geographically. The CRPD is a disability-specific treaty that recognises the interdependence of civil and political rights, and economic, social and cultural rights. By way of contrast, the ECHR is targeted at protecting civil and political rights, with the exception of its First Protocol (concerning the rights to property and education). Furthermore, as noted above, the ECHR does not contain any explicit protection for the rights of persons with disabilities.

The Strasbourg Court has shown 'significant weariness' in interpreting the ECHR as protecting socio-economic rights.[82] Nonetheless, the Court sometimes appears to be willing to recognise the interdependent nature of rights, particularly with regard to so-called vulnerable groups. The Court has made clear in *Airey* v. *Ireland* that 'whilst the Convention sets forth what are essentially civil and political rights, many of them have implications of a social or economic nature'.[83] Thus, 'the mere fact that an interpretation of the Convention may extend into the sphere of social and economic rights should not be a decisive factor against such an interpretation'.[84]

The CRPD has been deemed by O'Cinneide to adopt 'a particular conceptual view of the [s]tate's role', whereby States Parties have positive obligations that span all human rights, designed to ensure that a minimum level of support is accorded to persons with disabilities, compatible with their human dignity. That viewpoint is most clearly encapsulated in the human rights model of disability, which encompasses the duty to reasonably accommodate and the accessibility obligations under the CRPD. By way of contrast with the accommodation duty, the accessibility obligations laid out in Article 9 CRPD are

80 See, among others, ECtHR, *Glor* v. *Switzerland*, Application No. 13444/04, 30 April 2009, para. 53; ECtHR, *Jasinskis* v. *Latvia*, Application No. 45744/08, 21 March 2011, para. 40; ECtHR, *Seal* v. *United Kingdom*, Application No. 50330/07, 07 December 2010, paras. 41–3; ECtHR, *Kiyutin* v. *Russia*, Application No. 2700/10, 10 March 2011; ECtHR, *D. D.* v. *Lithuania*, Application No. 13469/06, 14 February 2012, para. 84.

81 ECtHR, *Pleso* v. *Hungary*, Application No. 41242/08, 2 October 2012; *Jasinskis* v. *Latvia*, note 80.

82 Liam Thornton, 'A Socio-Economic Rights Charter?', in Suzanne Egan, Liam Thornton and Judy Walsh (eds.), *Ireland and the European Convention on Human Rights: 60 Years and Beyond* (Dublin: Bloomsbury 2014), p. 227.

83 ECtHR, *Airey* v. *Ireland*, Application No. 6289/73, 9 October 1979, para. 26.

84 Ibid.

generalised obligations, requiring States Parties to make wide-ranging alterations to the built environment, transportation, goods and services, and information and communications, on a progressive basis. As discussed in Chapter 4 of this textbook, the reasonable accommodation duty is immediately realisable, being situated within the non-discrimination norm (a civil and political right). Combined with its immediate nature, the duty to accommodate is a positive obligation, but its scope of application is limited by the test of 'disproportionate burden'. While the ECHR does not share the CRPD's expansive view of the state's role and does not contain extensive positive obligations like the CRPD, it is clear that the ECHR applies equally to people with disabilities as it does to all other individuals. In order to give full effect to ECHR rights in the context of disabled people, positive measures will often be required.

4.2.2 *The Margin of Appreciation Doctrine*

The margin of appreciation doctrine refers to the realm of discretion left to national authorities in fulfilling their obligations under the ECHR. The Court-made doctrine allows Contracting States to the ECHR to pursue certain actions that the Strasbourg Court will not interfere with, provided that those actions fall within an acceptable margin (as adjudged by the Court). The margin of appreciation doctrine is traditionally only applied to some ECHR articles, most notably Articles 8, 10 and 14 ECHR, while other rights, such as Articles 2 and 3, are considered to be absolute rights and, accordingly, are not subject to the doctrine. It is noteworthy that, in determining a state's margin of appreciation, the Strasbourg Court may have due regard to the 'consensus and common values emerging from the practices of European States and specialised international instruments' as well as 'the evolution of norms and principles in international law'.[85] As outlined earlier in this chapter, the CRPD can be considered to represent an emerging consensus and a common standard on disability issues among CoE Member States. Moreover, the CRPD signals a paradigm shift in the understanding of disability equality. Since many CoE Member States are altering their laws and policies with a view to aligning them with the CRPD's provisions, this may impact on the interpretation by the

[85] ECtHR, *Opuz* v. *Turkey*, Application No. 33401/02, 9 June 2009, para. 164. See also, ECtHR, *Kiyutin* v. *Russia*, Application No. 2700/10, 10 March 2011, para. 67, where the ECtHR remarked as follows: 'the Court has consistently held that it takes into account relevant international instruments and reports in order to interpret the guarantees of the Convention and to establish whether there is a common standard in the field. It is for the Court to decide which international instruments and reports it considers relevant and how much weight to attribute to them'. See further Andrea Broderick, 'The United Nations Convention on the Rights of Persons with Disabilities and the European Convention on Human Rights: A Tale of Two Halves or a Potentially Unified Vision of Human Rights?' (2018) 7(2) *Cambridge International Law Journal* 199.

Strasbourg Court of the rights of persons with disabilities under the ECHR. However, in invoking the CRPD to guide the interpretation of ECHR rights, the Strasbourg Court will be careful not to erode the autonomy of CoE Member States, and the Court will seek to respect national resource allocation policies. When dealing with obligations that have a socio-economic nature, the ECtHR has generally ensured that Contracting States are afforded a wide margin of appreciation. Without doubt, the Court cannot incorporate all of the progressive CRPD obligations into its jurisprudence. It is constrained, *inter alia*, by the nature and scope of the ECHR itself. Notwithstanding this, it is arguable that the Strasbourg Court should draw on the spirit and tenor of the substantive provisions of the CRPD when interpreting ECHR rights for persons with disabilities, within the limits of the doctrine of the margin of appreciation.

4.3 Case Law of the European Court of Human Rights on Disability

The sub-sections below examine the development of disability rights in the Strasbourg Court's case law in relation to Articles 2 and 3 (the right to life and the prohibition on torture, inhuman and degrading treatment, respectively); Article 5 (the right to liberty and security); Article 6 (the right to a fair trial); Article 8 (the right to private and family life); Article 13 (the right to an effective remedy); and Article 14 ECHR (the right to non-discrimination). The case law of the Strasbourg Court is extensive, and the sub-sections below do not endeavour to be exhaustive; however, they present the most significant decisions of the Court to date in the field of disability.

4.3.1 *Article 2 and Article 3 ECHR: The Rights of Persons with Disabilities in Detention and Reasonable Accommodation*

ARTICLE 2 ECHR

1. Everyone's right to life shall be protected by law. No one shall be deprived of his life intentionally save in the execution of a sentence of a court following his conviction of a crime for which this penalty is provided by law.

2. Deprivation of life shall not be regarded as inflicted in contravention of this Article when it results from the use of force which is no more than absolutely necessary:

(a) in defence of any person from unlawful violence;
(b) in order to effect a lawful arrest or to prevent the escape of a person lawfully detained;
(c) in action lawfully taken for the purpose of quelling a riot or insurrection.

ARTICLE 3 ECHR

No one shall be subjected to torture or to inhuman or degrading treatment or punishment.

In many cases in which a violation of Articles 2 and 3 ECHR has been claimed, the ECtHR has acknowledged that prisoners with disabilities are confronted with numerous barriers that hinder their inherent dignity and impair their right to life. In several cases that have come before it, the ECtHR has not hesitated in finding a violation of Article 3 ECHR in circumstances where the special needs of a disabled detainee were not taken into account by the authorities in institutional settings. For example, in the case of *Price* v. *UK*[86] (a case that was decided before the coming into force of the CRPD), the Strasbourg Court ruled that the state in question had inflicted degrading treatment on the applicant (a disabled woman in state custody) contrary to Article 3 ECHR, by virtue of the fact that it had failed to accommodate her particular needs arising from her impairment. In *Price* v. *UK*, the Court did not use the language of 'reasonable accommodation', and it did not take the opportunity to frame the rights of the disabled applicant in terms of a right to non-discrimination. However, as de Schutter points out, 'it was the lack of any consideration of Ms. Price's special needs which led to the Court's finding that degrading treatment had taken place'.[87]

Several cases relating to *de facto* reasonable accommodation duties in the specific context of detention have come before the Court since the entry into force of the CRPD. In *Vincent* v. *France*,[88] for example, the Court ruled that detaining a disabled person in a prison (where he could not move around and could not leave his cell independently) amounted to degrading treatment. The Court did not refer to the concept of 'reasonable accommodation' under the CRPD. Nor did the ECtHR refer to the CRPD in *Engel* v. *Hungary*,[89] where the Court ruled that leaving a person with a serious physical disability to rely on his cellmates for assistance was sufficient to justify a finding that the conditions of detention at stake amounted to degrading treatment. Findings of *de facto* reasonable accommodation duties have been made in several cases of a similar nature.[90]

[86] ECtHR, *Price* v. *United Kingdom*, Application No. 33394/96, 10 July 2001.

[87] Olivier de Schutter, 'Reasonable Accommodations and Positive Obligations under the European Convention on Human Rights', in Anna Lawson and Caroline Gooding (eds.), *Disability Rights in Europe: From Theory to Practice* (London: Hart Publishing, 2005), p. 55.

[88] ECtHR, *Vincent* v. *France*, Application No. 6253/03, 24 October 2006, paras. 94–103.

[89] ECtHR, *Engel* v. *Hungary*, Application No. 46857/06, 20 May 2010, paras. 27–30.

[90] See, for example, the cases of ECtHR, *Khudobin* v. *Russia*, Application No. 59696/00, 26 October 2006; ECtHR, *Rupa* v. *Romania*, Application No. 58478/00, 16 December 2008; ECtHR, *Kupczak* v. *Poland*, Application No. 2627/09, 25 January 2009; ECtHR, *Xiros*

In other cases related to disabled individuals in institutional settings, there seems to be a greater emphasis by the Strasbourg Court on the CRPD's duty of reasonable accommodation. For example, *Jasinskis* v. *Latvia*[91] concerned the failure of the domestic authorities to provide medical assistance to a seriously injured deaf man, who was also unable to speak and died after being held in police custody for fourteen hours. Relying on Articles 2 and 3 ECHR, Mr Jasinskis' father alleged that the Latvian police had been responsible for his son's death and that the investigation conducted by the authorities had not been effective. The Court in *Jasinskis* demonstrated an awareness of the special needs of individuals with disabilities, noting that 'where the authorities decide to place and maintain in detention a disabled individual, they should demonstrate special care in guaranteeing such conditions as correspond to his special needs resulting from his disability'.[92] This finding is consistent with earlier cases,[93] such as *Price* v. *UK*.[94] The ECtHR cited Article 14(2) CRPD in the context of relevant international law.[95] In light of the fact that the applicant's son was deaf and unable to speak, the Court held that the police had a clear obligation, arising, *inter alia*, from the relevant standards of international law, to provide him with a pen and a piece of paper, in order to enable him to communicate his concerns. In sum, the Court concluded that the Latvian police were in violation of the substantive and procedural aspects of Article 2 ECHR,[96] since the police had not safeguarded the life of the applicant's son by providing him with adequate medical treatment. The ECtHR also held that the investigation into the circumstances of the death of Mr Jasinskis' son had not been effective, in further violation of Article 2 ECHR. Waddington notes that *Jasinskis* 'reflects two positive trends' in the case law

v. *Greece*, Application No. 1033/07, 9 September 2010; ECtHR, *Grori* v. *Albania*, Application No. 25336/04, 7 July 2009; ECtHR, *Raffrey Taddei* v. *France*, Application No. 36435/07, 21 December 2010; ECtHR, *Logvinenko* v. *Ukraine*, Application No. 13448/07, 14 October 2010; ECtHR, *Vasyukov* v. *Russia*, Application No. 2974/05, 5 April 2011; ECtHR, *Vladimir Vasilyev* v. *Russia*, Application No. 28370/05, 10 January 2012; ECtHR, *Artyunyan* v. *Russia*, Application No. 48977/09, 10 January 2012; ECtHR, *Grzywaczewski* v. *Poland*, Application No. 18364/06, 31 May 2012.

[91] *Jasinskis* v. *Latvia*, note 80. [92] Ibid. para. 59.

[93] See also ECtHR, *Farbtuhs* v. *Latvia*, Application No. 4672/02, 2 December 2004, para. 56.

[94] In *Price* v. *UK*, note 86, para. 30, it was held that 'to detain a severely disabled person in conditions where she is dangerously cold, risks developing sores because her bed is too hard or unreachable, and is unable to go to the toilet or keep clean without the greatest of difficulty, constitutes degrading treatment contrary to Article 3 of the Convention'.

[95] *Jasinskis* v. *Latvia*, note 80, para. 40. See above Chapter 7.

[96] In light of this finding, the Court considered that there was no need to examine Mr Jasinskis' complaint under Article 3 ECHR.

of the Strasbourg Court.[97] The first trend that she identifies concerns the 'willingness of the Court to refer to the [CRPD]',[98] and the second trend:

> relates to the willingness of the Court to recognise that states may be under certain additional (positive) obligations, which amount to *de facto* reasonable accommodation duties, when it comes to protecting the rights of individuals with disabilities, in recognition of the different, and sometimes particularly vulnerable, situation such individuals are in, in comparison with persons without disabilities.[99]

In *Z. H.* v. *Hungary*,[100] the ECtHR came closer than it had done in *Jasinskis* to acknowledging a duty to reasonably accommodate persons with disabilities under the ECHR – this time in the context of an alleged violation of Article 3 ECHR, read in conjunction with Article 5(2) ECHR (the right to be informed of the reasons for one's arrest and charge). The applicant was a Hungarian national who was deaf and had an intellectual disability. He was also unable to speak, to use sign language or to read or write. The applicant complained that, on account of his disabilities, he could not understand the reasons for his arrest on a charge of mugging, in alleged violation of Article 5(2) ECHR. The applicant further complained that his detention had amounted to inhuman and degrading treatment, in alleged breach of Article 3 ECHR. In interpreting the provisions of the ECHR, the Strasbourg Court referred to the CRPD in the context of relevant international law. Importantly, the Court cited Article 2 CRPD, which contains the definition of 'reasonable accommodation', and it also cited Article 14(2) CRPD, which requires the provision of reasonable accommodation to persons with disabilities in detention.[101] In addition, the Court cited Article 13 CRPD, which requires States Parties to provide 'procedural and age-appropriate accommodations' to disabled individuals in facilitating their access to justice. The Court read a *de facto* obligation to provide reasonable accommodation into Article 3 ECHR and stated that:

> given that the applicant undoubtedly belongs to a particularly vulnerable group . . . as such he should have benefited from reasonable steps on the side of the authorities to prevent situations likely to result in inhuman and degrading treatment.[102]

When considering the applicant's rights under Article 5(2) ECHR, the Court referred specifically to the CRPD when it stated that it was regrettable that the authorities 'did not take any truly "reasonable steps" – a notion quite akin to that of "reasonable accommodation" in Articles 2, 13 and 14 of the CRPD – to address the applicant's condition, in particular by procuring for him assistance by a lawyer or another suitable person'.[103] On the whole, the Court in *Z. H.* v.

[97] Waddington, 'Europees Hof voor de Rechten van de Mens, 21 december 2010, nr. 45744/08, Jasinskis tegen Letland', note 78, p. 564.
[98] Ibid. [99] Ibid. pp. 564–5.
[100] ECtHR, *Z. H.* v. *Hungary*, Application No. 28973/11, 8 November 2012.
[101] Ibid. para. 19. [102] Ibid. para. 31. [103] Ibid. para. 43.

Read *Price* v. *UK* and compare it to the later cases on disabled prisoners that were decided after the entry into force of the CRPD. Can you see a clear change in the ECtHR's approach to positive measures?

Hungary demonstrated a growing awareness of the individual provisions of the CRPD related to disability equality and, specifically, of the duty to accommodate under the CRPD.

Another relevant case is *Grimailovs* v. *Latvia*,[104] in which the Court cited the definition of 'reasonable accommodation' in Article 2 CRPD, together with the obligation to provide reasonable accommodation in detention (contained in Article 14(2) CRPD). The applicant in *Grimailovs* had alleged that there was a violation of Article 3 ECHR on account, *inter alia*,[105] of the unsuitability of prison facilities for persons with disabilities. The applicant complained that the prison facilities were unsuitable for him as a wheelchair user, as there was no social care or assistance in the prison to help him with his everyday activities and, as a result, he had to rely on the voluntary assistance of his cellmate.[106] The Court held that, while the ECHR does not guarantee a right to social assistance *per se*, the applicant's special needs were not sufficiently attended to by the State.[107] It ruled that:

> the help offered by the applicant's cellmate did not form part of any organised assistance by the State to ensure that the applicant was detained in conditions compatible with respect for his human dignity. It cannot therefore be considered suitable or sufficient in view of the applicant's physical disability.[108]

By recognising that this lack of organised assistance constituted degrading treatment contrary to Article 3 of the Convention,[109] the Court again reads a *de facto* reasonable accommodation duty into that same Article.

[104] ECtHR, *Grimailovs* v. *Latvia*, Application No. 6087/03, 25 June 2013.

[105] The applicant in *Grimailovs* v. *Latvia* also alleged a failure to examine adequately a complaint of alleged police ill-treatment. The Court found a violation of Article 3 ECHR in this regard. In addition, the applicant complained under Article 3 ECHR that, because of the lack of adequate medical assistance in the prison hospital and the prison itself, his state of health had deteriorated considerably, he had become paraplegic and had been certified as being Category 1 disabled, only being able to move in a wheelchair. The Court dismissed these allegations, ruling that the applicant did not lay the basis of an arguable claim in that regard.

[106] *Grimailovs* v. *Latvia*, note 104, para. 121. [107] Ibid. para. 161. [108] Ibid.

[109] Ibid. para. 162.

4.3.2 *The Potential Influence of the CRPD on the Interpretation of Articles 2 and 3 ECHR*

While the ECtHR has already drawn on the CRPD in many cases to inform its interpretation of ECHR rights for persons with disabilities in detention, the Court 'appears reluctant to specify the exact duty to accommodate which States bear in the disability context'.[110] In addition, the ECtHR analyses the claims of individuals with disabilities under the substantive provisions of the ECHR, primarily Articles 2 and 3 ECHR, and the Court does not seem to view the failure to provide reasonable accommodation in institutional settings as a form of discrimination.[111] However, while the ECtHR's approach is not always consistent, there is a clear recognition by the Court that some form of reasonable accommodation is necessary to ensure equal enjoyment of rights by persons with disabilities in detention. As demonstrated above, the Court has even likened the state obligations that it has read into ECHR rights for prisoners with disabilities to the CRPD's duty to accommodate. The development of the concept of 'reasonable accommodation', particularly by the CRPD Committee, may influence the Court to specify explicitly the scope of Contracting States' duties towards prisoners with disabilities under the ECHR. In contrast to the Court's restricted case law in this regard, Lord and Brown note that the CRPD 'offers a legal framework which can embrace both the substantive rights involved in these cases, and, crucially, adequately address the underlying discrimination, which has created or exacerbated the violations'.[112]

4.3.3 *Article 8 ECHR: Accessibility and Reasonable Accommodation for Persons with Disabilities*

ARTICLE 8 ECHR

1. Everyone has the right to respect for his private and family life, his home and his correspondence.

[110] Broderick, *The Long and Winding Road to Equality and Inclusion for Persons with Disabilities: The United Nations Convention on the Rights of Persons with Disabilities*, note 28, p. 346.

[111] Ibid, p. 343.

[112] Janet Lord and Rebecca Brown, 'The Role of Reasonable Accommodation in Securing Substantive Equality for Persons with Disabilities: The UN Convention on the Rights of Persons with Disabilities', in Marcia Rioux, Lee Ann Basser and Melinda Jones (eds.), *Critical Perspectives on Human Rights and Disability Law* (Boston: Martinus Nijhoff, 2011), p. 273, p. 284.

2. There shall be no interference by a public authority with the exercise of this right except such as is in accordance with the law and is necessary in a democratic society in the interests of national security, public safety or the economic well-being of the country, for the prevention of disorder or crime, for the protection of health or morals, or for the protection of the rights and freedoms of others.

Article 8(1) ECHR requires Contracting States to ensure respect for private and family life, home and correspondence. The Strasbourg Court has interpreted the constituent elements of Article 8 ECHR as well as the notion of 'respect' inherent to Article 8(1) quite expansively. It has developed a wide range of negative obligations (duties of the state not to interfere) and positive obligations (duties of the state to take action) under the ECHR.[113] In the disability context, three aspects covered by the concept of 'private life' are relevant: 'physical and psychological integrity', 'the right to autonomy or self-determination', and 'the right to establish relationships with other human beings'.[114]

The ECtHR appears to accept that Article 8 ECHR may, in exceptional circumstances, require positive measures for individuals who are particularly 'vulnerable'. In that connection, the Strasbourg Court's analysis of Article 8 incorporates two factors, namely the existence of a 'direct and immediate link between the measures sought by an applicant and the latter's private ... life' and the striking of a fair balance between individual interests and the general interests of society at large.[115] The Court has connected the concept of 'private life' with accessibility and reasonable accommodation in several cases, both pre- and post-CRPD. It has stated that the lack of access to public or residential buildings affects the lives of persons with disabilities in such a way as to interfere with the 'right to personal development' and the 'right to establish and develop relationships with other human beings and the outside world'.[116] The ECtHR has acknowledged that Contracting States have positive obligations to guarantee respect for the private life of disabled individuals. However, the Strasbourg Court has not always been consistent or coherent in

113 See, among others, ECtHR, *Van Kück* v. *Germany*, Application No. 35968/97, 12 June 2003; see also ECtHR, *L* v. *Lithuania*, Application No. 27527/03, 11 September 2007.

114 See Waddington, 'Europees Hof voor de Rechten van de Mens, 21 december 2010, nr. 45744/08, Jasinskis tegen Letland', note 78, citing Paul Bowen's analysis of the Court's case law in Paul Bowen, 'Article 8 and "Private Life": The Protean Right' (2010) *ALBA Seminar, Dought Street Chambers*, pp. 6–8.

115 ECtHR, *Botta* v. *Italy*, Application No. 21439/93, 24 February 1998; ECtHR, *Zehnalová and Zehnal* v. *the Czech Republic*, Application No. 38621/97, 14 July 2002; ECtHR, *Sentges* v. *Netherlands*, Application No. 27677/02, 8 July 2003.

116 *Zehnalová and Zehnal* v. *the Czech Republic*, note 115, para. 12.

the approach that it takes to assessing disability claims and in determining state liability for breaches of Article 8. The Court generally grants Contracting States a very wide margin of appreciation[117] when it comes to positive obligations. In particular, it is the financial aspect of claims[118] that has restricted the Court's intervention in cases giving rise to positive obligations.[119]

Case law on Article 8 ECHR has been criticised for the Strasbourg Court's fragmented approach,[120] which does not clearly define the limits of state responsibility and which does not analyse the rights of persons with disabilities in a coherent manner.[121] In two cases relating to general accessibility measures, *Botta* v. *Italy*[122] and *Zehnalová and Zehnal* v. *the Czech Republic*,[123] the applicants had claimed, respectively, that the right to private life inherent to Article 8 had been infringed when the relevant public authorities had failed to ensure that a private beach and public buildings were accessible to people with impaired mobility. The claim in *Botta* was rejected on the basis that the right asserted concerned 'interpersonal relations of such a broad and indeterminate scope'[124] that there was no conceivable direct link between the measures the state was urged to take and the applicant's private life.[125] Similarly, the Court declared that Article 8 ECHR was not applicable in *Zehnalova and Zehnal* v. *the Czech Republic*.[126] In that case, the applicant had complained about the inaccessibility of most of the public (government) buildings and buildings open to the public in her hometown, without giving details of the alleged obstacles that these buildings posed to her everyday life. The Court

[117] Colm O'Cinneide, 'Extracting Protection for the Rights of Persons with Disabilities from Human Rights Frameworks: Established Limits and New Possibilities', in Oddný Mjöll Arnardóttir and Gerard Quinn (eds.), *The UN Convention on the Rights of Persons with Disabilities, European and Scandinavian Perspectives* (Leiden/Boston: Brill, 2009), p. 184.

[118] The Court has expressly anticipated such an effect in the case of *Sentges* v. *Netherlands*, note 115 above and in ECtHR, *Pentiacova and 48 Others* v. *Moldova*, Application No. 14462/03, 4 January 2005.

[119] See the arguments by Dimitris Xenos, 'The Human Rights of the Vulnerable' (2009) 13(4) *The International Journal of Human Rights* 591, at 604.

[120] See, for example, de Schutter, 'Reasonable Accommodations and Positive Obligations under the European Convention on Human Rights', note 87; see also, Ellie Palmer, 'Protecting Socio-Economic Rights Through the European Convention on Human Rights: Trends and Developments in the European Court of Human Rights' (2009) 2(4) *Erasmus Law Review* 397, at 402.

[121] See further on this point, Andrea Broderick, 'The United Nations Convention on the Rights of Persons with Disabilities and the European Convention on Human Rights: A Tale of Two Halves or a Potentially Unified Vision of Human Rights?' (2018) 7(2) *Cambridge International Law Journal* 199.

[122] *Botta* v. *Italy*, note 115.

[123] *Zehnalová and Zehnal* v. *the Czech Republic*, note 115.

[124] *Botta* v. *Italy*, note 115, para. 35.

[125] Ibid. para. 35.

[126] *Zehnalová and Zehnal* v. *the Czech Republic*, note 115.

> Read *Botta* v. *Italy* and compare it with *Sentges* v. *the Netherlands*. Can you see why *Botta* is deemed to relate to accessibility measures, while *Sentges* concerns reasonable accommodation?

emphasised that positive obligations will only be found to exist in exceptional circumstances where a special link arises between the measure sought and the exercise of Article 8 rights.[127] The Court doubted the existence of such a link in *Zehnalová* on account of a lack of convincing evidence pointing to the daily use of the large number of buildings mentioned by the applicants.[128]

The 'direct link' was (eventually) found to exist[129] in the inadmissibility decisions, *Marzari* v. *Italy*[130] and *Sentges* v. *the Netherlands*.[131] As opposed to *Botta* and *Zehnalová* (where the applicants had requested the adoption of general measures for the benefit of a broadly defined community), in the cases of *Marzari*[132] and *Sentges*, it was claimed that the respective states had not adopted personalised accommodations for the benefit of the particular applicant in question.[133]

Sentges v. *the Netherlands*[134] concerned a man suffering from Duchenne Muscular Dystrophy, which made him completely dependent on others. The applicant asserted that the state had failed to discharge its positive obligations under Article 8 ECHR by refusing to provide him with a robotic arm, costing in the region of 36,000 euro. The applicant claimed that the domestic authorities

127 *Zehnalová and Zehnal* v. *the Czech Republic*, note 115, para. 12. 128 Ibid.

129 As noted by Waddington, the Court resolved the case based on the assumption that Article 8 ECHR was applicable (meeting the 'direct and immediate link' requirement), without actually finding this to be the case. See Lisa Waddington, 'Unravelling the Knot: Article 8, Private Life, Positive Duties and Disability: Rewriting *Sentges v. Netherlands*', in Eva Brems (ed.), *Diversity and European Human Rights: Rewriting Judgments of the ECHR* (Cambridge: Cambridge University Press, 2013), pp. 329–51.

130 ECtHR, *Marzari* v. *Italy*, Application No. 36448/97, 4 May 1999.

131 *Sentges* v. *the Netherlands*, note 115.

132 However, in *Marzari* v. *Italy*, the state demonstrated that, while the local authorities had tried to find adequate housing solutions for the applicant, Mr Marzari was never cooperative and did not use the venues that were available to him. In this light, the applicant's complaint was found to be inadmissible.

133 De Schutter, 'Reasonable Accommodations and Positive Obligations under the European Convention on Human Rights', note 87.

134 *Sentges* v. *the Netherlands*, note 115.

had breached his right to respect for private life and, more specifically, his right to establish and develop relationships with other human beings as well as his right to self-determination.[135] Notwithstanding this, the Court granted the state a wide margin of appreciation. It did so on the basis that some support had already been provided to the applicant and that providing further support would impose a stringent financial burden on the state.[136] The Court adopted an inconsistent approach to positive obligations in *Sentges*, as it did not consider whether a direct and immediate link had been established by the applicant between the measures sought and the right in question.[137] Instead, the Court went directly to the balancing stage of its analysis, balancing the rights of the applicant with those of the community at large.

Additionally, in *Molka* v. *Poland*,[138] the ECtHR declared the applicant's complaint inadmissible and granted the state a wide margin of appreciation in fulfilling its obligations. Mr Molka, who was a wheelchair user, had complained about the failure of the local authorities to provide him with appropriate access to the polling station where he intended to vote. The applicant had refused the reasonable accommodation proposed to him by the local authorities (entering the polling station with the assistance of a third person, either on a stretcher or in a wheelchair), as he felt that it would have been degrading for him. In light of the state's margin of appreciation, the ECtHR considered that the accommodation provided was adequate and, as a result, declared the applicant's complaint ill-founded.

Other relevant ECtHR judgments, adopted after the entry into force of the CRPD, focus on the violation of Article 8 ECHR read in conjunction with Article 14 ECHR. Those cases concern reasonable accommodations, rather than general accessibility measures. The case of *Bayrakcı* v. *Turkey*[139] involved a disabled employee who alleged a lack of suitable toilet facilities at his workplace. The Court examined whether the complaint fell within the scope of Article 8 and ruled that the notion of 'private life' is a broad one, which covers the physical and psychological integrity of an individual. The complaint was declared inadmissible for failure to exhaust domestic remedies. However, the ECtHR stated that the absence of toilets adapted to the applicant's disability at his workplace had the potential to have real and serious consequences for the applicant's daily life. In addition, the Court considered that the failure to install a toilet adapted to the applicant's needs may have

[135] Ibid. para. 5.

[136] The Court relied partly on the finding that the applicant had already received some assistance (i.e. an electric wheelchair with an adapted joystick), having met the applicable disability and income-based criteria.

[137] Waddington, 'Unravelling the Knot: Article 8, Private Life, Positive Duties and Disability: Rewriting *Sentges v. Netherlands*', note 129, p. 341.

[138] ECtHR, *Molka* v. *Poland*, Application No. 56550/00, 11 April 2006.

[139] ECtHR, *Bayrakcı* v. *Turkey*, Application No. 2643/09, 28 February 2013.

given rise to feelings of humiliation and distress that had the potential to affect his personal autonomy and, therefore, the quality of his private life.[140] This statement of the ECtHR suggests that the Court might have been willing to recognise a violation of Article 8 ECHR in conjunction with Article 14 ECHR if the complaint had not been deemed inadmissible.

Moreover, in *Kacper Nowakowski* v. *Poland*,[141] the Court considered (to a very limited extent and somewhat implicitly) the role of reasonable accommodation in the exercise of ECHR rights. In that regard, the Court referred to the specific needs of persons with disabilities in the context of an alleged violation of the right to respect for family life under Article 8 ECHR, read in conjunction with Article 14 ECHR. The case concerned the rights of a deaf and mute father to contact his son, who also had a hearing impairment. The applicant, Mr Nowakowski, complained that the dismissal of his request to contact his son had been based solely on his disability and had been discriminatory. The national court facilitated contact arrangements with the child's mother, since she was able to communicate both orally and in sign language, with a view to initiating contact between the applicant and his son. However, this solution ignored the existing animosity between the parents and the frequent complaints by the applicant (the father) that the mother had attempted to obstruct contact. The ECtHR highlighted that:

> the domestic courts should have envisaged additional measures, more adapted to the specific circumstances of the case ... Having regard to the specifics of the applicant's situation and the nature of his disability, the authorities were required to implement particular measures that took due account of the applicant's situation. The Court refers here to the second sentence of [Article 23(2) CRPD], which provides that 'State Parties shall render appropriate assistance to persons with disabilities in the performance of their child-rearing responsibilities'.[142]

4.3.4 *The Potential Influence of the CRPD on the Interpretation of Article 8 ECHR*

The wide-ranging rights in the CRPD are potentially relevant to the interpretation of Article 8 ECHR. In particular, the core obligations inherent to many CRPD rights, such as Article 19 (requiring States Parties to take effective and appropriate measures to facilitate full inclusion and participation in the community), have potential relevance to the interpretation of Article 8 ECHR. Waddington suggests that the CRPD may lead the ECtHR to find that states 'have a narrower margin of appreciation with regard to Article 8, to the extent

[140] Ibid. para. 26.

[141] ECtHR, *Kacper Nowakowski* v. *Poland*, Application No. 32407/13, 10 January 2017.

[142] Ibid. para. 93.

that the right protected by Article 8 is also protected by the CRPD'.[143] The scope of positive obligations under the ECHR, and particularly under Article 8, is not unlimited. This has been clearly demonstrated by the Strasbourg Court in many cases.[144] Thus, it is unlikely that the Court will accept more widespread claims by applicants for general accessibility measures. However, there is further potential for the introduction of the reasonable accommodation duty under Article 8 ECHR. The CRPD's duty to accommodate and its interpretation by the CRPD Committee might assist the Strasbourg Court in assessing the justifications put forward by Contracting States to the ECHR and in deciding whether a particular reasonable accommodation constitutes a disproportionate burden under the applicable thresholds in Article 8 ECHR.

4.3.5 *Article 14 ECHR: Discrimination on the Ground of Disability and Reasonable Accommodation*

Article 14 ECHR prohibits discrimination 'on any ground'. That Article specifically enumerates a list of grounds of discrimination, 'such as sex, race, colour, language, religion, political or other opinion, national or social origin, association with a national minority, property, birth or other status'. Notably, Article 14 ECHR cannot be invoked independently. It is accessory to the substantive rights contained in the Convention.

ARTICLE 14 ECHR

The enjoyment of the rights and freedoms set forth in this Convention shall be secured without discrimination on any ground such as sex, race, colour, language, religion, political or other opinion, national or social origin, association with a national minority, property, birth or other status.

Disability does not feature explicitly under the protected grounds contained in Article 14 ECHR, nor does it feature as a ground of discrimination in Protocol 12 to the ECHR.[145] Protocol 12 expands the scope of the prohibition of discrimination under the ECHR, by guaranteeing equal treatment in the enjoyment of any right, including rights protected under

[143] Waddington, 'Unravelling the Knot: Article 8, Private Life, Positive Duties and Disability: Rewriting *Sentges v. Netherlands*', note 127 above, p. 349.

[144] See ECtHR, *La Parola* v. *Italy*, Application No. 39712/98, 30 November 2000.

[145] Protocol No. 12 to the Convention for the Protection of Human Rights and Fundamental Freedoms, 4 November 2000, in force 1 April 2005, ETS No. 177.

national law. Notwithstanding the absence of disability as an explicit ground of protection under the ECHR, the Strasbourg Court has established, in *Glor* v. *Switzerland*,[146] that the ground of 'other status' in Article 14 also encompasses the prohibition of discrimination on the basis of disability. The *Glor* case revolved around the application of Swiss legislation concerning a military-service tax, the payment of which was required for those who did not carry out military service. Swiss law provided for a twin-track system, exempting from the payment of tax all those who were deemed to have a 'major' disability (i.e. a physical or psychosocial disability reaching a threshold of 40 per cent). Swiss law required the payment of the tax by all other individuals who were declared unfit to perform military service by virtue of a 'minor' disability. The applicant, Mr Glor, suffered from diabetes and was declared to be unsuitable for military service. Since his condition did not meet the threshold of 40 per cent physical or psychosocial disability laid down under Swiss law, he was required to pay the tax in question, by reason of his not carrying out military service. Mr Glor argued that the disability threshold set by Swiss law was discriminatory and violated Article 14 ECHR. The Strasbourg Court ruled that the Swiss authorities had failed to strike a balance between the protection of the interests of the community as a whole and respect for the rights of Mr Glor as a person with a disability. The ECtHR recognised that the list of grounds of discrimination contained in Article 14 is not exhaustive and that discrimination based on disability is included under the 'other status' ground contained in Article 14. The Court further held that the distinction made by the Swiss authorities between persons who are unfit for service (and not liable to pay the tax in question) and persons who are unsuitable for service (but still obliged to pay the tax) was not justified and constituted discrimination. Favalli highlights that, in *Glor* v. *Switzerland*, the ECtHR adopted a broad conceptualisation of what constitutes a disability, in line with the CRPD, and she argues that such a broad conceptualisation has been upheld in subsequent decisions in which the Court has extended the application of the non-discrimination norm under Article 14 of the ECHR to individuals affected by HIV, as a form of disability.[147] Moreover, the Court adopted a heightened standard of scrutiny in *Glor*, ruling that States have a 'considerably reduced'[148] margin of appreciation in establishing different

[146] *Glor* v. *Switzerland*, note 80 above.

[147] Silvia Favalli, 'The United Nations Convention on the Rights of Persons with Disabilities in the Case Law of the European Court of Human Rights and in the Council of Europe Disability Strategy 2017–2023: "from Zero to Hero"' (2018) 18(3) *Human Rights Law Review*, 517.

[148] *Glor* v. *Switzerland*, note 80 above, para. 84.

legal treatment on account of the 'need to prevent discrimination against people with disabilities and foster their full participation and integration in society'.[149] In narrowing the margin of appreciation of the state concerned, the Court enquired as to what prevented the authorities from 'setting in place special forms of service for people in a situation comparable to that of the applicant'.[150] The ECtHR gave examples of what it considered to be viable alternatives for the applicant, namely 'activities which, although carried out within the armed forces, required less physical effort and could therefore be performed by people like the applicant'.[151] This can be seen as an implicit recognition of some form of duty to accommodate within Article 14 ECHR. At the very least, 'it demonstrates the Court's willingness to consider the potential special measures which States can take in order to accommodate the needs of, and facilitate the rights of, disabled applicants'.[152] This illustrates a greater understanding of the social-contextual model of disability by the Court.

In a series of recent cases, decided under Article 14 ECHR in conjunction with Article 2 of Protocol No. 1 (on the right to education), the Strasbourg Court has 'shown itself to be cognisant of the educational disadvantage encountered by persons with disabilities'.[153] Of particular importance with regard to the Court's jurisprudence in the field of tertiary education for persons with disabilities is the case of *Çam* v. *Turkey*.[154] The applicant in that case had complained of a violation of her right to education under Article 2 of Protocol 1 and Article 14 ECHR, submitting that the respondent state had failed to provide disabled students with equal opportunities in accessing education. The Court in *Çam* found a violation of both Articles following the refusal of the Turkish National Music Academy to enrol the applicant on account of her visual impairment. The ECtHR focused on the importance of positive measures, to ensure that learners with disabilities could enjoy the right to education on a non-discriminatory basis. In that context, the Court referred to the reasonable accommodation duty enshrined in Article 2 CRPD.[155] Significantly, the Court considered that discrimination on the ground of disability extends to the refusal to provide a reasonable accommodation, in line with the CRPD.[156] This

149 Ibid. 150 Ibid. 151 Ibid. para. 94.

152 Broderick, *The Long and Winding Road to Equality and Inclusion for Persons with Disabilities: The United Nations Convention on the Rights of Persons with Disabilities*, note 28, pp. 322–3.

153 Andrea Broderick, Case Note: *Enver* v. *Sahin*, Verbod op discriminatie op grond van handicap, Recht op onderwijs, VN-Gehandicaptenverdrag, 'Doeltreffende aanpassingen', European Human Rights Cases EHRC 2018/106, EHRM 30-01-2018.

154 ECtHR, *Çam* v. *Turkey*, Application No. 51500/08, 23 February 2016. 155 Ibid. para. 65.

156 Ibid. para. 67. See Delia Ferri, 'L'accomodamento ragionevole per le persone con disabilità in Europa: dal "Transatlantic Borrowing" alla "Cross-Fertilization"' (2017) 2 *Diritto Pubblico Comparato ed Europeo* 151; Joseph Damamme, 'Disability Discrimination because of Denial

> Read *Çam* v. *Turkey* and *Enver Şahin* v. *Turkey*. Compare and contrast the two decisions of the Court.

was in spite of the fact that the applicant had not specifically requested a reasonable accommodation from the domestic authorities.[157] It is further noteworthy that the Strasbourg Court heavily criticised the national authorities for making no attempt to identify the applicant's specific needs and for not tailoring its music lessons to students with visual impairments.[158] The Court stated that, by refusing to enrol the applicant without considering ways to accommodate her disability, the national authorities had prevented her, without any objective justification, from exercising her right to education. In doing so, the Court interpreted the ECHR in light of the CRPD and held that persons with disabilities are entitled to reasonable accommodation, which 'helps to correct factual inequalities which are unjustified and therefore amount to discrimination'.[159]

A later case, *Enver Şahin* v. *Turkey*,[160] was brought before the Court by Mr Şahin – a student who had been rendered paraplegic following an accident in 2005. The facts of the case turned on the applicant's inability to access the building of Firat University in Turkey due to the lack of facilities adjusted to his impairment. The applicant alleged, *inter alia*, a discriminatory interference with his right to education under Article 2 of Protocol No. 1 in conjunction with Article 14 ECHR, on account of the fact that he had been obliged to give up his studies following the refusal of his request for adaptation of the relevant facilities. The Strasbourg Court placed heavy emphasis on the importance of the fundamental principle of non-discrimination in the exercise of the right to education, a principle which has been enshrined in several international instruments, including the CRPD. The ECtHR concluded that inclusive education is, unquestionably, a component of the

of "Reasonable Accommodations": A Very Positive Connection between the ECHR and the UNCRPD in *Çam v. Turkey*' (Strasbourg Observers, 1 April 2016), available at https://strasbourgobservers.com/category/cases/cam-v-turkey/.

157 Joseph Damamme 'Disability and University (Pragmatic) Activism: The Pros and Cons of *Enver Şahin v. Turkey*' (Strasbourg Observers, 9 March 2018), available at https://strasbourgobservers.com/2018/03/09/disability-and-university-pragmatic-activism-the-pros-and-cons-of-enver-sahin-v-turkey/.

158 *Çam* v. *Turkey*, note 153, para. 68.

159 Ibid. para. 65.

160 *Enver Sahin* v. *Turkey*, Application No. 23065/12, 30 January 2018.

international responsibility of states.[161] The ECtHR conceded that, in ensuring access for persons with disabilities to educational institutions, domestic authorities are in the best position to assess the margin of appreciation according to their available funds.[162] Nonetheless, the Court affirmed that Article 14 ECHR must be read in light of the CRPD's reasonable accommodation duty.[163] In finding a violation of Article 14 taken in conjunction with Article 2 of Protocol No. 1 to the Convention,[164] the Court ruled, *inter alia,* that the university had neglected to look for alternative solutions that would have enabled the applicant to resume his studies under conditions as close as possible to those provided to non-disabled students, without imposing an undue or disproportionate burden.[165] In many respects, the ECtHR's finding in *Şahin* 'consolidates' the approach adopted by the Court in the *Çam* case, highlighted above;[166] however, 'the Court goes even further than it did in *Çam* to assess the *suitability* of solutions proposed to the applicant, Mr Şahin, in light of his impairment and in order to ensure his autonomy and, ultimately, his participation in tertiary education'.[167] The *Şahin* judgment has been termed a 'welcome development' in the ECtHR's jurisprudence and has been deemed to constitute 'a strong endorsement of the right to inclusive education' contained in the CRPD[168] – one that adds 'considerable weight to the rights of persons with disabilities under the ECHR'.[169] In its judgment, the Court drew quite extensively on the CRPD, citing the accessibility duty (Article 9), the right to personal mobility (Article 20) and the right to education (Article 24), as well as the reasonable accommodation duty (Articles 2 and 5).

Outside the educational context, the ECtHR has also referred to the CRPD's duty of reasonable accommodation in *Guberina* v. *Croatia.*[170] That case arose

161 Ibid. para. 62. 162 Ibid. para. 64. 163 Ibid. para. 67. 164 Ibid. para. 75.

165 Ibid. para. 72.

166 Joseph Damamme, 'Disability and University (pragmatic) Activism: The Pros and Cons of *Enver Şahin v. Turkey*' (Strasbourg Observers, 9 March 2018), available at https://strasbourgobservers.com/2018/03/09/disability-and-university-pragmatic-activism-the-pros-and-cons-of-enver-sahin-v-turkey/.

167 Broderick, 'Case Note on *Enver* v. *Sahin*', note 152, para 8.

168 Oliver Lewis, 'Strasbourg Case: Disabled Student excluded from University Education' (Doughty Street Chambers, 2 February 2018), available at http://communitycare.doughtystreet.co.uk/post/102epfy/strasbourg-case-disabled-student-excluded-from-university-education.

169 Broderick, 'Case Note on *Enver* v. *Sahin*', note 152, para 13.

170 ECtHR, *Guberina* v. *Croazia,* Application No. 23682/13, 22 March 2016. See Delia Ferri, 'Reasonable Accommodation as a Gateway to the Equal Enjoyment of Human Rights: From New York to Strasbourg' (2018) 6(1) *Social Inclusion* 40; Silvia Favalli, 'L'Influenza sulla giurisprudenza di Strasburgo della Convenzione ONU sui diritti delle persone con disabilità: considerazioni a margine a Guberina c. Croazia' (2017) 11(3) *Diritti Umani e Diritto Internazionale*, 623–643. See further the analysis provided by Constantin Cojocariu, 'Guberina and Gherghina: The Two Sides of the Court's Disability Jurisprudence' (Strasbourg Observer, 17 May 2016), available at https://strasbourgobservers.com/2016/05/17/guberina-and-gherghina-the-two-sides-of-the-courts-disability-jurisprudence/.

from the complaint made by the father of a severely disabled child about the failure of the national tax authorities to take account of the needs of his child when determining his eligibility for tax exemptions on the purchase of property that was adapted to his child's needs. According to the national legislation applicable at the time of the judgment, tax exemptions were available to buyers who moved in order to solve their housing needs, when their previously owned property did not satisfy basic infrastructure requirements (i.e. when it did not satisfy basic hygiene and technical requirements). Arguing that his previously owned property did not satisfy such requirements, Mr Guberina requested a tax exemption on the purchase of the new property. In his request, he argued that accessibility constituted a basic infrastructure requirement and that his previous apartment did not satisfy his family's housing needs. However, the Croatian authorities dismissed his request, without taking into consideration his son's particular circumstances. After having exhausted domestic remedies, Mr Guberina took a case before the ECtHR, alleging a violation of Articles 8 and 14 ECHR in conjunction with Protocol 1 to the ECHR (the right to private and family life, the prohibition of discrimination, and the right to property, respectively). In its judgment, the Strasbourg Court reaffirmed the need to give an extensive interpretation to the concept of 'non-discrimination on the basis of disability', including that of 'discrimination by association'. Moreover, the ECtHR recalled the concept of 'reasonable accommodation', as defined in Article 2 CRPD. It found a violation of the prohibition of discrimination in Article 14 ECHR in conjunction with Article 1 of Protocol 1 to the ECHR, because the domestic authorities had failed to recognise the specificity of the applicant's situation with regard to the question of basic infrastructure and technical accommodation requirements.[171] In other words, the manner in which the Croatian legislation had been applied in practice had failed to accommodate the specific needs of the applicant, in breach of the CRPD. Notably, the ECtHR expressly considered that the denial of reasonable accommodation is a form of discrimination on the ground of disability, according to Article 14 ECHR, read in line with the text of the CRPD.

4.3.6 *The Potential Influence of the CRPD on the Interpretation of Article 14 ECHR*

The interpretation of Article 14 ECHR appears to be evolving in a manner that signals the Court's willingness to address systemic inequality and disadvantage with respect to vulnerable groups and individuals. Under the influence of the CRPD, the Court may move towards an approach whereby reasonable

[171] *Guberina* v. *Croatia*, note 170, para. 86.

accommodation and other positive obligations are perceived as a vital means by which to correct the many inequalities faced by persons with disabilities.

Arnardóttir has identified the magnifying effects that Article 14 can have in relation to other ECHR rights.[172] According to Arnardóttir, the first magnifying effect occurs when another ECHR article is applicable but the discriminatory element functions as an additional violation or as an aggravating factor. With regard to the Court's case law on Articles 2 and 3 ECHR, outlined above,[173] an increased focus on the non-discrimination norm in Article 14 may serve to highlight the discriminatory effect of the disadvantageous conditions to which prisoners with disabilities are subjected. This might encourage the Court to outline the scope of Contracting States' positive obligations under the ECHR in detention settings.

Another magnifying effect outlined by Arnardóttir concerns a situation where the claim in question does not come within the legal scope of an ECHR article, but where the invocation of Article 14 ECHR leads to an acknowledgement under the ECHR of an additional interest related to the right to non-discrimination. With regard to Article 8 ECHR, Fredman has argued that '[i]t is when allied with the equality guarantee in Article 14 that Article 8 has constituted the most potent source of positive duties'.[174] In the cases of *Botta* and *Zehnalovà,* outlined above, the applicants tried to rely on Article 14 in conjunction with Article 8. However, since the Court found, in both instances, that there had been no interference in the applicants' private lives (and, thus, that Article 8 was not applicable), their claims were unsuccessful. This meant that the applicants could not invoke Article 14 ECHR. Increased focus by the Strasbourg Court on Article 14 ECHR bodes well for the further development of positive obligations under both the ECHR's non-discrimination provision and also across the substantive articles of the ECHR, subject to the margin of appreciation doctrine.

4.3.7 *The ECtHR and Legal Capacity*

By way of contrast with the CRPD,[175] the ECHR does not include a specific provision on legal capacity. However, the ECtHR has commented on the legal capacity of persons with disabilities in several decisions in connection, in particular, with the following ECHR rights: Article 5 (the right to liberty and

[172] Oddný Mjöll Arnardóttir, 'Discrimination as a Magnifying Lens: Scope and Ambit under Article 14 and Protocol No. 12', in Eva Brems and Janneke Gerards (eds.), *Shaping Rights in the ECHR: The Role of the European Court of Human Rights in Determining the Scope of Human Rights* (Cambridge: Cambridge University Press, 2014), p. 330.

[173] See above section 4.3.1.

[174] Sandra Fredman, *Human Rights Transformed: Positive Rights and Positive Duties* (Oxford: Oxford University Press, 2008), at p. 207.

[175] See above Chapter 6 of this textbook.

security), Article 6 (the right to a fair trial), Article 8 (the right to respect for private and family life), Article 13 (the right to an effective remedy) and Article 14 (the prohibition of discrimination).

With regard to Article 5 ECHR, the Court held, in *Luberti* v. *Italy*, that, in deciding whether an individual should be detained as a 'person of unsound mind', national authorities have a certain margin of appreciation.[176] However, in a number of cases (concerning the compulsory confinement of persons with disabilities in psychiatric institutions or hospitals), the ECtHR confirmed that a 'person of unsound mind' must be allowed to be heard, either in person or, where necessary, through some form of representation. In *Winterwerp* v. *Netherlands*,[177] the Court also set out three conditions that must be satisfied in order for the detention of 'a person of unsound mind' to be lawful within the meaning of Article 5(1), and to avoid arbitrary confinement and institutionalisation of persons with intellectual and psychosocial disabilities. In particular, the ECtHR stated that: aside from emergency cases, the individual concerned must be reliably shown to be of unsound mind before a competent authority on the basis of objective medical expertise; the mental disorder must be of a kind or degree warranting compulsory confinement; and the validity of continued confinement depends upon the persistence of such a disorder.[178] In addition, the Strasbourg Court made it clear that the possibility to hold 'persons of unsound mind' in detention cannot be applied so as to undermine the right to a fair trial.[179]

In more recent cases, the influence of the CRPD and the recognition of the legal capacity of all individuals has led the Court to condemn more firmly the detention of persons with intellectual or psychosocial disabilities in psychiatric hospitals and the lack of domestic remedies available to them to challenge incapacitation decisions adopted by domestic courts. Among the most notable cases in that regard is *Shtukaturov* v. *Russia*.[180] Mr Shtukaturov, who had a psychosocial disability, had been deprived of his legal capacity without his knowledge and had been placed in a psychiatric hospital by his mother. The ECtHR found that the legal incapacitation of the applicant violated his right to a fair trial under Article 6 and his right to respect for his private life pursuant to Article 8 ECHR. The Court also found that the subsequent involuntary placement of the applicant in a psychiatric hospital, without court review, violated his right to liberty under Article 5. In particular, the Court ruled that, in line with Article 8 ECHR, domestic authorities must strike a fair balance between the interests of a 'person of unsound mind' and the other legitimate interests concerned. While the ECtHR noted that

[176] ECtHR, *Luberti* v. *Italy*, Application No. 9019/8023, February 1984.

[177] *Winterwerp* v. *Netherlands*, note 71. [178] Ibid. para. 38. [179] Ibid.

[180] ECtHR, *Shtukaturov* v. *Russia*, Application No. 44009/05, 27 March 2008.

Contracting States enjoy a wide margin of appreciation,[181] it also stated that 'the existence of a mental disorder, even a serious one, cannot be the sole reason to justify full incapacitation'.[182] As such, Russian law was considered not to be in line with the ECHR, in that it distinguished between full capacity and full incapacity without recognising any 'borderline' situation and without providing a 'tailor-made response' to the individual in question. According to the Court, this amounted to a disproportionate interference with the applicant's private life.[183] With regard to Article 5 ECHR, the Court held that the impossibility for Mr Shtukaturov to have the legality of his ongoing hospitalisation reviewed before the Russian courts amounted to a violation of Article 5(4), which specifically provides for the right of everyone deprived of their liberty to have the lawfulness of their detention decided upon speedily by a court. According to the Mental Disability Advocacy Center (MDAC), the *Shtukaturov* decision 'constitutes a milestone in the evolution of European human rights standards in relation to persons with mental disabilities', since it clarifies the relevance of the ECHR in the context of legal capacity and guardianship.[184]

Another very relevant case in this context is *Stanev* v. *Bulgaria*.[185] Mr Stanev, having been diagnosed with schizophrenia, was placed under partial guardianship against his will. He was placed in a home for individuals with psychosocial disabilities in a remote mountain location. His attempts (through his lawyer) to apply to the regional court to have his legal capacity restored and to put an end to his confinement were unsuccessful. Accordingly, he brought a case to the ECtHR, whereby he alleged a violation, *inter alia*, of Article 5 ECHR. The ECtHR acknowledged 'the growing importance' that international instruments accord to individuals with psychosocial disorders and their autonomy.[186] It also referred explicitly to the CRPD and to the necessity for adequate procedural safeguards to be put in place to protect legally incapacitated individuals to the greatest extent possible.[187] The Court also recognised the necessity to ensure periodic reviews of the status of those who reside in institutions and to make appropriate remedies available for breach of their rights.[188] The ECtHR concluded that Bulgaria had violated Article 5(1), since Mr Stanev had been illegally detained in the institution in question. Moreover, the Court held that there had been a violation of

[181] Ibid. para. 87. [182] Ibid. para. 94. [183] Ibid. paras. 95–6.

[184] MDAC, *Shtukaturov v. Russia – Recommendations on legislative measures required to achieve full implementation of the judgment of the European Court of Human Rights*, available at www.mdac.info/sites/mdac.info/files/English_Shtukaturov_V_Russia.pdf.

[185] ECtHR, *Stanev* v. *Bulgaria*, Application No. 36760/06, 12 January 2012. For a summary of the decision, see Joseph Dute, 'ECHR 2012/8 Case of Stanev v. Bulgaria, 17 January 2012, no. 36760/06 (Grand Chamber)' (2012) 19(3) *European Journal of Health Law* 305.

[186] Ibid. para. 244. [187] Ibid. [188] Ibid.

Article 5(4) ECHR because Mr Stanev could not bring proceedings to have the lawfulness of his detention decided speedily by a court, and a violation of Article 5(5) concerning the impossibility for him to apply for compensation for his illegal detention as well as the lack of review by a court of the lawfulness of his detention. The Strasbourg Court also held that there had been a violation of Article 6 ECHR, which provides for the right to a fair trial, in that the applicant had been denied access to a court to seek restoration of his legal capacity.

Another relevant case in which the issue of legal capacity was at stake is *D. D.* v. *Lithuania*.[189] The case concerned the placement of a Lithuanian woman in a social care home for persons with psychosocial disabilities. The ECtHR found that there was a violation of her rights under Article 5, with regard to the freedom from arbitrary detention, and Article 6 ECHR. Specifically, the Court held that Lithuania had violated Article 5(4) of the Convention, in light of the fact that where a person is deprived of liberty at the request of his or her guardian, he or she must be accorded the opportunity of contesting that confinement before a court (with independent legal representation).

In *Lashin* v. *Russia*,[190] the Court also found a violation of the legal capacity of the applicant. The applicant suffered from schizophrenia and had been legally incapacitated since 2000. In 2002, he applied to the relevant Russian authority in order to register his marriage. His request was refused, because the Russian Family Code prohibited people with intellectual or psychosocial disabilities who had been legally incapacitated from getting married. The ECtHR, referring to Article 12(4) CRPD, held *inter alia* that the maintenance of the applicant's status as an incapacitated person and his inability to have that status reviewed constituted a violation of Article 8 ECHR.

Other cases, while considering the procedural requirements necessary for a valid detention or institutionalisation procedure and the right to challenge guardianship regimes, focus on the consequences of a deprivation of legal capacity. For example, in *Ivinović* v. *Croatia*[191] and in *A. N.* v. *Lithuania*,[192] the Strasbourg Court held that the deprivation of legal capacity of the applicants disproportionately affected their right to private life and entailed a violation of Article 8 ECHR.

In *Kiss* v. *Hungary*,[193] the Court found a violation of the right to vote of persons with intellectual disabilities. The applicant was placed under partial guardianship in May 2005 and had, as a result, been taken off the electoral register. His request to be re-registered was unsuccessful, since, under the

[189] ECtHR, *D. D.* v. *Lithuania*, Application No. 13469/06, 14 February 2012.

[190] ECtHR, *Lashin* v. *Russia*, Application No. 33117/02, 22 April 2013.

[191] ECtHR, *Ivinović* v. *Croatia*, Application No. 13006/13, 18 September 2014.

[192] ECtHR, *A. N.* v. *Lithuania*, Application No. 17280/08, 31 May 2016.

[193] ECtHR, *Kiss* v. *Hungary*, Application No. 38832/06, 20 May 2010.

Hungarian Constitution applicable at the time of the decision, individuals placed under guardianship did not have the right to vote. The applicant submitted an application to the ECtHR, alleging the unjustified deprivation of his right to vote. The Strasbourg Court held that there had been a violation of Article 3 of Protocol No. 1 to the ECHR (concerning the right to free elections), finding that the indiscriminate removal of voting rights on the ground of psychosocial disability alone (and the ensuing partial guardianship) could not be considered compatible with the legitimate grounds for restricting the right to vote.

As can be seen from the foregoing cases, there is a growing body of jurisprudence within the ECtHR on issues related to the legal capacity of persons with intellectual and psychosocial disabilities. Although the doctrine of the margin of appreciation still leaves Contracting States some leeway in terms of the imposition of guardianship regimes (and *de facto* allows for full guardianship regimes), the Strasbourg Court's jurisprudence has slowly come to protect the exercise of legal capacity. According to O'Mahony, all of the cases discussed above show that 'the ECtHR has been edging closer to the core of legal capacity and has already explicitly invoked the CRPD as an interpretive aid' to the ECHR. In that vein, O'Mahony argues that the Strasbourg Court 'may further develop its case law requiring states to ensure that they provide a supported decision-making model that facilitates legal capacity and life and inclusion in the community'; however, most recent cases demonstrate that the issue of legal capacity is still a contentious one for the ECtHR and a field in which the Strasbourg Court is reluctant to fully embrace the relevant CRPD norms.[194]

Read *Ivinonic* v. *Croatia* and *A.N.* v. *Lithuania.* Compare and contrast those cases with the more recent cases of *A. -M. V* v. *Finland* and *Delecolle* v. *France.*

[194] Charles O' Mahony, 'Legal capacity and detention: implications of the UN disability convention for the inspection standards of human rights monitoring bodies' (2012) 16(6) *The International Journal of Human Rights* 883, at 892. However, see ECtHR, *A. -M. V.* v. *Finland*, Application No. 53251/13, 23 March 2017, and ECtHR, *Delecolle* v. *France*, Application No. 37646/13, 28 October 2018. In these cases, the Court appears to take a more conservative approach to legal capacity.

5 THE EUROPEAN SOCIAL CHARTER AND THE REVISED CHARTER

Alongside the ECHR, the other major human rights instrument adopted within the CoE is the ESC of 1961, which, unlike the ECHR, does contain a provision related specifically to the rights of persons with disabilities. This section examines the most relevant provisions of the ESC and the decisions of the ECSR concerning the rights of persons with disabilities.

5.1 The Provisions of the European Social Charter and the Revised Charter

The ESC lays down twenty-three fundamental rights. Pursuant to Article 15 of the ESC, States Parties to the Charter undertake to adopt adequate measures to provide training facilities to disabled persons and to adopt measures to encourage employers to employ individuals with disabilities. The concept of 'disability' contained in the ESC is based on the outdated medical model. In line with changes that took place at the international level, the ESC was revised. The Revised Charter updated the original provision on disability contained in the ESC, in order to reflect the human rights model of disability. Article 15 of the revised ESC provides for the right of persons with disabilities to independence, social integration and participation in the life of the community.

ARTICLE 15 REVISED EUROPEAN SOCIAL CHARTER

With a view to ensuring to persons with disabilities, irrespective of age and the nature and origin of their disabilities, the effective exercise of the right to independence, social integration and participation in the life of the community, the Parties undertake, in particular:

1. to take the necessary measures to provide persons with disabilities with guidance, education and vocational training in the framework of general schemes wherever possible or, where this is not possible, through specialised bodies, public or private;
2. to promote their access to employment through all measures tending to encourage employers to hire and keep in employment persons with disabilities in the ordinary working environment and to adjust the working conditions to the needs of the disabled or, where this is not possible by reason of the disability, by arranging for or creating sheltered employment according to the level of disability. In certain cases, such measures may require recourse to specialised placement and support services;

3. to promote their full social integration and participation in the life of the community in particular through measures, including technical aids, aiming to overcome barriers to communication and mobility and enabling access to transport, housing, cultural activities and leisure.

The explanatory report to the revised ESC highlights that it 'no longer applies only to vocational rehabilitation but to the right of persons with disabilities to independent social integration, personal autonomy and participation in the life of the community in general'.[195] The explanatory report describes the new scope of Article 15 as follows:

Parties must aim to develop a coherent policy for persons with disabilities. The provision takes a modern approach to how the protection of the disabled shall be carried out, for example by providing that guidance, education and vocational training be provided whenever possible in the framework of general schemes rather than in specialised institutions ... It not only provides the possibility, but to a large extent obliges Parties to adopt positive measures for the disabled.[196]

Despite its emphasis on community living, Article 15 of the revised ESC seems much less progressive than the CRPD. In the first instance, the Revised Charter uses medical model language (e.g. 'the disabled'), unlike the CRPD. It also provides that, where open labour market participation is not possible by reason of disability, States Parties should arrange for 'creating sheltered employment according to the level of disability. In certain cases, such measures may require recourse to specialised placement and support services'.[197] This is not in line with the CRPD's emphasis on open labour market participation, and the CRPD has a potential role to play in ensuring that the ECSR interprets the provisions of the Revised Charter in line with changing international norms for persons with disabilities.

In addition to Article 15, Article 10 of the revised ESC requires States Parties to ensure the effective exercise of the right to vocational training, including for persons with disabilities. Furthermore, Article 17 of the Revised Charter contains the right of children and young persons (including children with disabilities) to social, legal and economic protection. Of added relevance to persons with disabilities is the cross-cutting non-discrimination norm, contained in Article E of the Revised ESC.[198]

[195] Explanatory Report to the European Social Charter (Revised), para. 63, available at http://conventions.coe.int/Treaty/EN/Reports/HTML/163.htm.

[196] Ibid. para. 64.

[197] Article 15(2), European Social Charter (Revised).

[198] Article E, Revised European Social Charter, states that the enjoyment of the rights set forth in the Charter 'shall be secured without discrimination on any ground such as race, colour, sex,

5.2 The Role of the European Committee of Social Rights in Protecting the Rights of Persons with Disabilities

5.2.1 *The Role of the ECSR in a Nutshell*

The Revised Charter has two monitoring mechanisms. It is subject to a reporting system, and for the States Parties that have accepted it, they are bound by it. The reporting system is complemented by the Additional Protocol of 1995, providing for a system of collective complaints.[199] The collective complaints procedure was introduced to increase the effectiveness of the ESC and to enable NGOs (among others) to challenge the non-implementation of the Revised Charter. The main body that monitors compliance under the two existing monitoring mechanisms is the ECSR.

The ECSR has the power to examine national reports in order to decide whether or not the situations in the countries concerned are in conformity with the ESC and the Revised Charter. Its decisions, known as 'conclusions', are published every year. If a State Party takes no action following a decision of the ECSR to the effect that the State Party in question does not comply with the Charter, the CoM will address a recommendation to that State Party, urging it to change the situation in law and/or in practice. In addition, the ECSR can hear collective complaints alleging violations of the substantive rights contained in the ESC and the Revised Charter. The role of the ECSR naturally differs from that of the ECtHR, which is a judicial body. Unlike the Strasbourg Court, the ECSR cannot consider individual applications – it can only hear complaints raised by certain NGOs about general situations of non-compliance with the ESC and the Revised Charter. The organisations entitled to lodge collective complaints with the ECSR are the European social partners: for example, the European Trade Union Confederation (ETUC), Business Europe, the International Organisation of Employers (OIE), INGOs and national trade unions. States Parties to the Revised Charter may also grant domestic NGOs the right to lodge complaints against them to the ECSR, but, to date, only Finland has done so. Unlike applications to the ECtHR, collective complaints may be lodged without domestic remedies being exhausted and without the claimant organisation being a victim of the relevant violation. The decisions adopted by the ECSR establish whether a State Party is in compliance with one or more provisions of the Revised ESC, but they cannot be enforced in a domestic court.

language, religion, political or other opinion, national extraction or social origin, health, association with a national minority, birth or other status'.

[199] CoE, Additional Protocol of 1995 providing for a system of collective complaints, 9 November 1995, in force 1 July 1998, ETS No. 158.

Legal scholars have recognised that the ECSR seems to be very open 'to be guided by other standards and treaty body jurisprudence'.[200] Lord and Brown point to the fact that the ECSR has a 'fairly strong record of looking to treaty body jurisprudence to guide its work', and they cite in that regard the collective complaint of *Mental Disability Advocacy Center (MDAC)* v. *Bulgaria*,[201] in which the ECSR draws on the general comments of the UN Committee on Economic, Social and Cultural Rights (CESCR)[202] as an interpretive aid to the provisions of the Revised Charter. In the more recent decision, *Mental Disability Advocacy Center (MDAC)* v. *Belgium*, the ECSR mentions General Comment No. 4 of the CRPD Committee (on inclusive education)[203] in the context of international law that is relevant to the facts of the case at issue.[204]

5.2.2 *Pre-CRPD Collective Complaints*

Before the adoption of the CRPD, two important collective complaints came before the ECSR, seeking to enforce the right of children with disabilities to education under the Revised Charter. The first complaint of relevance is *Autism Europe* v. *France*,[205] which was decided by the Committee in 2003. In that case, there was evidence that the proportion of autistic children being educated in either general or specialist schools in France was disproportionately low in comparison to non-disabled children. The French authorities had passed relevant legislation[206] in that field as far back as 1975; however, it had failed to enforce the legislation in the interim. In view of that, the Committee ruled that France had not made sufficient provision for the education of autistic children and, as a result, a high proportion of autistic children were deemed not to have received an appropriate education.[207] The Committee ruled that France was in breach of Article 15(1) and Article 17(1) of the Revised Charter, relating to the right of persons with disabilities to education and the general right of children and young people to education, respectively. The Committee also found that France violated the non-discrimination principle

[200] Lord and Brown, 'The Role of Reasonable Accommodation in Securing Substantive Equality for Persons with Disabilities: The UN Convention on the Rights of Persons with Disabilities', note 112, p. 292.

[201] Ibid. p. 292, citing *Mental Disability Advocacy Center (MDAC)* v. *Bulgaria*, Complaint No. 41/2007, European Committee of Social Rights, 3 June 2007.

[202] Ibid. para. 37.

[203] UN Committee on the Rights of Persons with Disabilities, General Comment No. 4, 2 September 2016, UN Doc. CRPD/C/GC/4. See Chapter 9 above.

[204] *Mental Disability Advocacy Center (MDAC)* v. *Belgium*, Complaint No. 109/2014, European Committee of Social Rights, 16 October 2017, para. 24.

[205] *Autism Europe* v. *France*, Complaint No. 13/2002, European Committee of Social Rights, 7 November 2003.

[206] The Disabled Persons Policy Act (1975).

[207] In the instant case, 80–90 per cent of autistic children did not receive an adequate education.

(contained in Article E of the Revised Charter) in the enjoyment of Charter rights. The ECSR made an important pronouncement with regard to the progressive realisation of the right to education. It stated that the Revised Charter requires States Parties to take not merely legal action but also practical action to give full effect to the rights recognised in it.[208] The ECSR also asserted that when the achievement of a right is exceptionally complex and particularly expensive to resolve, States Parties must take measures to do so 'within a reasonable time with measurable progress and to an extent consistent with the maximum use of available resources'.[209]

Similarly, in the case of *Mental Disability Advocacy Center (MDAC) v. Bulgaria*,[210] the ECSR considered a collective complaint in which the applicants alleged that a group of children with disabilities, who were residing in certain social care home institutions in Bulgaria, had received no education or inappropriate education on account of their disabilities and that this constituted a violation of Article 17(2) of the Revised Charter. The complaint stated that legislation guaranteeing the right to education for all children had not been implemented in respect of the children who resided in the social care institutions. In that regard, the evidence adduced highlighted government data that indicated that only 6.2 per cent of children living in the relevant institutions had been enrolled in schools. It was further alleged that mainstream schools had not been adapted to accommodate the needs of such children, and that staff in those institutions had provided either no education at all or inadequate education. The ECSR found that the children in question had been denied an effective right to education on account of disability discrimination. The Committee held that, although the Bulgarian government had undertaken measures to respect the right to education for children with disabilities living in institutions, by putting in place legislation and action plans, those laws and policies had not been implemented effectively. The ECSR also found that Bulgarian educational standards were inadequate, because mainstream educational institutions and curricula were not accessible in practice.[211] The Committee considered, therefore, that the criterion of accessibility was not fulfilled.[212] The Committee also found that mainstream schools were not adapted to the specific needs of children with intellectual disabilities, teachers were not properly trained, and resources were not developed to cater to the educational needs of children with disabilities. In addition, the ECSR ruled that the schools were not suited to meet the needs of children with intellectual disabilities and that the criterion of adaptability of education was not met.[213] Moreover, due to the absence of primary education opportunities, children

[208] *Autism Europe* v. *France*, note 205, para. 53. [209] Ibid.
[210] *Mental Disability Advocacy Centre (MDAC)* v. *Bulgaria*, note 201. [211] Ibid. para. 43.
[212] Ibid. [213] Ibid. para. 44.

with disabilities were ineligible to enter secondary education.[214] In view of this, the Committee determined that the government had failed to fulfil the three core criteria consistent with progressive realisation of rights, namely: a reasonable timeframe; measurable progress; and financing that is consistent with the maximum use of available resources.

The two cases highlighted above raise many issues that have clear relevance to the types of concerns which the CRPD seeks to address in the areas of inclusion and equality in education for persons with disabilities. Lord and Brown argue that *Autism Europe* v. *France* and *MDAC* v. *Bulgaria* 'reflect a progressive trend in recogni[s]ing and applying the right to an education for children with disabilities and, further, in animating the non-discrimination and equality provision of the Charter'.[215] However, they acknowledge the fact that 'the framework for non-discrimination and equality and reasonable accommodation in education in the CRPD offers additional tools for the European Committee of Social Rights (and indeed other treaty monitoring bodies) to draw upon in such cases'.[216]

5.2.3 *Post-CRPD Collective Complaints*

Since the coming into force of the CRPD, two collective complaints alleging violations of the right to education for people with disabilities have been submitted to the ECSR. Significantly, both of those complaints cite the CRPD.

The first collective complaint of relevance is that of *European Action of the Disabled (AEH)* v. *France*.[217] Notably, the complaint brought by *AEH* before the ECSR outlined the changing international context and asked the ECSR to examine the rights set out in the Revised Charter in accordance with Article 24 CRPD. In its decision on the merits, adopted on 18 March 2013, the ECSR referred to the CRPD, and in particular to Article 24 thereof, in the context of relevant international standards. However, it did not refer to the CRPD in the rest of its opinion, and it did not invoke the provisions of Article 24 CRPD as an interpretive aid for the Revised Charter rights. Notwithstanding this, the views adopted by the ECSR in *AEH* reflect a positive outcome for children with disabilities. In the case, the Committee ruled that there was direct discrimination contrary to Article E of the Revised Charter taken in conjunction with Article 15(1), because families had no other choice than to leave the national territory in order to educate their children with autism in a specialised school.

[214] Ibid. para. 46.

[215] Lord and Brown, 'The Role of Reasonable Accommodation in Securing Substantive Equality for Persons with Disabilities: The UN Convention on the Rights of Persons with Disabilities', note 200, p. 292.

[216] Ibid.

[217] *European Action of the Disabled (AEH)* v. *France*, Complaint No. 81/2012, European Committee of Social Rights, 12 September 2012.

The Committee also found that there was a violation of the foregoing rights, because France had allocated limited funds in its budgets for the education of children and adolescents with autism, which the Committee deemed disadvantageous to those persons with disabilities.

Following on from the *AEH* decision, another opportunity arose for the ECSR to provide a contextualised interpretation of the provisions of the Revised Charter by considering the CRPD. In 2014, the MDAC had sent a collective complaint to the ECSR, entitled *Mental Disability Advocacy Center* v. *Belgium*, alleging a violation of the non-discrimination norm (Article E) in relation to Articles 15 and 17 of the Revised Charter. In that complaint, the MDAC drew on Article 24 CRPD as a clear basis for its argumentation in support of the education of children with disabilities in the mainstream in the Flanders region of Belgium.[218] The MDAC also quoted the concluding observations of the CRPD Committee, in which the Committee stresses the importance of establishing education policies that guarantee the right to inclusive education. In its decision, the ECSR concluded unanimously that there was a violation of Article 15 (1) of the Revised Charter on the ground that the right to inclusive education of children with intellectual disabilities had not been effectively guaranteed in the Flemish Community of Belgium. In addition, the Committee found that there was a lack of effective remedies concerning the refusal of enrolment in mainstream schooling for children with intellectual disabilities. Moreover, the ECSR cited Article 24 CRPD, the Concluding Observations of the CRPD Committee on the Initial Report of Belgium, adopted in 2014, and its General Comment No. 4 (on inclusive education) in the context of relevant international law. According to De Beco, the outcome of this decision is 'proof of the filtering of international developments into the Council of Europe'.[219]

SUMMARY

- **The core work of the institutions of the CoE entails promoting and protecting the human rights of all individuals, and upholding democracy and respect for the rule of law.**
- **The CoE's work is structured around binding conventions and treaties, which set out common legal standards for its Member States on a variety of different**

[218] *Mental Disability Advocacy Center* v. *Belgium*, Complaint No.109/2014, 27 May 2014, paras. 64–6. For the relevant parts of the decision see note 204, in particular paras. 23–4, 106–7 and 113–4.

[219] Gauthier de Beco, 'MDAC v Belgium before the European Committee of Social Rights: The Right to Inclusive Education Pushed by the UN Convention on the Rights of Persons with Disabilities', 1 June 2018, available at www.ejiltalk.org/mdac-v-belgium-before-the-european-committee-of-social-rights-the-right-to-inclusive-education-pushed-by-the-un-convention-on-the-rights-of-persons-with-disabilities/#more-16237.

matters, and soft law documents that promote compliance with those standards at the policy level. The most important instrument for the protection of human rights is the ECHR. Another relevant instrument within the CoE is the ESC, which is a treaty guaranteeing social and economic rights that is 'complementary' to the ECHR.

- **While the CoE has not yet adopted any specific binding instrument on the rights of persons with disabilities, those rights are protected, to varying degrees, by the ECHR, the ESC and the Revised ESC.**
- **The CoE has developed a significant disability policy, which has been progressively informed by the human rights model of disability.**
- **The first comprehensive action plan of the CoE was the Disability Action Plan 2006–2015, which aimed to serve as a practical tool to develop and implement viable strategies to bring about the full participation of people with disabilities in society.**
- **In 2016, the CoE adopted the Strategy on the Rights of Persons with Disabilities 2017–2023. The overall goal of the Strategy is to achieve equality, dignity and equal opportunities for persons with disabilities in all areas of the CoE's field of action. The Strategy identifies five priority areas, which echo the general principles of the CRPD. Those priority areas also mirror, to a certain extent, the European Disability Strategy 2010–2020, adopted by the European Commission within the EU context.**
- **The institutions of the CoE have also issued recommendations and issue papers that draw specific guidance from the concrete provisions of the CRPD and formulate recommendations to be employed by CoE Member States in their implementation of disability rights.**
- **The ECHR does not contain any express reference to disability. Only Article 5(1)(e) ECHR (on the lawful detention of 'persons of unsound mind') constitutes an indirect reference to psychosocial disability. However, the ECtHR has advanced the rights of persons with disabilities by interpreting ECHR provisions in a wide and evolving manner.**
- **The CRPD is proving to be of potential significance to the Strasbourg Court in its interpretation of the ECHR. At the very least, the CRPD is acting as a reference point for the Strasbourg Court, although it has not always been consistent in referring to the UN Convention.**
- **Alongside the ECHR, the other major human rights instrument adopted within the CoE is the ESC of 1961, which, unlike the ECHR, does contain a provision pertaining specifically to the rights of persons with disabilities.**
- **Article 15 of the Revised ESC provides for the right of persons with disabilities to independence, social integration and participation in the life of the community.**
- **There is potential for the CRPD to influence the ECSR's interpretation of the revised ESC, in light of the fact that the latter instrument aims at the protection of social rights (which are essential to increasing participation and inclusion of persons with disabilities in society) and contains specific provisions for disabled individuals.**

ACTIVITIES

REVIEW QUESTIONS

1. How has the CoE's disability policy evolved over time?
2. What are the main judgments of the ECtHR on disability discrimination?
3. What are the most relevant decisions of the ECSR in relation to Article 15 of the Revised ESC?

ESSAY QUESTIONS

1. Discuss the main tenets of the CoE Strategy on the Rights of Persons with Disabilities 2017–2023, and compare and contrast it with the European Disability Strategy 2010–2020.

2. 'The ECtHR and the ECSR have borrowed several principles and concepts from the CRPD, in particular that of reasonable accommodation.' *Discuss.*

GROUP PROJECT

John is a visually impaired person. In 2017, he wanted to enrol in a course at the Freedonia State University (FSU), in order to become a biologist. Before enrolling, he passed the entrance test, which was designed to assess his general knowledge and skills. However, the FSU refused to enrol him, stating that he could not attend lectures in the university because the laboratories were not accessible to blind people and because the chemical elements used in the laboratories could not be used by people with disabilities (for safety reasons). John challenged the refusal before the domestic courts, but he was unsuccessful. He then decided to consult a lawyer, to see whether he could bring a claim against Freedonia before the ECtHR.

Discuss the group project, taking into account that Freedonia is a Contracting State of the ECHR.

FURTHER READING

Broderick, A., 'The United Nations Convention on the Rights of Persons with Disabilities and the European Convention on Human Rights: A Tale of Two Halves or a Potentially Unified Vision of Human Rights?' (2018) 7(2) *Cambridge International Law Journal* 199.

Broderick, A., 'A Reflection on Substantive Equality Jurisprudence: The Standard of Scrutiny at the ECtHR of Differential Treatment of Roma and Persons with Disabilities' (2015) 15(1–2) *International Journal of Discrimination and the Law* 101–22.

Broderick, A., 'Emerging Trends in the Jurisprudence of the European Court of Human Rights: The Right to Education for Persons with Disabilities', in Quinlivan S., de Beco, G. and Lord, J. (eds), *The Right to Inclusive Education in International Human Rights Law*

(Cambridge: Cambridge University Press, 2019), pp. 424–46.

Favalli, S., 'The United Nations Convention on the Rights of Persons with Disabilities in the Case law of the European Court of Human Rights and in the Council of Europe Disability Strategy 2017–2023: "From Zero to Hero"' (2018) 18(3) *Human Rights Law Review* 517–38.

Ferri, D., 'Reasonable Accommodation as a Gateway to the Equal Enjoyment of Human Rights: From New York to Strasbourg' (2018) 6(1) *Social Inclusion* 40–50.

Lawson, A., 'Disability Equality, Reasonable Accommodation and the Avoidance of Ill-Treatment in Places of Detention: The Role of Supranational Monitoring and Inspection Bodies' (2012) 16(6) *The International Journal of Human Rights* 845–64.

Lewis, O., 'Advancing Legal Capacity Jurisprudence' (2011) 6 *European Human Rights Law Review* 700–14.

Lewis, O., 'Council of Europe', in L. Waddington and A. Lawson, *The United Nations Convention on the Rights of Persons with Disabilities in Practice: A Comparative Analysis of the Role of Courts* (Oxford/New York: Oxford University Press, 2018), pp. 89–130.

Lewis, O. and Campbell, A., 'Violence and Abuse Against People with Disabilities: A Comparison of the Approaches of the European Court of Human Rights and the United Nations Committee on the Rights of Persons with Disabilities' (2017) 53 *International Journal of Law and Psychiatry* 45–58.

Soboleva, A., 'Judges as Readers, Authors and Dialecticians: Legal Interpretation in the ECtHR Cases on Mental Disability' (2016) 29(3) *International Journal for the Semiotics of Law – Revue Internationale De Sémiotique Juridique* 557–75.

Waddington, L., 'Unravelling the Knot: Article 8, Private Life, Positive Duties and Disability: Rewriting *Sentges v. Netherlands*', in E. Brems (ed.), *Diversity and European Human Rights: Rewriting Judgments of the ECHR* (Cambridge: Cambridge University Press, 2013), pp. 329–51.

Wiesbrock, A., 'Disability as a Form of Vulnerability under EU and CoE Law: Embracing the "Social Model"?', in F. Ippolito and S. Sanchez, *Protecting Vulnerable Groups. The European Human Rights Framework* (Oxford/Portland: Hart Publishing, 2015), pp. 71–94.

14 Disability Law and Policy in the Inter-American Human Rights System

LEARNING OUTCOMES

- ✓ Trace the development of the Inter-American system for the protection of human rights.
- ✓ Understand the main instruments and mechanisms in the Inter-American system.
- ✓ Identify the significance of this regional system of international law in promoting disability rights.
- ✓ Gain an awareness of the differences in the norms and understanding of disability rights within the Inter-American system and under the CRPD.
- ✓ Demonstrate awareness of the decisions and case law generated in the Inter-American system, before and after the adoption of the CRPD, and its relevance to the protection of the rights of individuals with disabilities.
- ✓ Elaborate on the significance of the CRPD to the advancement of disability rights within the Inter-American system.
- ✓ Comprehend the main criticisms of the Inter-American system for the protection of human rights.

The Inter-American System has proved itself as a relevant mechanism for the protection of disability rights in the region ... Moreover, the Inter-American System has deepened its analysis of disability rights, going from the mere recognition that persons with disabilities are entitled to universal rights to a more detailed analysis of the way in which those particular rights could be exercised in order to comply with their specific needs.[1]

1 INTRODUCTION

The Inter-American system for the protection of human rights (IAHRS) is a subsystem within the Organization of American States (OAS). The OAS is comprised of thirty-five independent countries,[2] which form part of the Americas as a whole. Article 1 of the Charter of the Organization of American States (OAS Charter)[3] affirms that 'within the United Nations, the Organization of American States is a regional agency'. Thus, the IAHRS can be seen as a regional system of international human rights law. While it is distinct from the UN system (and from the CRPD itself), the link between the IAHRS and the UN is noted in the Preamble of the OAS Charter, which states that the OAS Member States are 'resolved to persevere in the noble undertaking that humanity has conferred upon the United Nations, whose principles and purposes they solemnly reaffirm'.

The formal beginning of the IAHRS was the approval of the American Declaration of the Rights and Duties of Man[4] (American Declaration) in the form of a resolution[5] at the Ninth International Conference of American States, held in Bogota, Colombia, in 1948. The American Declaration was the first regional human rights instrument to be adopted, more than six months before the Universal Declaration of Human Rights (UDHR) was adopted in the UN. At the conference in Bogota, the OAS Charter was also adopted. These two documents form the cornerstone of the IAHRS.

[1] Diana Guarnizo-Peralta, 'Disability Rights in the Inter-American System of Human Rights: An Expansive and Evolving Protection' (2018) 36(1) *Netherlands Quarterly of Human Rights* 43, at 62.

[2] The Member States of the OAS are: Antigua and Barbuda, Argentina, The Bahamas, Barbados, Belize, Bolivia, Brazil, Canada, Chile, Colombia, Costa Rica, Cuba, Dominica, Dominican Republic, Ecuador, El Salvador, Grenada, Guatemala, Guyana, Haiti, Honduras, Jamaica, Mexico, Nicaragua, Panama, Paraguay, Peru, Saint Kitts and Nevis, Saint Lucia, Saint Vincent and the Grenadines, Suriname, Trinidad and Tobago, United States, Uruguay, and Venezuela.

[3] Charter of the Organization of American States (OAS Charter), adopted on 30 April 1948, entered into force 13 December 1951. Since its entry into force, the OAS Charter has been amended by the Protocol of Buenos Aires of 1967, the Protocol of Cartagena de Indias of 1985, the Protocol of Washington of 1991, and the Protocol of Managua of 1993. See generally A. Glenn Mower, Jr, *Regional Human Rights: A Comparative Study of the West European and Inter-American Systems* (New York: Greenwood Press, 1991).

[4] OAS, American Declaration of the Rights and Duties of Man (American Declaration), adopted 2 May 1948, OAS Doc. OEA/Ser.L.V/II.82 doc.6 rev.1 at 17 (1992).

[5] OAS, Resolution No. XXX, Final Act of the Ninth International Conference of American States, adopted 30 April 1948.

The main goal of the OAS is to ensure the peaceful co-existence of the countries of North and South America. In that vein, and according to Article 2 of the OAS Charter, the objectives of the OAS are, *inter alia*: to strengthen the peace and security of the continent; to promote and consolidate representative democracy, with due respect for the principle of non-intervention; to ensure the pacific settlement of disputes that may arise among the Member States; to provide for common action on the part of those States in the event of aggression; to seek the solution of political, juridical and economic problems that may arise among them; to promote, by cooperative action, their economic, social and cultural development; and to eradicate extreme poverty.

The protection of human rights is clearly envisaged in the OAS Charter, which declares that one of the paramount principles of the OAS is to ensure respect for 'the fundamental rights of the individual without distinction with respect to race, nationality, creed or sex'.[6] The Inter-American system has developed a 'complex mechanism'[7] for the protection and promotion of human rights over the past fifty years. In addition to the American Declaration and the OAS Charter, two further instruments also comprise the core treaties of the IAHRS. The primary instrument through which disability rights are protected is the *Convención Interamericana para la Eliminación de Todas las Formas de Discriminación contra las Personas con Discapacidad*[8] – the Inter-American Convention on the Elimination of All Forms of Discrimination against Persons with Disabilities (CIADDIS or Inter-American Disability Convention), which entered into force in 2001. A further key document in the IAHRS is the American Convention on Human Rights (ACHR or American Convention),[9] which was adopted in 1969 and entered into force in 1978. The ACHR is a general human rights treaty that does not mention disability

[6] Current Article 3(l), OAS amended Charter.

[7] See Ariel Dulitzky, 'The Inter-American Human Rights System Fifty Years Later: Time for Changes' (2011) *Quebec Journal of International Law* (special edition), 127, available at: www.sqdi.org/images/volumes/HS_2011_Dulitzky.pdf. The Inter-American system of human rights protection (IAHRS) includes the: American Convention on Human Rights (1969); Additional Protocol to the American Convention in the Area of Economic, Social and Cultural Rights (1988); Protocol to the American Convention on Human Rights to Abolish the Death Penalty (1990); Inter-American Convention to Prevent and Punish Torture (1985); Inter-American Convention on Forced Disappearance of Persons (1994); Inter-American Convention on the Prevention, Punishment and Eradication of Violence against Women (1994); Inter-American Convention on the Elimination of All Forms of Discrimination against Persons with Disability (1999); Inter-American Convention against All Forms of Discrimination and Intolerance (2013); Inter-American Convention against Racism, Racial Discrimination and Related Forms of Intolerance (2013).

[8] OAS, Convention on the Elimination of All Forms of Discrimination against Persons with Disabilities (CIADDIS), adopted 6 August 1999, OAS Doc. AG/RES. 1608 (XXIX-O/99), entered into force 14 September 2001.

[9] OAS, American Convention on Human Rights (ACHR), adopted 22 November 1969, OAS Doc. OEA/SER. K/XVI/1.1 Doc. 65, entered into force 18 July 1978. To check the current status of ratifications to the ACHR, see the website of the IACHR, available at www.cidh.org.

explicitly. However, the protection of disability rights is ensured indirectly through the interpretation of the ACHR by the OAS organs. The American Convention has two additional protocols – one on economic, social and cultural rights, which refers to the protection of the rights of people with disabilities, and the other on the death penalty.

The Inter-American system is composed of two principal organs: the Inter-American Commission on Human Rights (IACHR or Inter-American Commission), set up under the OAS Charter, and the Inter-American Court of Human Rights (IACtHR or Inter-American Court), established under the ACHR. Both of these organs monitor the implementation of the ACHR, but while the IACHR is a quasi-judicial or non-adjudicatory body, the IACtHR is a judicial body. In addition to those organs,[10] the Inter-American Committee for the Elimination of All Forms of Discrimination against Persons with Disabilities (*Comité Interamericano para la Eliminación de Todas las Formas de Discriminación contra las Personas con Discapacidad* – CEDDIS), was established to monitor compliance with the CIADDIS.

This chapter provides an overview of the IAHRS, its key instruments that are relevant to the protection of disability rights and its core judicial and quasi-judicial mechanisms. Section 2 examines the IAHRS on the whole, while section 3 outlines the principal features of the ACHR. Section 4 analyses the salient features and provisions of the CIADDIS as well as the differences between the CRPD and the Inter-American Disability Convention. Section 5 discusses the composition and functions of the IACHR, before turning to an examination of the disability case law of the IACHR, pre- and post-CRPD. Section 6 conducts the same analysis with respect to the IACtHR. The latter two sections do not analyse the entire body of disability-related case law of the Inter-American Commission and Court; rather, they provide an overview of the most relevant cases.

2 THE INTER-AMERICAN SYSTEM AT A GLANCE AND ITS INTER-RELATIONSHIP WITH THE CRPD

In terms of the institutional set-up of the IAHRS, the most relevant bodies are the General Assembly of the OAS, the IACHR and its Executive Secretariat, as well as the IACtHR.

The General Assembly is the supreme organ of the OAS and is made up of the delegations of all OAS Member States. The functions of the General Assembly are defined in Chapter IX of the OAS Charter. Article 56 of the Charter delineates that all Member States are entitled to be represented at the General Assembly and have the right to one vote.

[10] Additional organs within the Inter-American system focus on specific rights or groups. These include the Inter-American Commission of Women (CIM, according to its Spanish initials); the Working Group on the Protocol of San Salvador; and the various Special Rapporteurs of the IACHR.

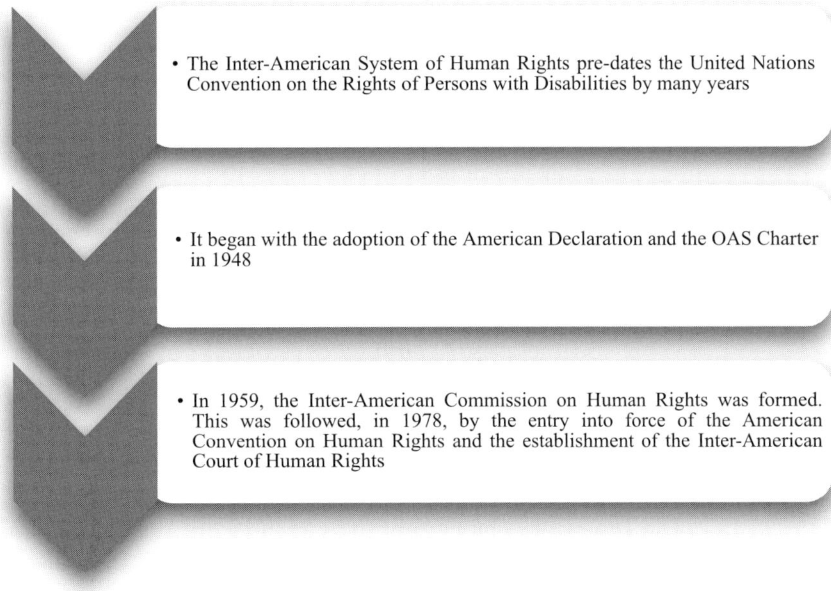

Figure 14.1 The Historical Development of the Inter-American System for the Protection of Human Rights

As outlined in the introduction to this chapter, the OAS system formed gradually – from its humble beginnings, with the adoption of the American Declaration and the OAS Charter, to its more elaborate institutional structure, with the creation of the IACHR and later the adoption of the ACHR that established the Inter-American Court. The historical development of the IAHRS is depicted in Figure 14.1.

Ten years after the adoption of the American Declaration and the OAS Charter, the Inter-American Commission was established by a resolution[11] and, a year later, in 1960, the Commission's Statute was drafted and approved by the Member States of the OAS. The IACHR is one of the two principal organs of the OAS, and its headquarters are in Washington D.C., in the United States of America. It has the competence to decide on individual complaints concerning alleged human rights violations and to make recommendations to Member States of the OAS on the adoption of progressive measures to realise their human rights commitments. It may also issue emergency protective measures when an individual or the subject of a complaint is at an immediate risk of irreparable harm. In addition, it has the competence to engage in a broad range of human rights monitoring and awareness-raising activities. Another way in which the IACHR carries out its mandate is through

[11] OAS, Resolution VIII of the Fifth Meeting of Consultation of Ministers of Foreign Affairs, Final Act, Santiago Chile (12–19 August 1959), OAS Doc. OEA/Ser.F/11.5, pp. 10–11.

conducting on-site visits to OAS Member States and drafting thematic and country reports. Although the Inter-American Commission was originally seen as having the primary role of human rights promotion, it has now taken on a much larger role, having become one of the monitoring bodies of the IAHRS (together with the Inter-American Court). In a quasi-judicial capacity, the Inter-American Commission supervises the implementation of human rights norms in States Parties to the ACHR and can refer cases to the Inter-American Court.

The Commission is attached to an Executive Secretariat, which provides legal and administrative support designed to assist the Commission in performing its functions. According to Article 13 of the IACHR's Rules of Procedure,[12] the Executive Secretariat prepares the draft reports, resolutions and studies of the IACHR, and it carries out other work entrusted to it by the Commission or the Commission's President. In addition, the Executive Secretariat processes the petitions that are addressed to the IACHR.

The Inter-American Court was created by the ACHR, and it is therefore officially deemed to be an organ of the American Convention and not of the OAS as such, unlike the Inter-American Commission. The IACtHR was formed in 1969 as the sole judicial monitoring body of the IAHRS, and its headquarters are in San Jose, Costa Rica. By means of the ACHR, the Inter-American Court was entrusted with the task of joining the Inter-American Commission in interpreting the American Convention. The Court has a broad judicial mandate in so-called contentious cases (in circumstances where States Parties to the ACHR have accepted the Court's contentious jurisdiction). In such cases, the Court has the power to declare a State Party in breach of its treaty obligations under the ACHR and to order reparations. The Inter-American Court may also, in cases of extreme gravity and urgency, and when necessary to avoid irreparable injury to individuals, order the adoption of provisional measures. With respect to a case not yet submitted to it and where precautionary measures are deemed to be required, the Inter-American Court may act at the request of the Inter-American Commission. Furthermore, the IACtHR is competent to issue advisory opinions on matters pertaining to the interpretation of all of the Inter-American instruments, at the request of any organ of the OAS or an OAS Member State.

The system of human rights protection in the OAS is quite complex, in that it encompasses two different 'sub-systems'.[13] While the IAHRS as a whole applies throughout all thirty-five Member States of the OAS, one can observe

[12] Inter-American Commission on Human Rights (IACHR), Rules of Procedure, approved by the Commission at its 137th regular period of sessions, held from 28 October to 13 November 2009.

[13] See Francisco A. Avalos, *The Inter-American System of Human Rights: A Research Guide* (2016), available at www.nyulawglobal.org/globalex/Inter_American_Human_Rights1.html#_ednref3.

'different levels of commitment' towards the 'common goal of promoting and protecting human rights'.[14] The IAHRS adopts a 'dual institutional structure': one sub-system having evolved from the adoption of the OAS Charter and the other having been created by the entry into force of the ACHR.[15] The first sub-system covers those OAS Member States that are subject 'to the law of the American Declaration of the Rights and Duties of Man vis-à-vis the OAS Charter, as well as to the recommendations issued by the [IACHR] under the American Declaration'.[16] The system based on the OAS Charter and the American Declaration is operated solely by the Inter-American Commission in relation to all OAS Member States. The second sub-system comprises the OAS Member States that are Parties to the ACHR and that have also accepted the Inter-American Court's contentious jurisdiction.[17] The latter States are subject to the binding judgments issued by the Court in cases referred to it by the Inter-American Commission and, at the same time, they are subject to the IACHR's resolutions and recommendations. States belonging to the second sub-system are bound by both the American Declaration and the American Convention.[18] The system based on the American Convention is, therefore, exercised by the Commission and the Court only towards States Parties that have actually ratified the ACHR.

The dual institutional structure of the IAHRS means that OAS Member States are governed by 'the interaction between soft and hard regional law'.[19] Avalos explains that primary soft law is represented by the content of the

[14] Ibid. [15] Ibid.

[16] Ibid. Eleven OAS Member States comprise this category: Antigua and Barbuda, The Bahamas, Belize, Canada, Cuba, Guyana, Saint Lucia, Saint Kitts and Nevis, Saint Vincent and the Grenadines, Trinidad and Tobago and the United States of America. In the case of Cuba, the IACHR has decided that although the government of Cuba was excluded from the organization, the OAS did not intend to exclude the Cuban people from the protection of international human rights law. Thus, the Inter-American Commission concluded that it retains jurisdiction *ratione materiae* to review individual petitions against Cuba that allege violations of a right or obligation contained in the American Declaration. See generally Claudio Grossman, 'American Declaration on the Rights and Duties of Man and The Inter-American Commission on Human Rights', in Rüdiger Wolfrum (ed.), *The Max Planck Encyclopedia of Public International Law*, available at www.mpepil.com.

[17] There are three OAS Member States that are parties to the American Convention but have not yet accepted the contentious jurisdiction of the Inter-American Court. Thus, Dominica, Grenada and Jamaica are subject to the law of the Inter-American Commission's resolutions with respect to both the American Declaration and the ACHR. See Francisco A. Avalos, *The Inter-American System of Human Rights: A Research Guide*, note 13.

[18] Ibid. Twenty-one OAS Member States belong to this category: Argentina, Barbados, Bolivia, Brazil, Chile, Colombia, Costa Rica, Dominican Republic, Ecuador, El Salvador, Guatemala, Haiti, Honduras, Mexico, Nicaragua, Panama, Paraguay, Peru, Suriname, Uruguay and Venezuela.

[19] Ibid.

American Declaration,[20] whereas primary hard law encompasses the provisions of the ACHR, its two Optional Protocols and other Inter-American human rights treaties. Secondary soft law of the IAHRS refers to the recommendations issued by the Inter-American Commission, whereas secondary hard law comprises the judgments and advisory opinions rendered by the Inter-American Court.[21]

Application of the human rights standards throughout the Americas has been described as being 'a heterogeneous process that moves forward slowly', one which 'requires specific, deliberate, and immediate efforts by states to close the gap between the human rights commitments they have assumed and full and real protection of human rights'.[22] An increasing number of cases related to disability rights have been examined within the judicial and quasi-judicial mechanisms of the IAHRS in recent years. The single instrument dealing with disability rights in the IAHRS – the CIADDIS – does not provide a very strong basis for disability rights, as explained later in this chapter. In addition, its monitoring body – the CEDDIS – has not been very active on the whole, when compared with other monitoring bodies in international human rights law. Thus, both the Inter-American Commission and the Inter-American Court have engaged in an 'expansive interpretation', in particular, of the ACHR, in order to protect the rights of persons with disabilities.[23] Both the Commission and the Court have adopted an 'indirect approach',[24] according to which the protection of certain rights is 'ensured not directly through the application of the right violated but indirectly through the application of other, better established, rights'.[25]

[20] Ibid. The American Declaration was originally adopted as a resolution (an instrument of soft law) and not as a treaty (an instrument of hard law). However, both regional monitoring bodies of the OAS, the IACHR and the Inter-American Court of Human Rights (IACtHR) have held that the American Declaration currently represents a binding source of international obligations for all OAS Member States. The Inter-American Court held that: 'The Court finds it necessary to point out that to determine the *legal status* of the American Declaration it is appropriate to look to the Inter-American system *of today* in the light of the evolution it has undergone since the adoption of the Declaration, rather than to examine the normative value and significance which that instrument was believed to have had in 1948.' See IACtHR, *Interpretation of the American Declaration of the Rights and Duties of Man within the Framework of Article 64 of the American Convention on Human Rights*, Advisory Opinion OC-10/89 of 14 July 1989, Series A No. 10, para. 37.

[21] Francisco A. Avalos, *The Inter-American System of Human Rights: A Research Guide*, note 13.

[22] IACHR, Legal Standards related to General Equality and Women's Rights in the Inter-American System: Development and Application, 3 November 2011, OAS Doc. OEA/Ser.L/V/II. 143 Doc. No. 60.

[23] Guarnizo-Peralta, 'Disability Rights in the Inter-American System of Human Rights: An Expansive and Evolving Protection', note 1, at 43.

[24] Ibid. [25] Ibid.

Notably, the CRPD has taken on an increased relevance in the IAHRS, in an attempt to inform the interpretation of the rights of individuals with disabilities within the OAS. Although the CRPD is not a treaty that can be applied directly by the organs of the OAS, according to Article 29(d) of the American Convention, both the IACHR and the IACtHR are authorised to use international instruments (other than the instruments stemming from the Inter-American system itself) to shed light on the meaning of the provisions of the ACHR. This would naturally include the CRPD, and both the Inter-American Commission and the Court have drawn on the CRPD at various junctures, as is discussed below in sections 5 and 6. Nonetheless, Guarnizo-Peralta claims that the Inter-American system 'has, in some aspects, progressively caught up with international standards of protection regarding disability rights', while, in other respects, 'it has developed a particular standard of interpretation that is in conflict with the CRPD's standards'.[26]

3 THE AMERICAN CONVENTION ON HUMAN RIGHTS

The ACHR entered into force on 18 July 1978. According to the first paragraph of its Preamble, the purpose of the Convention is 'to consolidate . . . within the framework of democratic institutions, a system of personal liberty and social justice based on respect for the essential rights of man'. This section details the structure and salient provisions of the ACHR, and it outlines in brief the content of the two additional protocols to the ACHR, namely the Additional Protocol to the American Convention on Human Rights in the Area of Economic, Social and Cultural Rights (Protocol of San Salvador)[27] and the Protocol to the American Convention on Human Rights to Abolish the Death Penalty.[28]

3.1 Structure and Key Provisions of the American Convention

Part I of the American Convention establishes the obligations of States Parties to respect the rights contained in the Convention as well as the

[26] Ibid.

[27] OAS, Additional Protocol to the American Convention on Human Rights in the Area of Economic, Social and Cultural Rights (Protocol of San Salvador), adopted on 16 November 1999, OAS Doc. A-52. See generally, Oswaldo R. Ruiz-Chiriboga, 'The American Convention and the Protocol of San Salvador: Two Intertwined Treaties – Non-Enforceability of Economic, Social and Cultural Rights in the Inter-American System' (2013) 31(2) *Netherlands Quarterly of Human Rights* 59. See also Tara Melish, 'Protecting Economic, Social and Cultural Rights in the Inter-American Human Rights System: A Manual on Presenting Claims' (2002) Yale Law School & CDES, SUNY Buffalo Legal Studies Research Paper No. 2002-001.

[28] OAS, Protocol to the American Convention on Human Rights to Abolish the Death Penalty, adopted on 8 June 1990, OAS Treaty Series, No. 73.

Draw up a list of rights in the CRPD that are mirrored in the ACHR.

duty to adopt the necessary legislative and other measures to give effect to those rights. The Convention focuses on civil and political rights. Chapter II of Part I of the ACHR contains twenty-three provisions, which list individual civil and political rights, including the right to juridicial personality, the right to life, the right to humane treatment, the right to a fair trial, as well as the right to privacy and the right to freedom of assembly, among others. Some of the articles of the ACHR have arguably been influenced by international human rights law. This is the case, for example, with Article 13(5) ACHR (on freedom of thought and expression), which prohibits 'any propaganda for war and any advocacy of national, racial, or religious hatred that constitute incitement to lawless violence or to any other similar action against any person on any grounds including those of race, color, religion, language, or national origin . . .'. That provision mirrors Article 20 of the International Covenant on Civil and Political Rights (ICCPR).

DID YOU KNOW THAT ...?

Many of the rights that are protected by the ACHR overlap with and mirror the rights protected in other instruments of international law, such as the ECHR. For example, the following rights are protected in both the ACHR and the ECHR:

- **The right to life (Article 4 ACHR; Article 2 ECHR);**
- **The right to humane treatment (Article 5 ACHR; Article 3 ECHR);**
- **The right to personal liberty (Article 7 ACHR; Article 5 ECHR);**
- **The right to a fair trial (Article 8 ACHR; Article 6 ECHR);**
- **Respect for private and family life (Article 11 ACHR; Article 8 ECHR);**
- **Freedom of expression (Article 13 ACHR; Article 10 ECHR);**
- **The right to property (Article 21 ACHR; Article 1 of Protocol 1 ECHR).**

Chapter III of the ACHR deals with economic, social and cultural rights, but it only contains a single article – Article 26 – which outlines the principle of progressive realisation in relation to socio-economic rights.

ARTICLE 26

The States Parties undertake to adopt measures, both internally and through international cooperation, especially those of an economic and technical nature, with a view to achieving progressively, by legislation or other appropriate means, the full reali[s]ation of the rights implicit in the economic, social, educational, scientific, and cultural standards set forth in the Charter of the Organization of American States as amended by the Protocol of Buenos Aires.

Chapter IV of the Convention addresses the suspension of rights, their interpretation and application, while Chapter V outlines the relationship between rights and duties.

Part II of the ACHR refers, in Chapter VI, to the organs that have competence to monitor the Convention, namely the IACtHR and the IACHR.

Chapter VII of the ACHR (Articles 34–51) details the organisation, functions, competence and procedures of the Inter-American Commission, whereas Chapter VIII (Articles 52–73) articulates the same aspects related to the Inter-American Court.

It is notable that the ACHR strengthened the Inter-American system, by broadening the Commission's competences. The entry into force of the ACHR in 1978 invested the Commission with a dual role. In the first instance, it retained its status as an organ of the OAS, thereby maintaining its powers to promote and protect human rights in the territories of all OAS Member States. In the second instance, it became an organ of the ACHR, and in that capacity it supervises human rights in the territories of the States Parties to the American Convention. The ACHR also created, for the first time, a Court, with a judicial mandate to monitor the observance of human rights in States Parties to the Convention.

Notably, Article 77 of the ACHR allows for the list of rights and freedoms that the American Convention protects to be gradually expanded by means of protocols. Two protocols have entered into force thus far, and they are discussed below in the next sub-section.

3.2 Additional Protocols to the American Convention

In 1988, the General Assembly of the OAS opened for signature the Additional Protocol of San Salvador. The Protocol entered into force on 16 November 1999. The adoption of the Protocol of San Salvador was intended to boost the protection of economic, social and cultural rights under the ACHR. In its Preamble, States Parties acknowledge the close relationship that exists between civil and political rights, on the one hand, and economic, social and cultural rights, on the other hand, 'in that the different categories of rights constitute an indivisible whole based on the recognition of the dignity of the human person, for which reason both require permanent protection and promotion . . .'. By ratifying the Protocol, States Parties:

> undertake to adopt the necessary measures . . . to the extent allowed by their available resources, and taking into account their degree of development, for the purpose of achieving progressively and pursuant to their internal legislation, the full observance of the rights recogni[s]ed in (the) Protocol.

The Protocol of San Salvador addresses the right to work, trade union rights, rights to social security, health, a healthy environment, food, education, the benefits of culture, the right to form a family, children's rights, the rights of the elderly, and the rights of persons with disabilities. Article 18 ACHR articulates the rights of disabled persons. That Article seems to be framed according to the outdated medical model of disability, and it is entitled 'protection of the handicapped'.

ARTICLE 18 ACHR

Everyone affected by a diminution of his physical or mental capacities is entitled to receive special attention designed to help him achieve the greatest possible development of his personality. The States Parties agree to adopt such measures as may be necessary for this purpose and, especially, to:

a. Undertake programs specifically aimed at providing the handicapped with the resources and environment needed for attaining this goal, including work programs consistent with their possibilities and freely accepted by them or their legal representatives, as the case may be;
b. Provide special training to the families of the handicapped in order to help them solve the problems of coexistence and convert them into active agents in the physical, mental and emotional development of the latter;
c. Include the consideration of solutions to specific requirements arising from needs of this group as a priority component of their urban development plans;
d. Encourage the establishment of social groups in which the handicapped can be helped to enjoy a fuller life.

Article 19 outlines the means of protection envisaged under the Protocol. It affirms that States Parties to the Protocol must submit periodic reports on the progressive measures that they have taken to ensure due respect for the rights that are set forth in the Protocol. Article 19(6) of the Protocol establishes that certain violations of rights (namely, of the right to education and trade union rights) may give rise, through participation of the Inter-American Commission and, when applicable, of the Inter-American Court, to a system of individual petitions. That system is governed by Articles 44–51 and 61–69 ACHR. According to Article 19(7) ACHR, the Inter-American Commission may also formulate such recommendations as it deems pertinent concerning the status of the economic, social and cultural rights established in the Protocol and can direct those recommendations to all or some of the States Parties to the Protocol.

The second additional Protocol to the ACHR, namely the Protocol to the American Convention on Human Rights to Abolish the Death Penalty addresses civil and political rights, which distinguishes it from the Protocol of San Salvador. It was approved by the General Assembly of the OAS at its twentieth regular session in Paraguay in 1990 and entered into force in 1991. The Protocol prohibits capital punishment, but it permits States Parties to reserve the right to apply the death penalty in wartime for extremely serious crimes of a military nature. It does not specify an enforcement mechanism, unlike the Protocol of San Salvador.

4 THE INTER-AMERICAN CONVENTION ON THE ELIMINATION OF ALL FORMS OF DISCRIMINATION AGAINST PERSONS WITH DISABILITIES

By way of contrast with the ACHR, the CIADDIS is a disability-specific treaty. Notably, the CIADDIS came into existence before the adoption of the CRPD, having entered into force on 14 September 2001. This means that it was the first regional international instrument that was adopted to provide a legal framework for the protection of disabled people. The sub-sections that follow highlight the structure and seminal provisions of the CIADDIS as well as the main differences that can be observed between the CIADDIS and the CRPD.

4.1 Structure and Key Provisions of the CIADDIS

The CIADDIS calls on OAS Member States to facilitate the full ‘integration’ of persons with disabilities in society, by means of legislation, social initiatives and educational programmes. The Convention is quite short, with only fourteen articles in total. Its provisions can be divided into four main categories, as depicted in Figure 14.2.

Article 1 contains the definition of ‘disability’ itself and the definition of the term ‘discrimination against persons with disabilities’. Those definitions are

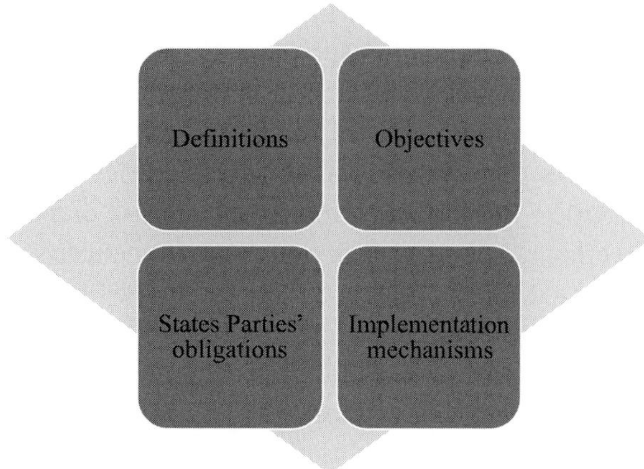

Figure 14.2 The Main Categories of Provisions in the CIADDIS

discussed in sub-section 4.2 below. Article 2 sets out the objective of the CIADDIS as being to prevent and eliminate all forms of discrimination against persons with disabilities and to promote their full integration into society. Article 3 enunciates the general obligations of States Parties to the Convention. Those obligations are outlined in Figure 14.3.

Article 4 CIADDIS appears to elaborate on the general obligations contained in Article 3 by requiring States Parties to 'cooperate with one another in helping to prevent and eliminate discrimination against persons with disabilities'. Article 4 expands on this non-discrimination mandate by requiring States Parties to collaborate effectively in:

i. Scientific and technological research related to the prevention of disabilities and to the treatment, rehabilitation, and integration into society of persons with disabilities.
ii. The development of means and resources designed to facilitate or promote the independence, self-sufficiency, and total integration into society of persons with disabilities, under conditions of equality.

Article 5 CIADDIS contains a similar obligation to that contained in Article 4 (3) CRPD, namely the obligation to include persons with disabilities, through their representative organisations, in the development, execution and evaluation of measures and policies to implement the CIADDIS.

Article 6 sets up the monitoring Committee for the Convention – the CEDDIS – which is composed of one representative appointed by each State Party. Article 6(3) CIADDIS affirms that States Parties must submit a report to the Committee once every four years. According to Article 6(4), that report should include details on measures adopted by States Parties pursuant to

States Parties undertake to adopt the legislative, social, educational, labor-related, or any other measures needed to eliminate discrimination against persons with disabilities and to promote their full integration into society, including, but not limited to:

- Measures to eliminate discrimination gradually and to promote integration by government authorities and/or private entities in providing or making available goods, services, facilities, programs, and activities such as employment, transportation, communications, housing, recreation, education, sports, law enforcement and administration of justice, and political and administrative activities;
- Measures to ensure that new buildings, vehicles, and facilities constructed or manufactured within their respective territories facilitate transportation, communications, and access by persons with disabilities;
- Measures to eliminate, to the extent possible, architectural, transportation, and communication obstacles to facilitate access and use by persons with disabilities; and
- Measures to ensure that persons responsible for applying this Convention and domestic law in this area are trained to do so.

States Parties undertake to work on a priority basis in the following areas:

- Prevention of all forms of preventable disabilities;
- Early detection and intervention, treatment, rehabilitation, education, job training, and the provision of comprehensive services to ensure the optimal level of independence and quality of life for persons with disabilities; and
- Increasing of public awareness through educational campaigns aimed at eliminating prejudices, stereotypes, and other attitudes that jeopardize the right of persons to live as equals, thus promoting respect for and coexistence with persons with disabilities

Figure 14.3 General Obligations of the CIADDIS

the Convention and on any progress made by States Parties in eliminating all forms of discrimination against persons with disabilities. The report should also indicate any 'circumstances or difficulties affecting the degree of fulfillment of the obligations' arising from the CIADDIS. In a similar vein to the CRPD Committee, the CEDDIS provides each State Party that submits a report with feedback in the form of a document containing the committee's conclusions, its observations, and its general suggestions for the realisation of the rights contained in the CIADDIS.

Notably, Article 7 CIADDIS affirms that no provision of the Convention 'shall be interpreted as restricting, or permitting the restriction' by States Parties of the enjoyment of the rights of persons with disabilities recognised by customary international law or the international instruments by which a particular State Party is bound. This includes the rights provided for under the CRPD.

Articles 8–10 outline the details pertaining to the entry into force of the Convention.

Article 11 provides that any State Party is entitled to propose amendments to the CIADDIS, whereas Article 12 affirms that States Parties may enter reservations to the Convention when ratifying or acceding to it. This is subject to the proviso that such reservations may not be incompatible with the aim and purpose of the CIADDIS and must relate to one or more specific provisions of the Convention. Article 13 allows States Parties to denounce the obligations that they have ratified in the CIADDIS.

Finally, Article 14 enunciates that the original instrument and any translations must be deposited with the General Secretariat of the OAS, which must send a certified copy thereof to the UN Secretariat for registration and publication pursuant to Article 102 of the UN Charter.

4.2 The CRPD and the Inter-American Disability Convention

While both the CRPD and the CIADDIS are international instruments designed to protect and promote disability rights, there are key differences between the two treaties. Aside from the obvious differences in their geographical scope, the treaties differ in terms of their respective understandings of disability, the scope of the rights protected (and obligations set forth) in each treaty and the mechanisms of protection provided for by each treaty.

The CIADDIS defines 'disability' in Article 1(1) thereof. That definition is highlighted in Figure 14.4.

Certain authors have emphasised the fact that the definition of 'disability' in the CIADDIS merges the medical model of disability, by referring to 'a physical, mental, or sensory impairment, whether permanent or temporary, that limits the capacity to perform one or more essential activities', with elements of the social model, by referring to economic and social factors.[29] Guarnizo-Peralta notes that the wording of the text of the CIADDIS 'gives the impression that the economic and social environment is relevant simply as a cause or factor of aggravation of the impairment, thus emphasising the impairment rather than the interaction with society as key elements of disability'.[30] The definition of 'disability' in the CIADDIS certainly does not reflect the CRPD's understanding

[29] See, for instance, Christian Courtis, 'Disability Rights in Latin America and International Cooperation' (2002–2003) 9 *Southwestern Journal of Law and Trade in the Americas*, 109, at 114–15.

[30] See Guarnizo-Peralta, 'Disability Rights in the Inter-American System of Human Rights: An Expansive and Evolving Protection', note 1, at 45.

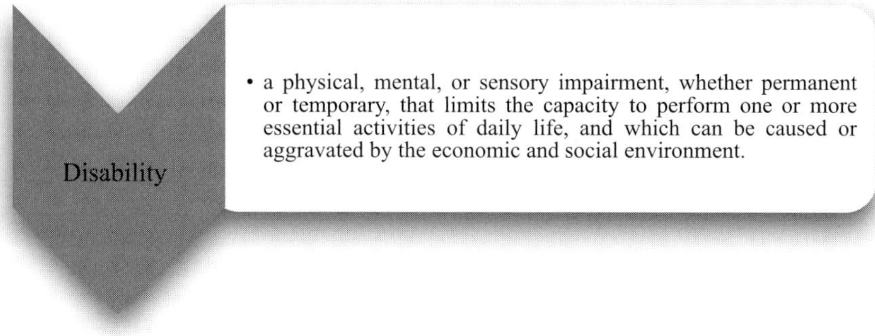

Figure 14.4 The Definition of 'Disability' in the CIADDIS

of that term. As outlined in Chapter 3 of this textbook, the CRPD articulates an open-ended conceptualisation of disability, both in the non-binding Preamble and in Article 1 of the UN Convention. Recital (e) to the Preamble of the CRPD affirms that '[d]isability is an evolving concept and that disability results from the interaction between persons with impairments and attitudinal and environmental barriers that hinders their full and effective participation in society on an equal basis with others'. Article 1(2) CRPD outlines the 'purpose' of the Convention, stating that:

> persons with disabilities include those who have long-term physical, mental, intellectual or sensory impairments which in interaction with various barriers may hinder their full and effective participation in society on an equal basis with others.

As outlined in Chapter 3, the CRPD incorporates a social-contextual understanding of disability,[31] recognising that 'disability stems primarily from the failure of the social environment to meet the needs and aspirations of people with impairments'.[32]

The different understandings of disability enshrined in the CRPD, on the one hand, and the CIADDIS, on the other hand, can be explained by the fact that the CRPD entered into force in 2008, seven years after the Inter-American Disability Convention. Thus, the UN Convention adopts a more progressive approach to disability.

The definition of 'discrimination' in the CIADDIS is not unlike that contained in the CRPD. It is outlined in Figure 14.5. The difference between the CRPD and the CIADDIS is that the latter treaty does not include the (unjustified) denial of reasonable accommodation as a form of discrimination,

[31] See Chapter 3 above.

[32] Lisa Waddington and Andrea Broderick, *Disability Law and the Duty to Reasonably Accommodate beyond Employment: A Legal Analysis of the Situation in EU Member States* (Luxembourg: Publications Office of the European Union, 2016), p. 38.

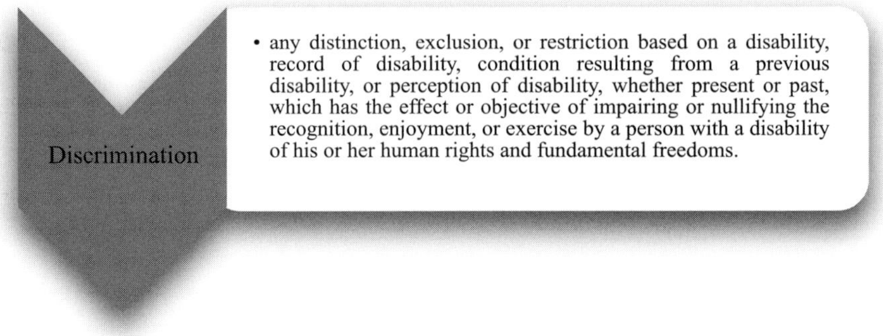

Figure 14.5 The Definition of 'Discrimination' in the CIADDIS

although it does include an explicit prohibition of discrimination on the basis of a past or perceived disability. As outlined in Figure 14.3, States Parties to the CIADDIS are required to adopt the 'legislative, social, education, labo[u]r-related, or any other measures needed to eliminate discrimination against persons with disabilities', in order to achieve the objectives of the instrument.[33] However, unlike the CRPD, the CIADDIS does not set out substantive rights in any great detail, and thus the prohibition of discrimination applies rather vaguely across the Inter-American Disability Convention. By way of contrast (and as outlined in Chapter 4 of this textbook), the equality and non-discrimination norms run through the UN Convention like a 'red thread',[34] underpinning its substantive rights, including civil,[35] political,[36] economic,[37] social[38] and cultural[39] rights. The CRPD recognises that the universal equality norm must be tailored to the specific needs of disabled people and specifies that the unjustified failure to provide reasonable accommodation is a form of discrimination. The CRPD also embraces a multidimensional or intersectional

[33] Article III(1) CIADDIS, note 8.

[34] Andrea Broderick, 'Harmonisation and Cross-fertilisation of Socio-Economic Rights in the Human Rights Treaty Bodies: Disability and the Reasonableness Review Case Study' (2016) 5 *Laws* 38, at 47.

[35] See the rights to life (Article 10 CRPD), liberty and security of the person (Article 14 CRPD), freedom from torture or cruel, inhuman or degrading treatment or punishment (Article 15 CRPD), freedom from exploitation, violence and abuse (Article 16 CRPD), protecting the integrity of the person (Article 17 CRPD), liberty of movement (Article 18 CRPD).

[36] See the rights to equal recognition before the law and access to justice (Articles 12 and 13 CRPD).

[37] See the rights to education (Article 24 CRPD), health (Article 25 CRPD), to access to comprehensive habilitation and rehabilitation services and programmes (Article 26 CRPD), to work and employment (Article 27 CRPD), and to an adequate standard of living and social protection (Article 28 CRPD).

[38] See the right to living independently and being included in the community (Article 19 CRPD).

[39] See the right to participate in cultural life, recreation, leisure and sport (Article 30 CRPD).

approach to discrimination. In that connection, Article 6(1) of the CRPD recognises that 'women and girls with disabilities are subject to multiple discrimination',[40] whereas the Inter-American Disability Convention does not mention multiple discrimination.

Similarly, to the CRPD, the CIADDIS includes a list of general obligations for States Parties to the Convention (elaborated in Figure 14.3). Unlike in the CIADDIS, however, the general obligations outlined in the CRPD are accompanied by more specific obligations throughout the UN Convention itself, focused on monitoring, the collection of statistical and research data, and the designation of focal points, in order to promote, protect and monitor the implementation of the Convention.

Another distinguishing feature of the CRPD, when compared with the CIADDIS, is the monitoring bodies of the two Conventions, discussed briefly in sub-section 4.3 below.

4.3 The Inter-American Committee

By way of comparison with the CRPD, which, as discussed in Chapter 3, includes an individual complaint mechanism, the CIADDIS includes a relatively weak enforcement mechanism. It does not establish a system of individual petitions, nor does it allow for the mechanisms contained in the ACHR to be applied.[41] Instead, it imposes a duty on States Parties to cooperate with one another in preventing and eliminating discrimination against people with disabilities[42] and to collaborate in scientific and technological research on the prevention and rehabilitation of disabilities.[43] Under the CIADDIS, and in a similar vein to the state reporting system in the CRPD, States Parties are required to submit periodic reports[44] to the CEDDIS every four years. The CEDDIS is composed of nineteen representatives – one representative being designated by each State Party to the CIADDIS.[45] The CRPD also establishes a committee that is designed to monitor compliance by States Parties with the UN Convention[46] and to decide on the individual communications presented by individuals or groups.[47]

[40] Article 6(1) CRPD.

[41] However, the rights of persons with disabilities have been protected through the expansive interpretation of ACHR rights. This is well exemplified by the interpretation of the right to health, as discussed by Steven Keener and Javier Vasquez, 'A Life Worth Living: Enforcement of the Right to Health through the Right to Life in the Inter-American Court of Human Rights' (2009) 40 *Columbian Human Rights Law Review* 595.

[42] Article IV(1) CIADDIS. [43] Article IV(2) CIADDIS. [44] Article VI(3) CIADDIS.

[45] Article VI(1) CIADDIS. [46] Article 35(1) CRPD.

[47] Optional Protocol to the Convention on the Rights of Persons with Disabilities (adopted 13 December 2006, entered into force 2 May 2008) A/RES/61/106, Annex II (OP-CRPD) Article 1.

Scholars point to the fact that the CEDDIS is less active than the CRPD Committee.[48] The first meeting of the Committee was held on 28 February and 1 March 2007 in Panama City, Panama. By July 2018, the CEDDIS had only held its ninth meeting,[49] which, according to Guarnizo-Peralta, 'reflects its limited impact on the definition of policies for disabled people in the region'.[50] By contrast, around the same time, the CRPD Committee had issued a large number of recommendations to States Parties to the CRPD and had examined more than a dozen individual petitions.

Notwithstanding the fact that the CEDDIS is less active than the CRPD Committee, it does convene meetings in which it examines the progress made by States Parties to the Inter-American Disability Convention in fulfilling their implementation obligations. For example, the eighth meeting of the CEDDIS took place between 24 and 28 April 2017 in Cali, Colombia, in order to consider the second group of national reports on the implementation of the CIADDIS. This entailed a detailed evaluation of several States Parties' reports on the situation of persons with disabilities under the Convention. At that meeting, the Committee also examined the progress made under the Program of Action for the Decade of the Americas for the Rights and Dignity of Persons with Disabilities (PAD), which had been launched in 2006[51] and ran until 2016, under the theme 'Equality, Dignity, and Participation'. The objectives of the PAD were to ensure the recognition and full exercise of the rights and dignity of persons with disabilities and their right to participate fully in economic, social, cultural and political life, and in the development of their societies, without discrimination and on an equal basis with others.

5 THE INTER-AMERICAN COMMISSION ON HUMAN RIGHTS

As highlighted in the introduction to this chapter, the IACHR is one of the two primary organs of the IAHRS. This section elaborates on the composition, functions and competences of the Inter-American Commission. It also

[48] See, for instance, Guarnizo-Peralta, 'Disability Rights in the Inter-American System of Human Rights: An Expansive and Evolving Protection', note 1, at 46.

[49] See generally www.oas.org/es/sedi/ddse/paginas/index-4_comite_reunion.asp.

[50] See Guarnizo-Peralta, 'Disability Rights in the Inter-American System of Human Rights: An Expansive and Evolving Protection', note 1, at 46.

[51] Program of Action for the Decade of the Americas for the Rights and Dignity of Persons with Disabilities (2006–2016) AG/RES 2230 (XXXVI-O/06). See www.oas.org/dil/AG-RES_2230_XXXVI-O-06_eng.pdf.

provides an account of the disability decisions adopted by the IACHR in the period before and after the adoption of the CRPD.

5.1 Composition, Functions and Competences of the Inter-American Commission

The Inter-American Commission is composed of seven members, who are elected by the OAS General Assembly. According to Article 34 ACHR, the members of the Commission must be 'persons of high moral character and recogni[s]ed competence in the field of human rights'. They are elected in their personal capacity, pursuant to Article 36 ACHR. In other words, they must have no connections to governmental agencies. Moreover, no two nationals of the same state may be members of the Commission (Article 37(2) ACHR).

The establishment of the Commission is detailed in Article 106 of the OAS Charter, which points to the fact that 'an inter-American convention on human rights shall determine the structure, competence, and procedure of this Commission, as well as those of other organs responsible for these matters'. The Commission's competence in relation to States Parties to the ACHR is established in the provisions of the American Convention itself (Articles 41–47).

The Commission's mandate has evolved through its practice over the years. The IACHR was originally conceived of 'as a study group concerned with abstract investigations in the field of human rights'.[52] However, the Commission soon began to accept communications from individuals about violations of human rights in their country. As Medina points out, the Commission's task at that point was not to examine 'isolated violations' but to document the existence of 'gross, systematic violations and to exercise pressure to improve the general condition of human rights in the country concerned'.[53] The Commission's competence to handle individual communications or petitions was formalised in 1965 when the OAS passed Resolution XXII,[54] which allowed the Commission to examine isolated human rights violations.

To this date, one of the primary competences of the Inter-American Commission remains the hearing of individual or state complaints that take the form of petitions or communications addressed to the Commission.[55] The

[52] Cecilia Medina, *The Inter-American Commission on Human Rights and the Inter-American Court of Human Rights: Reflections on a Joint Venture* (1990) 12(4) *Human Rights Quarterly* 439, at 440. See also Hugo Caminos, 'The Inter-American System for the Protection of Human Rights', in Janusz Symonides (ed.), *Human Rights: International Protection, Monitoring, Enforcement* (New York: Routledge-Unesco, 2017), pp. 165–211, at p. 187 et seq.

[53] Ibid.

[54] OAS, Resolution XXII of the Second Special Inter-American Conference, adopted in 1965, OAS Doc. OEA/Ser.E/XIII.I Doc. 150 Rev. (1965).

[55] In addition, the Commission may begin processing a case on its own motion.

individual petition is a quasi-judicial mechanism that may be initiated by any person, group of persons, or non-governmental entity legally recognised in one or more of the OAS Member States, regardless of whether the complainant is the victim of the particular human rights violation. Like all of the provisions of the American Convention, this right of individual petition under Article 47 is binding on all States Parties to the ACHR. By way of contrast, inter-state communications are dependent on an explicit recognition of the competence of the Commission to receive and examine them.

The procedures for determining the admissibility of complaints before the Commission resemble those set forth in the European Convention on Human Rights (ECHR). According to Article 47 ACHR, the Commission will judge any communication to be admissible if all of the following requirements are met:

i. The communication alleges a violation of a right or rights protected by the Convention.
ii. A communication on the same subject is not pending or has not previously been studied by the Commission or any other international organisation.
iii. The remedies under the state's domestic laws have been exhausted or the state does not respect the due process of law for the alleged violation.[56]
iv. The communication is brought in a timely manner.

The procedure for dealing with an individual communication is set out in Article 48 ACHR.

ARTICLE 48 ACHR

1. When the Commission receives a petition or communication alleging violation of any of the rights protected by this Convention, it shall proceed as follows:

   a. If it considers the petition or communication admissible, it shall request information from the government of the state indicated as being responsible for the alleged violations and shall furnish that government a transcript of the pertinent portions of the petition or communication. This information shall be submitted within a reasonable period to be determined by the Commission in accordance with the circumstances of each case.

[56] According to Article 46(2) ACHR, this rule is not applicable 'when: (a) the domestic legislation of the state concerned does not afford due process of law for the protection of the right or rights that have allegedly been violated; (b) the party alleging violation of his rights has been denied access to the remedies under domestic law or has been prevented from exhausting them; or (c) there has been unwarranted delay in rendering a final judgment under the aforementioned remedies'.

b. After the information has been received, or after the period established has elapsed and the information has not been received, the Commission shall ascertain whether the grounds for the petition or communication still exist. If they do not, the Commission shall order the record to be closed.
c. The Commission may also declare the petition or communication inadmissible or out of order on the basis of information or evidence subsequently received.
d. If the record has not been closed, the Commission shall, with the knowledge of the parties, examine the matter set forth in the petition or communication in order to verify the facts. If necessary and advisable, the Commission shall carry out an investigation, for the effective conduct of which it shall request, and the states concerned shall furnish to it, all necessary facilities.
e. The Commission may request the states concerned to furnish any pertinent information and, if so requested, shall hear oral statements or receive written statements from the parties concerned.
f. The Commission shall place itself at the disposal of the parties concerned with a view to reaching a friendly settlement of the matter on the basis of respect for the human rights recogni[s]ed in this Convention.

According to Article 49 ACHR, if a friendly settlement has been reached, the IACHR will draw up a report, which will be transmitted to the petitioner and to States Parties to the Convention. The Inter-American Commission must then communicate this to the Secretary General of the OAS for publication. If, on the other hand, a settlement is not reached, Article 50 provides that 'the Commission shall, within the time limit established by its Statute, draw up a report setting forth the facts and stating its conclusions'. Article 51 further affirms that the Commission (or the State Party concerned) can submit the dispute for settlement to the Inter-American Court.[57]

Among other functions and competences, detailed in Figure 14.6, the IACHR also has the competence to order the adoption of precautionary measures, which can be initiated on the request of a party or on the IACHR's own initiative. Pursuant to Article 25(2) of the IACHR's Rules of Procedure, it is

[57] Article 51 ACHR further states that: 'if within a period of three months from the date of the transmittal of the report of the Commission to the states concerned, the matter has not either been settled or submitted by the Commission or by the state concerned to the Court and its jurisdiction accepted, the Commission may, by the vote of an absolute majority of its members, set forth its opinion and conclusions concerning the question submitted for its consideration'.

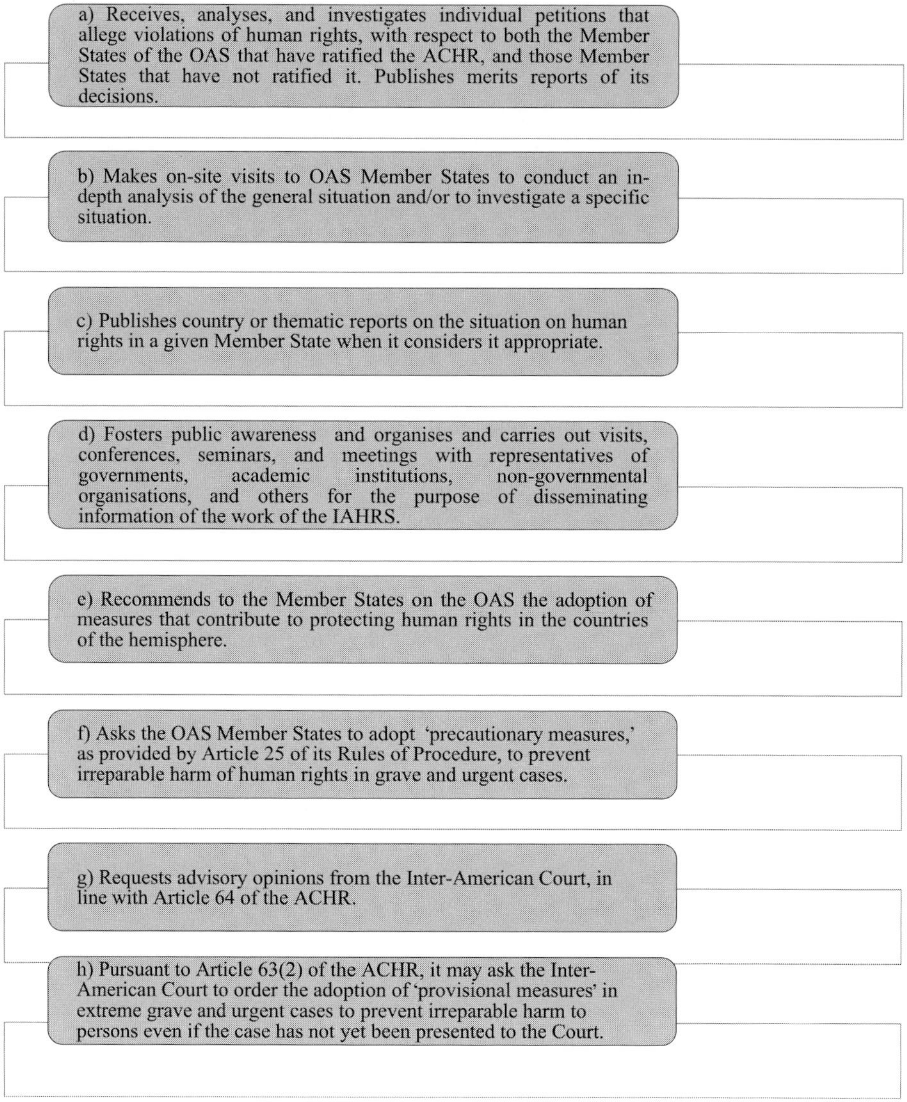

Figure 14.6 Main Functions and Competences of the Inter-American Commission on Human Rights

stated that 'such measures . . . shall concern serious and urgent situations presenting a risk of irreparable harm to persons or to the subject matter of a pending petition or case before the organs of the Inter-American system'.[58]

In addition to the functions and competences outlined above, a special mechanism of the Inter-American Commission is the Office of the Special Rapporteur. Article 15 of the Rules of Procedure of the IACHR grants the

[58] IACHR, Rules of Procedure, Article 25(2), note 12.

Commission the competence to create Special Rapporteurships and Working Groups or Committees. The Commission may create Country Rapporteurships or Thematic Rapporteurships. There are currently thirty-five Country Rapporteurships, one for each OAS Member State. There are also eight Thematic Rapporteurships, including a Rapporteurship on the Rights of Women, a Rapporteurship on the Rights of Migrant Workers and their Families, a Rapporteurship on the Rights of the Child, and a Rapporteurship on the Rights of Afro-Descendants and Against Racial Discrimination. Three new units were set up by the IACHR in May 2017, including a unit on the rights of persons with disabilities.[59]

5.2 Disability Decisions of the Commission Pre-CRPD

Before the entry into force of the CRPD (and the CIADDIS), the IACHR had dealt with very few individual communications on disability rights.[60]

In 1997, in *Víctor Rosario Congo* v. *Ecuador*,[61] the IACHR decided a complaint against the Ecuadorian state, in which it was alleged that the petitioner, Mr Víctor Rosario Congo (a prisoner at the Social Rehabilitation Center in Machala, Ecuador, who had a psychosocial disability), had died as result of maltreatment and attacks by officers at the centre. Specifically, it was alleged that, on 14 September 1990, the petitioner was assaulted by the security guards, causing a wound to his head. The applicant was placed in solitary confinement and denied medical care. The state authorities were alleged to have been neglectful in their obligation to investigate the events of 14 September 1990, and those that followed, culminating in the death of the petitioner.[62] The Commission concluded that the state was responsible for the violation of several rights set forth in the ACHR: the rights to life (Article 4), to humane treatment (Article 5), and to judicial protection (Article 25), in conjunction with the obligation established in Article 1(1) to respect the rights and freedoms set out in the American Convention without discrimination.[63]

[59] See IACHR, 'IACHR Creates New Thematic Units and Announces New Distribution of Rapporteurships', 24 May 2017, available at http://oas.org/en/iachr/media_center/PReleases/2017/066.asp.

[60] For further discussion on the Inter-American Commission on Human Rights regarding the rights of persons with disabilities, see: Analía Banfi and Sofía Galván, 'Los Derechos de las Personas con Discapacidad y la Comisión Interamericana de Derechos Humanos' (2014) *Revista Latinoamericana de Derecho Internacional*, available at www.revistaladi.com.ar/numero1-banfi-galvan/.

[61] IACHR, *Víctor Rosario Congo* v. *Ecuador* (1997), case 11.427, Report No. 63/99 (Petition).

[62] Ibid. para. 96.

[63] Ibid. para. 101. It recommended that the State of Ecuador should: i. Conduct a serious, impartial and prompt investigation to identify, try and punish the persons responsible for the violations specified in the conclusions of the report; ii. Take appropriate measures to compensate the family members of Víctor Rosario Congo; and iii. Provide medical and

However, the Commission did not engage in a detailed analysis of the rights of persons with disabilities in the merits report that it published following its decision (although it did refer to persons with psychosocial disabilities using the outdated term 'mental illness').

The next petition of relevance was brought on behalf of Maria Soledad Cisternas Reyes (who is now the UN Special Envoy on Disability and Accessibility).[64] The complaint had been filed by the Center for Justice and International Law in 1999 against the Republic of Chile. The petition alleged that Ms Soledad Cisternas Reyes, an attorney by profession and who is totally blind, asked her travel agent to make a reservation for her on a flight to the city of Montevideo, Uruguay. The airline made the reservation on the condition that the petitioner would not travel alone and that she would be accompanied by another passenger or by a guide dog. The petitioner alleged that she was the victim of a violation of her rights not to be subject to discrimination, to equal protection of the law, to have her mental and moral integrity respected, not to be subject to arbitrary interference in her private life, and to leave her country freely and without restrictions. Accordingly, it was alleged that the State Party had violated the provisions of Articles 5, 11, 22, 24 and 25 of the ACHR,[65] in conjunction with Articles 1(1) and 2 (on the obligations to respect rights and to give them domestic legal effect, respectively).[66] On 5 November 1998, the petitioner had filed a motion for constitutional protection before the Court of Appeals of Santiago against the airline, alleging that the facts constituted a violation of the right to equality. The motion was rejected, as was the appeal of that ruling. On 11 December 2003, the petitioner reached a Friendly Settlement agreement with representatives of the Chilean State. In the Friendly Settlement, the parties recognised that, in order 'to contribute to the progressive social integration of persons with disabilities'[67] and bearing in mind the CIADDIS, the state should facilitate the victim's meeting with the General Directorate of Civil Aviation in charge of reviewing the laws related to air travel of persons with disabilities. Except for this general reference to the CIADDIS, the Friendly Settlement did not elaborate in any detail on the right of persons with disabilities to non-discrimination.

psychiatric care for persons suffering from psychosocial illness and confined in penitentiary facilities.

[64] IACHR, *Maria Soledad Cisternas Reyes* v. *Chile* (2011), case 12.232, Report No. 86/11 (Friendly Settlement).

[65] On the rights to humane treatment, privacy, freedom of movement and residence, equal protection before the law, and the right to judicial protection, respectively.

[66] IACHR, *Maria Soledad Cisternas Reyes* v. *Chile*, note 64, para. 1.

[67] IACHR, *Maria Soledad Cisternas Reyes* v. *Chile*, note 64, para. 11(2).

In 2003, before the adoption of the CRPD, a request for precautionary measures was brought before the IACHR in *Patients at the Neuropsychiatric Hospital* v. *Paraguay*,[68] in order to protect the life and personal integrity of the patients detained in the psychiatric facility in Paraguay. The Commission's decision was issued in 2008, just after the CRPD came into force. The petitioners alleged that acts of physical violence and sexual abuse had been committed against over 400 individuals who were detained in the hospital and that the state did not take effective measures to investigate the facts and protect the patients. It was claimed that their internment was life-threatening because of the physical and sexual abuse that they had endured, the deplorable conditions at the facility and the lack of separation of adults and children at the institution. On foot of these allegations, the Commission granted precautionary measures, and it requested that Paraguay adopt actions to protect the life and personal integrity of the patients, such as making medical diagnoses, with special emphasis on women and children; and using solitary confinement according to the relevant standards of international law.

In the aftermath of the Commission's intervention, it continued to monitor the situation, which reportedly improved in favour of the disabled persons involved. In fact, the patient population at the institution decreased by approximately 33 per cent, the budget for community mental health increased, and community-based services were implemented.[69] This case has been deemed to represent 'in practice the main precedent of what it means to adopt measures to deinstitutionali[s]e persons with disabilities, through the implementation of community-based services'.[70]

5.3 Disability Decisions of the Commission Post-CRPD

Once the CRPD entered into force, the IACHR began examining more cases related to individuals with disabilities,[71] and it has even been suggested that

[68] IACHR, *Patients at the Neurosychiatric Hospital* v. *Paraguay* (2008), PM 277-07 (Decision on Precautionary Measures). For an explanation of that case, see Sofía Galván, 'Institutionalization and the Right of Persons with Disabilities to Live in the Community, within the Inter-American Human Rights System', *Human Rights Brief*, 18 April 2018, available at http://hrbrief.org/2018/04/institutionalization-right-persons-disabilities-live-community-within-inter-american-human-rights-system/. See also IACHR, *Ramon Martinez Villareal* v. *United States* (2002), case 11.753, Report No. 52/02 (Petition), where the Commission could potentially have addressed the disability aspects of the case, but it chose not to do so.

[69] Sofía Galván, 'Institutionalization and the Right of Persons with Disabilities to Live in the Community', note 68.

[70] Ibid.

[71] A similar trend can be observed at the European Court of Human Rights (ECHR), which has increased the number of landmark decisions on disability rights following the entry into force of the CRPD. On that point, see Chapter 13 of this textbook; see also Emily Hazlett,

> Pick two of the cases listed in this section. Can you identify whether the CRPD is relevant to the interpretation of the rights involved?

the Commission took a 'more decisive role' in the protection of disability rights.[72] The Commission did so by not only examining individual complaints or petitions, but also by granting increased levels of precautionary measures to applicants. Despite the existence of the CIADDIS (and perhaps because of the limited definition of 'disability' contained in that instrument), the Commission has relied mainly on the ACHR and, more recently, the Protocol of San Salvador, in order to protect the rights of persons with disabilities.[73] From 2009 onwards, the Commission published several admissibility reports related to individuals with psychosocial or physical disabilities, as in the cases of *Wellington Geovanny Peñafiel Parraga* v. *Ecuador*;[74] *Buzos Miskitos* v. *Honduras*;[75] *Luis Eduardo Guachala Chimbo* v. *Ecuador*;[76] *Maria Zambrano* v. *Ecuador*;[77] *Patients of the Psychiatric Hospital Santo Tomas* v. *Panama*;[78] and *Ronal Jared Martinez and Family and Marlon Fabricio Hernandez Fúnez* v. *Honduras*,[79] among others. However, with the only exception of the *Luis Fernando Guevara Diaz* case,[80]

'Disability Rights in a post-Convention Era: Protecting Legal Capacity at the European Court and Beyond' (2014) 2 *International Human Rights Internship Working Paper* 2, p. 11.

[72] Guarnizo-Peralta, 'Disability Rights in the Inter-American System of Human Rights: An Expansive and Evolving Protection', note 1, at 49. For further details on the petition system and to read about the decisions of the Inter-American Commission, see www.oas.org/en/iachr/docs/annual/2012/TOC.asp.

[73] Ibid. at 44.

[74] IACHR, *Wellington Geovanny Peñafiel Parraga* v. *Ecuador* (2009) Petition 4392/02, Report No. 73/09, para. 35.

[75] IACHR, *Opario Lemoth Morris and others (Buzos Miskitos)* v. *Honduras* (2009), Petition 1186-04, Report 121/09, para. 48.

[76] IACHR, *Luis Eduardo Guachala Chimbo* v. *Ecuador* (2010), Petition 247-07, Report 141/10, para. 42.

[77] IACHR, *Maria Zambrano* v. *Ecuador* (2010), Petition 11-513, Report 142/10, para. 35.

[78] IACHR, *Patients of the Psychiatric Service of Santo Tomas Hospital* v. *Panama* (2013), Petition 790-05, Report 94/13, paras. 36-7.

[79] IACHR, *Ronal Jared Martinez and Family & Marlon Fabricio Hernandez Fúnez* v. *Honduras* (2014), Petition 886-04, Report 56/14, paras. 29-30.

[80] The Commission indicated that it would refer to the Protocol of San Salvador and the CIADDIS for interpretive purposes. In that case, the Commission found that a person with a psychosocial disability, who gained first place in an entry exam for a State job, was not

in none of its reports did the Commission make any references to either the CIADDIS or the CRPD. While these were all simply admissibility reports, it might have been expected that the IACHR would have at least mentioned (one of) the two disability Conventions.

In 2013 and early 2014, the Commission published two reports on the merits of the petitions in *Clarence Allen Lackey et al.* v. *The United States*[81] and *Edgar Tamayo Arias* v. *The United States*,[82] where it analysed, for the first time, the rights of persons with psychosocial disabilities facing the death penalty to a fair trial, to due process, and not to be subjected to capital punishment. The Commission considered it to be a 'principle of international law' that 'persons with mental disability cannot be subjected to capital punishment, as these individuals are unable to comprehend the reason for or consequence of their execution'.[83] In reaching that conclusion, the Commission drew on the decisions of UN treaty bodies, among other sources of international law. The approach adopted by the Commission in its decisions in those cases reverts to a medical understanding of disability. The decisions appear to be at odds with Article 12 of the CRPD, which establishes the equal legal capacity of people with disabilities in all aspects of life. The decisions have also been deemed to be in clear contrast[84] with the approach adopted by the CRPD Committee in its General Comment No. 1 on legal capacity (although that General Comment was adopted shortly after the IACHR decisions), which would not appear to allow the denial of criminal responsibility based on a diagnosis of impairment. As Minkowitz observes, the denial of criminal responsibility exposes people with psychosocial or intellectual disabilities to acute stigmatisation and discrimination, since this group of people are deemed incapable of being treated as moral subjects, on the same basis with others.[85]

Later decisions of the Commission appear to take a somewhat more progressive standpoint on the rights of persons with disabilities. In October 2012, through a request for precautionary measures, the Commission was informed of the risk to life and integrity faced by patients interned in a long-term psychiatric institution in Guatemala, the Federico Mora National Mental

hired, due likely to discriminatory practices. The Court found that the facts could imply a potential violation of the rights to a fair trial, to equal protection before the law, and to judicial protection (Articles 8, 24 and 25 ACHR).

81 IACHR, *Clarence Allen Lackey et al.; Miguel Angel Flores; and James Wilson Chambers* v. *United States*, Report no. 52/2013 (2013), Cases 11.575, 12.333 and 12.341.

82 IACHR, *Edgar Tamayo Arias* v. *United States*, Report no. 44/14 (2014), Case 12.873.

83 See IACHR, *Clarence Allen Lackey et al.*, note 81, para. 218. See also ibid. para. 159.

84 Guarnizo-Peralta, 'Disability Rights in the Inter-American System of Human Rights: An Expansive and Evolving Protection', note 1, at 49.

85 Tina Minkowitz, 'Submission to Committee on the Rights of Persons with Disabilities on the Draft General Comment on Article 12' (2014), available at https://www.ohchr.org/EN/HRBodies/CRPD/Pages/DGCArticles12And9.aspx.

Health Hospital.[86] The Commission was informed of violations, such as physical and sexual abuse by medical and security staff, as well as by patients themselves, the abusive use of isolation rooms, degrading conditions and negligent medical care. A particular cause for concern arose from the fact that, at the time of the request, three hundred and thirty-four inpatients (including children) were sharing the same facilities as patients with psychosocial disabilities who had been convicted of a number of crimes.

In November 2012, the IACHR granted precautionary measures in favour of the patients at the hospital and required Guatemala to adopt measures to protect them and ensure their personal integrity. In particular, the IACHR asked Guatemala to take the following actions: to provide adequate medical treatment to the patients; to ensure the separation of children from adults; to separate the patients with psychosocial disabilities from the rest of the hospital patients; to ensure that custody of those patients be provided by unarmed hospital staff; to restrict the use of solitary confinement in accordance with international standards; and to prevent physical, psychological and sexual violence. The IACHR's grant of precautionary measures in this decision drew extensive national and international media coverage,[87] and led to pronouncements by other international human rights bodies.[88]

?

DID YOU KNOW THAT ...?

Since 2013, both the Office of the United Nations High Commissioner for Human Rights (OHCHR) and the UN Committee against Torture (CteAT) have voiced their concerns at the alarming conditions reportedly found to exist at the Federico Mora Hospital in Guatemala, including negligent medical care, deficient nutrition for the patients, and the lack of proper security (OHCHR – Guatemala, Report of the United Nations High Commissioner for Human Rights on the activities of the office in Guatemala, UN Doc. A/HRC/25/19/Add.1, 13 January 2014, para. 40). Specifically, the CteAT urged Guatemala to take effective measures to guarantee full and prompt compliance with the grant for precautionary measures, PM 370/12 (CteAT, Concluding Observations (COs) on the Fifth and Sixth Periodic Reports of Guatemala, 21 June 2013, UN Doc. CAT/C/GTM/CO/5-6, para. 21).

[86] IACHR, *Patients at the Federico Mora Hospital* v. *Guatemala* (2012) PM 370/12 (Precautionary Measures).

[87] See, among others, BBC, Inside the World's Most Dangerous Hospital, December 2014, available at www.bbc.com/news/magazine-30293880. See also Emisoras Unidas, 'Federico Mora es el peor hospital psiquiátrico de América, según BBC', 5 December 2014.

[88] See, for instance, the Office of the United Nations High Commissioner for Human Rights (OHCHR), Press Release, 'OACNUDH llama a garantizar los derechos humanos de pacientes del Hospital Federico Mora', 7 December 2014.

Since the date of granting the precautionary measures, the Inter-American Commission has followed up quite closely on Guatemala's progress in realising the rights of the disabled individuals concerned.[89] Five years after granting the measures, in August 2017, the Commission visited the Federico Mora Hospital during an on-site visit to Guatemala. The Commission observed and acknowledged two main changes: improvements in the institution's infrastructure and the separation of hospital patients from those charged with criminal offences. The IACHR was also informed of the increased budget allocation to the Federico Mora Hospital. However, the Commission expressed consternation at the fact that the state had not created alternatives in the community that enabled the social reintegration of patients.[90] For the first time in its history, the Commission called on an OAS state to guarantee the right of persons with disabilities to live in the community, by urging Guatemala to: define and expedite a strategy for deinstitutionalisation, with a timeline, sufficient resources and specific evaluation measures; ensure the participation of persons with disabilities, directly and through their representative organisations, in the design and implementation of the strategy; and allocate sufficient resources for the development of community-based support services.[91]

Other relevant decisions of the IACHR concened, *inter alia*, the rights to life and personal integrity, in *William Alberto Perez* v. *El Salvador*,[92] *Julio Cesar Molina* v. *Cuba*[93] and *Irene* v. *Argentina*.[94] In the *Perez* and *Molina* cases, a petition was brought by prisoners who had various health problems as well as psychosocial disabilities. The prisoners alleged that they did not have appropriate health care in the detention facilities. In both cases, the Commission ordered the states to adopt the necessary measures to guarantee their life and personal integrity and to provide the specialised medical care needed. In the *Perez* case, the IACHR cited the CRPD's definition of 'reasonable accommodation'[95] in its observation that the state had not furnished substantive

[89] IACHR, *Situation of Human Rights in Guatemala: Diversity, Inequality and Exclusion*, OAS Doc. OEA/Ser.L/V/II. Doc. 43/15, 31 December 2015.

[90] See www.oas.org/en/iachr/media_center/preleases/2017/114a.asp.

[91] IACHR, Report on the Situation of Human Rights in Guatemala, OAS Doc. OEA/Ser.L/V/II. Doc. 208/17, 31 December 2017.

[92] IACHR, *William Alberto Perez* v. *El Salvador* (2014), PM 442–12 (Precautionary Measures).

[93] IACHR, *Julio Cesar Molina* v. *Cuba* (2014), PM307–14 (Precautionary Measures).

[94] IACHR, *Irene* v. *Argentina* (2016), PM 376–15 (Precautionary Measures). Since the English version of the case was not accessible at the time of writing, the information on this case has been drawn from Diana Guarnizo-Peralta, 'Disability Rights in the Inter-American System of Human Rights: An Expansive and Evolving Protection' (2018) 36(1) *Netherlands Quarterly of Human Rights* 43.

[95] *Perez*, note 92, para. 18, footnote 5.

information on, among other things, 'the adoption of comprehensive measures and reasonable accommodations with regard to his mobility, ongoing monitoring of his health, special supports to meet his basic needs, among others'.[96] Under these circumstances, the IACHR considered that the petitioner was in a 'situation of defenselessness, inasmuch as a strategy designed to provide conditions that do not worsen his illness has failed to be implemented, taking into consideration his multiple special needs'.[97] Although it mentioned the CRPD's definition of 'reasonable accommodation', the Commission did not go further in *Perez* to engage in a thorough analysis of the petitioner's rights. Furthermore, it adopted a medicalised approach to the rights of the petitioner, viewing him as a vulnerable applicant.

In the subsequent decision of *Irene* v. *Argentina*, the Inter-American Commission conducted a more comprehensive analysis of the rights of the petitioner, a girl with cerebral palsy and visual and hearing impairments who required an assistant at school. The IACHR explicitly called for the recognition of a 'model of social integration for persons with disabilities on equal terms and under the principle of non-discrimination' and suggested that 'the way to achieve the psychophysical development of persons with disabilities is based on inclusive education'.[98] The Commission cited the definition of 'inclusion' put forward by the United Nations Educational, Scientific and Cultural Organization (UNESCO), a definition that was subsequently quoted by the CRPD Committee a few months later in its General Comment No. 4 on inclusive education.[99] The Commission ordered the state to preserve the life and integrity of Irene, taking into account her disability and health condition, in order to enable her to access all of the support recommended by the specialist in light of the relevant international standards.[100]

As mentioned above, the IACHR also addresses disability rights in some of its thematic and country reports. In the Report on the Situation of Human Rights in Jamaica (2012), for instance, the IACHR included a chapter on the rights of persons with disabilities.[101] More recently, in its 2013 report on The Right of Boys and Girls to a Family,[102] the Commission analysed the situation of boys and girls in vulnerable situations, such as those who have a disability. Notably, the Commission refers, at various junctures in the report, to the CRPD. In particular, it is noteworthy that when referring to the concept of

[96] *Perez*, note 92, para. 18. [97] Ibid. para. 25. [98] *Irene* v. *Argentina*, note 94, para. 25.

[99] See above Chapter 9.

[100] *Irene* v. *Argentina*, note 94, para. 31. Information taken from Diana Guarnizo-Peralta, 'Disability Rights in the Inter-American System of Human Rights: An Expansive and Evolving Protection' (2018) 36(1) *Netherlands Quarterly of Human Rights* 43, at 53.

[101] IACHR, *Report on the Situation of Human Rights in Jamaica* (2012), OAS Doc. OEA/Ser.L./V/II.144, Doc. 12, Chapter VIII.

[102] IACHR, *Report on The Right of Boys and Girls to a Family. Alternative Care. Ending Institutionalization in the Americas*, OAS Doc. OEA/Ser.L/V/II (2013).

'disability', the Commission followed the definition contained in the CRPD, instead of the one included in the CIADDIS.[103]

Overall, it is evident that increased attention is being paid by the Inter-American Commission to disability rights and relevant provisions of international law, particularly with the entry into force of the CRPD. However, the Inter-American Commission does not adopt a human rights model of disability, focusing instead on the perceived vulnerability of individuals with disabilities. In addition, as noted by Guarnizo-Peralta, the IACHR does not tackle the instances of discriminatory violations of rights directly, opting rather for an 'indirect approach', whereby it addresses well-established rights in the ACHR, such as the right to life and personal integrity, instead of delving deeper into the violation at issue.

6 THE INTER-AMERICAN COURT OF HUMAN RIGHTS

Alongside the IACHR, the Inter-American Court is entrusted with a monitoring role and, in that capacity, it engages in monitoring the activities of States Parties to the ACHR as the main judicial organ of the IAHRS. This section adopts a similar structure to the previous section, setting out the composition, functions and competences of the Inter-American Court, before providing an account of the disability case law adopted by the IACtHR in the period before and after the adoption of the CRPD.

6.1 Composition, Functions and Competences of the Inter-American Court

The Inter-American Court is formally an organ of the American Convention and not of the OAS. However, its members may be nationals of any Member State of the OAS, whether or not they are Parties to the American Convention. Chapter VIII of the ACHR sets out the Court's structure, jurisdiction and functions as well as its procedural aspects. According to Article 52 ACHR, the IACtHR is composed of seven judges, who are nationals of OAS Member States and are independent. They are elected in their individual capacity from among jurists of the highest moral authority and of recognised competence in the field of human rights. They must possess the qualifications required for the exercise of the highest judicial functions in conformity with the law of the state of which they are nationals or of the state that proposes them as candidates. According to Article 53 ACHR, the judges of the Court are elected by secret ballot by an absolute majority vote of the States Parties to the Convention, in the General Assembly of the OAS, from a panel of candidates

[103] Ibid. footnote 41.

proposed by those states. Judges are elected for a six-year term that is renewable only once. Article 55(1) ACHR permits judges who are nationals of OAS States Parties to sit in on cases that involve own countries. Moreover, Article 55(3) ACHR and Article 18 of the Court's Rules of Procedure[104] make provision for *ad hoc* judges.

The Court has contentious and advisory jurisdiction. OAS Member States can accept the Court's contentious jurisdiction in accordance with Article 62 ACHR.

ARTICLE 62 ACHR

1. A State Party may, upon depositing its instrument of ratification or adherence to this Convention, or at any subsequent time, declare that it recogni[s]es as binding, *ipso facto*, and not requiring special agreement, the jurisdiction of the Court on all matters relating to the interpretation or application of this Convention.

2. Such declaration may be made unconditionally, on the condition of reciprocity, for a specified period, or for specific cases. It shall be presented to the Secretary General of the Organization, who shall transmit copies thereof to the other member states of the Organization and to the Secretary of the Court.

3. The jurisdiction of the Court shall comprise all cases concerning the interpretation and application of the provisions of this Convention that are submitted to it, provided that the States Parties to the case recogni[s]e or have recogni[s]ed such jurisdiction, whether by special declaration pursuant to the preceding paragraphs, or by a special agreement.

In exercising its contentious jurisdiction, the Court's mandate is more limited than that of the Commission, since the Court may only decide cases brought against those OAS Member States that have specifically accepted the Court's 'contentious jurisdiction'. Cases taken under the Inter-American Court's adjudicatory jurisdiction must first be processed by the Commission. Additionally, only States Parties to the ACHR and the Commission may refer a contentious case to the Court, in line with Article 61 ACHR.

[104] IACtHR, Rules of Procedure, approved by the Court during its XLIX Ordinary Period of Sessions, held from 16 to 25 November 2000, and partially amended by the Court during its LXXXII Ordinary Period of Sessions, held from 19 to 31 January 2009. Notably, in 2009, the Inter-American Court of Human Rights (Court) substantially reformed its rules and regulations, making important changes to the procedures for the processing of petitions and contentious cases.

In order for the Inter-American Court to hear a case, it is necessary that the procedures set forth in Articles 48 and 50 have been complied with. Individual petitioners seeking redress for human rights violations (that are not addressed at the domestic level) do not have direct access to the IACtHR; instead, they must submit their complaint to the Inter-American Commission. Once a petition is processed through the Commission and the Commission decides to submit that case to the Court, the Court's Rules of Procedure provide individuals with the opportunity to take part in the case (through representatives chosen by the individual). While the judgment of the IACtHR is final and not subject to appeal, Article 67 ACHR provides that any of the States Parties to the ACHR may request the Court to interpret its decision (in circumstances where they do not agree with the meaning and scope of the judgment).

If a state has accepted the Inter-American Court's contentious jurisdiction, the Court can declare a State Party to the Convention in breach of its treaty obligations. If a right or freedom protected by the Convention has been violated, the Inter-American Court will rule that the injured party must be ensured the enjoyment of a right or freedom violated; that the breach must be remedied; and that fair compensation must be paid to the injured party (Article 63). It is notable that, in cases of an extremely serious or urgent nature, or when it is necessary to avoid irreparable damage to individuals, the Court can adopt provisional measures.[105]

As well as its contentious jurisdiction, the Court also has an advisory-jurisdiction that may be invoked by any Member State of the OAS and by the main bodies of the organisation, including the Inter-American Commission. In line with the Court's advisory jurisdiction, it has competence to interpret not only the ACHR but also any other treaty that relates to the protection of human rights in the OAS. The Court's advisory jurisdiction also extends to giving its opinion on the compatibility of the domestic laws of any OAS Member State with the requirements set down in the ACHR or any other human rights treaties to which the Inter-American Convention refers.[106] The advisory jurisdiction of the Court may be set in motion by any OAS Member State, whether or not it is a Party to the American Convention, or by any OAS organ listed in Chapter X of the OAS Charter.[107]

DID YOU KNOW THAT ...?

The Court began in operation in 1979 and soon issued several advisory opinions, but it did not begin exercising its contentious jurisdiction until 1986, when the Commission submitted the first contentious case: *Velásquez Rodríguez* v. *Honduras*, regarding

[105] Article 63(2) ACHR. [106] Article 64(2) ACHR. [107] Article 64(1) ACHR.

which the Court issued a judgment on the merits of the case in 1988. To date, the Inter-American Court has issued more than twenty advisory opinions on a wide variety of issues, including the rights of children in the context of migration (Advisory Opinions Nos. 17 and 21); due process (Advisory Opinion No. 19) and judicial guarantees in states of emergency (Advisory Opinions Nos. 8 and 9). In May 2018, the Inter-American Court published a landmark Advisory Opinion on the Environment and Human Rights (www.asil.org/insights/volume/22/issue/6/inter-american-court-human-rights-advisory-opinion-environment-and-human#_edn1).

6.2 Disability Case Law of the Court Pre-CRPD

In a similar vein to the Commission's approach, outlined above, the Court has generally considered the alleged violations of the articles contained in the ACHR in disability cases under what has been termed as an 'indirect approach'. As outlined in the introduction to this chapter, this means that protection for the rights of persons with disabilities is ensured through the application of well-established rights, rather than directly through the application of the right that has actually been violated.

Before the entry into force of the CRPD, the Inter-American Court had interpreted the rights of persons with disabilities in relation to, among others, the rights to life and humane treatment set forth in Articles 4 and 5 ACHR. The first pre-CRPD case on the rights of persons with disabilities to have been decided by the IACtHR was that of *Ximenes Lopes* v. *Brazil.*[108] While the case essentially concerned the right to health, that right is not directly justiciable in the Inter-American system, and so the Court relied on Articles 4 and 5 ACHR (among other Articles).

The case, decided in 2006, concerned an individual with a psychosocial disability who had been institutionalised at the *Casa de Reposo Guararapes*, a private psychiatric treatment centre that operated under the public health system of Brazil. It was alleged that violence was directed towards the patients of the centre and that there was a lack of training given to the employees of the home, who imposed control techniques on the patients. The applicant died of the injuries that he sustained after allegedly having been beaten by officers. Following his death, there was no substantive investigation of the facts which led to impunity on the part of the state. It was argued that the deficiencies in the medical care and the use of violence to control the patients were not exclusive to this particular case but were part of an 'atmosphere of violence, aggression, and maltreatment' at the centre.[109]

[108] IACtHR, *Ximenes Lopes* v. *Brazil* (4 July 2006), Series C No. 149.

[109] Ibid. para. 112(56).

The Court concluded that both the prevailing conditions at the centre and the medical care were sub-standard, and that the mistreatment of the applicant was unlawful. On the basis of the foregoing, the Court held that there was a violation of Article 1 (the obligation to respect rights); Article 1(1) (the duty of non-discrimination); Article 4 (the right to life); Article 5 (the right to humane treatment); Article 8 (the right to a fair trial); and Article 25 (the right to judicial protection).[110]

The Court ruled that, according to Article 1 ACHR, State Party liability may result not only from an act or a failure to act but also from the failure to prevent third parties from impairing the rights of an individual.[111] The Court further held that there is an obligation on all States Parties to the ACHR to protect the rights of individuals by regulating and supervising the health care services provided by private institutions.[112] The Court also emphasised the special attention that States Parties must pay to the rights of individuals with 'mental disabilities', who are particularly vulnerable.[113]

The case is relevant for the fact that the Court implied that the right to life includes both the right of every person not to be deprived of his life arbitrarily as well as positives duties for States Parties to the ACHR. Such duties entail the obligation to create a legal framework that counteracts any threat to the right to life and the duty to 'establish an effective system of justice which can investigate, punish and redress any act of deprivation of life' by state agents or private individuals.[114]

The Court established that States Parties to the ACHR have an obligation to guarantee the provision of effective health care services to all persons with psychosocial impairments[115] (although the Court used the outdated term 'mental illness' in that connection). The Inter-American Court emphasised that people with 'mental' disabilities are particularly vulnerable, and that any health treatment should aim at achieving the patient's welfare and the respect for his or her dignity as a human person.[116] The Court referred to UN standards,[117] namely the United Nations Principles for the Protection of People with Mental Health Illness and the Improvement of Health Care in this respect.[118]

While the decision of the Court represents a positive step in terms of acknowledging the importance of protecting the rights of persons with disabilities on an equal basis with others, the emphasis on vulnerability and the

[110] Ibid. para. 47. [111] Ibid. paras. 83–5. [112] Ibid. para. 99.

[113] Ibid. paras. 46, 123, 239. [114] Ibid. para. 125. [115] Ibid. para. 128.

[116] Ibid. para. 130. [117] Ibid. para. 47.

[118] UN Principles for the Protection of People with Mental Health Illness and the Improvement of Health Care, 17 December 1991, UN Doc. A/RES/66/119.

use of outmoded terminology to refer to disabled individuals would seem to diminish the actual findings of the case.

6.3 Disability Case Law of the Court Post-CRPD

Over the years, the Inter-American Court has referred to treaties from both the Inter-American and the UN systems[119] as well as soft law documents,[120] with a view to shedding light on the interpretation of the rights contained in the ACHR. Following the entry into force of the CRPD (and the CIADDIS), the Court has referred to those treaties as well as to other international standards as interpretive tools for the application of ACHR rights in the context of persons with disabilities.

In *Sebastián Furlán and Family* v. *Argentina*[121] the Court analysed the situation of the young applicant, who had developed difficulties in speaking and in the use of his upper and lower limbs following an accident at the age of fourteen. His father had filed a suit in the domestic civil courts against the state, claiming compensation for the damages that resulted from the accident. However, the state had failed to respond in a timely manner to the judicial authorities and had allegedly caused an excessive delay (twelve years) in the resolution of the action, on which Sebastián's medical treatment depended.

The facts outlined above gave rise to a case before the Inter-American Court, which held that States Parties to the ACHR have the duty to provide special protection to those who are in a 'vulnerable position', including people (and children) with disabilities. This implies that the state should adopt positive measures, in order to actively promote their social inclusion.[122] The Court engaged closely with the provisions of the CRPD and, in that vein, emphasised the obligations that states have regarding children with disabilities, as established in Article 7 CRPD,[123] as well as the duty of states to ensure effective access to justice for persons with disabilities in accordance with Article 13 CRPD.[124]

After having set out the UN framework, the Court went on to analyse the obligations to guarantee the rights to a fair trial and equal judicial protection contained in Articles 8 and 25 ACHR. The IACtHR considered that the state was not in a position to demonstrate that the delay of more than

[119] The Court included a reference to the Additional Protocol to the American Convention in the area of Economic, Social and Cultural Rights in order to interpret the right to property – see IACtHR, *Acevedo Buendia et al. (Discharged and Retired Employees of the Controller)* v. *Peru* (1 July 2009), Series C No. 198, footnote 72.

[120] IACtHR, *Ximénes-Lópes* v. *Brazil,* note 108, para. 47.

[121] IACtHR, *Furlán and Family* v. *Argentina* (31 August 2012), Series C No. 246.

[122] Ibid. para. 134. [123] Ibid. para. 136. [124] Ibid. para. 137.

twelve years in the proceedings was not attributable to the state authorities.[125] It also found that the delay in the proceedings and, therefore, in the compensation requested, had a 'significant and real' impact on the victim, as it did not allow him to access the necessary treatment.[126] The Court concluded that such an act constituted a violation of the rights to a fair trial under Article 8(1) and the rights of the child under Article 19(1) ACHR.[127] The Court also examined the decision of the domestic judge ordering the payment of compensation after a period of sixteen years had elapsed. According to the Court, this deferred payment of compensation implied a violation of the rights to judicial protection and property, according to Articles 25 and 21 ACHR.[128]

Throughout its judgment, the Court made references to both the CIADDIS and the CRPD in defining the concept of 'disability'. It underlined the attention paid in the UN Convention to societal barriers in order to draw out those same features of the definition of 'disability' in the CIADDIS.[129] In that regard, the Court concluded that 'disability' in the two treaties is 'not only defined by the presence of a physical, mental, intellectual or sensory impairment, but is interrelated with the barriers or limitations that exist socially for persons to exercise their rights effectively'.[130]

Since the entry into force of the CRPD, the Inter-American Court has also considered the rights of persons with disabilities to personal integrity, personal liberty, private and family life, as well as sexual and reproductive rights and the right to raise a family.[131] The case of *Artavia Murillo* v. *Costa Rica*[132] was brought before the IACtHR on behalf of nine infertile couples. The case related to the total ban on the practice of in vitro fertilisation (IVF) in Costa Rica after a decision enacted by the Constitutional Section of the Supreme Court of Justice in 2000. A group of patients later presented their case to the Inter-American Commission, and in its merits report issued in July 2011, the Commission held that, in imposing such a ban, Costa Rica had violated several rights under the ACHR, including the right to have one's private and family life respected, the right to start a family and the rights to equality and non-discrimination. Despite the Commission's decision, Costa Rica failed to make any significant progress towards compliance, and, in July 2011, the Commission submitted the case to

125 Ibid. para. 190. 126 Ibid. para. 203. 127 Ibid. para. 233. 128 Ibid. para. 223.

129 See Guarnizo-Peralta, 'Disability Rights in the Inter-American System of Human Rights: An Expansive and Evolving Protection', note 1, at 58.

130 IACtHR, *Furlán and Family* v. *Argentina*, note 121, para. 133.

131 See also IACtHR, *Gonzalez Lluy et al.* v. *Ecuador* (1 September 2015), Series C No. 298, which concerned the rights under the ACHR of a female student with HIV.

132 IACtHR, *Artavia Murillo et al. ('In vitro fertilization')* v. *Costa Rica* (28 November 2012), Series C No. 257.

Do you believe that there is room for further influence of the CRPD on the case law of the Inter-American Court?

the Inter-American Court with a view to resolving the situation for the individuals involved under its contentious jurisdiction.

The case before the Inter-American Court was considered under the obligation of non-discrimination (Article 1(1)) and, *inter alia*, under the rights to humane treatment (Article 5), personal liberty (Article 7), private and family life (Article 11), and to raise a family (Article 17(2)). Relying on Article 25 CRPD, which Costa Rica had ratified in 2008, the Court ruled that infertility necessitates access to treatment and techniques that can aid in resolving the resulting reproductive and health problems that arise for the individuals concerned.[133] The Inter-American Court drew on the social model of disability. According to the IACtHR, infertility is a type of disability that results from the interaction between reproductive health problems and the social barriers that hinder the exercise of rights by persons with disabilities.[134] The Inter-American Court also drew on the definition of 'infertility' laid down by the World Health Organization (WHO) as well as the opinion of expert witnesses who expressed the view that 'involuntary infertility is a disease'.[135] This seems to have prompted the Court to rule that reproductive health problems are a form of disability. It also allowed for the possibility that a reproductive disability could be considered as arising from a 'social condition' for the purpose of applying the grounds of discrimination enumerated in the ACHR.[136] The Court explained that societal barriers to infertility, such as the absolute ban on IVF, put infertile individuals in a more vulnerable position, meriting special protection from the state.[137] The Court found that the absolute ban prohibited infertile couples from accessing IVF treatments and from effectively exercising their right to private and family life, therefore having a disproportionate effect (from the perspective of disability, gender and the applicants' financial situation) on those couples. The Court ultimately made a finding of indirect discrimination and ordered Costa Rica to modify its legislation by taking out the prohibition on IVF and allowing couples to access IVF treatment without interference.

[133] Ibid. paras. 289 and 293.

[134] Ibid. para. 292.

[135] Ibid. para. 288. Some of the expert witnesses considered infertility as a form of disability only under certain conditions and presumptions and in determined cases. Ibid. para. 289.

[136] Ariel Dulitzky and Hannah Zimmerman, 'Case Note: Indirect Discrimination, Reproductive Rights and the In Vitro Fertilisation Ban' (2003) 10 *Equal Rights Review* 123, at 126.

[137] IACtHR, *Artavia Murillo et al. ('In vitro fertilization')* v. *Costa Rica*, note 132, para. 292.

This case is significant from the perspective of the references that the Inter-American Court makes to the relevant international standards on disability rights. Although the Court did not enter into an in-depth analysis of the rights contained in the CRPD, such as the right to sexual and reproductive health of people with disabilities in Article 25(a) CRPD, the case is nonetheless relevant in acknowledging infertility as a form of disability. Moreover, this case and the *Furlán* case demonstrate that the Court, in a similar vein to the Commission, is willing to expand the interpretation of the rights contained in the American Convention in order to take into account both the CRPD and the CIADDIS. This strategy reflects the international trend of 'globalisation of disability rights law'.[138] On the whole, the cases of the Court (and the decisions of the Commission) provide an important avenue through which to integrate universal standards on disability, with a view to a more comprehensive protection of the rights of people with disabilities in the OAS. However, both the Commission and the Court could make a greater effort in aligning the standards of the ACHR more closely with the tenor of the CRPD, where appropriate.

SUMMARY

- **The IAHRS is deemed to constitute a regional system of international human rights law. While it is distinct from the UN system (and from the CRPD itself), the link between the IAHRS and the UN is noted in the Preamble of the OAS Charter.**
- **The objectives of the OAS are, *inter alia*: to strengthen the peace and security of the continent; to ensure the pacific settlement of disputes that may arise among the Member States; to provide for common action on the part of those states in the event of aggression; to seek the solution of political, juridical and economic problems that may arise among them; to promote their economic, social and cultural development; and to eradicate extreme poverty.**
- **The formal beginning of the IAHRS was the approval of the American Declaration, which was the first regional human rights instrument to be adopted, more than six months before the UDHR was adopted in the UN. This was followed shortly thereafter by the entry into force of the OAS Charter.**
- **In addition to the American Declaration and the OAS Charter, two further instruments also comprise the core treaties of the IAHRS. The primary instrument through which disability rights are protected is the CIADDIS. A further key document in the IAHRS is the ACHR, a general human rights treaty that does not mention disability explicitly (although its Additional Protocol of San Salvador does mention the rights of persons with disabilities in Article 18).**
- **The quasi-judicial and judicial mechanisms of the IAHRS are the Inter-American Commission and the Inter-American Court, respectively.**

[138] Arlene Kanter, 'The Globalization of Disability Rights Law' (2013) 30 *Syracuse Journal of International Law & Commerce* 241.

- **The IAHRS adopts a dual institutional structure. The first system, based on the OAS Charter and the American Declaration, is operated in relation to all OAS Member States only by the Commission. The second sub-system comprises the OAS Member States that are Parties to the ACHR and have also accepted the Inter-American Court's contentious jurisdiction. The latter states are subject to the binding judgments issued by the IACtHR in cases referred to it by the IACHR and, concurrently, to the law embodied by the Inter-American Commission's resolutions and recommendations.**
- **The IACHR has the competence to decide on individual complaints or petitions concerning alleged human rights violations and to refer them to the Inter-American Court (where necessary). Moreover, it has the competence to engage in a wide range of human rights monitoring and awareness-raising activities. In addition, the IACHR carries out its mandate through conducting on-site visits to OAS Member States and drafting thematic and country reports.**
- **The IACtHR has contentious jurisdiction to decide cases brought before it and to order reparations, as well as an advisory jurisdiction that may be invoked by any Member State of the OAS and by the main bodies of the organisation, including the Inter-American Commission.**
- **Although the CIADDIS does not provide a strong tool for the analysis of individual claims in cases of violations of disability rights, both the Inter-American Commission and the Inter-American Court have interpreted the rights contained in the ACHR quite extensively, in order to protect disability rights.**
- **Since the entry into force of the CRPD, the Inter-American judicial and quasi-judicial mechanisms have paid increasing attention to disability rights. However, both the Commission and the Court could draw further on the tenets of the CRPD, in order to bring the standards of the Inter-American system in line with the progressive norms contained in the UN Convention, which views people with disabilities as holders of rights on an equal basis with others, rather than merely vulnerable subjects.**

ACTIVITIES

REVIEW QUESTIONS

1. **How has the Inter-American Commission's role evolved over time?**
2. **What are the key functions and competences of the IACtHR?**
3. **What are the most relevant decisions of the IACtHR on disability?**

ESSAY QUESTIONS

1. **'The differences between the content and thrust of the CRPD and the CIADDIS are substantial.'** ***Discuss.***

2. **'The CRPD's norms have the potential to influence the interpretation of the rights of persons with disabilities in the Inter-American system to a greater extent than they have to date.'** ***Discuss.***

GROUP PROJECT

A group of prisoners at the Confinement County Jail, in the state of Utopia, have severe psychosocial disabilities. They have been denied food by the prison guards, who consistently subject them to violence and abuse by using so-called control techniques. The prisoners have heard about several petitions that have been brought before the Inter-American Commission on Human Rights regarding similar issues, and, on the advice of their lawyers, they have decided to send a communication to the Commission immediately. They do not believe that they should wait too long before sending a petition to the Commission, since the domestic court system is not very effective and they want to resolve the situation sooner rather than later. They also believe that it would be a wise idea to bring a complaint before the CRPD Committee at the same time, alleging violations of their rights under the UN Convention, in order to bring increased visibility to their situation. The prisoners wonder whether they are entitled to proceed as planned and, furthermore, whether they can resort directly to any other mechanism in the Inter-American system.

Discuss the group project, assuming that Utopia is a Member State of the OAS as well as a State Party to the CIADDIS and to the CRPD.

FURTHER READING

Acuña Pereda, E., 'The Institutionalization of People with Mental Disabilities: Comparative Analysis between its Treatment under the Inter-American and the European Systems of Human Rights' (2012) 5 *Inter-American and European Human Rights Journal* 72–9.

Chouinard, V., 'Living on the Global Peripheries of Law: Disability Human Rights Law in Principle and in Practice in the Global South' (2018) 7(8) *Laws* 1–14.

Goldman, R. K., 'History and Action: The Inter-American Human Rights System and the Role of the Inter-American Commission on Human Rights' (2009) 31(4) *Human Rights Quarterly* 856–87.

Guarnizo-Peralta, G., 'Disability Rights in the Inter-American System of Human Rights: An Expansive and Evolving Protection' (2018) 36(1) *Netherlands Quarterly of Human Rights* 44–63.

Haris, D. J. and Livingstone, S., *The Inter-American System of Human Rights* (New York: Oxford University Press, 1998).

Kanter, A., 'The Globalization of Disability Rights Law' (2013) 30 *Syracuse Journal of International Law & Commerce* 241–69.

Medina, C., *The Inter-American Commission on Human Rights and the Inter-American Court of Human Rights: Reflections on a Joint Venture* (1990) 12 *Human Rights Quarterly* 429–64.

Sandoval, C., 'The Inter-American Human Rights System and Approach', in S. Sheeran and N. Rodley, *Routledge Handbook on International Human Rights Law* (New York: Routledge, 2013).

15 Disability Law and Policy in the African Human Rights System and in the Asian Transnational Regime

LEARNING OUTCOMES

- ✓ Identify the main turning points in the development of the disability policy of the African Union.
- ✓ Demonstrate awareness of the provisions of the African Charter on Human and Peoples' Rights that are most relevant to the protection and promotion of the rights of disabled people.
- ✓ Understand the core tenets of the Protocol to the African Charter on Human and Peoples' Rights on the Rights of Persons with Disabilities in Africa.
- ✓ Assess the role of the African Human and Peoples' Rights Commission in promoting disability rights.
- ✓ Comprehend the relevance of the CRPD in Africa and the particular challenges linked to the implementation of the Convention in that continent.
- ✓ Understand the provisions of the 2004 Arab Charter on Human Rights and Disability that are most relevant to the protection and promotion of the rights of persons with disabilities.
- ✓ Demonstrate awareness of the evolution in the protection of disability rights in Asia.
- ✓ Understand the role of the Association of Southeast Asian Nations in developing a pan-Asian disability policy.

Human rights for disabled people in the Global South are extremely complex and the lived reality is often distant from the legal rhetoric.[1]

1 INTRODUCTION

Over the last thirty years, the rights of persons with disabilities have received growing attention in the African and Asian regional and transnational systems.

The African Union (AU), formerly known as the Organisation of African Unity (OAU), has played a prominent role in advancing disability rights and in fostering a pan-African disability policy.[2] The African Charter on Human and Peoples' Rights (African Charter)[3] and other regional human rights treaties include several provisions that are relevant to disabled people. In January 2018, a new protocol to the African Charter concerning the rights of persons with disabilities was adopted at the AU Summit in Addis Ababa, and it is now open to ratification. It is entitled the Protocol to the African Charter on Human and Peoples' Rights on the Rights of Persons with Disabilities in Africa (RPDA Protocol).[4] As noted by the UN Special Rapporteur on the Rights of Persons with Disabilities, that protocol addresses 'some of the urgent issues that have the most disproportionate impact on people with disabilities, such as poverty, systemic discrimination and harmful practices'.[5] The African Commission on Human and Peoples' Rights (ACHPR or African Commission) – the body that monitors the implementation of the African Charter – has also addressed, albeit to a limited extent, the rights of persons with disabilities in its decisions, guidelines and concluding observations (COs).

[1] Helen Meekosha and Karen Soldatic, 'Human Rights and the Global South: The Case of Disability' (2011) 32(8) *Third World Quarterly* 1383.

[2] This chapter does not address sub-regional systems and treaties, such as the East African Community Treaty, the Treaty of the Southern African Development Community (SADC), the SADC Protocol on Gender and Development, the SADC Charter of Fundamental and Social Rights and the Treaty of the Economic Community of West African States. For a succinct overview of the foregoing instruments, see Rhona Smith, *Textbook on International Human Rights*, 7th edn (Oxford: Oxford University Press, 2016), pp. 148 et seq. Interestingly, those treaties, while focused on economic integration and development, include references to persons with disabilities, especially in the context of socio-economic rights and poverty reduction. See Japhet Biegon, 'The Promotion and Protection of Disability Rights in the African Human Rights System', in Ilze Grobbelaar-du Plessis and Tobias van Reenen (eds.), *Aspects of Disability Law in Africa* (Pretoria: Pretoria University Law Press, 2012), pp. 53–83.

[3] African Charter on Human and Peoples' Rights, adopted on 27 June 1981, OAU Doc. CAB/LEG/67/3 rev. 5, 21 I.L.M. 58 (1982), entered into force 21 October 1986.

[4] The text of the Protocol is available at https://au.int/sites/default/files/treaties/36440-treaty-protocol_to_the_achpr_on_the_rights_of_persons_with_disabilities_in_africa_e.pdf.

[5] See at www.ohchr.org/EN/NewsEvents/Pages/DisplayNews.aspx?NewsID=22661&LangID=E.

In addition to the AU, in Northern Africa and the Middle East, the League of Arab States (LAS)[6] has expressed its commitment towards the promotion of disability rights in the revised Arab Charter on Human Rights, which was adopted in 2004 and entered into force in 2008.

While a regional human rights system (comparable to the African and inter-American ones) does not exist in Asia and the Pacific, the Association of Southeast Asian Nations (ASEAN) has made considerable progress in advancing the protection of human rights alongside economic and political cooperation.[7] The ASEAN Charter,[8] which was adopted in 2007 and entered into force in 2008, includes explicit references to human rights and sets up the ASEAN Intergovernmental Commission on Human Rights (AICHR).[9] In the past ten years, the AICHR has addressed, to varying degrees, the rights of persons with disabilities. Moreover, the UN regional body – the UN Economic and Social Commission for Asia and the Pacific (ESCAP) – has also contributed to advancing the rights of disabled people in the region and to facilitating the exchange of good practices on accessibility and inclusion.

All of those regional developments in Africa and Asia are addressed in this final chapter of the textbook. Further to this introduction, section 2 presents the structure and functions of the AU and analyses the main tenets of the African human rights system. Section 3 outlines the key challenges faced by persons with disabilities in Africa and examines the development of a pan-African disability policy aimed at addressing those challenges. Section 4 discusses the extent to which the rights of persons with disabilities are protected and promoted in the core African human rights treaties. Particular attention is paid to the RPDA Protocol. The role of the ACHPR and of the African Court on Human and Peoples' Rights (African Court) in advancing disability rights is also examined. Section 5 goes on to discuss the main challenges associated with the implementation of the CRPD in Africa. Section 6 briefly addresses the role of the LAS in protecting and promoting the rights of disabled people, with a focus on the 2004 Arab Charter. Section 7 discusses the role of the ASEAN in advancing the rights

[6] Smith, *Textbook on International Human Rights*, note 2, p. 88.

[7] Ibid. p. 91. See also Mathew Davies, 'States of Compliance?: Global Human Rights Treaties and ASEAN Member States', (2014) 13(4) *Journal of Human Rights* 414, at 414. This chapter does not discuss the Pacific Islands Forum (PIF). The PIF is a political and economic policy organisation, which has limited engagement with human rights (https://www.forumsec.org/). In the last few years, the PIF has launched a few policy initiatives on disability, which are still in their infancy. The most relevant among those initiatives is the 2016–2025 Pacific Regional Framework for the Rights of Persons with Disabilities (PFRPD). The text of the PFRPD is available at http://www.forumsec.org/wp-content/uploads/2019/02/Framework-on-the-Rights-of-Persons-with-Disabilities-.pdf.

[8] The text of the ASEAN Charter is available at https://asean.org/storage/images/archive/publications/ASEAN-Charter.pdf.

[9] See at http://aichr.org/.

of persons with disabilities, while section 8 examines the ESCAP's actions on disability. This chapter does not address in any detail the debate on disability in the Global South.[10] However, the complexities related to extreme poverty and post-colonial contexts are highlighted, where appropriate, throughout the various sections.

2 THE AFRICAN REGIONAL SYSTEM AT A GLANCE

This section briefly describes the role and the structure of the AU and discusses the main features of the African human rights system.

2.1 The African Union: Objectives and Institutional Set-Up

Until the early 2000s, the OAU was the main regional organisation in Africa, having been established in 1963. It provided a forum for the adoption of coordinated positions on matters of common concern to the African population in the wake of decolonisation. However, since the measures adopted by the OAU in addressing pan-African socio-economic issues were deemed insufficient to boost the development of the continent, a new organisation, the AU, was set up in 2002, in order to replace the OAU.

The AU currently includes fifty-five Member States, after Morocco joined in January 2017.[11] It aims to boost economic and political collaboration among African states.[12] The AU has shifted its focus from decolonisation processes to 'spear-heading Africa's development and integration'.[13] Its overall vision is that of '[a]n integrated, prosperous and peaceful Africa, driven by its own citizens and representing a dynamic force in [the] global arena'.[14] The objectives of the AU, as Maluwa notes, are 'fairly expansive', going far beyond those of the former OAU.[15] Those objectives explicitly include the protection of human rights. In that regard, Article 3 of the Constitutive Act of the African

[10] Among others, see Shaun Grech and Karen Soldatic (eds.), *Disability in the Global South* (Cham: Springer, 2016). See also Helen Meekosha, 'Decolonising Disability: Thinking and Acting Globally' (2011) 26(6) *Disability and Society* 667.

[11] Morocco was a founder member of the OAU but withdrew in 1984. The fifty-five Member States of the AU encompass all the countries on the continent of Africa.

[12] Smith, *Textbook on International Human Rights*, note 2, pp. 136 et seq. See also Ngozi Mercy Opara et al., 'African Union and the Challenges of Development' (2016) 5(2) *Journal of African Union Studies* 67; Tiyanjana Maluwa, 'The OAU/African Union and International Law: Mapping New Boundaries or Revising Old Terrain?' (2004) 98 *Proceedings of the Annual Meeting* (American Society of International Law) 232; Yusuf Abdulqawi and Fatsah Ouguergouz, *The African Union: Legal and Institutional Framework: A Manual on the Pan-African Organization* (Leiden/Boston: Martinus Nijhoff, 2012).

[13] See at https://au.int/en/overview. [14] Ibid.

[15] Tiyanjana Maluwa, 'The Transition from the Organisation of the African Unity to the African Union', in Yusuf Abdulqawi and Fatsah Ouguergouz, *The African Union: Legal and*

Union (CAAU)[16] makes reference to the objectives of encouraging 'international cooperation, taking due account of the Charter of the United Nations and the Universal Declaration of Human Rights', and of promoting and protecting human and peoples' rights in accordance with the African Charter and other relevant human rights instruments. Respect for human rights is also listed in Article 4 CAAU, which lays down the guiding principles of the AU's work. In that connection, the principle of respect for human rights is listed alongside the promotion of gender equality, the respect for democratic principles, the rule of law, and the promotion of social justice.

The most important organs of the AU[17] are as follows: the Assembly; the Executive Council; the Pan-African Parliament; the Commission; the Court of Justice and the Economic, Social and Cultural Council. The Assembly is composed of Heads of State and Government or their representatives and is the supreme organ of the AU. Among other tasks, it is entrusted with determining the common policies of the Union and with receiving, considering and taking decisions on reports and recommendations from the other organs of the Union.[18] The Executive Council is composed of ministers or members designated by the governments of AU Member States. As established by Article 13 CAAU, the Executive Council must coordinate and take decisions on policies in areas of common interest to the Member States. Those encompass, among many others, 'social security, including the formulation of mother and child care policies, as well as policies relating to the disabled and the handicapped'.[19] The Pan-African Parliament ensures the full participation of the African peoples in the governance, development and economic integration of the continent. It addresses disability issues mainly through its Committee on Gender, Family, Youth and People with Disabilities.[20] Another primary organ of the AU is the Commission, which represents the Union as a whole and defends its interests; elaborates draft common positions; prepares strategic plans and studies for the consideration of the Executive Council; and elaborates, promotes and coordinates AU policies. The Economic, Social and Cultural Council is an advisory organ that is composed of different social and professional groups emanating from AU Member States. Finally, the Court of Justice is the judicial institution of the AU, which was set up and regulated by a Protocol that entered into force in 2009.[21]

Institutional Framework: A Manual on the Pan-African Organization (Leiden/Boston: Martinus Nijhoff, 2012), pp. 25–52, p. 42.

[16] See at https://au.int/en/constitutive-act.

[17] All of the AU organs are listed in Article 5 CAAU.

[18] Article 6 CAAU.

[19] Article 13(1)(k) CAAU.

[20] Biegon, 'The Promotion and Protection of Disability Rights in the African Human Rights System', note 2, p. 61.

[21] Protocol of the Court of Justice of the African Union, available at https://au.int/en/treaties/protocol-court-justice-african-union.

2.2 The Development of a Regional Human Rights System

The work of the former OAU revolved around various programmes for sustainable development and strategies to solve conflicts and promote peace on the African continent. On the whole, the OAU aimed to emancipate Africa from its long colonial history. Proposals for an African human rights instrument were put forward in the late 1960s, but it was only twenty years later, in 1981, that the African Charter was adopted by the OAU, in conjunction with the Grand Bay Declaration and Plan of Action on human rights.[22]

The African human rights system was established, alongside other programmes and policies, to overcome the detrimental consequences of colonialism.[23] In that vein, the African Charter has a unique 'anti-colonial slant'.[24] For example, it provides that 'all peoples shall freely dispose of their wealth and natural resources' and requires States Parties 'to eliminate all forms of foreign exploitation particularly that practised by international monopolies so as to enable their peoples to fully benefit from the advantages derived from their national resources'.[25] In addition, it explicitly lays down the right of all peoples to 'their economic, social and cultural development with due regard to their freedom and identity and in the equal enjoyment of the common heritage of mankind'.[26]

In accordance with Article 66 of the African Charter, which allows for 'special protocols or agreements', a number of other human rights instruments to supplement the provisions of the Charter have been adopted since the 1990s. The first agreement to be approved was the African Charter on the Rights and Welfare of the Child (1990),[27] which aims to protect and promote the human rights and fundamental freedoms of African children. In 1998, the Protocol to the African Charter on Human and Peoples' Rights on the Establishment of the African Court on Human and Peoples' Rights was adopted. After the entry into force of the Protocol in 2004, the African Court was set up, and it has jurisdiction over cases concerning the interpretation and application of the African Charter and other relevant AU human rights instruments.[28] With the advent of the AU, a series of treaties have addressed the rights of different categories of people: the Protocol to the African Charter on Human and Peoples' Rights on the Rights of Women in Africa (2003);[29] the African Youth Charter

[22] Grand Bay (Mauritius) Declaration and Plan of Action, 1999, available at www.achpr.org/instruments/grandbay/.

[23] Frans Viljeon, *International Human Rights in Africa* (Oxford: Oxford University Press, 2012), pp. 151 et seq.

[24] Eghosa Osa Ekhator, 'The Impact of the African Charter on Human and Peoples' Rights on Domestic Law: A Case Study of Nigeria' (2015) 41(2) *Commonwealth Law Bulletin* 253, at 254.

[25] Article 21(1) of the African Charter. [26] Article 22 of the African Charter.

[27] African Charter on the Rights and Welfare of the Child, OAU Doc. CAB/LEG/24.9/49 (1990).

[28] Article 3 of the Protocol.

[29] Protocol to the African Charter on Human and Peoples' Rights on the Rights of Women in Africa, adopted by the 2nd Ordinary Session of the Assembly of the Union (2003).

(2006);[30] and the AU Convention for the Protection and Assistance of Internally Displaced Persons in Africa (2009).[31] Moreover, in 2007, the African Charter on Democracy, Elections and Governance[32] was approved in order to further enhance the protection of democracy and the rule of law, and promote the exercise of civil and political rights in the African continent.

2.3 The African Charter and Its Monitoring Body

2.3.1 *Structure and Distinctive Features of the African Charter*

Aside from its Preamble, the African Charter contains sixty-eight articles, divided into three parts. The first part deals with rights and duties (Articles 1–29); the second part on measures and safeguards (Articles 30–63) concerns implementation and monitoring mechanisms; and the final part sets out general provisions on the ratification and entry into force of the Charter (Articles 64–68). As shown in Figure 15.1, the African Charter includes civil

Article 1: Obligations of Member States
Article 2: Right to Freedom from Discrimination
Article 3: Right to Equality before the Law and Equal Protection of the Law
Article 4: Right to Life
Article 5: Prohibition of Torture and Cruel, Inhuman and Degrading Treatment
Article 6: Right to Personal Liberty and Protection from Arbitrary Arrest
Article 7: Right to a Fair Trial
Article 8: Right to Freedom of Conscience
Article 9: Right to Receive Information and Free Expression
Article 10: Right to Freedom of Association
Article 11: Right to Freedom of Assembly
Article 12: Right to Freedom of Movement
Article 13: Right to Participate in Government
Article 14: Right to Property
Article 15: Right to Work
Article 16: Right to Health
Article 17: Right to Education
Article 18: Protection of the Family and Vulnerable Groups
Article 19: Right of All Peoples to Equality and Rights
Article 20: Right to Self-Determination
Article 21: Right to Free Disposal of Wealth and Natural Resources
Article 22: Right to Economic, Social and Cultural Development
Article 23: Right to National and International Security and Peace
Article 24: Right to a General Satisfactory Environment

Figure 15.1 Rights Included in the African Charter

[30] African Youth Charter, adopted during the 7th Ordinary Session of the Conference of Heads of States and Government (2006).

[31] Convention for the Protection and Assistance of Internally Displaced Persons in Africa, adopted by the Special Summit of the Union (2009).

[32] African Charter on Democracy, Elections and Governance, adopted during the 8th Ordinary Session of the Assembly of the AU (2007).

and political rights, as well as socio-economic rights. It recognises the indivisibility of all rights and does not allow for derogations.[33]

While reflecting existing international human rights treaties, the African Charter includes two main distinctive features: it sets out collective rights, and it lays down duties for States Parties as well as for individuals and peoples. Among the collective rights, Article 19 is particularly important. It enshrines the right of all peoples to equality, and provides that 'nothing shall justify the domination of a people by another'. In a similar vein to Article 21 on the right to free disposal of wealth and natural resources and Article 22 on the right to economic, social and cultural development, Article 19 reflects an anti-colonial sentiment. Among the duties of individuals, Article 27 is particularly significant. This provision affirms that individuals have duties towards their family, society, the state and other legally recognised communities, as well as towards the international community. Moreover, it requires that individual rights and freedoms are exercised 'with due regard to the rights of others, collective security, morality and common interest'.[34] The latter duty is corroborated by Article 28, which provides that every individual should 'respect and consider his fellow beings without discrimination', and 'maintain relations aimed at promoting, safeguarding and reinforcing mutual respect and tolerance'. Article 29 also highlights the responsibilities of the individual towards the family, the community and the state.

Another feature that distinguishes the African Charter from other regional human rights instruments, such as the European Convention on Human Rights (ECHR), is the reference to traditional values in various provisions. For example, Article 17(3) affirms that it is a duty of the state to promote and protect 'morals and traditional values recogni[s]ed by the community'. Additionally, Article 18(2) places an obligation on the state 'to assist the family which is the custodian of morals and traditional values recogni[s]ed by the community'.[35]

2.3.2 *The African Commission on Human and Peoples' Rights*

The ACHPR, established in 1987, is the main monitoring body entrusted with overseeing the implementation of the African Charter.[36] Every two years, in accordance with Article 62 of the African Charter, States Parties are required to submit a report to the ACHPR on the legislative or other measures taken with a view to giving effect to the rights and freedoms recognised and

33 ACHPR, *Media Rights Agenda* v. *Nigeria*, paras. 68 and 69.

34 Article 27(2) of the African Charter.

35 See also Article 29 of the African Charter.

36 For an overview of the ACHPR see, among others, Ilias Bantekas and Lutz Oette, *International Human Rights Law and Practice*, 2nd edn (Cambridge: Cambridge University Press, 2016), pp. 277 et seq.

guaranteed by the Charter. In addition, the ACHPR is empowered to receive and consider:

i. Communications submitted by one State claiming that another State Party to the Charter has violated one or more of the provisions in the Charter (Articles 48–49 of the African Charter).
ii. Communications submitted by individuals and/or organisations alleging that a State Party to the Charter has violated one or more of the rights guaranteed therein (Article 55 of the African Charter).

Moreover, Article 45 of the African Charter gives the ACHPR a mandate, *inter alia*, to undertake studies and research 'on African problems in the field of human and peoples' rights, organise seminars, symposia and conferences, disseminate information', and 'to interpret all the provisions of the present Charter at the request of a State Party, an institution of the [AU] or an African Organisation recognised by the [AU]'. In interpreting and applying the African Charter, the ACHPR relies on its own jurisprudence, and, as provided for by Articles 60 and 61 of the African Charter, it also relies on relevant international and regional human rights instruments, principles and standards.

3 THE EMERGENCE OF AN AFRICAN DISABILITY POLICY

This section presents, in a succinct manner, some factual information on the key challenges faced by persons with disabilities in Africa. It then discusses the role of the AU in developing a pan-African disability policy.

3.1 Disability in Africa: Key Regional Challenges

According to the UN, the number of persons with disabilities in Africa amounts to approximately 80 million.[37] In the region, physical disabilities are often related to impairments caused by malnutrition, diseases, environmental hazards, wars, conflicts, and landmines.[38] The number of people living with HIV/AIDS[39] is also extremely high in the African region. The World

[37] See at www.un.org/africarenewal/magazine/april-2010/africa%E2%80%99s-disabled-will-not-be-forgotten.

[38] Ibid. From all the African countries, Sudan and South Sudan are among the most affected by landmines. See Landmine and Cluster Munition Monitor, *Landmine monitor 2012*, available at www.the-monitor.org/lm/2012/resources/Landmine_Monitor_2012.pdf.

[39] The HIV condition, in interaction with external barriers, hampers the participation of the person concerned in society, and can be deemed to fall within the definition of 'disability' (although this connection between HIV and disability is not accepted by all scholars). In addition, the HIV condition can give rise to other long-term impairments that may result in a disability. The UN maintains that the close relationship between HIV/AIDS and disability is a

Health Organization (WHO) estimates that, in 2015, 90 per cent of the children living with HIV were in sub-Saharan Africa and that 70 per cent of AIDS-related deaths in the world occurred in the African region.[40] In addition, in 2015, of the 2.1 million new HIV infections worldwide, 1.37 million (i.e. 65 per cent) occurred in sub-Saharan Africa.[41] A large percentage of people living with HIV are women and girls with intellectual or psychosocial disabilities. Those individuals are more exposed to sexual violence and rape and, consequently, to HIV/AIDS,[42] than men with disabilities and non-disabled women. According to Djoyou Kamga, the vulnerability of women with intellectual disabilities is aggravated by the belief that sex with a person with a disability will cure AIDS.[43]

People with disabilities in Africa face specific and intertwined challenges, the most prominent of which is abject poverty. In particular, in the most deprived parts of the continent, disabled people are treated as objects of charity and placed under social welfare programmes, due to their 'inability to function in mainstream society and to provide for themselves'.[44] Poverty is inextricably linked to a lack of educational opportunities and employment, as well as to the impossibility to access health care and other social services. In several African countries, severe poverty not only hinders the possibility for people with disabilities to live in dignity but also seriously hampers their life expectancy and endangers their survival. Poverty and marginalisation are exacerbated in instances of forced migration from and within conflict-affected countries, such as the Congo, Liberia, Rwanda, Sierra Leone and Sudan. The 2017 Africa Report on Internal Displacement[45] recounts that, due to dictatorial regimes and civil wars, 12.6 million Africans were living in internal displacement at the end of 2016. A large number of internally displaced people are those with disabilities.[46] Among other scholars, Stein and Lord highlight

cause for concern, as persons with disabilities are often at higher risk of exposure to HIV. Additionally, there is a growing understanding that persons living with HIV or AIDS are also at risk of becoming disabled on a permanent or episodic basis as a result of their condition. See at www.un.org/development/desa/disabilities/issues/disability-and-hivaids.html. However, domestic laws in the African continent are contradictory. For example, section 3 of the HIV and AIDS Act 2006 (Mauritius) (Act No. 31 of 2006) expressly states that any person with HIV or AIDS shall not be considered as having a disability or incapacity, although it goes on to say that HIV status or presumed HIV status shall not be used as a ground for discrimination.

40 See at www.afro.who.int/health-topics/hivaids. 41 Ibid.

42 Serges Alain Djoyou Kamga, 'A Call for a Protocol to the African Charter on Human and Peoples' Rights on the Rights of Persons with Disabilities in Africa' (2013) 21(2) *African Journal of International and Comparative Law* 219, at 221.

43 Ibid. 44 Ibid.

45 The report is available at http://www.internal-displacement.org/publications/2017-africa-report-on-internal-displacement.

46 Ibid.

'the extremely precarious position' of such individuals with disabilities within this already vulnerable population.[47]

In rural areas, the marginalisation of persons with disabilities and the poverty that they encounter are recurrently the result of traditional or religious beliefs that consider disability to be a form of punishment from the gods. Since disability is seen as a 'burdensome affliction', a prevalent view is that it should be rooted out to ensure good health and well-being in society. In that regard, Biegon maintains that women who give birth to children with disabilities are prone to be blamed for such births and, consequently, abandoned by their spouses.[48] Ndlovu affirms that certain indigenous African beliefs portray virtually all types of physical and intellectual impairment as an affliction that must be counteracted by all means necessary and 'objectify and stigmatise disability as either punishment from divinities, or the ancestors, or as the embodiment of sin or social deviance'.[49] In particular, several African traditions 'depict people with [intellectual] impairment as victims of either witchcraft or ancestral anger due to their moral indiscretion'.[50] On the basis of Soko and Kubik's studies, Ndlovu reports that, for example, among the Thumbuka of Malawi, 'many people believe that serious ailments such as epilepsy and insanity are caused by *wachari* or witches'.[51] Taking Nigeria as a case study, Etieyibo and Omiegbe[52] suggest that 'religion and culture promote certain beliefs and attitudes about disability and people with disabilities that lead to discriminatory practices'.[53] They further highlight that people with intellectual disabilities are often killed as part of rituals, that women with

[47] Michael Ashley Stein and Janet Lord, 'Human Rights and Humanitarian Assistance for Refugees and Internally Displaced Persons with Disabilities', in Ilze Grobbelaar-du Plessis and Tobias van Reenen (eds.), *Aspects of Disability Law in Africa*, note 2, pp. 31–52, p. 32. The situation is particularly serious in South Sudan. The Report of the Office of the United Nations High Commissioner for Human Rights (OHCHR), published on 10 July 2018, documents the atrocities committed by government forces in the rebel-held areas, including shooting at fleeing civilians and the killing of persons with disabilities and children, through being hanged from trees and burned alive. The report can be downloaded at www.ohchr.org/EN/NewsEvents/Pages/DisplayNews.aspx?NewsID=23351&LangID=E.

[48] Biegon, 'The Promotion and Protection of Disability Rights in the African Human Rights System', note 2, p. 54.

[49] Hebron L. Ndlovu, 'African Beliefs Concerning People with Disabilities: Implications for Theological Education' (2016) 20(1–2) *Journal of Disability & Religion* 29, at 32.

[50] Ibid.

[51] Ndlovu, 'African Beliefs Concerning People with Disabilities: Implications for Theological Education', note 49, at 54. On the social and cultural context of mental issues in Africa, see also Mary Amuyunzu-Nyamango, *The Social and Cultural Aspects of Mental Health*, at www.commonwealthhealth.org/wp-content/uploads/2013/07/The-social-and-cultural-aspects-of-mental-health-in-African-societies_CHP13.pdf.

[52] Edwin Etieyibo and Odirin Omiegbe, 'Religion, Culture, and Discrimination against Persons with Disabilities in Nigeria' (2016) 5(1) *African Journal of Disability* 1, at 3.

[53] Ibid.

psychosocial impairments are frequently victims of rape and that children with disabilities repeatedly engage in 'alms-begging'.[54]

Among disabled people in Africa, persons with albinism[55] experience extreme forms of violence and discrimination.[56] They face physical attacks propelled by the belief that their body parts can be used in potions and in other witchery practices.[57] Even when persons with albinism do not face life-threatening attacks, they live in marginalised social conditions and in a state of economic vulnerability.[58] According to Ndlovu, in Swaziland (renamed Eswatini in April 2018), an additional tragic dimension of the lives of people with albinism is the rejection that they experience in their own families, where the birth of a child with albinism is viewed as a misfortune.[59] It is notable that, in 2015, the UN Human Rights Council, recognising the widespread violations against persons with albinism, designated a UN Independent Expert on the enjoyment of human rights by persons with albinism, with the mandate to combat stereotypes, prejudices and harmful traditional practices.[60]

In several areas of Africa, and particularly in Eritrea, Somalia, Guinea and Djibouti, women, including women with disabilities, are subject to female genital mutilation (FGM).[61] Rushwan reports that more than 90 million girls and women over the age of ten are estimated to have undergone FGM, with around 3 million girls at risk every year.[62] FGM is often carried out as part of a girl's initiation into womanhood within her community, but it can also

[54] Ibid.

[55] Albinism is an inherited genetic condition that reduces the amount of melanin pigment formed in the skin, hair and/or eyes.

[56] See the First regional forum for 'Action on Albinism in Africa' (17–19 June 2016), at www.ohchr.org/en/NewsEvents/Pages/DisplayNews.aspx?NewsID=20100&LangID=E.

[57] Ndlovu, 'African Beliefs Concerning People with Disabilities: Implications for Theological Education', note 49, at 34.

[58] Giorgio Brocco, 'Albinism, Stigma, Subjectivity and Global-Local Discourses in Tanzania' (2016) 23(3) *Anthropology & Medicine* 229.

[59] Ndlovu, 'African Beliefs Concerning People with Disabilities: Implications for Theological Education', note 49, at 35.

[60] UN Human Rights Council, Resolution No. 28/6 on the Independent Expert on the enjoyment of human rights by persons with albinism, 10 April 2015, UN Doc. A/HRC/RES/28/6. See at www.ohchr.org/EN/Issues/Albinism/Pages/IEAlbinism.aspx.

[61] FGM encompasses 'all procedures involving partial or total removal of the external female genitalia or any injury to them for socio-cultural and non-therapeutic reasons'. See at https://data.unicef.org/topic/child-protection/female-genital-mutilation/.

[62] Hamid Ruswan, 'Female Genital Mutilation: A Tragedy for Women's Reproductive Health' (2013) 19 *African Journal of Urology* 130, at 130. The WHO estimates an even larger number, and affirms that more than 200 million girls and women alive today have undergone female genital mutilation in the countries where the practice is concentrated. See at www.who.int/reproductivehealth/topics/fgm/prevalence/en/.

be perceived as a means by which to control a woman's sexuality.[63] It is well-established that FGM causes diseases, and several short- and long-term impairments.[64] Moreover, the WHO affirms that, although the direct association between FGM and HIV remains unconfirmed, the cutting of genital tissues with the same surgical instrument without sterilisation potentially increases the risk of transmission of HIV between girls who undergo FGM together.[65] Some studies have also shown an increased likelihood of post-traumatic stress disorder, anxiety, depression and psychosocial disabilities in women who underwent FGM.[66] Some authors have argued that FGM can be classified as a disability in itself. Adopting the social-contextual model, 'the social oppression of women who have undergone [FGM] in patriarchal societies takes the loss of some sex organs from the realm of impairment into the realm of disability'.[67]

Marginalisation, poverty, stereotypes and negative attitudes towards disability can, however, be contrasted with the African philosophy of '*ubuntu*' or '*batho*'.[68] The main feature of *ubuntu* is the 'respect for [the] diversity of what it means to be human'.[69] Cornell and Van Marle suggest that *ubuntu* is characterised by a sense of cooperation and interdependence and 'implies an interactive ethic ... in which who and how we can be as human beings is always being shaped in our interaction with each other'.[70] Such an approach has been invoked to foster respect for persons with disabilities and equality and to shape an 'African model of disability', in order to overcome traditional negative beliefs, but also to 'decolonise' the conception of disability from Western models.[71]

3.2 The Disability Policy of the AU

In the past thirty years, under growing pressure from international organisations, civil society and disabled people's organisations (DPOs), the AU has tried to combat the marginalisation faced by persons with disabilities, to address the

[63] Rajat Khosla et al., 'Gender Equality and Human Rights Approaches to Female Genital Mutilation: A Review of International Human Rights Norms and Standards' (2017) 14(1) *Reproductive Health* 1.

[64] See at www.who.int/reproductivehealth/topics/fgm/health_consequences_fgm/en/.

[65] Ibid. [66] Ibid.

[67] Michael Owojuyigbe, Miracle-Eunice Bolorunduro and Dauda Busari, 'Female Genital Mutilation as Sexual Disability: Perceptions of Women and Their Spouses in Akure, Ondo State, Nigeria' (2017) 25 *Reproductive Health Matters* 80, at 80.

[68] Ndlovu, 'African Beliefs Concerning People with Disabilities: Implications for Theological Education', note 49, at 35–6.

[69] Maria Berghs, 'Practices and Discourses of *Ubuntu*: Implications for an African Model of Disability?' (2017) 2 *African Journal of Disability* 292, at 292.

[70] Drucilla Cornell and Karin van Marle, 'Exploring *Ubuntu*: Tentative Reflections' (2005) 5(2) *African Human Rights Law Journal* 195, at 195.

[71] Berghs, 'Practices and Discourses of *Ubuntu*: Implications for an African Model of Disability?', note 69.

specific regional challenges highlighted above and to forge a pan-African disability policy. One of the most significant initiatives adopted by the former OAU was the first African Decade of Persons with Disabilities 1999–2009 (African Decade). It was launched in July 1999 and called upon African States to promote equality, full participation, inclusion and independence of persons with disabilities.[72] The mandate for organising the African Decade's activities was given to the African Rehabilitation Institute (ARI) – a specialised agency of the AU, which promotes rehabilitation programmes for people with disabilities. During the African Decade, the ARI's activities were of seminal importance to ensuring the exchange of information and good practices among African States and other countries. The ARI also assisted rehabilitation centres across Africa to harmonise their work strategies in the field of rehabilitation and to provide mutual assistance.

Towards the end of the African Decade, in 2007, the African Campaign on Disability and HIV/AIDS was launched.[73] That initiative brought together DPOs and organisations of people living with HIV to work for the integration of disability rights within HIV policies in Africa. It led to the development and signing of the 2008 Kampala Declaration on Disability and HIV/AIDS (2008 Kampala Declaration),[74] which called on African States to mainstream disability in all HIV programmes. The campaign was also one of the main drivers of the second African Decade of Persons with Disabilities for the period 2010–2019 (African Decade 2010–2019), which aimed to continue the activities undertaken during the first African Decade and to empower people with disabilities.[75] The proclamation of the African Decade 2010–2019 was accompanied by the adoption of the Continental Plan of Action of the African Decade of Persons with Disabilities 2010–2019 (Continental Plan),[76] which sets out eight strategic thematic areas for implementation at the national level, indicated in Figure 15.2.

For each thematic area, the Continental Plan includes priority actions that take into account the actual regional context and address, in a comprehensive fashion, specific marginalising factors concerning people with disabilities. For example, the Continental Plan requires AU Member States to 'combat harmful

[72] The launch of the first African Decade was accompanied by a Continental Plan 'aimed at implementing priority activities on disability', which is available at http://www.mhss.gov.na/documents/119527/432781/Continental+plan+of+action.pdf/2b9a9587-1942-4bcc-ab29-725befbfdc25.

[73] Djoyou Kamga, 'A Call for a Protocol to the African Charter on Human and Peoples' Rights on the Rights of Persons with Disabilities in Africa', note 42, at 246.

[74] An unofficial text of the Declaration is available at www.dhatregional.org/docs/kampala_declaration_hivaids_disability%5B1%5D.pdf.

[75] Djoyou Kamga, 'A Call for a Protocol to the African Charter on Human and Peoples' Rights on the Rights of Persons with Disabilities in Africa', note 42, at 246.

[76] Commission, 'Continental Plan of Action for the African Decade of Persons with Disabilities 2010– 2019', at https://au.int/sites/default/files/pages/32900-file-cpoa_handbook._audp.english_-_copy.pdf.

Figure 15.2 Thematic Areas of the Continental Plan of Action of the African Decade of Persons with Disabilities 2010–2019

traditional practices which result in disabilities'.[77] Furthermore, along the lines of the 2008 Kampala Declaration and, as recommended by the UN,[78] the Continental Plan acknowledges that persons with disabilities must be included in the national response to HIV/AIDS. It requires AU Member States, *inter alia*, to develop health care policies and strategies suitable for persons with disabilities living with HIV/AIDS; to ensure access for people with disabilities to HIV/AIDS prevention, treatment, care and support services available to the public; and to provide information on HIV/AIDS and other communicable diseases, in all accessible formats.[79] The

[77] Continental Plan, note 76, para. 2.5.1.3.

[78] See at www.un.org/development/desa/disabilities/issues/disability-and-hivaids.html.

[79] Continental Plan, note 76, para. 2.5.1.1.

Continental Plan also addresses the situation of persons with disabilities in armed conflicts and includes among its priorities the aim of protecting individuals with disabilities 'from all kinds of exploitation and violence during situations of conflict'.[80] Another distinctive feature of the Continental Plan is the significant attention that it pays to rehabilitation services and to the prevention of impairment. In that regard, the Plan requires AU Member States, *inter alia*, 'to allocate sufficient resources for the prevention of disease and chronic illness which result in disabilities', and 'to introduce a systemic landmine clearance program, where mines exist, or [to ensure the] strengthening of existing programs'.[81]

The Continental Plan includes several references to effective monitoring systems, in order to guarantee that the priority actions envisaged in it are actually implemented by AU Member States.[82] In addition, it proposes that AU Heads of State and Government appoint a Special Rapporteur on Disability 'to ensure implementation, monitoring and reporting of the implementation of the Continental Plan'.[83] However, at the time of writing of this textbook, the Rapporteur has not yet been designated. Significantly, and consistently with Articles 4(3) and 33(3) CRPD,[84] the Continental Plan provides for the inclusion of persons with disabilities in all monitoring systems, in all national decision-making structures and in all AU organs.[85] To that end, it requires AU Member States to 'promote and facilitate the establishment of DPOs at local and national levels'.

On the whole, the Continental Plan has been influenced, to a considerable extent, by the CRPD, which is referred to in the Plan as 'the most important international instrument to guide national action to address ... the situation of persons with disabilities'.[86] The Continental Plan also requires that AU Member States take all appropriate measures to ensure that AU human rights instruments and the CRPD are incorporated into domestic law, and it aims to be, at the same time, a supplement to, and a facilitator for, the implementation of the CRPD at the national level.

DID YOU KNOW THAT ...?

Since the 1980s, DPOs have started to become widespread in Africa, and have endeavoured to coordinate themselves and to make their voices heard. In 1986, the Southern Africa Federation of the Disabled (SAFOD – www.safod.net/home/) was set up to coordinate the activities of national DPOs in Southern Africa. However, it was

[80] Ibid. para. 2.2.1.5. [81] Ibid. para. 2.5.1.3. [82] Ibid. para. 2.9. [83] Ibid. para. 3.1.
[84] See above Chapter 3, section 10. [85] Continental Plan, note 76, paras. 2.9 and 3.1.
[86] Ibid. para. 1.1.2.

only in 2017 that Africa created its own legally recognised umbrella group of DPOs at the pan-African level. The African Disability Forum (ADF – www.africandisabilityforum.org/) was launched in 2014, but it was only formally registered on 15 March 2017 by Ethiopia's Ministry of Foreign Affairs. Currently the ADF has member organisations in thirty-four African countries. The ADF is committed to the implementation of the Sustainable Development Goals (SDGs) and the CRPD and is supported by the UN Partnership on the Rights of Persons with Disabilities (UNPRPD). Until the registration of the ADF, Africa was the only region of the world without its own legally recognised umbrella group of organisations of persons with disabilities.

4 DISABILITY RIGHTS IN THE AFRICAN REGIONAL HUMAN RIGHTS SYSTEM

This section examines, in the first instance, the protection of persons with disabilities provided for in various African human rights instruments, with particular emphasis on the RPDA Protocol. It then turns to discuss the role of the ACHPR and of the African Court in ensuring the rights of people with disabilities.

4.1 The African Charter and Disability

All of the civil and political rights and socio-economic rights as well as the collective rights that are formulated in the African Charter[87] are relevant to persons with disabilities and, according to Article 2, they must be applied without discrimination to all individuals.

ARTICLE 2 OF THE AFRICAN CHARTER

Every individual shall be entitled to the enjoyment of the rights and freedoms recognised and guaranteed in the present Charter without distinction of any kind such as race, ethnic group, colour, sex, language, religion, political or any other opinion, national and social origin, fortune, birth or other status.

[87] See above sub-section 2.3.

Disability does not feature explicitly under the protected grounds contained in Article 2. However, the reference to 'other status'[88] encompasses the prohibition of discrimination on the basis of disability. This was clearly established by the ACHPR in *Purohit and Moore* v. *The Gambia*.[89] The communication was submitted to the ACHPR by a DPO on behalf of patients detained in the Psychiatric Unit of the Royal Victoria Hospital, who alleged that the relevant Gambian legislation governing mental health (i.e. the Lunatics Detention Act – LDA) was, *inter alia*, in breach of Article 2 of the African Charter. In its decision, the African Commission clarified that disability is a prohibited ground of discrimination.[90] This understanding of Article 2 of the African Charter is consistent with the interpretation of Article 14 ECHR provided by the European Court of Human Rights (ECtHR), and it is in line with General Comment No. 5 of the UN Committee on Economic Social and Cultural Rights (CESCR).[91] The interpretation given by the ACHPR is also coherent with the whole wording of Article 2 of the African Charter. The words 'such as' in the text of Article 2 also imply that the list of prohibited grounds of discrimination is not exhaustive. Moreover, according to Abbay, 'the phrase "every individual" in that Article and throughout the Charter clearly signifies that the rights and freedoms recognised under the ACHPR are for all human beings, including persons with disabilities'.[92]

Article 2 must be read in conjunction with Article 3 of the African Charter. The latter provision contains the right to equality before the law[93] and guarantees the 'equal protection of the law' to all individuals.[94] According to the ACHPR, while Article 2 'lays down a principle that is essential to the spirit of the African Charter and is therefore necessary in eradicating discrimination in all its guises',[95] Article 3 'is important because it guarantees fair and just treatment of individuals within [the] legal system of a given country'.[96] The ACHPR also makes clear that the foregoing provisions are 'non-derogable'

[88] Different versions of Article 2 of the African Charter use varying terms – 'any status' and 'other status'. The version of Article 2 cited in the text above was taken from www.achpr.org/files/instruments/achpr/banjul_charter.pdf.

[89] ACHPR, 241/01, *Purohit and Moore* v. *The Gambia*, 15–29 May 2003, Niamey, Niger, available at www.achpr.org/files/sessions/33rd/comunications/241.01/achpr33_241_01_eng.pdf.

[90] Ibid. paras. 45–8.

[91] UN Committee on Economic, Social and Cultural Rights (CESCR), General Comment No. 5, 9 December 1994, UN Doc. E/1995/22, para. 5. See above Chapter 2.

[92] Futsum Abbay, 'An Evaluation of Disability Human Rights under the African Regional Human Rights System' (2015) 23(3) *African Journal of International and Comparative Law* 476, at 478.

[93] Article 3(1) of the African Charter.

[94] Article 3(2) of the African Charter. On the meaning of equality before the law, see above Chapters 4 and 6.

[95] ACHPR, *Purohit and Moore* v. *The Gambia*, note 89, para. 49.

[96] Ibid.

and 'must be respected in all circumstances, in order for anyone to enjoy all the other rights provided for under the African Charter'.[97]

One of the most relevant civil and political rights in the disability context is the 'right to the respect of the dignity inherent in a human being and to the recognition of his legal status', set out in Article 5. When interpreting that norm, the ACHPR has made it clear that:

> [h]uman dignity is an inherent basic right to which all human beings, regardless of their mental capabilities or disabilities ... are entitled to without discrimination. It is therefore an inherent right which every human being is obliged to respect by all means possible and on the other hand it confers a duty on every human being to respect this right.[98]

Among the economic, social and cultural rights provided for in the African Charter, Article 16(1) guarantees 'the right to enjoy the best attainable state of physical and mental health'. Abbay suggests that Article 16(1) encompasses the obligation to ensure medical care, rehabilitation services and psychological support to persons with disabilities as well as preventive medicine to avoid future impairments.[99] However, the words 'best attainable' seem to imply some leeway for economic considerations and limitations of the right by States.

Article 18(4) is the most relevant provision of the African Charter in so far as people with disabilities are concerned. It explicitly addresses the rights of persons with disabilities, alongside those of other categories of individuals considered to be 'vulnerable' (namely, women, children and elderly people).[100]

ARTICLE 18(4) OF THE AFRICAN CHARTER

The aged and the disabled shall also have the right to special measures of protection in keeping with their physical or moral needs.

Article 18(4) of the African Charter has the particular merit of making the rights of persons with disabilities visible. However, several authors argue that it is inspired by the medical model.[101] In this respect, Abbay maintains

[97] Ibid. [98] Ibid. para. 57.

[99] Abbay, 'An Evaluation of Disability Human Rights under the African Regional Human Rights System', note 92, at 478.

[100] Egypt expressed a reservation to Article 18, which 'must be implemented in accordance with ... Islamic Law ... as far as the Arab Republic of Egypt is concerned'.

[101] Abbay, 'An Evaluation of Disability Human Rights under the African Regional Human Rights System', note 92, at 479.

that, by requiring 'special measures of protection in keeping with their physical or moral needs', Article 18(4) is underpinned by the conception of disabled people as mere recipients of social welfare, care and rehabilitation services, rather than as holders of human rights.[102] The reference to 'physical and moral needs' does not encompass all human rights and fundamental freedoms and seems to allude to mere rehabilitation services. The wording 'specific measures of protection' is also considered to be vague and unclear.[103] This vagueness hampers the effectiveness of Article 18(4), which, to date, has never been enforced in front of the ACHPR. Another criticism that has been advanced by certain scholars concerns the fact that, by mentioning persons with disabilities and elderly people together in one provision, Article 18(4) '[mixes] the rights and contexts' of two different groups of people.[104] Viljoen and Biegon contend that '[a]lthough old age may often coincide with disability, disability has no necessary link to the ageing process', and that '[i]llness leading to disability may also develop at any phase of a person's life'.[105] Even though the foregoing critiques of Article 18(4) have merit, it should be noted that the African Charter was adopted in 1981[106] and was not influenced by the social-contextual model of disability, which gained momentum in later decades.[107] It can be argued that an evolutive interpretation of Article 18(4), read in conjunction with Article 2 of the African Charter, is possible (and desirable). In particular, Article 18(4) could be interpreted in a manner that is consistent with the CRPD, in such a way that it encompasses the right of persons with disabilities to be provided with reasonable accommodation when needed in an individual case. In addition, the wording 'special measures of protection' could be construed widely to encompass positive action, in line with Article 5 CRPD.[108]

[102] Ibid. at 479.

[103] Djoyou Kamga, 'A Call for a Protocol to the African Charter on Human and Peoples' Rights on the Rights of Persons with Disabilities in Africa', note 42, at 238.

[104] Abbay, 'An Evaluation of Disability Human Rights under the African Regional Human Rights System', note 92, at 479.

[105] Frans Viljoen and Japhet Biegon, 'The Feasibility and Desirability of an African Disability Rights Treaty: Further Norm-Elaboration or Firmer Norm-Implementation?', available at https://repository.up.ac.za/bitstream/handle/2263/42129/Viljoen_Feasibility_2014.pdf?sequence=1&isAllowed=y.

[106] In this respect, Abbay maintains that the African Charter 'was a pioneer among international and regional conventions that specifically deal with the rights of persons with disabilities' (Abbay, 'An Evaluation of Disability Human Rights under the African Regional Human Rights System', note 92, at 480).

[107] See above Chapter 2.

[108] See above Chapter 4.

4.2 Other Regional Human Rights Treaties and Disability

4.2.1 *The African Charter on the Rights and Welfare of the Child*

As with the African Charter, the 1990 African Charter on the Rights and Welfare of the Child (ACRWC), which entered into force in 1999, fails to mention disability explicitly as a ground of discrimination. Modelled on Article 2 of the African Charter, Article 3 ACRWC provides that every child is entitled to the enjoyment of the rights guaranteed by the ACRWC 'irrespective of the child's or his/her parents' or legal guardians' race, ethnic group, colour, sex, language, religion, political or other opinion, national and social origin, fortune, birth or other status'. Although Article 3 fails to refer expressly to disability, the phrase 'every child' includes children with disabilities,[109] and, consistently with the interpretation given to Article 2 of the African Charter, the words 'other status' must be construed as encompassing disability. The ACRWC also includes one provision on 'handicapped children' (Article 13), which echoes the wording of Article 18(4) of the African Charter.

ARTICLE 13 ACRWC

1. Every child who is mentally or physically disabled shall have the right to special measures of protection in keeping with his physical and moral needs and under conditions which ensure his dignity, promote his self-reliance and active participation in the community.

2. State Parties to the present Charter shall ensure, subject to available resources, to a disabled child and to those responsible for his care, assistance for which application is made and which is appropriate to the child's condition and in particular shall ensure that the disabled child has effective access to training, preparation for employment and recreation opportunities in a manner conducive to the child achieving the fullest possible social integration, individual development and his/her cultural and moral development.

3. The State Parties to the present Charter shall use their available resources with a view to achieving progressively the full convenience of the mentally and physically disabled person to movement and access to public highway buildings and other places to which the disabled may legitimately want to have access to.

[109] Abbay, 'An Evaluation of Disability Human Rights under the African Regional Human Rights System', note 92, at 480.

Under Article 13(1) ACRWC, a child with a disability has the right to special measures of protection. While Article 13(2) refers to care and assistance, it also makes clear that those 'special measures of protection' include providing effective access to training, preparation for employment, and recreational opportunities. Furthermore, those measures should allow the child to achieve the 'fullest possible social integration'. Article 13(3) also makes reference to accessibility, signalling a shift towards the social-contextual model of disability. The relatively wide formulation of Article 13 compared to Article 18(4) has led scholars to affirm that the ACRWC 'goes quite far in recognising and protecting disability rights and in shifting the approach to disability, although its scope is limited to children with disabilities'.[110]

4.2.2 *The Protocol to the African Charter on Human and Peoples' Rights on the Rights of Women*

The Protocol to the African Charter on Human and Peoples' Rights on the Rights of Women in Africa (African Women's Protocol), which was adopted in 2003 and entered into force in November 2005, further advances the protection of the rights of disabled people. In particular, its significance lies in the fact that it acknowledges the multiple and intersectional discrimination faced by women with disabilities. The African Women's Protocol requires States Parties to eliminate all forms of discrimination, harmful practices and violence against women and girls that negatively affect their fundamental rights and freedoms. It recognises that every woman has the right to dignity and respect as a person, and it condemns and prohibits all forms of exploitation, including medical or scientific experiments performed without their informed consent.[111] A unique feature of the African Women's Protocol is its groundbreaking provision guaranteeing the sexual and reproductive health of women. Article 14 gives all women (including women with disabilities) the right, *inter alia*, to terminate a pregnancy that results from incest or rape or where the continuation of the pregnancy will endanger the health or life of the mother. Under Article 14, women are also given 'the right to self-protection and to be protected against sexually transmitted infections, including HIV/AIDS'. The latter provision is clearly tailored to the African reality, considering that the majority of adults with HIV/AIDS in sub-Saharan Africa are women.[112] Moreover, the African Women's Protocol provides for measures

[110] Abbay, 'An Evaluation of Disability Human Rights under the African Regional Human Rights System', note 92, at 480.

[111] See, further, Christine Ocran, 'The Protocol to the African Charter on Human and Peoples' Rights of Women in Africa' (2007) 15(1) *African Journal of International and Comparative Law* 147.

[112] Ibid. at 149.

of 'special protection' for particularly disadvantaged groups of women: widows, elderly women, women in distress and women with disabilities. Article 23 of the African Women's Protocol focuses on the 'special protection of women with disabilities'.

ARTICLE 23 OF THE AFRICAN WOMEN'S PROTOCOL

The States Parties undertake to:

a) ensure the protection of women with disabilities and take specific measures commensurate with their physical, economic and social needs to facilitate their access to employment, professional and vocational training as well as their participation in decision-making;
b) ensure the right of women with disabilities to freedom from violence, including sexual abuse, discrimination based on disability and the right to be treated with dignity.

In mentioning both access to employment and freedom from violence, including sexual abuse, Article 23 addresses specific concerns of African women with disabilities.[113] However, that provision has been criticised for its limited scope and for being silent on access to education for girls with disabilities. Furthermore, Article 23 fails to tackle the specific barriers faced by women with disabilities in accessing health care, including reproductive health care (although this is provided for, to a certain extent, in Article 14, outlined above).

4.2.3 *Other Regional Human Rights Treaties*

Like the African Charter, the ACRWC and the African Women's Protocol, the African Youth Charter (AYC), adopted in 2006, fails to include disability among the prohibited grounds of discrimination. However, other provisions on equality mention disability explicitly. For instance, Article 15(4)(a) AYC requires States Parties to 'ensure equal access to employment and equal pay for equal work or equal value of work and offer protection against discrimination regardless of ethnicity, race, gender, disability, religion, political, social, cultural or economic background'. Moreover, Article 16, which guarantees the right to health, obliges States Parties to the AYC, *inter alia*, to '[p]rovide technical and financial support to build the institutional capacity of youth

[113] Djoyou Kamga, 'A Call for a Protocol to the African Charter on Human and Peoples' Rights on the Rights of Persons with Disabilities in Africa', note 42, at 241–2.

organisations to address public health concerns including issues concerning youth with disabilities and young people married at an early age'. Article 24 AYC specifically addresses the needs of 'mentally and physically challenged youth', an expression which, while somewhat vague and underpinned by the medical model,[114] alludes to young people with disabilities. In particular, Article 24 calls on States Parties to recognise 'the right of mentally and physically challenged youth to special care' and to ensure their 'equal and effective access to education' as well as 'training, health care services, employment, sport, physical education and cultural and recreational activities'. Furthermore, Article 24 also requires States Parties to 'work towards eliminating any obstacles that may have negative implications for the full integration' of young persons with disabilities.

In a similar vein to the AYC, the African Charter on Democracy, Elections and Governance (ACDEG), adopted by the AU in January 2007 and entered into force in 2012, includes references to disability in different provisions. The ACDEG aims to promote 'adherence, by each State Party, to the universal values and principles of democracy and respect for human rights' and to 'enhance adherence to the principle of the rule of law'.[115] It mentions persons with disabilities alongside other 'vulnerable social groups', such as ethnic minorities, migrants, refugees and displaced persons, in Article 8(2). That provision requires States Parties to adopt legislative and administrative measures to guarantee the rights of marginalised groups. In a similar vein, Article 43 ACDEG calls on States Parties 'to provide free and compulsory basic education' and to ensure 'the literacy of citizens above compulsory school age' to all, including people with disabilities. Furthermore, Article 31 ACDEG calls on States Parties to promote 'participation of social groups with special needs, including the [y]outh and people with disabilities, in the governance process'. That provision is particularly notable in that it highlights the need to involve disabled persons in decision- and policy-making processes. However, it fails to expressly mention accessibility and the need for States Parties to address specific barriers that hamper inclusion and participation.

The AU Convention on Internally Displaced Persons in Africa (Kampala Convention), which entered into force in 2012, includes only one reference to disability in Article 9. That provision requires States Parties to ensure 'special protection for and assistance to internally displaced persons with special needs, including separated and unaccompanied children, female heads of households, expectant mothers, mothers with young children, the elderly, and persons with disabilities or with communicable diseases'.

[114] Biegon, 'The Promotion and Protection of Disability Rights in the African Human Rights System', note 2, p. 65.

[115] Article 2 ACDEG.

On the whole, the human rights treaties and protocols that have been adopted within the African system include numerous references to disability or persons with disabilities. Although some of the provisions employ outdated terminology, a clear attempt to mainstream the rights of persons with disabilities in binding African instruments has been visible since the early 1990s and has paved the way towards the adoption of the RPDA Protocol, which is discussed below.

4.3 The Protocol to the African Charter on Human and Peoples' Rights on the Rights of Persons with Disabilities in Africa

The idea of a regional treaty on the rights of persons with disabilities in Africa had emerged long before the CRPD was adopted.[116] However, it was only in 2009 that the Focal Point on Older Persons in Africa, set up in 2007 by the ACHPR, was extended to persons with disabilities and transformed into the Working Group on Older Persons and People with Disabilities,[117] with the mandate to draft a treaty on the rights of persons with disabilities.[118] That working group elaborated a first draft protocol on the rights of persons with disability (the so-called 'Accra Draft') in 2011. However, the Accra Draft was put on hold for further reflection and consultation. The number of working group members was increased, to include key stakeholders, and a second draft treaty was adopted by the working group in March 2014, with an invitation for comments from members of the public. A further draft, which took into account the comments received, was adopted by the ACHPR in February 2016. The Protocol was then transmitted to the Secretariat of the AU. The RPDA Protocol[119] was finally adopted at the AU Summit in January 2018 and opened for ratification.[120]

[116] Djoyou Kamga, 'A Call for a Protocol to the African Charter on Human and Peoples' Rights on the Rights of Persons with Disabilities in Africa', note 42, at 241–2.

[117] ACHPR, Res. 143 (2009): Resolution on the Transformation of the Focal Point on the Rights of Older Persons in Africa into a Working Group on The Rights of Older Persons and People with Disabilities in Africa, at www.achpr.org/sessions/45th/resolutions/143/. See also Biegon, 'The Promotion and Protection of Disability Rights in the African Human Rights System', note 2, p. 72.

[118] The Working Group developed two draft protocols – one for the rights of older persons and the other one being the draft protocol on the rights of persons with disabilities. The Protocol to the African Charter on Human and Peoples' Rights on the Rights of Older Persons in Africa, which aims at promoting and protecting the rights of older persons and guaranteeing that they fully contribute and participate in society, was adopted by the AU in January 2016.

[119] The text of the Protocol is available at https://au.int/en/treaties/protocol-african-charter-human-and-peoples-rights-rights-persons-disabilities-africa.

[120] See at https://au.int/en/treaties/protocol-african-charter-human-and-peoples-rights-rights-persons-disabilities-africa.

Read the RPDA Protocol and compare and contrast it with the CRPD. What are the main differences? What are the main similarities?

The RPDA Protocol is intended to complement the African Charter and to address marginalisation, harmful practices and discrimination faced by persons with disabilities. It draws heavily on the CRPD in several respects, and its structure and content are modelled on the Convention.

The RPDA Protocol defines 'persons with disabilities' in a manner that is consistent with Article 1 CRPD, and it includes general principles and general obligations. There are also articles on accessibility, legal capacity and the right to live in the community, among others. The text also details, in a manner similar to the CRPD, the rights of persons with disabilities to: life, liberty, security of person, education, health, habilitation and rehabilitation, work, participation in political and public life, freedom of expression and opinion, and participation in recreation and culture. One of the distinctive features of the RPDA Protocol is that it contains references to specific regional issues. For example, Article 11 obliges States Parties 'to eliminate harmful practices perpetrated on persons with disabilities, including witchcraft, abandonment, concealment, ritual killings or the association of disability with omens'. Article 13 (on access to justice) requires, *inter alia*, States Parties to ensure that 'customary law processes are inclusive and should not be used to deny persons with disabilities their right to access appropriate and effective justice'. Article 16 stipulates that the education of persons with disabilities must be directed, among other things, to the 'preservation and strengthening of positive African values'. In addition, by including provisions on youth and older persons with disabilities, alongside provisions concerning women and children with disabilities, the RPDA Protocol adopts a wide intersectional approach. Article 29 (on youth with disabilities) extends and updates Article 24 AYC, and, in order to address specific regional issues, obliges States Parties, *inter alia*, to develop programmes aimed at overcoming 'social and economic isolation, and removing systemic barriers in the labour market'; to ensure access to credit facilities for youth with disabilities; and to promote sexual and reproductive health education for youth with disabilities. Significantly, the RPDA Protocol bans discrimination by association, by explicitly prohibiting discrimination against family members and caregivers of people with disabilities. Since caregivers are often women, this provision can be read as evidence of an intersectional approach to discrimination.

Another 'African' feature of the RPDA Protocol is that it includes a specific provision on duties. In particular, Article 31 requires States Parties not only to 'recognise that persons with disabilities have duties on an equal basis with other person as elaborated in the African Charter' but also to 'ensure that persons with disabilities are rendered the forms of assistance and support, including reasonable accommodations, which they may require in performance of such duties'.

At the time of writing this textbook, it is still too early to evaluate whether the RPDA Protocol will be effective in tackling the marginalisation experienced by persons with disabilities in Africa. The Protocol will enter into force only after the deposit of the fifteenth instrument of ratification, i.e. it will only become effective once it has been formally ratified by fifteen of the AU Member States that have accepted to be bound by the African Charter.

4.4 The Role of the African Commission on Human and Peoples' Rights in Promoting and Protecting the Rights of Persons with Disabilities

To date, the role of the ACHPR in protecting and promoting the rights of persons with disabilities has been quite limited, and several authors claim that disability rights are not a priority in the Commission's work.[121] Despite the ACHPR being active since 1987, references to persons with disabilities only started to appear in the ACHPR's body of soft law around the mid-2000s,[122] which was often still underpinned by the medical model. For example, the 2004 Pretoria Declaration on Economic, Social and Cultural Rights in Africa[123] stipulates that the right to work in Article 15 of the African Charter entails, among other things, '[e]quality of opportunity of access to gainful work, including access for refugees, disabled and other disadvantaged persons'.[124] The Declaration also mentions that 'access to humane and dignified care ... for persons with mental and physical disabilities' is encompassed by the African Charter.[125] However, it refers to the provision of 'special schools and facilities for physically and mentally disabled children'.[126] Until 2014, none of the thematic resolutions of the ACHPR had focused on disability

[121] Djoyou Kamga, 'A Call for a Protocol to the African Charter on Human and Peoples' Rights on the Rights of Persons with Disabilities in Africa', note 42, at 238.

[122] See e.g. ACHPR, Res.159 (XLV1) 09: Resolution on the Impact of the Ongoing Global Financial Crisis on the Enjoyment of Social and Economic Rights in Africa; ACHPR, Res.262 (LIV) 2013: Resolution on Women's Right to Land and Productive Resources; ACHPR, Res.335 (EXT.OS/XIX) 2016: Resolution on the Situation of Internally Displaced Persons in Africa. See also ACHPR, Res.109 (XXXXI) 07: Resolution on the Situation in Somalia.

[123] ACHPR, Pretoria Declaration on Economic, Social and Cultural Rights in Africa (2004).

[124] Ibid. para. 6. [125] Ibid. para. 7. [126] Ibid. para. 8.

rights.[127] A change in tone and attitude occurred in 2015, when the ACHPR adopted the Resolution on Accessibility for Persons with Disabilities,[128] which calls on States, the AU and its organs 'to take immediate and effective measures to ensure that all facilities and services open or provided to the public are accessible to persons with disabilities'.

ACHPR/Res.305 (EXT.OS/XVIII) 2015

Resolution on Accessibility for Persons with Disabilities

The African Commission on Human and Peoples' Rights, meeting at its 18th Extraordinary Session held from 29 July to 7 August 2015 in Nairobi, Republic of Kenya.

Recalling its mandate to promote and protect human and peoples' rights pursuant to the African Charter on Human and Peoples' Rights (the African Charter);

Reaffirming Article 2 of the African Charter on the entitlement of every individual to enjoy the rights and freedoms recognised in the African Charter without distinction of any kind;

Reaffirming Article 18 (4) of the African Charter which provides persons with disabilities with the right to special measures of protection;

...

Recognising the importance of enabling persons with disabilities to live independently and participate fully in all aspects of life;

The Commission:

[...]

2. ...calls on States Parties, the African Union and its Organs to ensure that meetings in which the public participate are held in places accessible to persons with disabilities;

3. Urges States Parties, the African Union and its Organs to ensure that all information intended for the general public is disseminated in accessible formats and technologies appropriate to different kinds of disabilities ...;

4. Urges those States Parties that have not done so to ratify the Marrakesh Treaty to Facilitate Access to Published Works for Persons Who Are Blind, Visually Impaired or Otherwise Print Disabled;

[127] Biegon, 'The Promotion and Protection of Disability Rights in the African Human Rights System', note 2, at 70. For a list of the resolutions adopted by the end of 2017, see at www.achpr.org/files/pages/resolutions/recomres_codified_1988_2017_eng.pdf.

[128] ACHPR, Res.305 (EXT.OS/XVIII) 2015: Resolution on Accessibility for Persons with Disabilities.

5. Calls on States Parties, the African Union and its Organs to recognise and promote the use of sign language at the national, sub-regional and continental levels; and

6. Requests the Working Group on Older Persons and People with Disabilities in Africa to remain seized of this matter and to provide any further advice or guidance as it may deem appropriate.

In 2016, the ACHPR passed another important resolution: the Resolution on the Right to Dignity and Freedom from Torture or Ill-Treatment of Persons with Psychosocial Disabilities in Africa.[129] That document has been deeply influenced by the CRPD, which is also explicitly mentioned in the Preamble. It calls on States Parties to ensure 'that persons with psychosocial disabilities enjoy legal capacity on an equal basis with others in all aspects of life', and 'to review and amend mental health laws which have been used as a basis for the torture or ill-treatment of persons with psychosocial disabilities'. It also encourages 'national institutions for the promotion of human rights and human rights non-governmental organisations (NGOs) to monitor on a regular basis, using effective mechanisms, institutions which provide services to persons with psychosocial disabilities'.

The growing emphasis on persons with disabilities in soft law has not yet been translated into a strict monitoring of States Parties' implementation of the rights of persons with disabilities under, in particular, Article 18(4) of the African Charter.[130] Despite several countries remaining silent on their implementation of disability rights, the ACHPR has not commented on this. Sometimes, the ACHPR commends the State Party in question for the changes that it has made to its domestic legislation on social protection measures for people with disabilities,[131] rather than highlighting the gaps. Only in some of its most recent COs has the Commission expressed concern regarding the absence of information on the measures adopted to combat discrimination on the ground of disability. In that connection, it has encouraged States Parties to enact legislation to ensure equality and inclusion of persons with disabilities in society.[132]

[129] ACHPR, Res.343(LVIII) 2016: Resolution on the Right to Dignity and Freedom from Torture or Ill-Treatment of Persons with Psychosocial Disabilities in Africa.

[130] See above sub-section 4.1.

[131] ACHPR, Concluding Observations on the 3rd Periodic Report of the Republic of Cameroon, 7 to 14 March 2014. See also Concluding Observations and Recommendations on the 8th to 11th Periodic Report of the Republic of Kenya, 16 to 25 February 2016.

[132] See e.g. ACHPR, *Observations conclusives et Recommandations relatives aux Rapports initial et périodique combinés de la République de Djibouti sur la Mise en Œuvre de la Charte africaine des Droits de l'Homme et des Peuples (1993–2014) – 21 avril–7 mai 2015, à Banjul, Gambie* (only in French).

The ACHPR's jurisprudence on the rights of persons with disabilities is also scant. To date, the most significant decision adopted further to an individual communication concerning the rights of persons with disabilities remains *Purohit and Moore* v. *The Gambia*.[133] As mentioned above, the complainants were mental health advocates who submitted the communication on behalf of patients detained at the Psychiatric Unit of the Royal Victoria Hospital. They claimed that the relevant Gambian law governing mental health (LDA) was outdated and did not establish any safeguards during the diagnosis, certification and detention of patients with psychosocial disabilities. The complainants also alleged that there was overcrowding in the psychiatric unit and that no consent to treatment was required. The African Commission considered the claims to be well founded and held that the Republic of the Gambia was in violation of, *inter alia*, Articles 2, 3, 5, 16 and 18(4) of the African Charter. Besides clarifying that disability must be considered as a prohibited ground of discrimination in the African Charter, the ACHPR affirmed that all human beings, regardless of their disabilities, are entitled to be treated with dignity.[134] The Commission also held that intellectually disabled persons cannot be detained arbitrarily and cannot be deprived of the right to participate in the electoral processes of the State of which they are a citizen.

ACHPR, Purohit and Moore v. The Gambia (2003)

61. The African Commission maintains that mentally disabled persons would like to share the same hopes, dreams and goals and have the same rights to pursue those hopes, dreams and goals just like any other human being. Like any other human being, mentally disabled persons or persons suffering from mental illnesses have a right to enjoy a decent life, as normal and full as possible, a right which lies at the heart of the right to human dignity. This right should be zealously guarded and forcefully protected by all States party to the African Charter in accordance with the well established principle that all human beings are born free and equal in dignity and rights.

62. The Complainants also submit that the automatic detention of persons considered 'lunatics' within the meaning of the LDA violates the right to personal liberty and the prohibition of arbitrary arrest and detention in terms of Article 6 of the African Charter.

. . .

[133] ACHPR, *Purohit and Moore* v. *The Gambia*, note 89.

[134] See above section 4.1.

64. Article 6 of the African Charter guarantees every individual, be they disabled or not, the right to liberty and security of the person. Deprivation of such liberty is only acceptable if it is authorised by law and is compatible with the obligations of States Parties under the African Charter.

. . .

73. The Complainants submit that the failure of the Respondent [s]tate to provide for and enable the detainees under the LDA to exercise their civic rights and obligations, including the right to vote, violates Article 13(1) of the African Charter . . .

. . .

75. The right provided for under Article 13(1) of the African Charter is extended to 'every citizen' and its denial can only be justified by reason of legal incapacity or that the individual is not a citizen of a particular [s]tate. Legal incapacity may not necessarily mean mental incapacity. For example a [s]tate may fix an age limit for the legibility of its own citizens to participate in its government. Legal incapacity, as a justification for denying the right under Article 13(1) can only come into play by invoking provisions of the law that conform to internationally acceptable norms and standards.

Purohit and Moore v. *The Gambia*, while ground-breaking in many respects, has remained an isolated decision. Although it had, in fact, the potential to prompt other individual communications on disability rights, those are yet to be submitted to the African Commission. It remains to be seen whether the new RPDA Protocol, should it enter into force, will serve as a catalyst to advance the jurisprudence of the ACHPR.

4.5 The Role of the African Court on Human and Peoples' Rights in Protecting the Rights of Persons with Disabilities

As mentioned above, the African Court is a regional court that was established to ensure the protection of the rights envisaged in the African Charter. It complements and reinforces the functions of the ACHPR. Cases can be submitted to the African Court by States Parties to the Protocol setting up the Court, by the ACHPR itself, or by individuals or NGOs. However, at the time of writing this textbook, only nine[135] of the thirty States Parties to the Protocol had recognised the competence of the Court to receive cases from NGOs and individuals on human rights violations.

To date, the African Court has not played a large role in protecting the rights of persons with disabilities. While it has considered the violation of Article 16

[135] The nine States are: Benin, Burkina Faso, Côte d'Ivoire, Ghana, the Gambia, Mali, Malawi, Tanzania and Tunisia.

(on the right to physical and mental health), in several cases (often in connection with conditions of detention),[136] none of those cases deals explicitly with disability. There are no decisions on Article 18(4) of the African Charter, nor is there case law on discrimination on the ground of disability. The case *Collectif Des Anciens Travailleurs du Laboratoire (ALS)* v. *Republic of Mali*,[137] concerning mining workers that had been contaminated, could have offered the possibility for the African Court to discuss the right to health and rehabilitation, but it was dismissed for procedural reasons. Although the case did not relate to disability itself, it could have led to interesting findings from a disability perspective, especially in relation to the issue of rehabilitation for long-term impairments. It might be argued that the dearth of cases on the rights of persons with disabilities in the African Court has been caused by the lack of visibility of those rights in the African Charter. However, that situation might change, should the RPDA Protocol enter into force.

5 THE CRPD IN AFRICA

As mentioned at the outset of this textbook, the CRPD serves as the global standard on disability rights and has been ratified by a large number of States, including African States. Having been negotiated within the realm of the UN, the Convention sets forth values that are shared by the worldwide community. As noted by Biegon, the CRPD inherently embodies African values and addresses a wide range of concerns that are relevant to Africa, such as the protection of persons with disabilities in situations of armed conflict, humanitarian emergencies, and the protection of disabled individuals from exploitation, violence and abuse.[138] However, current disability discourses are criticised for attempting to transpose the Western concept of 'disability', as framed in the CRPD, to other parts of the world.[139] It has also been suggested that the CRPD fails to address specific issues that are relevant to Africa.[140] First, the CRPD does not deal with the link between disability and HIV/AIDS. Secondly, the CRPD 'fails to comprehensively highlight the effect of harmful traditional practices and beliefs on the rights of persons with disabilities'.[141] Thirdly, it does not

[136] See e.g. African Court, *George Maili Kemboge* v. *United Republic of Tanzania*, App. No. 002/2016.

[137] African Court, *Collectif Des Anciens Travailleurs du Laboratoire (ALS)* v. *Republic of Mali*, App. No. 002/2015.

[138] Biegon, 'The Promotion and Protection of Disability Rights in the African Human Rights System', note 2, p. 77.

[139] Shaun Grech and Karen Soldatic (eds.), *Disability in the Global South*, note 10.

[140] Biegon, 'The Promotion and Protection of Disability Rights in the African Human Rights System', note 2, p. 77.

[141] Ibid. p. 78.

mention persons with albinism. Moreover, the emphasis on independence and autonomy of persons with disabilities can be considered to fall short of the African communal-based conceptions of 'society' and '*ubuntu*'.

Some of these pitfalls can be mitigated by a broad interpretation of the CRPD, with a view to addressing specific regional concerns. In that respect, the CRPD Committee plays a seminal role. For instance, in *X* v. *Tanzania*,[142] the CRPD Committee firmly condemned harmful practices against persons with albinism.[143] The author of the individual communication, a person with albinism, was the victim of a vicious attack in which two men cut off half of his left arm. The author claimed that, despite his complaint to the police, no investigation had been instituted by the competent authorities of the State Party and he also alleged a violation of Articles 5 (equality and non-discrimination), 15 (freedom from torture or cruel, inhuman or degrading treatment or punishment) and 17 CRPD (integrity of the person). The CRPD Committee held that the author had, in fact, been discriminated against on the basis of his disability, because the violence that he has suffered is a generalised practice in the State Party that only affects people with albinism.[144] The Committee also noted that the State Party's authorities 'have not taken the necessary measures to ensure an effective, complete and impartial investigation and prosecution of the perpetrators and that no preventive or protective measures have been implemented with regard to violence against persons with albinism'. With regard to the violation of Article 15 and 17, the CRPD Committee argued that the violent acts suffered by the author violated his physical and mental integrity and amounted to torture.[145] The Committee maintained that Tanzania did not take all necessary measures to prevent acts of violence similar to those suffered by the author and to efficiently investigate and punish those acts, and, according to the Committee, that amounted to a violation of the CRPD.

> Read the COs on the initial reports that have been submitted to the CRPD Committee by African countries. In your opinion, has the CRPD Committee sufficiently addressed regional concerns?

[142] CRPD Committee, *X* v. *Tanzania*, Communication No. 22/2014, UN Doc. CRPD/C/18/D/22/2014.

[143] See also above Chapter 3, sub-section 4.2.

[144] CRPD Committee, *X* v. *Tanzania*, note 142, para. 8.2.

[145] Ibid. paras. 8.5 and 8.7.

In its COs, the CRPD Committee also identifies specific concerns linked to the regional context. For example, it expresses concern that persons with disabilities are subjected to involuntary medical treatment by non-certified traditional healers.[146] The CRPD Committee also condemns 'the abandonment, malnutrition and exploitation through the use of children with disabilities for begging'.[147] It calls on States Parties to combat 'harmful stereotypes that consider women with disabilities asexual and pure and that suggest that having sexual intercourse with them might cure HIV/AIDS'.[148] Furthermore, on several occasions, the CRPD Committee has affirmed that FGM is in violation of the CRPD.[149]

It seems that the CRPD Committee's endeavours to encourage African states to address specific regional issues, such as traditional stereotypes, might prove extremely important in making the CRPD more effective in Africa. In the long run, the CRPD itself also has the potential to influence the jurisprudence of the ACHPR in a significant manner. Its provisions and underlying tenets could be used, alongside the RPDA Protocol, to advance the rights of Africans with disabilities.

DID YOU KNOW THAT ...?

In Africa, the implementation of the CRPD has been supported by the UN Partnership on the Rights of Persons with Disabilities (UNPRPD). As mentioned in Chapter 1 of this textbook, the UNPRPD brings together various UN entities, national governments, civil society and DPOs. The UNPRPD facilitates policy dialogue, coalition-building and capacity development at the country and regional levels, through providing various funding opportunities. In the first 'funding round', different projects were funded in Mozambique, Togo, and South Africa. The work of the UNPRPD in Mozambique created opportunities for several DPOs to play a more proactive role in demanding the full realisation of disability rights. A module on the collection of disability statistics was also developed by the project in collaboration with the Mozambique

[146] CRPD Committee, Concluding Observations on the Initial Report of the Sudan, 10 April 2018, UN Doc. CRPD/C/SUD/CO/1, para. 29.

[147] CRPD Committee, Concluding Observations on the Initial Report of Uganda, 12 May 2016, UN Doc. CRPD/C/UGA/CO/1, para. 30.

[148] Ibid. para. 32.

[149] Ibid. para. 31. See also CRPD Committee, Concluding Observations on the Initial Report of Ethiopia, 10 April 2018, UN Doc. CRPD/C/ETH/CO/1, para. 39; CRPD Committee, Concluding Observations on the Initial Report of Gabon, 2 October 2015, UN Doc. CRPD/C/GAB/CO/1, para. 40.

National Statistical Bureau. Furthermore, the UNPRPD project partnered with the Landmine Victims Assistance Network, the Ministry of Gender, Children and Social Action, the Ministry of Health and Handicap International to conduct a survey on the circumstances and aspirations of survivors of landmines in Mozambique. The findings of the survey, documented in the report 'Shattered Dreams – Living Conditions, Needs and Capacities of Mines and Explosive Remnants of War Survivors in Mozambique', significantly contributed to shaping the country's first National Plan of Action on Landmine Victim Assistance (UNPRPD, *Connections: An Overview of Results from the First UNPRPD Funding Round Building Partnerships for Disability Rights*, 2016). In the second 'funding round', the UNPRPD chose Ethiopia (among other countries) to implement a joint disability inclusion Project by the International Labour Organization (ILO) and the United Nations High Commissioner for Human Rights (OHCHR). By providing disability equality training to social partners and by organising disability workshops for law enforcement agencies, the project aims to raise awareness and advance key strategies for promoting inclusion (www.ilo.org/addisababa/technical-cooperation/WCMS_553933/lang–en/index.htm).

6 THE LEAGUE OF ARAB STATES AND DISABILITY

The AU embodies the principal human rights system on the African continent. However, in Northern Africa and in the Middle East, the LAS has also created a transnational regime for the protection of human rights, which revolves around the 2004 Arab Charter on Human Rights. While it is still in its infancy and has attracted significant criticism, that regime presents interesting features in relation to the rights of persons with disabilities. Those features are examined below, after a short introductory analysis of the institutional set-up of the LAS.

6.1 The LAS at a Glance

The LAS was established in 1945. Its six founding Member States were: the Kingdom of Egypt, the Kingdom of Iraq, Transjordan (renamed Jordan in 1949), Lebanon, Saudi Arabia and Syria. Yemen joined on 5 May 1945. Currently, the League has twenty-two members,[150] and some of them (such

[150] Syria's participation has been suspended since November 2011, as a consequence of government repression during the Syrian Civil War.

as Djibouti) are Member States of both the LAS and the AU. At the outset, the main purpose of the LAS was to develop closer relations between Arab countries. The LAS stands apart from other regional organisations with regard to the nature of its membership. While membership of the AU or the Council of Europe (CoE) is linked, first and foremost, to geographical factors, membership of the LAS is based on a shared culture and language.[151]

The LAS Charter, which defines the structure and functions of the organisation,[152] affirms that the main purpose of the LAS is the strengthening of relations between the Member States and the coordination of their policies. The Council of the League is the supreme decision-making body of the LAS. Since 1945, various treaties have been approved in the realm of the LAS, mostly in relation to economic cooperation and security. The LAS has also adopted a timid approach to putting in place a human rights system. In 1968, the creation of a Permanent Arab Commission on Human Rights, a consultative body,[153] was the first step taken towards the elaboration of a pan-Arabic human rights policy. In 1994, the first human rights treaty was approved, the Arab Charter on Human Rights (1994 Arab Charter); however, it never entered into force, failing to reach the minimum number of ratifications required. Ten years later, it was replaced by a revised Arab Charter on Human Rights (2004 Arab Charter), which entered into force in 2008.[154] In 2014, the LAS approved the Statute of the Arab Court of Human Rights, establishing a human rights court to enforce the provision of the 2004 Arab Charter. However, at the time of writing this textbook, the Statute is not yet in force.[155]

6.2 The Emergence of a Pan-Arabic Disability Policy

Disability has not been a major concern in the activities of the LAS. However, in the 2000s, the Arab Summit acknowledged the challenges faced by persons with disabilities and the need for concerted action. In response to the lack of data, the dearth of research and analysis, and with a view to fostering the exchange of good practices, the LAS launched the Arab Decade for Persons with Disabilities 2003–2012 (Arab Decade), under the auspices of the UN Economic and Social Commission for Western Asia (ESCWA). That decade

[151] Mohammad-Mahmoud Ould Mohamedou, 'Arab Agency and the UN Project: The League of Arab States between Universality and Regionalism' (2016) 37(7) *Third World Quarterly* 1219, at 1222. On the LAS see also Mervat Rishmawi and Marina Comandulli, 'The League of Arab States', in *Max Planck Encyclopedia of Public International Law – MPEPIL, ad vocem.*

[152] Charter of the League of Arab States, 22 March 1945.

[153] Konstantinos Magliveras and Gino Naldi, 'The Arab Court of Human Rights: A Study in Impotence' (2016) 29(2) *Revue Québécoise de Droit International* 147, at 150.

[154] See at www.lasportal.org/ar/sectors/dep/HumanRightsDep/Pages/Mechanisms.aspx#tab1.

[155] See at www.icj.org/arab-court-of-human-rights-comprehensive-amendments-required-before-ratification-new-report/.

established, for the first time, a set of regionally agreed principles and objectives in the field of disability, and it prompted the publication, in 2014, of a flagship report on Disability in the Arab Region.[156]

The Arab Decade has not been followed up to any great extent, and a pan-Arabic disability policy has yet to come to full fruition. This is partially due to the political instability in many of the countries of the LAS, after the Arab Spring.[157] However, collaboration among Arab States has been fostered under the ESCWA, which has recently published a second report that is entitled 'Disability in the Arab Region 2017: Strengthening Social Protection for Persons with Disabilities'. That report investigates the implementation of the CRPD in Northern Africa and the Middle East, in connection with the realisation of the Sustainable Development Goals (SDGs), with a view to advancing the rights of persons with disabilities.

CASE STUDY

The Promotion of the Rights of Persons with Disabilities in Tunisia

Tunisia, which has been a Member State of the LAS since 1958, was the first African country to be subject to the review of the CRPD Committee. The CRPD Committee's COs on the Tunisian report, published in 2011, recommended that the State Party should include DPOs within the Constitutional Council, the body designated to draft the new Constitution (CRPD Committee, COs on the Initial Report of Tunisia, 13 May 2011, UN Doc. CRPD/C/TUN/CO/1, para. 10). The UNPRPD supported the involvement of persons with disabilities in the period of political transition in the country, through the project 'The New Tunisia Won't Be Built Without Us', established in 2013 (UNPRPD, *Connections. An Overview of Results from the First UNPRPD Funding Round Building Partnerships for Disability Rights*, 2016). The project supported a large coalition of DPOs in drafting a Charter on the rights of persons with disabilities through a highly consultative process. Assistance was also provided in carrying out an advocacy campaign to secure political support for the Charter. Following that campaign, the President of the Tunisian Republic, Beji Caid Essebsi, formally committed to the principles outlined in the Charter. Moreover, the UNPRPD project supported

[156] ESCWA and LAS, *Disability in the Arab Region. An Overview* (2014) available at www.unescwa.org/sites/www.unescwa.org/files/page_attachments/disability_in_the_arab_region-_an_overview_-_en_1.pdf.

[157] The Arab Spring was a revolutionary wave of both violent and non-violent demonstrations, protests, and civil wars in North Africa and the Middle East that began on 18 December 2010 in Tunisia with the Tunisian Revolution. On the Arab Spring and its consequences, see, among many others, Bruno Nascimbene and Alessia Di Pascale, 'The "Arab Spring" and the Extraordinary Influx of People Who Arrived in Italy from North Africa' (2011) 13(4) *European Journal of Migration and Law* 341.

activities aimed at making elections more inclusive. As a result, during the 2014 legislative elections, 50 per cent of voting centres were equipped with Braille ballot forms and several voting centres were made accessible to people with reduced mobility.

6.3 Disability Rights in the 2004 Arab Charter on Human Rights

The 2004 Arab Charter constitutes an attempt to overcome the main weaknesses of its predecessor, which was considered fundamentally flawed and incompatible with international standards.[158] While it is drafted better than the 1994 version, the 2004 Arab Charter has also attracted a lot of criticism for being inconsistent with international human rights law and for its reference to Zionism.[159] It is composed of fifty-three articles that cover individual rights, States Parties' obligations, a supervisory mechanism and States Parties' reports, as well as procedural articles on ratification and entry into force. Article 1 affirms that, 'within the context of the national identity of the Arab States', the Charter aims to place human rights at the 'centre of the key national concerns' of Arab States and 'to entrench the principle that all human rights are universal, indivisible, interdependent and interrelated'. Significantly, Article 43 of the 2004 Arab Charter provides that the Charter cannot be construed or interpreted as impairing the rights set forth in the international and regional human rights instruments that the States Parties have adopted or ratified. The treaty body established to supervise the implementation of the Charter is the Arab Human Rights Committee.

The 2004 Arab Charter includes civil, political, cultural, economic, and social rights: the right to life (Article 5); freedom from torture (Article 8); the right to equality before the law and the equal protection of the law (Article 11); the right to privacy (Article 21); the right to political participation (Article 24); the freedom of movement and residence (Article 26); the prohibition of collective expulsions of aliens (Article 26); the right to nationality (Article 29); the freedom of thought, conscience and religion (Article 30); the right to own property (Article 31); the right to information and freedom of opinion and expression (Article 32); the protection, survival, development and well-being of the child (Article 33); the right of workers to enjoy just and

[158] Mervat Rishmawi, 'The Arab Charter on Human Rights and the League of Arab States: An Update' (2010) 10(1) *Human Rights Law Review* 169, at 169. See also Mervat Rishmawi, 'Arab Charter on Human Rights', in *Max Planck Encyclopedia of Public International Law – MPEPIL, ad vocem.*

[159] Ibid.

favourable work conditions (Article 34); the right to join or form trade unions (Article 35); the right to an adequate standard of living (Article 38); the right to health (Article 39); the right to education (Article 41); and the right to participate in cultural activities (Article 42).

Disability is mentioned several times in the text. Article 3(1) explicitly includes it as a ground of discrimination. Article 34(1) affirms the right to work and requires States Parties to ensure that right without distinction, *inter alia*, on the ground of disability, while Article 34(2) requires the protection of disabled persons in the workplace. Moreover, Article 40 of the 2004 Arab Charter explicitly protects and promote the rights of persons with disabilities.[160]

ARTICLE 40 OF THE 2004 ARAB CHARTER

1. The State Parties undertake to ensure that mentally or physically disabled persons should enjoy a decent life, in conditions which ensure dignity, promote self-reliance and facilitate their active participation in society.

2. The State Parties shall provide social services free of charge to all disabled persons, including material support for those in need, directly or through their family to enable the family to provide for them and do all necessary to keep them out of an institution. In all cases, the disabled person's best interest will be taken into account.

3. The State Parties shall take all necessary measures to fight disability by all possible means, including preventive health programmes, awareness-raising efforts and education.

4. The State Parties shall provide all educational services suitable for disabled persons, taking into account the importance of integrating these persons in the educational system, the importance of professional training and preparation for pursuit of a professional activity, and the creation of suitable job opportunities in public or private sectors.

5. The State Parties shall provide all health services for disabled persons, including rehabilitation services, to integrate them into society.

6. The State Parties shall ensure to disabled persons access to all public and private collective services.

Although Article 40(2) mentions dignity, participation in society and access to public services, it does not seem to comply with the CRPD. Contrary to

[160] An unofficial translation of the 2004 Arab Charter is published in the *Boston University International Law Journal* (2006).

> In your opinion, what are the strengths and weaknesses of Article 40 of the Arab Charter?

Article 12 CRPD, it mentions the 'best interests of the disabled person' as a leading principle, instead of the 'will and preferences' of the person with a disability. Moreover, Article 40(2) appears to permit institutionalisation, when the family cannot take care of a relative with a disability or when it is in the 'best interest' of the disabled individual. This seems to contradict the right to independent living enshrined in Article 19 CRPD.

7 THE ASSOCIATION OF SOUTHEAST ASIAN NATIONS AND DISABILITY

To date, the ASEAN represents the most developed transnational regime in Asia.[161] After having examined the main tenets and features of the ASEAN, this section succinctly addresses the most recent developments in the protection of the rights of persons with disabilities in the Asian region.

7.1 The ASEAN at a Glance

7.1.1 *The ASEAN: Objectives and Institutional Set-Up*

The ASEAN was created in 1967,[162] by means of the Bangkok Declaration,[163] in order to: 'accelerate the economic growth, social progress and cultural development in the region'; promote peace and stability in the region; and boost the 'collaboration and mutual assistance on matters of common interest in the economic, social, cultural, technical, scientific and administrative fields' among Southeast Asian nations.[164] The Bangkok Declaration represents the

[161] On the absence of a regional system in Asia and the Pacific, see, among many others, Smith, *Textbook on International Human Rights*, note 2, p. 90.

[162] The five original Member States (ASEAN-5) were Indonesia, Malaysia, Philippines, Singapore and Thailand. Brunei Darussalam joined on 8 January 1984, Vietnam on 28 July 1995, Lao PDR and Myanmar on 23 July 1997 and Cambodia on 30 April 1999.

[163] ASEAN Declaration (Bangkok Declaration) Bangkok, 8 August 1967, available at http://asean.org/the-asean-declaration-bangkok-declaration-bangkok-8-august-1967/.

[164] Ibid.

foundation stone of the ASEAN, whose action has been subsequently framed by different treaties, such as the Treaty of Amity and Cooperation in Southeast Asia (1976). The ASEAN was not founded as an organisation as such, rather it developed 'in an ad hoc fashion over the course of time'.[165] Until the early 2000s, the ASEAN undertook several initiatives with the aim of achieving economic convergence between Asian States, the most relevant of which was the ASEAN Free Trade Agreement (AFTA), set up in 1992. In 2007, only four decades after the Bangkok Declaration, a major step forward was achieved in the process of integration, namely the adoption of the ASEAN Charter, which formalised the structure of the organisation and gave it a 'collective identity'. The ASEAN Charter came into force in December 2008.

Article 2 of the ASEAN Charter lists adherence to the rule of law and democracy, as well as respect for, and protection of, human rights and fundamental freedoms, alongside the promotion of social justice, as some of the purposes and guiding principles of the ASEAN. The Charter also confers legal personality on the ASEAN and establishes the organs through which the ASEAN can act. Those include the ASEAN Summit, the ASEAN Coordinating Council, the ASEAN Community Councils and the Sectoral Ministerial Bodies. The ASEAN Summit includes Heads of States and Governments of the Member States, and is the 'supreme policy-making body' of the organisation as a whole. The ASEAN Coordinating Council is comprised of ASEAN Foreign Ministers and decides the criteria and rules for ASEAN engagement with external entities, including civil society organisations. The ASEAN Community Councils include the ASEAN Political-Security Community Council, the ASEAN Economic Community Council and the ASEAN Socio-Cultural Community Council. Those councils comprise of one ministerial representative per ASEAN Member State and must implement ASEAN Summit's decisions. The ASEAN Sectoral Ministerial Bodies gather the ministers of specific sectors (for example, the labour ministers of all ASEAN Member States will make up one sectoral ministerial body), and they are entrusted with the task of strengthening cooperation within their particular sector.

7.1.2 *The ASEAN and the Development of a Regional Human Rights System*

While the ASEAN's achievements in facilitating regional economic cooperation among its Member States have been remarkable, its human rights system is still in its early stages.[166] Despite the ASEAN Foreign Ministers having agreed that the ASEAN 'should coordinate a common approach on human

[165] Walter Woon, 'The ASEAN Charter Ten Years On' (2017) 39(2) *Contemporary Southeast Asia: A Journal of International and Strategic Affairs* 245.

[166] Hien Bui, 'The ASEAN Human Rights System: A Critical Analysis' (2016) 11(1) *Asian Journal of Comparative Law* 111.

rights and actively participate and contribute to the application, promotion and protection of human rights', no concrete action was taken until the early 2000s.[167] Until then, the ASEAN treaties and soft law instruments did not mention human rights. In fact, the first references to human rights can be seen in the Declaration Against Trafficking in Persons Particularly Women and Children[168] and the Declaration on the Elimination of Violence Against Women in the ASEAN Region,[169] both adopted in 2004. The entry into force of the ASEAN Charter represents the main turning point of the ASEAN transnational regime, as it includes the protection of human rights among the guiding principles of the regime as a whole and requires the establishment of a human rights body,[170] the AICHR, which was set up in 2009. The AICHR is a consultative body and its functions, as laid down in the Terms of Reference (TOR) of the AICHR, include: developing strategies for the promotion and protection of human rights and fundamental freedoms to complement the building of the ASEAN Community; enhancing public awareness of human rights among the ASEAN peoples through education, research and dissemination of information; encouraging ASEAN Member States to ratify international human rights instruments; providing advisory services and technical assistance on human rights matters to ASEAN sectoral bodies upon request; and preparing thematic studies on human rights issues.

After its establishment, the AICHR focused on the drafting of the ASEAN Human Rights Declaration (AHRD), which was then adopted in 2012. The AHRD is not formally binding. Nevertheless, it constitutes the main legal framework for human rights cooperation in the ASEAN regime, and its implementation by the Member States is overseen by the AICHR. As is further discussed in sub-section 7.3 below, the AHRD consists of forty articles, and it includes civil and political rights as well as economic, social and cultural rights.[171] It is divided into five main parts, outlined in Figure 15.3. The Preamble reaffirms adherence to 'the purposes and principles of ASEAN as enshrined in the ASEAN Charter' and 'a commitment to the Universal Declaration of Human Rights, the Charter of the United Nations . . . and other international human rights instruments to which ASEAN Member States are [P]arties'.

[167] See at http://aichr.org/about/.

[168] The text of the Declaration Against Trafficking in Persons Particularly Women and Children is available at http://asean.org/storage/2012/05/ASEAN-Declaration-against-Trafficking-in-Persons-Particularly-Women-and-Children-TPPWC.pdf.

[169] The text of the Declaration on the Elimination of Violence Against Women in the ASEAN Region is available at http://asean.org/?static_post=declaration-on-the-elimination-of-violence-against-women-in-the-asean-region-4.

[170] Article 14 of the ASEAN Charter.

[171] Catherine Shanahan Renshaw, 'The ASEAN Human Rights Declaration 2012' (2013) 13(1) *Human Rights Law Review* 557.

Figure 15.3 Structure of the AHRD

The AHRD is different from other UN instruments in several respects. For instance, similarly to the African Charter, it includes a provision on the duties of the individual.[172] Moreover, Article 7 AHRD, while reaffirming that all human rights are 'universal, indivisible, interdependent and interrelated', provides for them to be considered 'in the regional and national context bearing in mind different political, economic, legal, social, cultural, historical and religious backgrounds'. Significantly, the AHRD also contains a specific provision on persons living with HIV.[173] A further distinctive character of the AHRD is its emphasis on the right to development, which is also provided for in the ASEAN Charter. In particular, the AHRD appears to be in line with Article 1(9) of the ASEAN Charter, which lists among the goals of the ASEAN the promotion of 'sustainable development so as to ensure the protection of the region's environment, the sustainability of its natural resources, the preservation of its cultural heritage and the high quality of life of its peoples'.

7.2 The Emergence of the ASEAN Disability Policy

The ASEAN's engagement with disability issues is quite recent and can be traced back to 2011, when the ASEAN Decade of Persons with Disabilities 2011–2020 (ASEAN Decade) was proclaimed by means of the Bali Declaration on the Enhancement of the Role and Participation of the Persons with Disabilities in ASEAN Community (Bali Declaration).

[172] Article 6 AHRD states that: '[t]he enjoyment of human rights and fundamental freedoms must be balanced with the performance of corresponding duties as every person has responsibilities to all other individuals, the community and the society where one lives'.

[173] Article 29(2) AHRD.

Bali Declaration on the Enhancement of the Role and Participation of the Persons with Disabilities in ASEAN Community (2011)

We, the Peoples of the Member States of the Association of Southeast Asian Nations (ASEAN), represented by the Heads of State or Government of Brunei Darussalam, the Kingdom of Cambodia, the Republic of Indonesia, the Lao People's Democratic Republic, Malaysia, the Union of Myanmar, the Republic of the Philippines, the Republic of Singapore, the Kingdom of Thailand and the Socialist Republic of Viet Nam.

Recognising the enhancement of well-being and livelihood of the peoples of ASEAN by providing them with equitable access to opportunities for human development, social welfare and justice as stipulated in the ASEAN Charter;

. . .

Emphasizing the importance of mainstreaming disabilities issues as an integral part of relevant strategies of sustainable development;

DO HEREBY DECLARE TO:

1. Encourage ASEAN Member States to sign and ratify the Convention on the Rights of Persons with Disabilities and foster its implementation in the communities;
2. Proclaim the ASEAN Decade of Persons with Disabilities (2011– 2020) and its related initiatives as the theme is to promote disability-inclusive development within ASEAN;
3. Welcome the initiative of ASEAN Disabled People's Organisations for establishing the ASEAN Disability Forum, a joint efforts of multi-stakeholders, including ASEAN Member States, the ASEAN Secretariat, international development agencies, civil society organisations, media, business sector, academic groups, Disabled People's Organisations (DPOs), disability-related organisations and their parents/family organisations;
4. Urge that ASEAN Member States to promote the quality of life of the persons with disabilities in the context of poverty alleviation and develop regional statistical indicators in ASEAN to measure the development of vulnerable groups, particularly persons with disabilities;
5. Ensure the fulfillment of the rights of persons with disabilities in all aspects of life through mainstreaming disability perspective in the development and implementation of ASEAN policies and programmes across the economic, political security and socio-cultural pillars of the ASEAN Community;
6. Continue to raise awareness on disability issues and to increase outreach activities for all society ranging from local, national and regional levels by using various media and involving all components of the society;

. . .

13. Enhance sharing of information, good/best practices and experiences on issues concerning persons with disabilities as well as encourage the development of new knowledge through researches, analysis and trainings;

14. Work towards equal opportunities of persons with disabilities to education especially basic education and alternative means of communication including sign language, Braille and the like;

15. Emphasize the need of providing accessibility to public facilities and amenities, public transportation, education, employment, information communication and technology (ICT), recreation as well as sports for persons with disabilities in ASEAN;

16. Mainstream disability issues in disaster management policies and programmes at regional, national and community levels;

17. Develop social security schemes in ASEAN Member States for protecting persons with disabilities, especially those with severe disabilities;

18. Develop the social inclusiveness of persons with disabilities, which includes the development of leadership, community inclusive, gender-sensitive and socially inclusive business;

19. Encourage international development agencies and other international institutions to support the implementation of the disability policies and programs in the ASCC Blueprint;

20. Encourage the mass media, regardless of its scale and coverage, to be culturally and gender sensitive in promoting the accurate information and image of disability and persons with disabilities in ASEAN.

We hereby pledge our commitment to task the concerned Ministers of ASEAN Sectoral Bodies to implement this Declaration.

Adopted in Bali, Indonesia, this Seventeenth Day of November in the Year Two Thousand and Eleven.

The ASEAN Decade is intended to promote disability inclusive development and to reaffirm the ASEAN's commitment to equal opportunities for persons with disabilities. Its core tenets and guiding principles as well as its objectives have been laid down in the Mobilisation Framework of the ASEAN Decade (Mobilisation Framework), approved alongside the Bali Declaration.[174] The five fundamental principles that inform the ASEAN Decade are outlined in Figure 15.4.

The Mobilisation Framework makes several references to the CRPD, which is identified as the golden standard for the protection of the rights of

[174] The Bali Declaration and the Mobilisation Framework are available at http://asean.org/?static_post=bali-declaration-on-the-enhancement-of-the-role-and-participartion-of-the-persons-with-disabilities-in-asean-community.

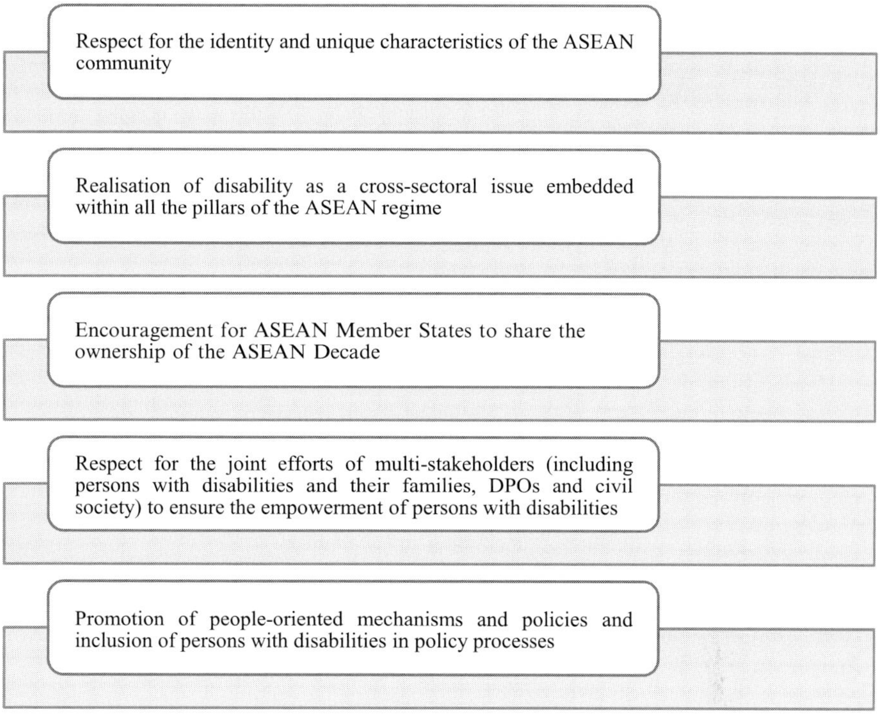

Figure 15.4 Fundamental Principles of the ASEAN Decade

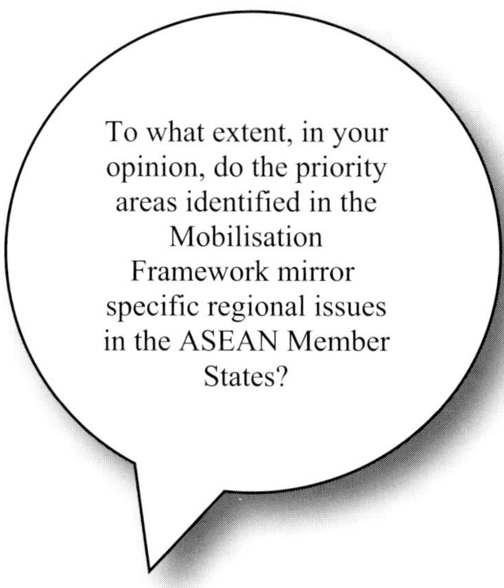

persons with disabilities, to be implemented by the ASEAN countries. Moreover, it sets out fifteen intertwined priority areas, which, for the most part, mirror CRPD provisions (outlined in Figure 15.5). In a similar vein to the AU Continental Plan, the Mobilisation Framework identifies specific regional issues, such as the protection and safety of persons with disabilities in situations of armed conflict, humanitarian emergencies and the occurrence of natural disasters. Notable among the priority areas is that of support for older disabled people.[175] The Mobilisation Framework also acknowledges 'the important role of family as the essential unit of society,

[175] Priority Area 11: Older persons with disabilities.

Priority Areas	1. Realisation and protection of fundamental rights and freedoms of persons with disabilities
	2. Development and effective implementation of disability discrimination laws and mainstreaming disability issues in policy and planning
	3. Employment and decent work
	4. Adequate and appropriate education
	5. Health care and rehabilitation, including community-based rehabilitation
	6. Political participation and access to justice of people with disabilities
	7. Livelihood, poverty alleviation, and social services
	8. Independent living and community inclusion
	9. Children with disabilities
	10. Women with disabilities
	11. Older persons with disabilities
	12. Participation in cultural life, recreation, leisure and sport
	13. Accessibility (e.g. ICTs, ATs, information, facility, transportation, services)
	14. Capacity building of government, Self-Help DPOs, and CSOs
	15. Persons with disabilities in emergencies

Figure 15.5 Priority Areas of the ASEAN Decade

communities, civil society, private sector and governments as well as the importance of inter-generational interdependence and solidarity in promoting active, self-care and healthy [people]'.[176]

Alongside the ASEAN Decade, which is the most important initiative of the ASEAN, other documents and activities contribute to shaping the disability policy of this transnational human rights regime. For instance, the 2014 ASEAN Declaration on Strengthening Social Protection seeks to foster inclusion of persons with disabilities and other vulnerable groups by ensuring 'equitable access to social protection' and adequate social assistance programmes. Significantly, the Preamble to the Declaration cites the CRPD, together with other human rights treaties, and makes explicit reference to

[176] Ibid.

accessibility and reasonable accommodation. The Declaration also mentions the role of the community (and of the family) in supporting the provision of services, but it fails to highlight the right to independent living, which is, by contrast, a cornerstone of the UN Convention.

7.3 Disability Rights in the ASEAN Human Rights System

The AHRD is a comprehensive document, encompassing the whole spectrum of civil, political, economic, social and cultural rights. However, references to disability within the document are scant. Disability is mentioned as a ground of discrimination in Article 2.

ARTICLE 2 AHRD

Every person is entitled to the rights and freedoms set forth herein, without distinction of any kind, such as race, gender, age, language, religion, political or other opinion, national or social origin, economic status, birth, disability or other status.

Similarly to the African Charter, Article 4 AHRD includes persons with disabilities alongside other vulnerable groups in its recognition, *inter alia*, of the indivisibility of human rights.

ARTICLE 4 AHRD

The rights of women, children, the elderly, persons with disabilities, migrant workers, and vulnerable and marginalised groups are an inalienable, integral and indivisible part of human rights and fundamental freedoms.

Article 29 is also extremely relevant from a disability perspective. That provision enshrines the 'right to the enjoyment of the highest attainable standard of physical, mental and reproductive health' and explicitly refers to the need to combat discrimination against persons living with HIV.

ARTICLE 29(2) AHRD

The ASEAN Member States shall create a positive environment in overcoming stigma, silence, denial and discrimination in the prevention, treatment, care and support of people suffering from communicable diseases, including HIV/AIDS.

Draw up a list of rights in the CRPD that are mirrored in the AHRD.

Despite the scant references to disability in the AHRD, the AICHR has engaged in several promotional activities, with a view to raising awareness of the rights of persons with disabilities and to supporting the implementation of the CRPD in ASEAN Member States. When it comes to disability, the ADHR is not, in fact, the main point of reference within the AICHR; rather, the CRPD or the policy documents adopted in the broader realm of the ASEAN form a central focal point. Illustrative in this respect is the five-year AICHR Work Plan for the period of 2016–2020 (WP 2016–2020),[177] which mentions the CRPD and includes among its main tasks for the period that of developing regional plans of action, recommendations or ASEAN policy frameworks. The AICHR has also set up the Task Force on the Mainstreaming of the Rights of Persons with Disabilities in the ASEAN Community, to advance the rights of persons with disabilities across the whole range of ASEAN activities.

8 REGIONAL DISABILITY POLICIES OF THE UNITED NATIONS IN ASIA AND THE PACIFIC

In Asia and the Pacific, the ESCAP serves as the UN's regional hub for promoting cooperation between countries in that geographical area, in order to achieve inclusive and sustainable development. It is the largest regional intergovernmental platform, with fifty-three Member States and nine associate members and having a geographical scope that stretches from Turkey to the Pacific island nation of Kiribati, encompassing the Russian Federation, China, India, Japan, Australia and New Zealand.[178] The work of the ESCAP addresses the implementation of the 2030 Agenda for Sustainable Development,[179] but it also has a strong focus on disability. In 1992, under the auspices of the ESCAP, the first Asian and Pacific Decade of Disabled Persons 1993–2002 was proclaimed. The ESCAP was then mandated with the task of implementing its activities.[180] That Decade aimed at raising awareness of the

[177] The report is available at http://aichr.org/documents/.

[178] See at www.unescap.org/about/member-states.

[179] See above Chapter 1, sub-section 3.4.

[180] ESCAP, Asian and Pacific Decade of Disabled Persons, 1993–2002: Mandates for Action, UN Doc. ST/ESCAP/1433.

need to create legislation, policies and programmes that address the many barriers faced by persons with disabilities. A second and third Asian and Pacific decade were also proclaimed (from 2003–2012 and 2012–2022, respectively) to follow up on the work done in the first Decade. During the High-level Intergovernmental Meeting on the Final Review of the Implementation of the Asia and Pacific Decade of Disabled Persons 2003–2012, the governments of the ESCAP region adopted the Ministerial Declaration on the Asian and Pacific Decade of Persons with Disabilities 2013–2022. In conjunction with that, they adopted a comprehensive regional strategy to support the implementation of the CRPD: the Incheon Strategy to 'Make the Right Real' for Persons with Disabilities in Asia and the Pacific (Incheon Strategy). The Incheon Strategy builds on principles of the CRPD, and it sets forth ten 'time-bound development goals' as well as targets and indicators. The goals, which are tailored to specific regional issues, include those of poverty reduction, employment generation, political participation, ensuring accessibility, social protection, early intervention, education and disability-inclusive disaster risk reduction. Improving the collection of disability statistics, increasing the number of ratifications of the CRPD, and improving the harmonisation of the UN Convention with domestic laws are also mentioned as key objectives of the Incheon Strategy. Furthermore, the Strategy promotes the realisation of the 2030 Agenda on Sustainable Development. A Working Group on the Asian and Pacific Decade of Persons with Disabilities 2013–2022 was established in early 2013 as an advisory body for the full and effective implementation of both the Decade and of the Incheon Strategy.

INCHEON STRATEGY TO 'MAKE THE RIGHT REAL' FOR PERSONS WITH DISABILITIES IN ASIA AND THE PACIFIC (2012)

7. In order to reali[s]e and protect the rights of persons with disabilities in the Asian and Pacific region, the Incheon Strategy underscores the following policy direction:

a. Legislative, administrative and other measures supportive of rights fulfilment are adopted, implemented, reviewed and strengthened so that disability-based discrimination is eliminated;
b. Development policies and programmes are disability inclusive and gender-sensitive and harness the potential of combining universal design with technological advancements for enabling persons with disabilities to fulfil their rights;
c. Development policies and programmes address the basic needs of persons with disabilities and their families who live in poverty;

d. Effective and timely collection and analysis of sex-disaggregated disability data are pursued for evidence-based policymaking;
e. National, subnational and local policies and programmes are based on plans that are explicitly inclusive of persons with disabilities and that also prioriti[s]e the active participation of persons with disabilities, through their representative organi[s]ations, in relevant decision-making processes;

...

h. National, subnational and local coordination, with subregional and regional linkages, ensure that disability inclusion in development policies and programmes is strengthened through intensification of multisectoral consultation and collaboration, to expedite and review Decade implementation and share related good practices;
i. Community- and family-based inclusive development is promoted in order to ensure that all persons with disabilities, irrespective of socioeconomic status, religious affiliation, ethnicity and location, are able, on an equal basis with others, to contribute to and benefit from development initiatives, particularly poverty reduction programmes;
j. Persons with disabilities are included in mainstream community life and are supported with life choices equal to those of others, including the option to live independently;
k. Persons with disabilities have access to the physical environment, public transportation, knowledge, information and communication, in a usable manner, through universal design and assistive technologies with reasonable accommodation provided, and taking into consideration the need to accommodate economic, geographic, linguistic and other aspects of cultural diversity, which altogether constitute a critical bridge to fulfilling their rights;
l. Diverse disability groups are empowered that include but are not limited to the following underrepresented groups: girls and boys with disabilities, young persons with disabilities, women with disabilities, persons with intellectual, learning and developmental disabilities, persons with autism, persons with psychosocial disabilities, persons who are deaf, hard of hearing and deafened, persons who are deafblind, persons with multiple disabilities, persons with extensive disabilities, older persons with disabilities, persons with disabilities living with HIV, persons with disabilities arising from non-communicable diseases, persons with disabilities affected by leprosy, persons with disabilities caused by medical conditions and intractable epilepsy, persons with disabilities caused by road traffic crashes, indigenous and ethnic minority persons with disabilities, persons with disabilities who are

> homeless and inadequately housed, persons with disabilities in situations of risk, including situations of armed conflict, humanitarian emergencies, and the occurrence of natural and human-made disasters, persons with disabilities who are victims of landmines, persons with disabilities who do not have legal status, persons with disabilities who are victims of domestic violence, particularly women and children, and family advocacy groups, as well as particularly marginali[s]ed persons with disabilities living in slums, rural and remote areas and atolls;
>
> ...

Overall, the ESCAP has played an important role in advancing disability rights in the region, mostly by facilitating the exchange of good practices and by supporting policy-makers across different ministries as well as civil society to advance disability-inclusive development strategies at the domestic level. The activities of the ESCAP have been supplemented by the UNPRPD, which supported different national projects and awareness-raising activities.

CASE STUDY

Indonesian Network of Inclusive Cities

The UNPRPD project in Indonesia supported the establishment of the Network of Inclusive Cities, a partnership of municipalities committed to the full realisation of the rights of persons with disabilities. The Network, which comprises seven cities representing a total population of 7.4 million, provides a platform for the exchange of good practices. Five high-level meetings were convened by network members over the course of the project and were attended by delegates from different Indonesian municipalities and DPOs.

SUMMARY

- **The number of persons with disabilities in Africa is extremely high. In the region, physical disabilities are often related to impairments caused by malnutrition, diseases, environmental hazards, wars, conflicts, and landmines. Individuals with disabilities are still extremely marginalised and excluded from mainstream African society. In rural areas, the marginalisation of people with disabilities and the** poverty they encounter are frequently the result of traditional or religious beliefs that consider disability as a punishment from the gods.

- Since the 1990s, the AU, formerly OAU, has played a prominent role in advancing disability rights. The African Decade 2010–2019 is one of the most recent initiatives of the AU. It is accompanied by a Continental Plan that identifies priority actions to address marginalising factors and discriminatory barriers faced by persons with disabilities.
- The African Charter and other core human rights treaties adopted in the realm of the African system include provisions that are particularly relevant to people with disabilities.
- One of the main bodies of the AU is the ACHPR. Its role in protecting and promoting the rights of persons with disabilities has been quite limited to date. However, this situation changed somewhat in 2015, when the ACHPR adopted the first thematic resolution on disability, namely the Resolution on Accessibility for Persons with Disabilities. That was followed, in 2016, by the Resolution on the Right to Dignity and Freedom from Torture or Ill-Treatment of Persons with Psychosocial Disabilities in Africa.
- The ACHPR's jurisprudence on the rights of persons with disabilities is scant. To date, the most significant decision in that regard is *Purohit and Moore* v. *The Gambia*.
- The CRPD Committee has addressed specific regional issues, such as FGM or traditional stereotypes in its COs. Moreover, in *X* v. *Tanzania*, the Committee considered the extreme violations that persons with albinism face. The CRPD Committee's decisions and COs might prove to be extremely important in making the CRPD more effective in Africa.
- Disability has not been one of the major concerns in the action of the LAS. However, in the early 2000s, the Arab Summit acknowledged the challenges faced by persons with disabilities and the need for concerted action on disability matters. In response to the lack of data, the dearth of research and analysis, and with a view to fostering the exchange of good practices, the LAS launched the Arab Decade for Persons with Disabilities 2003–2012.
- Since 1945, various treaties have been approved in the realm of the LAS. The primary treaty on human rights, the 2004 Arab Charter, entered into force in 2008. Disability is mentioned several times in the text of the 2004 Arab Charter. Article 3(1) explicitly includes it as a ground of discrimination. Article 34(1) affirms the right to work and requires States Parties to ensure the realisation of that right without distinction, *inter alia*, on the ground of disability, while Article 34(2) requires the protection of disabled persons in the workplace. Moreover, Article 40 explicitly protects and promotes the rights of persons with disabilities.
- The ASEAN's engagement with disability issues can be traced back to 2011, when the ASEAN Decade was launched. The ASEAN Decade was intended to promote disability inclusive development.
- Alongside the ASEAN Decade, other documents and activities contribute to shaping the ASEAN disability policy, including the 2014 ASEAN Declaration on

Strengthening Social Protection. That Declaration seeks to foster inclusion of persons with disabilities and other vulnerable groups by ensuring 'equitable access to social protection' and adequate social assistance programmes.

- The AHRD is a comprehensive document, encompassing the whole spectrum of civil, political, economic, social and cultural rights. However, references to disability within the document are scant. Disability is mentioned as a ground of discrimination in Article 2. Moreover, similarly to the African Charter, Article 4 AHRD includes persons with disabilities alongside other vulnerable groups in its recognition, *inter alia*, of the indivisibility of human rights.
- In Asia and the Pacific, the ESCAP serves as the UN's regional hub for promoting cooperation between countries in that geographical area, with the aim of achieving inclusive and sustainable development. The ESCAP's work addresses the implementation of the 2030 Agenda for Sustainable Development, and it has a strong focus on disability. The most important recent achievement of the ESCAP is the launch of the Incheon Strategy. That is the first regional strategy adopted in the realm of the UN, and it builds on principles of the CRPD, containing ten 'time-bound development goals' as well as targets and indicators.

ACTIVITIES

REVIEW QUESTIONS

1. What are the core tenets of the Continental Plan of Action of the African Decade of Persons with Disabilities 2010–2019?
2. What are the main provisions on the rights of persons with disabilities in the African human rights system?
3. What are the most important disability-related developments in Asia?

ESSAY QUESTIONS

1. 'The African Charter fails to mainstream disability rights and provides limited avenues for the protection of persons with disabilities.' *Discuss*.
2. 'The Incheon Strategy will enable the Asian and Pacific region to improve the quality of life of persons with disabilities and the fulfilment of their rights.' *Discuss*.

GROUP PROJECTS

Gender equality is promoted by Goal No. 6 of the Incheon Strategy, which aims to guarantee that women and girls with disabilities have equal access to development opportunities, are represented in decision-making bodies, have access to sexual and reproductive health services and are protected from violence and abuse.

Discuss the concrete actions which could be adopted by governments in the Asian and the Pacific region in order to achieve this goal on the basis of the indicators included in the Incheon Strategy.

FURTHER READING

Abbay, F., 'An Evaluation of Disability Human Rights under the African Regional Human Rights System' (2015) 23(3) *African Journal of International and Comparative Law* 476–502.

Berghs, M., 'Practices and Discourses of *Ubuntu*: Implications for an African Model of Disability?' (2017) 2 *African Journal of Disability* 1–8.

Carney, T., 'A Regional Disability Tribunal for Asia and the Pacific: Changing the Conversation to a Conversation' (2011) 7 *International Journal of Law in Context* 319–33.

Djoyou Kamga, S. G., 'A Call for a Protocol to the African Charter on Human and Peoples' Rights on the Rights of Persons with Disabilities in Africa' (2013) 23(2) *African Journal of International and Comparative Law* 219–49.

Enonchong, L. S., 'Mental Disability and the Right to Personal Liberty in Africa' (2017) 21(9) *The International Journal of Human Rights* 1351–77.

ESCAP, *Building Disability-Inclusive Societies in Asia and the Pacific: Assessing Progress of the Incheon Strategy* (2017), available at www.unescap.org/publications/building-disability%E2%80%91inclusive-societies-asia-and-pacific-assessing-progress-Incheon.

Hari, K. C., 'Disability Discourse in South Asia and Global Disability Governance' (2016) 5(4) *Canadian Journal of Disability Studies* 25–62.

Lamichhane, K., *Disability, Education and Employment in Developing Countries: From Charity to Investment* (Delhi: Cambridge University Press, 2015).

Perlin, M. L., 'Human Rights Law for Persons with Disabilities in Asia and the Pacific: The Need for a Disability Rights Tribunal: Human Rights Law for Persons with Disabilities' (2013) 10(2) *Journal of Policy and Practice in Intellectual Disabilities* 96–8.

Tesemma, S. T., 'Economic Discourses of Disability in Africa: An Overview of Lay and Legislative Narratives' (2014) 2 *African Disability Rights Yearbook* 121–50.

UNPRPD, *Connections. An Overview of Results from the First UNPRPD Funding Round Building Partnerships for Disability Rights* (2016), available at https://global-health.tcd.ie/assets/doc/UNPRPD%20REPORT-CONNECTIONS%202016%20(3).pdf.

Walsham, M., Kuper, H., Banks, L. M., and Blanchet, K., 'Social protection for People with disabilities in Africa and Asia: A Review of Programmes for Low- and Middle-income Countries' (2019) 47(1) *Oxford Development Studies* 97–112.

INDEX